CHALLENGES
OF
URBAN
EDUCATION

CHALLENGES OF URBAN EDUCATION

Sociological Perspectives for the Next Century

edited by

KAREN A. McCLAFFERTY
CARLOS ALBERTO TORRES
THEODORE R. MITCHELL

State University
of New York
Press

Chapter 1 appeared previously with the same title in the *British Journal of Sociology of Education* 17.2 (1996): 125–44. Copyright by Carfax Publishing, Ltd., 1996. Reprinted here with the kind permission of the publisher, Carfax Publishing (U.K.).

Chapter 8 comprises approximately forty-two pages from *Revolutionary Multiculturalism: Pedagogies of Dissent for the New Millennium*, ed. Peter McLaren. Copyright 1997 by Westview Press. Reprinted here with the kind permission of Westview Press.

Published by
State University of New York Press, Albany

Production by Susan Geraghty
Marketing by Patrick Durocher

Printed in the United States of America

For information, address State University of New York Press, State University Plaza, Albany, N.Y., 12246

Library of Congress Cataloging-in-Publication Data

Challenges of urban education : sociological perspectives for the next
  century / Karen A. McClafferty, Carlos Alberto Torres, Theodore R.
  Mitchell, editors.
        p.   cm.
    Includes bibliographical references and index.
    ISBN 0-7914-4433-3 (alk. paper). — ISBN 0-7914-4434-1 (pbk. :
  alk. paper)
      1. Education, Urban—Social aspects—United States. 2. Children
  of minorities—Education—United States. 3. Educational change-
  -United States. I. McClafferty, Karen A. II. Torres, Carlos
  Alberto. III. Mitchell, Theodore R.
  LC5131.C38 2000
  370'.9173'2—dc 21   99-24397
                                                                        CIP

10 9 8 7 6 5 4 3 2 1

CONTENTS

TABLES AND FIGURES

ACKNOWLEDGMENTS

In June 1996, sociologists from across the United States—as well as from Canada, Spain, South Africa, Hungary, and England—gathered at the University of California, Los Angeles. At that time, a three-day meeting of the Research Committee on Sociology of Education of the International Sociological Association was held to address the challenges that urban education presents to sociologists of education. This project could not have come to fruition without the support of the International Sociological Association. One individual, Ken Hale, also deserves mention here. We are grateful for his generous assistance and support in the preparation of the final version of this manuscript.

Two chapters have been reprinted here with the generous permission of the original publisher. Specifically, Michael Apple's piece, "Power Meaning and Identity: Critical Sociology of Education in the United States," originally appeared in the *British Journal of Sociology of Education* (1996, vol. 17, no. 2). Peter McLaren's piece, "Gangsta Pedagogy and Ghettocentricity: The Hip Hop Nation as Counterpublic Sphere," originally appeared in the Westview Press text, *Revolutionary Multiculturalism: Pedagogies of Dissent for the New Millennium* (1997).

The balance of the chapters contained in this volume represent a sampling of the papers presented at the 1996 conference, all of which were important contributions to the sociology of urban education. The editors are deeply indebted to each of the conference participants, whose determination and commitment to improving urban education should serve as an inspiration to educators everywhere.

PART I

Critical Issues in Urban Education and Challenges for the Sociology of Education

INTRODUCTION

Challenges of the New Sociology of Urban Education

Karen A. McClafferty, Carlos A. Torres, and Theodore R. Mitchell

According to a report by the National Center for Education Statistics (NCES), the proportion of all public school students in the United States who attend urban schools has been increasing slowly over time, to the point where the proportion of students in urban schools was at 28 percent in 1990. The report also points out that urban schools tend to be larger, with fewer resources, and located in areas with higher poverty rates. The student populations in urban schools are also more likely to be comprised of people of color[1] or of students who have difficulty speaking English. In addition, children in urban areas are more often exposed to conditions that endanger their health and well-being, such as limited access to medical care and increased exposure to violence and crime.[2]

Each of these factors alone presents a challenge to the student who must cope with it. These factors compounded present an even greater challenge. Hence, the perception that students in urban schools are "disadvantaged" or "at-risk" is not surprising. Indeed, the NCES found that even after controlling for poverty, students who attend urban schools are less likely than their suburban or rural counterparts to complete high school. Those who do graduate are more likely to be unemployed or living in poverty. Given these findings, the characterization of urban schools as in a "state of crisis"[3] seems reasonable and even necessary. This perception has been reinforced recently by works such as Jonathan Kozol's *Savage Inequalities*, which, through rich description and disturbing statistics, emphasizes the enormous inequities that exist in many urban schools.[4] The media attention received by Kozol's book and others like it has served to heighten awareness of the often drastic conditions of urban schools in the United States.

Another important point of the NCES report, however, is that the "often-cited bleak perceptions of urban schools and students may be overstated."[5] Indeed, the tendency in urban educational research to focus on problems and weaknesses is being challenged on many fronts, as researchers and practitioners alike realize the importance of highlighting both strengths and triumphs. In response, many researchers have begun to wrestle the spotlight away from the deficiencies of education, to shine it on the successes. Gloria Ladson-Billings, for example, describes the triumphs of teachers of African American students, calling them "dreamkeepers" because of their ability to enable their students to keep their dreams alive. She concludes her book by asserting her belief and hope that "if we can dream it, we can surely do it."[6] Similarly, Mike Rose argues that our criticism of public schools has become "one-dimensional . . . the humanity drained from it." In his contribution to a critique that "encourages both dissent and invention, fury and hope,"[7] Rose sets out on a journey to document the successes of public education. His rich descriptions of classrooms across the country highlight the greatest strengths of our efforts. It is in the voices of students and teachers—heard in works such as these—that an alternative vision of education can be found. Because these voices are often not easily heard through traditional positivistic research, the field of the sociology of education has begun to shift as well.

Viewed through a sociological lens, an analysis of contemporary urban education is increasingly an analysis of tensions, contradictions, and complexity. While both cities and the students in city schools have always been challenging and important subjects of inquiry, we are at a point in social history that increases this challenge enormously. More specifically, as the bodies of sociological theory for understanding cities become more complex, so too do the geographic and demographic structures of the cities themselves. As we begin to focus our theoretical frameworks more closely on making connections between the local and the global and the individual and the structural, these connections and characteristics become even more confounding.

CHANGING URBAN STRUCTURE

According to the U.S. Census, the proportion of people living in urban areas in the United States has been steadily increasing over the past fifty years.[8] Indeed, American cities—like cities everywhere—have been expanding and increasing in population and size since the end of World

War II. But as the cities change, so too do the ways in which we define them. To be sure, the definition of "urban" has never been simple or straightforward.

Urbanicity is perhaps most often discussed in terms of numbers. Frequently, this simply means population levels, with those of a certain size being deemed urban. Other distinctions have been based on population densities, with figures ranging from 1,000 to 10,000 persons per square mile serving as the line of demarcation. Although this type of analysis is important for many types of sociological inquiry that examine cities in broad scope, Louis Wirth, in a now classic discussion of the topic, notes its arbitrariness. He argues that this way of defining cities does not account for many of their significant social characteristics, and that attention to the many particularities of urban areas is necessary. With that in mind, he contends that "for sociological purposes a city may be defined as a relatively large, dense, and permanent settlement of socially heterogeneous individuals."[9] The result of this particular social structure, in his view, is the replacement of primary-group relationships with more impersonal, secondary relations, leading to lives more solitary and isolated than those of non–city dwellers.

In a response to Wirth's article, Herbert Gans makes an important, further distinction between "inner city," "outer city," and "suburban." He notes that Wirth's analysis seems to apply only to those residents of the inner city—the area that surrounds the central business district. It neglects the surrounding residential areas (or, the outer city) and the less population-dense suburbs. Gans notes both the importance of and difficulty in distinguishing between these different types of areas, because it may be economics, interpersonal relations, or something else entirely that sets them apart.[10]

Researchers must make distinctions somewhere, however, and in such instances, the criteria used by the U. S. Census are of some value. The Bureau of the Census defines "urban" as any area populated by 2,500 people or more. Clearly, this definition is still too vague to be of use to the sociologist studying urban education, but the broader Census category of "Metropolitan Statistical Area" (or MSA) is useful and applicable in this context. This refers to a city with 50,000 or more inhabitants or an urbanized area (defined by the Census bureau) with at least 50,000 inhabitants and a total metropolitan population of 100,000 (or 75,000 in New England). Using these criteria, "urban" can be understood as the central city of the MSA, suburban as the towns and cities outside of the central city, but still within the MSA. Any area outside of an MSA is considered rural.

The use of the Census category "MSA" is particularly relevant at this point in social history because it more fully captures a very significant shift in our city structures—the development of the megalopolis. As Robert Fishman notes, the largest cities at the beginning of the twentieth century typically measured one hundred square miles. The "new city" (the megalopolis) generally covers up to three thousand square miles. Encompassing both urban centers and suburban neighborhoods, these cities lack "what gave shape and meaning to every urban form of the past: a dominant single core and definable boundaries."[11] The difficulty in defining "urban," combined with this dramatic change in city structure, presents a great challenge to researchers. The city is no longer definable by geographic boundaries. Instead, it must be understood within the context of the surrounding region, which typically has characteristics quite distinct from the urban core.

The decentralization of cities, particularly evident in North America, is simultaneous with the gradual loss of the economic and political importance of the urban core (or "inner city").[12] The implications for urban education are enormous, as attention and resources shift away from the "city proper" and are dispersed to more affluent suburbs. Englert notes that this type of change results in a "severe concentration of poverty and social isolation of the inner-city from the mainstream of American life."[13] As more affluent residents depart for the outlying suburbs, the economy of the city becomes even more depressed. As a result, tax-supported services—such as schools—are at a great detriment. This is only compounded by problems with crime and violence, which are more common in cities than in suburbs or rural areas.[14]

As a result of the departure of the middle class from urban areas, some argue, the city is left with an impoverished "underclass." Often, this underclass is discussed in relation to people of color, most often blacks, because residential segregation is such a strong enforcer.[15] Residents of the ghetto, argues W. J. Wilson, have no ties to members of the middle and upper classes, because as individuals (in his analysis, blacks) move up the social ladder, there is an out-migration.[16] The end result is a lack of role models and "feelings of resignation originating from bitter personal experiences and a bleak future."[17] Massey and Denton echo this thought, arguing that "what set ghetto blacks apart from other Americans was not their lack of fealty to American ideals but their inability to accomplish them."[18] This concentration of "poor and minority children in inferior inner-city schools," it is argued, makes it difficult "for urban schools to respond effectively to the altered social context."[19]

Alternative analyses of urban life portray the city as space that is essentially at the mercy of dominant interests. For instance, Stephen Haymes argues that consumer capitalism "imposes structures of meaning on black narratives, consequently regulating how blacks come to know who they are as blacks."[20] The important aspect that these two perspectives share is the distinction between urban and nonurban, and the consequent weakness of the former when compared to the latter. Clearly, these issues of race and class become issues of power as well.

Another considerable factor related to the characteristics of urban areas is the significant demographic shift in recent years.[21] The almost constant flow of new residents has contributed to the development of the megalopolis, described above. Most recently, the accompanying demographic shift has been characterized by the relative increase in numbers of people of color. Englert, for example, notes that between 1993 and the year 2000, the overall growth rate of the Mexican American population in the United States is expected to be 46%. The growth rate in the African American population is projected to be 23%. In sharp contrast, the white population is expected to increase by only 7%.[22] Kretovics and Nussel paint the following picture of urban demographics:

> The minority population of Washington, DC is 73%; 66% of which are black. Detroit has 79% minorities; 76% of which are black. In these cities there are virtually no white children attending public schools. Those that remain are usually from economically depressed families. . . . Hispanic concentrations are noteworthy in other cities. In New York City, the total minority population is 56.8%; 29% black and the remainder mostly Hispanic. In San Antonio, the minority population is 64% of which 56% is Hispanic. In El Paso, the minority population is 74% of which 69% is Hispanic.[23]

Certainly, a portion at least of this demographic shift stems from increasing immigration—a phenomenon occurring worldwide. OECD reports the United Nations' estimate that, in 1993, "100 million people—almost one in fifty of the world's population—were living outside their native country, double the number in 1990."[24] Because the majority of immigrants arriving today settle in urban areas, cities are experiencing particularly dramatic population shifts.[25] The impact of these changes on one school district is described by Dworkin and colleagues in this volume.

The relationship between immigration and education has historically been a difficult one. As is often the case, schools have been seen as an antidote to the perceived related problems. Toward the end of the nineteenth century, for example, when immigration from non–northwestern European countries was on the rise, American schools took on the task of "Americanization." In 1909, Professor Ellwood P. Cubberley of Stanford University described the new wave of immigrants as "illiterate, docile, lacking in self-reliance and initiative, and not possessing the Anglo-Teutonic conceptions of law, order, and government . . . their coming has served to dilute tremendously our national stock, and to corrupt our civic life."[26] While it would be surprising to hear it in such crass terms today, similar sentiments relating to the need to "American-ize" the immigrant population still exist. The issue of language—a strong indicator of national identity—is a particularly relevant and poignant example of this persistence.

Consider, for example, the debate concerning bilingual education. Conservative supporters of bilingual education do not see it as a means to maintain the ethnic identity of a particular group (as liberal support-ers often do), but rather as "a means to speed the assimilation of non-English speakers."[27] Thus, students are often forced to surrender a vital part of their culture if they are to succeed in school. Similarly, Antonia Darder argues that schools serve to "civilize" marginalized students as they are taught their appropriate roles in the economic hierarchy.[28] They must find a way to mediate the differences between their home culture and the culture of the school in order to negotiate their education with any success. Thus, although the terminology and techniques may have evolved into something a bit more subtle, the "Americanizing" function of primary and secondary schools remains and, as a result, students of color "learn" their roles and experience increasing marginalization from the curriculum.

Bilingual education reforms are but one example of the many reform initiatives that characterize American urban education today. Politicians, policy experts, practitioners, and community members all contribute to the ongoing effort to allow city schools to thrive and suc-ceed. Their energies are directed to all levels, from the notion of a national curriculum to the emphasis on the importance of the individual student's engagement with her work. The following section provides a brief overview of some of these efforts.

CURRENT EDUCATIONAL REFORM

In recent years, a variety of educational reforms have addressed the problems with urban education in various ways. Curriculum, school governance, and teacher training—among others—have each received attention. Public interest in the topic has been increasing, arguably as a result of the release more than a decade ago of "A Nation At Risk: The Imperative for Educational Reform."[29] At the time, the report was the subject of intense media attention, as the "failure" of American schools was brought to our attention. By some estimates, more than six million copies have been circulated through direct distribution and journal reprints.[30] The report continues to receive attention as support for more recent reform initiatives such as Goals 2000 is sought.[31]

The goals laid out in "A Nation at Risk" address a wide range of factors including standards, curriculum, teachers, and school funding. It was a true "clarion call" for this country, appealing to the fears and concerns of public officials, educators, parents, and students. It warned that if something was not done, America was at risk of losing its stature as a world superpower. But the authoring committee's methods of fixing the schools served a particular purpose and, "all in all," Hlebowitsh argues, the report "was more of a political treatise than a thoughtful statement for the reform of American public schools."[32] Nevertheless, it had grabbed the nation's attention and created a framework for understanding educational reform. This framework is still evident in more current reform initiatives such as President Bush's America 2000 and President Clinton's Goals 2000. Both of these are rooted in top-down reform strategies and both, to varying degrees, push for a national curriculum. Despite widespread political support, the notion that standardization of curricula will make education more rigorous for both students and teachers is nevertheless problematic.

Many arguments for a standardized curriculum are clearly tied to those found in "A Nation at Risk"—education must be improved in order to maintain (or improve) this nation's stature. Michael Apple rightly argues that this push must be understood within the larger context if its implications are to be sufficiently appreciated. To be more specific, "a national curriculum and national testing needs to be situated within larger ideological dynamics in which we are seeing an attempt by a new hegemonic bloc to transform our very ideas of what education is." More precisely, Apple notes the current political context that prizes the market over the individual and "in which democracy becomes an economic, not a political, concept and where the idea of the public good withers at its very roots."[33] Indeed, this neoliberal ideology has enormous implications for urban education, some of which deserve attention here.

The call for more clearly defined standards comes simultaneously with a push for decreased federal intervention and increased privatization in schooling. Amy Stuart Wells and Jeannie Oakes refer to this as "simultaneous centralization and decentralization," noting that many believe freeing schools "of bureaucratic constraints while assuring that all students meet the same standards will lead to greater equality of opportunities across schools and districts."[34] At the root of today's reform efforts is the idea that if market principles are applied to education, schools will be forced to improve in order to survive. Most often, this manifests itself in debates concerning school choice, a principle which encompasses vouchers as well as magnet and charter schools.

The debate surrounding school choice is a heated one. The preface to a 1995 issue of *Daedalus*—devoted to the issue of equity in American schools—points out that there is a strong belief that public schools are expendable: "if schools do not quickly measure up to what are perceived to be yesterday's standards, parents will be invited to send their children to private facilities, helped to do so by some form of governmentally-supported voucher system."[35] In contrast, there are many who believe that the market is a biased system which cannot solve social, economic, and educational problems and, in fact, will only increase inequality.[36]

Chubb and Moe are strong supporters of the push for school choice. They, like many other neoconservative theorists and policymakers, see the choice as the impetus to school improvement. Specifically, they assert that

> schools of choice tend to be more informal, professional, and unified around a common mission than regular schools of assignment are. Their teachers are more autonomous, more excited about their work, more influential in decision-making, and happier with their overall situations. Students are more satisfied with their chosen schools; dropout and absenteeism rates are down; achievement scores are up. Parents are better informed, more supportive, and participate more actively.[37]

But as rosy as this picture sounds, critics and skeptics of school choice point to the inherent inequities in a market-driven educational system.

Opponents of school choice worry, for example, about the implications for those students not traditionally served by public education. Jonathan Kozol, for instance, worries that if we "strip away the fancy language" that schools will become "a triage operation that will filter off the fortunate and leave the rest in schools where children of the 'better' parents do not need to see them."[38] As Cookson warns, "markets as power structures are ill-suited to providing the kinds of human services that are needed in a stratified and deeply unequal society."[39]

Roslyn Mickelson (in this volume) draws attention to the importance of recognizing both the dangers and opportunities of one form of privatization—corporate interest in school reform. Through her description of one community's experience with these issues, the ways in which these more macrotrends manifest themselves at the local level become clear. Her analysis reveals that it is not a simple issue, and that it must be examined from all aspects before accepted or dismissed. Indeed, as Amy Stuart Wells (also in this volume) makes clear, the neoliberal agenda of privatization and market-driven policy plays differently in different contexts. Her comparative analysis of charter schools in the United States and grant-maintained schools in England highlights the struggle over the very meaning of these political contexts.

Inherent in many of the school choice reform movements is the idea that individual schools can and should be better-suited to local needs. Local control of schools (or decentralization) can be found in many successful cases including the recent school reform in Chicago. There, political leaders seeking to improve the city's public schools drew on "a well-established network of community-based organizations" and "opted for an unparalleled level of parent and community control."[40] The goal and result was that "the distance between the site of political activity and its consequences was radically reduced. Individual political accountability is now personal, immediate, and sharply drawn."[41] As Mirel notes, "no other reform effort has so clearly targeted the central bureaucracy as the source of the system's educational problems nor has any governance change given so much power to parents to oversee the education of their children."[42] The issue of decentralization, then, is obviously complex and worthy of careful attention.

Two chapters in this volume pay particular attention to issues of local control and reform. The first is a conversation with Ted Mitchell, who serves as advisor to Los Angeles Mayor Richard Riordan on educational matters. His insights into programs such as LA's LEARN (Los Angeles Educational Alliance for Restructuring Now), which emphasizes the importance of local control and school autonomy, bring these issues to a very concrete level. Similarly, a conversation with three former superintendents of schools in Los Angeles about their experiences and thoughts on urban education is presented in another chapter. Their ideas about educational research and practice—based on years of first hand experience as practitioners and policymakers—highlight the importance of critical reflection from the national policy level to the classroom.

Indeed, classroom-level urban educational reform, focused on curricular issues, is a critical component that must not be overlooked. Often, these initiatives take the form of multicultural education, a concept rooted in ideas about teaching students of color that has been expanded to include gender, sexual orientation, and a myriad of other student characteristics.[43] The concept has taken many forms through the years, often according to the political perspective of he or she who is advocating it. Sleeter and Grant, for example, have identified five categories of interpretation, ranging from teaching to bring students into the mainstream to preparing them to question and challenge the status quo.[44] The former is more acceptable to neoconservatives, who advocate a common culture and are therefore often skeptical of (or even adverse to) multicultural movements. The latter is more popular with those who perceive education as a means to social change. Each of these extreme positions is discussed in slightly more detail below.

Norman Podhertz, an early and notable neoconservative, referred to the integration of women and minorities into the curriculum as a "brazen assault on the entire concept of the classics." Furthermore, he called multiculturalism a "'vulgar' plot to undermine Western civilization itself."[45] Similarly, a 1992 article in *National Review* described multicultural education as "a systematic dismantling of America's unitary national identity in response to unprecedented ethnic and racial transformation."[46] According to Dorrien, the very term "multicultural" is rejected by neoconservatives who believe that this type of education is actually a rejection of all culture (i.e., the common culture) in favor of an empty "diversity." Many neoconservatives argue that the addition of these "other" voices overloads educators and thereby threatens the quality of education.

Neoconservative Diane Ravitch makes a distinction between pluralistic and particularistic forms of multiculturalism. Pluralistic multiculturalism, she argues, rejects the notion of the "melting pot" (which essentially erases ethnic differences) and rather emphasizes the idea that "we must listen to a diversity of voices in order to understand our culture, past and present."[47] Particularistic multiculturalism touts the idea of a "national culture," and posits that this culture is comprised of a diverse mix. Multicultural education allows for a richer, broader interpretation of that culture.

Pluralistic multiculturalism is typically acceptable to neoconservatives, who are amenable to highlighting differences and accepting diversity, provided those who are outside the mainstream assimilate and reshape themselves according to hegemonic ideals.[48] As noted above, neoconservatives advocate an "official knowledge" or a common culture to which others should be exposed, maintaining their own culture only for its folkloric character. In this sense, multicultural education does little to empower individuals, and a great deal to create conformity. Perhaps because there is room for such varied reconceptualization, multiculturalism has been criticized for being "mired in liberal ideology" and offering "no radical change to the current order."[49]

As noted above, however, there are numerous other theorists who do not perceive the potential of the curriculum as simply limited to elaboration on a canon. Educational theorists such as Paulo Freire,[50] Michael Apple,[51] and others warn that unless the curriculum encourages critical reflection, students merely serve as depositories of whatever "knowledge" the teacher chooses to impart. The curriculum, according to Apple, should be "a complicated and continual process of environmental design."[52] A concrete illustration can be found in the work of Ladson-Billings, who describes successful teachers in urban schools. Through culturally relevant teaching, she argues, students are empowered "intellectually, socially, emotionally, and politically by using cultural referents to impart knowledge, skills, and attitudes."[53] In order to be effective, the curriculum must be co-constructed, not prescribed from above, as in the case of reform initiatives such as the push for a national curriculum, for example.

What is clear from the initiatives described above is that educational reform is now being approached from a variety of perspectives and on numerous levels. At the national level, standards and testing are proposed as a means of "restoring rigor" to our educational system. At the state and community levels, school choice programs such as vouchers and charter schools are intended to decentralize control of the system. And at the classroom level, new curricula are being explored to engage and empower individual students and teachers. And just as reform efforts recognize and address numerous levels and perspectives, so too do the sociological theories that frame them.

THE NEW SOCIOLOGY OF URBAN EDUCATION

Like much social theory, the sociology of education has adopted and incorporated many of the tenets of what has come to be called postmodernism. As Henry Giroux has articulated, postmodernism is largely a reaction to the modernist notion that there is a referent point (or metanarrative) from which all individuals work and that truth exists independently of these individuals.[54] This idea is challenged by postmodernists as restrictive and totalizing. The claim is that in a diverse society such as ours, the wide range of cultures cannot possibly be explained or guided by a single, absolute truth. Essentially a challenge to the positivistic notion that there is an answer for us to work toward in one correct way, postmodernism has been instrumental in reshaping the direction of the sociology of urban education.

In recent years, sociologists of education have called not only for the incorporation and recognition of both qualitative and quantitative approaches, but also for the bridging of the two.[55] Apple (in this volume), in his in-depth discussion of the theoretical tendencies of the sociology of education in the United States, refers to the bridging of various traditions in theory, noting that "a little trespassing may be a good thing here." Similarly, Raymond Morrow (also in this volume) argues that we must develop a critical theory of methodology in order to allow for critical-emancipatory knowledge. Hence, in both theory and research, the trend toward making connections between what were previously seen as dualisms or oppositional concepts is increasingly common. As Wallerstein explains, "If we are to be serious about utopistics, we must stop fighting about nonissues, and the foremost of these nonissues is determinism versus free will, or structure versus agency, or global versus local, or macro versus micro."[56] Instead, if we are to work toward a more just society, our research must not be limited to one or the other, but dedicated to a broader, more all-encompassing scope.

Hence, the new sociology of education has an important role to play in the improvement of our urban schools. In his chapter included in this volume, for example, Geoff Whitty argues that sociology can and should be used to understand current educational policy. Through an analysis of contemporary social theory and current educational reforms such as school privatization and the reconceptualization of the teaching profession, Whitty argues that "sociologically informed studies of education policy can . . . help to provide lenses which are at some variance with the taken-for-granted assumptions of much contemporary education policy." And it is through these lenses that we may begin to perceive hope and, in turn, change.

Ayers and Ford argue that if city schools are to be improved (in their words, "saved"), we must "create the collective capacity to imagine a dramatically different world, and summon the collective courage to sustain that vision as we work toward making that imagined world real."[57] Indeed, this hope can be found in the voices of students, teachers, and administrators who have the power to bring about the change. This hope can also be found in research that respects these voices and seeks to understand them within a larger context.

Many of the chapters in this volume are presented within the framework of the incorporation of a plurality of voices and the bridging of gaps between research and practice, school and community. For instance, Dworkin and colleagues present an excellent example of the potential for universities to contribute to local school reform. Through their ongoing project assisting school districts with forecasting their changing demography, they have been able to help local school leaders better understand the implications of these important changes. Similarly, Fenning, Wilczynski, and Parraga conclude that if high school violence policies are to be effective and relevant, they must be formulated with a greater degree of input from both parents and students.

In slightly different ways, the chapters from David Keiser and Peter McLaren also give voice to the students of urban schools. Keiser's rich description of his students' lives and writing offers a compelling lens through which to understand the potential of critical pedagogy for combating nihilism in urban schools. Similarly, McLaren offers a thorough analysis of a very particular aspect of many urban students' lives—gangsta rap. Through his labeling of this genre as an oppositional practice, McLaren allows us to more fully understand the connections between the individual, culture, and society in the urban context.

Education is a source of both hope and frustration. Alternately portrayed as saviors and as scapegoats, schools are expected to please the body politic, serve individual students, and often work within unreasonable parameters, with insufficient funding and resources. This is particularly the case with urban schools, where political strength is often minimal, student populations are particularly diverse, and resources are especially scarce. Unless the conditions within these schools are better understood so that all of our students are being served, we will deny them their own successes and deny ourselves this vast and critical resource.

Recent sociological theory provides additional, useful lenses for understanding the issues particular to urban education. With increased attention to individual voice and to understanding the interconnectedness between the individual and society at large, sociologists of education have the potential to contribute to a project aimed at more equitable, just, and rewarding experiences for the students in our urban schools and the creation of more productive and prosperous members of our urban societies.

With this volume we seek to contribute to the evolving conversation surrounding these issues. Through the inclusion of sociological inquiry that is as diverse as it is rigorous, it is our intention to illustrate how critical it is that we begin to view urban education through a more complex and rich set of theoretical and empirical lenses. As we move into the next century, it is imperative that we recognize that it is only from this more comprehensive perspective that the sociology of urban education can sufficiently contribute to the improvement of our cities' schools and the empowerment of our cities' students.

NOTES

1. No terminology that differentiates between ethnic and/or racial categories is wholly acceptable. Ethnic or racial "minority" implies a numerical underrepresentation that is not necessarily accurate; use of the term "nonwhite" implies that "white" is a norm; and the phrase "people of color" implies that white is not, in fact, a color. We have chosen the phrase "people of color," however, because we believe it has greater political poignancy than the alternatives.

2. Laura Lippman et al., *Urban Schools: The Challenges of Location and Poverty* (Washington, D.C.: National Center for Education Statistics [Report 96–184], 1996).

3. H. Kantor and B. Brenzel, "Urban Education and the 'Truly Disadvantaged': The Historical Roots of the Contemporary Crisis, 1945–1990," *Teachers College Record* 94.2 (1992): 278–314.

4. Jonathan Kozol, *Savage Inequalities: Children in America's Schools* (New York: Harper Perennial, 1992).

5. Lippman et al., *Urban Schools*, p. xii.

6. Gloria Ladson-Billings, *The Dreamkeepers: Successful Teachers of African-American Children* (San Francisco: Jossey-Bass, 1994), p. 143.

7. Mike Rose, *Possible Lives* (New York: Houghton Mifflin, 1995), p. 4.

8. U.S. Bureau of the Census, *1990 Census of Population, Social and Economic Characteristics, United States* (Washington, D.C.: U.S. Government Printing Office, 1993).

9. Louis Wirth, "Urbanism as a Way of Life." 1938 essay reprinted in *Metropolis: Center and Symbol of Our Times,* ed. Philip Kasinitz (New York: New York University Press, 1995), p. 64.

10. Herbert J. Gans, "Urbanism and Suburbanism as Ways of Life: A Reevaluation of Definitions," 1991 revision in *Metropolis: Center and Symbol of Our Times,* ed. Philip Kasinitz (New York: New York University Press, 1995), pp. 170–95.

11. Robert Fishman, "Megalopolis Unbound," in *Metropolis: Center and Symbol of Our Times,* ed. Philip Kasinitz (New York: New York University Press, 1995), p. 398.

12. Philip Kasinitz, *Metropolis: Center and Symbol of Our Times* (New York: New York University Press, 1995).

13. Richard M. Englert, "Understanding the Urban Context and Conditions of Practice of School Administration," in *City Schools: Leading the Way,* ed. Patrick B. Forsyth and Marilyn Tallerico (Newbury Park, Calif.: Corwin Press, 1993), p. 20.

14. David C. Berliner and Bruce J. Biddle, *The Manufactured Crisis: Myths, Fraud, and the Attack on America's Public Schools* (Reading, Mass.: Addison-Wesley, 1995).

15. Douglas Massey and Nancy Denton, *American Apartheid: Segregation and the Making of the Underclass* (Cambridge: Harvard University Press, 1993).

16. William J. Wilson, *The Truly Disadvantaged: The Inner City, the Underclass, and Public Policy* (Chicago: University of Chicago Press, 1987) and William J. Wilson, *The Declining Significance of Race* (Chicago: University of Chicago Press, 1980).

17. Wilson, *The Truly Disadvantaged,* p. 159.

18. Massey and Denton, *American Apartheid,* p. 171.

19. Kantor and Brenzel, "Urban Education," p. 29.

20. Stephen Haymes, *Race, Culture, and the City: A Pedagogy for Black Urban Struggle* (Albany: State University of New York Press, 1995), p. 41.

21. Thomas J. La Belle and Christopher R. Ward, *Multiculturalism and Education: Diversity and its Impact on Schools and Society* (Albany: State University of New York Press, 1994).

22. Englert, "Understanding the Urban Context," p. 8.

23. Joseph Kretovics and Edward J. Nussel, *Transforming Urban Education* (Boston: Allyn and Bacon, 1994), p. 44.

24. Mike Duckenfield, *Schools for Cities* (Paris: Organisation for Co-Operation and Economic Development, 1995), p. 14.

25. See, for example, Dennis Carlson, "The Politics of Educational Policy: Urban School Reform in Unsettling Times," *Educational Policy* 7.2 (1993):

149–65 and A. Portes and R. G. Rumbaut, *Immigrant America* (Berkeley: University of California Press, 1990).

26. Lawrence Cremin, *The Transformation of the School* (New York: Vintage Books, 1964), pp. 67–68.

27. J. Citrin, B. Reingold and D. P. Green, "American Identity and the Politics of Ethnic Change," *Journal of Politics* 52.4 (1990): 1126.

28. Antonia Darder, *Culture and Power in the Classroom: A Critical Foundation for Bicultural Education* (Westport, Conn.: Bergin & Garvey, 1991), p. 6.

29. National Commission on Excellence in Education, *A Nation at Risk: The Imperative for Educational Reform.* [On-line.] Available: http://www.ed.gov/pubs/, 1983.

30. G. Holton, "A Nation at Risk Revisited." *Daedalus* 113.4 (1984): 1–27.

31. D. Tanner, "A Nation 'Truly' at Risk." *Phi Delta Kappan* 75.4 (1993): 289–97.

32. P. S. Hlebowitsh, "Playing Power Politics: How *A Nation at Risk* Achieved its National Stature," *Journal of Research and Development in Education* 23.2 (1990): 88.

33. Michael Apple, "The Politics of a National Curriculum," in *Transforming Schools*, ed. Peter W. Cookson Jr. and Barbara Schneider (New York: Garland, 1995), pp. 364–65.

34. Amy Stuart Wells and Jeannie Oakes, "Tracking, Detracking, and the Politics of Educational Reform: A Sociological Perspective," in *The Sociology of Education: Emerging Perspectives*, ed. Carlos A. Torres and T. R. Mitchell (Albany: State University of New York Press, 1998), p. 161.

35. American Academy of Arts and Sciences, "American Education: Still Separate, Still Unequal," *Daedalus*, Fall 1995, p. ix.

36. Gary Orfield and Carole Ashkinaze, *The Closing Door: Conservative Policy and Black Opportunity* (Chicago: University of Chicago Press, 1991).

37. John E. Chubb and Terry M. Moe, *Politics, Markets, and America's Schools* (Washington, D.C.: Brookings Institution, 1990), p. 209.

38. Jonathan Kozol, "The Sharks Move In," *The New Internationalist*, October 1993.

39. P. W. Cookson, *School Choice: The Struggle for the Soul of American Education* (New Haven: Yale University Press, 1994), p. 499.

40. Anthony S. Bryk, David Kerbow, and Sharon Rollow, "Chicago School Reform," in *New Schools for a New Century: The Redesign of Urban Education*, ed. Diane Ravitch and Joseph P. Viteritti (New Haven: Yale University Press, 1997), p. 168.

41. Ibid., p. 169.

42. Jeffrey Mirel, "School Reform, Chicago Style: Educational Innovation in a Changing Urban Context, 1976–1991," *Urban Education* 28.2 (1993): 117.

43. Gloria Ladson-Billings and William F. Tate, "Toward a Critical Race Theory of Education," *Teachers College Record* 97.1 (1995): 47–68.

44. C. E. Sleeter and C. A. Grant, "An Analysis of Multicultural Education in the U.S.A.," *Harvard Educational Review* 57 (1987): 421–44.

45. Gary Dorrien, *The Neoconservative Mind: Politics, Culture, and the War of Ideology* (Philadelphia: Temple University Press, 1993), p. 355.

46. Lawrence Auster, "The Forbidden Topic," *National Review* 44.8 (April 27, 1992): 43.

47. Dorrien, *The Neoconservative Mind*, p. 359.

48. Carlos A. Torres, "State and Education Revisited: Why Educational Researchers Should Think Politically about Education," *Review of Educational Research* 21 (1994): 255–331.

49. Ladson-Billings and Tate, "Toward a Critical Race Theory of Eduation," p. 62.

50. Paulo Freire, *Pedagogy of the Oppressed* (New York, Continuum, 1970).

51. Michael Apple, *Official Knowledge: Democratic Education in a Conservative Age* (New York: Routledge, 1993).

52. Ibid., p. 144.

53. Ladson-Billings, *The Dreamkeepers*, p. 18.

54. See, for example, Henry A. Giroux, *Living Dangerously: Multiculturalism and the Politics of Difference* (New York: Peter Lang, 1993), and Henry A. Giroux (ed.), *Postmodernism, Feminism, and Cultural Politics: Redrawing Educational Boundaries* (Albany: State University of New York Press, 1991).

55. See, for example, Scott Davies, "Leaps of Faith: Shifting Currents in Critical Sociology of Education," *American Journal of Sociology* 100.6 (1995): 1448–78; Hugh Mehan, "Understanding Inequality in Schools: The Contribution of Interpretive Studies," *Sociology of Education* 65 (1992): 1–20; and Immanuel Wallerstein, "Social Science and the Quest for a Just Society," *American Journal of Sociology* 102.5 (1997): 1241–57.

56. Wallerstein, "Social Science and the Quest for a Just Society," p. 1255.

57. W. Ayers and P. Ford (eds.), *City Kids, City Teachers: Reports from the Front Row* (New York: The New Press, 1996), p. 87.

CHAPTER 1

Power, Meaning, and Identity: Critical Sociology of Education in the United States

Michael W. Apple

INTRODUCTION

I trust that it comes as no surprise that answering the question "What is the state of sociology of education in the United States?" is not an easy task. The reasons for this are varied. First, surveying a field is itself an act of cultural production.[1] Like social and cultural activity in general, any field encompasses multiple dynamics, multiple and partly overlapping histories, and is in constant motion. Second, and equally important, what actually *counts* as the sociology of education is a construction. Academic boundaries are themselves culturally produced and are often the results of complex "policing" actions by those who have the power to enforce them and to declare what is or is not the subject of "legitimate" sociological inquiry. Yet, as Bourdieu reminds us, it is the ability to "trespass" that may lead to major gains in our understanding.[2] For these very reasons, I shall construct a picture of the state of sociology of education that is broad and that cuts across disciplinary boundaries—including important work in education in curriculum studies, history, gender studies, cultural studies, postcolonial studies, critical race theory, and so on.

Because of limitations of length, I shall only be able to give a sense of the multiple traditions and the constitutive tensions and agendas that are currently having an impact in the United States. Indeed, *each* of these traditions would require a book length investigation to do justice to the internal controversies and conceptual, empirical, and political assumptions and arguments contained in them.[3]

Further, the development of any field is not linear. Rather, it is characterized by untidiness and unevenness. Thus, what is important in the development of a field are the breaks in which previous traditions are disrupted, displaced, and regrouped under new problematics. It is these breaks that transform the questions to be asked and the manner in which they are answered.[4] In assessing these breaks, in some ways my contribution here by necessity will take the form of something like an enhanced bibliographic essay, in essence a series of snapshots specifying what I take to be particular examples of some of the most interesting work being done. It will also require that I say something about the current political situation in the United States.

MULTIPLE TRADITIONS

There are very real tensions within the multiple traditions of sociology of education in the United States, in part because of the historical trajectory of what might be called the "academic/scientific project." The attempt over time to make sociology of education into something other than "educational sociology"—that is, to gain recognition as a "science"—meant that quantitative, "value-neutral" orientations dominated here in very powerful ways. For some current interpreters, this had a chilling effect on those sociologists of education whose major interest was not a generalizable understanding of all schools but instead the development of thick descriptions of particularities.[5]

It also had other effects, some of which still are embodied as constitutive tensions within the field. Thus, the academic/scientific project:

> also generated the tension between knowledge production, the legitimated activity of the professorate in academe, and knowledge use as exemplified by social intervention to change and improve educational practice. . . . These tensions are at the very heart of rethinking the sociology of education. [Furthermore], questions of how best to understand how education works for different people in various settings, how best to evaluate educational outcomes, and how best to restructure schools to maximize the educational benefits for all students, must now begin with discussions concerning (a) whose knowledge is privileged most . . . and on what basis these competing knowledge bases are constructed . . . and (b) which role (observer vs. [active] participant) is most appropriate for the sociologist to adopt.[6]

In their own attempt to portray how these constitutive tensions are worked through—or ignored—Noblit and Pink point to five traditions existing simultaneously: empirical-analytic, applied policy, interpretive, critical, and postmodern.[7] These, of course, are no more than ideal types, since some of these can at times "trespass" onto the others' terrain. Yet it is the first two that characterize much of the sociology of education in the United States. That this is so is evident in the contents of the "official" journal of the field here, *Sociology of Education*. While the journal is a forum for some of the most technically sophisticated empirical work, and even though in the last decade and a half it has had editors such as Philip Wexler and Julia Wrigley who have themselves been part of the interpretive, critical, or postmodern traditions, it has been much less apt to publish ethnographic, theoretical, and critical material than, say, the *British Journal of Sociology of Education*. It has been an outlet for the empirical-analytic and applied policy perspectives, although more than before there will be an occasional interpretive study. (It would be even more unusual to find a serious article organized around more critical or postmodern frameworks.)

Speaking very generally, then, following a path that first came to wide public attention in the research of Coleman and Blau and Duncan, a large portion of research in the sociology of education continues to focus on the problematics of social stratification and status attainment. Its questions center around "the extent to which students from different social backgrounds have access to school experiences that foster academic and social success and on how success or failure in school affects later life chances."[8]

Further, a considerable portion of sociological research on education in the United States continues to devote its attention as well to systematic attempts at policy initiatives at the federal, state, and local levels, including such areas as the reform of finance, school "restructuring," accountability and assessment, and governance.[9]

Elsewhere, Lois Weis and I have engaged in an analysis of the strengths and weaknesses of these traditions and of the interpretive research that partly grew in response to them.[10] My critical evaluation of their basic orientations remains the same. Therefore, I shall spend less time on them here.[11]

Even though I shall not spend much time discussing the empirical-analytic, applied policy, and interpretive perspectives here, it is important to state that I do not wish to dismiss these traditions. Take the first two as examples. Weis and I have raised crucial theoretical, political, and empirical questions about their agendas—for example, their equating of socioeconomic status (SES) with class, their focus on the atomistic individual, their sometimes acritical stance on multiple relations of power, their vision of the disinterested researcher, their neglect of what actually counts as school knowledge and of cultural politics in general, their tendency to ignore or radically simplify issues of the state, and their neglect of what actually happens in the daily lives of teachers and students inside and outside of schools.[12] Yet, having said this, it is still crucial that we recognize the importance of their analytic and empirical sophistication.

All too many critical and postmodern researchers, for example, have too easily assumed that *any* statistical questions and representations by definition must be positivist, thereby giving over this terrain to conservatives or to methodological "experts for hire" who lend their technical expertise to any policy group willing to pay for it. This has proven to be disastrous in terms of our ability to raise and answer critical questions about the large-scale effects of the conservative reconstruction of education. It has also led to a partial deskilling of an entire generation of critically oriented researchers who, when confronted with quantitative analyses, simply reject them out of hand or do not have the analytic skills to deconstruct and criticize their specific arguments or their technical competence. While I have no wish at all to return to the days of unbridled positivism (there were *reasons* for the decades of critiques against it), we may need to take much more seriously the losses that accompanied the largely progressive move toward, say, qualitative work.

Having raised these cautions, however, I shall devote the rest of this article to recent developments within what I take to be some the most interesting movements in the sociology of education that have occurred following the breaks with the dominant traditions. I shall begin with a discussion of representative examples within the sociology of curriculum and its concern with the politics of meaning. In essence, the issue of the politics of meaning will be the thread that guides my entire analysis of the recent development of certain tendencies in the field and of the breaks that have been made. In order to accomplish this, I shall then take up work on critical discourse analysis, identity politics, political economy and the labor process, and racial formation. Finally, I shall conclude with a discussion of the continuing tensions within and between the critical and postmodern communities methodologically, conceptually, and politically.

OFFICIAL KNOWLEDGE AND POPULAR CULTURE

In the Noblit and Pink statement quoted above, a major question they point to is "Whose knowledge is privileged most and on what basis [are] these competing knowledge bases constructed." This involves complex issues of cultural politics, of the relationship between cultural legitimacy and state regulation, and of the power/knowledge nexus. It has also involved tensions between different models of understanding these issues from neo-Marxist, world-system, and poststructural/postmodern perspectives. In the sociology of curriculum, the relationship between culture and power has continued to receive considerable attention, with what counts as "official knowledge" being one of the foci and what does *not* receive the imprimatur of legitimacy also being subject to attention. Thus, the tradition represented in *Knowledge and Control* in the United Kingdom[13] and first articulated in coherent form in *Ideology and Curriculum* in the United States[14] has been widened and deepened, not only both in its scope and sophistication but in the number of ways in which the relationship between knowledge and power is interrogated. One of the prime emphases has been on that most common "pedagogic device," the textbook and other commodities actually found in classrooms. Influenced in part by Basil Bernstein's work on the processes of "recontextualization" of knowledge,[15] by the long European and American traditions of sociological studies of culture, and by newer models of textual analysis, considerably more sophisticated investigations of the political economy of texts (of various sorts), of the form and content of knowledge, and of readers' constructions of meanings have been produced.[16]

These issues have been examined historically in Teitelbaum's exceptional analysis of the development of socialist alternatives to the knowledge that was declared by the state to be official knowledge.[17] Olneck's series of studies on the symbolic crusade of "Americanization" and its influence on what was taught and on the larger politics of what schools were to do are very useful here.[18] David Labaree's investigation of class politics, credential markets, differentiated course offerings, and the contradictory pressures on schools provides an insightful discussion of the connections between curricular organization and larger political struggles in the development of secondary schools.[19] A growing concern with the role of the state is evident as well in Apple's treatment of the growth of state intervention into the process of the regulation, organization, and control of knowledge in textbooks. Here the activist state is seen as the contradictory result of social movements organized around class and race antagonisms and around regional politics.[20]

While a focus on textbooks as the embodiment of official knowledge is but one example of a much larger concern for the politics of culture in schools, there are a number of reasons why such things have been seen as important. First, textbooks and other curriculum material provide levers to pry loose the complex connections among economy, politics (especially the state), and culture. They are *simultaneously* commodities produced for sale, representations of what powerful groups have defined as legitimate knowledge that are at least partly regulated by the state, and they speak to ongoing struggles over cultural legitimacy. In the absence of an officially recognized national curriculum, though there are such proposals now being argued for,[21] they provide the material basis for the construction of legitimate content and form in schools. Further, they are the results of hegemonic and counterhegemonic relations and social movements involving multiple power relations, including but not limited to race, class, gender/sexuality, and religion.[22] Finally, they are subject to processes of interpretation as they are used and read by teachers, students, parents, and other community members. Thus, they are subject to multiple readings—in dominant, negotiated, or oppositional ways—depending on their form and content, the ways they position the reader, and on the person doing the reading.[23] In this way, such material provides one of the best examples for illuminating what Richard Johnson has called the circuit of cultural production.[24]

Yet the analysis of official knowledge has not only proceeded along such "critical" lines. Part of the research agenda in the sociology of curriculum has centered around a more world-system perspective. Thus, John Meyer and his colleagues have argued that most critical sociological studies of educational systems and of their curricula have overly emphasized the determining role of specific national or local needs and interests, assuming too readily that the curriculum "reflects" particular social histories, problems, and requirements that are the embodiments of entrenched powers. While recognizing that such research has contributed a good deal to our understanding of the relationship between power and school knowledge, Meyer and his colleagues emphasize the worldwide power of the idea of modernity as a distinctive project or vision.[25] In Meyer's words, "the overall structure of this vision—organized around great conceptions of the nation-state as moving toward progress and justice—is entrenched on a worldwide basis. Both the nation-state model, and the particular professions that define the nature and content of mass education within this model, have had worldwide hegemony throughout the modern period."[26]

Thus, for the tradition that Meyer and his colleagues wish to advance, the characteristics of mass education, and especially the curriculum in nations throughout most regions of the world, reflect worldwide forces. Local determinants and interests "tend to be filtered through such wider world cultural forces." For this very reason, the general outline of mass education and the curricula found in most nations are remarkably homogeneous around the world.[27]

This kind of approach is partly flawed by its unfortunate stereotyping and lack of knowledge of some of the best work within the more critical tradition, by its neglect of national and international class relations, and by its treatment of the state in undertheorized ways. Yet Meyer's analyses do raise a number of interesting issues about the internationalization of ideological visions that may cut across political economies.

Though less theoretically elegant than, say, Basil Bernstein's formulations, it is similar in some ways to Bernstein's emphasis in his later work on the similarities of pedagogic devices across economic systems.[28]

A third tendency represented in the United States is that organized around poststructural and postmodern forms of analysis of the power/knowledge nexus. Grounded in anti-essentializing tendencies, in a mistrust both of "grand narratives" and of calls for "emancipatory" curricula and pedagogy, and in broadening the traditional concern with particular kinds of power relations (in particular class, but also gender and race), these kinds of arguments have become increasingly influential. For example, Ellsworth's (1989) analysis of the politics of meaning and pedagogy in a college classroom[29] and of the ways in which multiple relations of power are constructed in that specific site, draws heavily on postmodern and feminist poststructural theories of multiplicity and difference. It suggests that previous critically oriented curricula and teaching smuggled in hidden assumptions about power as a zero-sum game that in actuality served to reproduce existing hierarchies and continued to privilege particular kinds of knowledge and experience centered around the power/knowledge relations of the academy and largely white, male, heterosexual assumptions.

This was an important intervention into the debate over "the" emancipatory project in critical educational activity, one that generated considerable debate.[30] Also representative of some of these tendencies is Popkewitz, who employs one particular reading of a Foucaultian approach to the study of the politics of educational reform and the relationship between power and knowledge.[31] While I have a number of concerns about what is lost as well as gained in the recent turn to postmodern and poststructural theories—for example, the tendency by *some* postmodernists and poststructuralists to see *any* focus on political economy and class relations to be somehow reductive, to analyze the state as if it floats in thin air,[32] to expand the linguistic turn until it encompasses everything, to embrace overly relativistic epistemological assumptions, and the stylistic arrogance of some of its writing[33]—and shall say more about this later on in this essay, it is important to note the emerging emphasis on these approaches and to recognize that there are a number of advances in them.

By and large, the orientations to curricula I have just discussed see official knowledge in two general ways. In the first, it is seen as the commodified result of a complex historical and political process in which particular knowledge, ways of knowing, and perspectives are made available. Hence, "legitimate" culture is seen as an object. In the second, culture is seen as lived.[34] A lived curriculum, a curriculum-in-use, that embodies multiple and contradictory power relations is produced in the bodily and linguistic interactions among texts, students, and teachers in educational institutions and between these institutions and other sites. Among the most significant ways of understanding such productions is critical discourse analysis, which is itself the result of the tensions, and sometimes the merger, of the interpretive, critical, and often poststructural tendencies I noted.

CRITICAL DISCOURSE ANALYSIS

Like sociolinguistics and ethnomethodology, critical discourse analysis begins with the assumption that language plays a primary role in the creation of meaning and that language use must be studied in social context, especially if we are interested in the politics of meaning. In a manner similar to interpretive research, it sees human subjects as constantly engaged in the negotiation of knowledge, social relations, and identity. However, it goes well beyond "mainstream" ethnographic research in that its primary focus is on how power, identity, and social relations are negotiated, are legitimated, and are contested toward political ends. In Luke's words, "Such an analysis attempts to establish how textual constructions of knowledge have varying and unequal material effects, and how these constructions that come to 'count' in institutional contexts are manifestations of larger political investments and interests."[35]

The focus here is on "systematic asymmetries of power and resources." Such asymmetries between speakers and listeners and between, say, writers and readers are then linked to the processes of the production and reproduction of stratified economic and political (in the broadest sense) interests. In essence, discourse in institutional life is viewed in a particular way. It is seen as "a means for the naturalization and disguise of power relations that are tied to inequalities in the social production and distribution of symbolic and material resources."[36]

Speaking broadly, Luke puts it this way.

> This means that dominant discourses in contemporary cultures tend to represent those social formations and power relations that are the products of history, social formation and culture (e.g., the gendered division of the workforce and domestic labor, patterns of school achievement by minority groups, national economic development) as if they were the product of organic, biological and essential necessity. By this account, critical discourse analysis is a political act itself—an intervention in the apparently natural flow of talk and text in institutional life that attempts to 'interrupt' everyday commonsense.[37]

The Bakhtinian influences here should be clear. Behind this position is the sense that critical discourse analysis should be involved in the destabilization of "authoritative discourse."[38] In the process, its task is to place at the very center of attention relations of domination, subordination, and inequality.[39]

This critical moment in critical discourse analysis is accompanied by a positive or constructive moment as well. Unlike some of the more aggressively postmodern positions that even deny its existence, one of the major aims of such critical research is to "generate agency." It wishes to provide tools to students, teachers, and others that enable them to see "texts"[40] as embodying both particular "representations"[41] of the social and natural world and particular interests. It wants to enable people to understand how such "texts" position them and at the same time produce unequal relations of institutional power that structure classrooms, staffrooms, and educational policies.[42]

Thus, some of these analyses are not only concerned with the active production of institutional power through a particular politics of meaning-making. They are also concerned with the ways in which knowledge is reconfigured, how new meanings are produced that challenge institutional regimes of power, not only in the classroom but in the structuring of daily economic and political relations. To take but one classroom example, in an insightful study Dyson analyses how young children in an urban primary school who are learning how to read and write construct and reconstruct stories to reveal and transform images of gender and power in their classrooms. The children constantly mediated and transformed images of gender relations that did not stand alone, but "were interwoven with race, class, and physical demeanor."[43] They reworked the material of the official curriculum and reworked material from popular culture (e.g., "superheroes" such as Ninja Turtles and the X-Men) that usually privileged male-dominated meanings and relations in ways that provided the possibility for counterhegemonic roles to be established in their classrooms.

There are many strengths in these kinds of approaches to the study of the politics of knowledge in schools, not the least of which is the activist component that takes a position on one of the tensions Noblit and Pink noted are deeply ingrained in the sociology of education in the United States. Yet there are a number of cautions that need to be taken seriously. Seeing the world as a "text" has a number of dangers if taken too far. It can lead to the neglect of the gritty materiality of the social world, of the materiality of the state, economy, and class/race/gender relations. It can ultimately embody what Whitty earlier called a "romantic possibilitarianism" in which changes in meaning and consciousness are the "new engines" of social transformation.[44] And it can make everything into a discursive construction.[45] On the other hand, used well such a research agenda and perspective can be extremely insightful in illuminating and acting on the complexities of the relationships between power and meaning in education.

The continuing attempt to think through the complex issue of the socio/cultural "determinants" of commodified and lived culture is not limited to official knowledge or discursive relations in schools. In fact, some of the most insightful advances have occurred in the area of popular culture. Though Giroux has recently called for more attention to be paid to popular culture,[46] an interest in this area predates this recognition and some of the best of current work goes well beyond his call in analytic and empirical sophistication.

Perhaps the best example of such work is Weinstein's analysis of the ways the "texts" of popular culture at a popular tourist museum are produced, made available, and then "read" by youth.[47] This investigation takes Johnson's earlier intuitions about the circuit of cultural production and Willis' interrogation of the multiple uses of popular culture to a new level by examining the processes by which culture is constructed, deconstructed, and "performed."[48] Its integration of material in cultural studies, political economy, and critical poststructuralist theory enables Weinstein to give us an analysis both of the ways in which popular culture is produced and consumed and of the sense-making practices of youth in and out of schools. Koza's recent discussion of rap music in schools and the larger society is also useful here,[49] as is Giroux's deconstruction of the popular cultural productions of Walt Disney.[50]

IDENTITY POLITICS AND SOCIAL MOVEMENTS

The intuitions that lie behind critical discourse analysis and the study of the politics of official and popular culture also underpin the recent growth of interest in various forms of narrative research in the United States. These include life histories, oral histories, autobiographies, largely feminist or antiracist "testimonies," work on popular memory, and narrative interviews. These approaches are distinctly interdisciplinary. While socially critical in intent, they selectively integrate elements from literary, historical, anthropological, psychological, sociological, and cultural studies.

As Casey documents in her recent review of such narrative approaches, what links these together is again a powerful interest in the ways people make meaning through language. While tracing out the history and contradictions of narrative research in education, and being duly cautious of some of its possible roots in the "bourgeois subject" and in the new middle-class's seeming infinite need for self-display, Casey demonstrates how such social and cultural research attempts to defy "the forces of alienation, anomie, annihilation, authoritarianism, fragmentation, commodification, depreciation, and dispossession."[51] In her words, those forms of narrative research that are culturally and politically *committed* "announce 'I am'('we are')."[52] Perhaps one of the best examples of such work is her own research on the collective biographies of politically active women teachers engaged in struggles over curricula, teaching, and larger relations of power inside and outside of schools.[53]

The issue of "I am" ("we are") speaks directly to the study of identity politics. While Casey's synthetic review of the emergence of narrative approaches is largely devoted to methodological and political issues, a considerable portion of the newest critical sociocultural work deals with the role of the school as a site for the production of identities. Here too there are benefits and problems. The poststructural emphasis on identity politics is visible in a number of areas, with for example Bromley arguing for much more attention to be paid to it and Wexler criticizing its evacuation of class dynamics as *the* primary determinant of identity formation.[54]

Wexler's ethnographic study of the "moral economy" of identity creation in different American secondary schools is a partial return to structural forms of analysis by him, but still within a partly poststructural understanding.[55] His argument that class is primary in the production of student identities is provocative, but his volume is too brief to fully develop his arguments about this. It is not just the issue of brevity that has been a concern here. Lois Weis, whose own research on the politics of identity formation provides important connections among political economy, identity in gender, class, and race terms, and social movements,[56] has raised a number of cautions about the centering of class as *the* fundamental dynamic.[57]

Weis's argument about Wexler's position is instructive in this regard. Both have some major concerns about the loss of a structural understanding of identity formation within some of the recent poststructural material. Yet, for Weis, rather than seeing race and gender as things that students bring in after their identities are structured in class terms by schools, the very structure of these institutions compellingly reflects raced and gendered—as well as classed—practices that are deeply implicated in identity formation.[58] I have sympathy with both positions here. It is unfortunate but clear that all too often class relations have been marginalized in much of the recent work on identity politics, in part because a concern with it is seen as somehow "too reductive." This position speaks more to the researcher's unfamiliarity with the best of class analysis and of the ways we might think through the contradictory tensions both within class and among multiple relations of power with class being one of them, than to the necessarily reductive nature of a concern with class itself. There is a world of difference between taking class as seriously as it deserves and reducing everything down to it.[59]

The Wexler/Weis discussion points to an important movement in the multiple critical communities within the sociology of education in the United States. It speaks to an attempt to widen the dynamics of power considered important, to look at the contradictory histories and relations within and among them, and at the same time to not ignore class dynamics—when thought about more elegantly—as truly constitutive.[60] In my mind, this is a crucial movement. There is perhaps a widening divide epistemologically, empirically, and at times politically between the "neos" and the "posts," with unfortunate stereotypes on both sides. Some of this is caused by, but not limited to, the rejectionist impulses, partial loss of historical memory, overstatements, and stylistic peculiarities of some postmodern and poststructural writings and some of it is caused by an overly defensive attitude on the part of some neo-Marxists.[61] In the midst of this, however, a tendency has begun to grow that seeks to let these traditions "rub against each other." The attempt is to let each one correct the emphases of the other and to see the tensions caused by their differences as *productive*—always provided that there is a clear political commitment behind each and always provided that the interest is not cynically deconstructive only.

Let me say more about this, since I believe it provides a context for one of the more significant breaks that I noted earlier were important. There have been attempts at combining neo-Marxist (specifically neo-Gramscian) and poststructural theories together. Thus Bruce Curtis, in a book that should be required reading for anyone involved in the history and sociology of education, integrates these two perspectives to illuminate the complex politics of state formation and the growth of school bureaucracies over time.[62] He examines the collective biographies of the groups of people who populated the newly emerging state, demonstrates the power of the conflicts over meaning and control and over the local and the more global, and insightfully shows the ethical and political nature of the search for centralization, standardization, and efficiency.

Perhaps some of my own recent works can also be useful here in providing an instance of the search for more integrative strategies. In *Cultural Politics and Education*, I demonstrate how a neo-Gramscian perspective—with its focus on the state, on the formation of hegemonic blocs, on new social alliances and the generation of consent, all within an economic crisis—and poststructuralism—with its focus on the local, on the formation of subjectivity, identity, and the creation of subject positions—can creatively work together to uncover the organizational, political, and cultural struggles over education.[63]

This work analyzes how authoritarian populist social movements are formed during a time of economic and ideological crisis and when the state engages in "policing" official knowledge. By examining a textbook controversy in a polarized local community undergoing an economic crisis and changes in class relations, it demonstrates how people can be pushed into rightist identities through their interactions with the state. Research such as this represents not only an attempted integration of neo and post positions, but an extension and reorientation of the material involving identity politics so that it focuses on the formation of *oppositional* identities and oppositional politics—the growth of rightist social movements.

In *Social Analysis of Education*, Wexler urged critical sociological work in education to devote more of its attention to the formation and power of social movements.[64] These social movements—both emergent and residual[65]—provide crucial elements in determining the stability and instability of the policies and practices involved in curricula, teaching, and evaluation and of beliefs about schooling, the state, and the economy in general. This insight is what has been taken up in work on the dialectical relationship between conservative cultural, religious, and economic movements on the one hand and schooling on the other. Struggles over schooling both participate in the formation of oppositional social and religious movements and are the subjects of these social and religious movements.

The research on the role of struggles over meaning in the formation of authoritarian populist movements represented in my own work is an attempt to take these issues seriously. It argues that most analyses of "the Right" assume (wrongly) a number of things. Too often they assume a unitary ideological movement, seeing it as a relatively uncontradictory group rather than a complex assemblage of different tendencies, many of which are in a tense and unstable relationship with each other. Even more importantly, many analyses also take "the Right" as a fact, as a given. This takes for granted one of the most important questions that needs to be investigated. How does the Right get *formed*? Thus, this research demonstrates how conflicts over state supported schooling—in particular the struggle over official knowledge and over the bureaucratic state—can lead to the formation of rightist movements that combine authoritarian populist religious elements (which in the United States are growing extremely powerful) and economic conservatism. In essence, oppositional political and cultural identities are formed among community members in interaction with local institutions such as schools, identities that are sutured into conservative movements in powerful ways.[66]

The Gramscian moment—his dictum that one must look to the role of commonsense in the formation of ideologies that organize and disorganize "a people"—is more than a little visible here in these analyses, as are the poststructuralist moments surrounding issues of identity and subjectivity. It is here where the sociology of curriculum and theories of state formation meet the sociology of identity, where a concern with the politics of meaning and the formation of new conservative hegemonic blocs meets the realities of the formation of subject positions and identity at a local level.

While I have focused on the building of oppositional identities and social movements, in no way do I wish to slight the research on identity politics inside schools in the lives of students and teachers. Although some of this research, like other elements of the postmodern and poststructural positions, is at times in danger of underplaying the very real structurally generated conditions of this society, as my comments on the Wexler/Weis positions indicate important work indeed is being done on the role of the school as a site of contested student and teacher identities along multiple dynamics such as race, class, gender, sexuality, and ability. Perhaps some of the best places to turn for examples of such research is in work by McCarthy and Crichlow, Weis and Fine, and Fine, Weis, and Wong.[67] Of considerable interest here as well is Bourgois, a detailed and sensitive study of the complex educational, economic, and personal lives of Latino drug dealers.[68] These issues are not only related to questions such as "I am" ("we are") among students, but also have surfaced in important ways in terms of the identities of researchers as classed, raced, gendered, sexed, and differently abled people as well, though at times in ways that again marginalize class issues a bit too much.[69]

POLITICAL ECONOMY AND THE LABOR PROCESS

The fact that there has been a growing interest in cultural politics and in the area of identity politics and an increasing influence (some of it warranted and some of it rather too trendy) of poststructuralist/postmodern theories and cultural studies does not mean that research on issues surrounding political economy and the labor process have not also had a significant presence. Exactly the opposite is the case.

Even though neo-Marxist sociology of education—especially the sociology of curriculum—advanced fairly sophisticated arguments against the reductive tendencies in base/superstructure models and developed alternatives to them, the current neoliberal attempts at reorganizing schooling around its ideological and economic agenda has stimulated a return to an emphasis on economic arguments. At times, this has meant a "return" in negative ways. That is, the material sounds not unlike the positions of an earlier generation influenced by Bowles and Gintis, *Schooling in Capitalist America*.[70] In this situation, there has been something of a loss of collective memory of the very real conceptual and empirical advances that were made surrounding such issues as the dialectical and contradictory relationships among the economic, political, and cultural spheres, on the nature of the state, on the "relative autonomy" of cultural practices, and so on.[71]

Yet, at other times, the reemergence of political economy has been accomplished through the incorporation of some of the best newer material in critical urban studies and on the social organization of class and race in spatial terms. Thus, Rury and Mirel provide an insightful discussion of the political economy of urban education that draws on David Harvey's analysis of the transformations of the political geography of space in advanced capitalism.[72] This is crucial. Rury and Mirel demonstrate how previous traditions of analyzing urban contexts are weakened in the extreme by their inability to situate the transformations of cities in the histories of class and race dynamics and by their lack of sophistication in *political* economy.[73]

A return to political economy,[74] and an increasing focus on the tensions and conflicts related to the crisis in the paid labor market and in income distribution, is also visible elsewhere. Thus, there have been comparisons of the claims made by neoliberals about the connections between schooling and the economy with demographic evidence about the current and future structuring of paid employment and the distribution of benefits. They show that such claims are at best based on very shaky evidence and at worst are simply incorrect.[75]

At the same time, approaches based on political economy have been used with counterintuitive results. For example, Gintis has recently argued in support of particular marketized voucher and choice plans for schools. He claims that there are political and economic justifications for such marketized initiatives, when they are incorporated into a larger program for the redistribution of economic assets.[76] As you would imagine, this suggestion has proven to be exceptionally contentious. It may document the fact that critical studies in the political economy of education may lead to surprising results. Or it may signify the loss of faith in democratic socialist alternatives among a number of scholars who were leaders in the early years of the political economy of education. It is not totally clear at this time which direction this kind of analysis will take. My own position is that such arguments may ultimately lend support to those marketized initiatives proposed under the conservative restoration that expressly *do not* have economically redistributive ends.

While analyses of political economy have once again gained momentum—in part stimulated by the evident crisis and the climate of conservative triumphalism here—there has also been a continuation and deepening of research on the labor process of teaching. This has followed up, expanded, corrected, and made more empirically substantial previous research on intensification, deskilling, reskilling, the contradictions of professionalism, and the daily lives of teachers.

Gitlin and Margonis may serve as an example here.[77] Taking account of previous work on intensification, resistance, and the contradictory elements of "good sense" and "bad sense" in teachers' understanding of their daily practices,[78] and situating their work within the past efforts at understanding the classed and gendered nature of teaching,[79] they examine the processes by which teachers interpret administrative attempts at "school reform." Gitlin and Margonis engaged in an intensive study of a site-based management reform and teachers' resistance to it. They demonstrate how what they call "first wave" research on such reforms and second wave investigators fundamentally misconstrue what is happening.[80] Both of these groups of social researchers "overlook the good sense embodied in teachers' resistant acts, which often point to the fundamental importance of altering authority relations and intensified work conditions."[81]

While there indeed is a recognition that teaching is a gendered occupation in Gitlin and Margonis, as Acker notes in her important synthesis of the literature on gender and teachers' work in the United States, Canada, the United Kingdom, Australia, and elsewhere, the increase in feminist scholarship in education over the past three decades has led to a significant body of recent work that makes gender central to the study of teaching.[82] She cautions us about the dangers of employing simple dichotomies (male/female) and urges us to think through the complexity that lies at the heart of teaching. Thus, there is a growing recognition here that not only do we need to integrate class and race into our discussions of gender, but we need to recognize the diversity *within* each of these groups. The research challenge facing those interested in teachers' work is clear in Acker's words: "how to keep gender considerations paramount, while simultaneously deconstructing the concept of teacher and still managing to achieve some generalizability about teachers' work."[83]

While less overtly connected to political economy and to studies of the labor process, the complexities of the racial structuring of teaching have provided important insights into the historical and current construction of teaching around racial dynamics.[84] Further, Ladson-Billings's recent ethnographic study of racial dynamics at the level of teaching and curricula—a study that highlights the potential of socially committed, largely African American, teachers to connect with students of color—gives us a sense of possibility in a literature that is too often characterized by a sense of defeat.[85]

RACIAL FORMATIONS

My previous section concluded with a statement about race and teaching. Yet it would be hard to overstate the constitutive role played by overt and covert racial dynamics historically and currently in the construction of teaching, evaluation, official knowledge, popular culture, identities, economic divisions, public policy, and the state itself in the United States. A sociology of education that does not recognize this lives in a world divorced from reality. For race is not an "add on." The realities and predicaments of people of color are neither additions to nor defections from American life. Rather, they are *defining* elements of that life.[86] In Omi and Winant's words, in what is considered to be one of the most impressive analyses of race and the state in the United States, "Concepts of race structure both state and civil society. Race continues to shape both identities and institutions in significant ways."[87]

Race is not a stable category. What it means, how it is used, by whom, how it is mobilized in social discourse, its role in educational and more general social policy—all of this is contingent and historical. Of course, it is misleading to talk of race as an "it." "It" is not a thing, a reified object that can be tracked and measured as if it were a simple biological entity. Race is a set of fully social relations.[88]

If race is not a thing, but what critical cultural analysts have called a "performance," neither is it an innocent concept. Real people's histories and collective memories, languages, and futures are at stake here. Understanding what race is and does has required a multidisciplinary approach including studies of popular culture, literature, the state, national and international political and economic structures, and the cultural politics of imperialism and postcolonialism, to name but a few areas.[89]

In fact, it has become abundantly clear that much of the conservative discourse about education—the supposed decline in standards, the call for a return to the "Western tradition," a reassertion of toughness and discipline, the call for privatization and marketization—lies a vision of "the Other." It symbolizes an immense set of anxieties, including cultural and economic ones, that are used to build a new hegemonic alliance around conservative policies.[90]

The increasing circulation of racial subtexts is heightened by the visibility of racist and racial discourse in the popular media and in (supposedly) academic books that receive widespread publicity. The recent popularity of the genetic arguments found in Herrnstein and Murray's volume, *The Bell Curve* (of which nearly 400,000 copies were sold) is an indication of this phenomenon.[91] This has occasioned a series of critical interrogations of its conceptual, empirical, and social assumptions and of the historical reasons behind its wide circulation and acceptance as plausible.[92] The fact that there have been a considerable number of such engaged critical social and historical analyses of positions such as Herrnstein and Murray's provides yet another example of the critical sociologist as "public intellectual" during a time of conservative restorational politics.

The growing acceptance of genetic arguments about race or of conservative restorational positions in general has led to even greater emphasis on the issue of the politics of race in the sociology of education, especially on the issue of "whiteness," that bears on my earlier discussion of identity. An assumption that has underpinned much of the research on racial identity is the belief that "white racial hegemony has rendered whiteness invisible or transparent."[93] Thus, whiteness becomes the unarticulated normative structure. It becomes so naturalized that "European-Americans" do not even have to think about "being white." It becomes the absent presence, the "there that is not there." As Roman puts it, race becomes a "reified synonym" that is applied only to racially subordinate groups.[94]

Yet the assumption of such invisibility is now more than a little problematic. Racial identities among, say, white students—partly formed out of a politics of commonsense during a period of conservative restructuring—are becoming increasingly powerful and volatile. Gallagher's research on the construction of white identities among university students provides an important example here, one that is worth examining.[95]

For many white working-class and middle-class students, there is now a belief that there is a social cost to being white. Whites are the "new losers" in a playing field that they believe has been levelled now that the United States is a supposedly basically "egalitarian, colorblind society."[96] These students constructed identities that avow a "legitimate, positive narrative of one's own whiteness . . . that negated white oppressor charges and framed whiteness as a liability."[97] Since "times were rough for everybody," but policies such as affirmative action were unfairly supporting "nonwhites," these students now claimed the status of victims.[98] As Gallagher puts it,

> Ignoring the ways in which whites "get raced" has the makings of something politically dangerous. A fundamental transformation of how young whites define and understand themselves racially is taking place. [They] have generally embraced the belief that the U.S. class system is fair and equitable. [They argue] that individuals who delay gratification, work hard, and follow the rules will succeed regardless of their color. . . . For many whites the levelled playing field argument has rendered affirmative action policies a form of reverse discrimination and a source of resentment. White students who believe social equality

has been achieved are able to assert a racial identity without regarding themselves as racist, because they see themselves as merely affirming their identity through language and actions—something racially defined groups do frequently.[99]

These arguments point to something of considerable moment in the politics of education in the United States and elsewhere. As it is being shaped by the political Right, whiteness as an explicit cultural product is taking on a life of its own. In the arguments of the conservative discourses now so powerfully circulating, the barriers to social equality and equal opportunity have now been removed. Whites, hence, have no privilege. Thus, "this ostensibly non-racist white space being carved out of our cultural landscape allows whites to be presented as just another racial contender . . . in the struggle over political and cultural resources and self-definition"—but always with an underlying belief that history has shown the superiority of "Western" political and cultural institutions and values.[100]

The implications of all this are profound politically and culturally. For, given the Right's rather cynical use of racial anxieties, given the economic fears and realities many citizens experience, and given the historic power of race on the American psyche, many members of the next generation now in school may choose to develop forms of solidarity based on their "whiteness." This is not inconsequential in terms of the struggles over meaning, identity, and the very characteristics and control of schools, to say the least. It underscores the movement toward marketized schooling in the United States and points toward a crucial terrain of research for socially committed sociological inquiry.

CRITICAL POLICY RESEARCH

While not totally explained by racial dynamics, the issue of the characteristics and control of schools has played an important role in one particular part of the sociology of education. Even though I have not gone into detail about the policy oriented tradition in the sociology of education in the United States, it should be noted that there has been an emerging focus on *critical* policy research.[101] As in the United Kingdom, the conservative restoration has attempted to redefine what is public as necessarily bad and what is private as necessarily good. The effects of this emphasis in educational policy have been predictable. This has included opening schools to even more corporate control and influence. The most powerful example is Channel One, in which schools sign contracts with a large corporation that gives them "free" equipment and a "free" news broadcast in return for converting their students into a captive audience for advertisements also broadcast over Channel One and which must be seen by the students in their schools. More than 40 percent of all private and public middle and secondary school students are currently enrolled in schools that receive Channel One. In reaction to this, research has critically examined the history, policy formation process, and ideological effects of such "reforms."[102]

Another major effect of such marketization initiatives has been the development of voucher and choice plans. While many of the empirical assessments are still being completed, there is growing evidence that such policies do not lead to higher achievement on the part of poor children and children of color. As Whitty has concluded in his review of what the American evidence has shown, "The stronger claims of choice advocates cannot be upheld . . . and choice needs to be carefully regulated if it is not to have damaging equity effects."[103] A number of analyses of the neoliberal project of marketization, and of the academic discourse that supports it, have been carried out. By and large, these too raise serious questions about its ideological vision and its differential effects.[104]

The neoliberal emphasis on the weak state has been accompanied by a neoconservative emphasis on strong state control over values, culture, and the body.[105] While there have been analyses of the cultural agendas of neoconservatives—especially of their visions of what and whose knowledge is legitimate[106]—it is only recently that investigations of their educational policies have been linked specifically to the ways in which they construct the meanings and histories of social problems and to the question of whether the empirical evidence supports such constructions.

Perhaps one of the more interesting examples of such an investigation is Burdell's analysis both of the social and cultural construction of the problem of teenage pregnancy and of the educational responses to it.[107] Using critical feminist tools, Burdell contextualizes the growth of teenage pregnancy as a *public* problem. She shows how these largely conservative constructions take on the power of "truth" and increasingly dominate discussions of the causes, effects, and solutions to the "problem of pregnant teens." In the process, she brings together historical and current evidence to counter the commonsense views of these causes, effects, and solutions, and suggests an alternative agenda for research and for educational policy and practice. Burdell's discussion provides another interesting example of the model of engaged research I noted earlier.

CONCLUSION

In this essay, by necessity I have had to be selective both in my discussion of the multiple traditions within the sociology of education and related areas in the United States and in my choice of research that exemplifies some of these traditions. I have sought to show how concerns with the politics of meaning, identity formation, the state, political economy, and the labor process intersect with concerns with multiple and contradictory dynamics of power such as race, gender, and class.

After reviewing the vast amount of material within these multiple traditions, especially within the critical and postmodern/poststructural elements of them, certain things become more obvious. There were clear silences, areas that were in considerable need of critical analyses of various kinds. For example, while a focus on identity politics is growing, it is much harder to find work on the best of recent theories of class. The *state* remains undertheorized and does not surface enough within critical analyses. Further, while the perspectives growing out of, say, cultural studies are growing, there is still a relative neglect of non-reductive theories of the political economy of culture. Consumption practices now too often "eat" production practices. And, even though there has been a partial "return" to political economy, in my opinion this is still too neglected and at times is less sophisticated than it might be. Finally, it is clear that there has been a growth of interest in postmodern and poststructural approaches in the United States.

In other places, I have raised a number of questions concerning this turn.[108] Yet, while I have real worries about the relatively uncritical acceptance of some aspects of these theories—and have noted a few of them briefly here—as I also indicated amongst the most positive signs on the horizon are the attempts at integrating the perspectives of the neo and post traditions and letting them interact with each other. At a time when we face a period of conservative triumphalism in the United States, too many neos and posts wind up arguing with each other rather than enabling the critical impulses of each to inform the other.

A good deal of the postmodern and poststructural emphases now emerging in "critical educational studies" has had a positive effect. It has increased the number of "voices" that need to be made public. It has helped legitimate or generate a welcome return to the concrete analysis of particular ideological or discursive formations, as well as the multiple sites of their elaboration and legitimation in policy documents, social movements, and institutions.[109] This focus on the concrete historical instance, without always having to search for "hidden" sets of determinations, in part does free us to understand the complexities of "the local" and contingent.

Yet, this said—and it must be—some of these studies suffer from the same silences as one of the major figures from whom they have often borrowed their emphases—Michel Foucault. As Hall reminds us, it has proven all too easy in scholarship and theory to accept Foucault's epistemological position whole and uncritically. There is a world of difference (and no pun is intended here) between emphasizing the local, the contingent, and non-correspondence and ignoring any determinacy or any structural relationships among practices. Too often important questions surrounding the state and social formation are simply evacuated and the difficult problem of *simultaneously* thinking about both the specificity of different practices and the forms of articulated unity they constitute is assumed out of existence as if nothing existed in structured ways.[110]

In my mind, it is exactly this issue of simultaneity, of thinking neo and post together, of actively enabling the tensions within and among them to help form our research, that will solidify previous understandings, avoid the loss of collective memory of the gains that have been made, and generate new insights and new actions. A little trespassing may be a good thing here.

NOTES

This article originally appeared as "Power Meaning and Identity: Critical Sociology of Education in the United States," in *British Journal of Sociology of Education* 17.2 (1996): 125–44. It is reprinted here with the generous permission of the original publisher (Carfax Publishing Limited, PO Box 25, Abingdon Oxfodshire, OX14 3UE, United Kingdom).

The author would like to thank Geoff Whitty for his perceptive comments on earlier drafts of this article.

1. G. Noblit and W. Pink, "Mapping the Alternative Paths of Sociology of Education," in *Continuity and Contradiction: The Futures of the Sociology of Education*, ed. W. Pink and G. Noblit (Cresskill: Hampton Press, 1995), p. 8.

2. P. Bourdieu, *In Other Words* (Stanford: Stanford University Press, 1990).

3. See, for example, R. Morrow and C. Torres, *Social Theory and Education* (Albany: State University of New York Press, 1995).

4. S. Hall, "Cultural Studies: Two Paradigms," in L. Grossberg, C. Nelson, and P. Treicher, eds., *Cultural Studies* (New York: Routledge, 1992), p. 520.

5. Noblit and Pink, "Mapping the Alternative Paths of Sociology of Education," p. 27.

6. Ibid., p. 27.

7. Ibid., p. 25.

8. B. Rowan, "Research on School Effects and Status Attainment," in *Continuity and Contradiction*, ed. Pink and Noblit, p. 34.

9. See the section on "The Policy Path," in *Continuity and Contradiction*, ed. Pink and Noblit, pp. 233–303.

10. M. W. Apple and L. Weis, "Ideology and Practice in Schooling," in *Ideology and Practice in Schooling*, ed. M. W. Apple and L. Weis (Philadelphia: Temple University Press, 1983).

11. For those readers who wish to examine the recent empirical and social agendas of such research programs, clear discussions can be found in the sections on "The Empirical-Analytic Path" and "The Interpretive Path," in *Continuity and Contradiction*, ed. Pink and Noblit, pp. 33–100 and 103–73.

12. Apple and Weis, "Ideology and Practice in Schooling."

13. M. F. D. Young, ed., *Knowledge and Control* (London: Collier-Macmillan, 1971).

14. M. W. Apple, *Ideology and Curriculum* (New York: Routledge, 1979; second edition 1990).

15. B. Bernstein, *The Structuring of Pedagogic Discourse* (New York: Routledge, 1990).

16. See, for example, M. W. Apple, *Teachers and Texts* (New York: Routledge, 1988); M. W. Apple, *Official Knowledge* (New York: Routledge, 1993); M. W. Apple, and L. Christian-Smith, eds., *The Politics of the Textbook* (New York: Routledge, 1991); L. Christian-Smith, ed., *Texts of Desire* (London: Falmer, 1993); A. Luke, *Literacy, Textbooks, and Ideology* (London: Falmer Press, 1988); and A. Luke, "The Secular Word," in *The Politics of the Textbook*, ed. Apple and Christian-Smith.

17. K. Teitelbaum, *Schooling for Good Rebels* (New York: Teachers College Press, 1995).

18. See M. Olneck, "Americanization and the Education of Immigrants, 1900–1925," *American Journal of Education* (1989): 398–423; M. Olneck, "The Recurring Dream: Symbolism and Ideology in Intercultural and Multicultural Education," *American Journal of Education* 98 (1990): 147–74; and M. Olneck, "Terms of Inclusion: Has Multiculturalism Redefined Inequality in American Education?" *American Journal of Education* 101 (1993): 234–60.

19. D. Labaree, *The Making of an American High School* (New Haven: Yale University Press, 1988).

20. Apple, *Official Knowledge*, and C. Cornbleth, *The Great Speckled Bird* (New York: St. Martin's Press, 1995).

21. Apple, *Cultural Politics and Education* (New York: Teachers College Press, 1996; London: Open University Press, 1996) and E. Eisner, ed., *Hidden Consequences of a National Curriculum* (Washington, D.C.: American Educational Research Association, 1995).

22. J. Delfattore, *What Johnny Shouldn't Read* (New Haven: Yale University Press, 1992).

23. Apple, *Official Knowledge*, and Luke, *The Secular Word*.

24. R. Johnson, "What is Cultural Studies Anyway?" *Social Text* 16 (1986/1987): 38–80.

25. J. Meyer, D. Kamens, and A. Benavot, *School Knowledge for the Masses* (London: Falmer Press, 1992).

26. Ibid., pp. 1–2.

27. Ibid., p. 2.

28. Bernstein, *The Structuring of Pedagogic Discourse*. It is unfortunate that Bernstein's work is now less well known in the United States among students and sociologists in education. As I have argued elsewhere for a largely American audience, it provides some of the most important elements of a serious and disciplined sociology of education. Given the popularity—and at times trendiness—of an all too often uncritical acceptance of postmodern and poststructural approaches in a number of areas in the United States, too many individuals have turned away from such work. I shall have more to say about this later. See M. W. Apple, "Education, Culture, and Class Power," *Educational Theory* 42 (1992): 127–45.

29. E. Ellsworth, "Why Doesn't This Feel Empowering?" *Harvard Educational Review* 59 (1989): 297–324. The focus on *pedagogy*, rather than *teaching*, in much of the new literature on "critical pedagogy," is an interesting case of the politics of linguistic usage I believe. Since teaching is seen as a low status occupation and taking it as worthy of scholarly criticism, hence, is also usually seen as low status within the academy and confined to low-status areas such as the field of education, higher-status academic inquiries into one's teaching must be reconfigured and reorganized around more "elegant" linguistic forms. In my mind, it is not an accident that much of the newer attention being paid to "critical pedagogy" (whatever that means, since it is a sliding signifier that shifts around the linguistic map) as a theoretical enterprise is to be found among academics in the humanities (see, e.g., D. Morton, and M. Zavarzadeh, eds., *Theory/Pedagogy/Politics*. [Urbana: University of Illinois Press, 1991]). All of this proceeds as if it was a new topic and as if the field of education and the very long tradition of dealing with the politics of teaching and curriculum did not exist. This would make a fascinating study in the politics of academic discourse and the construction of "new" fields.

30. C. Luke and J. Gore, eds., *Feminisms and Critical Pedagogy* (New York: Routledge, 1992).

31. T. Popkewitz, *A Political Sociology of Educational Reform* (New York: Teachers College Press, 1991).

32. For one example of this tendency, see I. Hunter, *Rethinking the School* (Boston: Allen and Unwin, 1994).

33. M. W. Apple, *Education and Power*, 2nd ed. (New York: Routledge, 1995); Apple, *Cultural Politics and Education*; and L. Zipin, "Emphasizing 'Discourse' and Bracketing People," in T. Popkewitz and M. Brennan, eds., *Foucault's Challenge* (New York: Teachers College Press, 1998).

34. Apple and Weis, "Ideology and Practice in Schooling."

35. A. Luke, "Text and Discourse in Education," in M. W. Apple, ed., *Review of Research in Education Volume 21* (Washington, D.C.: American Educational Research Association, 1996), p. 9.

36. Ibid.

37. Ibid.

38. M. Bakhtin, *Speech Genres and Other Essays* (Austin: University of Texas Press, 1986).

39. Luke, "Text and Discourse in Education," p. 9.

40. In this tradition, a "text" is not only a textbook, but is defined as language use—that is, as any instance of written and spoken language that has coherence and coded meanings. See Luke, "Text and Discourse in Education."

41. Of course, the very concept of representation and how it is used, and overused, is contentious. See ibid.

42. Ibid. See also K. Gutierrez et al., "Script, Counterscript, and Underlife in the Classroom," *Harvard Educational Review* 65 (1995): 445–71.

43. A. H. Dyson, "The Ninjas, the X-Men, and the Ladies," *Teachers College Record* 94 (1994): 219–39.

44. G. Whitty, "Sociology and the Problem of Radical Education Change," in *Educability, Schools and Ideology*, ed. M. Flude and J. Ahier (London: Halstead Press, 1974).

45. B. Palmer, *Descent into Discourse* (Philadelphia: Temple University Press, 1990).

46. H. Giroux, "Doing Cultural Studies," *Harvard Educational Review* 64 (1992): 278–308. See also P. McLaren, *Critical Pedagogy and Predatory Culture* (New York: Routledge, 1995).

47. M. Weinstein, "Robot World," Ph.D. dissertation, University of Wisconsin, Madison, 1995.

48. Johnson, "What is Cultural Studies Anyway," and P. Willis et al., *Common Culture* (Boulder, Colo.: Westview, 1990).

49. J. Koza, "Rap Music," *The Review of Education/Pedagogy/Cultural Studies* 16 (1994): 171–96.

50. H. Giroux, "Animating Youth," *Socialist Review* 94 (1994): 23–55. Giroux's analysis here does prove that he can write more clearly when he works hard enough at it. It is unfortunate that this is found much less often in the rest of the corpus of his work and in his overly defensive dismissal of such efforts to develop a less arrogant writing style.

51. K. Casey, "The New Narrative Research in Education," in *Review of Research in Education, Volume 21*, ed. M. W. Apple.

52. Ibid.

53. K. Casey, *I Answer with My Life* (New York: Routledge, 1993).

54. H. Bromley, "Identity Politics and Critical Pedagogy," *Educational Theory* 39 (1989): 207–23, and P. Wexler, *Becoming Somebody* (London: Falmer Press, 1992).

55. Wexler, *Becoming Somebody*.

56. L. Weis, *Working Class Without Work* (New York: Routledge, 1990).

57. L. Weis, "Qualitative Research in the Sociology of Education," in *Continuity and Contradiction*, ed. Pink and Noblit.

58. Ibid., p. 164.

59. See Apple, "Education, Culture and Class Power," and E. O. Wright et al., *The Debate on Classes* (New York: Verso, 1989).

60. See L. Weis and M. Fine, eds., *Beyond Silenced Voices* (Albany: State University of New York Press, 1993).

61. See Apple, *Education and Power*, and Apple, *Cultural Politics and Education*.

62. B. Curtis, *True Government by Choice Men?* (Toronto: University of Toronto Press, 1992).

63. Apple, *Cultural Politics and Education*. See also M. W. Apple and A. Oliver, "Becoming Right: Education and the Formation of Conservative Movements," *Teachers College Record* 97 (1996): 419–45.

64. P. Wexler, *Social Analysis of Education* (New York: Routledge, 1987).

65. R. Williams, *Marxism and Literature* (New York: Oxford University Press, 1977).

66. See Apple, *Cultural Politics and Education*; Apple, *Official Knowledge*; and Apple and Oliver, "Becoming right."

67. See C. McCarthy and W. Crichlow, eds., *Race, Identity and Representation in Education* (New York: Routledge, 1993); Weis and Fine, eds., *Beyond Silenced Voices*; and M. Fine, L. Weis, and W. Wong, eds., *Off White* (New York: Routledge, 1997).

68. P. Bourgois, *In Search of Respect* (New York: Cambridge University Press, 1995).

69. A. Gitlin, ed., *Power and Method* (New York: Routledge, 1994).

70. S. Bowles and H. Gintis, *Schooling in Capitalist America* (New York: Basic Books, 1976).

71. See, for example, Apple, *Education and Power* and M. Carnoy and H. Levin, *Schooling and Work in the Democratic State* (Stanford: Stanford University Press, 1986).

72. J. Rury, and J. Mirel, "The Political Economy of Urban Education," in *Review of Research in Education Volume 21*, ed. Apple and D. Harvey, *The Urban Experience* (Baltimore: Johns Hopkins University Press, 1989).

73. See also J. Mirel, *The Rise and Fall of an Urban School System* (Ann Arbor: University of Michigan Press, 1993).

74. Actually, "return" is not the appropriate word since while the tradition of political economy was never dominant in the United States in sociology of education, it also was never abandoned and continued to grow and to become increasingly nuanced.

75. See Apple, *Cultural Politics and Education*, especially chapter 4, and A. Sherman, *Wasting America's Future* (Boston: Beacon Press, 1994).

76. H. Gintis, "The Political Economy of School Choice," *Teachers College Record* 96 (1995): 492–511.

77. A. Gitlin and F. Margonis, "The Political Aspect of Reform," *American Journal of Education* 103 (1995): 377–405.

78. See Apple, *Teachers and Texts*; Apple, *Official Knowledge*; and Apple, *Education and Power*.

79. See, especially, S. Acker, "Gender and Teachers' Work," in *Review of Research in Education Volume 21*, ed. Apple.

80. They particularly and appropriately refer to A. Hargreaves, *Changing Teachers, Changing Schools* (New York: Teachers College Press, 1994).

81. Gitlin and Margonis, "The Political Aspect of Reform," p. 379. See also J. Anyon, "Teacher Development and Reform in an Inner-City School," *Teachers College Record* 96 (1994): 14–31; J. Anyon, "Race, Social Class, and Education in an Inner-City School," *Teachers College Record* 97 (1995): 69–94;

and D. Carlson, *Teachers and Crisis* (New York: Routledge, 1992).

82. Acker, "Gender and Teachers Work."

83. Ibid., p. 79. See also J. Rury, "Who Became Teachers?" in *American Teachers*, ed. D. Warren (New York: Macmillan, 1989).

84. See L. Perkins, "The History of Blacks in Teaching," in *American Teachers*, ed. Warren; and M. Fultz, "African-American Teachers in the South, 1880–1940," *Teachers College Record* 96 (1995): 544–68.

85. G. Ladson-Billings, *The Dreamkeepers* (San Francisco: Jossey-Bass, 1994).

86. C. West, *Race Matters* (New York: Vintage, 1993), p. 6. See also G. Ladson-Billings and W. Tate, "Towards a Critical Race Theory of Education," *Teachers College Record* 97 (1995): 47–68.

87. M. Omi and H. Winant, *Racial Formation in the United States* (New York: Routledge, 1995), p. viii.

88. Ibid.

89. Among the more interesting works of note here are E. Said, *Culture and Imperialism* (New York: Vintage, 1993); McCarthy and Crichlow, eds., *Race, Identity, and Representation in Education*; Weis and Fine, eds., *Beyond Silenced Voices*; and Fine, Weis, and Wong, eds., *On Whiteness*.

90. Apple, *Official Knowledge*, and Apple, *Cultural Politics and Education*.

91. R. Herrnstein and C. Murray, *The Bell Curve* (New York: The Free Press, 1994). This volume basically argues that African-Americans are genetically "less intelligent" on average. It had an immense advertizing budget and was given considerable resources to bring its case to the public by conservative foundations. It has also been reported in the national press that the authors received as much as $1,000,000 from conservative foundations to support the writing of the book. No reputable geneticist would make such arguments. But, as is often the case, conservative movements must find ways of explaining the destructiveness of their social policies that distance their own decisions from these consequences. Social Darwinist and biological arguments are often turned to here consciously or unconsciously as part of a legitimation strategy.

92. See, e.g., J. Kincheloe and S. Steinberg, eds., *Measured Lies* (New York: St. Martin's Press, 1996). Of considerable importance in situating these positions within larger historical dynamics is N. Fraser and L. A. Gordon "Genealogy of Dependency," *Signs* 19 (1994): 309–36.

93. C. Gallagher, "White Reconstruction in the University," *Socialist Review* 94 (1994): 167.

94. L. Roman, "White is a Color!" in McCarthy and Crichlow, eds., *Race, Identity, and Representation in Education*, p. 72. See also B. Hooks, *Black Looks* (Boston: South End Press, 1992).

95. Gallagher, "White Reconsruction in the University."

96. Ibid., pp. 175–76.

97. Ibid., p. 177.

98. Ibid., p. 180.

99. Ibid., pp. 182–83.

100. Ibid., p. 183.

101. The basis of both "mainstream" and critical policy research has been critically analyzed, using largely Bourdieuian and postmodern perspectives, in J. Ladwig, *Academic Distinctions* (New York: Routledge, 1996). While at times Ladwig overstates his case and is not always accurate chronologically, he does make a number of interesting arguments.

102. See Apple, *Official Knowledge*.

103. This evidence is clearly synthesized in G. Whitty, "Creating Quasi-Markets in Education," in *Review of Research in Education Volume 22*, ed. M. W. Apple (Washington, D.C.: American Educational Research Association, 1997).

104. Among these are J. Henig, *Rethinking School Choice* (Princeton: University Press, 1994); A. Wells, *A Time to Choose* (New York: Hill and Wang, 1993); and K. Smith and K. Meier, eds., *The Case against School Choice* (Armonk, N.Y.: M. E. Sharpe, 1995). Henig, in particular, shows the importance of technical and quantitative sophistication in his critical analysis of the empirical claims of research on marketization and choice plans.

105. Apple, *Cultural Politics and Education*.

106. S. Aronowitz and H. Giroux, "Textual Authority, Culture, and the Politics of Literacy," in Apple and Christian-Smith, eds., *The Politics of the Textbook*.

107. P. Burdell, "Teen Mothers in High School," in *Review of Research in Education Volume 21*, ed. Apple.

108. See Apple, *Official Knowledge*; Apple, *Education and Power*; and Apple, *Cultural Politics and Education*.

109. Hall, *Cultural Studies*, p. 537.

110. Ibid., pp. 537–38.

CHAPTER 2

Social Theory and Educational Research: Reframing the Quantitative-Qualitative Distinction through a Critical Theory of Methodology

Raymond A. Morrow

INTRODUCTION

The Problematic

As Robert Dreeben has noted, "In the 1960s and 1970s, the sociology of education, hitherto a sleepy and empirically underdeveloped subspecialty of the larger discipline, became embroiled in controversies over social stratification to an unprecedented extent. Education found itself at the center of them. . . . The subfield . . . grew in volume of research and in conceptual salience. It also moved out of its subdisciplinary backwater to become integrated into the larger sociological enterprise."[1]

The direct participation of critical social theory in the integration of education and sociology can only be dated in the Anglo-American context from the late 1970s.[2] In the context of educational research, critical theory—and here I refer to a theoretical program originating in the Frankfurt School tradition, but now ranging widely beyond it—is most often associated with critical pedagogy and related forms of curriculum theory.[3] Most recently, critical theory has also been defined in terms of a particular strategy for appropriating postmodernism for a theory of cultural politics.[4] In this context, critical theory is largely identified with critical pedagogy as an approach to curriculum theory and teaching practice, and the implications for empirical research largely restricted to a conception of ethnographic participatory action research.[5]

My task here is not to question directly these strategies of engagement and theorizing, which do indeed represent an important manner of extending the insights of the critical theory tradition. But I will contest the assumption that this *comprehensively* portrays the implications of critical theory for methodology, here with reference to educational research. Rather, I will be concerned with developing another—yet largely complementary—face of critical theory, one that more directly joins up with questions posed by empirical research in the sociology of education.[6] Though some of these issues have been addressed in the book written with Carlos Torres on *Social Theory and Education*,[7] which focuses on the problematic of social and cultural reproduction, here I would like to develop the more specific *methodological* issues involved. In particular I will attempt to justify the importance of social theory for the methodological concerns of the sociology of education today. To this end, I will sketch the way in which a critical theory of methodology, based on the metatheory of what I have termed in my *Critical Theory and Methodology*[8] as *interpretive structuralism*, provides a basis for reframing the quantitative-qualitative distinction. As well, this strategy opens the way for a more expanded conception of qualitative research, the primary focus of the present discussion.[9]

This essay will develop a position with respect to the notion of a critical theory of education that may take those familiar with critical pedagogy by surprise. The overidentification of the tradition of critical theory with two phases of its development (its origins in the 1930s and 40s; the antipositivist debates of the late 1960s), has culminated in a consistent stress on its antipositivism and anti-empiricism. But this antipositivist image of critical theory begs the question of its conception of the alternative, especially in a postmodernist context where there has been a proliferation of antipositivist standpoints.[10] The present essay might be read accordingly as a fraternal rejoinder and counterweight to the current postmodernist variants of critical theory associated with critical pedagogy. In the process, I attempt to sketch the framework for a more productive and inclusive methodological account of the actual and potential relationship between critical theory and educational research.

I found it instructive in developing this essay to return—with the vantage point of two decades—to the illuminating introduction by Karabel and Halsey to their *Power and Ideology in Education*.[11] On the one hand, one is struck by the continuity of the debates and issues. Even more true today is the general claim that "over the last generation educational research has come from the humblest margins of the social sciences to occupy a central position in sociology, as well as to receive considerable attention from economists, historians, and anthropologists."[12] Also familiar is their agenda of five "outstanding trends, theories and preoccupations":

1. Functionalist theories of education
2. The economic theory of human capital
3. Methodological empiricism (within which we attach a special importance to empirical studies of educational inequality)
4. Conflict theories of education
5. The interactionist tradition in educational research and the challenge of the "new" sociology of education.[13]

Equally striking, however, are the *additional preoccupations* that would inevitably also be a part of a similar agenda today:

- The revitalization and revisions of neofunctionalism and systems theory
- Gender inequalities and their epistemological ramifications in social science and culture in general
- The specific aspects of the interplay between race, gender, and class in educational reproduction
- The problematic of critical pedagogy and its intersection with postmodernist debates
- The emergence of cultural studies as an interdisciplinary space for rethinking culture, ideology, and educational knowledge in relation to class, gender, race, and so on
- Critical social theory as a conflict orientation increasingly distinct from neo-Marxist theory

Yet most of these shifts were prefigured in the agenda of two decades ago. Perhaps the revitalization of functionalism was most surprising given the mood of the mid-1970s. The gender and race questions were apparent in conflict theories of education, but what was missing here was the remarkable radicalization of these standpoints as epistemological interventions. Similarly, the problematic of critical pedagogy lurks in the background of various sections, for instance, references to the confrontational strategies of the New Left; the identification of a British form of "action-research";[14] and the problematization of school knowledge outlined by the "new sociology of education." Yet the radicalization of curriculum theory associated with critical pedagogy was just emerging despite the long-standing interest in Freire in adult education circles.[15] The diffusion of Freirean themes to education generally is a phenomenon of the 1980s, though a "reconceptualist" curriculum theory can be traced to the late 1970s.[16] Nor was there any hint of the remarkable explosion of one of the themes of the new sociology of education: its radical, relativist constructionism; or how these issues would be connected up with standpoint theories by feminist and postcolonial theorists. Paradoxically, aspects of the epistemological critiques of the new sociology of education have resurfaced and been reincarnated in a new and fleshed out form under the heading of postmodernism.[17]

Finally, neither the problematics of cultural studies nor critical theory are explicitly addressed in the Karabel and Halsey volume. The most obvious reason of course is that education was not an explicit part of the agenda of early critical theory[18] and education was just emerging as a site of cultural studies under the influence of Gramsci's theory of hegemony.[19] Further, the Anglo-American reception of Frankfurt critical theory had just got underway.

But, I would argue, it would have been only through engaging cultural studies and especially critical theory that Karabel and Halsey could have found some direction with respect to the metatheoretical and methodological dilemmas that underlie their introductory discussion, but do not get explicitly articulated. Such issues come to a head in their ambivalent critique of the "new sociology of education":

> What, then, is one to make of the claim that the "interpretative paradigm" that marks the beginning of a "scientific revolution" in educational research? . . . when the transformation of a discipline is announced *before* the event, there is reason to suspect that one is witnessing not a scientific revolution but a more familiar phenomenon of an attempt by an emergent school of thought to legitimate its approach. . . . Only if the "new" sociology of education were able to incorporate into its framework the contribution of "traditional" educational research could it lay claim to scientific revolution. This it has been unable to do.[20]

Though I would hesitate to use the somewhat grandiose terminology of "scientific revolutions" here, I would argue that now, a quarter century later, there has indeed been something like a paradigm shift in educational theory and research which has been documented indirectly in Carlos Torres' and my *Social Theory and Education* (1995). What I would like to address more directly and explicitly here, however, is the basis of the metatheoretical shifts underlying the reconfiguration of education around the problematic of social and cultural reproduction.

The frame of reference for developing this metatheoretical problematic is indicated by the title of my essay: "Social Theory and Educational Research: Reframing the Quantitative-Qualitative Distinction through a Critical Theory of Methodology." Let me anticipate my argument at the outset in somewhat oversimplified terms. From the later 1960s onward, metatheoretical and related methodological debates get formulated in terms of two basic, though overlapping polarizations: initially the confrontation of quantitative and qualitative research; and somewhat later—under the influence of European social theory—the parallel oppositions of "positivist social science" versus "interpretive social science," or "positivist social science" versus "critical social science." Though there were always voices that challenged these simplifications, there were things about the deep structure of the fields of social science—in the English-speaking world at least—that tended to reproduce these often unproductive and intellectual superficial characterizations. Whatever their theoretical deficiencies, such labels served to describe the actual splits that dominate training and research.

This essay will explore the origins and some of the problems of the way in which a critical theory of methodology reframes the problematic in terms of a threefold classification between *postpositivist empiricism*, *critical theory*, and *radical constructionism*. But even these distinctions must be used with care and some unresolved issues confronted, we shall see. The present discussion will only be able to provide an incomplete introduction to the complex agenda of issues and theses that can be described as follows.

The agenda:

- First, I will consider the remarkable persistence of the faulty quantitative-qualitative polarization and its surprising survival in Denzin and Lincoln's *Handbook of Qualitative Research*,[21] though this anthology's primary metatheoretical frame of reference is positivist versus interpretive methodologies.

- Second, I will trace the blindspots of Denzin and Lincoln's strategy to the ambiguities of the distinction between idiographic and nomothetic explanations and methodological strategies. As I will argue, this distinction is handled typically in a dichotomous way that obscures the variety of quasinomothetic or generalizing strategies found in social research.

- Third, I will sketch some of the key themes of what I have elsewhere termed a critical theory of methodology in order to reframe the preceding polarizations. The notion of what I have elsewhere termed *interpretive structuralism* will be used to identify the various ways in which efforts have been made to mediate between or transcend the idiographic-nomothetic polarization.

- Fourth, I will attempt to explore a set of distinctions that follow from a critical theory of methodology, that is, a differentiation of postpositivist empiricism; critical theory, and radical constructivism, especially in response to Egon Guba's formulations. In particular, this requires considering what can be called the "explanatory" moment of critical theory, a question that I will explore using the example of Daniel Liston's reconstruction of Claus Offe's account of selective mechanisms in state-capital relations.[22]

- Finally, I will argue against the tendency to reify this threefold classification, stressing the ultimate interdependence of these three strategies of inquiry, each of which suffers from internal tensions. In the context of educational research this argument forces the conclusion that critical pedagogy cannot be a self-sufficient political project; rather, it presupposes a theory of society—of social and cultural reproduction—and a critical theory of methodology that can serve as a unifying framework for much of the sociology of education.

THE QUANTITATIVE-QUALITATIVE POLARIZATION: FROM METHOD TO METATHEORY

Introduction

The most useful starting point for understanding the social sciences is the differentiation between three distinctive types of theoretical discourse: *metatheory, empirical theory,* and *normative theory.* The implication of such distinctions is that "theory" is not a logically unified symbolic form; instead, it assumes different modalities with complex interrelations. Most fundamentally, metatheory is *theory about theory* and incorporates the classical philosophical questions suggested by logic, ontology, epistemology, methodology, and so forth. Normative theory performs a distinctive role in social theory because it is about value and value claims, including their criticism and advocacy. As a consequence, normative theory has a kind of quasi-empirical status that makes it distinctive from metatheory generally, as well as from empirical theory, that is, explanatory and interpretive analyses of concrete sociohistorical relations. Though the distinction between is and ought is fundamental and cannot be ignored, this should not allow ideologically glossing over the continuity between

the two—there are contexts where is can imply ought—and the illusion of value-neutral concepts.

To make sense of the oppositions between quantitative and qualitative methods, or positivist and interpretive social science, we need to
turn to *metatheory*, a topic largely excluded or dogmatically treated in
traditional methods courses. The trouble with traditional discussions of
methodology is twofold. On the one hand, methodology is equated with
methods as techniques. Hence methodology is reduced to technical oper-
ations, for example, survey research, participant observation, and so on.
Second, the problematic of explanation is reduced to a single, deductive
form derived from the natural sciences, thus obscuring the significance
of the actual variety of productive explanatory strategies in social
research.[23]

As a consequence, the more general problematic of methodology is
handled within a largely taken-for-granted conception of scientific
knowledge, that is, a form of epistemology that is often labeled by critics as "*positivist.*" The basic positivist argument here is that the sciences
are logically unified in a way that can be identified by the *reconstructed
logic* of its most advanced forms (e.g., physics). The simplistic quantitative-qualitative distinction derives in part from the dominance of this
positivist model, which still reigns in many methods texts; but it is also
reproduced in qualitative methods texts that define themselves in opposition to positivism.[24]

As American pragmatists and historians of science have long
pointed out, however, analysis of the *logics-in-use* in research offers
more insight into the nature and practice of science than idealized reconstructions.[25] From this perspective, it is clear that there are indeed two
main types of social science with distinctive logics. The question then
becomes that of finding a vocabulary for these different ways of constructing social scientific knowledge, that is, a more adequate metatheory than classical positivism or a theory of qualitative methodology
based exclusively on *Verstehen* procedures, limited to interpretations of
meaning. Whereas positivism reduces inquiry to the natural science
model of a search for general laws, the purely interpretive approach
(now identified as hermeneutics) limits research to uncritical "readings"
of human experience.

The Persistence of a False Dichotomy

Despite interminable challenges to the quantitative-qualitative distinction, it persists for various practical reasons and, in a sense, has been
given a new lease on life with the advent of postmodernism in its guise
as epistemological and methodological critique.[26] For that reason I make

the problematic central to the problematic of methodology. In my *Critical Theory and Methodology* the more empirically oriented section of the book begins with a critique of the conventional methods discourse. On the one hand, it is argued that this contrast has been biased because structured in terms derived from the positivist tradition, thus marginalizing qualitative approaches as more or less defective because they fall short of the canonized "scientific" ideal.

On the other hand, this polarization also involves a false dichotomy that obscures more fundamental issues about the logics of research strategies. Such terminology is problematic for a simple, fundamental reason: so-called qualitative research does not preclude quantification, and quantitative analysis requires qualitative procedures. The mere presence of the quantitative is only an incidental feature of the contrast at stake. Qualitative research deprived of techniques of counting would be inconceivable.

Why does such problematic labeling then persist? Because it is a code word for two different strategies of theoretically constructing social facts.[27] So-called quantitative research is driven by statistical-causal modeling of variables (correlational analysis). In contrast, qualitative research is based on nonformalized accounts providing interpretive analyses of relations among structures and processes, whether at the symbolic (discourse analysis) or sociocultural levels (i.e., agency and structure relations).[28]

The Case of Denzin and Lincoln's Handbook: Old Wine in New Bottles?

Denzin and Lincoln's recent *Handbook of Qualitative Research*[29] is a useful point of departure for assessing the current status of the quantitative-qualitative problematic in social research. As we will see, though this volume updates the issues in "postmodern" terms, and claims to provide an international perspective,[30] it remains in the grips of the same problematic polarizations and binary oppositions.[31]

> The word *qualitative* implies an emphasis on processes and meanings that are not rigorously examined, or measured (if measured at all), in terms of quantity, amount, intensity, or frequency. Qualitative researchers stress the socially constructed nature of reality, the intimate relationship between the researcher and what is studied, and the situational constraints that shape inquiry. Such researchers emphasize the value-laden nature of inquiry. They seek answers to questions that stress how social experience is created and given meaning. In contrast, quantitative studies emphasize the measurement and analysis of causal relationships between variables, not processes. Inquiry is purported to be within a value-free framework.[32]

But is should be stressed that in the Denzin and Lincoln volume there has been a shift of emphasis away from the quantitative-qualitative distinction as a way of framing these issues toward a contrast between *objectivist* and *subjectivist* approaches, or "positivist" and "interpretive" strategies. Despite the title "qualitative" research, the Denzin-Lincoln anthology is not organized around a simplistic quantitative-qualitative distinction; rather it works with a version of the positivist versus interpretivist (or constructivist) opposition. Yet Denzin and Lincoln's *Handbook* illustrates clearly the continuing if latent hold of the quantitative-qualitative distinction as a kind of deep-structure of social scientific discourse. Their formulation simply codifies our taken-for-granted understandings.

This shift of metatheoretical language reflects the increasing influence of continental metatheory. But this language deriving from the subject-object distinction poses as many problems as that of contrasting pure techniques as quantitative and qualitative. Again this descriptive contrast quickly hardens into a binary opposition between incommensurable categories defined by the classic between *idiographic* and *nomothetic* explanations:

> Qualitative researchers are committed to an emic, idiographic, case-based position, which directs their attention to the specifics of particular cases . . . whereas quantitative researchers, with their etic, nomothetic commitments . . . use mathematical models, statistical tables, and graphs, and often write about their research in impersonal, third-person prose.[33]

Let us pause for a moment to consider this use of the *nomothetic-idiographic distinction*, as this is a question I will pursue in more depth later on. As the *Penguin Dictionary of Sociology* reminds us: idiographic is "a term used to describe methods of study of individual, unique persons, events or things. It contrasts with nomothetic methods in which the object is to find general laws which subsume individual cases."[34] As another dictionary adds more explicitly, "an *idiographic* focus is on cultural and historical particulars, using methods such as ethnography and biography; while a *nomothetic* focus seeks to establish general laws following an explicitly natural-science model of knowledge."[35]

Most problematic for my purposes is the resulting characterization of qualitative research, the form of inquiry the authors seek to justify. The *first* problem is whether such research can be consistently "idiographic," at least without the loss of crucial *theoretical* questions. How are we to analyze the historical origins, organization, and transformations of particular cases without *generalizing* concepts? How can we recognize the peculiarities of a case without reference to other cases as part of a comparative methodology?

Second, though reference is made to the study of *"processes"* and *"meanings,"* there is considerable ambiguity about the implications of the study of "processes"; if they are not to be studied nomothetically in terms of "causal relationships between variables," *how are they to be conceptualized?* In other words, what are the logics (whether reconstructed or as a logic-in-use) of processual analysis? This seemingly central question then disappears; there is only one reference in an excellent index to the term under the heading of "processual evaluations."

Perhaps the omission of the logic of processual analysis just reflects a terminological accident. Such issues may be explored under other headings. But again one looks largely in vain and quickly becomes aware that *important bodies of nonpositivist qualitative research have been inexplicably marginalized by this definitional strategy.* The comprehensive, detailed index provides some clues with respect to omissions and suggest that, *despite occasional claims to the contrary, methodology has been sharply separated from social theory.*

The problematic of *comparison* is briefly noted as a possibility for case study analysis.[36] There is no entry for *society, power,* or *political economy*; one each for *institutions* and *social structure*; one for *social theory*; *ideology* is mentioned in passing in three articles; *hegemony* is mentioned largely in passing in six. Neither *functionalism* nor *macrosociology* are referenced; *structuralism* is mentioned several times in relation to the original linguistic model (hence exclusively as a technique for analyzing meanings), but is only discussed in depth once in relation to semiotics. *Critical theory* and *Marxist* are mentioned often, but mostly as catchwords for "paradigms" that are not discussed in depth aside from one chapter on "Rethinking Critical Theory and Qualitative Research,"[37] which would have been more accurately titled "Critical Theory and Ethnographic Research as Praxis" given the focus of the discussion. I will return to this essay momentarily.

Why These Blindspots?

A key question arises from these symptomatic omissions: Why these blindspots with respect to qualitative research? I think there are two key sources of confusion that shape Denzin and Lincoln's editorial project. *First*, they remain constrained within the deep structure of the objectivist-subjectivist polarization, which inhibits their ability to recognize mediating forms of theory construction. The result is that various perspectives outside this polarization cannot be effectively assessed from within it. All qualitative research gets reduced by default or omission to the logic of idiographic interpretation.

Second, this same polarization opens the way for a relatively uncritical standpoint theory of knowledge that resonates with postmodernist critiques but contributes to a fragmented conception of contemporary theorizing. Subjective knowledge (i.e., idiographic knowledge) is by definition derived from and limited by its social positioning but expresses the authentic voices of experience; positivist knowledge is positionless and formal, hence a universalistic illusion. Whereas positivist theory had the tendency of dismissing such personal knowledge as "subjectivistic," postmodernist standpoint theories romantically and uncritically valorize it as "indigenous" knowledge, though somewhat arbitrarily restricting it to the dominated or those on the margins.[38]

The Inseparability of Methodology and Social Theory

What the Denzin anthology fails to do, despite its claims to the contrary, is to adequately link methodological questions to social theory. Though such possibilities are hinted at in some of the articles (e.g., in chapters on critical theory as well as historical methods; but especially Guba's discussion of paradigms, to which I will eventually turn), the editors largely work within a problematic objectivist-subjectivist framework that reinforces and reproduces the quantitative-qualitative polarization that already has long defined social research. As a consequence, qualitative research as a *methodological technique*—the interpretation of individual cases—is not differentiated from qualitative research as a *strategy of theory construction* oriented toward the historical-structural interpretation of the reproduction and transformation of social totalities.

RETHINKING THE NOMOTHETIC VERSUS IDIOGRAPHIC DISTINCTION

Windelband to Critical Theory

At this point I would like to digress a moment to reflect historically on a previously noted distinction that is often mentioned in passing, but rarely examined more closely, that is, the contrast between the nomothetic and idiographic. According to dominant interpretation of this distinction, the natural sciences are oriented to *Erklären* or explanation that takes the form of *nomothetic laws* (universal, ahistorical). On the other hand, the human sciences are limited to *Verstehen (hermeneutics)* and the ideographic interpretation of unique events and meanings.[39] Positivists, in contrast, follow John Stuart Mill and others in calling for a purely nomothetic account of society.

The key point to recognize is that there are *two nonpositivist stances* to take with respect to this distinction which originated in the work of the nineteenth-century German philosopher Wilhelm Windelband (1848–1915).[40] In one formulation, it leads to a fundamental divide between the natural and human sciences (*Naturwissenschaften* vs. the *Geisteswissenschaften*). The most well-known version is Wilhelm Dilthey's conception, which rejects nomothetic methods in the human sciences. This version has dominated interpretive and phenomenological research and continues to haunt the Denzin-Lincoln volume.[41] The second, known largely through the work of Max Weber, follows Heinrich Rickert in arguing that sociology could also selectively use nomothetic approaches. Most importantly, Weber sought to combine explanatory and interpretive techniques to provide both causal-adequacy and adequacy at the level of meaning.[42]

Bourdieu develops a complementary position based on a structuralist reinterpretation of this strategy, but one grounded in a theory of practice that incorporates a theory of action. As he puts it with respect to his *Homo Academicus,*

> One of the goals of the book is to show that *the opposition between the universal and the unique, between nomothetic analysis and idiographic description, is a false antinomy*. the relational and analogical mode of reasoning fostered by the concept of field enables us to grasp particularity within generality and generality within particularity, by making it possible to see the French case as a "particular case of the possible," as Bachelard (1949) says. Better, the unique historical properties of the French academic field—its high degree of centralization and institutional unification, its well-delimited barriers to entry—make it a highly propitious terrain for uncovering some of the universal laws that tendentially regulate the functioning of all fields.[43]

Aside from the problematic reference to "universal laws," I think this formulation effectively captures the essential features of a nonpositivist, interpretive structuralist perspective. Note that "laws" that tendentially regulate are not exactly "universal laws" in the strict nomothetic sense of covering-laws in hypothetico-deductive explanations. No, what is at stake here are typically structuralist notions of generative mechanisms that operate only historically and contextually as mediated by human agents. The shortcoming of most references to the nomothetic is that they implicitly restrict the conceptualization of generality to ahistorical, general laws; one of the most fundamental contributions of structuralism in social theory, on the other hand, is to provide a nonpositivist, historical account of social determination.[44]

Critical Qualitative Research

Now let us turn back to the implications of this interpretive structural-ist perspective as a way of approaching qualitative research's relation to social theory. By contrast, Denzin and Lincoln remain imprisoned within the logic of the Diltheyean (and later Husserlian) opposition between the nomothetic and idiographic. As a consequence, they find it difficult to focus on forms of qualitative research that go beyond this distinction. But there are several chapters in their anthology (e.g., the one on historical research by Tuchman[45]) that give some hints with respect to this hidden body of *marginalized qualitative research*. Most strategically, such issues are implicated in the critical theory article by Kincheloe and McLaren. Though focusing on critical ethnography ori-ented toward empowering the subjects studied, they begin with a list of assumptions of critical approaches which needs to be cited here:

> that all thought is fundamentally mediated by power relations that are social and historically constituted; that facts can never be isolated from the domain of values or removed from some form of ideological inscription; that the relationship between concept and object and between signifier and signified is never stable or fixed and is often mediated by the social relations of capitalist production and consump-tion; that language is central to the formation of subjectivity (con-sciousness and unconscious awareness); that certain groups in any soci-ety are privileged over others.[46]

I do not have any fundamental reservations with this statement as a general characterization. My point is only that the particular strategy they advocate *does not exhaust* the empirical tasks implied here. Most characteristic of their approach is the reduction of critical theory to the moment of practice without any indication of the complex explana-tory—and normative—problems that would have to be resolved *before* such knowledge is to inform transformative practice:

> Critical research can be best understood in the context of the empow-erment of individuals. Inquiry that aspires to the name *critical* must be connected to an attempt to confront the injustice of a particular soci-ety or sphere within the society.[47]

Two key issues are largely taken for granted in this formulation. *First*, the normative claim that the indentification of "injustice" can be authoritatively taken for granted, despite the increasingly chaotic babel identity and single-issue politics. Though this assumption is consistent with taking a standpoint within a social movement, it does not provide a frame of reference for mediating among standpoints. In other words, the dominant tendency in critical pedagogy is—despite much rhetoric to the contrary—to presume normative stances without pursuing the more complex strategy of a dialogical communicative ethics as suggested by Habermas and others.

And *second*, we are given no indication of how these power relations are to be studied qualitatively beyond an ethnography of the workplace; nor does the rest of the book provide much in the way of understanding how qualitative research is to deal conceptually and analytically with, say, concrete power relations and structures of domination. My argument is simply that it is difficult to talk about agency and emancipatory values without more explicit reference to agency-structure relations and the normative discourses that are to inform collective transformation. One of the central contributions of a critical theory of methodology is to more comprehensively frame the project of critical social research in relation to an integral theory of social and cultural reproduction.

THE ALTERNATIVE OF A
CRITICAL THEORY OF METHODOLOGY

Introduction: Reframing the Question

As I have formulated it, a critical theory of methodology is not a unique feature of critical theory; more precisely, it is an adaptation of the new philosophy of social science and pragmatic (contextual) account of methodology that gives critical theory a central, if not exclusive place.[48] Its point of departure is an interrogation of the dualism of the subject-object dichotomy.[49] I will highlight the following key features as follows:

- Reconstructing the subjectivist-objectivist polarization through interpretive structuralism
- A pragmatic conception of the interdependence of reflexive and empirical methods, both viewed as internally differentiated and selected contextually
- A distinction between three moments of inquiry and explanation: actional, systemic, and mediational, and a resulting refusal to reify the distinctions between positivist, interpretive, and critical social sciences

Reconstructing the Subjectivist-Objectivist Schema: Interpretive Structuralism

From the perspective of critical theory as qualitative research *the most fundamental dilemma of qualitative research is the problematic of ana-*

lyzing social processes in terms of both structures and meanings. In other words, the real question here is formulating a *nonpositivist* conception of objectivistic analysis.[50] The term interpretive structuralism attempts to link together the family resemblances between a variety of explanatory strategies that effectively analyze agency and structure.[51] Other terms can and have been used here: *hermeneutic* (Ricoeur) or *historicist structuralism* (Frankfurt tradition, Gramsci); *genetic structuralism* (Piaget, Bourdieu); *constructivist structuralism* (e.g., Bourdieu). In the context of the sociology of education, such strategies are evident in such diverse authors as: Margaret Archer, Bourdieu, Randall Collins, Raymond Murphy, and Michael Apple. I will return to this question in the next section where the explanatory moment of critical research is taken up.

Reflexive versus Empirical Methods

Further, a critical theory of methodology challenges the postmodernist tendency to allow reflexivity to become an end in itself, rather than a means. Indeed, much reflexive argumentation comes to replace empirical analysis, at times implying that the very desire to represent reality is an illusion. In contrast, I have argued that such reflexive procedures are heuristic procedures central to the research process, hence complementary to traditional empirical methods. Further, a number of different forms of reflexivity can be identified and should be made a part of research training: analysis of the *logics-in-use* in research, as opposed to formal, reconstructed logic; *historicist* and *deconstructive* analyses of inquiry; *existential reflexivity* deriving from diverse standpoints; and the reflexivity implied by *normative theorizing* (including ideology critique).[52]

In place of the quantitative-qualitative distinction, it is more fruitful to conceptualize empirical research in terms of a distinction between *extensive and intensive research designs*. Whereas the former defines its objects of study in terms of statistical samples that are then analyzed through correlational analysis, the latter involves a wide variety of qualitative strategies that goes far beyond the more restrictive framework of the Denzin and Lincoln anthology.[53]

Three Moments of Inquiry

Finally, an interpretive structuralist perspective differentiates between three interrelated modalities or moments of inquiry.[54] *Systemic inquiries* attempt to analyze the objective, structural properties of sociohistorical totalities; *actional accounts* interpret and explain the activities of agents and subjects as producers of and yet products of systemic relations; and *mediational analysis* attempts the illusive task of exploring moments of de-reification—the crises—where transformative potentials emerge, even if they are not successful in changing systemic relations. In this respect, a mediational perspective attempts to avoid the limitations of the macro-micro distinction that is embedded in a dualistic objectivist-subjectivist metatheory.

THREE FORMS OF SOCIAL SCIENCE?

Introduction

On the basis of the refinements implied by a critical theory of methodology as just outlined, it becomes possible to consider again the distinction between three forms of social science: positivist, interpretive, and critical.[55] Instead of reifying these as three, distinct, autonomous, stand-alone paradigms, critical theory is grounded on the assumption of their interdependence. That interdependence has a general logical form, but it is even more importantly historically contingent.

The general logical form of critical theory as a mediation between analytical empirical and hermeneutic knowledge has been elaborated in Habermas's theory of knowledge interests and Ricoeur's complementary critical hermeneutics.[56] For sociology, this problematic has been most insightfully and influentially confronted in Habermas' social theory. His point of departure in reconstructing critical social theory is a refusal of the subjectivist-objectivist polarization, or what he termed in his early book *On the Logic of the Social Sciences* as the confrontation between "analytic" and "hermeneutic" approaches:

> Whereas the natural and cultural or hermeneutic sciences are capable of living in a mutually indifferent, albeit more hostile than peaceful, coexistence, the social sciences must bear the tension of divergent approaches under one roof, for in them the very practice of research compels reflection on the relationship between analytic and hermeneutic methodologies.[57]

The most fundamental insight of *Knowledge and Human Interests*[58] is that social knowledge ultimately requires a mediation between the reflexive subjects and their potential capacity to become aware of the causal structures that constrain and enable action and the production of knowledge. Whereas the *empirical-analytical interest* relates to our need for instrumental control of nature and society, the *hermeneutic-historical interest* corresponds to our need to interpret and make sense of different cultural forms and meaning systems. What this polarization obscures, however, is that empirical-analytical knowledge is crucial to the processes of enlightenment, especially in the transformation and critique of tradition.

Only with the third, the *critical-emancipatory interest*, does it become possible to understand the forms of reflexive knowledge that take shape when we are confronted with forms of analysis that make us aware of distorted communication, that is, the effects of asymmetrical power relations on past understandings of social forms. To use a term from Paul Ricoeur, it is precisely the *distanciation* produced by structural knowledge that allows us to reframe our self and collective understanding.[59] *What has remained ambiguous in these formulations, however, is the status of the quasinomothetic generalizations that inform such nonpositivist empirical analysis.*[60]

What is most fully distinctive about critical theory is not merely its interpretive structuralist methodological stance, but also the closely linked substantive claim about the nature of society in which it is embedded: the notion of a theory of society as a system of domination, that is, as a mode of producing and reproducing power relations as mediated by processes of coercion and consent.

Paradigmatic Features of Critical Theory

More helpful than Denzin and Lincoln's introduction and conclusion is the effort by Guba and Lincoln to analyze "Competing Paradigms in Qualitative Research."[61] Four such paradigms are identified (*positivist, postpositivst, critical theory, constructivism*) and compared in terms of their central metatheoretical assumptions: ontology, epistemology, and methodology.[62] My concern here is primarily with the characterization of critical theory with which I generally concur:

> *Ontology: Historical realism.* A reality is assumed to be apprehendable that was once plastic, but that was, over time, shaped by a congeries of social, political, cultural, economic, ethnic, and gender factors, and then crystallized (reified) into a series of structures that are now (inappropriately) taken as "real," that is, natural and immutable. For all practical purposes the structures *are* "real," a virtual or historical reality.

> *Epistemology: Transactional and subjectivist.* The investigator and the investigated object are assumed to be interactively linked, with the values of the investigator (and of situated "others") inevitably influencing the inquiry. Findings are therefore *value-mediated.*

> *Methodology: Dialogic and dialectical.* The transactional nature of inquiry requires a dialogue between the investigator and the subjects of inquiry; that dialogue must be dialectical in nature to transform ignorance and misapprehensions (accepting historically mediated structures

as immutable) into more informed consciousness (seeing how the structures might be changed and comprehending actions required to effect change.[63]

Or later on critical theory's conception of knowledge:

Knowledge consists of a series of structural-historical insights that will be transformed as time passes. Transformations occur when ignorance and misapprehensions give way to more informed insights by means of a dialectical interaction.[64]

What is missing in Guba and Lincoln's account is a discussion of the *limitations* of such formulation as *reconstructed idealizations*. In reality, as a logic-in-use, even the production of critical knowledge is separated from the contexts in which it may take on transformative consequences. The communicative relations between knowledge creation and its many publics are historically diverse and continuously changing. For example, the current debates about the internet, the computer revolution and notions of an "information society" all point to novel contexts where knowledge and change interact.

It is quite misleading, therefore, to identify today critical theory exclusively with the classical model of the revolutionary proletariat coming to collective consciousness through the imbibing of revolutionary knowledge. Relaxing that model to address the diversity of the new social movements involves an important step in the right direction, but it still remains tied to a dangerously activist conception of knowledge that presumes in advance an understanding of how agents can respond to structural change. Critical theory cannot be identified exclusively with *participatory action research*, however effectively it may provide a rationale for it.

The Explanatory Moment: Power Relations and Structural Analysis

What is typically missing or at least glossed over in the Denzin-Lincoln anthology and most other characterizations of *qualitative methodology* is the status of structural accounts of power relations as found in political economy, state theories, organizational analysis, mass media analysis, the sociology of work, theories of hegemony, analyses of education and social change, and so on. Another way of putting this is that all such work is in important respects historical sociology concerned with the dialectic of power, agency, and structure. In the process, qualitative research ceases to become defined primarily as a tool kit of methodological techniques and becomes identified with the fundamental process of social theorizing.[65]

De facto, there has been a split in qualitative research that reflects this dilemma. The *Handbook* is devoted primarily to the *meaning-oriented forms of interpretive social inquiry*, whereas strategies more oriented toward *structural accounts of processes* are marginalized or rejected as involving a residual positivism (e.g., historical sociology, political economy, critical organization theory, much cultural sociology, etc.). What is consistently missing from the *Handbook of Qualitative Research* is attention to what is involved in analyzing those "*structural-historical insights that will be transformed as time passes*" (Guba and Lincoln's characterization of knowledge in critical theory). In this respect the tension between the purely *constructivist paradigm* (especially in its postmodernist reincarnations) becomes apparent, as well as some of critical theory's latent affinities with *postpositivist* approaches, at least in its concern with empirical evidence and causal hypotheses.[66]

It is in this context of justifying empirical claims that it is instructive to refer to Daniel Liston's discussion of the explanatory problems of Marxist theories of social reproduction in education. Though his analysis focuses primarily on models that suffer from a problematic functionalist correspondence assumption, his general strategy illuminates the claims that I have been making about the strategy of contemporary critical theory.[67] Not surprisingly, he uses the example of Claus Offe—an early collaborator with and influence upon Habermas—as the basis of an empirically justifiable account of state-school relations in capitalist society. I cannot summarize this complex argument here, which analyzes in detail problems of empirically identifying four levels of selective mechanisms: *structural, ideological, procedural,* and *repressive*.[68] The point I would like to stress is how Offe's strategy effectively illustrates the three moments of analysis that define critical theory, that is, systemic, actional, and mediational. To use Liston's terminology, the basis of an adequate explanatory strategy is a combination of what he calls a "mixed" functional claim (that only some "aspects of the selective curriculum persist because of the beneficial consequences for capitalism") and the "intentional claim" that selections are also "the direct outcomes of action that are unintentionally beneficial for capital." For example, "teachers may support tracking because of its positive effect for classroom order and not because tracking has beneficial consequences for capitalism."[69] In other words, this combination of a mixed functional explanation and an intentional analysis corresponds to relating actional and systemic moments of inquiry.[70] Finally, what I have referred to as mediational analysis takes the form of crisis analysis in Offe's strategy: "it is only when class conflict occurs that the implicit class options turn into empirical force, and it is only during these times of class conflict that the ruling class character of the state becomes evident. Offe's methodological route focuses on the eruption of class conflict, that is on times of crisis."[71] This example only illustrates one of the many possible forms of mediational analysis, but shares the essential feature of demonstrating the implications of the disruption of the smooth reproduction of agency-structure relations. This moment of analysis is the empirical foundation and focus of a critical theory of society, even though it cannot be ultimately separated from interpretive and structural analysis as a relatively autonomous research strategy.

THE DANGERS OF REIFYING RESEARCH STRATEGIES

Introduction: The Classic Standoff of Grand Narratives

Though the dichotomization of "positivist" versus "critical" social science is related to the quantitative-qualitative one, it is distinct in important ways. Above all, it is not a false dichotomy in the strong sense because this is a useful way of differentiating research strategies for many purposes. Furthermore, it is inevitably linked with a further distinction between positivist and interpretive research. The dilemma here is not that they are false or even inherently misleading distinctions; the problem is that they lend themselves to being reified and essentialized.

What is at stake here is what might be called the danger of the *chronic reification* of the otherwise useful distinction between three forms of social science: positivist, interpretive, and critical. Each of these terms is typically reified, essentialized, and superficialized in distinctive ways that obscures their interrelatedness, along with the contradictions within each of them. If I give critical theory a privileged place in this trio, it is because I think it provides the most powerful reflexivity for understanding these dilemmas. But it should be stressed that at the center of each strategy of inquiry lies a fundamental aporia or contradiction.

Positivism: Value Free or Liberating?

A fundamental aporia or immanent dilemma of positivism is that it wants to be value-free and yet not abandon its commitment to human enlightenment. The famous Popper-Adorno controversy would not have been possible otherwise.[72] Empiricist research has rarely sought to be fully value-free; its primary aspiration has been to claim a certain "objectivity" that legitimates empirical findings. Indeed, this aspiration for objectivity derived in part from the self-conscious value orientation and political passion that has driven empirical research. Nowhere has this been more apparent than in educational research on social inequality and status attainment.[73]

Critical Theory: Revolutionary or Unscientific?

A fundamental aporia of critical theory is that it wants to be both revolutionary and scientific.[74] Most idealized reconstructions of critical theory gloss over the practical tensions between its "scientific" and "practical" claims. One of the key rationales of much activist oriented critical research is that it is "empowering." Yet paradoxically, the rise of the new right to power largely coincides with the explosion of "empowering" research. For the theory that would place its claim to truth, its proof in the pudding of revolutionary praxis, this is a sobering paradox.

On the other hand, this totalizing identification with praxis runs the risk of jeopardizing any empirical truth claims. Here the attack on positivism confronts two choices: either identification with some metaphysical metanarrative (the residual Hegelianism of the older Frankfurt School) or the offering of an alternative account of social scientific knowledge. The dilemma is that this latter, empirical question gets lost with the reification of critical theory as a normative theory of praxis, just as positivism's normative impulses get buried in the reifications of reconstructed logic.

Constructivist Solipsism: The Paradoxes of Redneck Knowledge

A fundamental aporia of radical constructivism is the paradox of what I have come to call "redneck knowledge." In the context of the polarization between grand paradigmatic explanatory narratives such as the preceding opposition between positivist and critical theory, it is rather too easy for radical constructivism to proclaim itself as the ultimate alternative, now recast as poststructuralist and postmodern. But here again the reifications of totalization raise their ugly head in the reductionism of a constructivist fallacy: social reality is nothing but arbitrary linguistic forms and every standpoint has its own truth. Above all radical constructivism founders on the limits of any uncritical valorization of everyday standpoints. The dilemmas here are typically resolved in two ways. On the one hand, the response is an unflinching relativism that grants equal validity to diverse standpoints, however personally uncomfortable the consequences.

On the other hand, the more typical tendency for progressive intellectuals is to grant the perspectives of the dominated and marginal as having some kind of intrinsic superiority derived, presumably, from their victimized status. The dilemma of this position becomes apparent when claims are voiced by groups who fall outside the "progressive" pantheon, as would be apparent in the paradox of what I sometimes describe as "redneck knowledge." With this term I refer to the structures of feeling and indigenous knowledge that define the experiences and forms of oppression linked to experiences of a white working class (both rural and urban). Here lie the ultimate origins of the *ressentiment* that has redefined American politics. Here is a passionate knowledge of the disadvantages of limited educational opportunity, of being laughed at for signs of a culture of poverty, and of being used as part of a divide and rule strategy of using ethnic conflict, that is, splitting whites and blacks, thus averting class-based mobilization. To simply label this as nothing but racist, right-wing ideology is to beg the question of a theory of ideology which cannot be generated from with a relativistic, radically constructivist perspective. The "Bubbas" of the world have united too.

However important it is to get such suppressed and previously ignored voices heard, this general imperative does not dispense with *the need of every standpoint to develop its own critical hermeneutics*, that is, forms of historical reflexivity that facilitate an internal process of critique and transformation. A crucial component of this process of self-critique is cross-standpoint communication and the development of mediating categories that can link all perspectives. My most fundamental suggestion is that contemporary *critical theory provides the most important questions for answering this challenge.*[75]

In short the reification of these three forms of research produces equally absurd conclusions. For positivists, social reality becomes *nothing but* verifiable propositions. For critical theorists, reality becomes *nothing but* the imperative of utopian transformation. For radical constructivists reality becomes *nothing but* arbitrary linguistic play. Only through fully relational and pragmatically contextual thinking can these essentializing paradoxes be avoided.

CONCLUSION

My basic suggestion for critical theory as a research program in the context of education is twofold. *First*, each national and historical context, along with the increasing interplay between these as reflected in debates about globalization, must be specified with respect to the particular social formation, its political traditions, and the role of the social and human sciences within it. Within this context systemic, interpretive and mediational research all have a place in constructing an ever-changing understanding of concrete social totalities.

Second, within a specific tradition, it is necessary to identify the multiple sites of research practice, each of which defines distinctive priorities. Three of these may be taken as prominent in advanced, liberal democratic societies: the *relatively autonomous research* centers based primarily in universities; the forms of *policy-oriented research and social criticism* that define the debates within the media and the democratic public sphere; and the *participatory action research* that unifies theory and praxis in transformative social movements.

Though these metatheoretical reflections may be far from the everyday life struggles of East LA or Watts, I would hope that they could inform more self-consciously the research practices of those currently attempting to reveal the dynamics of agency, structure, and mediational crisis in urban educational settings. To do so requires the defense of contingently universal explanatory and normative principles. Social science may be a species of rhetoric, but its claim to knowledge—to persuade—is distinctively grounded in a world-historical story that cannot slide into postmodern "universal abandon" without abandoning its raison-d'être. In Andrew Ross's terms, "*In whose interests is it, exactly, to declare the abandonment of universals?*"[76] As he concludes, "To ask such a question is necessarily to survey the uneven effects of 'universal abandon' on our social and cultural landscapes. In asking that question, finally, we are obliged to fall back upon, not the faith, hope, and charity of History, but those resources at hand that can help a reconstructed agenda for our times, and a popular imagery of the future."[77]

My final point is simply that sociology as understood by a critical theory of methodology should have a place on this reconstructed agenda for our times; and that in grounding itself in the interpretive structuralist task of analyzing the universal in the particular *and* the particular in the universal, it mediates between the analytic and hermeneutic—between quasinomothetic generalizing and quasiideographic interpretive strategies, thus creating the formal *conditions of possibility of critical-emancipatory knowledge.*

NOTES

My general approach has been influenced for some time by collaboration with Carlos A. Torres and David D. Brown, though the latter has not had a chance to read this essay. Also, more recently I have become aware of the affinity of my strategy with Charles Ragin's general approach to methodology. (See Charles C. Ragin, *The Comparative Method* (Berkeley: University of California Press, 1987) and Charles C. Ragin, *Constructing Social Research* (Thousand Oaks, Calif.: Pine Forge Press, 1994). Though not explicitly oriented to critical theory, his approach provides a wider context complementary to a critical theory of methodology. Aspects of the general argument developed here were initially formulated in a guest lecture on "Rethinking Qualitative Research: An Interpretive Structuralist Alternative" (30 November 1995) in a paper presented to the Critical Methodologies Lecture Series organized by Ragin at Northwestern University.

1. Robert Dreeben, "The Sociology of Education: Its Development in the United States," in *Research in Sociology of Education and Socialization*, ed. Aaron M. Palls (Greenwich, Conn.: JAI Press, 1994), p. 7.

2. The primary exception here is the work of Ivan Illich dating from the late 1960s; key aspects of his critique of education can be traced to his relationship to the Frankfurt tradition (Morrow and Carlos Alberto Torres, "Ivan Illich and the De-Schooling Thesis Twenty Years After," *New Education* 12:3–17).

3. E.g., Stanley Aronowitz and Henry A. Giroux, *Education under Siege: The Conservative, Liberal and Radical Debate over Schooling* (South Hadley, Mass.: Bergin & Garvey, 1985); Michael W. Apple, *Official Knowledge: Democratic Education in a Conservative Age* (New York and London: Routledge, 1993); Henry Giroux and Peter McLaren, eds., *Between Borders: Pedagogy and the Politics of Cultural Studies* (New York and London: Routledge, 1994); Wilfred Carr and Stephen Kemmis, *Becoming Critical: Education, Knowledge and Action Research* (London and Philadelphia: Falmer Press, 1986).

4. Henry Giroux, ed., *Postmodernism, Feminism, and Cultural Politics: Redrawing Educational Boundaries* (Albany: State University of New York Press, 1991); Aronowitz and Giroux, *Postmodern Education: Politics, Culture and Social Criticism* (Minneapolis: University of Minnesota Press, 1991).

5. From Donald E. Comstock, "A Method for Critical Research," in *Readings in the Philosophy of Social Science*, ed. Michael Martin and Lee C. McIntyre (Cambridge: MIT Press, 1994) to Joe L. Kincheloe and Peter L. McLaren, "Rethinking Critical Theory and Qualitative Research," in *Handbook of Qualitative Research*, ed. Norman K. Denzin and Yvonna S. Lincoln (Thousand Oaks, Calif.: Sage, 1994).

6. This strategy is parallel to but more comprehensive than Forester's notion of "the applied turn in contemporary critical theory," but shares a concern with "concrete analysis of structure and of contingently staged social action" (John Forester, ed., *Critical Theory and Public Life* [Cambridge: MIT Press, 1985], p. xiii; see also Raymond A. Morrow (with D. D. Brown), *Critical Theory and Methodology* [Newbury Park, Calif.: Sage, 1994], p. 24).

7. Morrow and Torres, *Social Theory and Education: A Critique of Theories of Social and Cultural Reproduction* (Albany: State University of New York Press, 1995).

8. Morrow, *Critical Theory and Methodology*.

9. For a perspective that introduces the problematic of critical theory and methodology in a manner parallel to the present discussion, see Thomas S. Popkewitz, "Whose Future? Whose Past? Notes on Critical Theory and Methodology," in *Paradigm Dialog*, ed. Egon G. Guba (Newbury Park, Calif.: Sage, 1990).

10. Three distinctive features of the Frankfurt tradition should be stressed here. First, that it consistently retains a concern with a historical structuralist approach to social knowledge. Despite its critique of positivism and the disciplinary division of labor, the Frankfurt tradition never abandoned the principle of the social sciences as empirically accountable strategies of knowledge construction. Second, that in its later disillusioned "dialectic of Enlightenment"

phase it never succumbed to a full-blown nihilism. As a consequence it is misleading to equate Adorno's later work with postmodernism. And third, that Habermas's work represents a sharp break with respect to social science methodology given his eventual attempt to reconcile critical theory and American pragmatism. It is in the spirit of this latter strategy that I approach the question of a critical theory of methodology. Paradoxically, as Dahms stresses, Habermas in certain respects "switched sides" by moving to a pragmatist consensus theory of truth that had been previously rejected by the older Frankfurt School as "positivist" (Hans-Joachim Dahms, *Positivismusstreit: Die Auseinandersetzungen der Frankfurter Schue mit dem logischen Positivismus, dem amerikanischen Pragmatismus und dem kritischen Rationalismus* [Frankfurt am Main: Suhrkamp, 1994], p. 403; see also Hans Joas, *Pragmatism and Social Theory* [Chicago and London: University of Chicago Press, 1993]).

11. Jerome Karabel and A. H. Halsey, eds., *Power and Ideology in Education* (New York: Oxford University Press, 1977).

12. Ibid., p. 1.

13. Ibid.

14. Ibid., pp. 26–28.

15. Freire is cited peripherally twice.

16. E.g., Henry Giroux, *Ideology, Culture, and the Process of Schooling* (Philadelphia: Temple University Press, 1981).

17. This, of course, is a contentious thesis that I will not pursue further here.

18. In this context, discussions oriented toward the relationship between critical theory and education had only just emerged (e.g., Dieter Misgeld, "Emancipation, Enlightenment, and Liberation: An Approach Toward Foundational Inquiry into Education," *Interchange 6* (1975): 23–37). See also, Morrow and Torres, *Social Theory and Education: A Critique of Theories of Social and Cultural Reproduction* (Albany: State University of New York Press, 1995), p. 217ff.

19. Paul Willis's *Learning to Labor* (New York: Columbia University Press, 1981), a pioneering reference point for education and cultural studies, was first published in 1977, the same year as the Karabel and Halsey anthology. The question of the relationship between the Marxist tradition and education was still dominated by French structuralism and Bowles and Gintis's correspondence theory of educational reproduction (Samuel Bowles and Herbert Gintis, *Schooling in Capitalist America: Educational Reform and the Contradictions of Economic Life* (New York: Basic Books/Harper, 1977).

20. Karabel and Halsey, *Power and Ideology*, p. 59.

21. Norman K. Denzin and Yvonna S. Lincoln, eds., *Handbook of Qualitative Research* (Thousand Oaks, Calif.: Sage, 1994).

22. Daniel P. Liston, *Capitalist Schools: Explanation and Ethics in Radical Studies of Schooling* (New York and London: Routledge, 1988).

23. Daniel Little, *Varieties of Social Explanation: An Introduction to the Philosophy of Social Science* (Boulder, Colo.: Westview Press, 1991).

24. Nowadays, to be sure, there has been a partial toppling of positivist discourse under the heading of postmodernism, introducing new problems that

will not be the focus here. Suffice it to say that much postmodernism so under-cuts the project of disciplinary knowledge that it risks total relativism.

25. Abraham Kaplan, *The Conduct of Inquiry: Methodology for Behavioral Science* (San Francisco: Chandler, 1964).

26. As opposed to postmodernism as a theory of genres and styles or a periodizing concept for social and cultural change (e.g., Krishnan Kumar, *From Post-Industrial to Post-Modern Society* [Oxford: Blackwell, 1995]).

27. What I think is less often noted is that much confusion stems from the lack of identity, or perhaps the largely *negative identity* of so-called "qualitative" approaches that are united primarily by their opposition to constructing social facts as statistically defined variables. One of the central goals of our book was to recast the relationship between interpretive and statistical-causal research, making the latter merely a heuristic method ultimately dependent on the primary of interpretive (hence qualitative) theory and research. More recently, however, alternative criteria have elaborated for qualitative research (e.g., Joseph A. Maxwell, "Understanding and Validity in Qualitative Research," *Harvard Educational Review* 62 [1992]: 279–300).

28. The dominance of the quantitative-statistical model in North America can be attributed to a number of historical factors (above all, the rhetorical appeal of natural scientific models for legitimating social science) that need not concern us here. But it should be recalled that the emergence of the sociology of education in the 1960s can be traced in part to its effective use of statistical methods in stratification, mobility and status attainment research (Robert Dreeben, "The Sociology of Education: Its Development in the United States," in *Research in Sociology of Education and Socialization*, ed. Aaron M. Palls [Greenwich, Conn.: JAI Press, 1994]).

29. Denzin and Lincoln, *Handbook*.

30. Though the dust jacket boasts of contributors from "three continents," the connection is exclusively through American/Commonwealth hegemony of the English language, rather than any authentic cross-cultural concerns. And despite the North American focus, one would never guess that French Quebec and Mexico have highly developed traditions of qualitative inquiry.

31. I will not discuss extensively what it does well, let alone convey the range, diversity, and vitality of the forms of research touched upon. Above all, it brings the problematic of a poststructuralist or postmodernist (the terms are used virtually interchangeably) questioning of representational realism and scientific authority are brought to the center of attention, along with the inevitable value-laden and subjective basis of all inquiry. Further, this is a multicultural text that reflects the rainbow of standpoints competing for the limelight of attention and is truly interdisciplinary in orientation.

32. Denzin and Lincoln, *Handbook*, p. 4.

33. Ibid., pp. 5–6.

34. Nicholas Abercrombie, Stephen Hill, and Bryan S. Turner, *The Penguin Dictionary of Sociology*, 2nd ed. (Harmondsworth, England: Penguin Books, 1988), p. 119.

35. David Jary and Juali Jary, *Collins Dictionary of Sociology* (Glasgow: Harper Collins, 1991), p. 297.

36. Robert E. Stake, "Case Studies," in *Handbook of Qualitative Research*, ed. Norman J. Denzin and Yvonna S. Lincoln (Thousand Oaks, Calif.: Sage, 1994), p. 242.

37. Kincheloe and McLaren, "Rethinking Critical Theory."

38. There are several consequence for their strategy of defining qualitative research. *First*, the consequences of Denzin and Lincoln's relativistic standpoint epistemology is evident in their attempts to classify theoretical strategies. Difference is always privileged over similarity. Five theoretical-methodological "paradigms and perspectives" in qualitative research are covered in the editors' introduction: constructivist, critical theory (often reduced to Marxist), feminisms, ethnic (racial), and cultural studies. This classification obscures the more fundamental features of these modes of inquiry. Obsessed by the search for difference, each is portrayed monadically, monologically, and with only occasional, half-hearted reference to problems of validity or comparable approaches. *Second*, the problematic of qualitative research is to a great extent reduced to ethnography and textuality. Another strategy of classification is based on more specifically methodological criteria that identify qualitative research with what is variously referred to as ethnographic, field or participant observation research, or more peripherally particular techniques of analyzing symbolic materials. Despite a chapter on historical research, the problematic does not enter into the overall structure of the book and remains marginal to virtually all of the individual chapters. *Third*, contemporary critical theory loses its specific identity as a strategy for overcoming the very dualisms around which Denzin and Lincoln organize their anthology. If we look at the five-phase model of the research process presented, it appears that critical theory gets implicitly subsumed in either "Marxist models" or "cultural studies models"; moreover, these are reduced to "theoretical paradigms and perspectives" whose conceptual and empirical relation to "research strategies" remains largely unclassified (except for critical theory and a specific form of postmodernist ethnography privileged by the authors of the chapter in question). The editors are more concerned with a triumphal evolutionary model of approaches culminating in celebrating the differences within the postmodern here and now, rather than clarifying the relationships among methodology, social theory, and practice (Denzin and Lincoln, *Handbook of Qualitative Research*).

39. For the contemporary philosophical implications of this problematic, see Karl-Otto Apel, *Understanding and Explanation: A Transcendental-Pragmatic Perspective*, trans. Georgie Warnke (Cambridge: MIT Press, 1984).

40. Space limitations preclude a more extended exploration of this problematic here, but see Guy Oakes, *Weber and Rickert* (Cambridge: MIT Press, 1988).

41. Though the basic stance of interpretive structuralism has been sketched above with reference to Weber and Bourdieu, it is useful to refer as well to contemporary manifestations of the polarization they are criticizing. In the social sciences this polarization has been associated with contrasts between qualitative and quantitative, phenomenological and behaviorist, antipositivist and positivist, and so on. In the humanities this contrast has been defined more in terms of existentialism versus structuralism. Though aspects of poststructuralism

could be associated with overcoming this dualism, much work so labeled in fact slips backs into subjectivist standpoint theory.

42. I would argue that such a conception is also implicit in the early Marx and that such an interpretive structuralist strategy is a pervasive feature of much classical sociology (Simmel, Mannheim), and more recent reformulations (Mills, Berger and Luckmann, Giddens, Bourdieu, etc.).

43. Pierre Bourdieu and Loïc J. D. Wacquant, *An Invitation to Reflexive Sociology* (Chicago and London: University of Chicago Press, 1992), p . 75.

44. The most rigorous formulation of this argument can be found in the work of Roy Bhaskar (e.g., Roy Bhaskar, *Scientific Realism and Human Emancipation* [London and New York: Verso, 1986]).

45. Gaye Tuchman, "Historical Social Science: Methodologies, Methods, and Meanings," in *Handbook of Qualitative Research*, ed. Norman J. Denzin and Yvonna S. Lincoln (Thousand Oaks, Calif.: Sage, 1994).

46. Kincheloe and McLaren, "Rethinking Critical Theory," pp. 139–40.

47. Ibid., p. 140.

48. E.g. James Bohman, *New Philosophy of Social Science* (Cambridge: MIT Press, 1991); Ragin, *Constructing Social Research*.

49. Though Denzin's roots in pragmatism should have alerted him to other possibilities, his linguistic and postmodernist turn has attenuated his relationship to pragmatism in the direction of a Rorty's postmodernist neopragmatism.

50. See the clear and cogent exposition of Hekman who contrasts Althusser's structuralist Marxism and Habermas critical theory as objective analyses, arguing that though Althusser succumbs to objectivism, Habermas "comes so close to achieving a synthesis of the subjective and objective" (Susan Hekman, *Max Weber, the Ideal Type, and Contemporary Social Theory* [Notre Dame: University of Notre Dame Press, 1983], p. 145). As she concludes, if social science is to have a cognitive status beyond the language of everyday life, it must "define a conception of social scientific analysis which begins with actors' conceptions of their actions yet grants social-scientific understanding an explanatory status vis-à-vis those concepts. . . . Weber's attempt to define a conception of objectivity which avoids the pitfalls of both positivism and subjectivism is highly relevant to contemporary discussions" (p. 152). While I agree with her contention that Weber's concept of ideal types provides an essential bridge for mediating between interpretive and structural analysis, she does not address the crucial importance of structuralist concepts as non-nomothetic forms of generalization, a theme of interpretive structuralism as developed here.

51. The specific term can and should be contextualized with respect to what it opposes, as well as within a family of similar notions. Interpretive structuralism should first be contrasted with *empiricist structuralism*, on the one hand, and *hyperstructuralism* of the type proposed by Lévi-Strauss for a structuralist anthropology or Althusser for a structuralist Marxism. Both of these later strategies largely eliminate the subject and history from social inquiry. Interpretive structuralism shares some elements with poststructuralism in its rejection of the limitations of classic structuralism. Empiricist structuralism, on the other hand, originates in a very different conception of empirical regularities

and their relationship to "effects" or the production of social phenomena. Empiricist structuralism corresponds to the standard positivist strategy of a search for causal laws that probabalistically determine social actions. In contrast, forms of structuralism influenced by linguistic models point to generative mechanisms that define the rules that constrain human action, but do not determine its specific outcomes any more than a grammar determines what we might say, as opposed to how we must speak whatever we will.

52. Morrow, *Critical Theory and Methodology*, p. 226ff.

53. For a more detailed sketch of intensive research designs, see ibid., 248ff. and Andrew Sayer, *Method in Social Science: A Realist Approach*, 2nd ed. (London and New York: Routledge, 1992).

54. Morrow, *Critical Theory and Methodology*, p. 221ff.

55. Though originating in critical theory, these distinctions have been increasingly employed in the philosophy of social science (e.g., David Braybrooke, *Philosophy of Social Science* [Englewood Cliffs, N.J.: Prentice Hall, 1987]) and sociological methods texts (e.g., W. Lawrence Neuman, *Social Research Methods: Qualitative and Quantitative Approaches* [Boston: Allyn and Bacon, 1991]).

56. Paul Ricoeur, *Hermeneutics and the Human Sciences*, trans. and ed. John B. Thompson (Cambridge: Cambridge University Press, 1981).

57. Jürgen Habermas, *On the Logic of the Social Sciences*, trans. Shierry Weber Nicholsen and Jerry A. Stark (Cambridge: MIT Press, 1988), p. 3.

58. Jürgen Habermas, *Knowledge and Human Interests*, trans. Jeremy J. Shapiro (Boston: Beacon, 1971).

59. Paul Ricoeur, *The Conflict of Interpretations*, ed. Don Ihde (Evanston, Ill.: Northwestern University Press, 1974).

60. Fay terms this form of knowledge quasi-causal, but this aspect of critical theory remains ambiguous (Brian Fay, *Social Theory and Political Practice* [London: George Allen & Unwin, 1975]). His objective clearly is to avoid identification with the presuppositions of nomothetic and covering law models of causality. As he later concludes, "ultimately the nature of social-scientific theory (with its hereronomic generalizations, limitations in scope and specificity, and restriction to a particular [sort of] cultural setting) is shaped by the essential historicity of the objects it seeks to explain" (Fay, "General Laws and Explaining Human Behavior," in *Readings in the Philosophy of Social Science*, ed. Michael Martin and Lee C. McIntyre [Cambridge: MIT Press, 1994 (1983)]). I have sought to link non-nomothetic generalizing strategies to various forms of historicist structuralism found generally in classical sociological theory. In his early writings Habermas relied rather too much on positivist definitions of the empirical-analytical interest and had not yet fully incorporated the structuralist principles that inform his later social theory.

61. It is unclear where Lincoln stands on these issues, having participated in both formulations. This present formulation appears to originate from Guba (Egon G. Guba, ed., *The Paradigm Dialog* [Newbury Park, Calif.: Sage, 1990]).

62. The term "postpositivist" here refers to a form of empiricism (largely Popperian) that is sensitive to the pitfalls and limitations of classical positivism.

63. Egon G. Guba and Yvonna S. Lincoln, "Competing Paradigms in Qual-

itative Research," in *Handbook of Qualitative Research*, ed. Norman J. Denzin and Yvonna S. Lincoln (Thousand Oaks, Calif.: Sage, 1994).

64. Ibid., p. 113.

65. From this perspective, quantitative methods perform a similar, complementary heuristic role. Though they have the advantage of formal precision and in some cases more decisive evidential "tests," they are fundamentally limited because extensive research designs are inevitably abstracted out of concrete, historical social relations. The resulting artificiality does not make such research meaningless or unimportant in constructing comprehensive social explanations and interpretations, but it does make it something less significant than the classic positivist idealization of the cover-law model of explanation.

66. There are two fundamental differences, however. Critical theory approaches are more radically *historicist* in that causal structures are not reified as "causal laws" but are integrated into historically specific case studies. For example, Stinchcombe's (1968) justifiably famous discussion of causal imageries in demographic, functionalist and historicist explanations remains tied to the positivist search for general laws to be decomposed in terms of causal variables. As a consequence, agency and historicity gets suppressed within formalized causal loops and chains that may serve a certain heuristic purpose, but do not literally map contingent, open systems. The rhetoric of formalization runs the risk of self-deception. (Arthur Stinchcombe, *Constructing Social Theories* [New York: Harcourt, Brace & World, 1968]).

67. For a good sample of more recent work illustrating such an integral approach to a critical sociology of education, see the international contributions in Heinz Sünker, Dieter Timmermann, and Fritz-Ulrich Kolbe, eds., 1994. *Bildung, Gesellschaft, soziale Ungleichheit: Internationale Beiträge zur Bildungssoziologie und Bildungstheorie* (Frankfurt am Main: Suhrkamp, 1994).

68. Liston, *Capitalist Schools*, p. 114ff.

69. Ibid., p. 107.

70. In the work of Habermas and others this problematic is often referred to in terms of the distinction between systemic and social integration (e.g., Nicos P. Mouzelis, *Back to Sociological Theory* [London: Macmillan, 1991]).

71. Liston, *Capitalist Schools*, p. 118.

72. Theodor W. Adorno et al., *The Positivist Dispute in German Sociology*, trans. Glyn Adey and David Frisby (London: Heinemann, 1976).

73. The real dilemma of empiricist research has always been elsewhere: connecting its piecemeal and middle range findings with a theory of society. The alliance between Merton and Parsons can be traced to this question, as well as that between later researchers such as Bowles and Gintis and Marxist theory. Again, educational research is instructive because it is here where the fruitful interplay between empiricism and social theory has often been apparent. Researchers concerned with status attainment and mobility analysis often see their work as contributing to a general theory of social and cultural reproduction. Partly as a consequence, it would be hard to find representatives of critical or Marxist theory in education who reject in toto quantitative approaches to social research.

74. Alvin Gouldner, *The Two Marxisms* (New York: Seabury, 1980).

75. Nicholas C. Burbules, *Dialogue in Teaching: Theory and Practice* (New York: Teachers College Press, 1993).

76. Andrew Ross, "Introduction," in *Universal Abandon? The Politics of Postmodernism*, ed. Andrew Ross (Minneapolis: University of Minnesota Press, 1989), p. xiv.

77. Ibid., p. xvii.

CHAPTER 3

Sociology of Education and Urban Education Policy

Geoff Whitty

INTRODUCTION

Some of you will know that the chair I hold in the University of London is named after the sociologist Karl Mannheim. Karl Mannheim himself was appointed to a chair of education at the Institute of Education in 1946, just a year before his tragically early death in January 1947. I recently trawled the institute archives for material about Karl Mannheim in preparation for a lecture to mark the fiftieth anniversary of his death.[1] In the wartime archives, I came across a paper by the then director of the institute, Sir Fred Clarke, in which he argued the case for appointing someone like Mannheim—and he clearly had Mannheim himself in mind—to a position at the institute as soon as the war was over. He said the case could be related to "the uneasy awareness, now so widespread and yet so ill-defined, that great changes in the social order and the inter-play of social forces are already in progress—and that educational theory and educational policy that take no account of these will be not only blind but positively harmful."[2]

Fifty years later, there is a similar sense that significant but ill-defined changes in the nature of the social order are in progress. Unless gatherings of sociologists here are very different from those in England at the moment, it will no doubt be a matter of some debate among us as to whether we are living in late capitalism, postmodernity, high modernity, post-traditionalism, or whatever. Yet, just as in the days of Mannheim, too much education policy and even a great deal of contemporary educational research—not least within my own institute—has lost sight of Clarke's important insight that education policy needs to be informed by a sensitivity to the nature of these changes. Meanwhile the education press is full of advertisements for posts in educational administration and management, and more particularly school effectiveness and school improvement, but there is not exactly a glut of positions in the sociology of education.

Like Clarke, I believe this neglect of our discipline can be positively harmful, not just to our own career chances but to education policy and practice. In my chapter, I want therefore to explore two main themes. First, the ways in which sociology might help us to make sense of contemporary education policy. And, second, the ways in which sociology might be positioned in relation to future developments in education policy and practice. In doing so, I will draw mainly on two areas of education policy that I have been studying in some detail over the past few years—school reform and the reformation of teaching as a profession. Most of this work has been carried out in urban settings and, like Grace, I would argue that the contradictions that characterize modern state education are at their sharpest within urban contexts and impact upon the lives of teachers and students there in particularly intense ways.[3]

THEORETICAL INSIGHTS

To take the first question, what sociological accounts might, for instance, help us to make sense of the current trend in many parts of the world to restructure and deregulate state education systems? Central to these initiatives have been moves to disband centralized educational bureaucracies and create in their place devolved systems of schooling entailing significant degrees of institutional autonomy and a variety of forms of school-based management and administration. In many cases, these changes have been linked to an increased emphasis on parental choice and on competition between diversified and specialized forms of provision, thereby creating what we now call "quasi-markets " in educational services.[4]

Although such policies have received particular encouragement from New Right governments in Britain and the United States in the 1980s, and have subsequently been fostered by the International Monetary Fund and the World Bank in Latin America and Eastern Europe,[5] the political rhetoric of parties of the left has also begun to place increasing emphasis on diversity and choice in education. Even though these directions in education policy have not penetrated all countries,[6] and they have been mediated differently by the traditions of different nation states and different political parties, the similarity between the broad trends in many parts of the world suggests that education policy may be witnessing something sociologically significant—something perhaps rather more important than the passing political fashion of Thatcherism and the like.

Shilling argues correctly that too many analyses of education policy—and he includes some of my own work in his strictures—are characterized by a lack of theory and sociology.[7] So how far can contemporary social theory help us make sense of recent education policy? It is sometimes suggested that current shifts in the ways in which education is organized reflect broader changes in the nature of advanced industrial societies, characterized by some commentators as post-Fordism and by others as postmodernity.

Ball, for example, has claimed to see in new forms of schooling a move away from the "Fordist " school toward a "post-Fordist" one— the educational equivalent of flexible specialization driven by the imperatives of differentiated consumption replacing the old assembly-line world of mass production.[8] Kenway, though, regards the rapid rise of the market form in education as something much more significant than post-Fordism; she therefore terms it a "postmodern" phenomenon. In her own pessimistic version of postmodernity, "transnational corporations and their myriad subsidiaries . . . shape and reshape our individual and collective identities as we plug in . . . to their cultural and economic communications networks."[9] Her picture is one in which notions of "difference," far from being eradicated by the "globalization of culture," are assembled, displayed, celebrated, commodified, and exploited.[10] Such trends, she implies, can be detected in the current emphasis on both tradition and diversity in education policy.

In other accounts the rhetoric of "new times" seems to offer more positive images of choice and diversity, reflecting the needs of communities and interest groups brought into prominence as a result of complex contemporary patterns of political, economic, and cultural differentiation, which intersect the traditional class divisions upon which common systems of mass education were predicated. From this perspective, it is possible to contrast postmodernity to the oppressive uniformity of much modernist thinking—as "a form of liberation, in which the fragmentation and plurality of cultures and social groups allow a hundred flowers to bloom."[11]

It has been suggested that part of the appeal of the recent education reforms lies in their declared intention to encourage the growth of different types of schools, responsive to needs of particular communities and groups. Possibilities for community-based welfare, rather than bureaucratically controlled welfare, have sometimes been viewed positively particularly by women and minority ethnic groups. The concept of diversity seems to articulate with the ideas of radical pluralism and can seem more attractive than unidimensional notions of comprehensive schooling and, indeed, unidimensional notions of citizenship. Some aspects of the rhetoric of the new policies thus seem to connect to the aspirations of groups who have found little to identify with in the "grand narratives" associated with class-based politics. In this sense, the reforms might be viewed as a rejection of all totalizing narratives and their replacement by "a set of cultural projects united [only] by a self-proclaimed commitment to heterogeneity, fragmentation and differ-ence."[12] In other words, support for schools run on a variety of princi-ples may reflect a broader shift from the assumptions of modernity to those of postmodernity.

EMPIRICAL GROUNDING

Suggestive as they are, however, it is perhaps too easy to get carried away by these contemporary versions of "correspondence theory." Michael Apple warns us to be wary of overstating the move into post-modernity and to avoid the danger of "substituting one grand narrative for another." He also points to the need to ground our understandings in the lives of teachers and students in schools, another important aspect of the sociological enterprise.[13] And, when we start to interrogate theory with research, we encounter various problems with these "new times" theses. Not only are they "notoriously vague,"[14] they also tend to exag-gerate the extent to which we have moved to a new regime of accumu-lation. Insofar as recent changes in management practices represent an adjustment to the problems of Fordism rather than signifying an entirely new direction, neo-Fordism may be a more appropriate term than post-Fordism.[15]

Meanwhile, there is a growing body of empirical evidence that par-ticularly the more optimistic readings of postmodernity are dangerously naive. Rather than benefiting the urban poor, as many of the advocates of quasi-market systems of public education claim,[16] the emphasis on parental choice and school autonomy in recent reforms seems to be fur-ther disadvantaging the disadvantaged. It is certainly increasing the dif-ferences between popular and less popular schools on a linear scale—reinforcing a vertical hierarchy of schooling types rather than producing the promised horizontal diversity. For most members of disadvantaged groups, as opposed to the few individuals who escape from schools at the bottom of the status hierarchy, the new arrangements seem to be just a more sophisticated and intensified way of reproducing traditional dis-tinctions between different types of schools and between the people who attend them.[17]

Such evidence from a whole range of empirical studies suggests that to regard the current espousal of heterogeneity, pluralism, and local narratives as indicative of a new social order may be to mistake phenomenal forms for structural relations. Marxist critics of theories of postmodernism and postmodernity, such as Callinicos, who reassert the primacy of the class struggle, certainly take this view.[18] Even Harvey, who does recognize significant changes, suggests that postmodernist cultural forms and more flexible modes of capital accumulation may be shifts in surface appearance, rather than signs of the emergence of some entirely new postcapitalist or even postindustrial society.[19] At most, current reforms would seem to relate to a version of postmodernity that emphasizes "distinction" and "hierarchy" within a fragmented social order, rather than one that positively celebrates "difference" and "heterogeneity."[20] Thus, despite new forms of accumulation, together with some limited changes in patterns of social and cultural differentiation, the continuities seem as striking as the discontinuities.

THE STATE, CIVIL SOCIETY, AND "AUTONOMOUS" SCHOOLS

Yet, if some of the flights of fancy of contemporary social theory focus too much on the rhetoric and not enough on the reality of education reform, other less ambitious theories in the field of political sociology can help us to dig beneath the rhetoric and identify something significant going on. Thus, even if current policies are new ways of dealing with old problems, there clearly have been changes in the state's mode of regulation. With the delegitimation of conventional political and bureaucratic control by democratically accountable public bodies, there are more and more quasi-autonomous institutions with devolved budgets competing for clients in the marketplace—a system of market accountability sometimes assisted by a series of directly appointed agencies, trusts, and regulators. Such quasi-autonomous institutions, state-funded but with considerable private and voluntary involvement in their operation, appear to make education less of a political issue. But sociologically, the new arrangements for managing education and other public services can be seen as new ways of resolving the problems of accumulation and legitimation facing the state in a situation where the traditional Keynesian "welfare state" is no longer viable.[21] They are, if you like, an attempt to "export the crisis."[22]

So, although the extent of any underlying social changes can easily be exaggerated by various "postist" forms of analysis, both the discourse and the contexts of political struggles in and around education have been significantly altered by recent reforms. Not only have changes in the nature of the state influenced the reforms in education, the reforms in education are themselves beginning to change the way we think about the role of the state and what we expect of it. Green has pointed to the way in which education has not only been an important part of state activity in modern societies, but also played a significant role in the process of state formation itself in the eighteenth and nineteenth centuries.[23] The current changes in education policy may similarly be linked to a redefinition of the nature of the state and a reworking of the relations between state and civil society.

The new education policies foster the idea that responsibility for education and welfare, beyond the minimum required for public safety, is to be defined as a matter for individuals and families. Not only is the scope of the state narrowed, but civil society becomes increasingly defined in market terms. Although one of the many origins of the concept of civil society was the attempt by late-eighteenth-century liberal economists to protect an autonomous economic sphere from the growing administrative power of the state, political radicals used it as a context for democratic debate and the fostering of active citizenship.[24] However, Meehan suggests that, by the mid-twentieth century in Britain and some other countries, the establishment of political democracy led to a view in many countries that state bureaucratic regulation itself might serve as "a tool to improve the collective life of society."[25] This reliance on the state led to a decline in the autonomy and vitality of civil society.

Now, however, civil society is being reconstituted. But, as many of the responsibilities adopted by the state during the postwar period begin to be devolved to a marketized version of civil society, consumer rights increasingly come to prevail over citizen rights. So some aspects of education have been "privatized" not so much in the strictly economic sense as in the sense of transferring them to the private sphere. Meanwhile, others have become a matter of state mandate rather than local democratic debate. This can be seen as part of that broader project to create a free economy and a strong state[26]—a minimalist state in most respects but a more powerful one in defining its parameters. As far as democratic citizenship is concerned, this seems to produce the worst of both worlds—reducing the opportunities for democratic debate and collective action about education within both the state and civil society.

Thus, despite the rhetoric about "rolling back" or "hollowing out" the state, in many countries certain aspects of state intervention have been maintained, indeed strengthened. This is particularly noticeable in Britain, but has also been noted, in differing degrees, in other contexts such as New Zealand and parts of Latin America.[27] This may appear to be less the case in the United States than elsewhere, though in a federal state one would need to consider the combined powers of state and federal governments in relation to local government, so that (for example) state-sponsored charter schools may strengthen the role of the state government and the individual institution at the expense of local school boards.

McKenzie claims that British governments have actually increased their claims to knowledge and authority over the education system while promoting a theoretical and superficial movement toward consumer sovereignty.[28] It is certainly the case that a great deal of recent education reform, notably the National Curriculum, was as much to do with transferring power from the local state to the central state as with giving autonomy to the schools. This suggests that it is not merely that the contemporary state has devolved responsibility to a remarketized civil society. In the British case at least, it has abdicated some responsibility for ensuring social justice by deregulating major aspects of education, but in increasing a limited number of state powers it has actually strengthened its capacity to foster particular interests while appearing to stand outside the frame. In this situation, the removal or marginalization of the influence of interest groups (such as local authorities and trade unions) between the state and the individual institution may not have empowered the poor but actually made them more vulnerable.[29]

There are similar issues at the institutional level, where it is often claimed that self-management empowers teachers. Yet a number of studies have shown classroom teachers to be less positive about the recent reforms than headteachers.[30] While heads usually say that local management has increased the involvement of teaching staff in decision-making, a study of the effects of self-management on industrial relations in British schools by Sinclair and colleagues suggests that the very logic of the reforms is that "headteachers are no longer partners in the process of educating pupils—they become allocators of resources within the school, managers who are driven to ensure that the activities of employees are appropriate to the needs of the business, and givers of rewards to those whose contribution to the business is most highly regarded." At the same time, teachers' work is intensified in the name of the interests of the school community. In this situation, the celebration of flexibility and claims of enhanced professionalism can easily become a cover for the exploitation of teachers and worsening conditions of service.[31]

As Blackmore points out in an Australian review of the evidence, the self-managing school retains "strong modernist tendencies for a top-down, executive mode of decision-making . . . [alongside its] 'weaker' post-modern claims to decentralize and encourage diversity, community ownership, local discretion, professional autonomy and flexible decision-making."[32] Even the more genuinely participatory forms of teacher involvement in decision-making can have unintended consequences. One report on Minnesota charter schools, for example, commented that "as much as teachers appreciated being board members and making administrative decisions, wearing two hats required a great deal of time and effort" from which they would eventually require some relief.[33]

Strategies of neighborhood empowerment also have their limitations, since communities are far from equally endowed with the material and cultural resources for self-management of their schools, as Gordon has demonstrated in the case of New Zealand.[34] In the case of the Chicago reforms, Lewis and Nakagawa claim that "even if the model is implemented well, a tall order in and of itself, the exogenous factors that lead to the failure of the minority poor in school . . . would seem to require more than a change in school governance can deliver."[35] Certainly, such strategies are unlikely to succeed in the absence of changes in the broader distributive policies adopted by the central state.

Such research calls into question the frequent assumption in current policy discourse that it is the poor and the teaching profession who have the most to gain from recent reforms. Yet much of this remains opaque to those who regard the autonomous schools spawned by the recent reforms as genuinely empowered. Not only neoliberal rhetoric, but also much of the school improvement literature, takes the discursive repositioning of schools as autonomous agencies at its face value rather than recognizing that the atomization of schooling too often merely allows advantaged schools to enhance their advantages.[36] For those schools ill-placed to capitalize on their market position, the devolution of responsibility can often merely lead to the devolution of blame. And, particularly for schools in the inner city, there is a danger that too much emphasis upon the power of individual school faculty to seek their own salvation may only result in further damage to the morale of an increasingly exploited workforce.

IMPLICATIONS FOR POLICY

Sociologically informed studies of education policy can thus help to provide lenses that are at some variance with the taken-for-granted assumptions of much contemporary education policy.[37] We begin to move here into my second theme, which concerns the role of sociology in relation to future policies. Even if sociologists were able to agree on the epistemological status of our discipline, and that is unlikely, there would be a variety of ways in which sociology could be positioned in relation to other forms of practice. But, if few of us today believe that theorizing and charting changes in the social order and the interplay of social forces enables sociologists to provide solutions to urban educational problems in a direct or simplistic way, as Mannheim tended to assume in his later work,[38] does that mean that we should eschew engagement with policy altogether?

I would not want to argue, even if I once did, that there is some sort of imperative that requires all sociologists of education to forge explicit links with the world of policy and practice.[39] Nevertheless, many sociologists of education have, over the years, seen their work in these terms, particularly in relation to various forms of progressive policy and practice. Yet many sociologists of education seem somehow less engaged with social justice issues than they did, say, twenty years ago. Indeed, it is noticeable that, while sociologists of education seem to have become more isolated in the academy and increasingly disengaged from wider social movements, broader social theorists such as Giddens seem to be showing a greater willingness to address the political challenges posed by a changing social order.[40]

Of course, by no means have all sociologists of education abandoned engagement with the world of policy and practice. But some seem virtually to have abandoned their discipline, and more particularly its characteristically critical mode of engagement with the world of policy and practice, to engage more directly with technical issues of school effectiveness and school improvement.[41] Grace, who pioneered a sociological approach to urban education in Britain in the 1970s, has often dismissed the sort of "policy science" that typified American urban education in the 1970s on the grounds that it had become trapped within the assumptions of the particular policy context being studied.[42] Such work has laid itself open to the charge of "producing naive school-centered solutions with no sense of the structural, the political and the historical as constraints."[43] Much the same could be said of much of the work of the contemporary school improvement movement.

Grace's own alternative of "policy scholarship" maintains a sense of both theory and history that helps us to recognise the "bigger picture" and hints at the specific contribution that sociologists might make to our understanding of both the limits and possibilities of progressive policy and practice. Yet the term "policy scholarship" itself seems too detached to communicate the sort of relationship between critical theory and progressive practice that Grace, following Fay, envisages.[44] Whatever his own intentions, it could serve to reinforce that very disarticulation between the academy and the world outside that has led to a widening gulf between progressive educators and the communities they claim to serve—a gulf that is underscored by the juxtaposition of what, even after a period of retrenchment, is the relative affluence of the university with the devastation of the inner city.

This condition is, however, also a feature of other fields of professional and academic practice, including some in which the discourse seems unambiguously committed to an interventionist stance. Thus, it is not only sociology of education that, especially in Britain and the United States, has often become disarticulated from its object of study or engagement, so has education policy itself. Using Bourdieu's notion of social field, Ladwig argues that the field of education policy in the United States has developed a considerable degree of autonomy. He observes that the very fact that observations about the "failure" of education policy or its implications for particular groups pose no threat to the relatively autonomous field of education policy is indicative of the extent to which education policy as a field has become self-justifying and self-perpetuating.[45]

How, then, might sociologists who are dissatisfied with this condition not only re-engage with education policy but also help to re-engage education policy with the everyday experience of struggles in and around education while maintaining a critical stance? It would be comforting to think that we might rediscover what it means to be Gramscian organic intellectuals in the conditions of the late twentieth century. In this respect, neither the Mannheimian view of free-floating intellectuals or the Foucauldian concept of specific intellectuals is as appealing as the Gramscian one if we are concerned with the broad context of social injustice within which I have implied education is located. But what precisely this means in relation to new social movements is less clear than it was when, at least in the European context, there was a clearer notion of a labor movement with which to engage.[46]

DEVELOPING NEW CONTEXTS OF ENGAGEMENT

In *Sociology and School Knowledge*, I suggested that "the practical implications of [sociological] work for . . . political and educational practice [are] as much concerned with the ways in which policy is made as with specific substantive policies."[47] One area where I would argue that sociologists may potentially have an important role is in advocacy—not so much of specific interests, but of the importance of identifying and bringing together those constituencies that have conventionally been excluded from education policy and decision-making either intentionally or, just as often, as an unintended consequence of decisions made with the best of intentions. If, as much of the initial research evidence suggests, recent reforms are encouraging advantaged schools and advantaged families to maximize their advantage, then it is particularly important that there is an arena in which equity issues can be considered collectively by the various stakeholders in public education.[48]

Yet I suggested earlier that social relations were becoming increasingly accommodated in the notion of the strong state and the free economy. If that is the case, then neither the state nor civil society is currently much of a context for active democratic citizenship through which social justice can be pursued. How then might the field of education policy be reconstituted, reinvigorated, and rearticulated with political and professional struggles over education? The reassertion of citizenship rights in education would seem to require the development of a new public sphere somehow between the state and a marketized civil society, in which new forms of collective association can be developed. Foucault pointed out that what he called new forms of association, such as trade unions and political parties, arose in the nineteenth century as a counterbalance to the prerogative of the state, and that they acted as the seedbed of new ideas.[49] We need to consider what might be the modern versions of these collectivist forms of association to counterbalance not only the prerogative of the state, but also the prerogative of the market.

However, given what has been dismantled by New Right governments, creating a new public sphere in which educational matters can even be debated—let alone determined—poses a considerable challenge. Part of the challenge must be to move away from atomized decision-making to the reassertion of collective responsibility for education without recreating the very bureaucratic systems whose shortcomings have helped to legitimate the current tendency to treat education as a private good rather than a public responsibility. We need to ask how we can use the positive aspects of choice and autonomy to facilitate community empowerment rather than exacerbating social differentiation. The left has done little yet to develop a concept of public education that looks significantly different from the state education so often criticized in the past for its role in reproducing and legitimating social inequalities.[50] And even if the social democratic era looks better in retrospect, and in comparison with current policies, than it did at the time, that does not remove the need to rethink what might be progressive policies for the next century.

Nevertheless, Apple argues that we should recognize that there are some aspects of past practice in schools that should be defended as gains of collective struggles by progressive forces over the years.[51] Certainly, our fascination with recent neoliberal reforms can blind us to the potential of other ways of struggling to achieve social justice. As Henig rightly says, "the sad irony of the current education-reform movement is that, through over-identification with school-choice proposals rooted in market-based ideas, the healthy impulse to consider radical reforms to address social problems may be channeled into initiatives that further erode the potential for collective deliberation and collective response."[52]

But if new approaches to collective decision-making are to be granted more legitimacy than previous ones, what new institutions might help to foster them—initially within a new public sphere in which ideas can be debated, but potentially as new forms of democratic governance themselves? It is clear that careful consideration will need to be given to the composition, nature, and powers of new institutional forms if they are to prove an appropriate way of reasserting democratic citizenship rights in education in the late twentieth century and beyond. They will certainly need to respond to critiques of conventional forms of political association in most modern societies. While market forms are part of a social text that helps to create new subject positions that undermine traditional forms of collectivism, those forms of collectivism themselves often failed to empower many members of society, including women and minority ethnic groups.

Paradoxically, current forms of democracy in England may be even less appropriate than those associated with directly elected school boards in the nineteenth century, which used "an advanced form of proportional representation [which] ensured that all the major political and religious groupings could be represented on the School Boards, so that positive policies at this level achieved a genuine consensus."[53] We now have to ask what are the appropriate constituencies through which to express community interests in the late twentieth century? What do we mean by communities? What forms of democracy can express their complexity? How do we develop a radical pluralist conception of citizenship that involves creating unity without denying specificity?[54] If appropriately constituted and given real resources and powers, Community Education Forums, which have been floated but not hitherto really implemented by Labour parties in England and New Zealand, might provide one way forward.

And what implications do such issues have for teachers? In calling on teachers to foster the emergence of hitherto "silenced voices," Keith argues that we need a new discourse that joins the themes of collaboration, care, commitment, and community to those of difference, equity, rights, dialogue, and a wider sense of community."[55] This suggests that, as well as gaining genuine involvement in policymaking at the institutional level, teachers need to become more accountable to constituencies that have tended to be ignored in the past.

Both state control and market forces imply a "low trust" relationship between society and its teachers.[56] Media characterizations of teacher unions often tend to encourage popular suspicion of teachers. Furthermore, the defense of the education service has too often been conducted within the assumptions of the "old " politics of education, which involved consultation between government, employers, and unions but excluded whole constituencies—notably parents and business—to whom the New Right has subsequently successfully appealed.[57] It is clear that even now not all groups have been granted a legitimate right to be involved in developing education policy. It is perhaps indicative of the paucity of thinking on this that some of the leftist teacher educators who, twenty years ago, were criticizing the elitism of the professions should now be among those suggesting that teachers should adopt the modes of self-regulation traditionally associated with the conservative professions of medicine and the law. Are state control, market forces, or professional self-governance the only models of accountability—or can we develop new models of teacher professionalism, based upon more participatory relationships with diverse communities?

In the Australian case, Knight and colleagues argue for what they call "democratic professionalism," which seeks to demystify professional work and facilitate broader participation in decision-making.[58] Why is it, I wonder, that the evidence that teachers and educationists are not always concerned principally with the welfare of their clients has been so successfully used by public choice theorists to justify neoliberal consumer-oriented reforms rather than to justify greater inclusivity in democratic decision-making in education? It is to the discussion of just this sort of issue that sociologists might usefully contribute. While sociologists of education clearly cannot claim a privileged role in such discussions, we may bring a distinctive one. Of course, this does not mean that our perspective will always be welcomed or that our role in relation to policy can ever be a straightforward one, as is clear from the experiences of sociologists working in education policy units in the new South Africa.[59]

CONCLUSION

I have expressed some skepticism about the extent to which we are living under the postmodern condition, a skepticism that I have retained even when confronted with the reality of late-twentieth-century Los Angeles. But, whether or not those changes that are taking place in education do reflect fundamental changes in modes of accumulation and modes of social solidarity, signaled by terms such as post-Fordism and postmodernity, they do need to be confronted. At the level of rhetoric (though not reality), the recent reforms of the New Right have probably been more responsive than their critics usually concede to those limited, but nonetheless tangible, social and cultural shifts that have been taking place in modern societies. A straightforward return to the old order of

92 GEOFF WHITTY

things would be neither feasible nor sensible. Social democratic approaches to education that continue to favor the idea of a common school are faced with the need to respond to increasing specialization and social diversity. We have to remind ourselves that neoliberalism is but one response to this situation and one that effectively abandons the sort of social justice agenda implied by the call for papers of the conference at which this paper was initially presented.

But it seems clear that, if the only future for public education lies with the particular marketized forms that are currently fashionable, it will become increasingly difficult to articulate, let alone implement, such an agenda. Yet, while neoliberalism is increasingly regarded as part of the taken-for-granted world of education policy in many countries, it is but one possible response to current social conditions. If we are to avoid the atomization of educational decision-making, and associated tendencies toward fragmentation and polarization between schools and within schools, we need to create new contexts for determining appropriate institutional and curricular arrangements on behalf of the whole society. I have suggested that this will require new forms of association in the public sphere within which citizen rights in education policy—and indeed other areas of public policy—can be reasserted against current trends toward both a restricted version of the state and a marketized civil society. Otherwise education will become merely a private consumption good rather than a public issue.

In this context, I believe sociology of education still has a modest role to play in our understanding of the limits and possibilities of education policy in modern societies and in the future development of education as a public issue. In the 1940s, Mannheim argued that "no educational activity or research is adequate in the present stage of consciousness unless it is conceived in terms of a sociology of education."[60] Despite the hyperbolic character of this remark, I can see no case for going to the opposite extreme. Unlike Hammersley, I do not believe that we should be willing to accept the demise of our discipline on the grounds that what was once a distinctively sociological way of thinking about the world has somehow entered into the "common-sense" of other educators.[61] We have only to listen to the market advocates and the school improvement lobby to recognize that too often that is just not the case.

NOTES

This is a revised version of a paper presented to the ISA Sociology of Education Section Mid-Term Conference on "Urban Education: Challenges for the Sociology of Education" at UCLA, 20–22 June 1996.

1. Geoff Whitty, *Social Theory and Educational Policy: The Legacy of Karl Mannheim* (London: Institute of Education, 1997).

2. "Post-War Facilities for the Study of Education: Some Notes by the Director on the Essential Professorships," attached to Report B of the Delegacy for the Institute of Education, 18 March 1943. Sir Fred Clarke Archive, Institute of Education, University of London.

3. G. Grace, ed., *Education and the City: Theory, History and Contemporary Practice* (London: Routledge, 1984).

4. J. Le Grand and W. Bartlett, *Quasi-Markets and Social Policy* (London: Macmillan, 1993).

5. Robert Arnove, "Neo-Liberal Education Policies in Latin America: Arguments in Favor and Against," paper delivered to the Comparative and International Education Society, Williamsburg, Va., 6–10 March 1996.

6. A. Green, "Postmodernism and State Education," *Journal of Education Policy* 9.1 (1994): 67–84.

7. C. Shilling, "The Demise of Sociology of Education in Britain?" *British Journal of Sociology of Education* 14.1 (1993): 105–12.

8. S. Ball, *Politics and Policy Making: Explorations in Policy Sociology* (London: Routledge, 1990).

9. J. Kenway, "Marketing Education in the Postmodern Age," *Journal of Education Policy* 8.1 (1993): 105–22.

10. K. Robins, "Tradition and Translation: National Culture in its Global Context," in *Enterprise and Heritage: Crosscurrents of National Culture*, ed. J. Corner and S. Harvey (London: Routledge, 1991).

11. K. Thompson, "Social Pluralism and Postmodernity," in *Modernity and its Futures*, ed. S. Hall, D. Held, and T. McGrew (Cambridge: Polity Press, 1992).

12. R. Boyne and A. Rattansi, eds., *Postmodernism and Society* (London: Macmillan, 1990).

13. Michael W. Apple, *Cultural Politics and Education* (Buckingham: Open University Press, 1996).

14. M. Hickox, "Situating Vocationalism," *British Journal of Sociology of Education* 16.2 (1995): 153–63.

15. J. Allen, "Post-industrialism and Post-Fordism," in *Modernity and its Futures*, ed. S. Hall, D. Held, and T. McGrew (Cambridge: Polity Press, 1992).

16. See, for example, Terry Moe, "The British Battle for Choice," in *Voices on Choice: The Education Reform Debate*, ed. K. L. Billingsley (San Francisco: Pacific Institute for Public Policy, 1994) and S. Pollard, *Schools, Selection and the Left* (London: Social Market Foundation, 1995).

17. See T. Smith and M. Noble, *Education Divides: Poverty and Schooling in the 1990s* (London: Child Poverty Action Group, 1995); Geoff Whitty, S. Power, and D. Halpin, *Devolution and Choice in Education: The School, the State and the Market* (Bristol, Pa.: Open University Press, 1988); H. Lauder, D. Hughes, S. Watson, I. Simiyu, R. Strathdee, and S. Waslander, *Trading in Futures: The Nature of Choice in Educational Markets in New Zealand*, Smithfield Project, Victoria University of Wellington, 1995; and S. Gerwitz, S. J. Ball, and R. Bowe, *Markets, Choice and Equity* (Buckingham: Open University Press, 1995).

18. A. Callincos, *Against Postmodernism: A Marxist Critique* (Cambridge: Polity Press, 1989).

19. D. Harvey, *The Condition of Postmodernity: An Enquiry into the Origins of Cultural Change* (Oxford: Basil Blackwell, 1989).

20. S. Lash, *Sociology of Postmodernism* (London: Routledge, 1990).

21. R. Dale, *The State and Education Policy* (Milton Keynes, UK: Open University, 1989).

22. M. Weiss, "New Guiding Principles in Education Policy: The Case of Germany," *Journal of Education Policy* 8.4 (1993): 307–20.

23. A. Green, *Education and State Formation* (London: Macmillan, 1990).

24. Michel Foucault, *Politics/Philosophy/Culture*, ed. L. D. Kritzman (New York: Routledge, 1988).

25. E. Meehan, *Civil Society*, Contribution to an ESRC/RSA seminar series on The State of Britain (Swindon, UK: Economic and Social Research Council, 1995).

26. A. Gamble, *The Free Economy and the Strong State* (London: Macmillan, 1988).

27. See, for example, Robert Arnove, "Neoliberal Education Policies in Latin America" and L. Gordon, "Controlling Education: Agency Theory and the Reformation of New Zealand Schools," *Educational Policy* 9.1 (1995): 55–74.

28. J. McKenzie, "Education as a Private Problem or a Public Issue? The Process of Excluding 'Education' from the 'Public Sphere,'" presented at the International Conference on the Public Sphere, Manchester, 8–10 January 1993.

29. It is interesting in this connection that, in an American book on school choice, K. B. Smith and K. J. Meier (*The Case against School Choice: Politics, Markets and Fools* [Armonk, N.Y.: M. E. Sharpe, 1995]) present data that suggest that neither local democratic control nor strong trade unions are necessarily associated with those large impersonal bureaucracies that are seen by neo-institutional theorists as the symbol of the failure of conventional mass education systems.

30. For example, R. Bowe, S. J. Ball, and A. Gold, *Reforming Education and Changing Schools* (London: Routledge, 1992); A. Bullock and H. Thomas, *The Impact of Local Management of Schools* (Birmingham: University of Birmingham, 1994); and R. Levacic, *The Local Management of Schools: Analysis and Practice* (Buckingham: Open University Press, 1995).

31. J. Sinclair, M. Ironside, and R. Seifert, "Classroom Struggle? Market Oriented Education Reforms and Their Impact on Teachers' Professional Autonomy, Labour Intensification and Resistance," presented to the International Labour Process Conference, 1 April 1993.

32. J. Blackmore, "Breaking out from a Masculinist Politics of Education," in *Gender and Changing Education Management*, ed. B. Limerick and B. Lingard (Rydalmere, Australia: Hodder Education, 1995), p. 45.

33. S. Urahn and D. Stewart, *Minnesota Charter Schools: A Research Report* (St. Paul, Minn.: Research Department, Minnesota House of Representatives, 1994).

34. L. Gordon, "'Rich' and 'Poor' Schools in Aotearoa," *New Zealand Journal of Educational Studies* 29.2 (1994): 113–25.

35. D. A. Lewis and K. Nakagawa, *Race and Educational Reform in the American Metropolis: A Study of School Decentralization* (Albany: State University of New York Press, 1995), p. 172.

36. See, for instance, L. Angus, "The Sociology of School Effectiveness," *British Journal of Sociology of Education* 14.3 (1993): 333–45 and R. Hatcher, "The Limitations of the New Social Democratic Agenda: Class, Equality, Agency," in *Education after the Conservatives*, ed. R. Hatcher and K. Jones (Stoke-on-Trent, UK: Trentham Books, 1996).

37. G. Whitty, *Sociology and School Knowledge: Curriculum Theory, Research and Politics* (London: Methuen, 1985).

38. K. Mannheim, *Freedom, Power and Democratic Planning* (London: Routledge and Kegan Paul, 1951).

39. Geoff Whitty, "Left Policy and Practice and the Sociology of Education," in *Schools, Teachers and Teaching*, ed. L. Barton and S. Walker (Lewes, UK: Falmer Press, 1982).

40. Anthony Giddens, *Beyond Left and Right: The Future of Radical Politics* (Cambridge: Polity Press, 1994).

41. D. Reynolds, P. Sammons, L. Stoll, M. Barber, and J. Hillman, "School Effectiveness and School Improvement in the United Kingdom," *School Effectiveness and School Improvement* 7.2 (1996): 133–58.

42. See G. Grace, ed., *Education and the City*, and G. Grace, "Welfare Labourism versus the New Right," *International Studies in the Sociology of Education* 1.1 (1991): 25–42.

43. G. Grace, *Education and the City*, p. xii.

44. B. Fay, *Social Theory and Political Practice* (London: Allen and Unwin, 1975).

45. J. Ladwig, "For Whom This Reform? Outlining Educational Policy as a Social Field," *British Journal of Sociology of Education* 15.3 (1994): 341–63.

46. I am grateful to Suart Hall for this observation.

47. Geoff Whitty, *Sociology and School Knowledge*, p. 82.

48. See, for example, Geoff Whitty, "Creating Quasi-Markets in Education: A Review of Recent Research on Parental Choice and School Autonomy in Three Countries," *Review of Research in Education* 22 (1997): 3–47, and Whitty et al., *Devolution and Choice in Education*.

49. Michel Foucault, *Politics/Philosophy/Culture*.

50. M. Young and G. Whitty, eds., *Society, State and Schooling* (Lewes, UK: Falmer Press, 1977).

51. Michael W. Apple, *Cultural Politics and Education*, p. 52.

52. J. R. Henig, *Rethinking School Choice: Limits of the Market Metaphor* (Princeton: Princeton University Press, 1994), p. 222.

53. B. Simon, *The State and Educational Change* (London: Lawrence and Wishart, 1994), p. 12.

54. Chantal Mouffe, ed., *Dimensions of Radical Democracy: Pluralism, Citizenship, Democracy* (London: Verso, 1992).

55. N. Z. Keith, "A Critical Perspective on Teacher Participation in Urban Schools," *Educational Administration Quarterly* 32.1 (1996): 70.

56. K. Sullivan, "The Impact of Education Reform on Teachers' Professional Ideologies," *New Zealand Journal of Educational Studies* 29.1 (1994): 3–20.

57. Michael W. Apple and Anita Oliver, "Becoming Right: Education and the Formation of Conservative Movements," in *Cultural Politics and Education*, ed. Michael W. Apple (Buckingham: Open University Press, 1996).

58. J. Knight, L. Bartlett, and E. McWilliam, eds., *Unfinished Business: Reshaping the Teacher Education Industry for the 1990s* (Rockhampton, Australia: University of Central Queensland, 1993).

59. J. Muller and N. Cloete, "Out of Eden: Modernity, Post-Apartheid and Intellectuals," *Theory, Culture and Society* 10 (1993): 155–72.

60. K. Mannheim and W. A. C. Stewart, *An Introduction to the Sociology of Education* (London: Routledge and Kegan Paul, 1962), p. 159.

61. M. Hammersley, "Post Mortem or Post Modern? Some Reflections on British Sociology of Education," *British Journal of Educational Studies* 44.4 (1996): 394–406.

PART II

Empirical Perspectives on Urban Education

CHAPTER 4

Where Neoliberal Ideology Meets Social Context: A Comparative Analysis of U.S. Charter Schools and England's Grant-Maintained Schools

Amy Stuart Wells

Since the early 1990s, various researchers and commentators have compared educational reforms taking place in the United States and Britain, pointing out cross-Atlantic similarities and differences.[1] Two reforms in particular—charter schools in the United States and grant-maintained schools (or GM schools) in England—have been compared, and much has been made of the impact that the British grant-maintained schools policy had on the early thinking of U.S. reformers interested in starting charter schools.[2]

At first blush, there are many parallels between the two types of schools: grant-maintained schools operate with greater autonomy than their Local Education Authority (LEA) while still receiving public funds via direct grants from the central government. They were instituted by the Education Reform Act of 1988 as part of the Thatcher government's effort to weaken the role of the LEAs by providing greater opportunity for schools to operate free of LEA oversight and thus, in theory, to become more directly responsive to the needs of parents and to increase diversity of provisions of schools. Conservatives believed that such a policy would infuse free-market competition into an otherwise complacent educational system.[3] By 1997 when the Labour Party came to power and began to curtail the expansion of the policy, there were 1,188 GM schools.

Charter school policies in the United States were also developed to provide publicly funded schools with greater autonomy from local and state educational bureaucracies, thus infusing choice and competition into the public system. The first charter school law was passed in 1991 in Minnesota, and since then, thirty-two additional states have passed charter school legislation. As of fall 1998, an estimated 1,100 charter schools were operating and an additional 160 were approved to open.

This chapter looks more closely at the relationship between charter and GM schools policies[4] and argues that there are differences between the two that relate to distinctions in the social and political contexts of the two countries. Furthermore, I argue that these distinctions should not be overlooked because they help to illustrate how the neoliberal ideology of market-based reforms that has driven educational policymaking across the globe over the last decade interacts with and becomes reinterpreted by national and local contexts that have their own histories and cultures.

According to Whitty, Power, and Halpin: "Educational reform is being conducted within contexts with different histories, different constitutional and administrative arrangements and different political complexions. . . . Within the range of political rationales, it is the neoliberal alternative which dominates, as does a particular emphasis on market-type mechanisms."[5]

Through such comparative work, we can better understand the true hegemonic power of neoliberal ideology and thus the possibility of hope for an alternative vision of educational reform.

DEVOLUTION AND COMPETITION: THE SHARED POLITICAL PHILOSOPHY OF GRANT-MAINTAINED AND CHARTER SCHOOLS

Neoliberals advocate privatization of public institutions and services and increasing reliance on market forces, volunteerism, and individual demands to achieve social ends. The roots of this movement lie in classical political and economic liberalism in the eighteenth- and nineteenth-century laissez-faire sense, which "sees society as nothing more than a collection of atomistic individuals whose rational self-interested choices lead to optimal social efficiency."[6]

The rise of both the grant-maintained and charter school policies is due in large part to the political appeal of these neoliberal or free-market economic arguments to dismantle the welfare state, break up the public education monopoly, technically "free" schools from government bureaucracies and force them to compete for clients and thus state funds in the educational marketplace. This educational market theory, or the economic metaphor for school improvement has, for the last fifteen years, been the dominant ideology in both the United States and the United Kingdom and has fueled reforms that emphasize both devolution and competition.

Devolution, in theory, allows for placing more power and decision-making authority in the hands of parents and educators at the school sites; competition means breaking up the public school "monopoly" and forcing individual schools to compete with each other for pupils, public funds, and survival.[7]

Within this neoliberal framework, a competitive market system of education will maximize efficiency while assuring individual choice and freedom.[8] Thus, critics of neoliberalism and its privatization efforts note that it provides an ideological shift in which democracy is framed in terms of individualism, and education is framed in terms of consumerism. According to Kenway:

> markets require a shift in focus from the collective and the community to the individual, from public service to private service, and from other people to the self. Clearly, in promoting the marketization of education, policy makers seek to promote and tap into a cult of educational selfishness in the national interest. Educational democracy is redefined as consumer democracy in the educational supermarket.[9]

In a postmodern age in which global markets transcend and often dominate political nation states, the substitution of market forces for government-run services becomes a "natural" evolution. And thus, the educational system is increasingly reified, as social relationships between educators and families become material objects in the sphere of market exchange. Furthermore, the increasing reliance on market forces in providing educational services naturally lessens the impact of public policy in redistributing resources, such as educational opportunity, to those who most need it. According to Handler, "Privatization shifts power to those who can more readily exercise power in the market."[10]

Both charter schools and grant-maintained schools, with their autonomy from their local education authorities and state governments and their need to attract clients in order to stay in "business" fit this neoliberal paradigm, although, both also embody other reform ideologies and histories.

Members of the Thatcher and Major Conservative governments argued that competition between grant-maintained schools would not only lead to greater parental choice of schools, but also that the autonomy of these GM schools from their LEAs would enable them to be more directly responsive to parents' demands. This effort to simultaneously extend parental choice and foster a direct relationship between education's providers and consumers, it was argued, "will encourage healthy competition between schools in those LEAs directly affected and, as a result, lead to a gradual improvement in 'standards' throughout the educational system."[11]

Similarly, in the United States, charter schools have been seen as a new brand of specialized choice schools, designed to devolve educational governance by "freeing" schools of bureaucratic constraints and forcing schools to compete for parents and students in a more deregulated educational marketplace for their own survival.[12]

For instance, in a set of interviews conducted with policymakers in six states, my colleagues and I learned that neoliberal policymakers often connected charter schools philosophically to tuition voucher proposals, which would offer public money to students attending private schools. According to a gubernatorial aide in one state, charter schools and the voucher proposal together "link the continuing existence of a school to its ability to attract students and enroll students."[13]

Despite these common neoliberal political roots, both grant-maintained and charter schools were shaped by other political forces, including neoconservatives who sought more centralized control over curriculum, particularly in England, and so-called progressives and even radical liberals in the United States who have sought greater community control over schools for decades. Thus, in both countries, the simple theory of neoliberalism is redefined, rewritten, and resisted within these more complicated contexts. Still, neoliberalism's appeal lies in its call for individualism and consumerism—two prominent themes in both British and American society. These popular themes have allowed neoliberalism to define complex social issues in highly simplistic terms. And according to Apple: "One of the most crucial aspects of politics is the struggle to define social reality and interpret people's inchoate aspirations and needs."[14]

NEOCONSERVATIVES AND ENGLAND'S NATIONAL CURRICULUM

From 1979 and 1997, when the Conservative Government was in power in Great Britain, the national agenda was dominated by the programs of the political "New Right," which incorporates two main political strands: neoliberalism, described above as the call to roll back the state and infuse market forces, and neoconservativism, or an emphasis on traditional and often nationalist and religious moral values. The neoconservative wing of the New Right represents a coalition of interests—

namely the religious right, fractions of disgruntled working- and middle-class whites, and cultural elitists—that see the salvation of Western society from its current decline embedded in "ideal forms of institutions" such as the patriarchal family and religion.[15]

The neoconservative/neoliberal strands within the politics of the New Right have led to what is referred to as "free market" and "strong state"—the seemingly contradictory efforts by the state to be rolled back and rolled forward simultaneously. The theory is guided by the notion that reforms should be non-interventionist and decentralized in some areas and highly decentralized in others.[16]

The free-market, strong state approach to educational governance is best portrayed in the Thatcher government's establishment of a highly centralized national curriculum and national assessment for England and Wales along with decentralization and deregulation via open enrollment plans, Local Management Schools (LMS), and grant-maintained schools. The central political argument of the New Right reform agenda as applied to education is that high-stakes competition within a system of centralized standards helps assure accountability because parents will compare schools based on their ability to teach students the national curriculum and therefore prepare them for national exams. The testing program is overseen by the National Schools Examinations and Assessment Council (SEAC) charged with devising and administering tests to all students age 7, 11, and 14.[17] These test scores are then published in the popular press.

At the same time, schools, especially the grant-maintained schools, are assumed to be "free" to figure out the best, most efficient way for them to deliver this curriculum and thus compete with other schools.

The government formed the National Curriculum Council (NCC) to oversee the design and implementation of the National Curriculum, which, not surprisingly, reflected traditional conservative values with much emphasis on traditional academic subjects and content.[18] As Hughes explains, while the New Right political groups were divided over the degree to which they thought a national curriculum was necessary, those who advocated such a curriculum saw it as "means of maintaining traditional standards and values."[19]

Another justification for the National Curriculum was that it would reduce variation between schools and thus between students' curricular experiences. This is an "equity argument" for centralized standards that is often heard in the United States as well.

Several researchers studying the impact of England's grant-maintained schools have concluded that the National Curriculum has interacted with neoliberal market ideology of choice and competition in some unpredictable ways. For instance, Halpin, Power, and Fitz[20] found that in part due to the National Curriculum, that far from "breaking the mold," grant-maintained schools (or opted-out schools as they are also called) seem to celebrate past visions of educational practice. This finding, they note, implies a trend toward "opting into the past." They argue that if GM schools, with their extra autonomy and resources, are unable to generate innovative practices, we need to consider from where alternative visions of state schools can be generated.

Similarly, Walford found that often parents and students see no difference between grant-maintained and other schools, except for the better facilities and attention to symbols of academic elitism.

> Indeed, one of the seeming paradoxes of government policy [GM schools] is that, although it claims to wish to increase diversity of provisions, its other policies act to greatly constrain the content of teaching that schools can offer. The imposition of the National Curriculum and regular inspection of all schools by the Office for Standards in Education (Ofsted) has ensured a greater uniformity in curriculum content and methods of teaching than even existed before.[21]

In fact, Whitty and Power write that rather than being academically innovative, some GM schools reverted to being overtly academically selective and only those schools that had clearly failed on traditional academic criteria in the past are likely to risk deviating significantly from the dominant definition of excellence in their curriculum offerings.[22]

Stearns argues that the standardization of the National Curriculum in England had not spurred the creation of academically superior schools overall, rather it led to a "pecking order" of schools, in which the least popular are the least able to improve and compete.[23]

Thus, the neoconservative push for a traditional national curriculum in England interacted with the neoliberal push to create a quasi-market of autonomous and competitive schools in a way that exacerbated the existing inequalities in the system as opposed to spurring all schools to improve.

NEOCONSERVATIVES AND STANDARDS-BASED REFORM IN THE UNITED STATES

In the United States, the "New Right" political movement has slightly different connotations. As Giddens and others have pointed out, the term "New Right" has been used more to describe the socially conservative or religious right in the United States as opposed to a coalition of neoconservative and neoliberal forces. This is due in part to the fact that American conservatives have traditionally been fairly neoliberal or pro–capitalist, anti–welfare state.[24]

Furthermore, the term "neoliberal" has been more problematic, given the popular use of the word "liberal" in U.S. politics to describe supporters of the New Deal policies who subsequently favored the expansion of the welfare state and thus a more pro-active redistributive role of the government.[25] At the same time, many U.S. liberals have also been fairly libertarian when it comes to individual rights and freedoms.

The rise of the New Right in U.S. politics can be traced back to Goldwater, but seems to have coalesced around Reagan's vision of "New Federalism" or the shift of power from the national government to the state and ultimately the local level. The idea was to return greater control to local governments or individual schools and their constituents while getting "big government" out of their lives.[26] To the extent that this was appealing to both the socially conservative or neoconservatives and the pro-capitalist neoliberals, there was a convergence of "the right" in the 1980s and 90s that had seemed perhaps more fractured before.

In a similar vein, Edsall argues that Reagan's political popularity was due in large part to his ability to convince white working-class voters that the federal government's welfare state had gone too far in its efforts to redistribute wealth from "hard-working" taxpayers to the "undeserving" poor and to protect the rights of racial minorities, women and gays.[27] According to Carl, "Neoconservative rhetoric reserves special disdain for the 1960–era social movements, especially the counterculture, feminism, black power, and gay rights, in part because these movements threaten traditional conceptions of family and nation."[28]

Thus, Reagan's symbolic politics of "welfare queens" and useless bureaucrats fanned the flames of a deep resentment toward the federal government and a broader antigovernment rhetoric that is evident today in many political movements—from the call to end affirmative action to the bombing of the Oklahoma City federal building.

Antigovernment neoconservatives resent educational "regulations"—that is, legislation and court orders—that helped create educational bureaucracies at the federal, state, and local district level and thus a centralization of policymaking over the last thirty years. Many of these regulations and government mandates were designed to address the unequal access that certain students—that is, racial minorities, handicapped students, and non-English speakers—had to quality educational programs in more locally controlled schools.[29]

Carl also notes that both the United States and United Kingdom have long histories of marginalized groups—especially racial minorities and women—organizing within the state in order to redress grievances, with the schools being one of the most important sites for this organization. This historical perspective on the redistributive and regulatory role of the federal government is important to understanding the current political backlash against "big government" and the call for more parental choice and control.[30]

Harmer, a neoconservative who favors deregulated tuition voucher plans, argues that too much education funding is wasted on "narrowly focused categorical programs"—that is, Title 1, bilingual education, and special education—controlled by "administrators at the top of the top-heavy system." He adds that "These programs take money that should be spent on the academic basics."[31]

In addition to the antigovernment rhetoric of the New Right in the United States, there are aspects of this agenda that are reminiscent of the "free market-strong state" paradox of the United Kingdom. For instance, according to Jonathan, while the neoconservatives want less state intervention in most areas of their lives, they want the state to be sufficiently strong to maintain property relations and the current unequal distribution of wealth.[32] In education policy, as in the United Kingdom, the neoconservatives have in the past demanded that the state remain strong in the area of "standards" while at the same time getting out of the way of parents who want to choose schools for their children and have more say in how these schools are run and whose values are taught.

Carl argues that under Chubb and Moe's tuition voucher or "scholarship" plan in which students receive funding directly from the state, the authority of the state governments that would distribute and monitor the scholarships would be enhanced at the expense of district autonomy. "Bureaucracy disappears and reappears; New Right bureaucrats replace those officials who, to some extent, represent social groupings that struggled, often successfully, for more egalitarian educational policies."[33]

He adds that "the 'rolling back' of a generic state is not the issue. Rather, the New Right targeted for reorganization structures that had emerged in the New Deal and post–World War II accords . . . as a result, the state is reshaped in ways that eliminate venues where formerly dispossessed groups shared some power."[34]

BIPARTISAN SYSTEMIC REFORM

Despite the strong connection between the New Right and deregulatory reforms, including but not limited to charter schools, the political landscape of the educational reform movement in the United States is more complicated, with many so-called liberals also supporting both devolution of governance systems and the creation of more centralized academic standards. Thus, the political support for centralized standards and decentralized governance structures for schools (the strong state–free market paradigm) would be bipartisan in nature and not just supported by those who fit politically into the New Right framework.

In the United States, the "free market" and "strong state" approach is described as "systemic reform"—a strategy that was largely popular on both sides of the political isle in the early 1990s. This reform effort included setting national goals, standards, and assessment measures while delegating implementation of reform to the states and their decentralized, autonomous districts and schools. On the state level, complementary systemic reforms were to take place, with state policymakers mandating standards, curriculum frameworks, and new student performance tests while calling for devolution of decision-making, school-based management, and greater parental choice.[35]

Ultimately, this systemic reform approach is embodied in the 1994 federal Goals 2000 legislation sponsored by the Clinton administration. This legislation originated in the Bush administration's policy proposal, called "America 2000." Interestingly, the Clinton administration did not dramatically alter Goals 2000 from its original form as it was drafted by the Bush administration. The main difference between the Bush and Clinton administrations regarding school reform is that President Bush favored taking the concepts of deregulation and competition to the extreme, arguing for privatization and voucher plans, whereas the Clinton administration stops short of such proposals, calling for greater parental choice and deregulation within the public sector—and thus providing federal support for charter schools.

Under this major piece of federal legislation, passed with bipartisan support in 1994 before the Congressional election, schools and districts are held accountable for students' performance by centralized, "world-class standards." Meanwhile, greater authority is decentralized to the local level, allowing educators, parents and students to decide how best to meet the standards. The legislation advocated the creation of charter schools and subsequent legislation supported by the administration provided federal funding for charter schools.

More specifically, Goals 2000 offers states funding to develop state curriculum frameworks and complementary assessment programs that would meet or surpass the rigor of the voluntary national standards in twelve subject-matter areas. Simultaneously, Goals 2000 called for states to grant greater autonomy and flexibility to schools as they implement the state frameworks.[36]

Yet when the federal legislation was first proposed, educators, researchers, and advocates argued that efforts to hold all schools accountable based on standards and student outcomes were being cast onto an uneven playing field in which some schools were less able to provide students with the "opportunities to learn" content reflected on the state tests.[37] The final legislation half-heartedly attempted to address these concerns by expanding the bill to include voluntary opportunity-to-learn standards to assess student access to educational resources and high-quality instruction.[38]

Thus, the concepts of national and state standards in the United States, unlike the National Curriculum in the United Kingdom, have enjoyed bipartisan support. In fact, after 1994, they have been more strongly supported by Democrats than Republicans.

The 1994 elections brought additional equity issues related to decentralization into clearer focus. Republican politicians, once the champions of educational standards, launched a political assault on the national standards movement. Robert Dole, 1996 presidential candidate and Senate majority leader, attacked the proposed history standards, calling them un-American: "The purpose of the national history standards seems not to be to teach our children certain facts about our history, but to denigrate America's story while sanitizing and glorifying other cultures."[39]

Overall, Congressional support for the national standards and systemic reform has dissipated, as is illustrated in the House of Representatives' 1995 legislative proposal to fold Goals 2000 and several other federal programs into one large block grant to the states while eliminating the opportunity-to-learn standards. Meanwhile, conservative groups lobbied Republican members of Congress to end federal involvement in standards setting of any kind.[40]

Conservatives have not, however, abandoned the goal of decentralization and deregulation of the educational system as they desert the standards movement. The same 1995 House proposal would allow states to use federal block grants for school choice programs that involve private schools, deregulated charter schools, and for-profit private management firms to run public schools.[41]

At the state level, the movement toward centralized standards has also encountered political roadblocks, particularly in California, where the implementation of standards-based systemic reform presaged the national movement by nearly a decade. In 1994, state funding was discontinued for the new state testing system, the California Learning Assessment System (CLAS), designed to test students on the content of the state curriculum frameworks. The demise of CLAS began with a political backlash by conservative religious groups over the content and morality of the test. Recent efforts to revise and reinstate CLAS have failed in the California Assembly.[42] Similar political protests have erupted in other states and districts implementing standards-based or outcomes-based reforms designed to hold schools accountable for student learning in an increasingly decentralized educational system.[43]

Still, in the state houses as in Congress, the backlash against standards has not lessened the enthusiasm for massive decentralization of decision-making and deregulation of the education system from government equity-based mandates or the infusion of market forces to foster greater competition between schools.

THE SOCIAL AND POLITICAL CONTEXTS OF GRANT-MAINTAINED AND CHARTER SCHOOLS

Some of these U.K.-U.S. distinctions are related to major structural and cultural differences in the two countries' political and educational systems. For instance, the highly decentralized U.S. public educational system has nearly 16,000 school districts and the much smaller, more nationalized British system has about 120 Local Education Authorities.

Centralized and Politicized Reform in England

Education in England and Wales was traditionally seen as a national system, locally administered through these LEAs, although the 1988 Reform Act and the National Curriculum "nationalized" the system to a much greater extent.[44] Public education in the United States, on the other hand, has always been considered a state and local concern. Children's guarantee of a free, public education is found in the state and not the federal constitution, and the federal government in the United States plays a rather minuscule role in funding public education—on average, only 6 percent of the total cost.

This structural and political difference means that in England, reforms of the central government can be mandated and quickly implemented in every educational authority, whereas in the United States, most major reforms are legislated by the state governments. Still, given the history of local control in U.S. education, even sweeping state reform efforts have limited impact on districts and schools.[45]

Related to these structural differences in the United States and England is the more direct political and ideological confrontation between the Conservative and Labour Parties in Britain. Although the Republican and Democratic Parties in the United States also battle—intensely at times—over specific legislation and educational reform efforts, these confrontations take place on various levels of educational policymaking—federal, state, and local—with local levels less clearly linked to specific party agendas.

Also, unlike the United States, where legislative process is generally meted out through a series of political compromises, the parliamentary system in Britain leads to policymaking that is more clearly identified with the party in power. Thus, the movement in Britain toward a more comprehensive secondary education for all children ages 5–16 during the decades following World War II, is clearly identified with the Labour (socialist) government's brief series of reigns in 1945–54, 1964–71, and 1974–79. The strict allocation of students to schools by the LEAs based on geographic location and school size was also part of the Labour Party's agenda, as the party fought against selectivity in the state-supported system and for greater "comprehensivisation," mixed ability groupings, social education, and the removal of inequality and discrimination in education.[46]

The more partisan bent to educational reform in Great Britain appears to have intensified when Thatcher came to power in 1979. Since that time, most of the education legislation passed by the central government is perceived a direct attack on the mostly Labour-controlled LEAs. For instance, the 1980 Education Act, which provided for open enrollment, gave parents the statutory right to request seats for their children in schools outside their designated attendance areas and empowered the Education Secretary to regulate the balance of planning and choice between LEAs and parents. The act also required LEAs to publish brochures describing their schools, including information on curriculum and policies concerning homework, uniforms, and school discipline, as well as exam results.[47]

This 1980 act along with the major, 1988 Education Reform Act are perceived by Labour Party leaders and leftist academics as the Thatcher government's measures to undermine the powers of the LEAs to organize education. In this way, these acts were also seen as conservative attacks on more "egalitarian" reforms that had been the trademark of the Labour Party's educational policy since 1944. The move then toward competition, decentralized, autonomous schools, greater parental choice, and a national curriculum against which individual child's progress can be measured ties in with the Conservative government's effort to increase streaming or tracking and the general thrust toward identifying and highlighting differences—a clear backlash against the prior Labour Party reforms.[48] According to Ball, "The path which the UK has hewn is far more radical in the undiluted application of ideologically driven policy."[49]

Decentralized and Politicized Reform in the United States

In the United States, similar attacks have been made on the so-called "educational establishment," which includes the teachers unions, school and district administrators, and anyone else associated with educational bureaucracy. But because of the legislative process in the United States these very groups continue to play an important role in the debates over education policy.

When educational change occurs in the United States, it often seems to take longer and is messier than in England, and specific reforms are often, but not always, less clearly identifiable with one of the main political parties. Charter schools in the United States are a good example of such a reform, because it is perceived by policymakers on both ends of the political spectrum as a compromise between maintaining a more regulated public education system and the annihilation of public schools through privatization schemes and voucher plans.[50] According to Pipho, the growth of the charter movement and more general support of efforts to reform education by using ideas from the consumer marketplace reflects "bipartisanship" in the United States.[51]

In fact, there has been ongoing, if uneven teacher union support for charter schools in the United States since their inception. For instance, in 1988 Budde wrote a report entitled *Education by Charter* in which he envisioned a group of teachers designing instructional programs.[52] Shortly afterward, the late Al Shanker, then-president of the American Federation of Teachers, presented an adaptation of Budde's vision to the National Press Club in Washington. The original discussions of the charter school concept in the United States then was directed by people who were most interested in eliminating regulations that prevent teachers from attempting more innovative practices.

Also, in the United States for the last thirty years liberal progressive and more radical reformers who are anti-authoritarian and anti-establishment, have argued for decentralization of state-run schools, greater parental choice, and nonselective, independent "alternative" schools. In urban areas, where large numbers of low-income students of color have been subjected to impoverished and politically bankrupt schools and poorly trained educators, activists have fought for greater community control of their schools.[53]

In more recent years, these advocates for urban school children have often sided with more economically conservative and libertarian reformers fighting for tuition voucher programs within a selective and highly competitive setting.[54] This "strange bedfellows" situation in the U.S. school choice debates has made party-specific politics on this issue more tentative, although conservative Republicans are more likely to favor deregulation and competitive private school choice whereas liberal Democrats generally are more supportive of public school choice plans.

Still, charter legislation in the United States is state legislation, not federal, which means that partisan politics and power struggles between state and local policymakers can play out in fifty different ways, depending on the political makeup of the statehouses and communities. In some states, such as Arizona, charter school reform, as most reform in that state, has been part of the conservative agenda. In other states, including Hawaii and Georgia, they are seen as more closely tied to the Democratic Party's vision of systemic reform.

The contrast between the United States and United Kingdom along these structural, political, and historical lines contributes significantly to differences between the grant-maintained schools in England and charter schools in the United States. These distinctions include the different roles that English LEAs versus U.S. local school districts play, the curricular focus of charters and GM schools and the amount of funding available for charter and GM schools.

Still, I argue that the power of an overarching neoliberal ideology is pushing charter school reform in the United States toward a more right-wing agenda, while in Britain, the election of the Labour Party in 1997 is pushing grant-maintained schools slightly in the opposite direction.

THE ROLE OF THE LEAs AND LOCAL SCHOOL DISTRICTS

Efforts on the part of the Conservative government in Britain to strip the LEAs of political power and to eliminate them as organizing bodies for schools is evident in the design of the grant-maintained policy in both the 1988 and 1993 Education Reform Acts. Under the guidelines of the 1988 act, schools seeking grant-maintained status were to apply directly to the national Secretary of Education and if successful they received their funding from the central government and not through the LEAs.[55] Grant-maintained schools became accountable to the Department for Education, as the policy was designed to help these schools circumvent the bureaucracy of the LEAs.[56]

Also, under the original act, all grant-maintained schools were existing LEA schools that converted or opted out into GM status. (The 1993 act allowed groups of parents of independent sponsors to create GM schools.) Existing LEA schools that opted out were able to determine their own admissions policies, although they were required to retain LEA designated character in terms of size, selection criteria, religious basis, and age-range. Grant-maintained schools could, however, after a period of five years, apply to the central government to change their character.[57] This option to change the character of a grant-maintained school inhibited the LEAs' efforts to equalize access for all students who live within their regions and to reduce the level of "creaming" that some schools are able to accomplish.

Furthermore, because GM schools applied directly to the central government, schools facing closure or change of character by their LEA opted out as a way to overrule the local authorities and avoid closure. In fact, more than half of the comprehensive schools and one fourth of the grammar schools that achieved GM status in the first years of implementation had been identified for closure or redesignation by their LEAs.[58] When schools identified for closure or consolidation opted out or threatened to, the LEAs were unable to reorganize and try to balance enrollment at a time of falling secondary numbers and per pupil funding.[59]

In the United States, while charter school legislation is considered part of an overall agenda to decentralize and free schools from bureaucratic constraints, it is not usually perceived to be as much of a directed political attack on local school districts as the English grant-maintained reform. As mentioned earlier, in many states there has been bipartisan support for charter school legislation, and generally, state policymakers from both parties praise charter school reform as a way to help schools escape the burdensome regulations of both the state and local government.

This varies obviously from one state to the next, and with thirty-three different state charter school laws it is difficult to generalize. However, in most states, charters can be granted through the local school districts as well as other entities, such as the state board of education or a university. In California, for instance, the state with the second highest number of charter schools (156), virtually all charters are granted by local school districts. Thus, unlike England's grant-maintained schools that bypass the LEAs, many of the schools in the United States that apply for charter status do so through their local school districts.

By naming school districts as the sponsor or one of the sponsoring organizations for charter schools, state policymakers in the United States have allowed local school boards to maintain a degree of control over which schools are able to "opt out" of the public system and which are required to remain. Still, the more conservative and neoliberal supporters of charter schools in the United States favor charter school laws that allow for multiple charter granting agencies—either instead of or in addition to local school districts.[60]

Furthermore, when charters are granted through local school districts to existing public schools that apply to "convert" into charters, some of these schools remain highly dependent on their districts and do not break away to become fiscally independent. In fact, a study of charter schools in California found that only 27 percent of the charter schools in the state had financial autonomy—or full control over staff salaries and benefits and other budgetary expenses. About 85 percent of "start-up" charter schools were more financially autonomous, while only 15 percent of the "converted" charter schools—or those converted from public schools—were fiscally autonomous. About half of the 156 charter schools in the state are start-ups and half are conversion schools.[61]

Still, despite the relatively strong position that U.S. school boards find themselves in with regard to charter school legislation, they do in some ways feel threatened by these new laws and the burden placed upon them when they are caught between the demands of the new, "autonomous" charter schools for more flexibility and freedom and the demands of the state department of education that still holds the district accountable to the state education code. According to a school board member in Los Angeles, the state legislation sends mixed messages telling the school districts to let the charters go, but at the same time saying that the school's district is going to be held liable and responsible for how well they do.

> [The state says] let the charter schools operate without the restrictions of the state education code, without the restrictions of all the directives that come from the state department of education, but you [the district] are going to be responsible for them operating out of compliance with what the state code says ought to be standard for public schools.

In this way, the closer relationship between charter schools and their local school districts is more of a bane than a blessing. While the school districts maintain greater control over the charter proposal and granting process they also inherit the ambiguity of state legislation designed to deregulate individual schools while leaving their districts responsible *for* these schools and *to* their state education departments.

THE CURRICULAR FOCUS OF
CHARTERS AND GM SCHOOLS

The distinctions between England's grant-maintained and U.S. charter schools become even more clear in an examination of the stated reasons why schools want to opt out—for the flexibility to change curriculum and pedagogy or simply for flexibility to do as they please, whatever that may be. English schools, for instance, that decide to opt out of LEA control are not required to provide the Education Secretary with any reason for wanting to do so other than the desire to gain greater independence. GM schools are not required, therefore, to present a plan for teaching methods to be used, techniques to improve education at the schools or anything to do with curriculum.[62]

Obviously, the mandated National Curriculum greatly limits the degrees of freedom that grant-maintained schools have in devising innovative curricula and instruction. Grant-maintained schools, like all schools in England, are obligated to teach to the National Curriculum.[63] If the National Curriculum is not enough to dissuade schools from becoming overly innovative in the educational approach, the national testing and evaluation program, designed to assess student progress in learning the required curriculum, will.

Thus, in a competitive educational marketplace of deregulated schools fighting for survival, it is not in most schools' best interest to stray too far from the mandated curriculum. As I mentioned above, the ability to change their instructional program does not appear to be the central motivating factor behind opting out for the grant-maintained schools. Other factors, including becoming more selective, do seem to be important. There is evidence that schools are opting out to maintain the status quo—avoid closure or to fend off LEA efforts to change their current character—rather than to reform. This means that rather than extending parental choice by creating different schools, a grant-maintained school may simply preserve an existing choice.[64]

In the United States the many reasons why schools opt out and become charter schools do sometimes include the desire to create new educational programs. In fact, the charter proposal process in most states requires schools to spell out desired outcomes for students and the instructional strategies that will help the schools achieve those goals. Many states also ask charter school applicants to include a detailed plan including teaching and learning approaches as a key aspect of the charter proposal.[65]

Because the United States has no mandatory national curriculum, and few states have yet to implement state standards and matching assessment systems, individual schools have far more flexibility in what they teach and how it is taught. In fact, most of the states' charter school legislation explicitly states that the charter schools' central purpose should be to improve student learning outcomes through their focus on adopting innovative or different teaching methods.[66]

Some charter schools are innovative, blurring the institutional lines between schools and work or higher education. In Minnesota, a teamsters' local is working with a new vocational school and a utility company is helping to finance a year-round school requiring students to do community work. In California, about 15 percent of the charter schools in the state are home-schooling programs that provide support and guidance to parents who want to educate their children at home.

While all of this focus on curriculum and instruction sounds good in theory, the reality is that some charter schools are interested in serious reform while others are interested in continuing what they have been doing within the existing system and obtaining a charter for other reasons—for example, to establish stricter discipline standards, to maintain greater control over who gets in and who stays in the school, or to use their resources more flexibly. Other schools we studied were established to serve students of a particular racial/ethnic group and the curriculum was designed to reflect the history and culture of that group.[67]

It appears that charter schools in the United States have more flexibility to use their autonomy in different ways. And in states such as California that have not had a state assessment in place during the implementation of charter school reform, efforts to hold charter schools accountable to a single set of student outcomes have been futile.[68]

Thus, the range of possibilities of what charter schools can accomplish with their devolved status appears to be greater than what grant-maintained schools are able to do.

THE AMOUNT OF FUNDING AVAILABLE FOR CHARTER AND GM SCHOOLS

Another striking difference between England's grant-maintained schools and U.S. charter schools is the substantial funding available to GM schools in Britain and the absence of public funds available for the U.S. charter schools. In part because of the partisan battles between the Conservative central government and the Labour-dominated LEAs for control of English education, grant-maintained schools are offered considerable financial inducement by the central government to take on that status. Former Prime Minister John Major stated that his government has made no secret of the fact that GM schools get preferential treatment in allocating grants for capital expenditure. The government clearly looks favorably on GM schools.[69]

Although the money available for GM schools in England has been cut back with the election of the Labour Government in 1997, at the peak of the reform, GM schools were eligible for two seed grants—known as transitional grants and special purpose grants—that could be used during the transitional period made immediately after grant approval.

Also, nonfinancial start up resources in the form of planning time for anywhere from a year to two months and outside consultation, mainly information, guidance, and advice to schools from the time of their approval for GM status were available to schools through the Grant-maintained Schools' Centre (GMSC). The center was established by the government and was supported during the 1993–94 school year by more than $1.35 million. GMSC ran professional development workshops and on topics such as adapting and setting up administrative and financial systems at the school site. It also promoted and encouraged grant-maintained schools by disseminating information about the opting-out process and, in an ongoing capacity, negotiating terms for various services and products on behalf of the schools. The center, in essence, took over many of the LEA responsibilities.[70]

In addition to the seed money available, all GM schools receive an annual allocation for capital structural repairs from the Department for Education. During the 1992–93 school year, each school received $18,000 plus an additional $36 per student. For major capital improvement programs, GM schools may bid for grants to finance the purchase of capital equipment and building work. For 1993–94, nearly $140 million was allocated for GM schools' capital development projects.[71]

In sharp contrast to all of funds available to GM schools in England, charter schools in the United States are generally poor. In California as well as most other states, charter schools are clearly "unfunded mandates"—educational decentralization without resources. While charter schools in California are technically funded on a per-pupil basis according to their school districts' averages, all of their funding is funneled through their local school districts. Thus, the exact amount that each school receives varies from one district to the next and even from one charter school to the next within a single district. Furthermore, new, start-up schools that are not already housed in a district-owned building must pay their rent out of their per-pupil operating budget. This means these schools are in reality receiving less public funding per pupil than the regular public schools.[72]

According to the former state senator who authored the California charter school legislation, "My bias is that if there is a will there is a way. I'm sounding very cliché [but] I really don't think resources is the primary obstacle to charters being established."

The education advisor to the governor was even more blunt: "If teachers and parents have the desire and the determination, they can do it without the special funds."

While there have been federal funds available—up to $100 million for 1999—these are generally dispersed through each state department of education and thus the size of the grants varies widely.

Yet perhaps the greatest danger of an unfunded state mandate to decentralize education is that some local school communities are in a better position to take advantage of them than others because they can muster the resources to fund unfunded mandates themselves, leading to inequities in who can and cannot participate. In this way, charter school legislation has led to increased privatization of public education as charter schools in more affluent communities scramble to raise private funds and write grant proposals to pay for their new programs.[73] This is how the highly educated, upper-middle-class leader of the parent council at one cluster of charter schools explained her group's fundraising efforts: "There is only one grant I've written so far that is going through the district and the others, we're going either through the booster clubs or the [parent council], which is becoming more and more just the financial arm of the charter schools."

The California charter school law allows for schools to raise private funds to pay for their public school programs. In fact, in the legislation, after the section that explicitly forbids private schools from applying for charters, the law clearly states: "This part shall not be construed to prohibit any private person or organization from providing funding or other assistance to the establishment or operation of a charter school."

Thus, while charter schools are completely free of state and district regulations related to instruction, they are also free of district regulations regarding private fundraising for public schools. With no additional government funding, each charter school is left to its own devices to find money to support new and innovative programs. The notion that some schools may be in a better position to do that than others—that is, some schools can draw upon the expertise of parents who are lawyers or the networks of parents who are executives in large corporations— did not seem to be of any great concern to most policymakers in Sacramento. But at the local level, advocacy groups and educators worry about the long-term implications of entrepreneurial charter schools in wealthy communities that are able to support exceptional programs through private funds while their counterparts in less affluent neighborhoods are left to survive on dwindling public resources.

THE NEOLIBERAL HEGEMONY: SIMILARITIES BETWEEN THE UNITED KINGDOM AND UNITED STATES

According to Johnson, it is important to see the 1988 Education Reform Act in England as the product of many frustrations within the Conservative Party—"Aspirations were modified by external opposition and internal disagreement and by the need to take account of the past. The Act must not be read as a New Right blueprint or ideal. It is 'vouchers' which occupy this space in most of the writing. The Act is a more interesting and formidable thing: a transformative mechanism, a plan for transition in the long run."[74]

Similarly in the U.S. charter school–voucher plan connections are illustrated quite clearly in Mintron's study of the role of policy entrepreneurs in the development of charter school legislation. He reports that in Michigan, a coalition of voucher proponents strongly backs the charter school legislation as an "incremental" and "non threatening" way of introducing school choice–type innovations to the general public in hopes of building broader support for a constitutional amendment to allow vouchers. Thus, in Michigan, the charter school idea was seen as a useful measure for laying the groundwork for vouchers.[75]

As I mentioned above, the interviews that I conducted with colleagues reveal that state policy makers often view charter laws as laying the groundwork for voucher plans.[76] For instance, in Arizona, the governor's advisor for education noted that charter schools are helping people feel more comfortable with various options—"that it is okay to go to a school that's not part of the public system. [Charter schools] will begin to break down this attitude we have that we have to protect the public system at all costs or else our whole way of life is going to be crumbled."

An Arizona senator who likened public schools to prisons noted that charter schools offer the promise that new types of schools will evolve within an increasingly competitive environment. "As they [charter schools] move out into the future, I think what I'd see evolving is sort of a hybrid school that is supported both by the state and also might be able to . . . from an economist's standpoint, be able to, you know, in a sophisticated way, charge tuition."

Conceptually, legislators are linking charter schools and voucher plans, as is evident in the following quote from a California assemblyman: "when the charter school concept came along the Republicans right away said this is good . . . this is not a private school but it is the closest thing you are going to get to a private school and maintain public funding."

Thus, despite these vast differences in the social and political contexts of English grant-maintained and U.S. charter schools, research suggests that similar trends might have developed in both countries, or at least in England and certain states within the United States depending on the specifics of their legislation. For instance, in California, where charter schools are allowed to have admissions criteria and where charter schools are allowed to raise their own private funds, disturbing similarities between England and California can be seen even in this early stage of implementation.

The first similar trend appears to be that in both England and California the opting-out policies tend to have favored those who were politically empowered to begin with. Despite the rhetoric of charter school legislation as an act to empower the disempowered, the fact that no start up funds are available in California means that only those communities that are able to garner private and in-kind resources will survive.[77]

Furthermore, since the Labour government was elected in 1997, the extra funding for GM schools has been eliminated and the status of GM schools has been changed, through the 1998 School Standards and Framework Act, to "foundation schools," which receive grants from the government to operate. To the extent that the former GM schools have become highly dependent on their extra funding, those that have the connections may now turn to private donors to raise the extra funds.

The second emerging cross-Atlantic finding or trend is that greater competition between schools does not appear to benefit the losers of that competition. Despite political rhetoric about how competition will pull the bottom up by subjecting all schools to higher standards and putting them in a situation in which they must fight for their survival, in both England and California, evidence suggests that schools that lose in this competitive environment are not benefiting from this new deregulated system. For instance, in the UCLA study of charter schools, my colleagues and I found that the noncharter public schools were not spurred to action to dramatically improve because of the competition presented by the charter schools. Instead, due to overcrowding in many of the school districts we studied, these schools were not in a position to compete for students, and at the same time, they felt that the charter schools had an unfair advantage in this competition because they were able to establish admissions criteria and require parents and students to sign contracts.[78]

In England, the schools that did not opt out were left behind in LEAs that are less able to meet their needs because of the resources that had been drained off to pay for the more expensive GM schools. Furthermore, any increase in exam results for GM schools appeared to be the result of their increased selectivity rather than their success in improving student outcomes.[79]

And finally, evidence from both sides of the Atlantic suggests that GM and charter schools do increase choices for parents and students, but more importantly, they allow these schools to be more selective and thus to have more choices in terms of who they serve.[80]

These similarities between former GM schools and charter schools suggest that these reforms, both of which were inspired at least in part by neoliberal ideology, may be more successful in pushing the educational system toward privitization and increased stratification than they are at pushing the entire educational system toward "excellence."

CONCLUSIONS

Although the neoliberal economic metaphor for educational improvement—that is, the notion that deregulation and competition will force positive reforms to take place—sounds powerful and convincing, there is virtually no empirical evidence to support its assertions in the real educational world. Emerging trends in the data being collected on both grant-maintained schools in England and on charter schools in the United States do not support the economic metaphor. Rather, in these two very different countries with their dissimilar political and social contexts, some of the same disturbing trends are emerging from reform efforts based on the idea that competition and deregulation will improve the educational experiences of all students.

Given this preliminary evidence, two things should occur: researchers should continue to study the impact of legislation predicated on this neoliberal ideology, with a particular focus on the three issues mentioned above. And second, policymakers and the general public need to think more carefully and critically about the usefulness of economic theory as a guiding principal to improving a fundamentally socialistic educational system in the United States and Britain.

As Whitty and Power point out, despite the negative impact of neoliberal educational policy, the left has done little yet to develop a concept of public education that looks significantly different. They write, "Even if the social democratic era looks better in retrospect, and in comparison with current policies, than it did at the time, that does not remove the need to rethink what might be progressive policies for the next century."[81]

NOTES

1. Liz Bondi, "Choice and Diversity in School Education: Comparing Developments in the United Kingdom and USA," *Comparative Education* 27.2 (1991): 125–34; Tony Edwards and Geoff Whitty, "Parental Choice and Educational Reform in Britain and the United States," *British Journal of Educational Reform* 40.2 (May 1992): 101–17; and David Halpin and Barry Troyna, "Lessons in School Reform from Great Britain? The Politics of Education Policy Borrowing," paper presented at the annual meeting of the American Educational Research Association, New Orleans, La. (1994).

2. Priscilla Wohlstetter and Leslie Anderson, "What Can U.S. Charter Schools Learn from England's Grant-Maintained Schools?," *Phi Delta Kappan* 75.6 (February 1994): 486–91; Geoff Whitty, "Creating Quasi-Markets in Education: A Review of Recent Research on Parental Choice and School Autonomy in Three Countries," *Review of Research in Education* 22 (1997): 3–47; and Amy Stuart Wells, Cynthia Grutzik, Sibyll Carnochan, Julie Slayton, and Ash Vasudeva, "Underlying Policy Assumptions of Charter School Reform: The Multiple Meanings of a Movement," *Teachers College Record* 100.3 (Spring 1999): 513–35.

3. David Halpin, John Fitz, and Sally Power, "Local Education Authorities and the Grant-Maintained Schools Policy," *Educational Management and Administration* 19.4 (1991): 233–42.

4. This article will focus primarily on GM schools in England only because these are the schools most carefully studied by researchers. While Wales also has GM schools, educational reforms in Scotland and Northern Ireland are different and thus outside of the scope of this article.

5. Geoff Whitty, Sally Power, and David Halpin, *Devolution and Choice in Education* (Buckingham, UK: Open University Press, 1998), p. 35.

6. Richard Jonathan, "State Education Service or Prisoner's Dilemma: The 'Hidden Hand' as Source of Education Policy," *British Journal of Educational Studies* 38.2 (May 1990): 116–32, at 117–18.

7. John E. Chubb and Terry M. Moe, *Politics, Markets and America's Schools* (Washington, D.C.: Brookings Institution, 1990); David Hellawell, "Structural Changes in Education in England," *International Journal of Educational Reform* 1.4 (October 1992): 356–65; Whitty, "Creating Quasi-Markets in Education: A Review of Recent Research on Parental Choice and School Autonomy in Three Countries"; and Whitty, Power, and Halpin, *Devolution and Choice in Education.*

8. Anthony Giddens, *Beyond Left and Right: The Future of Radical Politics* (Stanford, Calif.: Stanford University Press, 1994).

9. Jane Kenway with Chris Bigum and Lindsay Fitzclarence, "Marketing Education in the Postmodern Age," *Journal of Education Policy* 8.2: 105–25, at 116.

10. Joel F. Handler, *Down from Bureaucracy: The Ambiguity of Privatization and Empowerment* (Princeton, N.J.: Princeton University Press, 1996), p. 9.

11. David Halpin and John Fitz, "Researching Grant-Maintained Schools," *Journal of Education Policy* 5.2 (1990): 167–80, at 167.

12. Chris Pipho, "Bipartisan Charter Schools," *Phi Delta Kappan* 75.2 (1993): 10–11.

13. Wells, Grutzik, Carnochan, Slayton, and Vasudeva, "Underlying Policy Assumptions of Charter School Reform."

14. Michael W. Apple, *Cultural Politics and Education* (New York: Teachers College Press, 1996), p. 22.

15. Jim Carl, "Parental Choice as National Policy in England and the United States," *Comparative Education Review* 38.3 (1994): 294–322.

16. Hellawell, "Structural Changes in Education in England," and Whitty, Power, and Halpin, *Devolution and Choice in Education.*

17. Hellawell, "Structural Changes in Education in England," p. 363.

18. Ibid.

19. Martin Hughes, "The National Curriculum in England and Wales: A Lesson in Externally Imposed Reform?" *Educational Administration Quarterly* 33.2 (April 1997): 183–97, at 185.

20. David Halpin, Sally Power, and John Fitz, "Opting into the Past? Grant Maintained School and the Reinvention of Tradition," in *Choice and Diversity in School: Perspectives and Prospects,* ed. R. Glatter, P. Woods, and C. Bagley (London: Routledge, 1996).

21. Geoffrey Walford, "Diversity, Choice, and Selection in England and Wales," *Educational Administration Quarterly* 33.2 (April 1997): 158–69, at 166.

22. Geoff Whitty and Sally Power, "Quasi-Markets and Curriculum Control: Making Sense of Recent Education Reform in England and Wales," *Educational Administration Quarterly* 33.2 (April 1997): 219–40, at 227.

23. Kathryn Stearns, *School Reform: Lessons from England* (Princeton, N.J.: The Carnegie Foundation for the Advancement of Teaching, 1996), p. 85.

24. Giddens, *Beyond Left and Right*.

25. Ibid.

26. Jeffrey Henig, *Rethinking School Choice: Limits of the Market Metaphor in Education* (Princeton, N.J.: Princeton University, 1994), p. 84.

27. Thomas B. Edsall (with Mary Edsall), *Chain Reaction: The Impact of Race, Rights, and Taxes on American Politics* (New York: Norton, 1991).

28. Carl, "Parental Choice as National Policy in England and the United States," p. 300.

29. Dan A. Lewis and Kathryn Nakagawa, *Race and Educational Reform in the American Metropolis: A Study of School Decentralization* (Albany: State University of New York Press, 1995); David N. Plank and William L. Boyd, "Antipolitics, Education, and Institutional Choice: The Flight from Democracy," *American Educational Research Journal* 31.2 (Summer 1994): 263–81.

30. Carl, "Parental Choice as National Policy in England and the United States."

31. David Harmer, *School Choice: Why You Need It—How You Get It* (Washington, D.C.: CATO Institute, 1994), p. 44.

32. Jonathan, "State Education Service or Prisoner's Dilemma."

33. Carl, "Parental Choice as National Policy in England and the United States," p. 303.

34. Ibid., p. 305.

35. Jennifer A. O'Day and Marshall S. Smith, "Systemic Reform and Educational Opportunity," in *Designing Coherent Education Policy*, ed. Susan H. Fuhrman (San Francisco: Jossey-Bass, 1993), pp. 250–312.

36. O'Day and Smith, "Systemic Reform and Educational Opportunity."

37. See, for example, Linda Darling-Hammond, *Standards of Practice for Learner-Centered Schools* (New York: National Center for Restructuring Schools and Teaching, Teachers College, Columbia University, 1992). And Jeannie Oakes, "Opportunity to Learn: Can Standards-Based Reform Be Equity-Based Reform?" Paper presented at "Effects of New Standards and Assessment on High Risk Students and Disadvantaged Schools," a Research Forum of New Standards Project (Cambridge: Harvard University, 1993).

38. Anne C. Lewis, "Winds of Change Are Blowing," *Phi Delta Kappan* 75.10 (1994): 740–41. And United States Department of Education. "The Goals 2000: Educate America Act: Making American Education Great Again" (Washington, D.C.: Author, 1994).

39. Mark Pitsch, Dole Decries History Standards for Dwelling on the Negative," *Education Week*, September 13, 1995), p. 1 (from downloaded story).

40. January 11, 1995, pp. 1 and 12. And K. Diegmueller, "Running Out of Steam: Special Report, Struggling for Standards," *Education Week*, April 12, 1995, pp. 4–8.

41. Mark Pitsch, "House Republicans Unveil Bill to Ax E.D., Create Block Grants," *Education Week*, May 31, 1995.

42. Drew Lindsay, "Panel Puts Brakes on Bill to Rebuild California Testing System," *Education Week*, September 13, 1995.

43. Diegmueller, "Running out of Steam."

44. Hughes, "The National Curriculum in England and Wales."

45. David Tyack. "'Restructuring' in Historical Perspective: Tinkering toward Utopia," *Teachers College Record* 92.2 (1990): 170–91.

46. Walford, "Diversity, Choice, and Selection in England and Wales," and Bill Inglis, "The Labour Party's Policy on Primary and Secondary Education 1979–89," *British Journal of Educational Studies* 39.1 (February 1991): 4–16.

47. See Andrew Stillman, "Legislating for Choice," in *The Education Reform Act 1988*, ed. Michael Flude and Merril Hammer (London: The Falmer Press, 1990), pp. 87–106.

48. Hellawell, "Structural Changes in Education in England.," p. 364.

49. Stephen J. Ball, "Education Markets, Choice and Social Class: The Market as a Class Strategy in the UK and USA," *British Journal of Sociology of Education* 14.1 (1993): 3–19, at 8.

50. Wells, Grutzik, Carnochan, Slayton, and Vasudeva, "Underlying Policy Assumptions of Charter School Reform."

51. Pipho, "Bipartisan Charter Schools," p. 102

52. Priscilla Wohlstetter and Lesley Anderson, "What Can U.S. Charter Schools Learn from England's Grant-Maintained Schools?" Paper presented at the Annual Meeting of the American Educational Research Association, San Francisco, 1992.

53. See Lewis and Nakagawa, *Race and Educational Reform in the American Metropolis*; Maurice R. Berube and Marilyn Gittell, *Confrontation at Ocean Hill-Brownsville: The New York School Strikes of 1968* (New York: Frederick A. Praeger, 1969).

54. Amy Stuart Wells, *Time to Choose: America at the Crossroads of School Choice Policy* (New York: Hill and Wang, 1993).

55. Hellawell, "Structural Changes in Education in England."

56. Halpin and Fitz, "Researching Grant-Maintained Schools."

57. Michael Flude and Merril Hammer, *The Education Reform Act, 1988* (London: The Falmer Press, 1990).

58. David Halpin, John Fitz, and Sally Power, "Local Education Authorities and the Grant-Maintained Schools Policy, *Educational Management and Administration* 19.4 (1991): 233–42.

59. Flude and Hammer, *The Education Reform Act, 1988*.

60. Center for Education Reform, www.edreform.com (1998).

61. SRI International, *Evaluation of Charter School Effectiveness* (Menlo Park, Calif.: Author, 1997).

62. Lori Mulholland and Mary Amsler, *The Search for Choice in Public Education: The Emergence of Charter Schools* (Tempe, Ariz.: The Morrison Institute of Public Policy, 1992), p. 14.

63. Wohlstetter and Anderson, "What Can U.S. Charter Schools Learn from England's Grant-Maintained Schools?"

64. Halpin, Power, and Fitz, "Opting into the Past."

65. Mulholland and Amsler, *The Search for Choice in Public Education*, p. 14.

66. Brunno V. Manno, Chester E. Finn, Louane A. Bierlein, and Greg Vanourek, "How Charter Schools are Different: Lessons and Implications from a National Study," *Phi Delta Kappan* (March 1998): 489–98. And Mulholland and Amsler, *The Search for Choice in Public Education*, p. 3.

67. UCLA Charter School Study, *Beyond the Rhetoric of Charter School Reform: A Study of Ten California School Districts* (Los Angeles: Author, 1998).

68. Ibid.

69. Hellawell, "Structural Changes in Education in England."

70. Wohlstetter and Anderson, "What Can U.S. Charter Schools Learn from England's Grant-Maintained Schools?," p. 488.

71. Ibid.

72. UCLA Charter School Study, *Beyond the Rhetoric of Charter School Reform: A Study of Ten California School Districts*.

73. Ibid

74. Richard Johnson, "Thatcherism and English Education: Breaking the Mold or Confirming the Patterns?" *History of Education* 18.2 (1989): 91–121, at 110.

75. Michael Mintron, "Policy Entrepreneurs and the Diffusion of Innovation," *American Journal of Political Science* 41 (1997): 738–70.

76. Wells, Grutzik, Carnochan, Slayton, and Vasudeva, "Underlying Policy Assumptions of Charter School Reform."

77. UCLA Charter School Study, *Beyond the Rhetoric of Charter School Reform: A Study of Ten California School Districts*.

78. Ibid.

79. Bob Doe, "Tory Competition Fails to Raise Standards," *The Times Educational Supplement* (9 January 1998).

80. Sharon Gewirtz, Stephen J. Ball, and Richard Bowe, *Markets, Choice and Equity in Education* (Buckingham, UK: Open University Press, 1995); UCLA Charter School Study, *Beyond the Rhetoric of Charter School Reform: A Study of Ten California School Districts*.

81. Whitty and Power, "Quasi-Markets and Curriculum Control: Making Sense of Recent Education Reform in England and Wales," p. 236.

CHAPTER 5

Corporations and Classrooms: A Critical Examination of the Business Agenda for Urban School Reform

Roslyn Arlin Mickelson

The campus of IBM's Palisades, New York Executive Conference Center was the site of the March 1996 Education Summit. Cosponsored by IBM, the National Governors' Association, and the Education Commission of the States, the two-day meeting was a response to IBM Chief Executive Officer Louis V. Gerstner Jr.'s exhortation to governors and business leaders to join ongoing efforts to restructure American public education. The summit highlighted the very public role of business leaders today in setting agendas for school reform and in commanding the attention of state educational decision-makers.

This chapter examines a local manifestation of the corporate role in educational restructuring. It is a case study of one community's experiences with a decade of intense business involvement in school reform. The community is Charlotte, North Carolina where national and local leaders of IBM and other firms participate intimately in the reform process. Using the city and its schools as a strategic case study, this chapter seeks to theorize more fully the corporate role in contemporary school reform. Its conceptual contributions lie in an explication of different kinds of business involvement and empirical illustrations of these. By approaching the corporate role in school reform from this perspective, the work mediates between abstractions of general social processes and microanalyses of conflicts within the educational system.[1]

The chapter provides an integrative analysis of corporate participation in educational policy formation and implementation in two distinct ways. First, it presents a typology of business involvement in school reform and the multiple motivations for these interventions. Next, it applies the typology in a concrete fashion to specific education policy initiatives in Charlotte. Rather than merely describing the reforms and key actors, the study analyzes various events and actions in terms of for whom and in whose interests local schools are being reformed. The case study serves as an example for examining and theorizing the contemporary corporate role in school reform more generally.

The chapter will focus primarily upon two reform initiatives sponsored by IBM, although related activities of other firms will be discussed as well. The first reform is ProjectFirst, a collaboration between IBM and the Charlotte-Mecklenburg Education Foundation (CMEF). ProjectFirst, staffed with Americorps volunteers, was designed to bring technology specialists into the district's nonmagnet middle schools. The second is a planned complex of four technology-rich schools adjacent to the Charlotte IBM facility. Originally called the Education Village, but renamed the Governors' Village following the bitter controversy that will be discussed in this chapter, this project was partially funded by a grant to the school district through IBM's Reinventing Education initiative. The third example describes the involvement of a prominent real estate developer in an educational policy decision that had broad implications for the wider school district. The relationship between corporations, their leaders and the Charlotte-Mecklenburg school system is instructive for understanding the larger ideological, political, and educational policy significance of corporate involvement in the school reform process. By tracing how various policies and reform initiatives were developed and contested, we gain insights into their meaning and theoretical significance, as well as the opportunities and dangers that accompany them.

BACKGROUND

Since the early 1980s, business representatives across the United States have renewed their focus on public schools. How can we best understand the intimate involvement of firms and their leaders in educational reform? The answer most likely lies in the larger contemporary corporate environment that has been likened to turbulent, white water rapids. There are three critical features of this fierce environment: (1) intense globalization that demands both national and international competitiveness; (2) the growing, changing diversity of the modern workforce; and (3) the technological revolution that sets the stage for an information and communication-driven economy. Unable to control the course of macro economic trends like globalization or the advance of technology, corporate leaders appear to have turned their attention to elements of the broader social environment that may be more susceptible to their influence than the business cycle—for example, the public schools that prepare their domestic workforce. By focusing concern on the public schools, corporate leaders deflect attention from their own contributions to domestic and international productivity problems.

During the 1980s, business leaders' assignment to the flawed public school system of blame for the crisis in international competitiveness gained widespread acceptance among parents, school leaders, and policymakers. As this new definition of the situation facing the United States became standard, corporate actors intensified their involvement in the development and implementation of the solutions to the problems they helped to define. American corporate leaders attributed their reinvigorated involvement to the need to resolve the crisis in the U.S. educational system that, from their perspective, was responsible for the crisis in U.S. productivity and international competitiveness.[2]

The country's educational failings enumerated in *A Nation at Risk* reflected this perspective, as did former Secretary of Education Lauro Cavazos who observed in 1989 that the United States faced three deficits—the budget, trade, and education deficits—and that the first two would only be remedied after the last one was resolved.[3] The Reagan and Bush administrations embraced both market principles and the precept that privatization is the antidote to flawed, inefficient governmental bureaucracies. Encouraged by these administrations, the business critique of public education acquired even greater legitimacy. It also found systematic institutional strength through advocacy organizations like the Business Roundtable, the Conference Board, and chambers of commerce across the nation.[4] Furthermore, business leaders indirectly shaped the course and direction of school reform through their pivotal role in the first National Education Summit in 1989.[5]

In the 1990s, the U.S. economy regained its position as the most productive in the world. That return negated the argument that flawed public schools were responsible for lagging U.S. competitiveness in international markets. So corporate leaders adjusted their construction of the problems with public schools. Now they say that public schools are failing to prepare students for future information age jobs that will require advanced knowledge of technology.

There is perhaps no clearer expression of current corporate influence than the second nationwide education summit held during March 1996, at IBM's Executive Conference Center in Palisades, New York. It highlighted the very public role of business leaders today in setting agendas for school reform and in commanding the attention of state educational decision-makers.[6] Cosponsored by IBM, the National Governors' Association, and the Education Commission of the States, the two-day meeting was a response to IBM Chief Executive Officer Louis V. Gerstner Jr.'s exhortation to governors and business leaders to join ongoing efforts to restructure American public education. On March 26 and 27, 1996, forty-three governors, each joined by a CEO of his or her choice, met at IBM's Palisades conference center. The hosts were IBM's CEO, Louis V. Gerstner Jr. and Governor Tommy Thompson of Wisconsin. The summit was envisioned as a bipartisan effort, so Secretary of Education Richard Riley attended and President Clinton addressed the group on the second day of the conference. In addition to the governors and their honored corporate guests, thirty education experts were invited as resource people.

There are disagreements over the appropriateness, importance, motivation, and results of corporate involvement in school restructuring whether at summits or in school partnerships. However, there is no disagreement that that corporate financial and symbolic capital have stimulated programmatic innovation and technical support for local and national reform efforts. Some analysts and practitioners consider business leadership and involvement to be integral to reforming schools; others see corporate efforts as nothing more than feel-good gestures that do little systematically to reform public education. Other more critical observers contend that corporate philanthropy is a conscious venture into school reforms that will ultimately serve corporate long- and short-term interests more than improve public education. It is indisputable that business leaders have more than just a place at the table where restructuring is planned. Current reform efforts are intimately linked to the widely accepted corporate critique of the schools. Executives representing their corporations or acting as individual citizens are actively involved at local, state, and national levels in agenda-setting, formulation of reform designs, and the implementation of reforms.

Raymond Morrow and Carlos Alberto Torres observe that the key to a theory of educational reproduction lies in a theory of public policy that can analyze educational policy formation in specific empirical terms, thus mediating between abstractions of general social processes and microanalysis of conflicts within the educational system.[7] This chapter seeks to illuminate these general processes with a detailed case study of the corporate agenda for school reform in Charlotte, North Carolina. It introduces a comprehensive typology of corporate involvement in school reform. The typology distinguishes among types of corporate involvement and the multiple motivations that underlie business participation, and identifies the various consequences of that participation.

Using this typology we can examine the activities of corporate actors in Charlotte to see how business involvement and its consequences in Charlotte-Mecklenburg Schools (CMS) are emblematic of wider practices, political struggles, and contested policy processes and outcomes in communities across the nation.

CORPORATIONS AND SCHOOL REFORM IN CHARLOTTE-MECKLENBURG, NORTH CAROLINA

Recent History of Reform

Charlotte, North Carolina, is a rapidly growing sunbelt city known for its landmark *Swann v. Charlotte-Mecklenburg Schools* decision wherein the Supreme Court upheld within-district busing as a remedy for segregated schooling.[8] Scholars and lay observers cite early and widespread business support for peaceful implementation of the plan as a crucial element in the creation of a communitywide consensus that desegregated education was good for the city. For almost twenty years, CMS served as a model for other systems of how to undertake the process of desegregation of public education using busing and other tools. The district remains under court order today, although much of the reform effort during the last decade has altered the manner in which the system desegregates its schools.[9] In the 1996–97 school year, the district had about 93,000 students who attend 130 schools scattered across a countywide district that covers 528 square miles. The student population was 52.5 percent white and 41 percent black. The remaining 6.5 percent of students were from Asian, Hispanic, and American Indian backgrounds.

This case study draws from a decade-long investigation of school reform in Charlotte-Mecklenburg. The data used in this chapter come from over 150 semistructured interviews conducted by the author with corporate and civic elites and educational policymakers in Charlotte and across the nation; interviews with educators and parents in Charlotte; field notes from observations of local task forces, community forums, and other public meetings about education; and official documents from business, government, and the schools. Direct quotations are attributed to an identified person, unless the individual specifically requested confidentiality. Initial drafts of this chapter were reviewed by local corporate executives, Americorps volunteers, citizen activists, and educators who were interviewed. Several activists and educators who were not interviewed also read earlier versions. All comments were considered in the subsequent revision of the chapter. The names of schools used in the chapter are pseudonyms.

Beginning in the late 1980s, Charlotte corporate leaders ceased to be the vocal, public champions of the school system that they had been for the previous fifteen years.[10] They began publicly to express their dismay over the city's scarcity of qualified entry-level workers, a problem for which they largely blamed the schools. Critics paid little attention to the contributions of rapid economic development and a low unemployment rate to the labor shortage during the last fifteen years. Instead, looking to the schools as both the source of and solution to their problems, corporate leaders began to shape the direction of reform with the explicit purpose of improving schools in order to enhance both the business climate and the future workforce.[11] Since the late 1980s, corporate involvement in CMS has been both formal (i.e., membership on task forces and the school board) and informal (i.e., creating political action committees that identify and fund school board candidates compatible with the business agenda).

About this time, the school system began reform in response to external pressure from corporate critics and dissatisfied parents many of whom were new to the district. Disappointed with initial efforts, in 1991 the school board hired a new superintendent, John Murphy. Shortly after arriving in Charlotte, Superintendent Murphy convened a panel of experts to advise him on systemic reform.[12] After he released the panel's report to the public, the superintendent launched a number of reform initiatives using the panel's recommendations to argue for their necessity and wisdom. Interestingly, Murphy's most controversial and sweeping reform—the end of mandatory busing for desegregation—was not a subject of the panel's deliberations. On March 31, 1992, the Charlotte-Mecklenburg school board voted to replace its historic countywide busing plan with a desegregation plan largely built around parental choice among magnet schools. Local corporate and civic leaders who found their corporate recruitment efforts hampered by the districtwide busing plan and the nascent nationwide reputation of the school system as mediocre supported this reform vigorously. Many middle-class parents from all racial backgrounds did as well.[13]

It is impossible to understand the push for reform in Charlotte without considering the spreading distaste for desegregated schooling among the business leaders and middle-class families who relocated to Charlotte since 1985. While improving the quality of the entry-level workforce was the formal goal of business leaders engaged in early reform efforts, ending busing for desegregation was at the heart of their informal agenda. This goal was not publicly articulated until the mid-1990s when it became more politically acceptable to support neighborhood schools. Despite these pressures, in 1997 the school district still formally maintained its commitment to becoming the nation's premier urban integrated school system. However, in each of the first four years since the adoption of the magnet desegregation plan, the district became modestly more segregated.[14] Overall levels of desegregation stabilized during the fifth year of the magnet plan, 1996–97, but levels of racial isolation intensified in a number of elementary schools in the central city and in prosperous white outlying suburban areas.

Until the last six months of his four and one half year tenure in CMS, Murphy enjoyed strong personal and organizational support from local business leaders. The relationship between the business community and the new superintendent was mutually supportive. For example, when the Chamber of Commerce was in the process of recruiting Transamerica Reinsurance for relocation to Charlotte, it dispatched Superintendent Murphy to the firm's headquarters. He assured employers that the local public schools were good and improving and that relocated employees purchasing homes in certain subdivisions could expect to attend nearby schools.

Two events are emblematic of business support for Murphy. In the summer of 1992, the chairman and CEO of First Union, one of the nation's largest banks and one of the most influential corporations in Charlotte, personally lobbied the school board on behalf of a substantial raise for Murphy, pacing the hallway outside the board room while personnel matters were discussed in executive session.[15] At the end of Murphy's first year as superintendent, an anonymous group of corporate leaders collected $30,000 as a bonus. The school board did not permit the donors to give him their gift; instead, the school board awarded him a smaller bonus.

Major corporate actors who have been critical of CMS's performance also have been highly supportive of reform efforts. Executives have served on numerous task forces, donated their facilities for educational functions, given money and equipment to the schools, and supported the creation of an educational foundation (the Charlotte Mecklenburg Education Foundation [CMEF]). CMEF's goals include raising community awareness of educational matters and supporting educational innovations with small grants they called venture capital. Executives have supported bond issues and lobbied the legislature on behalf of the public schools. Corporations have loaned executives to the schools and to CMEF; they have adopted schools, and their employees have volunteered in classrooms. To varying degrees, CMS's school leaders cultivate the support of corporate leaders, socialize with them, and consult with key individuals before launching important initiatives.[16] The executive president of the Charlotte Chamber of Commerce characterizes this as "an *aggressive* partnership with the school system [his emphasis]."[17]

IBM has been one of the most prominent and active forces in national and CMS school reform during the last decade. The prominent role of IBM's leaders makes the study of the nature of their involvement, their motivations, and examples of their activities in CMS useful for examining a number of general issues about corporate involvement in educational reform. IBM mid-level executives serve in a number of capacities on educational task forces and the executive in charge of the local facility was an active member of the Charlotte-Mecklenburg Education Foundation. The corporation's support of the local schools is most evident in two specific programs, ProjectFirst and the Education Village.

ProjectFirst

In the early 1990s, IBM funded a ProjectFirst (Fostering Instruction Through Service and Technology) program in Charlotte, Atlanta, and New York. IBM's formal purpose was to assist schools in bringing technology into classroom instruction. In Charlotte, the IBM grant paid for computer hardware in ten nonmagnet middle schools and a limited training program for the technology specialists who were to bring computer expertise to classroom teachers. Charlotte's ProjectFirst personnel were Americorps volunteers.[18] The Charlotte-Mecklenburg Education Foundation received one of the first Americorps grants awarded by the federal government. CMS placed the Americorps volunteers in ten nonmagnet middle schools as technology specialists. The expectation was that technology specialists would help teachers integrate technology into their instruction.

The choice of these particular nonmagnet middle school as ProjectFirst sites involved more than an empirical assessment of which schools had the greatest need. The superintendent's choice of nonmagnet middle schools was also a response to criticism that new magnet schools diverted district resources from older, inner city schools. Soon after the district replaced its mandatory desegregation plan with a voluntary one built around choice among magnet schools, it became apparent to many parents and other citizens that there were gross inequalities in resources available in magnets, newer schools, and older schools primarily in the urban core. They noted that the magnet strategy for reform left many schools in dire need of attention and additional resources. In the view of some critics, these inequities exacerbated existing race and class disparities in opportunities to learn.[19] People complained that the magnet program, rather than addressing educational inequality, was exacerbating it by draining funds that could be spent for all school. School district personnel explained that the magnet program was funded initially by federal desegregation monies, not local funding intended for all schools. However, critics insisted that in the future, magnet schools' special needs would likely create financial speed bumps when federal funding ended.

In his presentation to the August 1994 CMEF board meeting, the superintendent reported on his plans for improving technology in the schools. He mentioned a planned technology-rich educational complex (the formal announcement of the Educational Village was a few weeks away), and described ProjectFirst. In introducing ProjectFirst, he intimated that his choice of nonmagnet middle schools as ProjectFirst sites was strategic. First, ProjectFirst would bring technology specialists into schools desperately deficient in these tools. Second, it held the potential to mollify critics who charged that newly created magnet schools drained disproportionate shares of the district's resources and contributed to greater educational inequities.[20]

In fact, there was no way that ProjectFirst could balance the inequality of resources between magnet and nonmagnet middle schools. For example, in 1993 the science and technology magnet middle school, Sherwood, received $750,000 in resources. It was transformed from a highly segregated minority school into a racially integrated showcase magnet. A nonmagnet middle school, Westway, received an Americorps volunteer and several IBM computers. Westway and other nonmagnet ProjectFirst middle schools remained largely racially unbalanced and dilapidated. Furthermore, many of them could not use the ProjectFirst equipment effectively because of infrastructure problems like wiring inadequate to support computers and personnel problems like high teacher turnover and little teacher knowledge about computers and educational software.

CMEF staff touted IBM's ProjectFirst as an important, technology-based innovation that was making important contributions to staff development and students' learning in the nonmagnet middle schools where Americorps volunteers were placed. The validity of this claim remains unverified. The author's repeated requests to CMEF for program evaluation documents were ignored. However, a series of interviews with Americorps volunteers, teachers, and principals from these nonmagnet middle schools, revealed a picture of ProjectFirst's educational value at odds with CMEF's account.

The characterization of Americorps volunteers as technology specialists in the nonmagnet middle schools accurately described neither their qualifications nor what they were able to accomplish throughout most of the first year the project was in schools. Apparently, Americorps volunteers were not screened for either knowledge of computers or experience with educational technology. Consequently, volunteers had uneven technological backgrounds. Some had degrees in computer science, some had business backgrounds, but none had direct experience or any training in teaching computer technology or computer skills to others. Most volunteers anticipated that any gaps in their backgrounds, skills, and knowledge would be filled during their two weekend training sessions with IBM. However, midway through their first official training in the IBM's New York headquarters, the volunteers realized that they were not going to get from IBM any information or training about either computers or how to teach about computers. Instead of technology training, they were given a quick overview of schooling in America. Concerned, they formed a self-study group during that weekend.

> AUTHOR. Did they [IBM] give you technology training?
>
> AMERICORPS VOLUNTEER. No. If you were to talk to any of the ten [original Americorps volunteers], and ask them what was the biggest disappointment [of the IBM training] it would have been there was no training in technology. . . . They didn't talk about how to integrate technology into the curriculum. And there even was no basic stuff like, "Here's the latest technology that we have, here's how the technology works. This is what a hard drive is. This is some of the old technology that you're going to run into. You may know a lot about the latest Macs, but do you know what to do when you go to [your school]. You're going to see a whole bunch of old IBM PC's from 1984 and this is how to work with them." No, it was very disappointing. By Saturday night, when we realized there wasn't going to be anything, a group of us from New York and Charlotte got together and said, "let's just hold our own little training tonight." Two of the volunteers from New York sat down and went through the whole entire guts of a computer and told us about the Internet.

After the training sessions in New York, Americorps volunteers returned to Charlotte where they continued learning about technology on their own. During the first six months in their schools, Americorps volunteers were caught in a difficult situation: dedicated to public service and to improving public education, they were initially ill-equipped to do the very job for which they were placed in the schools. A number of them worked in fear that they would be asked a question by an educator before they had had the opportunity to learn about it on their own. During the first year, when asked a computer-related question by a teacher, one volunteer would say "Let me get back to you on this" and would then spend the next few days furiously researching the question. By the time the volunteer gained some clarity about the answer, the teacher's need for it had generally disappeared. ProjectFirst's Americorps volunteers were by-and-large unable to provide the technological support teachers needed for a very long time. Some were never able to do so.

The observations of a principal newly assigned to a troubled middle school midway through the period of the IBM grant underscored the dubious educational value of ProjectFirst.

I arrived at Crozier Middle School . . . and met with the Americorps volunteer to ascertain his responsibilities at the school. He had not been given "directions" from the previous principal who "did not believe in technology." There was little interest in technology by the previous principal and even less support and resources from CMS to provide needed hardware and upgrades to the [school] facility. The Americorps volunteer identified five computers purchased through the project, of which three computers were used by the administration. There was no accounting for these computers on school inventory lists.

The volunteer had limited skills and knowledge in technology and even less in instruction. Teachers expressed concerns that the volunteer was unable to assist or to train them. Consequently, the school computer teacher "trained" the volunteer. The volunteer spent a great deal of time "finding" someone who could help him relative to technical knowledge and curricular issues. Americorps volunteers served several schools, hence there was limited availability of the volunteer at my school. Finally, the placement of Americorps volunteers in nonmagnet needy schools wasn't equivalent to a band-aid; it was a cotton swab.

Overall, Americorps volunteers encountered widespread resistance to the use of computers among teachers and principals in many other ProjectFirst nonmagnet middle schools. This is in part because educators with knowledge, skills, and appreciation for computer technology tend to self-select themselves into schools with the best equipment. When the CMS magnet program began, the schools with technology themes drew technologically inclined educators from other schools across the district. Teaching staffs who remained in the ProjectFirst middle schools were therefore disproportionately computer illiterate or even computer phobic. Despite repeated opportunities for staff development during ProjectFirst's first year, most teachers in these schools resisted volunteers' efforts to teach them computer skills. Complicating matters, many of the ProjectFirst schools were older and physically unable to support the technology donated by IBM because their wiring was too antiquated to be updated.

The second year, most ProjectFirst Americorps volunteers were new, and the large turnover in the volunteers was matched by the teacher turnover in many of the ProjectFirst nonmagnet middle schools. Once teachers received training in technology, a significant number of them transferred to more desirable schools in the district. Consequently, much of what little ProjectFirst accomplished in the first year left the school with these teachers. A volunteer summed up this dilemma:

What I see is that groundwork that you lay is not going to stay because at the nonmagnet schools there is such a high turnover rate, not only in teachers but also in principals—that they [Americorps volunteers] can come in there and build a foundation, but then next year, it's going to change because you have new people coming in and you've got others leaving [to go to better schools].

This description of ProjectFirst raises doubts that IBM's grant to CMS had measurable positive effects on either teachers or students. Certainly ProjectFirst did not contribute to measurable, systemic reform in CMS. ProjectFirst suffered from (1) initial poor planning, (2) implementation in schools ill-equipped to support additional computers, (3) gross differences in Americorps volunteers' technical and instructional skills, (4) a lack of understanding of schools as organizations on the part of its project director (a young assistant at the Charlotte-Mecklenburg Education Foundation), (5) an overestimation of the power of technology to solve entrenched, complex educational problems, (6) little to no long-term staff development in ProjectFirst schools, and (7) staff instability. Examination of the project illustrates the more general proposition that, at a minimum, without teacher professional development in integrating technology into the curriculum, faculty stability, and a physical plant that can sustain modern technology, computers themselves cannot improve teaching and learning.

The Charlotte-Mecklenburg Education Village

Perhaps the most significant point about the example of the Education Village is that during the time the village was designed, the CMS school board in office—the entity with responsibility for policy decisions—was never formally presented the details of any plans. This fact became important in the political struggle that unfolded beginning in January 1996. The school board learned of the Education Village when, in fall 1994, IBM's Gerstner and Superintendent Murphy announced to the community the award of a $2,000,000 IBM grant to support an Education Village, the first of ten Reinventing Education grants awarded nationally by the corporation. IBM's Reinventing Education initiative is aimed at funding systemic reforms in public schools. In the program's first round of gifts, $2 million grants also were awarded to public schools in Philadelphia, Vermont, Chicago, Dallas, West Virginia, Broward County, Florida, San Francisco, San Jose, and Cincinnati.[21]

The village's plans were designed by Superintendent Murphy and Stanley Litow, IBM's Vice President of Corporate Community Relations. The village was designed as a four-school complex (two elementary, one middle, and one high school) to be built on 200 acres of land adjacent to the IBM facility in the University Research Park (URP). The land was purchased by CMS in 1993 for $6 million. The IBM site executive who participated in the negotiations described the sale of the land to the district at $32,000 per acre as "a straight business transaction of an IBM asset."[22] The construction of the actual schools is financed by $82 million in public bonds approved narrowly by citizens in the fall of 1995.

University Research Park is located in northern Mecklenburg County close to the University of North Carolina, Charlotte. It is designed to replicate the renowned Research Triangle Park associated with Duke University, North Carolina State University, and University of North Carolina, Chapel Hill. This area is a rapidly growing, prosperous section of Mecklenburg County (see figure 5.1). Its adjacent neighborhoods—largely affluent and white—tend toward bucolic suburbs, rather than dense multiethnic urban neighborhoods. In addition to IBM, Verbatim, and First Union National Bank, a number of other high-tech and financial institutions have major installations there.

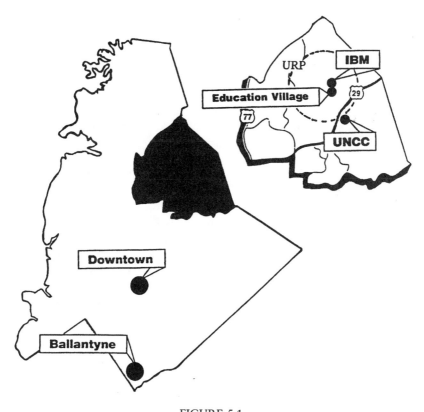

FIGURE 5.1
Charlotte-Mecklenburg School System with the
University Research Park Area and the Education Village in Relief

A defining feature of the Education Village was its designation as a workplace magnet. Parents of children who attend Education Village schools were to pledge to volunteer one hour per week in their children's school, and parents' employers were to be required to agree to this commitment of time. Classrooms were to have business mentors. When the four-school complex is completed, students were to learn in multi-age classrooms, were to experience a curriculum integrated from kindergarten through the twelfth grade, and were to use state-of-the-art technology. Parents were to be connected to the school with IBM's Wired for Learning educational software. Once admitted to a village school, children were to be able to attend one of its schools until they graduate from high school. Their siblings were to be permitted to attend as well.[23]

The development of Wired for Learning software utilizes over half of the IBM grant to CMS. In addition to software development, the grant supports a project manager, staff development, some network hardware, and computers in nearby libraries, the local science museum (Discovery Place), and the community center in the inner-city neighborhood. IBM retains the copyright for all software and intellectual property developed as part of the $2 million Reinventing Education grant awarded to the Charlotte schools.[24]

The Educational Village's original plans describe a partnership remarkably similar to the Downtown School, a workplace magnet in Winston-Salem, North Carolina. Gerstner, now the CEO and chairman of IBM, was the head of RJR Tobacco at the time the Downtown School was developed. The Downtown School was created with funding from the RJR Nabisco Foundation's Next Century Schools program in 1992.[25] The Downtown School's business partners are RJR Tobacco, RJR Tobacco International, and Planters LifeSavers. These firms give their employees, who are parents of students in the magnet, one hour of released time per week to volunteer in the schools "to tie learning to the business perspective."[26] Children who attend the school are selected by lottery. Sixty percent of the seats are allocated to children of full-time regular employees of the three business partners and 40 percent of seats are available to inner-city children who live in the immediate area.

The similarities between the Downtown School in Winston-Salem and the original plans for the Education Village are apparent. As outlined in a series of letters between Murphy and Litow, the Education Village was to be a partnership between IBM, other URP firms, and the school system. Murphy and Litow's original design allocated one third of the seats to children from University Research Park firms (of the URP's approximately 12,000 employees, about 4,000 worked for IBM at that time), one third from adjacent subdivisions, and one third for children who live in a specific inner-city neighborhood. In the original proposal for the Educational Village, Superintendent Murphy wrote:

> a number of seats will be reserved for children of employees who work in the immediate area (our private sector partners) [parentheses in the original].[27]

Seats for children of employees of URP firms and adjacent subdivisions were to be filled by lottery. The remaining third of the seats would be filled by inner-city children assigned to the schools in order to desegregate them.

In January 1996 a new CMS school board was seated. Its first task was to begin the search for a new superintendent (Murphy resigned effective the day the board took office); its second was to address pupil assignment for the coming 1996–97 school year. Because the district still operates under the terms of the 1971 *Swann* ruling, any pupil assignment decisions must take into account issues of racial balance. Although the school board had never voted to approve or accept the Education Village plans, the first of the four schools in the village was scheduled to open in fall 1996. Decisions about its attendance area were therefore part of the January discussion of pupil assignment. Members of the newly elected school board were very frustrated by the apparent *fait accompli* laid at their feet. They viewed the creation of the Education Village—especially the designation of who could attend it—as an usurpation of their statutory rights to make pupil assignment decisions. Moreover, when the details of the Education Village's original attendance formula became public knowledge, an intense controversy erupted, polarizing numerous sectors of the Charlotte-Mecklenburg community. The original attendance formula appeared to privilege employees of certain firms in the small geographic area of the URP (those referred to by Murphy as "our private sector partners"), while shutting out a majority of families who worked in other firms elsewhere in the school district. This was especially aggravating to county residents because they had just passed a large bond in part to support the building of these much-touted technology-rich magnet schools. Reacting to both the public outcry and their own anger over being bypassed in the planning, the school board canceled the Education Village's attendance plan crafted by IBM's Litow and the former superintendent.

The stakes were high: IBM and its URP neighbors were facing the loss of a plum amenity if the original plan were amended—a third of the prized 5,200 "workplace magnet" seats. Speaking confidentially, the CEO of a major employer in Charlotte described the Education Village as "a First Union[bank]-IBM-John Murphy deal." He elaborated:

Let me put it this way, . . . First Union had a tremendous desire to develop that area—tremendous desire to develop that area because they had already planned to come and build two million square feet [in URP]. And they wanted a place where their employees could be happy. They could encourage employees to get out of downtown and go north, and plus they had—they were doing some development on the rest of their land and so they had tremendous interest in that new development. And so education was a critical element of that. And so to get that done, they worked their magic. That is what corporations do. My understanding is . . . that they were investing in *their* amenity for *their* employees [italics added for emphasis].

From the point of view of the IBM and other URP corporate leaders, the school system had given its word and was now breaking it. Explanations from the new school board that previous oral agreements between IBM and the superintendent were not legally binding under North Carolina law only angered corporate actors. During a conference call following the board's revision of the Education Village design, a furious Litow insisted: "That's *not* how businesses operate." In Charlotte, URP leaders believed that school board revisions in the Educational Village plans amounted to "bureaucratic interference" with agreements previously concluded. The president of the URP association wrote in an editorial published in the *Charlotte Observer*:

> These companies [that donate money to schools] do not need to have their motives questioned. They do not need to be hassled. They do not need to be set straight by public officials. They need to be persuaded to offer even more support. Like me, people in other businesses are watching the Education Village situation unfold. If our school board can't understand the grant's purpose, won't honor agreements and can't act graciously, other companies will think twice before extending new offers of support.[28]

On the other side of this controversy were many other parents and employers in the countywide school district who were excluded from the lottery for seats by the original design because they neither worked in a URP firm nor lived in an adjacent subdivision. The public, which had just agreed to foot the bill for the four schools when they approved $82 million in bond money for the Education Village in November 1995, was outraged. Sentiments expressed at several open forums during school board meetings, in letters to the editor of the *Charlotte Observer,* and local talk radio programs indicated that citizens across the political spectrum and from all racial/ethnic backgrounds believed that provisions to allow only URP employees to apply for the Education Village workplace portion of the seat lottery amounted to an unfair advantage for IBM and other URP firms. A local conservative activist captured the resentment of many:

So, at a cost of $2 million, they [IBM] bought a seat for the children of their employees at the newest, highest (sic) technology school in the county. To put their $2 million in perspective, consider that the total Education Village will cost in the neighborhood of $80 to $100 million. That means that IBM is putting up 2 to 2.5 percent of the total cost of the village to buy one-third of the seats there for the children of their employees—not a bad investment part.[29]

To set the public record straight, the recently elected chairperson wrote an essay for the *Charlotte Observer* clarifying the school board's position. She argued that, while the board welcomed corporate partners and their resources, pupil assignment is the statutory responsibility of the school board and not within the purview of superintendents or business leaders.

I remember a call from a particular stay-at-home mom. This woman rightfully considers herself a working mother. She lives next door to someone who works in the URP and has children. Under the original proposal, the stay-at-home mom wouldn't be allowed to apply for a slot in the Village [lottery], but her neighbor's children could attend. The inequity of this situation was being repeated all over the county. . . . The political reality was fast becoming apparent. Our citizens didn't want a school that favored employees of a select group of businesses.[30]

On January 29, 1996, the school board exercised its statutory duty and opened one third of the Education Village seats—the workplace magnet portion—to all working families in the county with the proviso that each family commit one hour weekly of parental time (or its equivalent over the course of the school year) to school involvement and that employed parents obtain their employers' guarantee to cooperate. Reactions from URP companies, particularly IBM, were swift and severe: IBM froze its grant to CMS pending further negotiations.

A month of intense exchanges of letters and face-to-face meetings between the school system representatives and IBM ended with an agreement that broadened the original workplace magnet theme so that it included stay-at-home parents, too. The Village became a parental involvement magnet. Eligibility to enter the lottery for the third of the seats allocated to the magnet theme portion of the Village was expanded to all families in the county. Parents of Governors' Village (the Education Village name was changed) students must sign a pledge to volunteer in their child's school an average of one hour per week or the equivalent over the course of the school year. Employed parents are required to obtain a statement of support from their employer. The revised plan also broadened the residential catchment area to include more suburbs in the northeast portion of the county. The final agreement stipulated that :

IBM maintains the rights to any new products or intellectual property developed as result of the grant. The grant does not include future upgrades of the [yet-to-be-developed] software.[31]

IBM then released the $2 million in grant funds.

The head principal of the Governors' Village, Ann Clark, described how the grant was implemented: $500,000 was spent on training, a network server, and 240 IBM computers for community sites and teachers in the schools. The principal is given a budget and can allocate these funds for furniture, fixtures, equipment, and technology in classrooms. The remaining $1,000,000 of the grant went to the development of the software that will link homes to schools. Eventually Wired for Learning software will permit parents to have round-the-clock access to their child's classroom via their home computer. Families with an IBM computer that has at least a 486 processor and Windows95 software can readily access their child's record. In the first year of the grant, families with less powerful computers or no computers were be able to access their children's classrooms from community centers and libraries during the first year of the village's operation. Families with Macintosh home computers gained access to their child's school through the school's home page on the Internet.[32]

Reflecting on his colleagues' reaction to the Education Village imbroglio, the CEO of a Fortune 500 firm headquartered in Charlotte, speaking confidentially, confirmed that [URP] business leaders

> were very upset that the school board got involved, if you will, you know. It is business. It was business. It really was not an issue of quality education, it was an issue of developing University Research Park. And making that thing come to life. Making that new [area] in the north part of town come to life. [Corporate executives] were saying, "You want my money, play the game my way. We have a deal here. A deal has been struck and you're messing with this deal. How dare you undo our deal!" It [the school board's action] wasn't as much of a threat, as an affront [to corporate leaders]. . . . Bureaucrats got involved—the people who got involved, however, they were the people whose job it was to be there. And they [members of the school board] *had* been excluded.

Even after the settlement, the scent of corporate favoritism lingered over the community. A school board member, George Dunlap, expressed the concerns of many parents and citizens:

> What's to say some other company won't come into the area and want to buy into public education? What do you say to them? Do you say no? I don't think so.[33]

Ballantyne

Fears that the village's original arrangement sets a dangerous precedent whereby certain businesses, through their donations, could, in effect, "purchase" their own public schools were not idle speculation. In fact, what many believe was exactly such a scenario unfolded only a few months after the rancorous debate over the Education Village. In the late 1980s, the school system voted to take an option on land in a then-undeveloped part of the county that was donated by a politically-connected real estate developer. Unless schools were built on the donated parcels, they would revert back to their owner. When the Ballantyne neighborhood eventually developed in the 1990s, it emerged as an almost all-white enclave with average home prices of $500,000. The combination of the development's extremely expensive homes and its location in the most southerly corner of the county near the South Carolina state line made the prospects for desegregating the proposed schools exceedingly difficult (see figure 5.1).

In January 1995, the new school board confronted enormous pressure to exercise its option on the land from both the growing population in the Ballantyne area that required schooling, and from county and state officials because building schools on the donated parcels would obviate the need to use tax funds for the purpose of land acquisition. Faced with the need to obtain County Commissioners' approval to place a $400 million school bond measure on the November 1997 ballot, school board members feared the commissioners would refuse to approve the new bonds if the board turned down the "free" land. However, building schools on this land was tantamount to providing public schools for what would almost certainly become a segregated white, upper-income subdivision. This arrangement also violated the school board's own guideline for building new schools only in neighborhoods with 10 percent or greater minority populations. The donation of land for schools thus became a de facto school siting decision by a corporate actor.

Board members reluctantly accepted the Ballantyne land in spring, 1996. A condition of their acceptance, however, was that both elementary and middle schools would be magnets. Both would be constructed in such a manner as to minimize the likelihood that the schools would later revert to a neighborhood school (for example, a performing arts magnet would have space for theaters, recital halls, and recording studios that can only be used for these purposes). Eighteen months after the school board made the difficult and contentious decision to accept the land-for-schools deal, the ground had not yet been broken for construction. Ironically, there will be no school on the donated Ballantyne land designated for the elementary school; the seventeen-acre site was deemed unsuitable for a school because it is contaminated. It sits adjacent to a methane-producing landfill.[34] School system officials will likely build the elementary school on a second site originally designated for a middle school and a public park. The second site is slightly closer to the rest of the city and will be somewhat easier to desegregate by race and class.

A TYPOLOGY OF CORPORATE INVOLVEMENT

The preceding section described several examples of business participation in reform efforts in Charlotte-Mecklenburg. To assist in theorizing these, table 5.1 presents a typology of corporate involvement in educational reform. The table identifies by type who the corporate actors are, what the nature of their involvement is, and their motivations, and it illustrates each type with examples. The first four types range from the activities of large philanthropic organizations to those of individual volunteers acting directly or indirectly in concert with the school officials who provide actual educational services. The fifth type specifies how corporate leaders can become state actors with regard to education. The sixth type reflects educational services purchased from a for-profit firm by state actors who themselves no longer provide the service. Because there is very little type I and VI activity in Charlotte, the case study focused primarily upon the activities and motivations of Charlotte corporate actors in types II, III, IV, and V.

- *Type I: Large Independent Foundations.* Large foundations can be considered corporate actors because their boards of directors are selected from the highest ranks of the corporate world. Foundations conceptualize and fund broad reform initiatives consistent with their worldview and political ideals. These initiatives often begin as support for a national task force or for empirical studies. Their empirical studies have been central to the nation's normative understanding of the condition of American schools. The Ford, Rockefeller, and Spencer Foundations are examples of this type.

- *Type II: Corporate Leaders.* They serve in largely symbolic roles on high-profile national task forces or use the respect and attention they command to advocate for systemic reforms. Corporate leaders at this level are able to commit their firm's resources. Combined with their corporation's material and financial support, their bully pulpit inspires national, state, and local reform efforts. The activities of IBM's Louis Gerstner and BellSouth's John Clendenin at the

Palisades summit illustrate this type of activity at the national level. IBM and Gerstner's involvement in Charlotte represents this type at the local level, as are the activities of the real estate developers involved in the Ballantyne land-for-schools deal.

- *Type III: Mid-level Corporate Actors*. They do much of the actual day-to-day labor on high profile task forces that design educational reforms at the state and local levels, but they rarely are able to commit their firm's resources to reform. Typically these mid-level executives have some experience with education (sometimes they are former educators), and they liaise with local and state school personnel as reforms are implemented. In some cases, they may served as executives-on-loan to a school system or an education foundation, or they may serve as the corporation's educational expert. A key actor in Charlotte's Education Village is IBM's Stanley S. Litow, Vice President of Corporate Community Relations. He is a former educator.[35]

- *Type IV: Corporate Employees, Hourly Wage Earners Working in Ongoing Reform Programs*. These men and women regularly volunteer as tutors or mentors in particular schools. They contribute thousands of hours in classrooms working directly with teachers, aides, and students in programs designed by their corporate leaders. They are guest speakers in classrooms, or they spend their weekends hard-wiring schools for the internet, or coaching student groups. Volunteers represent the majority of business people involved in the schools. Their dual status as parent and employee often underlies their attachment to particular schools.

- *Type V: Business Leaders as Educational Decision-Makers*. Individual men and women appointed or elected to positions in federal education bureaucracies, or state and local education authorities hold formal state power. Usually they are appointed to these positions or run for office because of their credentials as business people with a perspective quite different from professional educators. School boards are the most common forum in which business leaders exercise authority as educational decision-makers.

- *Type VI: For-profit Companies as Systemic Reform*. These firms sell their products (Channel One) or services (Education Alternatives, Inc. [EAI], the Edison Project) as systemic reform. They are not the same as vendors who sell specific services (drivers education instruction, maintenance, bus driving) or products (paper, sports equipment, computers, blackboards) to school systems. For example, the Edison Project is a prospective chain of for-profit private schools that markets its educational services as a cheaper, more efficient,

TABLE 5.1

Typology of Corporate Involvement in and Motivation for Educational Reform with Examples from Charlotte, NC

Type	Nature of Involvement	Motivation	Examples in Charlotte*
TYPE I Large, independent foundations	donations of millions through foundation grants	altruism; shape national debate; eleemosynary impulses; advance political goals	Carnegie, Pew, Ford, Lilly, Bush, Casey, Annenberg, MacArthur, Rockefeller, Spencer, Olin, Bradley, Johnson
TYPE II Elite corporate heads, individual firms, business organizations	donations of corporate resources; service on boards; chairing task forces; bully pulpit in support of school reform	strategic self-interest; shape national and local debate; advance symbolic values	IBM's Gerstner; Bell South's Clendenin; CED; Business Roundtable Conference Board; Charlotte Chamber of Commerce: Charlotte-Mecklenburg Education Foundation
TYPE III Mid-level executives, small business owners	service on task forces designing business/education collaborations; exec on loan to schools; corporate exec in charge of educational division in local firm	altruism; improve schools in one's nation or community; career advance; personal dedication to children and education	IBM's Litow; Susan Q. Corporate VP for Community Relations; John Q. Small Entrepreneur; Leslie Q. Regional Manager

(continued on next page)

TABLE 5.1 (continued)

Type	Nature of Involvement	Motivation	Examples in Charlotte*
TYPE IV Corporate employees, hourly wage earners working in ongoing reform program	volunteers in classrooms, tutors, mentors, guest speakers on company or own time	personal dedication to children and education; altruism; career advance	Americorps volunteers; Susan Q. and John Q. Public
TYPE V Corporate leader as state actor	elected or appointed status in federal bureaucracy	altruism; improve schools in one's nation or community; shape direction of reform consistent with ideology; advance corporate long-term interests	Xerox's David Kearns as Deputy Secretary of Education; Chicago School Finance Authority; corporate leader as school board member
TYPE VI For-profit firms as reform	for-profit schools; management, products, and school services for purchase	profit	Edison Project; EAI; Channel One; Vendors of educational products and services

*There is very little evidence of type I and type VI activity in Charlotte.

and more effective educational delivery system than the public schools. It currently operates twenty-five public schools either in partnership with districts or with local charters. EAI sells its management services to school systems on much the same basis.

The third column in table 5.1 distinguishes among the varying forms of motivation underlying corporate involvement. Individuals or corporations may act for quite different reasons. And any involvement by corporate or individual actors may serve a number of purposes. To claim that mixed motivations exist is not meant to discount genuine eleemosynary impulses; altruism clearly stimulates much of what is done across the first four types of activities. Large foundations express their civic responsibility to the nation through their gifts. Business leaders and their firms express pride in and commitment to the larger social good of the communities in which they are located through their involvement and donations. Many business people, as human actors, care passionately about children and hold almost reverential personal values about the importance of education for individual and social betterment. Many individual actors across all five types of corporate involvement in reform approach their education work with missionary zeal and dedication. Service to children as tutors and mentors or to the school reform process (as members of task forces) is often personally satisfying and genuinely altruistic.

It is no secret, however, that business involvement in school reform, especially at the highest levels, springs as well from no small amount of long- and short-term strategic self-interest. Philanthropic ends are self-evident: schools do obtain human, material, and symbolic support from benefactors. Other motivations are much less obvious. For example, corporate actors' short-term strategic self-interests are served when improved school-to-work education transfers training costs from the private to the public sector or when better schools generate better appraisals of local infrastructures by mobile capital seeking an area for relocation.

Long-term strategic self-interest can be both ideological and material. For example, a long-term strategic interest is served when leaders shape the terms of the national debate over the putative educational crisis facing this nation. They influenced the social construction of the economic crisis of the last decade as largely the responsibility of the flawed public schools—a view essentially unchallenged until recently when the obvious economic recovery made it difficult to blame schools for a crisis that no longer existed. Now that the U.S. economy has regained its international competitiveness, corporations no longer hold public schools responsible for their international competitive standing. Firms now charge schools with failing to produce workers for future high-tech information-age jobs. Research suggests that the new charge of corporations may be as poorly focused as their earlier charge. For example, skill requirements for future jobs are expected to be highly variable and it is not at all clear if most high-tech information-age jobs will require highly skilled workers. Furthermore, evidence indicates no systematic shortage of appropriately skilled workers for contemporary jobs. Rather, employers are dissatisfied with the work ethic of their less skilled employees.[36] And technology cannot address that dissatisfaction.

There is one crucial negative latent consequence of corporations' continuing attribution to the public schools of responsibility for whatever they dislike in the attitudes and training of their workforce. If the derisive characterization of public schools as "ineffectual government schools" is accepted as conventional wisdom, it lays the foundation for widespread penetration of public education by the the private sector. In addition, it advances the neoliberal position that all that is public is suspect, while that which is private or market-driven is good.[37]

COMPLEXITIES OF CORPORATE INVOLVEMENT

Table 5.1 presented a typology of corporate involvement in order to examine the full range of activities in which individuals and firms engage. ProjectFirst and the Education Village activities primarily fell within types II, III, and IV. It is useful to specify these types more fully in order to understand and theorize their contributions to systemic reforms in public education. The next section of this chapter will discuss the varieties of involvement that fall within each of the five types.

Gifts from Independent Philanthropic Foundations

Without question, material support for reform from large independent philanthropic foundations has been critical both for stimulating reforms and in financing them across the nation. Without the material support of these foundations, it is unlikely that reform efforts would have gained broad-based constituencies or achieved the momentum they have since the 1980s. By definition, this form of involvement is unique to type I. Large independent philanthropic foundations have played a minor role in Charlotte reform efforts.

Roundtables and Task Forces

Local, state, and national business roundtables or task forces raise questions, identify problems, and suggest (sometimes set) reform agendas.

Their public advocacy of school reform brings visibility and legitimacy to the needs of school systems, students, and their families. The Committee for Economic Development, the National Alliance of Business, the Business Roundtable, and the Conference Board are examples of prominent national organizations of this type. National task forces and roundtables provide crucial political and factual scaffolding for national and local reforms. Local task forces play a similar role in laying groundwork for reform at the school district level. An example is the Charlotte Chamber of Commerce's 1987–88 Task Force on Education and Jobs. This body's deliberations marked the critical moment when educational restructuring began in Charlotte. These activities fall within type II and Type III.

Partnerships, Compacts, and Collaborations

Local partnerships between a business and a specific school can take numerous forms. These typically involve adoption of a school or a school district; direct donations of funds, equipment, and other materials, and opportunities for employees to volunteer in schools as tutors or mentors. As of 1992, over 200,000 businesses in the United States had partnerships with over 40,000 elementary and secondary schools.[38] Currently, there are about 250 different business partnerships with some of Charlotte's approximately 130 schools. This number includes individual partnerships with specific schools or systemwide initiatives. These activities also fall within type II and type III.

Education Foundations

Education foundations are another form of corporate involvement in school reform. These organizations raise private money that is then given to fund specific innovative programs. The New American Schools Development Corporation's (NASDC) "break-the-mold" projects are examples of the reforms financed by such national-level foundations. Charlotte participated briefly in the Hudson Institute's Modern Red School House, one of NASDC's first eleven projects. Local educational foundations are nonprofit organizations that raise venture capital to support local innovations. Representatives of the most powerful businesses typically sit on their boards. Local education foundations such as the Charlotte-Mecklenburg Education Foundation serve a symbolic function as well in that the existence of these and their prestigious boards of directors lend legitimacy and status to local public education. They support various activities such as summer institutes for teachers, grants to teachers for innovative course development, or the purchase of equipment for specific schools. Increasingly, many have broadened their scope to focus upon governance issues. For example, a number of education foundations have become involved in nonpartisan civic actions in support of school board elections.[39] These activities fall within type II and type III.

Business-Oriented Consultants

A national cadre of consultants with a neoliberal economic perspective and long-standing connections to corporate America participate in reforms efforts often as support personnel. Many are employed by conservative think tanks where they generate position papers that are then disseminated widely. They also serve as consultants to educational organizations where they help plan, design, and implement reforms. Their activities fall also within type II and type III.

Denis P. Doyle is an example of a business-oriented consultant. Through his writing and consulting, he serves as an intermediary between conservative ideology and corporate actors on the one hand and on the other, among educational practitioners around the country. Widely published in the business and education popular press, he works with school districts, business task forces, think tanks, and conservative foundations. He has co-authored two books about the necessity of corporate involvement and leadership in school restructuring. Doyle served as a consultant to the authors of the education chapter of the Heritage Foundation's congressional briefing book for new members,[40] and Doyle was one of several dozen experts who joined the governors and business leaders in Palisades, New York, in 1996.

In many important ways, school reforms initiated during the tenure of John Murphy were shaped by Doyle. He consulted extensively in Charlotte during the months before John Murphy became superintendent, and during the first few years of Murphy's tenure in CMS. (Between January 1991 and the end of 1995, he received compensation as a consultant to the Charlotte-Mecklenburg schools twenty-six times.[41]) Doyle helped to write the district's NASDC grant proposal (Charlotte-Mecklenburg Schools was one of the original districts participating in the Hudson Institute's Modern Red School House where Doyle was a research fellow), and he participated in the World Class Panel of educational experts convened by Superintendent Murphy to advise him on reform. Doyle developed the district's grant proposal to the RJR Foundation's Next Century Schools. At the time, Doyle was a member of the board of the RJR Foundation.[42] When in 1996 Murphy became a consultant to Chicago schools' CEO, Paul Vallas, Doyle collaborated again with Murphy.[43]

Volunteers

This variety of involvement occurs in types II, III, and IV. Most volunteers come from the ranks of corporate workers, not leaders. They may be hourly blue-collar workers who regularly volunteer as tutors or mentors in particular schools or specialists who lecture students about their own jobs. Many times they are parents whose employers encourage them to work regularly with teachers, aides, and other students in their child's classrooms. In 1996, 3,300 employees from 250 companies volunteered 52,000 hours in CMS.[44] These type IV volunteers represent the majority of all business workers involved in the schools. Type III mid-level executives and small business owners who serve on task forces or work with local educational collaborations or partnerships are volunteers, too. Type II corporate leaders who serve on high profile national task forces or local foundations are also in some respects volunteers.

Business Leaders as Educational Decision-Makers

Business leaders often serve as formal state actors in federal, state, and local educational bureaucracies. This form of involvement is unique to type V. The former CEO of Xerox, David Kearns, served as the Deputy Secretary of Education during the Bush administration. Thereafter, he took the helm of NASDC. Another example, the five-person Chicago School Finance Authority, composed of businessmen and attorneys, from 1979 to 1995 held statutory power to oversee school finances and approve all major budgetary decisions.[45] More often, corporate leaders serve on local school boards where they are able to have direct influence on educational reform. An extensive literature has documented the continued presence and influence of business leaders on school boards since George Counts[46] first demonstrated this in the early part of this century.

Business influence on school boards is informal as well. Bishop George Battle, the former chairman of CMS's board of education, illustrated this in remarks he made at a dinner honoring Bill Lee, the late chairman of Charlotte-based Duke Energy Corporation. Battle joked that, "Some of you thought I was chairman of the school board, while Bill Lee was probably the chair." Another member of the Charlotte school board commented that the downtown business interests "really sort of infiltrated the Board of Education so that we sometimes behave like a little Chamber of Commerce."[47]

Whether what is good for business is good for schools is both an empirical and ethical question. As is evident in Charlotte, business involvement both offers great opportunities and poses potential dangers for public education. The material, human, and symbolic resources brought to schools from corporations and their employees are consequential. A number of observers believe that without the support of the corporate sector, public schools and their reform would be stagnant or lost. At the same time, some aspects of the broader corporate reform agenda and its implementation bring a host of contradictions and questions about equity, fairness, accountability, and the wisdom of the reform trajectory implicit in certain policy choices. The blurry line between strategic self-interest and eleemosynary impulses makes it difficult to distinguish potential dangers from valuable opportunities. The following sections will attempt to make that distinction through an analysis of the actions, motivations, and consequences primarily of type II and type III corporate actors.

OPPORTUNITIES PRESENTED BY BUSINESS INVOLVEMENT

Resources

Corporate leaders have shared some of their firms' enormous material resources with large numbers of schools and entire districts. Philanthropy takes the form of individual gifts (like those of Walter Annenberg who gave millions to NASDC and to the Chicago public schools), or corporate gifts either as direct grants to schools or through business/education foundations. Donations of financial capital and land have provided needed resources to many schools and districts. So, too, have material donations like computers and the human capital made available to selected schools in the form of employee volunteers, tutors, pro bono technical assistance, and mentors who volunteer in schools on company time. Nevertheless, donated resources constitute a small portion of school budgets. Lewis C. Solmon, economist and one of the educational experts who attended IBM's 1996 National Education Summit, estimates only 6 percent of the total technology in the nation's schools has been donated by the private sector.[48] Some observers point to the financial speed bumps that lie ahead when current technology becomes outdated and school systems, having committed to a particular platform or software program, are required to upgrade. For example, future upgrades of Wired for Learning were specifically excluded from the finalized Reinventing Education grant to CMS.

Symbolic Capital

The high profile of corporate leaders in local and national reform efforts raises the public's awareness of educational reform needs and helps to place education at the center of public discourse regarding the welfare of the nation, of states, and of local communities. In the case of urban districts surrounded by separate suburban systems to which many middle-class families escaped, business serves as a visible constituency in support of large urban public schools. Their advocacy in support of the public schools can fill the vacuum left by the flight of the middle class to the suburbs.

In certain large cities with corrupt and inefficient bureaucracies, business groups have at times aided school reformers by serving on task forces, conducting management and financial audits, and fighting long-established but educationally dubious practices that are entrenched either in administrative decisions and/or some union contracts. As Elizabeth L. Useem notes, often it is difficult for reformers to engage in struggles with teacher unions and educational bureaucracies but with business leaders as allies, reformers' chances of initiating reform are enhanced.[49] Useem's observation, however, says nothing about the direction, utility, equity, or value of a particular reform or set of reforms.

Welfare of Children and Families

Corporate actors have placed on the reform table a host of broader issues pivotal to human learning and to successful school reform. In conjunction with renewed attention to public education, the related issues of early childhood education and the health and welfare of children and their families have become, by necessity, issues of legitimate public discourse. The Committee for Economic Development's (CED) widely disseminated reports illustrate how advocacy legitimates the need for public policy to attend to schools, students, and their families.[50] The Annie E. Casey and W. T. Grant foundation reports have been instrumental in identifying poverty and its attendant social dislocations as barriers to school success. Their reports brought widespread attention and support at the state levels for early childhood education, vaccination, and nutrition, and to parenting education as concomitant needs that must be addressed if schools are to be successfully reformed.

Transition from School-to-Work

Business leaders' insistence that secondary schools must provide better prepared entry-level workers has resulted in renewed attention to the school-to-work transition for non-college-bound youth, an area many analysts describe as frequently slighted by educators.[51] Until recently, the post-graduation focus of secondary schools was on college preparation and neglected other avenues. Business complaints about the schools' failure to prepare the entry-level workforce have helped to push schools to reexamine, reinvigorate, and renew their school-to-work education programs. Today, there are cooperative efforts between local employers, local schools, and state departments of employment to build the pathways from school to work in many communities.

The Charlotte-Mecklenburg School system and a group of business leaders from small and medium firms have spent the last two years developing crucial linkages between the workplace and the schools. Their activities include a coordinating body named the School-to-Career Partnership; a planning task force for a prospective technical high school; the sponsorship of internships, apprenticeships, job-shadowing, and the mentoring of youngsters interested in certain careers; and several industry-specific training programs in certain schools (for example, one program trains Novell network administrators). The network of business actors, typically those characterized as type IV in table 5.1, serve as a broad base of support, information, and resources for CMS's efforts to enhance the programmatic offerings available to secondary students. For the youths who will not go directly to college, the results of the network's activities are designed to serve as the bridge from school to postsecondary work force participation.

Support for Parental Involvement

Corporations that encourage their employees to participate on company time in their children's schools provide an important opportunity for schools. Employees in these firms suffer fewer conflicts between their job, and their parental responsibilities when they must attend a parent-teacher conference or want to volunteer in their child's school. By establishing a formal mechanism whereby parents can participate in their children's schools, corporations support family involvement in education.

DANGERS OF BUSINESS LEADERSHIP AND INVOLVEMENT

A problem for public schools is that while the possibilities of positive contributions by business are usually easy to see, any potential dangers they pose may not be visible until long after the contributions have been accepted uncritically. To complicate the matter more, corporate involvement in local reform can be at once an act both of altruism and of strategic self-interest. And that self-interest may, in the long run, harm the schools and the communities in which the reforms are located. It is important, then, to analyze why and when certain types of corporate involvement pose potential harm to public education.

Data-Free Ideologues with a Bully Pulpit

Some prominent business leaders and consultants do harm to public education when they make errors about American schools in their pub-

lic pronouncements and writings. An example is IBM's Louis V. Gerstner Jr., lead author of *Reinventing Education: Entrepreneurship in
America's Public Schools*. Gerstner's core argument is that public education, insulated from the discipline of the market, is a failure and that
solutions lie in educational entrepreneurship of all kinds—choice among
vouchers, magnets, charters, and other forms of privatization. To make
the case, Gerstner uses anecdotes that describe schools or districts that
have broken out of the strictures of government control and allowed
market forces of some kind to flower. The book proclaims American
public education "a wasteland."

A major problem with the book is that the evidence Gerstner and
his coauthors use to make their case is frequently incorrect or taken out
of context.[52] The book's errors regarding Charlotte reflect the often
loose relationship among arguments and empirical data. For example,
Gerstner and his coauthors wrote in 1994

> Charlotte-Mecklenburg school district was the first large district in the
> nation to fall under court order to integrate. Twenty-five years later the
> *Swann* decision has been lifted because Charlotte has successfully inte-
> grated.[53]

In fact, five years after the publication of Gerstner's book, the *Swann*
decision has not been lifted. It was officially inactive until the original
plaintiffs reopened the case on October 9, 1997. And the Charlotte-
Mecklenburg school district's renown stems from its legacy as the first
district to use mandatory busing to integrate its schools, not that it was
the first large district under court order to desegregate. What is worse,
the authors use their errors of omission and of fact to advance an argument that in marketization lies the answer to problems that plague
American schools:

> What are the new terms that made it possible for the court to lift
> *Swann?* Schools of choice.[54]

Gerstner's conclusion that the implementation of choice in CMS made
it possible for the federal court to lift *Swann*, therefore, rests on errors
in his reporting of historical fact. However, his erroneous assertion is
consistent with the reforms he advocates.

The book also ignores a host of respected scholarly publications and
widely available reports that present the strengths and weaknesses of
U.S. education, but also research that analyzes the institutional, organization, and cultural reasons for difficulties in achieving reform.[55] Gerstner and his colleagues do not engage the evidence or the debates that
critically examine claims that market-based reforms are the silver bullet
for all that ails the schools.[56] Gerstner's prominence as a national advo-

cate of school reform who can mobilize governors and presidents to attend summits in his training facilities lends credibility to his arguments and thereby makes his errors in fact and inference that much more potentially harmful to public education.

Romanticizing the Market

The influence of business leaders in defining the nature of the problems facing education and in shaping the terms of the debate over their solutions leads to a growing public acceptance of market principles as an appropriate mode for school reform. This influence is perhaps most evident in statements by the most ardent advocates of school choice. It is fair to ask what articles of faith market romantics bring to the reform table when they are employed by public school systems as reform consultants. For example, Denis P. Doyle, whose extensive consulting work in CMS was described earlier, lamented the absence of any discussion of school choice at the 1996 National Education Summit at the IBM facility in New York.

> The alternative to command and control, is a market, whether it is purely private, as many of us would like it to be, or regulated, a mix of public and private providers. Markets have two overwhelmingly important characteristics. First, they are exquisitely calibrated communication systems, letting willing buyers and sellers know what good or service is available at what price in what quantity and quality, and letting each know what the other would be like; second, as Schumpeter declared, they permit "creative destruction." Inefficient, corrupt, and ineffectual organizations disappear. That's what markets are all about. That is why in a market the consumer is sovereign. To create a system of high academic standards, and schools which are safe and disciplined, there must be choice among schools.[57]

Doyle's highly idealistic description of how markets operate only loosely relates to the actual workings of the commodities, health care, real estate, airline, or higher education markets. Despite what market-reform romantics assert are the powers of the market to cure the ills of public schools, a host of empirical studies of choice in education challenge such unqualified claims.[58]

The point here is not to enumerate the perils of privatization to public education. A vast literature on this subject already exists. The purpose of this discussion is to juxtapose the arguments made by market-romantics with their location in the larger vista of school reformers. Early in the current round of the privatization movement, prominent choice advocate Chester A. Finn Jr. admitted that claims that choice will bring about improved achievement "spring more from ratiocination and conviction than from airtight research." Eight years later, Finn urged conservatives to "look into our own blind spots" in order to accomplish more sound educational reform. Two among the eleven blind spots that he identified are that "private schools are doing fine if only more children could attend them" and that "vouchers will fix it."[59]

Jeffrey Henig argues that the market metaphor functions in two ways to make privatization more palatable. First, it bridges the gap between this radical way of providing education by linking it to familiar market arrangements in other spheres of life. Second, the market metaphor assists advocates in bridging the gap between evidence and their prescription. Lacking an empirical basis on which to support their claims, advocates assume school choice, magnets, and vouchers will act "like free markets."[60] Public discourse that romanticizes the market and understates its troubled track record in school reform sets the stage for educational entrepreneurs, like the Edison Project and Education Alternatives, Inc. (EAI), to step through the privatization door wedged open by local political skirmishes over school reform.

Missing Evaluations of Business Interventions

Perhaps the most serious danger business interventions pose is that there are few if any systematic evaluations of these program. In the absence of evaluations of business partnerships, programs, and gifts, there is very little reliable evidence that these, in fact, lead to positive school outcomes for students. Timpane and McNeill label such partnerships feelgood associations that do not reform schools. In their estimation, with only modest exceptions, there has been no widespread impact of business involvement on educational outcomes.[61] Many partnerships and collaborations may well be diversions of valuable resources, opportunities, and participants' time. In such cases, the feel-good aspect of the interventions conveys the patina of genuine reform while it distracts people from effectively addressing the core problems facing their schools. ProjectFirst is a prime example of an unevaluated feel-good reform that, to at least a limited degree, diverted public attention from systemic reforms needed by CMS nonmagnet middle schools.

Masking Business Contributions to Educational Problems

There is indeed heavy irony in the fact that the generous donations by corporations and their leaders of money, materials, and time to educational reforms often deflect attention from the far more serious damage they do to education through their actions to restructure the American economy. Firms contribute both directly and indirectly to educational problems by the way that they conduct their own business affairs—

extracting maximum profits from workers and communities. Since the recent economic expansion began, there has been a huge transfer of wealth from middle-class Americans to owners of capital assets. The owners of financial assets have been the overwhelming beneficiaries of the current economic expansion. At the same time, the wages of most working American families have stagnated. Furthermore, the spread between the pay of the typical worker and the chief executive has increased from 30–to-1 in the 1960s to more than 100–to-1 today. Often the actions of corporate leaders must negatively affect the families of precisely those students who are most at-risk for educational failure and whom they mean to benefit by their contributions to education.

Corporations indirectly contribute to educational problems when their policies undercut the economic health of entire communities or families. Certain demographic groups (poor racial and ethnic minorities) and geographic regions (inner cities, rural areas) continue to suffer from acute poverty despite the economic boom of the late 1990s. The outright disappearance of jobs paying livable wages in inner cities and rural areas has had profoundly negative consequences for families there. Children of the jobless poor and of IBM's downsized middle-class workers are at an increased risk for educational problems. For example, IBM world-wide employment stood at 241,000 in 1997, down from a high of 406,000 in 1985. Gerstner presided over the layoff of 60,000 workers beginning in 1993. In Charlotte, IBM has reduced its total workforce from a high of about 5,100 in the late 1980s, to 3200 by 1997.[62]

Business contributes to the economic problems facing communities and schools in other ways. Tax breaks that state and local governments often negotiate with corporations to induce them to remain in or relocate to a region often directly diminish for decades the tax bases that fund public education. Furthermore, such agreements often draw corporations and their employees to poorer regions where schools already suffer from inadequate funding. That influx of employees and their children increases the population of school-age children at the same time that the companies' negotiations limit the revenues necessary for the schools to provide for both new and continuing students. Critics of these agreements note that tax abatements distort the marketplace and shift the tax burdens unfairly to homeowners and consumers. Many of the corporate leaders who criticize schools for being inadequate also negotiate away their company's share of the community property taxes. In Westchester County, New York, state and local officials offered IBM tax incentives and a $75 million low-interest loan in 1995 after the firm considered leaving its Armonk headquarters.[63]

State actors help deflect public scrutiny from corporate culpability for these problems when they effusively praise corporate philanthropy while uncritically accepting business assessments of the public schools as seriously flawed. The effects are the same whether they are the functional by-products of the reform process or are due to the conscious agency of business leaders and state actors. Educational decision-makers and other state actors who privilege firms and their leaders by giving them more than merely a place at the educational reform table often hinder the public's awareness of business contributions to educational problems.

Threats to Public Accountability in Public Education

Geoff Whitty argues that the practical implications of political and education practice are as much a matter of the ways in which policy is made as is the specific substantive policies.[64] In the case of the Education Village, by the time the reform initiative was announced, corporate actors had already shaped its terms. Because corporations are private entities, there is no legal imperative for public disclosure of their goals, processes, and resources. As corporate actors become more deeply involved in educational policy design and implementation, their *means* as well as policy ends must be scrutinized. For example, based on her analysis of corporatism in contemporary Chicago reform, Shipps concludes that the informal influence of parent and community groups is no match for the massive influence of business. In Chicago, there is no public debate to determine if business values and practices are appropriate for the schools; business actors have no accountability to the public. Once citizens in Charlotte scrutinized the proposed Education Village, they found that what appeared to be a tidy integration of work, school, and family was a reform initiative shaped to a considerable degree by the strategic interests of private corporations.

DISCUSSION AND SUMMARY

The central points that emerge from the description and analysis of corporate involvement in Charlotte's school reform are summarized in table 5.2. The table is useful for theorizing the intersection of human agency with social structure with respect to corporate involvement in school reform. It delineates how corporate actors in certain structural locations are able to act in ways that offered limited benefits to CMS, while positioning their firm to realize future benefits of considerable potential value. The IBM reform initiatives and the Ballantyne gift to CMS illustrate how a single project may serve a number of purposes that simultaneously advance philanthropic, strategic self-interest, and symbolic ends. The examples also reveal how corporate involvement can have unanticipated negative consequences for the school system and the community at large.

ProjectFirst

The philanthropic core of ProjectFirst is IBM's material support for Americorps volunteers working as technology specialists in CMS non-magnet middle schools. The funds provided badly needed computers for the schools and some training for the volunteers. But ProjectFirst also served the strategic self-interest of IBM. It helped the firm to garner a larger share of CMS's educational computing market. Symbolically, ProjectFirst promoted the image of IBM as a good corporate citizen and furthered the acceptance of the notion that in technology lies the solution to many educational problems.[65]

Were an objective evaluation done, it likely would show program outcomes were at best negligible and at worst, counterproductive. The program undercut a growing public demand for more equitable distribution of middle school resources across the district. In the instance of ProjectFirst, there was little public knowledge of and no debate over the program. Furthermore, by privileging technology as the key solution to poor quality middle schools, ProjectFirst partially derailed the attention of parents and educators from genuine, systemic reforms in the areas of curriculum, instruction, staff development, and infrastructural improvements—all desperately needed by ProjectFirst middle schools.

The Education Village

By far the most far-reaching and important of the three examples analyzed in this chapter, IBM's role in the original design of the Education Village speaks directly to the central issues under investigation here. It illustrates how powerful corporate actors sought to use public schools for private ends. The entire episode demonstrates the necessity for citizens and democratically elected educational leaders to exercise oversight of school reform planning and implementation. The $2 million Reinventing Education funds offered the district a unique opportunity to develop a four-school complex, rich in technology and parental involvement. As a prototype, the successes of the village could be replicated across the district and the nation. Yet the grant cost the district dearly. The countywide struggle over access to the prized magnet school complex undermined community confidence in the fairness of the system's pupil assignment plan (in itself, a wound the district could ill-afford to suffer). It also generated rancor among citizens, parents, firms not included in the original plan, and the school board. This struggle

TABLE 5.2

Conceptual Analysis of Corporate Involvement in Three Philanthropic Educational Reform Projects in Charlotte, NC

	Project First (as implemented)	Ballantyne (as designed)	Education Village (as designed)
Philanthropic activities	provides computers, media specialists' training for Americorps volunteers	donation of land to be used for elementary schools	$2 million grant for teacher, staff training software development & hardware, project and staff salaries
Strategic self-interest (short and long term)	advances use of technology in schools, increases IBM share in educational computer market	"private" public school in subdivision	R&D tax write-off for software development; software testing in real schools; diversion of public scrutiny from corporate restructuring's contribution to social, education problems

(continued on next page)

TABLE 5.2 (continued)

	Project First (as implemented)	Ballantyne (as designed)	Education Village (as designed)
Symbolic value	strategic placement mollifies magnet critics who believe magnets get more resources than nonmagnet schools; promotes good citizen image; legitimizes business role in educational reform	deal too good to forego, "saves" tax payers from purchasing expensive land; promotes good corporate citizen image	legitimizes use of technology in education; promotes good corporate citizen image; legitimizes business role in educational reform
Latent consequence	undercuts movement for equitable resources in all CMS schools; privileges some students in some schools; masks resource inequities between magnets and older, nonmagnet schools	contributes to resegregation of schools by race and social class; privileges wealthy subdivision parents; generates good will for developer who creates exclusive enclave that exacerbates racial and class isolation in public schools	undermines community confidence in fairness of pupil assignment; privileges some firms and neighborhoods; masks corporate layoff of engineers, managers, that contradicts "skill deficit" claims; masks relatively small material corporate contribution in relation to enormous potential returns

unfolded just weeks after the new board was seated, at a time when it was important to build community support. In fact, the way the new board resolved the dispute garnered respect and trust from most of the community. The exception was the corporate leaders whose original design for the Education Village was revised. In the short run, however, IBM still enjoys tax and publicity benefits, the chance to develop and test an educational software program in a real school setting, and an increase in the local educational computer market. In the long run, it will earn profits from the software it developed in Charlotte. Perhaps the most crucial long-term benefit to IBM is the grant's advancement of Louis Gerstner's vision of educational technology's leading American schools into the high-tech, information-age twenty-first century. This was, of course, a pivotal goal of the Palisades summit.

Ballantyne

On its face, the gift of land to the school system appears to be an act of generosity that would benefit all citizens of the county whose taxes will not be used to acquire very expensive land for new schools. But if a school is built in the most southerly tip of the county, it will in a sense become what John Goodlad warned against—public schools used for private purposes.[66] Given the difficulty of racially integrating three elementary schools at least five miles closer to the center of the county than is the Ballantyne development, the school board abandoned its efforts in 1996 (board members refer to McCloud, McAndrews, and Montgomery elementary schools as the 3M problem). Only extraordinary efforts and long bus rides will permit the Ballantyne elementary school to be utilized by any children living outside the subdivision. By donating land, the developer in effect gained the amenity of a de facto private school for those who can spend an average of $500,000 on their homes. The donation exacerbated community tensions over both equity of resource allocations and sharing of the burden for racial balance across the district. Moreover, it set a precedent. Building upon the Ballantyne precedent of land-for-schools, a conservative politician who advocates neighborhood schools began to discuss with other developers the possibilities of setting aside land-for-schools in new subdivisions, some only one mile from the South Carolina border in areas that are nearly impossible to integrate.[67]

CONCLUSION

It is possible to draw several general conclusions from this case study of corporate involvement in Charlotte school reform. First, it shows how political struggle and public contestation over the actions of corporate leaders, in some instances, can move the educational policy process and its outcomes away from serving a more narrow corporate agenda toward broader public goals. Second, this chapter demonstrates why we must neither universally praise corporate involvement in educational reform nor uniformly condemn it as pernicious. Many instances are quite helpful; others are rather benign; some are potentially ruinous to public education. Each corporate initiative, program, or donation plots along continua of philanthropic altruism and strategic self-interest; latent and manifest consequences; and dangers and benefits to communities, schools, individual and corporate actors. It is necessary to specify how and when each initiative offers opportunities and dangers for schools and communities. Third, the chapter shows that we cannot assume that every attempt by corporate actors to shape and implement educational policies and programs in ways that narrowly serve their strategic self-interest will be wholly successful. The three initiatives described in this chapter show how political contestation by citizen groups, individual parents, and elected members of the school board can undermine attempts to use public education for more narrow private ends.

NOTES

1. An earlier version of this chapter was presented at the Urban Education Conference, Graduate School of Education and Information Science, University of California, Los Angeles, June 20–23, 1996. This research is supported by a grant to the author from the National Science Foundation (RED-9550763). Stephen Samuel Smith, Dorothy Shipps, Annelle Houk, and several confidential reviewers made helpful and incisive comments on earlier versions of this essay. Susan Masse and Damien Heath provided technical assistance in transcribing interviews; and Hillary Edwards, Anne Velasco, Angela Wadsworth, Debra Wakefield, and Matthew Walker assisted with research. Stella Nkomo provided valuable insight into the contemporary business climate.

2. David Kearns and Denis P. Doyle, *Winning the Brain Race: A Bold Plan to Make Our Schools Competitive* (San Francisco: ICS Press, 1988); Carol. A. Ray and Roslyn A. Mickelson, "Restructured Students for Restructured Work: The Economy, School Reform, and Noncollege-bound Youth," *Sociology of Education* 66 (1993): 1–23.

3. Lauro Cavazos, Address to Charlotte Conference on Parental Choice.(Charlotte, North Carolina, November 1989).

4. Kathryn L. Borman and K. Gallagher, "Business Involvement in School Reform: The Rise of the Business Roundtable," in *Politics of Education Yearbook*, ed. Catherine Marshall (London: Falmer, 1994).

5. S. R. Martin, "The 1989 Education Summit as a Defining Moment," in *Changing American Education. Recapturing the Past or Inventing the Future?*

ed. Kathryn Borman and Nancy P. Greenman (Albany: State University of New York Press, 1994).

6. The summit's formal purpose focused upon putative needs of corporations to assure a better skilled workforce for future high-tech information-age jobs. Prior to the summit, participants received a two-inch thick briefing book containing commissioned essays and other materials on standards, technology, and topics related to systemic school reform (1996 National Education Summit, Presummit Briefing Materials, Armonk, N.Y.: IBM Corporation, 1996). The topics in the pre-summit briefing book reflected this formal goal and the preferred means to this end. The informal agenda was clear as well. According to Denis P. Doyle, one of the resource persons,

> While the meeting's larger purpose was to reinvigorate the standards movement and highlight education technology, its real function was to solemnize the fact that the federal role in education is virtually at an end. (Denis P. Doyle, "A Personal Report from the Education Summit: What Does It Mean for Education Reform?" *The Heritage Lectures* [Washington, D.C.: The Heritage Foundation, 1996], p. 6)

7. Raymond Allan Morrow and Carlos Alberto Torres, *Social Theory and Education: A Critique of Theories of Social and Cultural Reproduction* (New York: State University of New York Press, 1995), pp. 343–44.

8. *Swann v. Charlotte-Mecklenburg Board of Education,* 402 U.S. 1 (1971).

9. Roslyn A. Mickelson and Carol A. Ray, "Fear of Falling from Grace: The Middle Class, Downward Mobility, and School Desegregation," *Research in Sociology of Education and Socialization* 10 (1994): 207–38. In the spring of 1999, CMS returned to court to defend its efforts to desegregate the school system. Sued by white plaintiffs who desire a return to neighborhood schools, and black plaintiffs who desire greater desegregation and equity, the school system's position is that while it has made progress since 1971, many schools remain segregated and unequal.

10. Ibid.; Roslyn A. Mickelson, Carol A. Ray, and Stephen Samuel Smith, "The Growth Machine and the Politics of Urban Educational Reform: The Case of Charlotte, North Carolina," in *Education in the Urban Context,* ed. Nelly Stromquist (New York: Praeger, 1994).

11. Carol A. Ray and Roslyn A. Mickelson, "Restructured Students for Restructured Work: The Economy, School Reform, and Noncollege-bound Youth," *Sociology of Education.* 66 (1993): 1–23; Carol A. Ray and Roslyn A. Mickelson, "Corporate Leaders, Resistant Youth, and School Reform in Sunbelt City: The Political Economy of Education," *Social Problems* 37 (1990): 178–90.

12. The group of experts, christened the World Class Panel by the superintendent, met three times between December 1991 and April 1992. In May 1992, the Chamber of Commerce sponsored a communitywide forum at the Charlotte Convention Center to present the findings of the panel. Members of the panel included Chester A. (Checker) Finn Jr., William Bennett, Denis P. Doyle, James Comer, M.D. (although he did not participate until the May 1992 public forum), Patricia A. Graham, Matina Horner, Donald Steward, and Ernest

Boyer. James Kelly was the moderator. The author observed at three of the four meetings, analyzed tapes of all three panel deliberations, and conducted in-depth interviews about the panel experience with six of the eight panel participants in the cities in that they lived. An analysis of the interviews, the proceedings of the panel, and related CMS documents revealed that the panel's deliberations and final report were largely generic and symbolic and had little to do specifically with reform in Charlotte. Nonetheless, for many of the reform initiatives he proposed, Superintendent Murphy invoked the imprimatur of the world-class panel to legitimize his actions. This was not true of his most controversial and far-reaching initiative: the recommendation to end mandatory busing and replace it with parental choice of magnet schools made independent of and prior to the panel's work. That reform was designed and enacted during the panel's deliberations, yet it was never a topic of discussion. Panelists occasionally referred to school choice in general, and all agreed with Patricia A. Graham's observation that with respect to school choice, "the devil is in the details."

13. Mickelson and Ray, "Fear of Falling."

14. Ibid.; Allison Marantz, "Desegregation at Risk: Threat and Reaffirmation in Charlotte," in *Dismantling Desegregation: The Quiet Reversal of Brown v. Board of Education*, ed. Gary Orfield, Susan E. Eaton, and the Harvard Project on School Desegregation (New York: The New Press, 1996); Roslyn Arlin Mickelson, "Expert Report to the U.S. District Court for the Western District of North Carolina in the Case of Capacchione v. Charlotte-Mecklenburg Schools et al.," December 1998.

15. Stephen Samuel Smith, "Hugh Governs? Regime and Educational Policy in Charlotte, North Carolina," *Journal of Urban Affairs* 19 (1997): 247–74.

16. Ibid.

17. Carroll Gray, Remarks to Technical High School Task Force (Charlotte, N.C., July 1997).

18. Americorps is President Clinton's volunteer service program. Volunteers work in their communities for two years. During their commitment they receive a minimal stipend but are entitled to grants for additional education once they complete their service.

19. Committee of 25, *Resource Subcommittee Report to the Board of Education* (Charlotte, N.C.: Charlotte-Mecklenburg Board of Education, April 1994); Committee of 25, *Pupil Assignment Subcommittee Report to the Board of Education* (Charlotte, N.C.: Charlotte-Mecklenburg Board of Education, July 1994).

20. John Murphy, Remarks to Charlotte-Mecklenburg Education Foundation board meeting (Charlotte, August 1994).

21. Stanley S. Litow, "IBM Introduces New Corporate Philanthropy Initiative; Charlotte Schools are First to Benefit," Press release (Armonk, N.Y.: IBM Corporation, September 14, 1994).

22. Herbert Watkins, Interview with the author, Charlotte, N.C., August 1995.

23. Litow, Letter to Superintendent John Murphy, September 12, 1994; Litow, Letter to Superintendent John Murphy, April 5, 1995; John Murphy, "The Charlotte-Mecklenburg Education Village: The Next Step in Reforming America's Schools" (Charlotte: Charlotte-Mecklenburg Schools, n.d.).

24. Litow, September 14, 1994.

25. RJR Nabisco's Next Century Schools program provided $32 million to forty-three schools nationwide (Gerstner). At the same time, RJR under Gerstner's stewardship, Camels became the most highly identified cigarette among children. The Joe Camel character helped RJR's share of the cigarette market rise from 1 to 32.8 percent, and this increase brought RJR an estimated $476 million in sales (see Derrick Jackson, "Louis Gerstner's Double Standards," *Rethinking Schools*, Summer 1996). The purpose of juxtaposing these two actions by one corporation is to illustrate how a firm can be motivated simultaneously by narrow self-interest (in this case, greater market share and greater profits) while it engages in what many consider to be child-centered philanthropy. Recent books by Alex Molnar (*Giving Kids the Business: The Commercialization of America's Schools* [Boulder, Colo.: Westview, 1996]) and Alfie Kohn (*Education, Inc.: Turning Learning into a Business* [Arlington Heights, Ill.: IRI Skylight Press, 1997]) describe and analyze these bipolar practices toward children among many other American corporations.

26. Winston-Salem/Forsyth County Schools, The Downtown School Information Sheet (1996).

27. Murphy, *The Charlotte-Mecklenburg Education Village*, p. 3

28. Seddon "Rusty" Goode Jr., "Don't Botch the Education Village," *Charlotte Observer*, February 29, 1996, p. A10.

29. Joe Miller, "Grants Are Not Free as IBM Has Shown the BOE," *Conservative Views: NC Free Society Foundation* 3 (1996): 1.

30. Susan Burgess, "IBM and the Education Village: Setting the Record Straight," *Charlotte Observer*, February 22, 1996, p. A7.

31. Stanley Litow, Letter to Acting Superintendent Dennis Williams, March 13, 1996.

32. Ann Clark, Interview with the author, Charlotte, North Carolina, June 3, 1997.

33. John Minter, "IBM Grant Not Worth as Much as Taxpayers Put," *Charlotte Post*, January 30, 1996: p.1A.

34. "The Famed Ballantyne School Could be a Dump," *The Leader*, October 31, 1997, p. 5. This is not the first time that this developer sought to donate land in the hopes of future profits. In the early 1990s, Sears Roebuck and Company announced its intentions to move from Chicago to the Sunbelt. The developer offered to sell the corporation land for its new headquarters for $1.00 (the land later became part of the Ballantyne development). Sears Roebuck negotiated a more satisfactory fiscal agreement with Cook County and, instead, moved from its famed tower to the Chicago suburbs. Rumors circulated that the loss of Sears was due, in large part, to the poor quality of Charlotte's schools. Many observers in Charlotte believe that the loss of Sears inspired the downtown business elite to ratchet up their pressure on CMS to improve.

35. Clark. Litow declined to answer a written request for an interview.

36. Roslyn. A. Mickelson,"The Need to Build Bridges from School to Work . . . and Much, Much More." *Advances in Educational Policy* 3 (1997): 158–89; National Center on Education and the Economy, *America's Choice: High Skills or Low Wages!* (Rochester, N.Y.: NCEE, 1990); National Center on

Educational Quality of the Workforce, *Educational Quality of the Workforce: National Employer Survey* (Philadelphia: University of Pennsylvania, 1995); Ruy Teixeira and Larry Mishel, "Whose Skill Shortage—Workers or Management?" *Issues in Science and Technology*, Summer 1993, 69–74.

37. Philip Wexler, *Social Analysis of Education* (Boston: Routledge and Kegan Paul, 1987).

38. National Association of Partners in Education, *Handbook of Education Partners* (Alexandria, Va.: National Association of Partners in Education, 1995).

39. See Elizabeth. L. Useem, and R. C. Neild, "A Place at the Table: The Changing Role of Urban Public Education Funds," paper presented at the meetings of the American Educational Research Association, New Orleans, April 1994. At times, however, an educational foundation's actions challenge this characterization of nonpartisan civic-mindedness. For example, at its August 1994 board meeting, the Charlotte-Mecklenburg Educational Foundation (CMEF) announced that one of its 1995 projects would be the identification of appropriate candidates to run for the next school board election when, for the first time, six of the nine seats on the board were to be selected by district rather than at-large.

A school board member explained why corporate elites felt this initiative was necessary. She described the fear the anticipated switch from at-large to school board election by district had engendered among the corporate elites:

Well, now districts are scaring the Chamber of Commerce to death. And they are already really actively working on getting, recruiting their own candidates in the districts. And talk about throwing money at them, I think that you will see that a lot. . . . [The Chamber] is scared they are going to get a group of people out of the districts that they cannot control. (Quoted in Stephen Samuel Smith, "Education, Race, and Regime Change in Charlotte-Mecklenburg," paper presented at the annual meeting of the Urban Affairs Association, New York, March 1996)

40. Allison Tucker and W. F. Lauber, "Chapter 6. Education," *Briefing Book for Newly Elected Members of Congress* (Washington, D.C.: Heritage Foundation, 1994).

41. Charlotte-Mecklenburg Schools, *Financial Ledger, Accounts Payable* (Charlotte, N.C.: Charlotte-Mecklenburg Schools, 1991–95). Doyle was paid a little under $77,000 in expenses and consulting fees during this period.

42. Denis P. Doyle, Personal interview with the author, (Charlotte, N.C., March 1993); Denis P. Doyle, Personal interview with the author (Washington, D.C., June 1993).

43. Dorothy Shipps, personal communication, January 1999.

44. Neil Mara, "Schools Weigh Business Impact," *Charlotte Observer*, March 10, 1996), p. 1B.

45. Shipps, "The Invisible Hand: Big Business and Chicago School Reform," *Teachers College Record* 99 (1997): 73–116.

46. George Counts, *Social Composition of School Boards: A Study in the Social Control of Education* (Chicago: University of Chicago Press, 1927).

47. Peter Sola, "The Corporate Community on the Ideal-Business School Alliance: A Historical and Ethical Critique," in *The New Servants of Power*, ed C. M. Shea, E. Kahane, and P. Sola (New York: Praeger, 1990); "Insider," *Charlotte Observer*, (September 29, 1997), p. 14D.

48. Lewis C. Solmon, Interview with the author, Santa Monica, Calif., June 1996.

49. Thanks to Elizabeth L. Useem for this bringing this and many other insight to my attention.

50. Committee for Economic Development, *The Unfinished Agenda: A New Vision for Child Development and Education* (New York: CED, 1991); Committee for Economic Development, *Children in Need. Investment Strategies for the Educationally Disadvantaged* (New York: CED, 1987); Committee for Economic Development, *Investing in Our Children: Business and the Public Schools* (New York: CED, 1985).

51. Ivan Charner, "School to Work Opportunities: Prospects and Challenges," in *Implementing Educational Reform: Sociological Perspectives on Educational Policy* ed. Peter Cookson, Kathryn Borman, Alan Sadovnik, and Joan Spade (Norwood, N.J.: Ablex, 1996); Gary Orfield and Faith G. Paul, *High Hopes, Long Odds: A Major Report on Hoosier Teens and the American Dream* (Indianapolis, Ind.: Indiana Youth Institute, 1994).

52. In his article,"The Right's Data-Proof Ideologues," *Education Week*, January 25, 1995, p. 42, Gerald Bracey uses the moniker "data-proof ideologues" to characterize those who dismiss evidence contrary to their positions and continue to advance in their public speeches and writings the claim that American education is stagnant and ineffectual. Several of the data-proof ideologues were consultants to the authors of the Heritage Foundation's 1994 Briefing Book for new members of Congress (Tucker and Lauber). The briefing book's gross inaccuracies in fact and interpretation of educational matters prompted the Department of Education to prepare a document that rebuts each point (see U.S. Department of Education, *Setting the Record Straight: Responding to Key Factual Errors and Assertions in the Heritage Foundations' Brief for Congress*, Office of the Undersecretary, Washington, D.C.: U.S. Department of Education, 1994). This rebuttal was then sent to all new members of Congress.

53. Gerstner et al., *Reinventing Education*, p. 45.

54. Gerstner et al., *Reinventing Education*. For a detailed discussion of Gerstner et al.'s numerous errors in fact and interpretation, see Roslyn Arlin Mickelson, "Opportunity and Danger: Understanding Business Involvement in School Reform," in Borman, Spade, and Cookson.

55. See David C. Berliner and Bruce Biddle, *The Manufactured Crisis.* (Reading, Mass.: Addison-Wesley, 1995); Bracey; Larry Cuban, "The Great School Scam," *Education Week*, June 15, 1994, p. 44; Lawrence C. Stedman, "The Achievement Crisis is Real: A Review of *The Manufactured Crisis. Educational Policy Analysis Archives* 4.1 (1996), http://seamonkey.ed.asu.edu/

56. Peter Cookson, *School Choice. The Struggle for the Soul of American Education.* (New Haven: Yale University Press, 1994); Jay Greene, Paul E. Peterson, and Jiangtao Du, "Effectiveness of School Choice: The Milwaukee Experiment," paper presented at the Annual Meeting of the American Educa-

tional Research Association, Chicago, April 1997; Jeffrey Henig, *Rethinking School Choice. Limits of the Market Metaphor* (Princeton: Princeton University Press, 1994); Edith Rasell and Richard Rothstein, *School Choice. Examining the Evidence* (Washington, D.C.: Economic Policy Institute, 1993); John Witte, A. Bailey, and C. Thorn, *Fifth Year Report. Milwaukee Parental Choice Program*, Robert LaFollette School of Public Policy (Madison: University of Wisconsin, 1996); Geoffrey Walford, "Educational Choice and Equity in Great Britain," *Educational Policy* 6 (1992): 123–38.; Douglas Willms and Frank Echols, "The Scottish Experience of Parental Choice of Schools," paper presented at "Choice: What Role in American Education?" (Washington, D.C.: Economic Policy Institute, 1992).

57. Doyle, *A Personal Report*, p. 9.

58. See note 56; Alexander W. Astin, "Educational 'Choice': Its Appeal May Be Illusory," *Sociology of Education* 65 (1992): 255–60.

59. Chester A. Finn Jr., "The Choice Backlash," *The National Review*, November 10, 1989, pp. 30–32; Finn, "Blind Spots on the Right," *The National Review*, September 25, 1995, 68–69.

60. Jeffrey Henig, *Rethinking School Choice: Limits of the Market Metaphor* (Princeton: Princeton University Press, 1994).

61. Michael Timpane and L. M. McNeill, *Business Impact on Education and Child Development Reform* (New York: Committee for Economic Development, 1991), p. 32.

62. David Boraks, "IBM Trims Workforce," *Charlotte Observer*, October 18, 1997, p. 1D; Harry Greyard, "IBM Cuts New for Charlotte," *Charlotte Observer*, July 11, 1987, p. 10A; Greyard, "IBM's Charlotte Facility May Shrink," *Charlotte Observer*, August 8, 1992, p. 1D; Douglas Massey and Mary Denton, *American Apartheid: Segregation and the Making of the Underclass* (Cambridge: Harvard University Press, 1993); Louis Uchitelle, "1995 Was Good for Companies and Better for a Lot of CEOs" *New York Times*, March 29, 1996; William Julius Wilson, *When Work Disappears* (New York: Alfred A. Knopf, 1996).

63. Kerry A. White and Robert C. Johnston, "Schools' Taxes Bartered Away to Garner Jobs," *Education Week*, March 12, 1997, p. 1f.

64. Geoff Whitty, *Sociology and School Knowledge: Curriculum Theory, Research, and Politics* (London: Methuen, 1985), p. 82.

65. See Larry Cuban, "High-Tech Schools and Low-Tech Teaching," *Education Week*, May 21, 1997, p. 38.; Douglas D. Noble, "Selling the Schools a Bill of Goods: The Marketing of Computer-Based Education," in *Education, Inc.*, ed. Kohn and Todd Oppenheimer, "The Computer Delusion" *The Atlantic Monthly*, June 1997, pp. 45–65, for trenchant critiques of both the underlying conceptualization of the role of technology in education and current practices that implement it.

66. John Goodlad, "Making Democracy Safe for Education," *Education Week*, July 9, 1997, p. 56.

67. John Deem, "Okay, So Now Who Controls School Siting?" *The Leader*, November 7, 1997, pp. 4–5.

CHAPTER 6

A Comparative Analysis of Existing Secondary School Discipline Policies: Implications for Improving Practice and School Safety

Pamela Fenning, James D. Wilczynski, and Marianela Parraga

Violence is increasingly a concern in schools and surrounding communities. While some researchers explain that schools remain relatively safe places in comparison to other environments, safer even than their own homes,[1] the fact still remains that an increasing number of students are reporting, witnessing, or being exposed to acts of violence within school halls and in surrounding communities. Statistics indicate that between 43 percent and 55 percent of inner-city adolescent males have witnessed a robbery, assault, or shooting. Ten percent of adolescent inner-city females have been raped, while up to 16 percent have been threatened with rape.[2] Furthermore, increasing numbers of students are bringing weapons to school. According to the U.S. Centers for Disease Control, it was estimated that 5 percent of students brought a gun to school at least once a month.[3] Since many students report that they bring weapons to school for protection, one may wonder if these numbers will increase now that some states have passed concealed weapons laws in which adults may carry concealed weapons in public.

Violence and the threat of violence dramatically impact the school routine and the learning of youth in urban communities. A case example in Chicago involves a school for youth with emotional disorders. The administrative personnel have changed the school hours to allow the students to leave the building earlier than the usual Chicago Public School dismissal time. This decision was made because of continual victimization of these youth as they boarded their buses at the end of the day. Many students also fear for their own safety while at school. Just as a poor child who is perpetually hungry may not learn well in school, one will expect a child who is fearful of being injured or killed to also have difficulty learning. For instance, 80,000 children stay home from school at least one day a month due to fear of being hurt at school.[4] The U.S. Department of Education reinforces that even being forced to cope with the constant risk of violence interferes with learning. At times, violence impacts our youth to such an extent and in so many ways that students' education is completely halted.

To address issues of violence and related urban issues, educators have taken a number of theoretical approaches. Recent classroom management approaches, such as responsive classroom management, have focused on teaching children responsibility within a specific context.[5] General guidelines and standards guide classroom activity versus enforcement of specific rules. The focus within the classroom management approach is to develop students' internal control through acceptance of logical consequences for behavior.

Attention has been given to the presentation of curriculum in the creation of an accepting learning environment for all students. Cooperative learning is effective in promoting student discovery in learning, social skills, and positive classroom behavior.[6] Proactive classroom management, which focuses on teacher skills that prevent or de-escalate behavioral difficulties, has documented success in creating a supportive learning environment and reduction of behavior problems.[7]

Ancillary schoolwide interventions, involving peer mediation and conflict resolution, focus specifically on reduction of violence.[8] Schools have also begun to adopt violence prevention curricula, which tend to involve problem solving and role-playing alternatives to aggression.[9]

But the previously described interventions fail to consider the larger social context in which violence and school discipline issues emanate. Poverty and social marginalization are factors that contribute to the proliferation of violence.[10] Few researchers have examined the multiplicity of larger societal variables that impact the display of aggressive behavior in school settings. An extensive review of the literature related to the causes of aggression in school settings and the efficacy of programs to address school violence was completed by Tolan and Guerra.[11] The authors cited a variety of cultural and social factors that increase the risk of aggression and violence. These cultural and social factors include socioeconomic status, peer influences, family resources, and coping skills.[12] School culture and the social context in which schools operate may actually be contributing to violence seen in schools. Schools attempt to exert a great deal of control in managing behavior. When these school expectations and the social context of the school are not consistent with the social norms of the student, problem behaviors may emerge.[13] Individual student behavior is not in isolation, but within the context of each specific school.[14] Punitive behaviors of teachers, in addition to discipline policies themselves, may contribute to the proliferation of violence seen in schools.[15] For example, harsh verbal abuse and, in some states, corporal punishment, contribute to an abuse of power between teacher and student. This, in turn, contributes to the establishment of a negative social context in which students are expected to function.

Without considering the social context and sociological variables that promote aggression, teachers and school administrators have relied on reactionary interventions as an attempt to achieve immediate reductions in violence. For example, metal detectors and in-house police have been placed in all Chicago secondary public schools. Many school districts across the nation boast of a "zero tolerance policy" in which violent students are removed from public schools and are placed in an alternative private school setting. Another common, but controversial, strategy is to conduct searches of students if they are suspected of possessing drugs or weapons.[16]

Many schools are attempting to adopt "get tough" approaches and are becoming more punitive in their efforts to illustrate how they do not tolerate violence. Effective efforts, however, address the specific problems children have within a larger social context and do not solely focus on a specific violation.[17] Hyman and colleagues explain that there are few simple solutions and "the best solution must take into account the total ecology of the school situation."[18]

Schools can address violence and problem areas effectively by implementing good discipline policies. There is a body of literature suggesting that effective discipline policies possess many similar features. The most basic feature is that discipline policies must clearly state what behaviors are violations and what consequences will result if violations do occur.[19] Therefore, an effective policy does not leave any room for inconsistent messages regarding acceptance or nonacceptance of behavior and subjective application of consequences. Each violation, however, may have different circumstances surrounding it, and would necessitate some latitude in applying the policy. This is because each specific school has larger community needs, and the behavior must be placed within the social ecology in which it operates. Students would be treated equitably, but not necessarily in the same manner for every circumstance. For instance, if a policy simply indicates that stealing will result in a two-day suspension, it would seem illogical to give the same consequence to a student who has committed his or her first offense and another student who has committed his or her fifth offense. These situations are plausible scenarios and should be handled differently, with a consideration of the specific needs of the student within the school community. In order to adequately address the multitude of scenarios in schools, a range of possible consequences for each offense is provided so that the disciplinarian can consider specific mitigating circumstances of an incident.[20] The range of consequences is clearly specified and an explanation of why there is a range should be provided. Again, this procedure must be implemented with sensitivity to the social context in which the student is operating.

Another major factor believed to relate to effective discipline policies is the degree to which they are consistently and fairly enforced.[21] If teachers attempt to make examples out of some students while allowing others to break rules, students will quickly learn that the discipline policy is a farce and the important lesson to learn is which teachers or staff allow which infractions.

Rubel and Blauvelt also believe it is important for a policy to delineate between violations of school rules and violations of state laws.[22] Students also need to be aware of when outside authorities, such as police, will be contacted. For instance, if two students are fighting, a criteria for police involvement versus internal handling of the incident needs to be specified. In some schools, police are called only if a weapon is involved. However, what constitutes a weapon is unclear as a gun, knife, lock, book, or any object used with an intent to injure could potentially be defined as a weapon. These issues need to be explicitly clarified within the policy. Some states also require a school to report certain incidents to law enforcement authorities.[23] Consequently, not only do students need to be aware, but staff must know when to refer the incident to authorities outside the school.

Discipline policies tend to be more effective when the school is sure that students have read and understand the policy.[24] In some schools, students are required to read the policy or handbook and pass a test measuring their understanding of the rules and consequences.[25] If a student fails, he or she receives additional instruction and is later retested. While the emphasis thus far has been placed on the students, teachers and staff also need to be fully aware of the policy so that they can consistently enforce the rules and apply consequences fairly.[26]

Effective policies generally reflect the values of the community and can be adapted to meet the specific needs of the school. This aspect suggests that very large school districts need to be flexible and, possibly, individualized policies need to be developed for each school building. Some schools within large cities like Chicago, for example, have had success in forming a "discipline committee" consisting of school staff, parents, and students who develop the policy and determine the proper consequences.[27] However, according to a national survey, school principals feel that they and the district personnel are most responsible for developing discipline policies. Only 18 percent of principals said teachers should share responsibility in setting the policy.[28] The principals were not even asked if members of the community should be involved in developing the discipline policies. This is counter to consideration of these behaviors within the social context in which they are expressed.

While prior research has reviewed discipline policies in terms of what makes a general policy effective, there are several neglected areas in light of recent educational trends concerning violence prevention and intervention. The degree to which discipline policies vary in relation to the setting of service (e.g., urban versus suburban and public versus private) and in terms of the student population serviced (students referred for emotional or behavioral problems versus students in general education settings) has not been examined. We believe it is imperative to examine such policies within a cultural context and to individualize the policy for the diverse needs of the student population. We need to focus on clear communication among school personnel, students, and families in our establishment of standards for school behavior and subsequent development of formal policies. This is particularly pressing as a major component of our attempt to grapple with complex, larger social issues related to violence and in our mission to create a safe environment for all within public schools. These issues must be considered in the development of discipline policies which are not a means of control, but address the deeper sociological issues that contribute to school violence.

METHODOLOGY

As an attempt to begin addressing these larger questions regarding the content of discipline policies across settings, we chose seven discipline policies in a variety of secondary school settings. We engaged in the technique of purposive sampling. This technique involves choosing subjects because of known parameters of interest.[29] We were interested in obtaining discipline policies from schools that had a range of socioeconomic levels, specialized services, and economic support (public versus private). Our settings included large city public schools, a public school bordering the city, a large private city school with a religious affiliation, a large private high socioeconomic status (SES) suburban school with a religious affiliation, a public high SES suburban school, a private school for students with emotional and behavior disorders and a public school for adjudicated students.

In the city, all public secondary schools utilized a uniform discipline code. This policy is established for use across the variety of neighborhoods and settings. However, there is a qualification to school personnel that modifications can be made for the individual school site, with the understanding that any changes should not replace the uniform guidelines.

The developed school policies also followed basic regulations established by the Illinois School Code and the Illinois Criminal Code. The Illinois Criminal Code applies most directly to mandated reports of illegal activities of students to the Bureau of Safety and Security. However, the policies varied in terms of their interpretations of the legal guidelines.

The qualitative data-reduction technique of grounded theory was utilized in the development of a coding system. In this approach, the data drives the development of the categories, which are collapsed as common themes emerge.[30] Advantages of this approach are the generation of hypotheses for the variables of interest. A weakness of this approach is the lack of experimental control, and related threats to internal validity.

Two female psychologists, one Ph.D. and one M.Ed. level, created and utilized the coding system, based on their analysis of the content of the existing discipline policies. Their backgrounds are in applied psychology, including learning theory, assessment and evaluation of school-aged children and adolescents. They have experience across all school settings examined in the current study. The purpose of the coding system was to examine behaviors and the range of consequences referenced by each specific school discipline policy.

Specifically, behaviors related to violence or a negative school climate were examined within the school policy. Behaviors such as truancy, tardiness, and proper dress were not examined. The coding system was continually altered to encompass the extensive range of behaviors specified in the various policies. Initially, broad categories were created and were expanded to include specific subcategories, enabling a more detailed analysis of frequently addressed behaviors across all policies.

When the behaviors were coded, each specific instance of a behavior was tallied as a separate frequency. For example, if using slanderous verbalizations was mentioned more than once within the policy, it was coded each time it occurred. A decision was made regarding whether the behavior met the criteria for one of the larger categories or a specific subcategory. In this example, slanderous verbalizations could be classified under the broad categories of harassment and academic disturbance. Depending on the situation and content, one would make a decision regarding which classification to follow. In this case, whether the focus of the behavior was on an individual student/staff or the larger school context would determine which code was chosen. If the statement within the policy closely matched the defining features of a category/sub-category, it was classified as such, and did not have to match the prose in the code verbatim. During the coding process, the examiners discussed behaviors that could not clearly be categorized, and made a joint decision after deliberation.

The minimum and the maximum consequences for each behavior were coded if they were identifiable within the policy. Some behaviors within the discipline policies did not have a stated consequence, and this was indicated within our coding system. In addition, some behaviors listed only one consequence. If this occurred, the stated consequence was coded without an indicated range.

RESULTS

Findings across All Policies

We examined all discipline policies in terms of the relative importance given to each of the discipline categories. The percentage of total attention that each category obtained in relation to the overall percentage is displayed in table 6.1 for all school settings. Our main finding was that every school policy, with the exception of one, focused mainly on student misconduct relating to possession, distribution or use of prohibited objects on school grounds. Prohibited objects were defined either as being illegal by a state or federal mandate, or deemed unacceptable by school authorities. Schools tended to be specific and elaborate regarding the type of object(s) that were prohibited. The subcategories included narcotics, alcohol, tobacco, destructive devices, electronic devices, and weapons. This generally increased the number of codes within this category, yielding a higher percentage in relation to the overall policy.

However, an examination of physical aggression indicated that this broad category received much less attention, with the exception of one school. This relative lack of attention is evidenced in both the relatively lower resulting percentages of attention to physical aggression in relation to the overall categories, and with regard to the lack of specificity to defining features. Physical aggression was defined only in terms of whether or not it resulted in a physical injury, or involved individuals or groups. There was virtually no attention to sexual assault, and only one policy mentioned molestation or rape.

Apart from the dominant category of possession, distribution and use of prohibited objects, there was a general trend across all policies for relatively higher levels of attention to the categories of academic distur-

TABLE 6.1
Percentage of Attention in Discipline Policies
for Behavioral Categories: All Schools

	Public, Urban	Urban Detention Center	Private, Urban, Religious Affiliation	Public, Suburban High SES	Private, Suburban with Religious Affiliation High SES	Private School for Children with Emotional and Behavioral Disorders	Public School on Border of City, Low SES
Possession/ distribution of prohibited objects or substances	32	27	53	63	45	26	22
Academic disturbance	19	18	11	10	5	19	22
Physical aggression	12	15	5	3	3	3	11
Theft	10	4	16	3	0	6	4
Insubordination	10	6	5	3	3	3	4

(continued on next page)

TABLE 6.1 (continued)

	Public, Urban	Urban Detention Center	Private, Urban, Religious Affiliation	Public, Suburban High SES	Private, Suburban with Religious Affiliation High SES	Private School for Children with Emotional and Behavioral Disorders	Public School on Border of City, Low SES
Academic dishonesty	7	7	0	3	11	0	0
Harassment	6	8	0	6	21	23	11
Group offenses	2	4	5	3	2	0	7
Disruptive bus behavior	2	0	5	0	2	4	0
Display of affection/ physical conduct	0	1	0	0	0	6	0
School damage/ destruction	0	10	0	6	8	10	19

bance, harassment, and school property destruction. While each school tended to emphasize one of these categories more than another, based on the specific mission of the school, these categories emerged as the next major area of school policy focus.

In terms of consequences and alternatives to traditional discipline procedures, none of the policies that were reviewed formally stated the need for student participation.

Comparisons among Specific School Settings

A comparison was made between the various school policies in terms of the emphasis placed on specific categories, subcategories of behavior, and consequences. The policies presenting the most significant differences will be emphasized within the chapter.

Variations among Public Urban versus Public Suburban in High SES Settings

In comparing a high SES suburban public school with the uniform policy for the city public schools, as depicted in table 6.2, we found a much greater focus by the suburban school (63 percent) toward the discipline categories of possession, distribution, and use of objects than the city policy (32 percent).

TABLE 6.2
Percentage of Attention in Discipline Policies for Behavioral Categories:
Public Urban vs. Public Suburban in High SES Setting

	Public, Urban	Public, Suburban High SES
Possession/distribution of prohibited objects or substances	32	63
Academic disturbance	19	10
Physical aggression	12	3
Theft	10	3
Insubordination	10	3
Academic dishonesty	7	3
Harassment	6	6
Group offenses	2	3
Disruptive bus behavior	2	0
Display of affection/ physical conduct	0	0
School damage/destruction	0	6

With regard to physical aggression, more attention was given to this area by the city policy code (12 percent). However, these two settings varied in terms of the consequences given for these behaviors. In the city policy, the minimum consequence was a teacher, resource person, and administrator conference, while the suburban policy chose suspension as its minimal consequence for physical aggression. The maximum consequence for physical aggression was expulsion for both policies.

The policies also varied significantly in terms of other stated consequences for behavior. The suburban policy outlined an alternative to traditional consequences for alcohol consumption and use, identifying a specific program of service to students, and the option to obtain an approved outside counselor of student/parent choice. The city policy mentioned the mandate for free and appropriate counseling services as students' rights, but did not identify a specific program or procedure for obtaining services.

Related to consequences, a specified procedure for students with grievances and perceptions of unfair treatment was outlined in the suburban policy, while the city policy mentioned the necessity of due process rights without a delineated procedure.

Variations among Public Urban versus Private Urban with Religious Affiliation

While there were no major differences in the relative emphasis of categories and subcategories of behavior, we found some differences for the consequences. Please see table 6.3. In the public urban (city) policy, a range of consequences were stated with every behavior. However, in the private urban policy, possible consequences were listed, but not in association with any specific behavior. In general, there was much discretion given to the private school administrators regarding the application of consequences and grounds for removal of the students.

Variations among Public Suburban in High SES versus Private School for Students with Behavior/Emotional Disorders

The private school that was examined, as can be seen from table 6.4, placed more of an emphasis on behaviors involving harassment than the public suburban school. There was a notable difference regarding the consequences given for behaviors such as physical aggression and threats of physical aggression. In the private school, consequences were unique to the setting and involved time-out from the school activity, and problem-solving, although suspension was listed as a potential consequence. Within the public school, consequences focused more on traditional procedures, and emphasized in-school suspension, out-of-school suspension, and expulsion.

TABLE 6.3

Percentage of Attention in Discipline Policies for Behavioral Categories:
Public Urban vs. Private Urban with Religious Affiliation

	Public, Urban	Private, Urban, Religious Affiliation
Possession/distribution of prohibited objects or substances	32	53
Academic disturbance	19	11
Physical aggression	12	5
Theft	10	16
Insubordination	10	5
Academic dishonesty	7	0
Harassment	6	0
Group offenses	2	5
Disruptive bus behavior	2	5
Display of affection/ physical conduct	0	0
School damage/destruction	0	0

TABLE 6.4

Percentage of Attention in Discipline Policies for Behavioral Categories:
Public Suburban in High SES Setting vs. Private School
for Students with Behavioral/Emotional Disorders

	Public, Suburban High SES	Private School for Children with Emotional and Behavioral Disorders
Possession/distribution of prohibited objects or substances	63	26
Academic disturbance	10	19
Physical aggression	3	3
Theft	3	6
Insubordination	3	3
Academic dishonesty	3	0
Harassment	6	23
Group offenses	3	0
Disruptive bus behavior	0	4
Display of affection/ physical conduct	0	6
School damage/destruction	6	10

Another remarkable difference concerned the use of counseling as a consequence. Within the private school, counseling was specified, but not in relation to any one specific behavior. In the public school, counseling was tied to a specific behavior of concern, such as alcohol or narcotics abuse.

Public Urban versus Urban Detention Center School

There were no general differences between the policies in terms of relative attention to major categories of behavior, as can be seen in table 6.5. However, one slight difference was the mention of security issues and related behaviors within the urban detention policy (e.g., walking down the hall, and having an adult escort at all times).

Public Urban versus Public Suburban Border School

The comparative analysis of these two policies is demonstrated in table 6.6, and reveals no major differences in terms of the relative importance given to specific categories of behavior. However, the secondary school bordering the city had a broader range of consequences, which varied in severity as well as mention of appeal for most behaviors. The city policy did not discuss levels of appeal.

TABLE 6.5
Percentage of Attention in Discipline Policies for Behavioral Categories:
Public Urban vs. Urban Detention Center

	Public, Urban	*Urban Detention Center*
Possession/distribution of prohibited objects or substances	32	27
Academic disturbance	19	18
Physical aggression	12	15
Theft	10	4
Insubordination	10	6
Academic dishonesty	7	7
Harassment	6	8
Group offenses	2	4
Disruptive bus behavior	2	0
Display of affection/ physical conduct	0	1
School damage/destruction	0	10

TABLE 6.6
Percentage of Attention in Discipline Policies for Behavioral Categories:
Public Urban vs. Public School on Border of City

	Public, Urban	Public School on Border of City, Low SES
Possession/distribution of prohibited objects or substances	32	22
Academic disturbance	19	22
Physical aggression	12	11
Theft	10	4
Insubordination	10	4
Academic dishonesty	7	0
Harassment	6	11
Group offenses	2	7
Disruptive bus behavior	2	0
Display of affection/ physical conduct	0	0
School damage/destruction	0	19

DISCUSSION

The main finding regarding the emphasis given by all schools to the categories of possession, distribution, and use of prohibited objects, and the relatively less attention focused on physical aggression is somewhat surprising, in light of recent regional and national movements calling for school prevention and intervention efforts in the area of violent behaviors.

Suarez emphasizes the need for discipline policies to have clear and established guidelines for behavior and consistent application of consequences across incidents.[31] Given our knowledge of the relatively vague descriptions of physical aggression across all policies examined, it would seem appropriate that clearer definitions of physical aggression need to be established. The definition of physical aggression needs to be understood within the context of the school. This would assist in the consistent and fair application of the policy to all individuals, including those who experience social marginalization. The greater attention to the distribution, possession, and use of prohibited objects, such as weapons and narcotics, is encouraging in that these issues relate to violence. However, the actual issue of violent actions is not directly addressed.

The discipline policies address, to some degree, external methods of control and intervention when misbehavior occurs. However, this focus could be greatly expanded by attending to other interventions that are also associated with problematic behaviors within the classroom. These approaches are based on teacher behaviors that influence the expression of positive and negative social behaviors, and include the responsive classroom management model,[32] curricular modifications, and proactive classroom management.[33] These approaches consider the need to develop teacher competencies in addressing behavior. These interventions go beyond considering the student's behavior in isolation, but address the role of the teacher in discipline issues.[34]

Another significant finding involves the absence of any written content in the policies regarding violence prevention and intervention activities within the schools. Indeed, the Goals 2000 program, which has mandated violence prevention and intervention efforts, has not forged its way into formal written and established policies governing the behavior of students in school settings. While many schools are beginning to assume an active approach in the provision of these services, written communication about them within the discipline policy has not occurred. From a sociocultural and organizational perspective, this lack of attention may provide some evidence that these programs have not been formally sanctioned within the school institution, or integrated into the daily functioning of the school. Possibly, these programs do not follow traditional school norms, which tend to focus on punitive, reactionary means of control to the exclusion of flexibility in meeting the student's individualized broader social needs.

A third conclusion concerns the relatively few alternatives offered to traditional discipline practices across all school settings. Basically, formal counseling options were mentioned only in a specialized school focusing on children with emotional and behavior disorders. This intervention was also a component of the discipline policy within a bordering city school, and a high SES suburban school. In the higher-income setting, a well-defined program is offered within the school to students at no cost, and students have the added option of obtaining a school-approved outside counselor at parent expense. Unfortunately, while counseling services were mentioned as an option for students in the city schools, a procedure for obtaining them was not specified. It would seem important that accessible services be provided for students in the city environment, as they may or may not have the personal resources or referral information to obtain them. This finding would be consistent with economic issues that impinge on a student's behavioral functioning within the school setting.

Qualitative observations within specific policies revealed several areas for further study. It is important to note that sexual assault was seldom addressed within the policies, and was scarcely coded in our current system. Only one policy mentioned rape or molestation within the school setting, and police involvement was not clearly indicated as a consequence. The need to consider acts of sexual exploitation as aggression would seem to be important as part of the teaching strategy of a discipline policy.

Another qualitative observation concerned the relatively few schools that explicitly involved parents, students, support personnel, and community leaders in the development of the policies. Schools that did involve community members through a committee or advisory board tended to encourage active participation in all phases of the policy, ranging from its inception to grievances brought forth by students. This collaboration is beneficial in bridging the gap between community, social, and family factors, and the need for schools to operate in a safe, supportive environment. In the city public school codes, one uniform policy was the main blueprint for conduct across all participating secondary schools, decreasing the possibility of involvement from those in the surrounding neighborhood. These observations would match a national study, indicating that school administrators feel primarily responsible for the establishment of discipline policies.[35]

IMPLICATIONS

The primary implication of this study is the recommendation that discipline policymakers integrate the larger body of literature focused on student development of internal control and responsibility versus solely relying on external control. Further, attention to proactive classroom management and related teacher behaviors needs to be considered in the implementation of discipline policies and procedures. It is imperative that discipline policies be considered within the larger social context in which schools operate if they are to have any chance for success. Schools must consider themselves as part of the larger social context and community in which they operate, and cannot continue to function as isolated entities.

A second implication involves the need for increased involvement of parents, community members and support staff in the development and implementation of discipline policies within a culturally appropriate context. The discipline policies need to consider the norms of the neighborhood and community regarding appropriate behavior. Currently, the uniform discipline policy that was evaluated within the city public schools is applied across a range of school settings, without regard to socioeconomic status, size of school, age of school, ethnic composition of students and faculty, and a range of other demographic variables. Although modifications are allowed, schools are required to follow the basic tenets of the uniform policy, which may or may not fit the needs and concerns of the specific neighborhood. While principals tend to feel ultimately responsible for discipline within their schools, it is imperative that parents are provided an opportunity to participate in the initial development, implementation, modification and evaluation of discipline policies within their children's schools. This is essential if students' behavior is to be viewed within an ecological context. Possibly, a regional committee could be developed with representation from parents, students, school personnel, related agency members, and community residents. The charge of this committee would be the development of general guidelines that would serve as a framework for each individual school district to adopt and modify as needed. The general guidelines would serve as a benchmark for developing specific competencies to be achieved by students at various levels. However, the guidelines would be flexible enough to be adapted to the specific needs of the diverse population within each school district.

An additional outcome of this study is that school policies need to include more specific and comprehensive definitions of physical and related aggression. Specifically, attention to types of aggression, such as sexual and physical assault need to be attended to in the consideration of discipline policies. It is imperative that policymakers agree on what is meant by violence or violent acts. Otherwise, students will not learn consistent expectations for nonviolent behavior, and will have no opportunity to internalize these guidelines.

An additional implication relates to the lack of consistency between policies in relation to alternative interventions, such as counseling, and related alternatives to traditional disciplinary measures. Policy makers, particularly within urban environments, need to make efforts at developing mental health interventions for youth. These interventions must consider the range of sociological variables rarely addressed within the literature.

LIMITATIONS OF THE STUDY AND
IMPLICATIONS FOR FUTURE RESEARCH

The limitations of the current study involve the small sample number of discipline policies that were used in the analysis. This limits the generalization of the study to other school districts, and the findings could be related to specific parameters and irrelevant characteristics of the discipline policies that were chosen. However, the study represents an initial

attempt to examine the content of discipline policies, with a consideration of variables rarely studied in the school violence literature. These
sociological variables include socioeconomic status, school resources,
and specialized services.

Another limitation concerns the reliability and validity of the coding system. While initially useful for pilot studies and the development
of specific hypotheses, the current system should be replicated with a
larger sample size, and continually validated for the purpose of examining discipline policies across a wider range of settings. Future work
should conduct inferential statistical analyses of the data to expand the
findings of the current study.

The current study was an initial attempt at examining larger social
and community variables in which students exist. Future research
should empirically evaluate the degree to which the social context, and
larger community influence the development and implementation of discipline policies. A major hypothesis developed in the current study indicates that discipline policies must vary by community to be effective. A
follow-up study of greater depth in examining this issue would be an
important area for future research.

Implications for practice and policy development suggest the need
for empirical evaluation of multi-dimensional programs which address
the social and familial context in which discipline concerns arise. The
involvement of parents and community members in the development
and implementation of discipline policies needs to be a focus of further
study.

NOTES

1. I. A. Hyman et al., *Policy and Practice in School Discipline: Past, Pre-
sent and Future.* Paper presented at Safe Schools, Safe Students: A Collaborative
Approach to Achieving Safe, Disciplined and Drug-Free Schools Conducive to
Learning Conference, Washington, D.C., October 1994.

2. R. Gladstein et al., "A Comparison of Inner-City and Upper-Middle-
Class Youths' Exposure to Violence," *Journal of Adolescent Health* 13.4
(1992): 275–80.

3. W. Landen, "Violence and Our Schools: What Can We Do?" *Updating School Board Policies* 23 (1992): 1–5.

4. Ibid.

5. J. A. Queen, B. B. Blackwelder, and L. P. Mallen, *Responsible Classroom Management for Teachers and Students* (Upper Saddle River, N.J.: Mer-
rill, 1997), pp. 18–35.

6. R. E. Slavin, *Educational Psychology: Theory and Practice* (Needham
Heights, Mass.: Allyn and Bacon, 1997), pp. 266–303; C. R. Greenwood, J. J.
Carta, and R. V. Hall, "The Use of Peer Tutoring Strategies in Classroom Man-

agement and Educational Instruction," *School Psychology Review* 17 (July 1988): 258–75.

7. M. Gettinger, "Methods of Proactive Classroom Management," *School Psychology Review* 17 (July 1988): 243–57.

8. G. S. Heller, "Changing the School to Reduce Student Violence: What Works?" *NASSP Bulletin* 80 (1996): 1–10; D. W. Johnson and R. T. Johnson, "Reducing School Violence through Conflict Resolution Training," *NASSP Bulletin* 80 (1996): 11–18; K. E. Powell, L. Muir-McClain, and L. Halasyamani, "A Review of Selected School-Based Conflict Resolution and Peer Mediation Projects," *Journal of School Health* 65 (1995): 426–31.

9. D. Prothrow-Stith, *Violence Prevention Curriculum for Adolescents* (Newton, Mass.: Education Development Center, 1987); R. Pesce, personal communication, August 19, 1996.

10. C. Burnett, "School Violence in an Impoverished South African Community," *Child Abuse and Neglect* 22 (1998): 789–95; P. Bourgois, "Confronting Anthropology, Education, and Inner-City Apartheid," *American Anthropologist* 98 (June 1996): 249–58.

11. P. H. Tolan and N. G. Guerra, *What Works in Reducing Adolescent Violence: An Empirical Review of the Field* (Boulder, Colo.: Center for the Study and Prevention of Violence, Institute for Behavioral Sciences, University of Colorado, Boulder, 1994).

12. P. C. Kratcoski, "Perspectives on Intrafamily Violence," *Human Relations* 37 (1984): 443–54; S. K. Steinmetz, "The Violent Family," in *Violence in the Home: Interdisciplinary Perspectives*, ed. M. Lystad (New York: Brunner/Mazel, 1986), pp. 51–70; M. A. Strauss and R. J. Gelles, "Societal Changes in Family Violence from 1975 to 1985 as Revealed by Two National Surveys," *Journal of Marriage and Family* 48 (1986): 465–79.

13. J. A. Baker, "Are We Missing the Forest for the Trees? Considering the Social Context of School Violence," *Journal of School Psychology* 36 (1998): 29–44.

14. I. A. Hyman and D. C. Perone, "Introduction to the Special Theme Section on School Violence: The Ecology of School Violence," *Journal of School Psychology* 36 (1998): 3–5.

15. I. A. Hyman and D. C. Perone, "The Other Side of School Violence: Educator Policies and Practices That May Contribute to Student Misbehavior," *Journal of School Psychology* 36 (1998): 7–27.

16. T. M. Suarez, *Creating Safe Environments for Learning in North Carolina's Public Schools* (Chapel Hill, N.C.: North Carolina Educational Policy Research Center, ERIC Document ED 373 406, 1992).

17. Ibid.

18. Hyman and Perone, "Introduction to the Special Theme Section," p. 3.

19. R. Linquanti and B. Berliner, *Rebuilding Schools as Safe Havens: A Typology for Selecting and Integrating Violence Prevention Strategies* (Portland, Or.: Western Regional Center for Drug Free Schools and Communities, ERIC Document ED 376 600, 1994).

20. Suarez, *Creating Safe Environments*.

21. R. J. Rubel, and P. D. Blauvelt, "How Safe Are Your Schools?" *Amer-*

ican School Board Journal 181 (1994): 28–31; U.S. Department of Education, *Safe, Disciplined, Drug-Free Schools: A Background Paper for the Goals 2000: Educate America Satellite Town Meeting, July 20, 1993* (Washington, D.C.: Department of Education, ERIC Document ED 366 103, 1993).

22. Rubel and Blauvelt, "How Safe Are Your Schools?"
23. Suarez, *Creating Safe Environments.*
24. Ibid.
25. U.S. Department of Education, *Safe, Disciplined, Drug-Free Schools.*
26. Rubel and Blauvelt, "How Safe Are Your Schools?"
27. U.S. Department of Education, *Safe, Disciplined, Drug-Free Schools.*
28. U.S. Department of Education. *Who Runs the Schools? The Principal's View* (Online). Available: http//www.ed.gov/pubs/OR/ResearchRpts/prinview. html (September 1, 1996).
29. F. N. Kerlinger, *Foundations of Behavioral Research* (New York, New York: CBS College Publishing, 1986), pp. 120.
30. B. G. Glaser, *Grounded Theory* (Mill Valley, Calif.: Sociology Press, 1995).
31. Suarez, *Creating Safe Environments.*
32. Queen, Blackwelder, and Mallen, *Responsible Classroom Management.*
33. Gettinger, "Methods of Proactive Classroom Management."
34. Hyman and Perone, "Introduction to the Special Theme Section."
35. U.S. Department of Education, *Who Runs the Schools?*

CHAPTER 7

Modeling of the Effects of Changing Demography on Student Learning: Applications Designed to Change School District Practices

Anthony Gary Dworkin,
Laurence A. Toenjes, Margaret K. Purser,
and Ayman Sheikh-Hussin

In 1968, the U.S. Congress amended the Title XI Higher Education Act of 1965 to create the Urban Community Service Program, which called for universities to provide expertise to enable cities to address their urban problems, particularly in the field of education. The 1968 program was initiated to attempt to redress some inequalities that had led to several years of urban revolts in minority communities. However, the legislation was passed without appropriation by Congress and signed by then President Lyndon Johnson. In 1986, the legislation was up for renewal and was again passed without funding by Congress and the Reagan administration. Finally, in 1992, out of concerns for urban revolts occasioned by the Rodney King beating in Los Angeles and worries over a reelection bid, President Bush encouraged funding of the program. Congress passed the enabling legislation and grant applications were accepted in May 1992.

Our Urban Community Service project called for us to assist school districts in the metropolitan area to improve their forecasting of the changing demography of their student bodies and to develop models to explain the impact of that changing demography on student learning.[1] With the completion of the project, our center remains committed to

195

working with the districts beyond the funding period and has established research relations with several districts to continue our work. The congressional elections of 1994 and subsequent federal budget impasses have resulted in the effective termination of the Urban Community Service Program. Allocations have been made only to complete projects that were approved during the 1995 fiscal year. Consequently, the U.S. Department of Education solicited nonfederal strategies to continue the services created by the program. We offer our approach as an example of how social science and sociology in particular can maintain a research/service relationship with urban school districts in the absence of continued federal funding. While there are a plethora of available models for the conduct of urban education, we have found this one to be successful for us and for the school districts with which we work. In the course of this chapter, we shall describe the forecasting project and findings, as well as our activities that have led to an ongoing relationship with school districts. In so doing, we can specify some of the elements that work in redefining one role of sociology of education in urban school districts. The chapter is divided into three parts: (1) the development of a forecasting model and summary of findings; (2) the creation, testing, and summarized findings of our student learning outcomes model; and (3) the establishment of a set of ongoing deliverables to districts to retain a working research relationship with urban schools. This final element resembles an urban education equivalent of the "agricultural experiment station" model. This third element further raises issues of role ambiguity and conflict associated with the multiple expectations of school districts, the academic community and our standards for research, and the needs of assorted stakeholders in the public schools, including the students and their parents.

BACKGROUND OF THE FORECASTING MODEL

The Need for Better Forecasting

It is estimated that in the United States, by the year 2000, more than four fifths of all first-time workers entering the labor market will be women, minority group members, or persons with limited facility in English.[2] To date, the public schools have met with limited success in promoting the needed reforms to insure that the new labor force will be able to maintain the effort to keep the United States economically competitive. Concerns over the products of the public schools generated the 1983 report of the President's Commission on Excellence in Education known as *A Nation at Risk*[3] and more than three hundred task force reports since then.[4]

Conditions in Houston, Texas, are no different. Houston is the fourth largest city in the United States and its metropolitan area ranks fifth. The Houston area, even more than many other large urban communities, is at a crossroads in its thinking about development, growth, and service provision, especially in the area of public education. Houston has a history of being the epitome of a "free-enterprise city" under a laissez-faire government. Oilmen, bankers, and developers controlled Houston's future, as they controlled its past. Money flowed freely and public sector agencies often had fiscal surpluses at the end of the year. Growth was so rapid that public agencies, including public schools, had no time to respond adequately, much less to plan for change. During the 1980s, however, the rapid decline in oil prices coupled with the severe overbuilding of retail, office, and residential space led Houston into the worst economic recession seen by a major city since the Great Depression following the 1929 stock market crash. Despite the recession of the mid-1980s, however, Texas, California, and Florida are expected to absorb over 50 percent of the nation's total population growth.[5] As a result of sustained population growth coupled with economic decline in the 1980s, both public and private sectors began rethinking the need for accurate accounts of existing economic and demographic conditions, accurate predictions of Houston's general future and the future of individual neighborhoods, and solid objective rationales for implementing programs to respond to and direct emerging trends.

Trends in Houston and Harris County

The Houston Primary Metropolitan Statistical Area (PMSA) is comprised of some 5,400 square miles (8,775 sq. km.) or nearly one half the area of Belgium, of which 1,775 square miles (2,863 sq. km.) are in Harris County. Harris County, of which Houston is the principal city, grew from 1.741 million people in 1970 to 2.818 million in 1990 or an increase of nearly 62 percent over the two decades. Harris County changed from 30 percent minority in 1970 to 47 percent minority in 1990. Houston, which includes 35 percent of the public school children in the county and one third of Harris County's land, is the largest city in the nation without zoning or a comprehensive plan. In the past, when school districts in the metropolitan area have attempted to estimate future student populations, they have relied upon relatively simple cohort survival models, or have surveyed the parents of current students to determine whether there are other children at home who might be attending school in the future. These surveys have not been tied to community-based data and do not enumerate community dynamics, the major driver of changing enrollment patterns. In addition, using enrollment patterns in lower grades to predict enrollment in middle and higher grades is effective only when the neighborhoods within the school attendance zones are stable and homogeneous. In Houston, not only are families becoming more diverse and more mobile, the vast number of immigrant (from Latin America and Asia) and in-migrant (U.S.-born from other states) students precludes use of the previous enrollment patterns to predict future ones.

Houston area school districts experienced dramatic and often unforeseen changes in enrollment and composition during the 1980s, with no apparent end in sight. Three area districts grew by over 80 percent between 1980 and 1990, with another six increasing in student enrollment by more than 40 percent. Two districts lost more than 20 percent of their student body during the same time period due to a redistribution of the population. Every suburban district but one decreased in the percentage of Anglo or white students, with seven losing more than 20 percentage points in Anglo enrollment. Black enrollment increased significantly in two districts (increasing between 5,000 to 7,500 students), but decreased by nearly 14,000 in the Houston Independent School District, as the middle-class African American population migrated from the inner city to the suburbs. Asian and Hispanic enrollment has increased across all district lines, with the exception of one district that is overwhelmingly black and has experienced an overall decline in enrollments. In addition to changes in the minority student populations, school districts have been facing alarming increases in the numbers of underserved populations—those school-aged children who are not enrolled in school at all—as well as increases in the percentages of children enrolled in private schools or who are home schooled. The consequence is that by 1990, the enrollment rate among children between the ages of 6 and 17 was well under 95 percent, a decline from 1980.

To illustrate the nature of changing ethnic characteristics in Houston area schools, we turn to a middle school on the western edge of the Houston Independent School District. The attendance zone for this school is a group of neighborhoods which were built in the 1960s and contain some small apartment complexes that were traditionally family-oriented housing for Anglos and Hispanics; more than ten thousand apartment units that were previously adult only and predominantly Anglo; and several large middle-income, Anglo neighborhoods of single-family homes. In the 1974–75 school year, the student body was 86 percent Anglo, 8 percent Hispanic, 4 percent black, and 2 percent Asian. By the 1981–82 school year, the neighborhoods had become desegregated, but only a few had opened family sections by 1982. The ethnic distribution of the students was 52 percent Anglo, 18 percent Hispanic, 17 percent black, and 13 percent Asian. By 1990, the U.S. Supreme Court had outlawed adult-only complexes, the real estate market plummeted, and the multifamily complexes in this school's attendance zone were virtually 100 percent minority—mostly Hispanic. The student body was 12 percent Anglo, 70 percent Hispanic, 14 percent black, and 4 percent Asian. With the majority of the students being Hispanic, and of that 70 percent, a majority being new immigrants from Central America, the middle school was faced with an unanticipated educational crisis. While middle schools in stable communities can look to the enrollment patterns of the feeder elementary schools to forecast enrollments, schools that have a large percentage of students who were not previously served in Houston, in the United States, or at all during their elementary school years must employ other methods for anticipating change.

Changing Demographics Lead to Changing Programs

School reform efforts are driven by population dynamics operating in schools, neighborhoods, and communities. Urban and increasingly suburban communities are characterized by greater degrees of diversity and heterogeneity, which, in turn, change demands upon the public schools.[6] As housing stocks change and as birth rates among populations are modified, the schools become recipients of children with needs that differ from those of earlier cohorts. Borman and Spring report that schools are affected by some twenty-eight different demographic variables that display four factor patterns.[7] Changes in housing mix and housing condition, changes in neighborhood makeup, changes in employment patterns in and around the neighborhoods, and changes in the quality of schools or the emergence of alternative school options each affect the likely composition of the student bodies of school districts, as well as, obviously, individual campuses.

  In practice then, transformations of neighborhoods through the aging of the housing stock or other ecological patterns are likely to lead to shifts in the social makeup of the neighborhood and the magnitude of needs and resources that individuals attending schools from the neighborhood are likely to bring with them to school. Changing student bodies with different needs make obsolete some educational programs, while calling forth programs not previously implemented. Administrative and teaching styles, course offerings, the scheduling of school events, length of school day and year, and the extent to which the schools can depend upon parental support and involvement are all modified by changing school demographics, which are driven in part by changing neighborhood demography. The demographic shifts and changed organizational structures, along with changes in programmatic offerings are likely to affect patterns of interaction among teachers, students, and the parents of the students. They will also affect the extent to which schools can depend upon traditional curricular formats to produce desired student learning outcomes. Finally, student self-esteem, retention rates, and student dropout behavior are likely to be affected by the goodness of fit of programs and personnel as they mesh with organizations and population dynamics.

Thus, a transition from single-family, middle-class housing in which the majority of the residents are white and are in intact families—the image around which the schools of the 1950s were built—to multifamily housing in which the residents are ethnically diverse and in which there are a substantial proportion of single-parent families reflects a major distributive or demographic change that will have profound organizational consequences for schools and that will also affect interpersonal relationships in schools. It is not our intent to suggest that changing demography and changing diversity are negative factors. Rather, the difficulties itemized arise when school districts fail to anticipate change and continue outmoded practices, policies, and procedures. Below is only a partial list of the school factors affected by changing demography and about which school districts must focus efforts for changes in administrative and teaching practices.

Organizational consequences for schools include:

1. Increased population density will affect the ability of existing buildings to house increased student body size, which will affect:
   a. The need for new classrooms;
   b. The need for new campuses;
   c. The employment and deployment of additional teaching and support staff;
   d. The need to obtain waivers from the state on the classroom enrollment limits enforced in Texas law.

2. Changes in the student body mix and the ethnic and socioeconomic status of the families served by the school will affect:
   a. The extent to which extended day programs are needed for latch key children;
   b. The level of intergroup relations training needed by the instructional staff;
   c. The amount of resources needed to be spent on free and reduced lunches;
   d. The deployment and employment of bilingual and special education teachers;
   e. The need to apply for Chapter I funding;

   f. The proportion of time spent by instructional and administrative staff on remediation;
   g. The level of community relations efforts needed to be made by the principal;
   h. The degree to which the school can rely upon parental support for PTO or PTA activities;
   i. The extent to which the schools can expect the parents to support them in maintenance of discipline at home and in insuring that the students do their homework;
   j. The content of instruction and the extent to which traditional teaching methods can be used.

3. Failure of the school to adjust to the changing demographic makeup of the student body may lead to:
   a. Unanticipated negative changes in student academic performances;
   b. Increased student dropout rates;
   c. Diminished student attendance;
   d. Difficulties in getting parents to participate in their children's education and to be supportive of their children's teachers;
   e. Diminished student self-esteem;
   f. Increased student reliance upon gang activities as a source of esteem enhancement and identification;
   g. Increased levels of school-based violence, vandalism, and threats against school personnel.

4. Declines in student performance and parental support for the schools may lead to:
   a. Greater difficulties in passing tax increases and floating school bonds;
   b. Greater migration of middle income families to the suburbs and increased enrollment in private schools;
   c. More difficulty in attracting and retaining qualified teachers in urban schools.

5. Increased student problems, diminished support for schools, and increased suspicion about the capacity of schools to meet needs may lead to:
   a. Increased administrator stress and depersonalization of students and staff;
   b. Higher rates of teacher burnout and diminished morale;
   c. Increased teacher absenteeism;
   d. Greater reliance upon substitute teachers and the attendant effect upon student achievement;

e. Higher turnover rates among teachers as well as higher rates of entrapment of certain groups of teachers (those who hate their jobs but have no salable skills to permit them to leave teaching);

f. More litigation against school districts by teachers.

In turn, school districts that fail to address demographic changes that challenge current policies, programs, and practices are likely to experience lowered student achievement and diminished public confidence in public schools; in turn the negative consequences will have a cumulative, circular effect.[8] Clearly, then, it is in the best interest of school districts to engage in short-, intermediate-, and long-range planning for changes in neighborhoods that are likely to affect schools. The future of public education, the labor force needs of the coming century, and the continued societal well-being depend upon school systems that adequately address the dual demands of equality of educational opportunity and academic excellence for all of their children.

The benefits of changing demography and the progressive response to that change are manifold. The changes in demographic characteristics of student bodies can result in greater student diversity, rather than new forms of segregation. This diversity can offer what Leon Warshay once described as "the breadth of perspective" to all that experience that diversity.[9] Expanded perspectives enhance adaptation skills in a more global society. Thus, all benefit when students, teachers, administrators, and educational stakeholders come to draw upon the plethora of distinct insights that diversity can offer.

Generally speaking, a large district such as Los Angeles, California, which developed the Los Angeles Unified School District Forecasting Model, have begun to monitor Census data.[10] The Houston Independent School District is in the process of beginning to use census data to establish attendance area boundaries. However, most small school districts, including those adjoining large cities, have access to no such tools for forecasting student body changes. Further, most of the forecasting models project only one or two years into the future.[11] Further, when the models are built upon census data (as was the case with the Los Angeles County Planning Council), they are not updated between decennial censuses. Thus, the models become increasingly inaccurate over time. Models are needed that are subject to updating and validity checks.

The traditional forecasting by school districts relies upon variants of the cohort-survival model, which has been associated with as much as ten percent error over three years.[12] Shaw describes the usual format for the cohort survival approach as generally used as a short-range (1–7) years forecasting tool and is based on the calculation of a series of survival rates that indicate the fraction of students in one grade in a given year who "survive" to the next grade the next year. The survival ratios encompass all of the individual factors influencing enrollments, such as death, in-migration, out-migration, retention, annexation, housing changes, and employment changes. Enrollments in the initial grade, most typically kindergarten, are calculated independently on the basis of past birth data.[13]

The University of Houston (through cooperation between the Center for Public Policy [CPP] housed in the College of Social Sciences and the Texas Center for University School Partnerships then housed in the Office of the University President and now part of the College of Education) and Harris County Department of Education have been creating a set of viable forecasting equations and models that will assist local school districts in their planning efforts and will allow for replication in other urban areas in the nation. The process involves the mapping of Census data to attendance zones for the schools within each of the participating districts, followed by the matching of student-level data (according to home address) and block- and block group–level statistics from the Census. Forecasting occurred initially using a "shift-share" model, which is simply the tracking of the shifting shares in population that each sub-area has been of the region and moving that trend forward in time. It takes into account saturation of sub-areas and the reallocation of growth when the sub-areas reach maximum potential. The Census data are then augmented by more current data provided by the Houston-Galveston Area Council and the local utility companies and finally a small area model is built, using twelve equations driven by ten local and national exogenous variables. This aspect of the forecasting was completed by the Center for Public Policy of the University of Houston, a coprincipal investigative partner in the project.

The collaborative effort has been directing services to school districts in Harris County by providing:

- Detailed 1990 Census data by school district, census tract, and census block group
- Biennial estimates of population by age and ethnicity by school district and census tract
- Biennial estimates of land use and land value by district and census tract
- Biennial estimates of employment by Standard Industrial Classification and employee location

- Forecasts for 5-, 10-, 20-year horizons of population and school age population by school district and census tract
- Forecasts for five-year horizon of population by age and ethnicity by school district
- Models for translating current and predictive data into quantifiable forecasts of school-aged children by student status, socioeconomic status (SES), and program needs

Forecasts for Schools in the Houston Metropolitan Area

The 1990 Census for the school-aged population reported that 536,512 children between the ages of 6 and 17 lived in the attendance boundaries of the twenty-five school districts in the study area, with 180,494 living in the central city district's attendance boundary. Since some portion of children under six and some portion of those over seventeen attend school, these figures are conservative. The forecast model developed under the aegis of the grant indicated that by 1995, the population of potential students between the ages of six and seventeen years old living in the attendance boundaries of all districts would grow to nearly 567,000, while the central district would expand to almost 181,000. This metropolitan area figure could be incremented by a portion of the 329,000 children under the age of six estimated to be living in the attendance boundaries of the twenty-five school districts by 1995, while the central school district figure could be increased a portion of the nearly 116,000 children under age six forecast for its attendance zone. By the year 2000, the forecast for six to seventeen year olds is almost 625,000 for all of the districts and 181,000 for the central district, and by the year 2030, the forecasts estimate that over 772,000 children between the ages of six and seventeen will live in the boundaries of the sum of the districts and 173,000 will live in the central district. Again, the 2030 estimates can be incremented by some portion of the children under six in the districts; those figures being over 370,000 across the twenty-five districts and 111,000 in the central district. The purpose for restricting the forecasts to ages six to seventeen was that this population had the highest probability of actually being in school. School participation is voluntary for children under six, and graduation, retention, GED programs, and dropout behaviors make figures for those over seventeen more unstable. Actual enrollments of all ages in the twenty-five districts, as reported by the Texas Education Agency (AEIS reports for 1990 and 1995) amounted to over 574,000 in 1990 and 623,000 in 1995.

The figures that were forecasted for the period between 1990 and 2030 summarize the following trends: growth in the central school district will initially increase slowly through the early years of the new century and then decline; growth in the eastern suburbs will be small, with some districts experiencing slight declines over the time period before regaining their population; growth in the northern and western suburbs will be substantial. The growth in the west and north is occasioned by the availability of land, the relocation of jobs to those areas, and the continued decline of the central business district. The limited growth to the east is a function of limitations on available land and the status of the petrochemical industry. The engines that will drive the total population and ethnic makeup of the region over the ensuing decades is foremost a dramatic increase in the Hispanic population both from natural increases and internal and external immigration, and to a considerably lesser degree, some continued white and Asian American flight, primarily from the central school district and those districts immediately contiguous to it. Beginning in the 1970s, the central urban district changed from predominantly one with a white plurality and a small Hispanic population, to one in which Hispanics currently represent half of the total student body, and whites represent less than 12 percent.

STUDENT LEARNING OUTCOMES MODEL

Estimates of changes in student demography are by themselves important to school districts, as administrators need to establish plans for new campuses, teacher hiring, and programs to meet the needs of students from diverse backgrounds. However, changing demography also has ramifications for test performance and the state-mandated accountability standards to which districts are subjected. Dramatic shifts in student bodies can result in schools that were seen as exemplary at one time period becoming low performing at another. Not only are there financial rewards offered to districts and campuses that have high standardized test scores, there are the possibilities of severe costs, including the loss of accreditation, wholesale firing of staff, and the failure of school bond elections that accrue from continued low student performance. The Texas Education Agency is mandated by the legislature annually to report the passage rates on the Texas Assessment of Academic Skills (TAAS) of all districts and to indicate which districts are exemplary or recognized (both high-performing categories), which are acceptable, and which are low performing. In turn, districts are required to make public the TAAS passage rates of students disaggregated by campus, grade level, and ethnicity. TAAS passage rates within districts frequently appear on the front page of local newspapers, fueling the debate over public confidence in public education. A significant aspect of our work with schools has been to develop models of the factors that affect student learning in each district. Not only do the models estimate the effect of student, campus, and community factors on student achievement, they also provide indications of the potential impact on TAAS performance of future demographic mixes in the districts as estimated by the forecasts. We have used a common core of variables to account for aggregate TAAS performance in reading and mathematics among students in the districts in the metropolitan area, and then have run separate versions of the models on data on individual districts and campuses.

Our general models reflect those adopted by researchers since the release of *The Equality of Educational Opportunity* by Coleman and his associates[14] and are further informed by a myriad of studies that have attempted to isolate factors associated with effective educational practices and student learning. Early studies isolated blocks of student, peer, neighborhood, campus, and teacher effects that are influential in explaining the academic performances of students.[15] More recent work has suggested additional blocks of variables that we found useful in our model.[16]

Common among many of the contemporary models are blocks of variables representing factors that a student brings to the school setting, demographic factors associated with the school itself, peer group factors associated with classmates of the individual student, teacher factors that are experienced by all students in the classroom, as well as neighborhood and even school district effects. Increasingly common is the use of hierarchical analyses to understand the complexity of the different levels of effects on student learning. Early work tended to aggregate campus and teacher demographics to all students, as if all students experienced the mean or median characteristics of teachers or schools identically (such as the percentage of teachers with M.A. degrees or the per capita funding at the school or the district).

The widely used *High School and Beyond* and the *National Educational Longitudinal Survey* have provided researchers with many of the attitudinal effects, but such data sets are national random samples and do not permit the modeling of the classroom experience.[17] By contrast, our longitudinal data consist of all information contained in the permanent record cards and test score tapes; such records do not contain attitudinal information. Our task was then to model some of the effects, without losing significant blocks of data.

The data we used to assess student performance include extensive demographic information on every student in the participating districts for up to four years (1990–91 through 1993–94) and five years in two districts (1994–95 data also included) and TAAS scores and related information on all students tested between 1990 and 1995. Since the 1992–93 TAAS administration, annual test score data are available on one half of all enrolled students. Grades three through eight and ten are routinely tested, while in years prior to 1992–93, selected grades were tested. The population sizes varied from roughly 3,000 students in the smallest district to 202,000 students in the largest. The total database consisted of 506,000 students.

In our reports to school districts, we attempted to capture some of the relevant variables useful in explaining standardized test performances of students in the Houston metropolitan area. Data limitations often necessitated that we utilize surrogate measures for some of the constructs identified in national studies. This was particularly the case when reference group effects, usually measured in other studies in terms of peer attitudes, were included in analyses of data contained in student records. In the reports, we presented a test of a general model, gleaned from our review of current research and based on a demonstration using a less circumscribed data set that includes both student and teacher information collected by the Texas Center for University School Partnerships (TCUSP) in 1992. Finally, we presented a test of the model to each district, using their own data. The intent of the presentation strategy was to permit school district personnel to see what analyses were possible given data resident in the district.

TAAS Scores as the Dependent Variable

Because of its salience to school districts, the dependent variables in our student learning outcome model are the student's performances in mathematics and reading on the state-mandated achievement test. Under pressure from the Texas State Legislature, the Texas Education Agency commissioned National Computer Systems and its subcontractors, the Psychological Corporation and Measurement Incorporated, to develop a criterion-referenced test intended to assess both the problem-solving and critical-thinking skills of the children of Texas public schools in reading, mathematics, and writing. The test, known as the Texas Assessment of Academic Skills (TAAS), was intended to deviate from the previous state practice of testing only minimal or basic skills. Implementation of testing began in October 1990. Beginning in 1994, an attempt was made to develop a vertical scale score system for the TAAS, thereby permitting direct comparison of student progress, year by year. The attempt was abandoned and replaced by a metric known as the Texas Learning Index (TLI), which, like a z-score, gives the relative standing of students, year by year, compared with others. TLI scores have a theoretical maximum of 100, but the empirical maximum at some grade level tests may have maximum scores as low as 91. Further, the content of earlier TAAS tests was not equivalent to later ones. Thus, a passing score on earlier tests was 1500, with a range from around 500 to somewhat over 2200, depending upon year and grade level, while a passing score in later years was 70. The content of the tests also changed. As a result, we often present longitudinal data on TAAS in terms of z-scores.

Selected Empirical Generalizations from the Student Learning Outcome Model

1. The amount of variance explained by the campus and student structural variables and peer variables differed by districts. In some districts, the over-all model could account for more than 50 percent of the total variance, while in others it could account for only ten percent. Factors such as tracking, exemptions from testing of some LEP (Limited English Proficiency) populations, the magnitude of the special education population, and intergenerational stability of minority populations seemed to account for many of the differentials. Districts that have had stable populations and those where the class structure is flattened and where ethnicity and social class are not highly correlated tended to have lower R^2 values than districts that have experienced dynamic population shifts and substantial inequality. Consequently, variances are smaller and hence, less variance could be captured.

2. In most districts, African American children consistently score lower than other children even with the introduction of controls for poverty and other factors. This may be a function of the limitations with the measure of poverty and the persistence of racism in a Southern city. There is a notable exception: in one predominantly African American district with the highest poverty rate in the county, African American student passage rates among students in the lower grades outstrip other high poverty districts and nearly equal that of some relatively affluent, predominantly white districts. This district, once with the lowest test scores and placed in receivership by the state, hired a dynamic superintendent who replaced all the principals and many of the teachers, supplanting them with talented people from all over the state.

3. Some of the smaller, working-class districts, especially those in the eastern part of the county, where the "urban cowboy" stereotype prevails, produce generally lower and more homogeneous test scores. After controlling for LEP status, Hispanic test scores equal those of Anglo students. In these eastern districts parents and even grandparents attended the same schools as their children do, and all expect to continue the family traditions of working in blue-collar jobs in the petrochemical industry. Graduation rates are high in

these districts, as the oil companies require a high school diploma for employment, but parents do not aspire to have their children attend college or attain above-average test performances. Nevertheless, in these districts, African American students had lower TAAS scores than either the Hispanic or Anglo children by as much as one full standard deviation.

4. Asian American academic advantages, even in math, are not uniform across the districts. In districts that have recently experienced a substantial influx of Asian American students who are recent immigrants, Asian Americans are associated with lower performances than other groups.

5. Stability of enrollment (attending the same school until graduation) and family (not being shifted from parent to grandparent each year, for example) universally raises achievement, even if family stability consists of remaining in a single-parent family. We have urged districts to work with social service agencies to encourage parents not to change residences frequently and not to shift children from parent to parent or parent to grandparent if possible. School districts are also working with owners of large apartment complexes to change from offering free rent for the first month to offering free rent for the last month.[18]

6. Poverty and being older than one's classmates generally lower achievement, but in some districts this effect washes out because of enrichment programs directed toward the economically disadvantaged and because of strategies designed not to stigmatize children who are older than their classmates.

7. Students in higher grades perform less well than those in lower grades, reflecting the impact of more recent innovations that have been applied earlier rather than later in a student's career. Additionally, as school districts take more seriously the accountability mandates, they teach more to the test, a test that now more accurately measures the critical skills established by the state. Additionally, early intervention clearly is more effective than intervention in later grades.

8. In a related fashion, test scores have been rising since the implementation of the accountability system, but some of this can be explained by the tendency for some districts to exempt more students from having their tests scored and counted. While exemptions are permitted for LEP and special education students, some districts test fewer of their students than others. Exemption rates sometimes exceed 70 percent of all students in a grade.

9. Gain scores for LEP and special education students and some minorities have been greater than for non-LEP, non-special education, and majorities. This pattern tends to be more common in the suburban districts, especially the smaller suburban districts, than in the large central district. It may reflect the ability of such districts to integrate such students into the campus community because of the smaller scale of such districts and the higher probability that teachers, students, and parents live in the same communities and have established a "functional community."[19] Alternatively, it may reflect the overall lower performance of all students in these small suburban districts.

10. In more working-class districts, girls and boys do not differ in reading performance, but boys perform better in math than girls. In many more middle-class districts, girls perform better in reading than do boys and perform equally to boys in math, at least through the fifth grade.

11. By aggregating the achievement scores for classmates in the same grade and campus, we were able to create a surrogate measure of peer effects. We further created same race peer influence by aggregating only the test scores of classmates of the same race as the individual student. This measure proved to be very interesting. For third graders, the scores of all classmates better predicted individual test performance, but beginning with fourth grade for African American students, the better predictor of individual performance was African American peers. Hispanic peers were a better predictor for Hispanic students from the fifth grade onward, while the whole class remained the better predictor for Anglo and Asian American students across all grades. The results are suggestive of the findings of Ogbu and Mickelson regarding the "cultural myths" about the value of schooling.[20] They may well be passed on from classmate to classmate, especially within ethnic groups.

Poverty, Campus Demography, and Achievement:
A Cross-District Comparison

Presented in table 7.1 are the 1993–94 year TAAS results aggregated across fourteen districts in the Houston area expressed as Texas Learning Index (TLI) scores. Poverty for the children was defined as participation in the free or reduced lunch program, while poverty level for campuses was the percentage of students on a campus participating in the free or reduced lunch program. The analysis links the TAAS performances of individual children with the poverty rate on the campus attended by those children. Unfortunately, reliance upon the free lunch

TABLE 7.1
Elementary School TAAS Performance in TLI Mean Scores by
Poverty Level of Child and Campus for Urban and Suburban Districts

		Urban Districts		*Suburban Districts*	
		TAAS		*TAAS*	
Child	*Campus*	*Math*	*Reading*	*Math*	*Reading*
Subsidized	High Poverty	63.9	72.8	50.3	55.2
lunch	Med. Poverty	62.5	70.2	57.7	64.4
	Low Poverty	66.9	74.8	60.0	66.9
No	High Poverty	65.3	70.9	65.3	72.2
subsidized	Med. Poverty	66.8	74.8	68.5	76.3
lunch	Low Poverty	75.7	83.2	77.5	84.1

measure does not permit us to distinguish between children from relatively low-income families, but whose income is just enough above the poverty line not to qualify for the lunch supplement, and children from much more affluent families. Both would be coded as not on free or reduced lunch. As there is a substantial fall-off in participation in the program after elementary school, only data on elementary school children are presented. The urban district was the central city district, while the suburban districts included all others. The analysis is based upon the scores of nearly 195,000 students who took the TAAS. The aggregated poverty levels of the campuses were trichotomies in which high-poverty schools had two thirds or more of their students on free or reduced lunch, medium-poverty schools had less than two thirds and more than one third of their students on free or reduced lunch, and low-poverty schools had one third or fewer of their students on free or reduced lunch. The cutting points of the trichotomy were chosen to permit both sufficient numbers in each cell while considering the relatively high levels of poverty extant in many school districts.

Table 7.1 displays mean TLI scores in math and reading for the students whose tests were scored (many of the nonscored tests were from students with LEP exemptions and students with significant levels of retardation). To explore the nature of the interaction, the data were analyzed for simple main effects using successive one-way analyses of variance. Scheffe tests revealed that any difference of one or more TLI points was statistically significant. Passing a section of the TAAS test requires a score of 70 TLI points or higher. Thus, in math, the mean score for children on free or reduced lunch was a failing grade in high-, medium-, and low-poverty schools in both types of districts, and a failing grade for children not in poverty for all schools but the low-poverty campuses in both the urban and suburban districts. Children, regardless of their lunch subsidy status, performed better in reading than in math. Higher reading than math scores characterizes TAAS performance throughout the state. The mean scores in reading for all combinations of students and schools in the urban district is a passing grade, but a failing grade for children in poverty in the suburban districts.

With one exception, that being the reading scores in high-poverty urban schools, children in poverty scored lower than those not in poverty at each kind of campus. This exception could be a function of the amount of teachers' time allocated to a child not in poverty in an overwhelmingly low-income school. In addition, in reading in the urban district, children in poverty in the high-poverty urban campuses performed as well (no statistically significant difference) as children not in poverty in the medium-poverty school. There were also no differences in reading in the urban district between children not in poverty in the medium-poverty campuses and children in poverty in the low-poverty campuses.

Children in poverty performed better on the reading and math tests in each type of school poverty level in the urban district than in the suburban districts. On the other hand, children not in poverty performed better in the suburban districts than the urban district, with the exception that there were no differences in math scores between children not in poverty in the high-poverty urban and suburban campuses.

There are several possible explanations for the overall advantage of the urban district over the suburban districts in the teaching of children in poverty. Many of the children in poverty in all of the districts are minority group members. The urban district has vastly greater numbers of minority teachers who can serve as role models than do any of the suburban districts. In addition, the suburban districts have only recently had substantial numbers of children in poverty in their schools. This rapidly changing demography was one of the motivations for school districts to participate in the University of Houston's Urban Community Service project. The suburbs have had less of a history of teaching low-income children who bring to school few educational resources from home than has the urban district. Teaching children who bring few resources to school requires different kinds of teaching skills, many of which have not been expected of suburban teachers. Gary Orfield once commented on the difficulties that many middle-class teachers experienced when they began teaching low-income minority children after the implementation of desegregation plans:

I met many white teachers who said that they didn't realize that they didn't know how to teach because they were teaching in a very pleasant middle-class professional neighborhood. All the kids came in and all the kids went out and went to college, and they all got C's. Then when they had children who came from a more troubled background who needed to be taught, they found that they didn't know how.[21]

Until the influx of minority and low-income children to their districts, many of the suburban schools were able to ignore the small pockets of suburban poverty. The children on free or reduced lunch did not need to excel for suburban districts to show high aggregate passage rates on the tests. By contrast, for decades the urban district has had to educate large numbers of minority children, many of whom live in poverty. Two suburban districts that most resembled the urban district's student body also resembled the urban district's TAAS performance for children in poverty (see table 7.2). One is a predominantly African American district with the highest percentage of children on free or reduced lunch in the metropolitan area (66.4 percent compared to the urban district that has 57.7 percent). The second suburban district has the third highest percentage of children on subsidized lunch (54.7 percent) and has a higher percentage of minority teachers than any suburban district other than the predominantly African American district, and nearly as high a percentage as the urban district. All three districts have had a long history of teaching children in poverty and have had to rely upon the academic performance of the poor to satisfy their accountability mandates.

TABLE 7.2
Elementary School TAAS Performance in TLI Mean Scores by Poverty Level of
Child and Campus for Urban, Diverse, and Other Suburban Districts

Child	Campus	Urban District		Diverse Suburban Districts		Other Suburban Districts	
		TAAS		TAAS		TAAS	
		Math	Reading	Math	Reading	Math	Reading
Subsidized lunch	High Poverty	63.9	72.8	69.8	75.7	44.0	48.6
	Med. Poverty	62.5	70.2	65.1	72.8	52.9	58.8
	Low Poverty	66.9	74.8	72.7	79.2	58.8	65.8
No subsidized lunch	High Poverty	65.3	70.9	72.7	79.1	62.0	69.1
	Med. Poverty	66.8	74.8	70.5	78.8	67.2	74.7
	Low Poverty	75.7	83.2	78.2	85.7	72.1	79.8

Finally, many of the children in poverty also have little stability in their lives. We have been told that some of the schools that have a predominant number of children in poverty on their campuses and also have high TAAS scores rely upon greater amounts of structured instruction, which serves as a kind of anchor for these children. Structured instruction and set routines add predictability and regularity to the lives of the children, many of whom are shuffled from relative to relative. Suburban districts are used to working with children who have much more stability in their lives (even the divorce and abandonment rates in the suburbs are a fraction of those in the inner city) and who can thrive in the absence of structured instruction.

Table 7.2 represents a disaggregation of the data presented in table 7.1. The suburban districts with high percentages of children on subsidized lunches, a relatively long history of teaching children in poverty, and a high percentage of minority faculty are separated out from the other suburban districts. The table lends support to the previous contention that the urban district's advantages stem from experience with children in poverty and a high percentage of minority faculty. As evident in table 7.2, the urban district even more substantially outperforms those suburban districts with few minority faculty and a limited history of working with children in poverty in reading and math among children in poverty. In fact, the children not in poverty in the low poverty schools even outperform their suburban counterparts. By contrast, the suburban districts with a history of teaching children in poverty outperform the urban district and greatly outperform the other suburban districts. Even children not in poverty do better in these suburban districts than comparable children do in the other suburbs. Perhaps the reduced organizational scale and complexity that allows for the quick adoption of innovations, conjoined with a history of working with a diverse student body result in academic benefits for all.

The findings presented in tables 7.1 and 7.2 have implications for the issues of school choice and voucher plans discussed in Texas. If children living in poverty perform less well in most suburban school districts than in the urban district, and the reasons are associated with the inability of many suburban schools to meet the needs of these children, voucher plans that send inner-city children to the suburbs may actually lower the test performances of the children. These findings are tentative and will require further analysis.

ONGOING ROLES IN SOCIOLOGY OF EDUCATION BEYOND FEDERAL FUNDING: A RESEARCH SHOP FOR SMALLER DISTRICTS

In an effort to support our continued research interests, fund our students, and serve the research needs of some of the districts in our

Urban Community Service Program, we have become an off-site research department for smaller school districts. These smaller districts in the metropolitan area do not have the operating budgets to hire a full-time research staff, often costing $30,000 to $50,000 per year plus fringe benefits per staff member. Districts have often relied upon the regional educational service centers operated by the state education agency. However, district employees often complain that the state agency is either unresponsive to their needs or is overworked to the extent that they cannot address the district's research issues. A few districts have banded together to form a collaborative, but by its very nature the collaborative can address only issues held in common by the participating districts. With increased state and corporate demands for school accountability, especially as it relies almost exclusively on the TAAS, districts are in greater need for quantitative research on student learning. TCUSP has signed research contracts with several districts to serve as their research departments. A standard package includes the use of our student learning outcome model to explain achievement results, the assessment of nonschool factors, such as neighborhood demographics and community resources to predict passage rates on the test and to isolate policies, practices, and programs that may affect TAAS passage, and the presentation of the findings to the school board, the superintendent, community and corporate groups, and to appear at press conferences for the districts. Itemized below are a few of the additional services we have provided for the districts. These represent aspects of our "urban extension," or "off-site research department" model.

Determining District Capture Rates

The availability of updated Census data linked to school attendance boundaries allows us to compare the number of school-aged children living in an attendance zone with school data (from the aggregated PEIMS [Public Education Information Management System] database maintained by the Texas Education Agency) to determine what percentage of the school-aged population was being captured by the districts. Since the Census information and those data supplied by the National Center for Educational Statistics also had information on public and private school enrollments, as well as numbers of children of school age not enrolled in schools, districts could then assess how effective they had been in attracting children of school age to their campuses. In general, districts captured 70 to 80 percent of the eligible students, although low-performing districts tended to capture a much smaller percentage of Anglo American and Asian American school-aged children who lived in the attendance zones. Likewise, as the percentage of African American and

Hispanic students in a district increased, the capture rate for Anglo and Asian Americans diminished, even in districts where test scores were comparable to those districts with smaller minority populations. Such discrepancies in capture rates reflect prejudice and stereotyping about the "educational costs" of sending one's children to districts with high minority populations. The largest urban district captured 94.6 percent of the Hispanic students, 94.6 percent of the African American students, 85.0 percent of the Asian American students, and 63.3 percent of the white (Anglo) students living within the attendance zone boundaries. Further inspection revealed that in the largest district approximately 4 percent of those not in school, but of school age, were in neither public nor private schools. Some districts have viewed these results as a challenge to locate and enroll students not currently in any school by targeting neighborhoods where student undercounts were highest. It must be recognized that there the student enrollment data used in the analysis lag behind the Census data by six months, as the 1990 Census enumeration was conducted in April and the PEIMS count was in October. This introduces some marginal amount of error in the estimation of the "capture rate."

Parental Educational Resources

Another analysis incorporated the Census data on percentages of adults without any college education as one of a group of predictors of student achievement. A few of the districts in the eastern part of the county are in communities where generation after generation of adults have worked in the local petrochemical plants as blue-collar workers. While income levels are high enough to produce smaller than average percentages of children on lunch subsidies, test scores are generally not commensurate with income or even property tax revenues generated. Parents often did not strongly urge their children to consider going to college, except to obtain technical training at a community college, as they and their parents had not attended college. They assumed that the children would graduate from high school and enter the same petrochemical jobs that they had. Unfortunately, many forecasts suggest that many of these jobs will disappear in the next century, seriously handicapping the children in the labor market of the twenty-first century. Students were not taking advanced courses and gifted and talented children were not enrolling in the accelerated programs. Our analyses have permitted school district personnel to explain the lower than expected test performance to petrochemical executives, while identifying strategies to increase advanced course taking and college applications in these districts. The districts are going to work with the employers to convince parents of the educational needs of the future labor force. The expectation is that test scores will eventually rise as the curriculum becomes more challenging and as more students have college goals. While the model building using school and Census data has the potential of providing school districts with an "out" to explain away low student performance, we have viewed our role as not merely to explain results, but to isolate practices that may attenuate achievement.

Interdistrict Comparisons on TAAS Passage Rates

We have established regression lines for TAAS passage, locating campuses within districts that are performing above, at, or below expectation given the rates of poverty on the campus. Error bands are computed to locate similarly performing campuses. Next, the rate of exemption from having a test scored is determined. This permits districts to compare their passage rate, that is, poverty levels with similar districts, and to discern whether some districts are taking advantage of the regulations that allow the exemption of some LEP and special education students. Districts that test all students tend to appear to perform below expectation, while districts that selectively exempt potential low scorers who fit the established categories tend to perform above expectation. Further analysis has revealed which of the exempted students actually would have performed well enough to pass the test, thereby permitting districts to reclassify children and end the labeling of such children as LEP or special education students.

Locating Underserved Populations

The socioeconomic status of children in school districts is most commonly measured by free or reduced lunch status. Annually, districts send out applications for lunch subsidies to parents and when verified, the children become eligible for benefits beyond meals, including Title I activities, compensatory education resources, and the like. However, because free lunch status is often stigmatizing to middle and high school students, there is a substantial fall off in participation beyond the elementary grades. For example, in the largest school district in our study (student body size is 202,000), over 70 percent of the elementary school students were in the free/reduced lunch count, but fewer than 40 percent of the middle and high school students were so registered. In many of the smaller districts, the free lunch count for high school juniors and seniors fell to less than 22 percent of the participation rate among first and second graders. The consequence is that there exists a severe underestimation of poverty rates in higher grades in schools, especially as there is considerable reason to expect that poverty is fairly uniform within a family. Not only does the undercount affect statistical model-ing of the impact of poverty on student learning and diminish the oppor-tunities for low-income students to eat during the school day; it also reduces the state compensatory educational funding for the school dis-tricts. Under the Texas school finance system, property-poor districts receive up $800 per child per year in funding for resources for disad-vantaged children on the lunch subsidy roll, while property-rich districts avoid up to $1,000 per child per year in state recapture payments for each child on the roll (Texas Education Agency). These monies are sep-arate from the lunch subsidy per se, but their funding formula is driven by the lunch subsidy count. It is not actually necessary for students to receive the subsidized lunches for a district to receive the state compen-satory education funds, which can then be used to hire additional staff, purchase computers for the classrooms, augment the campus library, or meet any other educational purpose.

We utilize our data on every child enrolled in the districts to locate children whose siblings are on the free/reduced lunch count. Matching students by address alone has increased the estimated free/reduced lunch count by about 8.6 percent per district, or by as many as 10,100 students in the largest district and by 150 to 2,200 students in most of the other districts. A more refined technique that we have identified as "Operation Child Find," has been conducted for districts that have agreed to contact each parent and certify the children using the current year's data matches students on combinations of same surname, same address, and same tele-phone number. Triple matches (same surname, address, and phone num-ber) provide almost certain additions to the count. Double matches pro-vide somewhat lower probabilities of success in adding to the count. That is, matches by surname and phone number may involve a mismatch by address because of differences in the spelling of the address or data entry errors; matches by surname and address may involve a mismatch by phone number because one child used a parent's work phone, while another used a parent's home phone; and matches by address and phone number may involve a mismatch by surname because the children had different fathers. Other factors which may reduce the chance of compen-satory funding might include the possibility that the previously unidenti-fied child has already dropped out of school, has moved to another dis-trict, no longer is in the custody of a low-income parent, or lives with a parent who refuses to grant the district permission to certify the child. As such, rarely will the technique add more than one quarter of the identi-fied children to the free/reduced lunch count for the district, and thus, districts are likely to receive between 10 and 30 percent of the compen-satory education funding from the state. Nevertheless, to date this has brought in over $1 million to a group of smaller districts.

More accurate free lunch counts also improve the explanatory power of that variable in accounting for student achievement. The zero-order effect of free/reduced lunch status as determined from the school district data has been $b = -.210$ ($s.e. = .030, t = -7.06$). By contrast, reclassifying the siblings of children on free/reduced lunch status has increased the effect size of poverty on student achievement to $b = -.310$ ($s.e. = .037, t = -8.20$). With the very large data sets, the increment in b is statistically significant.

An additional component of our work with the free/reduced lunch count has been to advise districts on ways of increasing eligible student participation in the subsidized lunch program. Older students are frequently afraid that participation in the program will lead to teasing by classmates. To reduce the stigma of lunch subsidies we have urged school districts to eliminate separate lines for free or reduced lunch students, issue all students meal cards that bear no indication that the meals have been subsidized or purchased by parents, and eliminate the practice in middle and high schools of having teachers ask students to come forward and request lunch subsidy application forms during class. One district has installed a computer-activated debit card system so that all students and even teachers use an identical card. Only key administrators know whether the individual or the subsidy pays the funding of the card's balance.

Another underserved population that can be located using our database are LEP students who are not enrolled in programs. In many urban areas, up to 10 percent of the LEP students are not in bilingual or ESL programs and have not received waivers to be placed in regular programs. They simply get lost in the system. As we have data on every student in the school districts, we can locate such students and notify the districts. Districts then initiate the paperwork to determine the preferences of the children's parents and then assign students to programs. The slippage in assignment of LEP children is a serious problem, one in which the parents of the children, many of whom are immigrants and are themselves non-English speakers, have little voice in the schools. There are few advocates for either the children or the parents and too often the schools appear not to care. In part this is because the schools are overwhelmed by the numbers; in part, it is because immigrants and minorities often have much less political and social capital; and finally, it is because surveys conducted by the school districts repeatedly reveal that Hispanic parents, especially those who are relatively recent immigrants, are most likely to report that the schools are doing an excellent job in teaching their children. Reductions in Title VII funding are likely to mean that even more LEP students will get lost in the system. It has become one of our assumed responsibilities to goad school districts by reporting the slippage.

CONCLUSIONS, CONCERNS, AND RECOMMENDATIONS

The Urban Community Service Program was developed to enable universities to assist public agencies, including public schools, to create plausible responses to the plethora of problems present in urban areas. As the program ends, many of the funded projects are seeking strategies to continue their work, as well as continue the funding of their staffs. During the course of the project we developed a forecasting model for urban schools, projecting enrollment characteristics through the year 2030. The urban district utilized the forecasts to determine siting of new campuses that would have been funded by a $390 million school bond election (unfortunately, the voters defeated the bond election). Other districts are using the forecasts to plan for the substantial demographic change they are experiencing, especially large increases in minority and low-income students and students with limited proficiency in English. To understand the impact of the changing demography on state-mandated accountability standards, we developed a student learning outcome model, containing the variables usually associated with sociological research on student achievement.

Since the end of federal funding, we have adopted the role of research department for many of the smaller school districts. Work with small districts has its pitfalls. Often the districts have been infrequent consumers of research. They may not know how to phrase researchable questions, or they expect us to tell them what questions they need to raise, or they may raise questions that can not be answered with existing data, but do not want to fund the collection of new data. However, as district administrators become more familiar with the benefits of research into their students' performances, some districts develop limitless interest in asking questions, but no awareness of how much data analysis costs. It is advisable to develop a research contract that specifies what can be done for a given quantity of funds. A research contract that specifies what is to be delivered, when, and for how much is a necessary protection of the research shop. Additional services then become defined as needing additional compensation. Finally, the transition from research funded by the federal project and the research contracted by the school districts is sometimes a difficult one to negotiate. Small districts may not have budgeted for the research services and sometimes will attempt to redefine the research as merely part of the federal project. One district administrator pointed out that he had no funds to pay for the contracted services and had assumed that we were not really going to charge him for the services. It is an ongoing problem, although some districts later allocated funds for the research services in their future budgets.

The student learning outcomes model that we developed, with its inclusion of neighborhood and parental resource factors, has the potential of creating new dilemmas, including those associated with split loyalties. Specifically, below the surface are always issues of "whose side are you on?" Nonschool factors permit school districts to shift the onus of blame for low achievement from themselves to their communities, students, and the parents of their students. While schools have often explained poor achievement by looking to parental involvement and student commitment, we offer the potential of hard data to support their claims. When faced with corporate stakeholders who ask why the students of their district have low passage rates on the TAAS, despite relatively high property tax rates in a district, school boards and superintendents appreciate a model that incorporates nonschool variables that have substantial explanatory power.

In fact, three variables describing communities that have significant effect sizes on the percentage of students in a district that pass the TAAS include the percentage of children on free or reduced lunch ($b = -.44$), percentage of female parents with no college experience ($b = -.60$), and percentage of male parents with college degrees ($b = .68$). Thus, for each increment of a percentage point in the poverty rate of children, there is a drop of almost a half of a percentage point in the passage rate of the TAAS; while each increment in the percentage of female parents without college lowers the passage rate by sixth tenths of a percent; and each increment in the percentage of male parents with college degrees raises the percentage rate of TAAS passage by over two thirds of a point.

While these community resource effects do account for a significant amount of the variance in student achievement, they enable schools to report to taxpayers, state governmental bodies, and the business community that they can only do a limited amount with the resources and students they have.

The desire for school districts to shift blame is understandable. Elsewhere, we have written about the hierarchy of distrust that has become more pervasive since the recent waves of school reform.[22] The public has reported decreasing confidence in public education, as exemplified by two decades of Phi Delta Kappan polls conducted by the Gallup Organization (See any of the Phi Delta Kappan "Annual Gallup Polls"). States have enacted school reform legislation in terms of new curricular standards, competency testing of teachers, more stringent graduation standards, and heightened demands for public school accountability. In Texas, as in many other states, the new accountability systems gave decision-makers access to information on how well schools were doing in serving their students. The accountability system further had built-in rewards and punishments, making it imperative to school administrators that their children perform well on standardized tests, not drop out, and graduate within a prescribed period. Competency testing of teachers begun in the 1980s resulted in the removal of teaching certificates and forced resignations of several thousand teachers, many from minority groups.[23] Districts in which student performances on the standardized tests have been consistently low have been taken over by the state education agency, had their superintendents and boards removed, and campuses where students consistently failed the standardized tests have been reorganized into charter schools or have experienced the wholesale termination of faculty and principals.

Later waves of school reform and restructuring included state-mandated site-based management plans and decentralized decision-making, which often resulted in vesting much more power in the hands of principals, while simultaneously holding them more directly responsible for the test score performances of their children. Since the state education agency authorized exemptions of some categories of LEP and special education students, principals had the means to determine which students took the test, and hence, how well their campuses performed. Not uncommon was the practice in some schools and districts of exempting a majority of the students in a grade from taking the TAAS (one of the participating districts was subject to a TEA investigation because of excessive numbers of exemptions). It was understandably the case that those children exempted either had been low scorers on the previous year's exam, or were expected to perform poorly on the exam that was to be administered. Decentralization of decision-making meant that central district offices were frequently unaware why test scores on some campuses rose dramatically from year to year. The use of our database provided districts with insights into campus practices.

Blame shifting is rampant. In our research relationship with the districts we have attempted to focus upon programs and practices that could nevertheless facilitate student learning, even in the presence of the community demographics. That is, we sometimes function as an external gadfly, reminding the smaller districts of resources available to them that could enhance student learning and some of their practices that have tended to diminish outcomes. Additionally, we have employed a rule that we will never willingly help a school district get around the state accountability criteria. Rather, we often explore with district administrators changes in practices that might help to raise student achievement in order to meet the state's accountability standards. It is important to recognize that the ultimate beneficiary of the research endeavor ought to be the children in the schools.

An example of our gadfly role occurred in the districts in the eastern part of the county. Low rates of parental college attendance significantly accounted for the lower than expected TAAS performances of the students. The districts also had lower than expected participation rates of their students in gifted and talented programs and in advanced courses in high school. The superintendent noted that the parents do not expect their children to go to college and seem satisfied with the education their children get. These districts are linked to the petrochemical industry and the children expect to follow their parents and grandparents into blue-collar jobs in the communities. We pointed out the forecasted downturn in employment in high-paying blue-collar jobs and expectation that good jobs, even in the petrochemical industry will require college degrees and even graduate training. We then urged the superintendent to speak to the petrochemical stakeholders to offer to inform their employees of the need for their children to go to college.

This chapter began with the promise that we would address three issues relevant to urban education. First, the use of forecasting models for school districts that are experiencing rapid demographic change, and this clearly typifies most districts in metropolitan areas, is essential. Without the ability to anticipate new populations school districts are likely to continue to offer programs and curricula that increasingly fail to address the needs of their students. Simple cohort survival models, as are used by many urban districts, are inadequate, as they utilize recent student populations to predict future ones. If new populations are entering neighborhoods as a result of changing housing characteristics and political and economic forces in the region or the nation, then data based upon neighborhood dynamics will be more useful than school-based information. While the school districts in metropolitan Houston could not anticipate future civil wars and monetary crises in Latin America and Asia, they could take into consideration the state of housing stocks, and transportation systems, and should be attentive to recent changes in neighborhood compositions. Each of the school districts in which we work now concerns themselves with more accurate and more frequent forecasts.

Second, we offered a student learning outcomes model that revealed numerous unexpected results. The sociological and educational literature is replete with national studies that aggregate data across school districts and do not capture entire districts, campuses, and classrooms. Our work does not suffer in that sense; yet, there is sufficient interdistrict diversity that common structural variables applied across different parts of the metropolitan area have substantially different effect sizes. Knowing the ethnicity, the level of poverty, or the family constellation of students in different districts in the county will not assure one of capturing similar amounts of variance. The effect sizes of these structural variables are greater for new residents than for children whose parents and grandparents attended the same schools.

Most interesting and potentially most disturbing are the differing effects of poverty status on student achievement among children in urban and suburban districts. The issue appears to be whether the district considers the teaching of children in poverty as its prime mandate. The data suggest strongly that urban schools and those suburban districts with large numbers of minority faculty and an extensive history of serving low-income students should not be abandoned to the more affluent suburbs, especially by low-income parents hoping to use vouchers to purchase a quality education for their children. Nevertheless, all suburbs are experiencing the influx of a more diverse student body, including children from more economically disadvantaged backgrounds. It is vital that those suburbs view the academic success of all of their students as central to their mandate. There is a great need for increased ethnic diversity among the teaching populations in the suburbs and there is much that the suburbs can learn from the urban districts. Quite simply, the suburbs will not remain bastions of privilege.

Finally, we recommend our "outsourced" research department approach as a strategy for academic researchers. We have recently had our contracts with our districts renewed. Districts find that sociologists can offer structural explanations for the dynamics that affect their campuses and welcome our efforts to explain how TAAS works in their districts. We are not always bearers of good news. While some in academia believe that school districts will not want to work with researchers who find that programs are not working or that district performances are significantly below the regression lines, the reality is that most superintendents want accurate information and not glowing myths. Eventually, the myths are shattered by the dynamics of demographic change.

NOTES

1. The research presented in this chapter was supported in part by a U.S. Department of Education, Urban Community Service grant (P252A20004–94).

2. K. Geiger, *The Cost of Excellence* (Washington, D.C.: National Education Agency, 1992).

3. National Commission on Excellence in Education, *A Nation at Risk: The Imperative for Educational Reform* (Washington, D.C.: U.S. Government Printing Office, 1983).

4. M. Haberman, "Urban Schools and the Problems They Face," in *A Framework for Educational Excellence*, ed. The Greater Houston Partnership (Houston, Tex., 1990), pp. E1–3.

5. J. Waldrop, "2010," *American Demographics* 11 (1989): 53–55.

6. K. M. Borman and J. H. Spring, *Schools in Central Cities: Structure and Process* (New York: Longmann, 1984); W. J. Wilson, *The Truly Disadvantaged: The Inner City, the Underclass, and Public Policy* (Chicago: University of

Chicago Press, 1987); and M. D. LeCompte and A. G. Dworkin, *Giving Up On School: Student Dropouts and Teacher Burnouts.* (Newbury Park, Calif.: Corwin/Sage, 1991).

7. Borman and Spring, *Schools in Central Cities.*

8. A. G. Dworkin, *Teacher Burnout in the Public Schools: Structural Causes and Consequences for Children* (Albany: State University of New York Press, 1987).

9. L. Warshay, " Breadth of Perspective," in *Human Behavior and Social Process*, ed. A. Rose (Boston: Houghton Mifflin Company, 1962), pp. 148–76.

10. T. Hart and L. Lumsen, *Demographic Analysis: Using Today's Data to Plan for Tomorrow's Schools* (Portland: Oregon School Study Council, 1990).

11. Ibid.

12. See, e.g., R. C. Shaw, "Enrollment Forecasting: What Methods Work Best? *NASSP Bulletin* 68 (1984): 52–58, and W. B. Strong and R. R. Schulz. "Models for Projecting School Enrollment," *Educational Evaluation and Policy Analysis* 3 (1981): 75–81.

13. Shaw, "Enrollment Forecasting," pp. 52–58.

14. J. S. Coleman, E. Q. Campbell, C. J. Hobson, J. McPartland, A. M. Mood, F. D. Weinfeld, and R. L. York, *The Equality of Educational Opportunity* (Washington, D.C.: U.S. Government Printing Office, 1966).

15. See, e.g., S. S. Bowles and H. M. Levin, "More on Multicollinearity and the Effectiveness of Schools," *Journal of Human Resources* 3 (1968): 393–400; M. T. Katzman, *The Political Economy of Urban Schools* (Cambridge: Harvard University Press, 1971); E. A. Hanuschek, *Education and Race* (Lexington, Mass.: Lexington Books, 1972); C. Jencks, Smith M., H. Acland, M. J. Bane, D. Cohen, H. Gintis, B. Heyns, and S. Michelson, *Inequality: A Reassessment of the Effects of Family and Schooling in America* (New York: Basic Books, 1972); and R. J. Murnane, *The Impact of School Resources on the Learning of Inner City Children* (Cambridge, Mass.: Ballinger, 1975).

16. See, e.g., more recent work by Dworkin, *Teacher Burnout*; LeCompte and Dworkin, *Giving Up On School*; and national studies by J. S. Coleman, T. Hoffer, and S. Kilgore, *High School Achievement* (New York: Basic Books, 1982); G. Cohen and R. A. Lotan, "Can Classrooms Learn?" *Sociology of Education* 62 (1989): 75–94; J. S. Coleman and T. Hoffer, *Public and Private High Schools: The Impact of Communities* (Basic Books: New York, 1987); D. R. Entwisle and L. A. Hayduk, "Lasting Effects of Elementary School," *Sociology of Education* 61 (1988): 147–59; Gamoran, "The Stratification of High School Learning Opportunities," *Sociology of Education* 60 (1987): 135–55; C. L. Garner and S. W. Raudenbush, "Neighborhood Effects on Educational Attainment: A Multilevel Analysis," *Sociology of Education* 64 (1991): 251–62; M. T. Hallinan and R. A. Williams, "Students' Characteristics and the Peer-Influence Process," *Sociology of Education* 63 (1990): 122–32; V. E. Lee and A. S. Bryk, "Curriculum Tracking as Mediating the Social Distribution of High School Achievement," *Sociology of Education* 61 (1988): 78–94; V. E. Lee and A. S. Bryk, "A Multilevel Model of the Social Distribution of High School Achievement," *Sociology of Education* 62 (1989): 172–92; J. D. Willms, *Monitoring School Performance: A Guide for Educators* (Washington, D.C.: The Falmer

Press, 1992); V. E. Lee and J. B. Smith, "Effects of School Restructuring on the Achievement and Engagement of Middle-Grade Students," *Sociology of Education* 6 (1993): 164–87; and K. Namboodri, R. G. Corwin, and L. E. Dorsten "Analyzing Distributions in School Effects Research: An Empirical Illustration," *Sociology of Education* 66 (1993): 278–94.

17. See especially, Coleman, Hoffer, and Kilgore, *High School Achievement*; and Lee and Bryk, "Curriculum Tracking."

18. Greater Houston Partnership, eds., *A Framework for Educational Excellence* (Houston, Tex., 1990).

19. Coleman and Hoffer, *Public and Private High Schools*.

20. J. U. Ogbu, "Minority Status and Schooling in Plural Societies," *Comparative Education Review* 27 (1983): 168–90; and R. A. Mickelson, "The Attitude-Achievement Paradox among Black Adolescents," *Sociology of Education* 63 (1990): 44–61.

21. G. Orfield, "Examining the Desegregation Process," *Integrated Education* 13 (1975): 127–30.

22. Dworkin, *Teacher Burnout*; LeCompte and Dworkin, *Giving Up On School*; and A. G. Dworkin. "Coping with Reform: The Intermix of Teacher Morale, Teacher Burnout and Teacher Accountability," in *The International Handbook of Teachers and Teaching*, ed. B. J. Biddle, T. L. Good, and I. F. Goodson, (Dordrecht, The Netherlands: Kluwer Academic Publishers, 1997).

23. Texas Education Agency, "Performance on the Texas Examination of Current Administrators and Teachers: March 1986 Administration," Austin, Texas, mimeograph.

CHAPTER 8

Gangsta Pedagogy and Ghettocentricity: The Hip-Hop Nation as Counterpublic Sphere

Peter McLaren

Race is the modality in which class is lived.
      —Eric Lott, "Cornel West in the Hour of Chaos"

I was beautiful; after all, my skin was as rich and as dark as wet, brown mud, a complexion that any and every pale white girl would pray for. . . . My butt sat high in the air and my hips obviously gave birth to Creation.
                    —Sister Souljah, *No Disrespect*

>   Black athletes . . . white agents
>   Black preacher . . . white Jesus
>   Black entertainers . . . white lawyers
>   Black Monday . . . white Christmas
>   —Chuck D, "White Heaven . . . Black Hell"

When Harvard scholar Henry Louis Gates Jr. defended the imagery and lyrics of 2 Live Crew at their highly publicized 1990 trial, claiming that the group's album, *As Nasty as They Wanna Be,* was not obscene on the grounds that the lyrics and imagery were derived from the venerable African American tradition of "signifying" and "playing the dozens," no doubt many critics were thinking that the controversy over rap would probably go the way of the debates over rock 'n' roll in the 1950s: it would generally "fade away." At the time of the trial it was difficult to imagine not only the public furor over rap music—gangsta rap in particular—but also the extent to which Washington would develop its anti-rap campaign, signaling a "moral panic" destined to become one of the lightning rods in the 1996 presidential campaign and a flashpoint in the current debate over race relations. As former Secretary of Education and Drug Czar William J. Bennett joins forces with C. DeLores Tucker, the conservative activist with the National Political Caucus of Black Women, to publicly denounce gangsta rap as a seductive, immoral force, presidential candidates, Bob Dole, Phil Gramm, and Pat Buchanan have decided not only to join in the condemnation of Time Warner (which up to the time of this writing owns interests in a number of rap record labels) but also to launch a frontal assault on Hollywood's entertainment industry and all those liberals who were likely to defend affirmative action, government assistance programs for nondocumented workers, or gay-rights initiatives.

Despite the fact that the Geto Boys' lead rapper, Bushwick Bill, recently thanked Dole for $300,000 worth of publicity,[1] the attacks have had a considerable negative effect on the rap industry, prompting Time Warner to fire record executive Doug Morris and to be reportedly (as of this writing) negotiating its way out of a $100 million share in Interscope Records, distributor of Snoop Doggy Dogg, Dr. Dre, and Tupac Shakur.[2]

Gangsta rappers follow a long line of musicians denounced by the moral custodians of U.S. culture as prime instigators of juvenile delinquency—a list that includes, among others, Frank Sinatra, Elvis, the Beatles, the Sex Pistols, Metallica, and Prince. Members of my generation, puzzling over the 2 Live Crew trial or reflecting on the earlier public debates surrounding the subliminal messages purportedly inserted into songs by Judas Priest and Ozzy Osborne, are perhaps reminded of earlier controversies that accompanied the Rolling Stones' hit "Satisfaction," or the two-and-a-half-year analysis by J. Edgar Hoover's G-men of the Kingsmen's 1963 hit, "Louie, Louie."[3] The investigation by FBI sound technicians and cryptographers of this pop chant (which merely recounts a lovesick sailor's return to his Jamaican sweetheart) seems ironic now, given the fact that the teen anthem has since appeared as the backdrop of numerous films, charity telethons, and wine cooler ads.[4] The debate over gangsta rap has captured the public imagination at a time when the nation is vigorously reevaluating public policies surrounding affirmative action and urban reform. This has given gangsta rap an urgency and public visibility far greater than earlier debates over rock 'n' roll and morality. Sister Souljah had been criticized by President Clinton and others for inciting violence against white people when in fact she had told a journalist only that she could understand why some black people might want to kill white people: "In the mind of a gang member, why not kill white people? In other words, if you've been neglected by the social and economic order of America, and you've become casual about killing, you would have no hesitancy about killing somebody white."[5] In providing a sociological insight she was roundly condemned—unfairly—as a hate-monger. Rapper Chuck D maintains that rappers themselves don't necessarily feel violent toward whites. Rappers are contemporary urban messengers from God: "It's not me, or Ice Cube, or Sister Souljah's feelings—we're just the messengers, and how you gonna kill the messenger? The best thing about rap is it's a last-minute warning, the final call . . . a last plea for help on the countdown to Armageddon."[6] Chuck D sees rap as the 'hood's equivalent of CNN.

As I complete some final editing to this essay, which takes the form of an interrogative excursion into the subject of gangsta rap, the *Los Angeles Times* reports that rap singer Dasean Cooper (J-Dee), a member of Da Lench Mob, was recently sentenced to twenty-nine years to life for the 1993 murder of his girlfriend's male roommate at a party in Inglewood.[7] Terry (T-Bone) Gray, another member of Da Lench Mob, has also been charged with murdering one individual—and wounding another—at a Los Angeles bowling alley. Da Lench Mob's 1992 single, "Who You Gonna Shoots Wit Dat," was cited in the Cooper case by the prosecuting attorney in an attempt to paint murders by rap artists as "life imitating art." Criminal charges have recently been filed against Snoop Doggy Dogg (who is awaiting trial for allegedly driving the getaway car during a murder) and Tupac Amaru Shakur, San Francisco Bay Area rapper and former member of the Digital Underground (arrested for sexually assaulting a nineteen-year-old woman whom he and his friends had held captive in a hotel room). The widow of slain Texas police officer Bill Davidson has sued Tupac for allegedly inciting a nineteen-year-old car thief, Ronald Ray Howard, to murder Davidson with a nine-millimeter pistol. After listening to the mantra-like lyrics of Shakur's song "Crooked Ass Nigga," from his album *2Pacalypse Now,* which describes a drug dealer on a rampage with a nine-millimeter pistol and contains a reference to "droppin' the cop," Howard claims that he "snapped" and shot Davidson as a result of being instructed by the lyrics. Dan Quayle cashed in on the media attention by visiting Davidson's grieving daughter and announcing that Tupac's music 'has no place in our society." These events have induced the breach birth of the gangsta rap media elite and have added to hip-hop's hype as hard-edged urban drama muscled onto a compact disc. (As the original printing of this chapter went into production, Tupac lay dead of gunshot wounds that he received in Las Vegas after attending the Mike Tyson–Bruce Seldon boxing match. He was shot while driving in a car with Death Row

Records co-founder and president, Marion "Suge" Knight.) Although he bragged defiantly about the tough life in the 'hood, and had "Thug Life" and an AK-47 assault weapon tattooed across his abdomen, his Grammy-nominated 1995 hit single, "Dear Mama," was a tender ballad written for his mother. Tupac's mother, Afeni Shakur, was a member of the Black Panther Party and was pregnant with Tupac while she was serving time in a New York prison for allegedly plotting to blow up department stores and police stations. He sang: "Even as a crack fiend always was a black queen." The name Tupac Amaru comes from a sixteenth-century Incan chief whose name means "shining serpent." Tupac Amaru was the last Incan leader to be defeated by the Spanish. He was executed in 1572. The Tupac Amaru Revolutionary Movement led by Nestor Cerpa Cartolini is currently holding hundreds of international diplomats hostage in the Japanese embassy in Lima, Peru. Tupac's posthumous *The Don Killuminati: The 7 Day Theory* is expected to replace the Beatles' *Anthology 3* as the nation's best-selling album.

Eazy-E's recent death from AIDS (Eazy-E was a former member of NWA, a financial contributor to the Republican Party and the head of Ruthless Records, the first significant rapper-owned record label) has left the hip-hop nation stunned. Early this April, the Los Angeles Police Department joined with FBI agents in Operation Sunrise, sweeping through a thirty-block area of South Central Los Angeles, arresting gang members of the Eight-Tray Gangster Crips, a gang that came into public prominence during the 1992 uprising with its involvement in the attack on truck driver Reginald O. Denny and other motorists at the intersection of Florence and Normandie. East LA Chicanos are still recovering from the news of the slaying of Selena, superstar of Tejano music and heroine of Molinatown's Chicano barrio in Corpus Christi. Among gangsta rappers, the mood of the city felt all too familiar.

By late October, when jury selection in the murder trial of Snoop Doggy Dogg, his bodyguard, and his friend began in Los Angeles, defense attorneys (including Johnnie L. Cochran Jr.) were preparing to "play the LAPD card" in their attack on police evidence tampering. In the post-Simpson era, the lawyers representing Snoop Doggy Dogg (a.k.a. Calvin Broadus, former member of the Long Beach Insane Crips) and his associates stand a good chance of landing further blows to the credibility and integrity of the police. A few months earlier Snoop Doggy Dogg was praised by President Bill Clinton and Ice-T for writing a letter to sixty gang sets in Los Angeles and honoring their efforts to "keep the peace." As Snoop Doggy Dogg's words of thanks were sounded at a celebration at the International House of Blues in West Los Angeles, sets from the Imperial Courts, Jordan Downs, and Nickerson Gardens housing projects in Watts sat down with the Fruit Town Pirus of Compton and sets from Long Beach, the Pueblo Bishops 5 Duce Mid-City Gangsters, the 5 Duce BCG, the Santana Block Crips, the V-13s and Shoreline Crips of Venice, and the Parkside Manor Circle City Pirus of Los Angeles. When, at this afternoon gala, a Crip, a Blood, and a Latino gang member cut a cake in unison, gangsta rappers had symbolically joined forces with Bill Clinton's four-member Color Guard, present at the ceremonies as a sign of "respect."

For someone who grew up listening to Robert Johnson's Delta Blues, who used to frequent the Colonial Tavern on Toronto's Yonge Street to hear musician friends jam with Muddy Waters, who idolized Lightning Hopkins, and who wanted to play the blues harp like Little Walter, rap music was not a natural transition for me. Ska, rock-steady, and reggae helped to broaden my musical sensibilities, but, even so, rap was a taste that was difficult to acquire at first. In recent years I have grown to greatly appreciate gangsta rap as an oppositional political practice, but despite its possibilities for articulating an oppositional performative politics, gangsta rap remains, in some senses, a problematic cultural practice. In this article I am generally referring to *gangsta rap* and do not wish to conflate this term with those of *rap* or *hip-hop*. When I speak generally about rap music as a form of black cultural address, without specifically calling it gangsta rap, I am emphasizing rap music's situatedness within hip-hop culture, its criticism of the dominant white culture's racial and economic discrimination, and the contradictory urban expressions of African American economic and racial marginality. Here I share Tricia Rose's perspective that rap "is a black idiom that prioritizes black culture and that articulates the problem of black urban life."[8] I am referring to rap artists as cultural workers engaged to a large extent in "the everyday struggles of working-class blacks and the urban poor."[9] Jeffrey Louis Decker refers to such cultural workers as "hip hop nationalists" who function in the manner suggested by Gramsci's description of organic intellectuals.[10]

With what some rap critics might call its numbing psychorealism; its fixing of "in-your-face" rhymes to social meltdown and bass rhythms to urban disaster; its commodification of black rage through high-volume and low-frequency sound; its production of sexualizing fugues for an imploding Generation X; its ability to provoke a white hellification of black youth with "attitude"; its seventh sons in blue or red bandanas and ten-dollar gold tooth caps "droppin science" and warning their homeboys against "tell-lie-vision," the "lie-bury," and public school "head-decay-tion"; its dance culture of the Handglide, Flow, Headspin, King Tut, Windmill, Tick, Float, Wave, and freestyle; its production of affective economies of white panic around a generalized fear of a black planet; its sneering, tongue-flicking contempt of public space; its visceral intensity and corporal immediacy; its snarling, subterranean resistance; its eschatological showdown of "us" against "them"; its "edutainers" down with the brothas in the street; its misogynist braggadocio; its pimp-inspired subjectivity; its urban war zone counternarratives; its home-brewed polymerized anarchism; its virulent autobiographical hype; its Five Percenters flashing their ciphers, 7s, and crescent moon and star within a large sun, praising "Father Allah"; its irreverent first-person narratives powered by gats and urban souljahs high on malt liquor; its rhythmic macho boastfests by brothas in Carhartt jackets; and its dissentious themes and high-pitched contempt for the white petit bourgeoisie and the yuppie heirs of the overclass who can afford to sidestep the frenetic dizziness of reality, gangsta rap has occasioned much public debate over the last few years. Gangsta rap is merely the latest incarnation of the rap music industry in general.

Tricia Rose notes that rap music was "discovered" by the music industry, the print media, the fashion industry, and the film industry during the five years after music entrepreneur Sylvia Robinson released "Rapper's Delight" in 1979.[11] Rose further declares that rap music needs to be situated within Afro-diasporic traditions and cultural formations of the English- and Spanish-speaking Caribbean and in the context of specific historical musical junctions such as urban blues, be-bop, and rock 'n' roll. Further, rap needs to be considered in light of such factors as the creation of the postindustrial city and the larger social movement of hip-hop. For instance, rap music can be traced to, among other cultural and social elements, the hip-hop nationalism of the 1960s, such as the Black Panthers, Malcolm X, gender politics; New York City's political context of the 1970s; postindustrial shifts in economic conditions, including access to housing, the formation of new communication networks; blaxploitation films such as Melvin Van Peebles's *Sweet Sweetback's Baadassss Song;* deindustrialization; the relocation of people of color from different parts of New York City into the South Bronx; city planning and projects such as the Title I Clearance program; the system of crews or posses as means for alternative youth identities: disco music and the cross-fertilization among rapping, break dancing, and graffiti writing.[12]

In the 1980s we started to see rap music emerging in other urban ghettos in major cities such as Houston's fifth ward, Miami's Overtown, Boston's Roxbury, and South Central, Watts, and Compton, in Los Angeles. The Los Angeles rappers have spawned a specific rap style that, Rose notes, must be seen in the context of narratives specific to poor, young, black, male subjects in Los Angeles. Rose writes that Los Angeles rappers "defined the gangsta rap style."[13] and "spawned other regionally specific hardcore rappers such as New Jersey's Naughty by

Nature, Bronx-based Tim Dog, Onyx, and Redman, and a new group of female gangsta rappers, such as Boss (two black women from Detroit), New York–based Puerto Rican rapper Hurricane Gloria, and Nikki D."[14] When examining the roots of rap, or rap's inflection into gangsta rap genres, we need to examine the conjunctural specificity of many factors, including those listed above.

White and black listeners alike are drawn to this surly form of urban apostasy, fashionable deviancy, and stylized outlawry, whose message and transgressive status dig pretty close to the eschatological roots of holy war. Gangsta rap has been accused by some middle-class whites as well as some black professionals of fomenting the anger, racial hatred, and lawlessness that led to the LA uprising of 1992. Of course, in tandem with such dispatches from the bourgeoisie was a studied ignorance about the irreversible structural unemployment faced by many blacks in the inner city, the dismantling of social services, and the progressive hardening of racial lines.

The LA media have not been known for their celebration of rap as a musical genre since the heyday of its Compton rappers: MC Ren, Dr. Dre, Yella, Ice Cube, and Eazy-E (who left groups such as The CIA and World Class Wreckin Cru in order to work collaboratively as NWA— Niggas With Attitude—from 1987 to 1992). Instead, the media have preferred to demonize and hellify the genre that these young Angelenos from Watts, Compton, and South Central—"the nihilistic school of Los Angeles–centered gangsta rappers"—helped to create.[15] Following their more politicized hard-core and hard-beat counterparts in New York (such as Run-DMC and KRS-1) on the East Coast (such as Notorious B.I.G.), in the footsteps of New York's Grandmaster Flash and the Furious Five, and fellow Angelenos Gil Scott-Heron, the Watts Prophets, and the Last Poets (a group of black nationalist lyricists), LA rap artists provided the space for the development of a new form of social criticism. This form of social criticism was apotheosized in Ice Cube's *The Predator*, which offered a potent commentary on the LA uprising of 1992. The cultural power and promise of rap resided in its powerful dramatization of white racism. In "We Had to Tear This Motherfucker Up" Ice Cube (a.k.a. O'Shea Jackson) sentences former LAPD officers Stacey Koon, Laurence Powell, and Timothy Wind to death for the beating of Rodney King.

Like their New York counterpart, Afrika Bambaataa, former member of the Black Spades street gang and founder of the hip-hop community, Zulu Nation (made up of African American, Puerto Rican, Afro-Caribbean, and Euro-American youths and based on the Zulu military system), LA rappers Ice-T, Tone Loc, Ice Cube, and Eazy-E were also former gangbangers. Many of these rappers were products of the economic and cultural upheavals that had assaulted and displaced numerous multiethnic urban communities; their futures were bound up in the dimming job market by inner-city trade vocational schooling. For instance, hip-hop originator DJ Kool Herc (whose original rap style was influenced by prison "toasting") attended Alfred E. Smith auto mechanic trade school; Grandmaster Flash studied electronic repair work at Samuel Gompers vocational high school; and Salt 'n' Pepa both worked as telemarketing representatives at Sears and were intent at one time on nursing school.[16] These working-class black youths were able to escape the uncertain futures constructed for them in an era of deindustrialization. They are some of the lucky few to succeed as part of a financially lucrative musical phenomenon. However, it is a phenomenon often accused of fomenting racial panics and urban youth criminality. Just ask Charlton Heston and Oliver North.

Emerging in the 1970s from the epicenters of hip-hop culture—the blue-collar housing units of America's postindustrial cities—rap music developed among relocated black and Puerto Rican male youths of the South Bronx who celebrated break dancing, graffiti, B-Boy, and wild style fashions.[17] Puerto Rican rap has incorporated inflections from salsa, variations of which are drawn from *Santéria* rhythms, as is the case of the music of Tito Puente (himself a priest of *Santéria).*

Some of the major strands of hip-hop culture (in which rap, style, and politics become mutually informing inflections) can be traced from the jive talkers of the be-bop era to the reggae-based sounds of Jamaican DJ Kool Herc in the West Bronx in 1973 and Jah Rico in north London around 1976. Hip-hop youth in the Bronx and London sympathized with the economic and social struggles of young people in Jamaica and Soweto, wore dreadlocks ("Funki Dreds") with shaved back and sides created by Jazzy B and Aitch for the Soul II Soul crew, or combined the Philly Cut or skiffle with shaved diagonal lines, bleaching, or perms.[18] Shifts in clothes displayed a taxonomy of funky sartorial motifs, from Teenybopper to Home Boy to hard-rocker to Afrocentric; and from Hustler to Superfly to Daisy Age to Cosmic (via Rifat Ozbek). With styles eventually shifting to athletic and leisure wear, Home Boys and Fly Girls started sporting sweatshirts, cropped shorts, "pin-tucked" baggy jeans, baseball caps, chunky gold chains, Dukie Ropes, and leather pendants.[19] Then came the "hoodies" and the "triple fat" goose-down jackets.

Influenced by the music of Curtis Mayfield, the funk of James Brown, be-bop, and rhythmic jazz, rap is an impressive amalgam of complex musical formations. Some ethnomusicologists consider such formations to be extensions of African expressive forms such as "playing the dozens" and "signifying" as well as the praise songs of the

African storyteller, or *griot*.[20] In saying this, however, I am reminded of Tricia Rose's important admonition that hip-hop not be reduced to its African musical origins as oral traditions.[21] Hip-hop needs to be understood, argues Rose, as a "secondary orality" bound up in an electronically mediated reality that is conjuncturally embedded in relations of power and politics. Rose further notes that "rap musicians are not the only musicians to push on the limits of high-tech inventions. Yet the decisions they have made and the directions their creative impulses have taken echo Afro-diasporic musical priorities. Rap production resonates with Black cultural priorities in the age of digital reproduction."[22]

Tricia Rose's discussion of mass-produced repetition undercuts perspectives by Adorno, Attali, and Jameson by arguing that repetition in rap is not always connected to the commodity system of late capitalism in the same way as other musical forms. She argues that repetition in mass-cultural formations can also serve as a form of collective resistance.[23]

The operational or performative logics of gangsta rap vary but what is constant is what Lawrence Grossberg calls "affective agency"—its ability to articulate "mattering maps" in which agency is defined as brushing up against the prison of everyday life.[24] Michael Dyson describes the emergence of rap within a context that emphasizes its situatedness as a cultural form of resistance. According to Dyson,

> Rap music grew from its origins in New York's inner city over a decade ago as a musical outlet to creative cultural energies and to contest the invisibility of the ghetto in mainstream American society. Rap remythologized New York's status as the spiritual center of black America, boldly asserting appropriation and splicing (not originality) as the artistic strategies by which the styles and sensibilities of black ghetto youth would gain popular influence. Rap developed as a relatively independent expression of black male artistic rebellion against the black bourgeois *Weltanschauung,* tapping instead into the cultural virtues and vices of the so-called underclass, romanticizing the ghetto as the fecund root of cultural identity and authenticity, the Rorschach of legitimate masculinity and racial unity.[25]

Tricia Rose describes hip-hop culture, from which rap and eventually gangsta rap evolved, in a more global context:

> Hip hop is an Afro-diasporic cultural form which attempts to negotiate the experiences of marginalization, brutally truncated opportunity and oppression within the cultural imperatives of African-American and Caribbean history, identity and community. It is the tension between the cultural fractures produced by postindustrial oppression and the binding ties of Black cultural expressivity that sets the critical frame for the development of hip hop.[26]

Rap's beginnings as highly politicized and powerfully eclectic music can be seen in such songs as "Rapper's Delight" by the Sugarhill Gang in 1979, Brother D's (Daryl Asmaa Nubyah) "We Gonna Make the Black Nation Rise," recorded in 1980, and Afrika Bambaataa and Soul Sonic Force's 1982 recording of "Planet Rock." According to Dick Hebdige, Bambaataa "has been known to cut from salsa to Beethoven's Fifth Symphony to Yellow Magic Orchestra to calypso through Kraftwerk via video game sound effects and the theme from *The Munsters* television series back to his base in James Brown."[27] Bambaataa—who ran a sound system at the Bronx River Community Center—would also mix the theme from the *Pink Panther* with bits and pieces of songs from the Monkees, the Beatles, and the Rolling Stones.[28]

Poison Clan, AMG, Hi-C, Nu Niggaz on the Block, Compton Cartel, 2nd II None, Mob Style, and Compton's Most Wanted did not emerge in a social vacuum. When former LAPD Chief of Police Darryl Gates proclaimed that "we may be finding that in some Blacks when [the chokehold] is applied the veins or arteries do not open up as fast as they do on normal people," he was reflecting the sentiments of the white dominant culture of law enforcement in Los Angeles.[29] Not only was he demonizing African Americans as biologically subnormal, he was adding to the criminalization of black youth in general, corralling connotations of black masculinity into the operative lexicon of unimpeachable white common sense. The LAPD term describing "African Americans in the vicinity" as "Gorillas in the Mist" provoked Da Lench Mob to title their album *Guerrillas in tha Midst*. Some cultural critics were beginning to view rap artists as agents of revolutionary consciousness. When Operation HAMMER sent Chief Gates and his minions into the streets of South Central to pick up "suspicious looking" black youth, harass them, and build up the data base of the LAPD's task force, gangsta rappers were portraying the practice of law enforcement as a form of racial and class warfare.

After the release of NWA's 1988 debut album, *Straight Outta Compton*, white audiences were treated to urban nightmares of white throats being slit in midscream. NWA's hit crossover recording, "Efil4zaggin"—"niggaz 4 life" spelled backward—was the first hardcore rap collection to reach number one on the pop charts. Then "Cop Killer" hit the airwaves, with Ice-T's hard, pounding, and pimpified lyrics smashing through listeners' ribs like a brass-knuckled fist, tagging a "don't fuck with me" on their hearts with an aerosol can of his digitized blood. The media went ballistic in condemnation of this new transgressive musical form known as "gangsta rap," which was even propelling white audiences into adopting black inflection and "ghetto" identification. Ice-T became buoyant after President Clinton publicly criticized "Cop Killer" and sixty congressmen signed a letter condemning the song: "Very few people have their names said by the president, especially in anger. It makes me feel good, like I haven't been just standing on a street corner yelling with nobody listening all the time. . . . It lets you know how small this country is."[30]

Ice Cube's 1990 hit "Endangered Species," from the album *Amerikkka's Most Wanted,* captures the attitude that many gangsta rap lyrics reflect with respect to law enforcement agencies:

> Every cop killer ignored
> They just send another nigger to the morgue
> A point scored.
> They could give a fuck about us
> They'd rather find us with guns and white powder
> Now kill ten of one to get the job correct.
> To serve, protect and break a nigga's neck.

This was heavy stuff in a society too preoccupied with consolidating its hegemony through frontal assaults on the welfare state and labor coalitions to concern itself with a bunch of "lowlifes" singing about their crime-ridden hoods. Latino rap didn't really become popular until 1990, during a groundswell of public panic surrounding the growing Latino population in the United States and amidst the reactionary tactics of the English Only Movement. Mellow Man Ace went gold with *Mentirosa,* and Kid Frost's (a.k.a. Arturo Molina) Chicanismo-inspired debut album, *Hispanic Causing Panic,* became the rap anthem of La Raza.[31] Chicano rapper ALT (a.k.a. Al Trivette) fuses insights of barrio life in El Monte and Rosemead into African American rap in albums *ALT* and *Stone Cold World.*

The amazing thing about the disjunctive barrage of ghetto moments known as rap was that it sold, turning inner-city homeys such as Mixmaster Spade into deities in gold chains, hawking their rap wares on the very mean streets that they rapped about. Since those early days, gangsta rap has even gone platinum with Dre's *The Chronic* and Snoop's *Doggystyle.*

In the eyes of many ghetto youth, society is going under and gangsta rappers and hepcats from the barrios are the new prophets, sounding their nationalist warnings over a Roland TR 808 drum synthesizer as the world about them swirls into the urban vortex, like DeNiro's ex-convict character in *Cape Fear,* whose savaged and tattooed body writhes while his soul speaks in tongues as both sink beneath the foaming waters.

Death Row Records, run by Andre (Dr. Dre) Young and Marion "Suge" Knight, is the nation's most profitable producer of gangsta rap, grossing a total of $90 million from tape, CD, and merchandise sales in 1993 and 1994.[32] Affiliated with media giant Time Warner, this West-wood-based firm boasts a corporate logo of a hooded man in an electric chair. Death Row Records has not escaped the controversies surround-ing its stars' involvement in criminal violence. At a party for its out-of-town retailers and promoters held hours after Snoop Doggy Dogg (Calvin Broadus) took top honors at the Soul Train Music Awards, a fan was brutally stomped to death. Young is currently serving a five-month term in Pasadena City jail for parole violation. (In 1992 he was con-victed of breaking another rap producer's jaw and hitting a New Orleans police officer in a hotel brawl.) A year earlier he was convicted of slamming a TV talk-show host into a wall at a Hollywood club. Knight was also convicted of assault with a deadly weapon. According to Dre, "America loves violence. America is obsessed with murder. I think murder sells a lot more than sex. They say sex sells. I think mur-der sells."[33] However, Death Row Records publicly denounces gang vio-lence, and the firm has donated $500,000 to a South Central antigang program.

Russell Simmons, CEO of Def Jam Recordings (the largest African American–owned company in the record business) defends rap as a way to reach kids in Beverly Hills:

> And the most important thing is this. It's very, very important that there be communication between kids that would generally not talk to each other. Your kids may not be bad, but it's pretty sure they know some who are. Your kids are surrounded by those kids. So maybe some kid in Beverly Hills listens to rap and gets a better idea of what some kids in Crenshaw are thinking. And as that kid in Beverly Hills grows up and goes to college, maybe he'll keep a little bit of that in his con-sciousness, and maybe even grow up to do something about it.[34]

Simmons's justification for rap and gangsta rap as the contempo-rary hope for shaping the consciousness of rich white kids in Beverly Hills certainly overestimates rap's potential for political resistance and social transformation through the mobilization of Generation X. Yet it vastly underestimates the power of capitalist hegemony to produce, pro-mote, and protect the vested interests of dominant culture in Western society, and what it takes to construct counterhegemonic social prac-tices.

Shortly after the 1992 LA Intifada, pop singer Michelle Shocked and freelance writer Bart Bull mounted a powerful (if not profoundly misguided) denunciation of gangsta rap in an issue of *Billboard*. Claim-ing it to be a contemporary recoding of a turn-of-the-century white racist stereotype, a racist revival of the minstrel tradition as embodied in the nineteenth-century "coon song," they proclaimed that the "chicken-thieving, razor-toting 'coon' of the 1890s is the drug-dealing, Uzi-toting 'nigga' of today."[35] Ice Cube is criticized by Shocked and Bull as a "greed artist" who, through albums such as *The Predator,* is profiting from the conditions that produce the underclass through his production of a "Zip Coon Toon Town" version of Los Angeles, "a coon song fantasyland." This perspective is echoed by New York essayist and music critic Stanley Crouch, who calls gangsta rap "the selling of coon images" and who compares record executives who produce gangsta rap to "high tech slave traders."[36] Crouch condemns gangsta rap for portraying black people as wild savages and as badges of black authenticity, as the "real" voices from the hood. Taking issue with Crouch's position, the Geto Boys' lead rapper, Bushwick Bill (whose physical status as a one-eyed midget has not been lost on rap's media critics) describes rap as an "opera to people in the ghetto."[37] Rock critic Dave Marsh argues that the attack on rap is directed at new access to the mainstream media by America's underclass. He condemns the anti-rap campaign by William Bennett and C. DeLores Tucker as 90s-style McCarthyism. Former *Wall Street Journal* writer and critic Martha Bayles blames the offensive lyrics in much of today's music not on African American music but on the avant-garde European art school thinking that she calls "perverse modernism."[38]

In Mexico border towns like Tijuana, *narcocorrido* ballads (historically derived from the narrative style of Nahuatl epic poetry and Andalusian romantic verse from the sixteenth century) tell stories of drug dealers who prevail in the face of the authorities. Narcocorrido balladeers have provoked the wrath of anti-drug spokespeople such as Marta Rocha de Diaz, president of Housewives of Playas de Tijuana. The public debate is similar to that surrounding gangsta rap. Los Tucanes sing narcocorridos about smugglers who take heroin, cocaine, and marijuana across the border into the United States. The popularity of Los Tucanes and Los Tigres del Norte has provoked critics to condemn narcocorridos for mimicking U.S.-style gangsta rap.

David Troop's *Rap Attack: African Jive to New York Hip Hop,* Houston Baker's *Black Studies: Rap and the Academy,* and Tricia Rose's brilliant *Black Noise: Rap Music and Black Culture in Contemporary America*[39] are just a few of the burgeoning scholarly commentaries on rap that offer a much more congenial account of rap's potential for developing forms of counterhegemonic resistance than the account of gangsta rap that is offered by Shocked and Bull. For these critics, it is important to understand how and why the terms governing the popular responses to rap have come into being and how they have, to a large extent, become naturalized. Accordingly, these writers maintain the need to see hip-hop in a much broader context: as a global cultural practice that is articulated through the tropes and sensibilities of the African diaspora and the history of Afro-America, and that creates a "diasporic interchange" and "diasporic intimacy" among struggling black peoples the world over who are fighting racism and capitalist exploitation.[40] As Nick De Genova emphasizes, "rather than as an expression of social pathology, gangster rap's imaginative empowerment of a nihilistic and ruthless way of life can be better understood as a potentially opposi- tional consciousness—albeit born of desperation, or even despair."[41] Common subjective understandings of alienation among oppressed groups are articulated through rap; as a cultural force it is integral in providing black urban youth with both an expression of race and with codes of solidarity. As De Genova puts it, "gangsta rap can be found to transcend the mere reflection of urban mayhem and enter into musical debate with these realities, without sinking into didacticism or flatten- ing their complexity."[42] Rap needs to be understood not so much for its musical poaching through "sampling" as for the way that it is premised on what Tricia Rose calls "transformations and hybrids"—developing "a style that nobody can deal with." She writes that

> transformations and hybrids reflect the initial spirit of rap and hip hop as an experimental and collective space where contemporary issues and ancestral forces are worked through simultaneously. Hybrids in rap's subject matter, not unlike its use of musical collage and the influx of new, regional and ethnic styles, have not yet displaced the three points of stylistic continuity to which I referred earlier: approaches to flow, ruptures in line and layering can still be found in the vast majority of rap's lyrical and music construction. The same is true of the critiques of the postindustrial urban America context and the cultural and social conditions which it has produced. Today, the South Bronx and South Central Los Angeles are poorer and more economically marginalized than they were ten years ago.[43]

Strutting apocalyptically across the urban landscape, today's gangsta rappers have, for some listeners, become the new black super- heroes invested with dangerous, ambiguous, uncontrolled, and uncon- trollable powers, the force of nature bound up with self-conscious and grandiose marginality. You don't fuck with these brothers and sisters and live to tell about it. Shocked and Bull's dismissive appraisal of gangsta rap as a message primarily mediated by whites eager to be titil- lated by the thrilling despair within aggrieved black urban communities in the form of "bad nigga" narratives and hyperbolic masculinism underscores their view that the production and performativity of rap is directly at the expense of the structurally subordinated black subject. But is gangsta rap really "an exaggerated defiance feigned for commer- cial purposes," signifying steroids for sculpting rage, or perhaps a "mock nihilism that parallels the ambiguous accommodationism displayed in subversive forms of minstrelsy"[44] or, to borrow a phrase that Charles Pierce used in another context, a "phony menace that is little more than Tomming with your hat turned backward"?[45]

Some gangsta songs, for instance, promote a stereotypical (re)framing that depicts the gangsta rapper as both sociopath and criminal. Stereotypes are recast and refigured so that the negative connotations (of laziness, violence, etc.) become positive attributes of strength, of power, and of resistance to white domination. While the mock nihilism in gangsta rap "is an inherently resistive element," it has also "been a key element in its commercial exploitation."[46] While Angela Davis has decried the sexism of rap, she comments, somewhat reluctantly, on the power evoked by the image of the black man—as gun-toting revolutionary—that is offered up to the public by gangsta rap: "Many of the rappers call upon a market-mediated historical memory of the black movement of the sixties and seventies. The image of an armed Black man is considered the 'essence' of revolutionary commitment today. As dismayed as I may feel about this simplistic, phallocentric image, I remember my own responses to romanticized images of brothers (and sometimes sisters) with guns."[47]

Bell hooks argues that much of the sexism and misogyny that riddles rap songs is based on an assertive patriarchal paradigm of competitive masculinity and its emphasis on physical prowess. Decker presents Sister Souljah's role as a member of Public Enemy between 1990 and 1992 as deflecting gender-based criticism away from Public Enemy and constructing "an alibi for the stereotypical hypermasculinity of black men"[48] through her exclusive emphasis on racial politics and her allegiance to a hip-hop nationalism that tends to objectify the black woman as a sign of "Mother Africa."[49] However, black female rappers have done much to present affirming images of black women outside the binary couplet of good girl/bad girl that dominates the patriarchal culture of gangsta rap. For instance, Queen Latifah (Dana Owens) has challenged racist white America's view of black women as "welfare queens" and unwed mothers as well as challenged the view of some black nationalists that women accept roles subordinate to men. For Latifah, women are not the "bitches" signified by some male rap artists. According to Steven Gregory,[50] the welfare mother (defended by Queen Latifah and other female rappers)

> is a privileged site, where the brutalities of racism, patriarchy, and post-Fordist economic restructuring are mystified and, indeed, eroticized as the reproductive pathologies of black poverty. It is precisely this displacement of a politics of real bodies for a biopolitics of patriarchal desire that renders the iconography of the welfare mother and

the inner city serviceable to a wide spectrum of cultural and political projects, ranging from the misogynist beats of gangsta rappers, to the more sober, but no less phallocentric, politics of welfare reform. What these projects share, whether as an appeal for a more "paternalistic" state authority . . . the aggressive policing of "group home turnstiles" or the selective re-tooling of black masculinity à la *Boyz 'N the Hood,* is the conviction that patriarchy is the bedrock of nation-building.[51]

Queen Latifah refuses the role given to the black woman within hip-hop nationalism—that of Isis—which merely symbolizes the imperialist glories of Egypt and the African empire. Latifah's Afrocentric expression is remarkable, not only because it is devoid of the concomitant sexism of nationalism but because it challenges the masculine logic of the idea of nation as well.[52]

Rose believes that it is hypocritical of black middle-class critics of rap lyrics not to launch the same level of moral criticism at black urban poverty as well as sexism and racism. She asserts that

the problem is: one, that technology brings these vernacular practices, the practices most vulnerable to middle-class outrage, into spaces where they might never have been heard twenty-five years ago; and two, rappers are vulnerable, highly visible cultural workers, which leaves them open to increased sanctions. But sexism, at the level of the toast and the boast, is only a subset of structurally sanctioned sexism. In that way, all manner of cultural practices and discourses that do not challenge the structures upon which these ideas are based wind up confirming them. Why, then, is the concern over rap lyrics so incredibly intense, particularly from Black middle-class guardians? Why not the same level of moral outrage over the life options that Black folks face in this country? It seems to me we need a censorship committee against poverty, sexism, and racism.[53]

Few cultural formations exist within popular culture that are stronger and more potent politically than gangsta rap. According to Kristal Brent Zook, "To say that rap is no more than a sad by-product of oppression is to take an explanatory, defensive stance when, in actuality, rap is a fundamental component of what may be the strongest political and cultural offensive gesture among African Americans today."[54] Rap is a powerful offensive medium in the way that it raises havoc with white middle-class complicity in and complacency with institutionalized racism; its dialogic pulsions disarticulate white supremacist governing narratives; it ruptures consensual images of blacks whom middle-class whites wish would "know their place." As De Genova argues,

for its white listeners, gangster rap truly reconstitutes "the tyranny of the real"—both by musically and lyrically reconfiguring the real

tyranny of the ghetto-space of death and destruction, and by recon-
firming, *through* these phantasms of the "other," the sanitized comfort
(and privilege) that comes with the tyrannical tedium of suburban,
middle-class reality. It is here that we can discern a shared "culture of
terror," a musical conjunction of the terror lived in Black ghettoes, and
the enchanting terror *dreamed* in white suburbia.[55]

Rap unmakes feelings of security and safety in middle-class homes and
neighborhoods. It indexes areas of concrete rage and generalized despair
that are normally hidden from the official view of American democracy.
De Genova powerfully captures this reality when he argues that gangster
rap evokes

> a bilateral "culture of terror" in a dislocated "space of death": hege-
> monic (racist) fantasies about stereotypical "Blackness" and the self-
> destructive ("savage") violence of the urban ghetto-space, are con-
> joined with the nihilistic, lawless (oppositional) terror-heroism of
> proud, unapologetic self-styled "niggers"—Niggas With Attitude, Geto
> Boys, Compton's Most Wanted, et al.—who fulfill the prophesy and
> the promise of systemic violence and orchestrated destruction. Thus,
> gangster rap serves up white America's most cherished gun-slinging
> mythologies (heroic American dreams) in the form of its worst and
> blackest nightmares, while it empowers Black imaginations to negate
> the existential terror of ghetto life (and death) by sheer force of the
> will.[56]

Following Kobena Mercer, George Lipsitz notes that rap is not a
radical form in itself but has to be understood as a function of culture.
He remarks that "culture functions as a social force to the degree that it
gets instantiated in social life and connected to the political aspirations
and activities of groups. It is here that hip hop holds its greatest significance and its greatest challenge to interpreters."[57]

Bell hooks lucidly illustrates that the context out of which rap has
emerged is intertwined with the public stories of black male lives and the
history of the pain suffered by black men in a racist society. She is worth
quoting at length:

> Rap music provides a public voice for young black men who are usu-
> ally silenced and overlooked. It emerged in the streets—outside the
> confines of a domesticity shaped and informed by poverty, outside
> enclosed spaces where . . . [black bodies] . . . had to be contained and
> controlled. . . . The public story of black male lives narrated by rap
> speaks directly to and against white racist domination, but only indi-
> rectly hints at the enormity of black male pain. Constructing the black
> male body as site of pleasure and power, rap and the dances associated
> with it suggest vibrancy, intensity, and an unsurpassed joy in living. It
> may very well be that living on the edge, so close to the possibility of

being "exterminated" (which is how many young black males feel) heightens one's ability to risk and make one's pleasure more intense. It is this charge, generated by the tension between pleasure and danger, death and desire, that Foucault evokes when he speaks of that *complete total pleasure* that is related to death. Though Foucault is speaking as an individual, his words resonate in a culture affected by anhedonia—the inability to feel pleasure. In the United States, where our senses are daily assaulted and bombarded to such an extent that an emotional numbness sets in, it may take being "on the edge" for individuals to feel intensely. Hence the overall tendency in the culture is to see young black men as both dangerous and desirable.[58]

The most politically astute rappers take the racist and sexist stereotypes of black males and recontextualize them so that within popular culture, criminalized and hypersexualized black youths now become fearless rebels "standing up" heroically to the white man's exploitation. This fusion of heroism and criminality, of pleasure and pain, occurs without denying the endemic effects of institutionalized racism, patriarchal structures, heterosexist relations, and class exploitation. De Genova captures this point when he notes that "gangster rap exposes the multivalence and equivocation of racial essentialism: it evokes all of the conflicted meanings and opposed values which congeal simultaneously around a shared set of socially charged signifiers that comprise a single racial nomenclature."[59] Matthew Grant argues that gangsta rap results from the relationship between the criminalized underclass and the overclass reaching a point "where they can mutually benefit from the destabilization of the middle-class majority."[60] According to Grant, what makes gangsta rap so attractive to the middle-class white consumer is not its attempt to develop a revolutionary consciousness among its listeners, but rather the actively transgressive character of its assaults on middle-class taboos against violence. Gangsta rap provides white consumers who yearn to be part of the hip-hop nation with shocking images in which "the norms of bourgeois liberality are violated in an orgy of paradoxically subaltern elitism."[61] Through the politics of voyeurism, white youth can become the menacing urban *baaadman*.

Far from being a dispiriting successor to rhythm and blues, gangsta rap occupies a formidable yet not unproblematic space of resistance to racial oppression. A more productive account of gangsta rap, Grant argues, would examine its "celebration of insanity based as a singularly gendered obsession"—what he calls "the insane investment of the real."[62] Grant writes that

> the fantasy of losing it, of stepping over the limit of reason and civility, of surrendering oneself to the intoxication and ecstasy of violence uninhibited by the strictures of reason, is an important component of

male subjectivity (which herein seems to cross boundaries established by class or skin color). Madness, among men, is something that must be endured or overcome (unless one is completely overwhelmed and obliterated by it). The flip side of this adventurist relation to the insane is the wholesale projection of insanity onto women as one legitimation of their exclusion from certain segments of the social order.[63]

Maintaining that the criticism leveled at rappers—that they wildly sensationalize urban life—is wrongly dependent upon holding rappers to the same ineluctable standards that inform the genre of social realism. Grant offers a spirited defense of gangsta rap, noting that the

insanity that speaks through the voice of rap music is not simply a brand of psychic exoticism: it is the mental state produced by the process of racist oppression to which these bodies are subjected. The radical decentering of the subject, either through the use of drugs or through the use of semiautomatic weapons (and what could be more decentering than "a hole in your fuckin' head"?), which finds its expression in rap, a decentering celebrated by poststructuralists and postmodernists everywhere, results from an intensely decentering material configuration of the real. The insane distortions of gangsta rap actually make their representations realistic. It's just a psychorealism thing.[64]

Representation, as Grant points out, is not just about adducing an accurate or realistic depiction of an event from many possible interpretations. It also speaks to forms of political advocacy that, in the case of gangsta rap, deal primarily with the Kafkaesque and carceral universe of the black urban male. (There are also "hard-core" female rappers such as Manhole, a Latina from LA, and Boss, a classically trained African American musician who did not grow up in the hood but raps about it as if she did.)

Echoing the music of Dr. Dre and Snoop Doggy Dogg, Grant remarks that prison has become the educational alternative for black men: "the generalized form of social space for the underclass." Moreover, he argues that "hard-core" gangsta rap constitutes a political program that he describes as an urban guerrilla movement. As a social force, however, gangsta rap overwhelmingly fails in its attempt to organize effectively, since, according to Grant, it has at its disposal only an "anarchofascist politics of drug dealership and gang-bangerism."[65] After all, NWA's drug dealing was decidedly "precapitalist" and, Grant maintains, no match for "the internationally organized capitalist bloc with its huge armies, advanced armaments, and high-tech domestic security systems."[66] Despite its failure to bring forth the hegemonic articulations that would make Gramsci proud, gangsta rap does present what I would call a contingent or provisional utopian longing—a trace, within a

tapestry of violent imagery, of what is needed to bring about social justice. Grant puts it this way: "Gangsta rap, in spite of its contradictions,
in spite of what is retrograde in it (like its often vicious sexism and
homophobia), at least contains elements that give us a glimpse of what
a radically oppositional culture could look like."⁶⁷ De Genova echoes a
similar sentiment when he remarks that "rap music flourishes in the
contradictory interstices of hegemonic appropriation and a fairly self-
conscious and articulate politics of oppositional maneuvering."⁶⁸

I locate gangsta rap as an "oppositional practice" in the sense that
Michel de Certeau uses the term. While de Certeau is referring to the
actions of the Amerindians, I believe his ideas are applicable to many
contemporary groups—for example, African Americans—who find
themselves exploited and oppressed. According to de Certeau,

> even when they were subjected, indeed even when they accepted, their
> subjection . . . often used the laws, practices, and representations that
> were imposed on them by force or by fascination to ends other than
> those of their conquerors; they made something else out of them; they
> subverted them from within—not by rejecting them or by transform-
> ing them (though that occurred as well), but by many different ways of
> using them in the service of rules, customs, or convictions foreign to
> the colonization which they could not escape. They metaphorized the
> dominant order; they made it function in another register.⁶⁹

For instance, Shocked and Bull's criticism of rap overlooks rap's oppositional possibilities. It overlooks the fact that, among other things,
gangsta rap has conflated the image of the "real nigga" and the "bad
nigger" of black urban folklore. However, this distinction is admittedly
unclear at times and, as Tommy Lott himself notes, the mass media's
politicizing of the "bad nigger" idiom has led to a "troublesome conflation" of the "heroic badman" of folklore and the "bad nigga" of rap.⁷⁰

The politics of resistance in gangsta rap needs to be located within
the globalization of capital, the international circuit of debt and consumption, the deindustrialization, deskilling, and de-unionization of
work in the expanding service sector. For instance, while it points to the
structural instability of capitalist America and the production of urban
rage, and while it wages political war against the white sentinels of the
status quo, it remains ideologically aligned with capitalist interests, glorifying crass materialism and celebrating conspicuous consumption. As
such, rap as a form of resistance can be conflictually located along a
series of semantic axes; it varies, in other words, from song to song,
from artist to artist, and from listener to listener, depending upon the
performative moments that are meant to be signified. In other words,
gangsta rap does not constitute a master trope of urban criticism, an ur-

text of cultural resistance but is read differently by different groups. Oppressed minorities are more likely to resonate with rap for its political critique, while middle-class white groups are more likely to be drawn to rap for its aestheticization of transgression. De Genova makes an important point when he claims that "what emerges in gangster rap, like the figure of Bigger Thomas, is 'a snarl of many realities.' Gangster rap would seem to provide a very different kind of 'therapy' for those who live its nihilism, than the shock treatment it provides for those who live in mortal terror of it."[71] Tommy Lott notes, for instance, that "with the commercializing of gangsta rap we can no longer speak in a totalizing manner of rap music. Instead, this designation must be reserved for specific rap tunes."[72]

I believe that it is instructive to locate rap as a challenge to the bourgeois political and racialized structures that discursively articulate what counts as the quintessential American experience. Elsewhere I have argued that the cultural logic of late capitalism has reinscribed the moral order within the United States around the practice of consumption and the secular redemption of acquiring wealth.[73] The structural unconscious of American popular culture (the term *structural* is meant to draw attention to the fact that the social structure is folded into individual and collective forms of subjectivity that operate through the language of myth) has been occupied by the figure of the serial killer as the last frontiersperson, the last autonomous subject, the last "true" American who can act.

America—Europe's other—has often been considered the promised land.[74] But when all the old myths based on America as the promised land are demythologized, when the Protestant millenarianist project to recreate Zion in the streets of Los Angeles end in the Intifada of 1992, then the quintessential apocalyptic moment becomes the act of random murder. America is exporting this myth through film *(Love and a .45, Natural Born Killers, Pulp Fiction)*, music, and other cultural formations.

The gangsta rapper serves in this context to remind white audiences that utopia is lost, that the end of history has arrived (but not in the way Francis Fukuyama predicted), that the logic of white utopia is premised upon white supremacy and exploitative social relations, and that whites have mistakenly pledged their loyalty to the Beast. Gangsta rap reveals the white millenarianist project of democracy to be grounded upon a will to sameness, a desire to drive out people of color from the mythic frontier of the promised land. In this sense, gangsta rap transforms the "brothas" into avenging angels who call upon whites to redeem themselves or face the wrath of God—a God who will send forth not locusts or floods but angry black urban dwellers taking to the streets.

Just as the black subject has always operated as a metaphor for chaos and instability, the Los Angeles uprising of 1992 literalized this metaphor as one of physical terror. In a world where history has already been purchased by the wealthy, the losers have no choice but to steal some of history back again. The agents of leadership will not be the good Rodney Kings on television but the "bad niggaz" in the streets.

Before we can answer the question of whether hip-hop culture itself is preventing gangsta rap from evolving into a social movement, we need to gain a deeper understanding of the semantic orbit surrounding the politics of difference in gangsta rap. Do we accept, for instance, the resistive elements of gangsta rap only in the context of the production of aesthetic pleasure, rather than the promotion of a political agenda only because acts of resistance can be defused as well as diffused into a politics of the sublime? Has the commercialization of gangsta rap imploded into the political such that these two characteristics are indistinguishable? Does the conflation of gangsta rap's commodification and political project effectively cancel both rather than dialectically reinitiate a productive political tension around a project of social justice and a praxis of liberation? Does rap's repackaging of oppositional codes along aesthetic lines merely reduce gangsta rap to a more marketable form of cultural capital that can be traded within existing capitalist frameworks of power and privilege? Can the same questions be raised about hip-hop movies such as *Krush Groove, A Thin Line between Love and Hate, Set It Off*, and *Booty Call*?

De Genova argues that gangsta rap does escape the nihilistic aestheticism of which it has been accused by linking such aestheticism with the politics of the street:

> Gangster rap, even more than other types of hip hop, raises the free-for-all aesthetic far above and beyond the music's formal level: gangster rap celebrates a free-for-all in the streets. Here it becomes possible to imagine the transcendence of a merely aesthetic nihilism which can be contained by commodification to imagine an articulation of this highly public nihilist aesthetic with the street, the place where the sideshow can become the main event.[75]

The street or neighborhood, it should be pointed out, becomes a liminal site: "The symbol of 'the ghetto' in gangster rap becomes its fire-brand of 'authenticity.' The ghetto comes to be valorized not only as a 'space of death' (and destruction) but also as a space of survival and transcendence; not merely a 'heart of darkness,' it is also the heart of 'Blackness.'"[76]

Gangsta rap is concerned with the articulation of experiences of oppression that find their essential character among disenfranchised urban black and Latino populations. Rap helps to communicate symbols and meanings and articulates intersubjectively the lived experience of social actors. The ontological status of the gangsta rapper resides in the function of the commodity of blackness, but a certain quality of blackness that is identified through the expressive codes of the rapper is the "inner turmoil" of the oppressed black subject of history. Here, blackness (or Latino-ness) marks out a heritage of pain and suffering and points to the willingness and ability of oppressed groups to fight against injustice "by any means necessary." Gangsta rap songs are able to demonstrate how popular white constructions of black men and women ultimately seek to instantiate control over people of color in order to contain them culturally as well as physically. Rap exposes the hidden and hardened fissures and faultlines of democratic social life, revealing the underpinnings of social justice to be little more than a convenient cultural fiction.

Much of the hard-core political gangsta rap provides a type of hallucinatory snapshot of everyday life on America's mean streets—a video canvas of Fortress USA—that evinces fearful images of black rage and destruction, images that typically endure in gangsta rap videos but unfortunately do little to transform the social and material relations that produce them. Violence in gangsta rap has become an Adamic ritual that creates a world of order through disorder that performatively constitutes both the gangsta himself or herself and the object of their violence. In other words, the founding language of the gangsta is violence. It is within this rationality that the image of the gangsta circulates like a political sign within an imagined community of oppressed and resisting subjects. Invading the space of other gang bangers or that of dominant groups in binary-coded struggles (black vs. white, male vs. female, cops vs. black community) helps to stabilize the subjectivity of the gangsta rapper and to contingently anchor identity through a negative interjection of the Other, a negation of whatever threatens it: bitches, rival gangs, the police, and so on. The paramount hegemonic voice that gangsta rappers struggle against—and this is true for its eastern Caribbean and East London counterparts—is law and order. Gangsta rappers challenge the hegemonic modes of thought that are embedded in formal conventions—educational, legal, sexual, and others.

It is important to understand that while gangsta rap suffers from problems of misogyny and nihilism and while the capitalist culture industry amplifies the aesthetic dimension of rap at the expense of its political pronouncements, rap also produces important forms of nationalistic thought that work to nurture forms of coalition building and community. For instance, Zook notes that both the form and content of rap express black autonomy, self-determination, and cultural pride. But what is perhaps most fascinating is not only the way that rap confirms a sense of imagined, metaphorical community, but rather, the fact that this fantasy of "home" is simultaneously constructed materially through the very modes of production, marketing, and the critical discourses which surround it. In other words, just as [Benedict] Anderson argues that literary forms such as the newspaper and the novel made European nationalisms possible, I would say that the forms of television, music videos, film, literary works, and the networks involved in producing these forms are also nurturing a heightened sense of racial collectivity, group solidarity, and even political responsibility—all of which are important elements of nationalist thought.[77]

Gangsta rappers assume a contradictory attitude to black nationalism. On the one hand, they identify with the liberation struggles in Africa, yet on the other hand, they are wary of focusing too much attention on Africa and Afrocentrism for fear of deflecting concern from the serious problems in America's inner cities. According to Robin D. G. Kelley, rappers "contend that the nationalists' focus on Africa—both past and present—obscures the daily battles poor Black folk have to wage in contemporary America."[78]

While it does little to offer a project of transformation, gangsta rap manages, by bursting through the representational space of whiteness and by advancing political solidarity in the form of an imagined community of struggle, to depict what Grant describes as the "proprietary position that whites occupied during the days of slavery (and *mutatis mutandis* still enjoy today)."[79] Whites who are most threatened by gangsta rap's aggressive and adversarial masculinity attempt to consolidate their opposition in a white woman/black beast symbolic order mythologized in white supremacist discourses that have lately been discursively reinforced by prominent politicians such as Newt Gingrich, Jesse Helms, Pat Buchanan, and Pete Wilson. It is possible, too, that white consumers of gangsta rap are drawn to a self-consciously exaggerated display of sexuality, much the same way that rhythm and blues artists captured white audiences in the fifties. As Medovoi notes,

> Of course, sexuality had long been a principal theme of rhythm and blues, but the youthful white audience now took an interest in exaggerating and redirecting its sexual themes symbolically across the race line. Chapple and Garofalo quote R&B artist John Otis recalling: "We found that we moved the white audiences more by caricaturing the music, you know, overdoing the shit—falling on your back with the saxophone, kicking your legs up. And if we did too much of that for a black audience they'd tell us—'Enough of that shit—play some music!'"[80]

While hard-core rap artists such as Snoop Doggy Dogg, Da Lench Mob, Ice Cube, Eazy-E, Niggas with Attitude, and Naughty by Nature unquestionably create politically motivated music, the politics can often be traced to a black nationalist focus. A key issue emerges here. It has to do with the fact that the aesthetic power of the music creates a pleasure among listeners that may even be against the values of the progressive listeners. Tommy Lott reports on a similar issue when he notes that the rap group Public Enemy (which often expresses black nationalist imperatives) is the favorite rap group in some racist white communities such as South Boston.

The controversial rap single "Fuck Rodney King" by former Geto Boy Willie D., makes the powerful claim that during the LA uprising of 1992, "Rodney King so willingly took the moral low ground and turned himself into an establishment ad for social harmony" through his plaintive plea, "Can we all get along?"[81]

> Fuck Rodney King, and his ass.
> When I see the motherfucker I'm a blast
> Boom in his head, boom boom in his back
> Just like that
> Cause I'm tired of the [ ] niggers
> Sayin' increase the peace
> And let the violence cease
> When the Black man built this country
> But can't get his for the prejudiced honkey . . .
> But when it's time for the revolution
> I'm a click click click, fuck this rap shit
> Cause money ain't shit but grief
> If ya ain't got no peace
> Gotta come on with it
> Get down for my little Willies
> So they can come up strong and live long
> And not be scared to get it on![82]

Rather than identifying the song as an example of black nihilism—the image typically conjured by the lyrics—Lott suggests that it constitutes an incisive political critique. In Lott's view, Willie D.'s song "demands the autonomy and agency wards of the state lack."[83] Willie D.'s rap demands the type of political change that would make the violence he calls for unnecessary.

Tommy Lott's analysis of the term *nigga* is instructive. He claims, rightly in my view, that gangsta rap has creatively reworked and recoded in a socially transgressive and politically retaliatory manner the social

meaning of the term in ways that distinguish it from the taboo term used
by white racists and from the often self-hating inflections of the term
expressed by black professionals.[84] Not only is the racist meaning of the
term *nigga* recoded by the gangsta rappers but its ambiguity now shifts,
depending on the contexts of its enunciation and reception. When
gangsta rappers revise the spelling of the racist version of the word *nigger* to the vernacular *nigga* they are using it as a defiant idiom of a resistive mode of African American cultural expression which distinguishes
it from the way that, for instance, white racists in Alabama might
employ the term. Further, Lott notes that the vernacular *nigga* permits
a form of class consciousness among the black urban "underclass" or
lumpen proletariat in the sense that it distinguishes black urban working-class youth from those middle-class black professionals who feel
denigrated whenever the term is used. According to Robin D.G. Kelley,

> Nigga speaks to a collective identity shaped by class consciousness, the
> character of inner-city space, police repression, poverty, and the con-
> stant threat of intraracial violence. . . . In other words, Nigga is not
> merely *another* word for black. Products of the postindustrial ghetto,
> the characters in gangsta rap constantly remind listeners that they are
> still second-class citizens—"Niggaz"—whose collective experiences
> suggest that nothing has changed *for them* as opposed to the black
> middle class. In fact, Nigga is frequently employed to distinguish urban
> black working class males from the black bourgeoisie and African
> Americans in positions of institutional authority. Their point is simple:
> the experiences of young black men in the inner city are not universal
> to all black people, and, in fact, they recognize that some African
> Americans play a role in perpetuating their oppression. To be a "real
> nigga" is to be a product of the ghetto. By linking identity to the
> "hood" instead of simply skin color, gangsta rappers implicitly
> acknowledge the limitations of racial politics, including black middle-
> class reformism as well as black nationalism.[85]

Within the sociohistorical conjuncture of current U.S. urban centers, the gangsta has become a sign of immanence, an alteration of signification between *nigger* and *nigga* relayed to infinity. Through its cultural fusions, intercultural encounters, and expressive articulations, we
are invited by gangsta rap to visit spaces we have never lived physically,
nor would ever wish to—spaces that function significantly in the manufacturing of identity. George Lipsitz remarks that "music not only
shapes and reflects dominant and subordinate social and cultural relations, but . . . music making and other forms of popular culture serve as
a specific site for the creation of collective identity."[86] Rap artists continue to move within Henri Lefevbre's "theatrical or dramatized space"
by creating a new legacy of insurgency and struggle, one that menaces

the prestige hierarchies of white supremacy, that constructs critical aperçus about human dignity and suffering, and that sets itself in opposition to melioristic reform and on the side of revolutionary transformation. As such, it serves as a "social force."[87] Yet I wish to underscore that it cannot be celebrated as a form of oppositional consciousness by uncritically attributing political consciousness to rap artists merely because of their social location as urban "underdog" musicians. Nor can we, as Lipsitz maintains, after Kobena Mercer, argue that music is in itself politically transgressive. Rather, music becomes a "social force" only "to the degree that it gets instantiated in social life and activities of groups."[88] The political inflections of music need to be understood in terms of their cultural, historical, and geopolitical specificity. Lipsitz further argues that the expansion of transnational capital does not, prima facie, sound the death knell of political resistance but rather that "the reach and scope of transnational capital" can make indigenous musical forms more powerful as forms of resistance.

Gangsta rap is essentially a diasporic cultural politics and positions itself as such against cultural displacement and capitalist exploitation. For this reason we can't unproblematically articulate white rappers ("wiggers" or "white niggers") into the rap resistance movement. Cultural borrowings by white rappers are not necessarily problematic but can be seen as troublesome when consideration is given to the way gangsta rap is cognitively mapped by white rappers: the cultural circuits along which such borrowings travel and how these borrowings become fused to dominant Euro-American "universal" meanings, knowledge claims, and social conventions addressed to "the other." Imitation *of* the other doesn't necessarily mean identification *with* the other, yet at the same time it doesn't necessarily exclude such an identification. The Beastie Boys and House of Pain are examples of white rappers with some crossover appeal to black audiences. However, Lipsitz warns that "powerful institutions attach prestige hierarchies to artistic expressions in such a way as to funnel reward and critical attention to Euro-American appropriators, and because ethnocentric presumptions about the universality of Western notions of art obscure the cultural and political contexts that give meaning to many artifacts from traditional cultures that are celebrated as pure form in the West."[89] While there is, to be sure, a depoliticizing aspect to commodification, this contradiction is also a primary condition of gangsta rap's political enablement. Following bell hooks, Grant underscores the fact that because consumers could ignore the political message or information disseminated throughout the music that it also implies the contrary: consumers could pay attention to precisely that element.[90] Gangsta rap creatively exploits the contradictions brought on by commodification to construct a guerrilla warfare of the airwaves—a war waged through what I have called elsewhere the media's "perpetual pedagogy."[91] Grant speaks to this issue when he writes that

> we could thus conceive of a diffuse war of resistance and liberation being waged against the forces of white supremacy with rap music serving as its communication system. . . . Rap music, as the objectified representative of the gangsta, invades the white world and steals white kids. . . . Ice-T also understands his intervention, his invasion, pedagogically. He teaches white kids about racism and power. In addition, he maintains that this music supplies the white youth with an alternative vocabulary in which to articulate their rebellion against the parental authority structure.[92]

At its best, gangsta rap urges the creation of cooperatives of resistance, zones of freedom, where strategies and tactics of liberation can emerge, where the opposite of local struggles does not collapse into some abstract universalized call for emancipation in the form of a master narrative that brings premature closure to the meaning of freedom, where the opposite of local struggles brings to mind not the master trope of the universal but rather the concept of reciprocal relations at the level of the social. This alternative points to the idea of peoples' collective struggle to advance a project of hope lived in the subjunctive mode of "as if" yet grounded in the concreteness of everyday life. It is within the dialectical relationship between local and more broad, collective struggles that gangsta rap accelerates the anger and rage that is the very condition of its existence. Unlike more mainstream musical forms such as heavy metal or rock, which tend to displace issues dealing with relations of power between black and white populations onto quarantined spaces, and which often elide conflicting and contradictory relations premised upon racialized and differential relations of power and privilege, gangsta rap troubles the certainty and unsettles the complacency of existing power arrangements between blacks and whites. I would argue that the multicultural nihilistic hedonism that Newt Gingrich's authoritarian populist millenarianism hates with such a frenzied passion is really one of the few sources of oppositional popular discourses remaining in a nation morally flattened by the weight of the New Right's rhetorical cant that demonizes, hellifies, and zombifies African Americans, Latinos, the poor, and the disenfranchised.

Yet in saying this there is evidence that gangsta rap is running its course within the circuits of capitalist commodification. In a recent issue of *The Los Angeles Reader*, Steve Appleford[93] writes that "another album cover with a gun thrust in your face is as shocking and dangerous now as Madonna without clothes."[94] He cites M. C. Ren as saying that "we wanted to put Compton on the map, so we rapped about what went on in Compton. . . . But now it's like everybody's talking the same shit, people talking about shit we did years ago, you understand? You've got to advance, man. . . . Everybody right now is just stuck."[95] Ren remarks that "you got all these fools coming out now, they think all you got to do is just cuss, talk about weed, low ridin', shit like that, and you can get a record deal, you know what I'm saying? Rap is fucked up, man. It started a few years ago when somebody realized this shit is making money."[96]

According to Appleford, Ice-T now rejects the gangsta label, preferring to describe his music as "reality rap." When gangsta rap restricts itself to the politics of the ghetto, white viewers see it as a threat that is constrained to certain areas of life that they can avoid at the everyday level. When you have easy access to the "black threat" for entertainment purposes, it becomes more familiar and therefore less intimidating. On the other hand, ghettocentricity is a constant reminder to white viewers that they themselves are white. Whiteness—that absent presence that outlines the cultural capital required for favored citizenship status—becomes, in this instance, less invisible to whites themselves. The less invisible that whiteness becomes, the less it serves as a tacit marker against which otherness is defined.

There have been some recent alternative movements within rap, such as G-funk and rap/be-bop fusion. For instance, R&B artists such as Me'Shell Ndegéocello are experimenting with aspects of hip-hop and soul. Recently in the *LA Weekly,* Donnell Alexander[97] surveyed some alternative rap, arguing that while hard-core gangsta rap (Big Mike, M. C. Eiht, Jeru, Treach) is now mainstream, alternative rap groups such as Digable Planets, Spearhead, Justin Warfield, the Broun Fellinis, and Michael "Basehead" Ivey haven't been able to develop much of a following outside of white college students. And there is the question of the powerful forces of commodification from the marketplace. Is rap's restricted code of black solidarity against oppression being elaborated for financial gain by the white-dominated culture industry? Is it being diffused into an aesthetic style that can be danced to or played because of its growing availability as a cultural code?[98] Is it being depotentiated because it is being wrenched away from the cultural contexts that made it meaningful?

The politics of commodification and appropriation that have been confronting gangsta rap artists in the face of the hypermobility of capital is reminiscent of the phenomena occurring with salsa and *rockero* in the context of Puerto Rico. For instance, Javier Santiago-Lucerna[99] discusses how artists like Ruben Blades and Willie Colon, whose earlier musical productions resonated with a progressive politics, have been absorbed into the politics of the marketplace. According to Santiago-Lucerna, salsa music and the cultural *comarrona* have been transformed into spaces constituted with the cynical sign of consumer culture. In fact, the music being produced in the local rock scene and among local punk bands is currently far more hard-edged politically than salsa, *nueva trova,* and *musica campesina,* as the bands Whisker Biscuit, Kampo Viej, Descojon Urbano, La Experiencia de Tonito Cabanillas, and Sin Remedio can attest. For instance, in "Urban Fuckup," Descojon-Urbano sings:

> Oye es que me da gusto
> Cada vez que cogen a un politico corrupto
> Que cabroneria, que barbaridad
> el pobre se jode y el rico tiene mas
>
> [It gives me so much pleasure
> every time they catch a corrupted politician
> What shit, what an atrocity
> the poor are fucked, while the rich have more][100]

The issue of political domestication and product commodification is on the surface somewhat different in the case of gangsta rap because oppositional political rap is now mainstream. Therefore, it is hard to see what other kinds of music might soon replace rap's hard-edge political critique. Perhaps forms of rap will develop that are not coded in the image of the hypersexualized gangbanger and that begin to address issues of economic exploitation, misogyny, and homophobia.

Critics of gangsta rap need to take seriously Rosemary Hennessy's[101] suggestion that "in postmodern consumer culture the commodity is a central means by which desire is organized."[102] In other words, listeners of gangsta rap affectively invest in the music and video productions. The music produces certain structures of feeling, particular economies of affectivity. But the logic of the commodity conceals certain invisible social relations that need to be considered. The commodity, argues Hennessy, after Marx, is not material in the physical sense alone but rather in the sense that "it is socially produced through human labor and the extraction of surplus value in exchange."[103] Commodity fetishism refers to the "illusion that value resides in objects rather than in the social relations between individuals and objects."[104] In other words, commodity fetishism "entails the misrecognition of a structural effect as an immediate property of one of its elements, as if this property belonged to it outside of its relation to other elements."[105]

Gangsta rap as a commercial product needs to be understood not simply in terms of the way it transgressively signifies social life but in terms of the exploitation of human labor and the way in which the social relations of production and consumption organize everyday human life: in short, in terms of its commodity fetishism. De Genova notes that

> commodified rap music was able to proliferate through the virtual pillage of an ever-expanding universe of already-existing commodified music—instantiating the semblance of something like a parodic auto-cannibalization of the commodity form. The very essence of hip-hop music, as a musical genre which begins with the unabashed appropriation of pre-recorded, mass-produced, commodified music, demonstrates that "public culture" is inevitably and unassailably "public-access culture"—a free-for-all.[106]

Gangsta rap's relation to the corporate marketplace, its potential for expropriation, and its reproduction of ideologies historically necessary to commodity exchange—such as patriarchal ones—is an important issue that needs to be addressed. In other words, gangsta rap needs to be viewed not merely as an ideological formation, cultural signifier, or performative spectacle, but also as the product of historical and social relations. Gangsta rap needs to be seen not only in discursive terms but rather in terms of the materiality of discourse. By materiality of discourse I refer to "the ways culture constructs subjectivities, reproduces power relations, and foments resistance" insofar as these relations and practices are "shaped by social totalities like capitalism, patriarchy, and imperialism as they manifest differently across social formations and within specific historical conjunctures."[107] This is not to say, however, that gangsta rap at the level of the oppositional spectacle is not an important popular counterdiscourse.

Thomas Cushman's important work on understanding the diffusion of revolutionary musical codes raises some important questions about rap (which, unfortunately, exceed the scope of this essay). These questions demand an analysis of the social evolution of gangsta rap as a musical style as it is situated within the world capitalist system. This suggests examining gangsta rap as a restricted code (condensed, context-specific cluster of symbols and meanings) that articulates the existential experience of subordinate groups of African Americans and Puerto Ricans and their everyday dissent. It also means tracing rap's diffusion into an elaborated code (context-free, universal) across time and space into new social contexts and analyzing how its original, organic, revolutionary expression as a means of addressing race and class exploitation has been diffused.[108] For instance, what is to prevent gangsta rap from becoming, in Cushman's terms, a casualty of "a highly developed, world-wide culture industry that operates precisely by scanning the world environment for disturbances, selectively amplifying and altering certain aspects of those disturbances and re-presenting them to large audiences who receive them as entertainment commodities"?[109]

Gangsta rap creates identity through a racial system of intelligibility that produces binary distinctions between blacks and whites, an us-against-them discursive matrix. As a performative signification anchored in the context of the urban ghetto, it constitutes part of the regulatory practices of the dominant culture while at the same time resisting and critiquing this culture.

Diane Fuss, following Frantz Fanon, argues that under conditions of colonialism, blacks are "forced to occupy, in a white racial phantasm, the static ontological space of the timeless 'primitive.'"[110] In this "imaginary relation of fractured specularity," blacks are denied by the white Imperial Subject, the alterity or otherness necessary to achieve subjectivity. Interpellated and fixed into a static objecthood, blacks become neither an "I" nor a "not-I," becoming instead a degraded and devalorized signifier, a fragmented object, a form of pure exteriority.

The transcendental signifier "white," according to Fuss, is never a "not-black," but rather operates from its own self-proclaimed transparency, as a marker that floats imperially over the category of race, operating "as its own Other" and independent from the sign "black" for its symbolic constitution. In terms of the colonial-imperial register of self-other relations, which, as Fuss notes, operates in psychoanalysis and existentialism on the Hegelian principle of negation and incorporation in which the other is assimilated into the self—the white subject can be white without any relation to the black subject because the sign "white" exempts itself from a dialogical logic of negativity. But the black subject must be black in relation to the white subject.

For instance, whereas white rap singer Vanilla Ice was once referred to as "the Elvis of rap," the black singer Al B. Sure was referred to as "the Black Elvis." Lionett cites remarks made by Patricia Williams, who points out the parodic nature of these labels: "Elvis, the white black man of a generation ago, reborn in a black man imitating Elvis." Lionett adds that Elvis is "reborn in Vanilla Ice, a white man imitating the black rapper imitating Elvis: a dizzying thought." The point here is that in the depiction of each rap artist, the major point of reference is white culture.[111]

Imperialist acts of assimilation and incorporation are located at the level of the unconscious. The gangsta is simultaneously a mimicry of subversion and subjugation. Drawing on Homi Bhabha's notion that colonial mimicry possesses the possibility of resisting and subverting dominant systems of representation (through the possibility of mimicry slipping into mockery) as well as subtending them, I want to argue that when it ironizes the role of the incorporated black subject, gangsta rap (at least in its video incarnations) undermines the image of the impotent black subject, de-transcendentalizing it and rendering it unstable.[112] However, when the gangsta rapper undertakes a "parodic hyperbolization" (to borrow Fuss's term) of the subjugated black man—in the figure of the gangsta with a gun—but does not connect it to a larger political project of liberation, this may rupture the image of the subjugated black subject but fail to unsettle the exploitative relations connected to white supremacist patriarchal capitalism. By not connecting its subversion to a larger politics of possibility, gangsta rap runs the risk of ironizing its own act of subversion and parodying its own performance of dissent in such an I-don't-give-a-fuck fashion that, rather than erode dominant social relations of exploitation and subjugation, it may actually reinforce them.

The social realism that accompanies much of the gangsta rap of Ice Cube, Ice-T, and others is situated within a larger political agenda and sets the context for portraying the role of the rapper (qua oppositional cultural forms) as a "truth sayer" and noble revolutionary subject fighting the injustices of the white-controlled megastate. It also builds the ground for a more sustained critique of racist and capitalist social relations.

But in some of the rap videos of, say, Sir Mix-A-Lot or 2 Live Crew, unrealistic portrayals occur of the dissenting black male subject, depicting him as living in ostentatious luxury, surrounded by black and white women massaging their breasts on his car window ("put 'em on the glass") or swaying their G-stringed buttocks in his welcoming face. In this instance, there is a tendency to recuperate a reversionary politics, because the lifestyle of the black hepcat dissenter appears to be exaggerated to the point of parody. Such a parodic representation of the successful black consumer (where women are presented as thong-clad commodities to be plucked from swimming pools) tends to defray and to occlude a larger politics of liberation outside of commodity culture. In this case, the landscape of rap is defoliated in terms of race, class, and gender issues, while dissent is defused into issues of who has the most "babes who got back." In another sense, however, it's also possible to look at 2 Live Crew's videos in a different light. It's possible to overlook the sexism and the hyperbolizing of the black male-as-womanizer by focusing on the consumer trappings of the black rapper—swimming pools, fancy cars, beautiful houses, and available sex. Acquiring these "trappings" becomes a form of resistance because they are not available to the average white or black subject. The problem here is rap's apparent legitimation of capitalist social relations of consumption. Do rappers—including gangsta rappers—just want to make the pleasures of patriarchal capitalism available to all black males?

Can gangsta rap move beyond Benjamin's shock effects, its decontextualization as an effect of its mechanical reproducibility, beyond the space of its own commercial structures, beyond its ideological prohibitions, its structures of expectation, its demarcations of despair—all of which create a locus of signifying phantasms and perverse forms of the "other," which, in turn, collaborate with neoliberal approaches to politics that ultimately wrest away rap's oppositional potency? To create a praxis of both opposition and possibility, gangsta rap needs to undertake the construction of new identities that are refractory to commodification. It must continue to perturb society, to shape culture on a deeper level. Hip-hop culture must provide spaces of resistance and transgression, without succumbing to political incoherence. Only in this way will it be able to prevent its revolutionary potential from being articulated to the terms of the official culture of consumption that defuses adversarial codes into the cultural logic of the aesthetic.

Despite the always-present threat of commodification, gangsta rap still poses a serious challenge to the formation of new identities of resistance and social transformation. The new identities surrounding various articulations of gangsta rap hold both unforeseen promises and potential dangers. As Lipsitz remarks, "to think of identities as interchangeable or infinitely open does violence to the historical and social constraints imposed on us by structures of exploitation and privilege. But to posit innate and immobile identities for ourselves and others confuses history with nature, and denies the possibility of change."[113]

The challenge that confronts gangsta rap in particular and hip-hop culture in general is the extent to which it contributes to the defamiliarization of the Western sovereign subject, the Euro-American imperial subject, and the extent to which it can become self-conscious of the relations of power and privilege that create the context for and overdetermine its cultural exchanges. This means, as I have argued above, linking a politics of semiotic subversion to a critique of the material social relations of exploitation that have been largely responsible for the problems faced by people of color in the United States.

Manning Marable speaks to a new articulation of the concept of blackness that is defined not in racial or ethnic/cultural terms but as a political category that speaks to new forms of political mobilization:

> We must find new room in our identity as people of color to include all other oppressed national minorities—Chicanos, Peurto Ricans, Asian/Pacific Americans, and other people of African descent. We must find the common ground we share with oppressed people who are not national minorities—working-class people, the physically challenged, the homeless, the unemployed, and those Americans who suffer discrimination because they are lesbian or gay. I believe that a new mul-

ticultural America is possible, that a renaissance of Black militancy will occur in concert with new levels of activism from the constituencies mentioned above. But it is possible only if we have the courage to challenge and to overturn our own historical assumptions about race, power, and ourselves. Only then will we find the new directions necessary to challenge the system, to "fight the power," with an approach toward political culture that can truly liberate all of us.[114]

In its most politically enabling formations, gangsta rap is able to create a space of resistance in which black identity is not dependent upon whiteness to complete it. It escapes colonial mimesis through a series of cultural relays that keeps identity fluid and shifting. The particular liberatory values that are affirmed in gangsta rap need, however, to coreside with other resonant values rooted in the contingency and radical historicity of oppressed groups throughout the globe. For white folks this means not simply a *tolerance of* difference but rather a critical *engagement with* difference on a global scale.

The recent death of Tupac Shakur provides a bitter lesson about the best and worst of gangsta rap. Tupac's reputation as one of the most hard-core of the gangsta rappers and his obsession with living the "authenticity" of the streets as a "real nigga" eventually rebounded against him as he brought together his own brand of what Mike Dyson calls "thuggery and thanatopsis."[115] Dyson remarks that "the Real Niggas are trapped by their own contradictory couplings of authenticity and violence. Tupac's death is the most recent, and perhaps most painful, evidence of that truth."[116] Dyson further notes that Tupac's own project constituted "a sad retreat from a much more complex, compelling vision of black life that gangsta rap and hard-core hip-hop, at its best, helped outline."[117] In his art of "celeterrogation" (what Dyson calls "the deft combination of celebration and interrogation") Tupac embodied the best and the worst of gangsta rap. Dyson eloquently comments:

> by joining verbal vigor to rage—about material misery and racial hostility, about the avalanche of unheard suffering that suffocates black lives before they wake, walk or will their own survival—hard-core rappers proved that theirs was a redemptive vulgarity. At their best, they showed that the real vulgarity was the absurd way too many black folk perish on the vine of fruitless promises of neighborhood restoration, of racial rehabilitation. The hard-core hip-hopper proved that the real vulgarity was the vicious anonymity and punishing silence of poor black life, with which they broke faith every time they seized a mike to bring poetry to pain. . . . But, in the end, despite all his considerable gifts, Tupac helped pioneer a more dangerous, even more destructive, trend in hard-core hip-hop that, ironically, draws from the oral energy of the orthodox black culture from which he sought thuggish refuge.

Tupac yearned to live the life he rapped about in his songs. That golden ideal was the motive behind gospel passions in black culture to close the gap between preaching and practice, between what one said and what one did.[118]

As long as African Americans and other historically marginalized social groups are perceived by whites to be artificial constructions—in effect, artificial white people—who exist largely to be economically exploited or else reinvented and rewarded by whites in the sphere of leisure culture for their own entertainment, then it is unlikely that democracy will ever be achievable. As long as the rules by which society functions continue to be defined by the white majority, and the interpretation of such rules continues to be controlled by a dominant capitalist elite, then the concept of equality is nothing but a hollow term. As long as the liberal pluralistic society in which we all participate is controlled a priori by our failure to address the problem of material exploitation, then gangsta rap will operate out of necessity as a serious critique of U.S. cultural life. As long as the politically unifying cultural understanding that pluralists posit as the framework for democratic social life continues to read narratives such as gangsta rap as necessarily threatening to social harmony, then success in our society will always be racially determined.

Equal access to shared symbols of nationhood do not spell democracy for any group when such symbols are discouraged from being interrogated, reanimated, and transformed. More importantly, equal access to the material necessities of human survival and dignity must be made a fundamental prerequisite for democracy. Anything less than this makes a mockery of the ideal of social justice. In this context, the "brothas" and "sistahs" of gangsta rap are demanding that democracy live up to its promises. They challenge—by any means necessary—democracy to rearticulate its mission in view of the current urban nightmare in which the melting pot itself has melted in a postpluralist firestorm. How must we rethink identity when the container can no longer contain, when the ladle dissolves in the mixture, when the signifier ceases to signify?

If British sociologists Scott Lash and John Urry are correct in asserting that "we are not so much thrown into communities, but decide which communities—from youth subcultures to new social movements—we shall throw ourselves into," then what sort of aesthetic (hermeneutic) reflexivity is required in the case of gangsta rap?[119] What is at issue when the ideographic mode of gangsta-ing is counterposed to conduct regulated by the abstract norm-governed social structure of the state? Is this a question of what Lash and Urry call "race-baiting neotribes" or the beginning of "new communitarian social movements"? What happens when the wild zones of information flows and networks of the so-called underclass enter into a marriage with the new informational bourgeoisie?

In an era in which the subject is located as ambivalent and grounded in lost referents and instabilities within signifying chains, gangsta rap draws needed attention to the importance, not only of disidentifying with the cultural obvious but also of recognizing that the difference rendered most invisible in the production of postmodern cultural representations is the difference between rich and poor. We are viscerally reminded by gangsta rappers that cultural identities and practices remain tied to capital's drive to accumulate profits through the appropriation of labor that relies historically on forms of racism, patriarchy, and imperialism.[120]

EPILOGUE

The casket carrying the body of Notorious B.I.G. (Christopher Wallace, a.k.a. Biggie Smalls) rests in a hearse winding its way past 226 St. James Place in the rapper's old Brooklyn neighborhood toward the Frank E. Campbell Funeral Chapel in Manhattan's Upper East Side. Two black Cadillacs filled with flowers—the letters B.I.G. are spelled out in brilliant red carnations—are spotted driving through Bedford-Stuyvesant. At the open casket service, fans stricken with grief catch a glimpse of Junior M.A.F.I.A., Flavor Flav, Dr. Dre, Spinderella, and Sister Souljah. For the postmodern theorist, there is a whole lot of signifying going on. For the people lined up outside the funeral home—who don't have the consolation of the sociology seminar room—the issue is not one of semiotics but of survival. It is not an event that calls for interpretation. It is an event that calls for a commitment to struggle.

NOTES

This chapter comprises approximately forty-two pages from *Revolutionary Multiculturalism: Pedagogies of Dissent for the New Millennium*, ed. Peter McLaren. Copyright 1997 by Westview Press. Reprinted here with the generous permission of Westview Press.

Special thanks to Carlos Tejeda. Ash Vasudeva, Warren Crinchlow, Makeba Jones, Karl Bruce Knapper, Michelle Knight, Mike Seltzer, and Nicole Baker for their helpful suggestions.

1. Jesse Katz, "Rap Furor: New Evil or Old Story," *Los Angeles Times,* August 5, 1995, pp. 1, 18, 19; Steve Proffitt, "Russell Simmons: Defending the Art of Communication Known as Rap," *Los Angeles Times,* August 27, 1995, p. M3.

2. Time Warner Inc. has formally abandoned its $115 million stake in Interscope Records, blaming the split on contractual provisions that prevented the company from monitoring the content of Interscope's gangsta rappers such as Dr. Dre and Snoop Doggy Dogg. Bob Dole claimed responsibility for this development claiming he "shamed" Time Warner into dropping their gangsta rappers ("Time Warner to Abandon Gangsta Rap," *Los Angeles Times,* September 28, 1995, pp. 1, 13).

3. Katz, "Rap Furor." Richard Berry's original hit in 1955, "Louie Louie," was Afro-Calypsonian yet was influenced by the Rhythm Rockers, a Chicano-Filipino band from Orange County, California. Band members had introduced Berry to René Touset's "Loca cha cha," which provided Berry with the model for "Louie Louie." See George Lipsitz, "The Bands of Tomorrow Are Here Today: The Proud, Progressive and Postmodern Sounds of Las Tres and Goddess 13," in *Musical Aesthetics and Multiculturalism, ed. Steven Loza* (Los Angeles: University of California, Department of Ethnomusicology and Systematic Musicology, 1994), pp. 139–47. "Louie Louie" has been recorded by more than three hundred artists, for example, Ike and Tina Turner, the Kinks, the Beach Boys, Tom Petty and the Heartbreakers, Frank Zappa, Iggy Pop, and even the Rice University Marching Owl Band. A resident of South Central Los Angeles, Berry contributed vocals to the Robins' "Riot in Cell Block No. 9" and Etta James's "Roll with Me Henry (the Wallflower)."

4. Ibid.

5. Cited in Douglas Rushkoff, *Media Virus* (New York: Ballantine Books, 1996), p. 163.

6. Ibid.

7. John L. Mitchell, "Third Trial Ruled out in Slaying by Officer," *Los Angeles Times,* February 4, 1995, pp. B1, B8. See also Rosalind Muhammad, "LA Gangs Honored in Keeping the Peace," *Final Call* 14.21 (Aug. 16, 1995): 4, 10.

8. Tricia Rose, *Black Noise: Rap Music and Black Culture in Contemporary America* (Hanover, N.H.: Wesleyan University Press, 1994), p. 4.

9. Jeffrey Louis Decker, "The State of Rap: The Time and Place of Hip Hop Nationalism," in *Microphone Friends: Youth Music, Youth Culture,* ed. Andrew Ross and Tricia Rose (New York: Routledge, 1994), p. 101.

10. Ibid.

11. Rose, *Black Noise.*

12. Ibid.

13. Ibid., p. 59.

14. Ibid.

15. Tommy Lott, "Black Vernacular Representation and Cultural Malpractice," in *Multiculturalism: A Critical Reader,* ed. David Theo Goldberg (Cambridge, Mass.: Basil Blackwell, 1994), p. 246.

16. Tricia Rose, "A Style Nobody Can Deal With: Politics, Style, and the Postindustrial City in Hip Hop," in *Microphone Friends,* ed. Ross and Rose, pp. 71–88.

17. George Lipsitz, *Dangerous Crossroads: Popular Music, Postmodernism, and the Poetics of Place* (London: Verso, 1994).

18. Carol Tulloch, "Rebel without a Pause: Black Street Style and Black Designers," in *Chic Thrills: A Fashion Reader*, ed. Juliet Ash and Elizabeth Wilson (Berkeley: University of California Press, 1993), pp. 84–98.

19. Ibid.

20. Kristal Brent Zook, "Reconstruction of Nationalist Thought in Black Music and Culture," in *Rockin' the Boat: Mass Music, and Mass Movement*, ed. Rebee Garofalo (Boston: South End Press, 1992), p. 257.

"Playing the dozens" and "signifying" are variations of African American linguistic practices or traditions that can be characterized as ritualized verbal contests or wars of words. The "dozens" are confrontations of wit, intellect, and repartee played out in lingual games of one-upmanship that are distinguished by lexical originality and creativity, mental dexterity, and verbal innovation and agility in the effective deployment of clever and sarcastic insults or put-downs. A continuation of a rich African diasporic oral tradition that has been distilled through the lens of the African American experience, playing the dozens and signifying are the ultimate expression of brains over brawn—spoken word showdowns that have transformed and elevated a marginalized community's collective humor, anger, joy, and pain in the face of adversity into a game of survival, a ritualized form of entertainment, and a highly valued and respected sociocultural art form. See James Percelay, Monteria Ivey, and Stephan Dweck, eds., *SNAPS* (New York: Quill/William Morrow, 1994), pp. 8–9, 16–23, 27–35, 161–67.

21. Rose, *Black Noise*.

22. Tricia Rose, "Give Me a (Break) Beat! Sampling and Repetition in Rap Production," in *Culture on the Brink: Ideologies of Technology*, ed. Gretchen Bender and Timothy Druckrey (Seattle, Wash.: Bay Press, 1994), p. 251.

23. Rose, *Black Noise*, p. 4.

24. Lawrence Grossberg, "Is Anybody Listening? Does Anybody Care? On 'The State of Rock,'" in *Microphone Friends*, ed. Ross and Rose, pp. 41–58.

25. Michael Dyson, "The Politics of Black Masculinity and the Ghetto in Black Film," in *The Subversive Imagination: Artists, Society, and Social Responsibility*, ed. Carol Becker (London: Routledge, 1994), pp. 159–60.

26. Rose, "A Style Nobody Can Deal With," p. 71.

27. Dick Hebdige, *Cut 'n' Mix* (London: Comedia, 1987).

28. Ibid.

29. Robin D. G. Kelley, *Race Rebels: Culture, Politics, and the Black Working Class* (New York: Free Press, 1994), p. 184.

30. Cited in Rushkoff, *Media Virus*, p. 164.

31. Juan Flores, "Puerto Rican and Proud, Boyee! Rap, Roots, and Amnesia," in *Microphone Friends*, ed. Ross and Rose.

32. Jack Cheevers, Chuck Philips, and Frank B. Williams, "Violence Tops the Charts," *Los Angeles Times*, April 3, 1995, pp. 1–18.

33. Ibid., p. 18. Young and Knight have since broken up their partnership. With a record eight criminal convictions (mostly for assault and weapons charges), Marion "Suge" Knight is currently serving time in a Chino prison while awaiting a Superior Court hearing. In 1995 he entered no-contest pleas to two accounts of assault that involved the beating of two rappers in a Hollywood

recording studio. Under a plea bargain he was given a suspended nine-year prison term and five years probation. Since it was discovered that Knight had cut a record deal with the original prosecutor's eighteen-year-old daughter and had lived in the prosecutor's Malibu Colony house through the summer of 1996, the prosecutor was dropped from the case. At the MGM Hotel in Los Vegas, just hours before Tupac Shakur was fatally wounded in a car driven by Knight, a surveillance videotape showed Knight and several Death Row employees attacking a Crips gang member. This led to the revoking of Knight's parole. Death Row Records is currently under investigation by the Federal Bureau of Investigation, the Internal Revenue Service, the Bureau of Alcohol, Tobacco and Firearms and the Drug Enforcement Administration for funding crimes by the Mob Piru set of the Bloods street gang, for allegedly engaging in business deals with "drug kingpins" Michael Harris and Ricardo Crockett, and for dealing with entrepreneurs linked to organized crime factions that included New York Mafia figures Joseph Colombo Jr. and Alphonse "the Whale" Mellolla (Chuck Philips and Alan Abrahamson, "U.S. Probes Death Row Record Label's Money Trail," *Los Angeles Times*, December 29, 1996, pp. A1, A34, A35).

34. Proffitt, "Russell Simmons," p. M3.

35. Matthew T. Grant, "Of Gangstas and Guerrillas: Distance Lends Enchantment," *Appendx* 2 (1994): 44.

36. Katz, "Rap Furor," p. 18

37. Ibid.

38. Ibid.

39. David Troop, *Rap Attack: African Jive to New York Hip Hop* (London: Pluto Press, 1984); Houston Baker, *Black Studies: Rap and the Academy* (Chicago: University of Chicago Press, 1993); Rose, *Black Noise*.

40. Lipsitz, *Dangerous Crossroads*.

41. Nick De Genova, "Gangster Rap and Nihilism in Black America: Some Questions of Life and Death," *Social Text* 13.2 (1995): 113.

42. Ibid., p. 114.

43. Rose, "A Style Nobody Can Deal With," p. 83.

44. Tommy Lott, "Black Vernacular Representation," p. 247.

45. Charles P. Pierce, "Sunshine Is Back!" *Los Angeles Times Magazine*, April 23, 1995, pp. 12–15, 35, 36.

46. Tommy Lott, "Black Vernacular Representation," p. 246.

47. Angela Davis, "Discussion," in *Black Popular Culture*, ed. Gina Dent (Seattle, Wash.: Bay Press, 1992), p. 327.

48. Decker, "State of Rap," p. 109.

49. Ibid., p. 110.

50. Steven Gregory, "Race and Racism: A Symposium," *Social Text* 13.1 (1995): 16–21.

51. Ibid., p. 20.

52. Decker, "State of Rap," p. 116.

53. Tricia Rose, "Black Texts/Black Contexts," in *Black Popular Culture*, ed. Dent, p. 226.

54. Zook, "Nationalist Thought," p. 256.

55. De Genova, "Gangsta Rap and Nihilism," p. 111.

56. Ibid., p. 107.

57. Lipsitz, *Dangerous Crossroads*, p. 38.

58. bell hooks, *Black Looks: Race and Representation* (Boston: South End Press, 1992), pp. 35–36; emphasis in original.

59. De Genova, "Gangsta Rap and Nihilism," p. 107.

60. Grant, "Gangstas and Guerrillas," p. 45.

61. Ibid. See also the important work of Stephen Haymes, *Race, Culture, and the City: A Pedagogy for Black Urban Struggle* (Albany: State University of New York Press, 1995).

62. Grant, "Gangstas and Guerrillas," p. 47.

63. Ibid.

64. Ibid.

65. Ibid., p. 51.

66. Ibid.

67. Ibid.

68. De Genova, "Gangsta Rap and Nihilism," p. 105.

69. Michel de Certeau, *The Practice of Everyday Life* (Berkeley: University of California Press, 1984), pp. 31–32.

70. Tommy Lott, "Black Vernacular Representation," p. 249.

71. De Genova, "Gangsta Rap and Nihilism," p. 116.

72. Tommy Lott, "Black Vernacular Representation," p. 246.

73. Peter McLaren, *Critical Pedagogy and Predatory Culture* (London: Routledge, 1995).

74. Jon Stratton, "The Beast of the Apocalypse: The Post-Colonial Experience of the United States," *New Formations* 21 (Winter 1993): 35–63.

75. De Genova, "Gangsta Rap and Nihilism," p. 106.

76. Ibid., p. 119.

77. Zook, "Nationalist Thought," p. 263.

78. Kelley, *Race Rebels*, p. 212.

79. Grant, "Gangstas and Guerrillas," p. 52.

80. Leerom Medovoi, "Mapping the Rebel Image: Postmodernism and the Masculinist Politics of Rock in the U.S.A.," *Cultural Critique* 20 (Winter 1991–92): 165.

81. Eric Lott, "Cornel West in the Hour of Chaos: Culture and Politics in *Race Matters*," *Social Text* 12.3 (1994): 41.

82. Ibid., pp. 41, 43.

83. Ibid., p. 42.

84. Tommy Lott, "Black Vernacular Representation," p. 246.

85. Kelley, *Race Rebels*, p. 210; emphasis in original. Kelley also points out that the term *nigger* made a "comeback" at the height of the Black Power movement of the 1960s when a distinction was made between *nigger* and *negro*—the latter signified a sellout or a brainwashed black person.

86. Lipsitz, *Dangerous Crossroads*, p. 127.

87. Ibid., p. 89.

88. Ibid., p. 90.

89. Ibid., p. 58.

90. Grant, "Gangstas and Guerrillas," p. 40.

91. McLaren, *Critical Pedagogy.*

92. Grant, "Gangstas and Guerrillas," p. 41.

93. Steve Appleford, "The Rise and Fall of Gangsta Rap," *Los Angeles Reader,* March 3, 1995, pp. 8–11, 56.

94. Ibid., p. 9.

95. Ibid.

96. Ibid., p. 11.

97. Donnell Alexander, "Closed Border: The Hip-Hop Nation Deports Alternative Rap. Michael Ivey's B.Y.O.B.," *LA Weekly* 17.17 (March 24–30, 1995): 39–40.

98. Thomas Cushman, "Rich Rastas and Communist Rockers: A Comparative Study of the Origin, Diffusion, and Delusion of Revolutionary Musical Codes," *Journal of Popular Culture* 25.3 (1991): 17–61.

99. Javier Santiago-Lucerna, "Nothing's Sacred, Everything's Profane: Rock Isleno and the Politics of National Identity in Puerto Rico," paper presented at York University, Toronto, March 1995, pp. 16–17.

100. Ibid.

101. Rosemary Hennessy, "Queer Visibility in Commodity Culture," *Cultural Critique* 29 (Winter 1994–95): 31–76.

102. Ibid., p. 52.

103. Ibid., p. 53.

104. Ibid.

105. Ibid.

106. De Genova, "Gangsta Rap and Nihilism," pp. 105–6.

107. Hennessy, "Queer Visibility," p. 33.

108. Cushman, "Rich Rastas," pp. 17–61.

109. Ibid., p. 48. According to Christian Parenti, prisoners are being exploited as cheap labor and their wages are used to pay for their incarceration. He notes that "the California Department of Corrections is also trying to find a niche in Japan's jeans market with its new line of 'Gangsta Blues.' Thus, the much deplored hip-hop culture of African-American and Latino youths—which has embraced the look of denim workclothes—is being imitated, glorified, and sold back to the public by the very criminal justice system that claims to wage war on Gangsta culture" (Parenti, *New Statement and Society,* November 3, 1995, pp. 20–21).

110. Diane Fuss, "Interior Colonies: Frantz Fanon and the Politics of Identification," *Diacritics* 24.2–3 (Summer–Fall 1994): 21.

111. Françoise Lionett, *Postcolonial Representations: Women, Literature, Identity* (Ithaca, N.Y.: Cornell University Press, 1995), p. 10.

112. Homi Bhabha, "Of Mimicry and Man: The Ambivalence of Colonial Discourse," *October* 28 (1984): pp. 125–33.

113. Lipsitz, *Dangerous Crossroads,* p. 62.

114. Manning Marable, "Race, Identity, and Political Culture," in *Black Popular Culture,* ed. Dent, p. 302.

115. Michael Eric Dyson, "Tupac: Living the Life He Rapped about in Song," *Los Angeles Times,* Sunday October 22, 1996, p. 3.

116. Ibid.

117. Ibid.

118. Ibid.

119. Scott Lash and John Urry, *Economies of Signs and Space* (London: Sage, 1992), p. 316.

120. Teresa Ebert, "The Surplus of Enjoyment in the Post-al Real," *Rethinking Marxism* 7.3 (1994): 137–42.

CHAPTER 9

Battlin' Nihilism at an Urban High School: Pedagogy, Perseverance, and Hope

David Keiser

The proper starting point for the crucial debate about the prospects for black America is an examination of the nihilism that increasingly pervades black communities. . . . Nihilism is to be understood here not as a philosophical doctrine that there are no rational grounds for legitimate standards or authority; it is, far more, the lived experience of coping with a life of horrifying meaninglessness, hopelessness, and (most important) lovelessness. The frightening result is a numbing detachment from others and a self-destructive disposition toward the world. Life without meaning, hope, and love breeds a cold-hearted, mean spirited outlook that destroys both the individual and others.[1]

What Cornel West and others describe as a culture rooted directly in violence, whose defining principles are homicide, cultural suicide, and social decay, touches many students living in inner cities. Nihilism within urban communities in the United States gravely affects schools. Students bring their lived experiences to school; if students live amid nihilist conditions, their schools will feel the ripples. Students preoccupied with pressing problems such as violence, drugs, and poverty may see school less as a stable social institution than as an additional stress on their lives. Schools need to at least acknowledge these problems, if not make them explicit in curriculum; if students fail to see school as a place where they can grapple with and interrogate their life circumstances, they will be less likely to invest in school.

They may see teachers as indifferent to their problems, and consequently feel alienated and detached from the institution. Some students' alienation may manifest as truancy, defiance, or illicit behavior on school property.[2] Teachers may react defensively, and treat students as unteachable. If students have learning disabilities as well, the problem is compounded, for despite a recent spate of "full-inclusion" rhetoric, many students with learning disabilities or behavioral problems remain ostracized and marginalized within public schools.[3]

INTRODUCTION

The Corner Campus is a 160 student high school in northern California. It is significantly smaller than other local high schools. The Campus enrolls students who do not succeed in other schools, and, according to the school brochure, "who are looking for or need an alternative to the traditional high schools." While some students face arduous conditions outside school, the policy inside the Campus is to promote critical thinking and agency; even if Campus students live amid nihilist threats, their school tries to provide meaning, hope, and love.

This chapter is about the students of the Corner Campus and the issues they face and make salient in school. The methods used by the Campus teachers and staff in reaching and teaching their students deserve recognition and emulation; my contribution to such recognition is the impetus for this paper. In my first seven months at the school, I noticed a distinctive and intentional critical pedagogy. The teachers make societal inequity explicit, relearn curricula with students, incorporate student experiences, and teach dialogically.[4] Such methodology may counter student nihilism, the loss of hope that school can provide meaning and nurture possibility. Many students see the school as listening to their stories and accepting and educating them despite prohibitive conditions such as gang affiliation, past or present incarceration/probation, and illicit extracurricular activity like drug dealing.

I frame this paper around the collision of critical pedagogy and student nihilism; the possibility that a critical pedagogical perspective may mitigate student attrition and disinvestment in school. In this chapter I ask the following questions: What makes this alternative school work for its students? Given that students can talk freely about their experiences,[5] what do they talk about? What are the problems or frustrations of teaching critically amid violent and impoverished conditions? Lastly, I wonder to what extent teachers can validate student voice without encouraging or condoning illicit behavior? I address these questions through the themes of violence, drugs, and rap music and culture, as manifest both through previously published empirical literature and through student work samples.

RESEARCH SETTING

The school is centrally located in a busy urban neighborhood. It is located across from an outpatient hospital, and within walking distance of several bus stops. It is surrounded by a parking lot, a rarely used basketball court, and a vacant lot. The actual campus of the Campus consists of the steps in front of the school. A hot dog vendor sells franks and sodas diagonally across the street, and several eateries are within two city blocks.

The regular school day consists of three seventy-five minute periods between nine and one, and tutoring, makeup work, or workshops after school. The extended class periods are almost double those in regular high schools, and provide curricular flexibility and greater time for dialogue between students and teachers. Furthermore, fewer class periods means fewer bells and fewer student transitions between classrooms.

The school is located in an old and spacious school building with twelve classrooms and several offices. Unlike other overcrowded schools in the district, size is not a problem, save the lack of a lunchroom, auditorium, or gym. Behind the school, there are netless basketball hoops amid unremarkable asphalt. The structural problems are leaky, wood-exposed ceilings, walls with chipping plaster, no doors on bathroom stalls, and old gas spigots sticking out of some classroom floors. The hallways of the two floors are partially lined with student writing samples and school murals. On the second floor, a double door is covered with sexy hip hop lyrics and photos from Ebony and Vibe magazines and the acronym LIFE; Ladies in Full Effect.[6] Inside these doors, a part-time school counselor sees students throughout the day, and teaches a class about female empowerment[7] once a week. But the doors themselves connote an urban adolescent spirit bespeaking physical and sexual maturity.

CORNER CAMPUS KIDS

The school brochure describes the students of the Campus as being

> of all racial, ethnic, and cultural groups. They come from neighborhoods from (this) and other cities in the area. . . . Students come to the Campus for many reasons. Some prefer an alternative to the traditional high school. Some have fallen behind in earning their credits and want to catch up. Others have dropped out of school for personal reasons and now want to resume their studies. They are referred by counselors, friends, and family.

Also in the pamphlet is the rejoinder that all new students must be interviewed by their peers and teachers. Accountability is overt: "Students must also show a commitment to the right of others to learn." Every student agrees to this prior to admission. Thus, the staff expects that students come to school ready and eager to learn, but clearly, this idealistic expectation is mitigated, because some students attend the Campus for reasons ranging from truancy to behavior problems.[8] Some, however, choose the Campus for its small size and pedagogical strengths.

Nina, a fourth-year language arts teacher, posits that while most students attend because they take school seriously, others are persuaded to attend a school cited by the state as a "model dropout prevention program."

> Some come from a small safe environment or 'cuz they've heard its a good small school with an alternative curriculum or they knew somebody who came here. . . . A few people come just cuz they live in the neighborhood. . . . I think 95% of them here think that being in school is important and a step to success—that's reflected in their being here. I think that some of them are under some form of coercion by their parents or their p.o.[9] or something.

RESEARCH QUESTIONS AND PAPER PARAMETERS

My original research question was 'What makes students invest in the Corner Campus?' But I think that given small classes, caring teachers, and a shorter school day, a better question would ask why some students don't invest. However, I changed my focus when I realized the answer to this question might vary greatly between students. Considering the heterogeneous student populace, my "answer" doubtless would conflate with issues too large for this project.[10] I was still interested in my question but guessed the answer would revolve around the size of the school and the dedication and flexibility of the teachers.

Early in the study I worried about the role of the Campus in its students' lives; later I began to worry about the students. When I got to know the students, and read their work, I became interested in how they made sense of their world verbally and in writing. That is, what were salient themes in their life? In a school clearly focused on student voice, emancipation and agency, what themes emerge?

Rather than simply take notes and interview staff, I taught a basic skills writing workshop, and in seven months, countless themes surfaced, many of which interest me as much as those I chose to write about here. In thinking about nihilism within schools and students, and about the human spirit vis-à-vis education and society, I wonder when and how students decide to sell drugs for a quick profit rather than stay in school for a diploma. I wonder as well, what awaits my students five or ten years from now if they invest in school? And if they don't?

From one workshop's worth of student stories, I focus on violence, drugs, and hip-hop culture only because these themes seemed most salient at the time. My title, "Battlin' Nihilism," pays homage to the students and teachers of the Corner Campus who resist the temptation to give up amid drugs, violence, and social and economic inequities. The teachers do this by struggling with critical pedagogy in practice; the students by attending school to obtain a high school diploma.

CRITICAL PEDAGOGICAL POSSIBILITIES

Critical pedagogy, with its goals of empowering the powerless and transforming social injustice through schooling, represents one strategy for elucidating inequity within a curricular context.[11] All students need to learn to think critically about society and themselves. Human agency is innate, and it is up to schools, among other sites, to nurture student agency, and to inspire students to praxis.[12] If schools and classrooms do not serve as pressure valves from the craziness permeating many urban communities, and if they no longer represent possibilities for change and betterment for students, the nihilist threat will increase. If the pay-off, the result of attending school is meaningless, why go to school? That is, teachers need to better understand and incorporate their students' realities in order to keep student hope alive.

As a former special education teacher, where critical pedagogy is harder to implement, I was excited to do research and work at a school without labels, one which espouses students reading the word *and* the world.[13] Campus teachers learn about students' worlds through dialogic teaching methods, where students' stories become part of the curriculum.[14] Their stories bespeak current urban adolescent realities, several of which are addressed in this paper. Within the Campus, students study current social issues that directly impact their lives. Thus, teachers often focus on issues such as drugs, violence, sex, teen pregnancy, rape, and domestic violence.

STUDENT TEACHERS AND TEACHER STUDENTS: THE ACTS OF KNOWING AND REKNOWING

Teachers, students, and researchers must be jointly active in the learning process. All must have chances to learn and to construct and revise theories about what and how they know. They must be free to use the language of give-and-take to negotiate ideas, to build knowledge, and to acquire new skills to prepare for lifelong learning.[15]

The above quote addresses critical pedagogy and dialogic teaching, and calls on teachers to learn from students.[16] While many teachers still resist "the language of give-and-take" and maintain "chalk and talk" classrooms, others challenge didactic pedagogy.[17]

In his seminal book *Pedagogy of the Oppressed,* Paulo Freire contrasts the models of banking versus problem-posing education. In the former, students are passive receptacles of knowledge and "accounts" into which teachers deposit knowledge that may be withdrawn for tests, papers, or not at all. The latter model posits teachers and students learning and relearning units of study together, while posing critical questions along the way to gaining knowledge. This problem-posing model assumes both that teachers think their students' knowledge worthwhile, and that they are willing to adapt their teaching style to student needs.

Building on the Freirean model, James Cummins constructed a pedagogical continuum ranging from "reciprocal, interaction-oriented" to "transmission-oriented."[18] Thus, teachers perceive students either as coparticipants in the act of learning or as passive recipients of the instructor's knowledge. Both Freire and Cummins identify the variability of power relations within classrooms. If teachers see students as "bank accounts," or empty vessels needing a "transmission of knowledge," the modes of instruction and themes for analysis will be quite different than if teachers see students as active educational participants or agents of change.

ONE EXAMPLE OF HOW TEACHERS CAN SQUELCH STUDENT AGENCY

In my work as a special education teacher and supervisor, I saw how teacher expectations and attitudes affect student performance and readiness to learn. I visited schools throughout the Bay Area, and witnessed some demoralizing pedagogical practice. This was manifest through uncreative and demeaning assignments, multiple student expulsions, hostile rapport and even rudeness. But low teacher expectations especially hinder praxis and agency: when students perceive that teachers don't care about their presence or their education, excitement to learn converts quickly to hostility. Students get expelled from class for hours or sometimes days at a time for being loud, or because they are literally misunderstood. They learn that questioning authority may be tantamount to forfeiting opportunities to learn.

For example, the phrase "why ya gotta be bitin' on my caps?" is urban literate;[19] it is neither profane nor disrespectful to the teacher, but I saw a student expelled for two hours for saying that within a middle school classroom. The comment was actually subtle closure to a two to three insult exchange that the teacher missed entirely. But she reacted to what she perceived as threatening, or simply too loud for her class, which had not yet even begun. Antagonism toward students—especially ones already labeled "special" or "at risk" learners—is counterproductive. It affects the other students and their possibilities as well. Pervasive apathy between students, teachers, support staff, and even administration can snowball into complacency and negligence. This chapter concerns an antithetical snowball.

SOME REASONS WHY STUDENTS FAIL AT OTHER SCHOOLS

While most educators might agree that public schools need help, larger questions are why do they need help? Or, what can be done? We need to examine schools not as autonomous institutions, but as agents of social and academic reproduction.[20] Students learn in school, but also learn to "do" school. Students conforming to expectations of teachers, schools, and society do better in school. But what does society expect from schools? Or from students? In this nexus of student and school expectations, the role of cultural capital is crucial. For the purposes of this chapter, I employ Henry Giroux's definition of student cultural capital: the amalgamation of differing cognitive, linguistic, and dispositional or behavioral attributes that students bring to school.[21]

Dispositional attributes are of course inseparable from their cognitive and linguistic attributes. How and why students behave or misbehave in school may well be related to cognitive and linguistic competence, and especially how this competence is perceived by school and society. Students who do not conform, assimilate, and succeed within schools may be labeled learning disabled, culturally deficient, emotionally disturbed, behaviorally disordered, or simply "too loud." Thus, students learn that resistance is often tantamount to educational exclusion, and may internalize their placement; that is, they belong in special, or alternative, or remedial education.

In addition to behavioral norms, students and indeed their schools, are held to state-imposed curricular standards. One problem with "standardizing" curricula is that schools are not neutral, and knowledge is not objective. Recent revived policy battles over teaching evolution, book banning, sex education, and "multicultural" historical perspectives bear witness. But current educational policy and debate focuses on "the basic curriculum," not on basic human needs of security, safety, and health. Emphasizing curricular standards precludes and prevents treating larger societal ills such as racism and rampant poverty. A 1996 *New York Times* op-ed piece offers this summation on the eve of a second national education summit:

> The public schools offer perhaps the clearest picture of our nation's economic and social health. President Clinton and other leaders are often heard worrying about the poor performance of American students, especially compared to students in other industrialized countries. But they must remember that this poor performance is and always had been partly a symptom of our neglect of the many social crises that afflict our nation.[22]

A critical pedagogy illuminates these symptoms instead of neglects them, because when students bring "social crises" into classrooms, it affects their capacity and desire to learn academic material, and teachers are left between a rock of school bureaucracy and the hard place in which their students exist. That is, schools choose whether "back to basics" means basic human needs or basic academic skills. They need not be mutually exclusive, but teachers must be willing to make social crises and their impact on students an explicit part of curricula and further analyze the "relationship between classroom objectives and cultural capital":

> crucial to the development of progressive classroom social relationships is the opening of channels of communication which allow students to use those forms of linguistic and cultural capital though which they give meaning to their everyday experiences. If students are subjected in the classroom to a language as well as a set of beliefs and values whose implicit message is that they are culturally illiterate, students will learn very little about critical thinking, and a great deal about what Freire has called the "culture of silence."[23]

One manifestation of the "culture of silence" is that students learn that if they don't disrupt the teacher, they will pass the class; if they resist their teacher or their schoolwork, they will handicap their progress. Critical pedagogy opposes the culture of silence, and posits that student experience is the curriculum, and should determine what is prioritized in classrooms. For many public school students, particularly in large urban areas, student experience is laced with violence, but teachers ultimately decide how fully to incorporate such experience into their teaching and curricula.

VIOLENCE WITHIN STUDENTS' LIVES

In a special issue of *The Harvard Educational Review* on youth and school violence, Pedro Noguera posits that schools need to adapt different approaches to curtailing and containing violence. He criticizes traditional approaches for their over-reliance on punitive measures and institutional controls to ebb violence, and instead calls for a more humane and culturally proactive response:

> The urban schools that I know that feel safe to those who spend their time there don't have metal detectors or armed security guards, and their principals don't carry baseball bats. What these schools do have is a strong sense of community and collective responsibility. Such schools are seen by students as sacred territory, too special to be spoiled by crime and violence, and too important to risk one's being excluded.[24]

While the Corner Campus has neither metal detectors nor security guards, if students fight, they are expelled without exception. The students and staff feel safe for two main reasons: they assume that students come to school to learn, and all agree to the unbendable rule that if you fight, regardless of who started the fight, you will be expelled. For many Campus students, the risk of expulsion outweighs any propensity toward fighting. Teachers identify the one-punch rule as crucial to the success and survival of the school:

> [I]t feels like a safe place. I think the kids feel safe at school. (A student) didn't go to his other school because there were fights every day and drive-bys in the school yard . . . at Corner Campus people feel safe, you know, cuz if you fight you're out, and I think that provides a good basis. (First-year teacher, interview)

> [T]hat school rule—if there's one rule that they know and they know well . . . is that if you start it or finish it, you're gone, you're out of school . . . our students really like that. (Second-year teacher, interview)

While a zero-tolerance policy may have immediate or even lasting effects on a school environment, what about the rampant violence many students face outside school? That is, how can schools deal effectively with violence in their students' lives? Should this task be up to schools? Does continual exposure to violence and death inhibit student readiness to learn? Teachers have used their students' experiences with death as an integral part of their curriculum. Another urban researcher in northern California incorporated student voice and expertise within her classroom, and embodies both sensitivity and critical pedagogy in practice.

> I came to realize that connecting school knowledge with the students' real-life issues is essential in my classroom. . . . Death is one example of students' life experiences that enters the classroom whether a teacher chooses to acknowledge it or not. It is also one of many student experiences that debunk the notion of classroom teaching and education as neutral spaces or endeavors.[25]

This researcher allots nearly half her article to student work samples. This testifies to her commitment to incorporating student voice both in her classroom and within educational research. She raises huge issues in the day-to-day life in urban schools, and inherent subjectivity within teaching and education. She invites teachers to teach holistically, treating the student as an organic whole, not a removed receptor of knowledge.

Teachers need to acknowledge that certain life circumstances outrank academic achievement in their students' lives, and that they can provide a forum for students to express these circumstances. In a recent issue of *English Journal*, Nancy Hudson wrote about the amount of violence within her students' writing. She encapsulates the value of providing a forum for such expression:

> It is partly my job as teacher to understand that this violence exists in almost all my students' lives and seriously affects their socialization and readiness for education. It affects my class, my relationship to my students, and their relationship to each other. We as English teachers must also realize the transformative power of writing and the importance of respecting our students' voices.[26]

Hudson provides a valve for the pressure her students endure living amid violence, and while they may be marginalized by society in terms of access to power, equal opportunity, and money, in her class they speak from places of authority and expertise, rather than from the margins.[27] Thus, violence in their lives is neither ignored nor minimized, but made explicit within scholastic activities.

In the film *Dangerous Minds*, based on the book *My Posse Don't Do Homework*, Louanne Johnson asks her students to analyze death references within the poetry of Dylan Thomas and Bob Dylan.[28] While both Hudson and Johnson promote using classic, or white mainstream literature to get students thinking critically about violence or death, such curricular complacency may be problematic.

Why focus only on white European authors? Why not incorporate voices closer to the students own? After addressing salient and pressing issues, the next step is to incorporate student cultural forms and preferences within curricula. While Johnson points to Bob Dylan's "code words" for drugs and drug dealers in *Mr. Tambourine Man* as a way of getting her students' attention, she uses nothing relating to the rap music her students listen to in and out of her classroom, and she makes little attempt to understand her students' codes and code words. She finds school rules deferring to street codes when she breaks up a fight, and assumes the students will keep their word and not fight again. She is wrong.

SCHOOL CODES VERSUS STREET CODES

In *The Code of the Streets*, Elijah Anderson explicates the importance of respect and 'juice' to many African-American males living in inner-city communities. His article is about survival amid violence. It compels urban teachers to understand the various obstacles their students must overcome to *attend* school, and to take seriously the nihilist threat in their lives.

> The inclination to violence springs from the circumstances of life among the ghetto poor—the lack of jobs that pay a living wage, the stigma of race, the fallout from rampant drug use and drug trafficking, and the resulting alienation and hope for the future. Simply living in such an environment places young people at special risk of falling victim to aggressive behavior.[29]

At the Campus, student experience is manifest and explored within their curricula; as one teacher told me, "we don't ask them to check their lives at the door." Violence permeates many Campus students' lives, and they are encouraged to deal with it constructively at school through writing, discussing, and acting their experiences. For example, in one English class, *Language Arts through Social Issues*, students choose themes to study each quarter; invariably, they select violent ones. One recent class chose rape, child abuse, and serial killers to write about.

I asked my workshop students to write a few sentences on their feelings about violence, and to differentiate between real and perceived violence. Does violent imagery in media influence student violence? I worry about this relationship, and wonder if students do also; that is, is a gangsta rapper on MTV raping women real or perceived? I hoped we could then critically interrogate societal violence, but soon realized I was perhaps too detached from it to fully understand their perspective. I needed to listen to them before assuming they were as critical of violence as I was.

We talked about proliferation of violence in media and in their communities. I asked how they felt about escalating and incessant violence in society and in their communities especially. Several of their responses to "The way I feel about violence" illustrate nihilism, or de facto acceptance of violence as a normal part of day-to-day life. While student responses ranged from approving. . . .

- I really don't care just as long as it's not affecting me or my family. But if it is we shall retaliate. (Female)
- I can't really talk bad about violent people, because if somebody did something that made me real mad, I would get violent . . . so I see myself as half violent and half nonviolent. (Female)

to abhorring . . .

- I hate that violence happens everyday . . . my cousin was killed and he wasn't violent. (Male)
- I had a friend who joined a gang, he wasn't really violent. . . . He died three months after joining. He got a bullet through the head. (Male)

. . . the consensus was that violence was one means of solving problems, and an inescapable part of life

- [I]t does affect some of the communities because a lot of loved ones get killed or hurt . . . some people think it's a game, but when it comes to losing a life, they find out it's not. (Male)
- Sometimes I feel very brave about violence and other times I feel very scared. (Female)

Unlike other schools, the Campus deals with this reality proactively through academic exercises, discussions, and daily conferences between students and their homeroom teachers. They attempt to at once address and minimize the threat of violence within the school. The student responses indicate both an acceptance and an abhorrence of violence. While some students disavow violence, most realize they might not have a choice. As a follow-up question, I asked whether or not they considered themselves violent. I wondered how living amid violence affects behavior and self-identification. Do my students consider themselves violent?

- Violence is really a thing to be considered by all people so we can stop it. I don't consider myself violent . . . as you know I'm a lover not a fighter. (Male)
- [Y]es, sometimes . . . I see myself being violent when it's needed. (Male)
- I wouldn't hurt nobody unless they started a fight with me. . . . I don't mess with guns because that's an automatic death. (Male)
- I see myself as a violent person when my temper goes off, and that does not take much time . . . other than that, no. (Female)
- I can get a little violent, but I would have to be really mad at somebody. (Female)

These responses illustrate both a de facto acceptance of violence as a reality in day-to-day existence and an encouraging resistance to perpetuating violent behaviors themselves. But even if my students are not prone to violent behaviors, they must deal with the violence of others. Their awareness of violence and need for street smarts is essential for survival in their communities. When I asked one student about nonviolence, or his desire to live peacefully, he offered "Sure, but what's the point? You can't do anything about anything." This is one manifestation of the nihilist threat; loss of hope for a nonviolent world. While letting students talk about violence may not lessen its impact, it shows students that teachers can be responsive and sensitive and may be an incentive for students to attend and invest in their education.

The violence affecting the students of the Corner Campus reflects urban blights such as drugs, poverty, and gang turf wars.[30] When teachers are ignorant or scared of these realities, they may not reach and teach students as effectively. I do not believe teachers need to be from violent areas to relate to students who are, but they do need to listen. In *Dangerous Minds*, Ms. Johnson needed to learn about her students' personal lives before they opened up to her. She then incorporated her students' themes—death and drugs—into her teaching. Teachers can choose whether to allot classroom time to students' life experiences, but avoiding class discussions of violence does not negate its reality for students; if anything it makes it seem shameful, as if it's their fault that violent obstacles distract them from learning in school. Teachers I interviewed identified violence as one of the major obstacles facing the students, and a student teacher at the Campus was somewhat shocked.

> When I was teaching the social issues class last year, we had this unit on gang violence and almost every kid in the class had been affected in some way, not necessarily by gang violence, but some kind of street violence. For all of them, it's touched their lives in some way. You know, they don't feel safe in their neighborhoods or they know someone who's been killed, or you know, that kind of stuff. And that is so foreign to my experience you know I can't even imagine having that kind of stuff hanging over you on a daily basis.

Teachers at the Campus acknowledge that social issues such as violence "hang over" many students on a daily basis, and try to construct curricula which deal with issues proactively. For example, in the aforementioned *Language Arts through Social Issues* class, a unit on rape included excepts from novels, plays, current articles, and a film, and compelling student testimony. Violence in Campus students' lives will not disappear because of empathic instruction, but in acknowledging and incorporating relevant themes, teachers employ critical pedagogy and allow their students to bring lived experiences into classes.

DRUG USE AMONG STUDENTS

Many young adults use or abuse drugs. Notwithstanding the paternalistic *Just Say No* campaign of Nancy Reagan and others, many high school students continue to use drugs. While some Corner Campus students only use drugs such as marijuana, others deal drugs as well. A recent student poll, published in the quarterly school newsletter, showed that 35 percent of Campus students smoke weed. I asked Ike, a third year teacher at the school, about drug use and abuse among students. His comments both enlighten and frighten:

> One thing that's scaring me, that's really kinda hard to accept . . . is the amount of drugs in their lifestyles and their culture. . . . I found out it's not only them who are abusing it, but their parents . . . they want to quit but they can't because . . . their uncles, their mother, their father, everybody's doing it . . . it's scary . . . here have been a couple of cases where parents have even forced their kids to sell in order to subsidize their income.

During my time at the Campus, I noticed a tacit student acceptance of drug use and drug culture. While not all students use drugs, they acknowledge their classmates using. In fact, marijuana is now seen by many as less a drug than a vice on par with alcohol or cigarettes. The aforementioned poll showed that only 20 percent of students smoke cigarettes, about half the number who smoke weed.

While Campus staff know students smoke, they are sometimes at a loss concerning what to do about it. In drug awareness presentations, teachers acknowledge that students who get high before school are probably "coming down" during class. But the Campus teachers relate to students with language and attitudes that do not seem righteous and alienating to students. While students may not wear pro-drug T-shirts to school, they wear the marijuana leaf icon on earrings, nose rings, caps, and shoelaces. I learned from teacher interviews that dealers and heavy users keep weed referents to a minimum and students who seem preoccupied with "the leaf" do so just to impress others. One day I gave a grammar quiz in which students were to complete sentences with correct subject-verb agreement. Here is one student's paper, with the given grammatical phrase in italics:

> *None of the contestants* won the contest because they smoked bomb.[31]
> *The children and Helen* smoked hella bomb.
> *Everyone in the house* smokes bomb.
> *Margaret and Susan* smoke a lot of bomb.
> *Ellen and Jean, and I* smoked bomb.

A few of the exercises involve smoking bomb.
Either Jim or the twins have the bomb.
Part of the movie showed people smoking bomb.

During a poetry unit, the same student continued his theme in a seventeen-syllable haiku poem:

> I smoke hella bomb
> The bomb is so good to me
> Bomb relaxes me.

This student doesn't care whether his teachers think he smokes weed. But juxtaposed with the teacher's indication that such preoccupation is only a facade, what does the quiz connote? Does it mean the student smokes incessantly, or does it simply reek of indignant disclosure?

Students' feelings about drugs are often more subtle, but equally telling. During a unit on faith and spirituality, I asked my students to write a letter to God, whoever he or she represents to them. While many letters dealt with issues of thankfulness for family and health, one stuck out for its stark honesty and classification of drugs. From teacher interviews I learned that this student comes from a supportive family, but lives in a particularly dangerous housing project, where drug use is rampant. Here is his letter:

> Dear God,
> I have not been doing anything bad. No drugs or anything. I have been going down the right path, but I have been drinking and smoking weed but that is a habit that is hard to break, and I'm not trying to right at this time.

Seeing an opportunity to listen without lecturing, I responded:

> I'm very moved by your honesty—I would say that both alcohol and marijuana are drugs, but this matters less than your awareness that you are trying to do the right thing. Keep trying and do let me know if there's anything I can do.

He never sought my help but he never missed a class. He also wrote a haiku poem about drugs:

> I see his red eyes
> I hear him breathing deeply
> I hate my brother

I think I learned more about my students by allowing them to struggle with unsavory or illegal themes in writing. By accepting street vernacular and illicit stories in writing, I felt as if I was validating student cultural capital, but also wondered to what extent this was in their best interests. I feared that if I mandated proper English usage and forbade drug stories, attendance would fall. Since my class was accredited but voluntary, I thought students would stay and participate more if I eased up on discourse restrictions.

While I agree with Lisa Delpit[32] that students need to learn rules of school and society, I believe that, to some extent, school rules are changeable and should provide a forum for student vernacular. Furthermore, many students know societal rules and disavow them. For example, selling drugs provides an excellent example of a thriving and illegal enterprise that students defend as necessary and worth the risks involved:

- I think it's okay to deal drugs for a while but only if you really need the money. . . . To me it is better and safer to steal and sell what you got than to sell drugs because if you steal the right shit then you make almost as much as you do in drug sales. (Male)

- To a certain extent it is (okay to sell) because I can understand the fact that people are without and they really have nothing to lose. . . . I also feel that most of the people have families to take care of and the $4.25 an hour just is not going to get it. (Female)

- If you can make over $500 a night selling 50 little pieces of rock cocaine, you can become rich. . . . If you was to work at a fast food place it would take four or five weeks just to make $500, and the drug dealer is just taking the easiest way. (Male)

- I think it is okay to deal drugs . . . because people have to support their kids. (Female)

All four of these responses cite money as the reason and redemption for selling drugs. Students sell drugs for pocket money, so they don't have to get a "real" job paying much less money, but many sell to help support their families. Some students, however, felt that dealing was wrong, or at least too dangerous:

- I think that it's dumb to be standing on the corner, many bad things can happen to you out there, and you cannot depend on the people you grind with. (Male)

- No, I don't think it good to sell drugs because you are putting your life on the line and half of the time you got to watch our for the cops or the people you selling with because they could get two face and smoke you in a minute. (Female)

Again, teachers acknowledge this dilemma, and try to empathize with students who either fight the urge to deal drugs, or must contend with parents who do. There was no consensus as to whether dealing or using drugs was desirable behavior; the right of people to choose to sell, however, was defended by all. Drugs are so pervasive as to immobilize most "just say no" arguments. This poignant yet disturbing comment from a second-year teacher illustrates the dilemma many Campus teachers struggle with:

> I think that their dealing is more like an income—subsidizing income—in terms of just survival. I know a couple of kids here who need to sell it in order not to have a job in order to have enough time to study . . . some of our students do sell it just for survival wise. . . . Some kid last year—he came to me and he was all happy and he said "Ike, my dad doesn't make me sell coke now, it's just pot." And I'm like shit, what do I tell him? I'm like "Good for you. Congratulations!" You know? In terms of condoning the behavior . . . it's just so hard to tell because you can't tell them one thing like "it's not right to smoke" and then they go home and their parents and everybody in the world is doing it. Or when we take a trip to the park and see two nurses at the bus stop lighting up. I mean the medical profession just doing it right in public like it was nothing. How can you reinforce your rules here, if they're not enforced as soon as they step out the door?

In terms of rules, then, those of the Campus can be stricter than those of society. Drug use and drug dealing permeate Campus students' lives, and Campus teachers encourage students to stay off drugs and alcohol, but above all, to be careful.[33] Tantamount to understanding the depth of the problem is some familiarity with street vernacular and cultural markers or code words for drugs; that is, rock, bud, bomb, dank, and bammer. Campus teachers make such code words their business, and try to reach and teach in the language of their students. Knowledge of codes shows teacher interest in student culture and may enable teachers to better address student nihilism, as manifest through violence and drug use.

STUDENTS' CULTURAL CAPITAL

Hip-hop clothing, graffiti tags, and vernacular represent some current urban adolescent markers. A few years before my study, Susan Katz Weinberg studied Latino middle school students in an English as a Second Language class in San Francisco. Her students utilized street slang, nicknames, and graffiti both as handwriting practice and gang affiliation. She explains her students' making sense of their world through nonacademic forms of literacy:

Language and literacy were ways in which students were trying to take control over their lives—to communicate in their own style. Graffiti and tag names represented forms of critical literacy-reshaping written language for one's own purposes. To understand the meanings embedded in graffiti, one must be a member of a particular literacy community. Not everyone can "read" graffiti; you must be taught by an insider who can decipher the codes—the nicknames, the acronyms, the use of Roman numerals. In these ways, Julio and the other students brought the streets into the classroom. They expressed much alienation from school as an academic world. They did not want to read any books that were linked to school in any way, even if a former gang member wrote them. To gain a place for themselves in school, the students created an alternative cultural identity. This identity was based on oral and written language forms from the streets, the world in which they felt included.[34]

Weinberg validated and incorporated her students' gang culture, identity, and indeed literacy into her classroom to increase student participation, but her project begs further questions: How do we validate student culture and voice if that voice is violent or illegal? If we allow students to talk about guns and drugs openly in class, are we simply validating voice, or legitimating licentious behavior? Student language is one front on which this battle plays out.

In Philadelphia, Miriam Camitta studied literate practices among high school students in Philadelphia, and discovered student literary investment outside her curriculum. She found vernacular writing such as love letters, poems, and journal entries happening both in and out of class. Her description of the students' covert behaviors connotes a playful subversion:

In the classroom, vernacular writing flourishes on a surreptitious basis. Here, students write during times when they have finished the assigned work, and sometimes, instead of doing it. Among the one hundred students whom I met daily in my classes, I observed, as in non-assigned student time, that students were writing in their diaries, composing letters, and copying song lyrics into their notebooks.

Thus, private and personal writing, such as diary and letter-writing, can be carried out at the same time as teacher-assigned writing is supposed to be taking place, because superficially it looks the same to the teacher.[35]

Camitta argues for validating adolescent vernacular writing and for recognizing adolescent writers as experts within given literate communities. She analyzes and codifies her students' creations as "patchwork" and "mosaic" compositions appropriating, in part or whole, previously written, recorded, or heard texts in order to recreate an additional text.[36] Students use patches, or samples, both to convey meaning and as status markers of cultural capital. Examples of verbal samples include words, rhythms, and rhymes connoting life in "da hood."[37] Current adolescent slang evolves quickly with popular culture, and meanings change. I usually know what most street slang means, and ask for clarification if I don't. For example, I recently learned the meaning of "bitch made."[38]

Critical teaching demands teachers listen to students, even if their responses are unnerving and irreverent. Current vernacular connotes unsavory themes such as violence against women, but must be interrogated rather than ignored. This is not to say that students should not learn "standard" English needed for scholastic and vocational endeavors, or that offensive language should go unchallenged, but if teachers ask them to code switch from slang to standard English, teachers should as well; that is, using slang in class to make a point, but then translating.

Here is a poem written by a Corner Campus student that conveys the ubiquity and power of current Californian urban vernacular, with translations in parentheses.

Crazy

It was a hot sunny day
I was like parlayin   (speaking or acting with confidence)
In the muthafuckin' Bay   (slang used for emphasis)
About to get sideways   (stoned)
to the summer jam.   (outdoor concert with several
                                hip-hop bands)

rippin up the mic   (rapping or singing smoothly)
wit something tight   (lyrics are strong and marketable)
That hit and slam.   (and powerful and danceable)
So we hit the high way   (unsure if high means on dope . . .)
puffin' on a Phillie   (smoking a cigar . . .)
stuffed wit some bomb   (with marijuana inside)
That'll have yo ass goin crazy.

VERNACULAR AS "ALL THAT AND A BUCKET O' CHICKEN"

In current urban vernacular, the expression "all that" is a superlative term for success, proficiency, confidence, or arrogance. It is most often used in the second or third person; for example, "He was all that," or "You thinking you all that." *All that and a bucket o' chicken* is from a play written by a female high school student at the Campus. The phrase in its original context—a dialogue between two female characters—describes a girl's feelings toward a male date, specifically: "He was thinking he was all that and a bucket o' chicken." Translated from vernacular, it means that the girl speaking was quite critical of the boy's arrogance, hence the "He was thinking" preface. Without the preface however, it connotes praise rather than criticism; that is, "You *think* you are special, don't you?" versus "You *are* special."

When the student read her play aloud, the dialogue received laughter and affirmation—similar to an Amen! response. Students praised the playwright for her poignant vernacular usage and for its dialogical context within the story. The female protagonist was out with a man—who thought he was "all that"—and she reported on his cockiness. In one sentence, the writer encapsulated female disempowerment within current urban vernacular. The play was one of several narratives read that day, all written by girls and all depicting rape or murder of young women. The plays were profane, sexually explicit and validated substance use among teens—that is, drinkin' forties and smokin' weed as part of a cool party scene—but also represented hard work such as composing, editing, typing, and performing. In this example, students engaged in literate behaviors demonstrating diligence, perseverance, and courage by reading their prose aloud, but with behaviors and dialogue outside the curricular canon.

The ability of the Campus to go outside "canons" is one of its strengths. Teachers do not use work sheets or many formal textbooks, and encourage students and parents to help plan curriculum. Such openness to student opinion and input yields greater student investment.

HIP-HOP CORNER: RAP, DAP, AND MAKIN' DUCKETS[39]

Many Corner Campus students come from tough urban neighborhoods, and are encouraged to make sense of their world through schoolwork. For students in rough neighborhoods, respect is often hard-won, and backing down from challenges, whether from teachers or not, is not an option. Saving face far outweighs deferring to authority.[40] Saving student face in urban secondary schools means listening to their stories and language and challenging them to learn school codes as well as street codes. A first step, however, is providing accessible avenues for student participation, such as incorporating rap music into language arts curricula to increase student engagement.

Rap music applies to language arts curricula on several levels: as poetry, where students compose and edit original raps, or analyze previously recorded raps; as resistance commentary, where students discuss and hypothesize about information and messages within the music;[41] and as dialogic teaching and learning, in which students consciously make sense of their world in order to read "the word."[42] Unfortunately, much hip-hop, or rap music elucidates a violent and difficult world. Recent media hype about gangsta rap focused on its anti-establishment lyrics, irreverence, and espousal of drugs, and misogyny. The question is whether artists can ever abridge their first amendment right to free speech, even if their lyrics incite others to act destructively. The rap group *2 Live Crew* won a lawsuit several years ago, after their album *As Nasty as They Wanna Be* was pulled from record store shelves. Most current hip-hop fans don't follow the legal history much; they do, however, listen to and repeat lyrics and themes from current songs and artists. The dilemma for educators is how to incorporate salient themes without promoting or validating negativity or even nihilism.

For example, a recent hit single, *I Got Five on It*, sounds softer and more harmonious than most gangsta rap, and does not espouse violence. It does, however, romanticize the act of splitting a dime bag ($10) of weed from a corner drug dealer. I believe that teachers can frame discussions and analyses around generative themes and genres from students' lives, but we must be ready for difficult dialogue.[43] I have a problem with the proliferation of misogynist lyrics in hip-hop, but I want to hear what my students think and hear when interacting with this medium. In short, I am far less affected by "thug life"[44] than my students. It is in their struggle with this text and with their current reality, that critical thinking can emerge; unlike much standardized curricula, hip-hop media is something popular.

In one classroom, student essays about this lifestyle line the walls. Some essays embrace the lifestyle, others warn to stay off drugs and crack "rocks." The Corner Campus deals with students' experiences proactively, by validating students' voices and experiences, even if they are profane, violent, or otherwise controversial.

THE CORNER CAMPUS: A CASE STUDY
IN STUDENT-CENTERED PEDAGOGY

At the Corner Campus, teachers make concerted efforts to "hook" students into school, and to make curricula exciting and relevant to students' lives. In an English class, a teacher solicits generative themes for study from her students; in a history class, the teacher allows students to work together to raise a collective quiz grade; and in a political economy class, a student blames the teacher for passive discussion management and specifies that he would have learned more in class had the facilitation been better.[45] In these three examples, teachers shared their power and control over students to increase student involvement and investment. Whether through thematic choice, teacher criticism, or grading negotiation, the Corner Campus students are encouraged and expected to engage and determine their educational activities.

Such encouragement is one component of critical pedagogical practice—others found at the Campus include dialogic teaching, exposure of societal inequalities, and promotion praxis—reflection and action upon the world in order to change it.[46] This chapter examined salient student issues at a school that employs critical pedagogical practice amid abject nihilist threats. That is, the Campus attempts to hook students' into school by giving them more attention and voice than they would receive in a school five times as large. Most importantly, the school doesn't ask its students to leave problems outside, but rather to critically interrogate them inside. This method may not eliminate threats of violence and drug use, but it doesn't repress them either.

I offered student work samples to illustrate nihilist threats facing students outside school in terms of violence and drug use, but I wish to emphasize that Campus students face difficult situations but usually make the choice to attend school and participate. They persevere within a school that engenders agency and hope, and many do obtain a diploma. For those that do, half choose to attend college. Those that do not face a plethora of futures ranging from entrepreneurship to incarceration. While teachers compel students to stay in school—they can leave legally at sixteen—and get a diploma, many simply cannot or do not make the time. Corner Campus staff work hard to make school worthy of their students' time. Sometimes, however, for varied reasons, they lose students. Still they retain a collective consciousness of hope. Their actions and pedagogies embody their belief that despite it all, Corner Campus students are "all that."

Can student nihilism—loss of hope and absence of meaning—be combatted with critical pedagogy? If student attitudes like "you can't do anything about anything" permeate schools and promote apathy, can teachers reach them anyway? Amid a violent and drug infested urban America, can a small school succeed? After working at the Corner Campus for almost a year, I answer all three questions with cautious optimism. The battle against nihilism and apathy rages in a small alternative high school in California.

APPENDIX: HOW I LANDED AT THE CAMPUS

I met several Campus teachers and students when they visited one of my doctoral classes. After having an encouraging conversation with one of the visiting teachers, I lined up an interview with the principal. She told me to come to the next staff meeting: if the staff liked me and okayed my involvement there, I could return and if not we couldn't work together.

I chose this site for my research in part because of that screening: to me it shows good judgment, particularly about a full-time graduate student who may extract data and leave. The staff is very tight, and with only nine teachers and two administrators, they work and choose researchers collectively. When I told the principal I taught special education, she told me the school had no special ed kids. That the school eschewed labels attracted me.

For the interview I prepared a one-page list of my interests and experience and schooling, and defended it and myself to a room of committed teachers. After a twenty-minute group interview, I was thanked and told to call back. Thus began a relationship that continues as of this writing. I observed and took notes in classrooms, particularly the two language arts classrooms, for two hours a week for three months. I then began teaching an after school writing workshop two hours a week with ninth and tenth graders. The students receive half the credit of a regular language arts class. Those low in credits or skills are encouraged to take my workshop, but enrollment is voluntary, so I try to make it worth their time. During my first quarter, two of fifteen students were expelled, one eloped and dropped out, and one dropped my class. Eleven others received high school credit.

NOTES

1. Cornel West, *Race Matters* (New York: Vintage Press, 1993), pp. 22–23.

2. For analyses of how street culture differs from and affects schools and classrooms, see Elijah Anderson, "The Code of the Streets," *The Atlantic Monthly*, May 1994, pp. 81–94; Lawrence Baines, "Fistfights, Guns, and the Art of Teaching English," *English Journal* 84 (September 1995): 59–64.

3. For recent work regarding the ostracization of "tough-to-teach" students, see Lisa Delpit, *Other People's Children: Cultural Conflict in the Classroom* (New York: The New Press, 1995), and Jonathan Kozol, *Savage Inequalities* (New York: HarperPerennial, 1991).

4. For a theoretical explanation of dialogic teaching, see Ira Shor and Paulo Freire, *A Pedagogy for Liberation: Dialogues on Transforming Education* (New York: Bergin & Garvey, 1987).

5. Though the school is legally required to report intimations of violence or crime, students are not discouraged from revealing other illicit realities, such as the need to deal drugs to help support their family.

6. Full effect = thriving in life. This and all subsequent slang translations

emanate from clarifying conversations I had with students, as well as from listening to current radio and reading current hip-hop publications.

7. The counselor was not on staff during the writing of this chapter, because funding could not be found to continue her position. Since I wrote this chapter, I have begun a young men's group, analogous to LIFE.

8. A full explication of the pedagogical implications of this term is superfluous here; in this instance it refers to fighting, not following directions, talking back to teachers, or being loud in class.

9. Parole/probation officer.

10. In this chapter I do not deal explicitly with students' family background, race, ethnicity, previous or current gang affiliation, religious faith, self-esteem, and so on. That is, I address the students, vis-à-vis the issues they brought to my workshop, rather than try to correlate student behaviors with demographic variables.

11. Shor and Freire, *A Pedagogy for Liberation*.

12. Praxis-reflection and action upon the world. Paulo Freire, *Pedagogy of the Oppressed* (New York: Herder and Herder, 1970).

13. Paulo Freire and Donaldo Macedo, *Literacy: Reading the Word and the World* (New York: Bergin & Garvey, 1987).

14. Shor and Freire, *A Pedagogy of Liberation*.

15. Shirley Brice Heath and Leslie Mangiola, *Children of Promise: Literate Activity in Linguistically and Culturally Diverse Classrooms* (Washington, D.C.: National Education Association, 1991).

16. Freire and Macedo, *Literacy*.

17. Jim Cummins, "Empowering Minority Students: A Framework for Intervention," in *Transforming Urban Education*, ed. J. Kretovics and E. J. Nussel (pp. 327–46) (Boston: Allyn and Bacon, 1986). For a description of critical pedagogy in practice, at the university level, see bell hooks, *Teaching to Transgress: Education as the Practice of Freedom* (New York: Routledge, 1994).

18. Ibid.

19. It means "you need new lines, you're just copying my insults."

20. See, for example, Henry Giroux, "Doing Cultural Studies: Youth and the Challenge of Pedagogy," *Harvard Educational Review* 64 (Summer 1994): 278–308.

21. Henry Giroux, *Teachers as Intellectuals: Toward a Critical Pedagogy of Learning* (Granby, Mass.: Bergin & Garvey, 1988).

22. Stephen O'Connor, "Problems Schools Can't Solve," *The New York Times*, March 26, 1996, p. A19.

23. Giroux, "Doing Cultural Studies," pp. 292–93.

24. Pedro Noguera, "Preventing and Producing Violence: A Critical Analysis of Responses to School Violence," *Harvard Educational Review* 65 (Summer 1995): 189–212.

25. J. Alleyne Johnson, "Life after Death: Critical Pedagogy in an Urban Classroom," *Harvard Educational Review* 65 (Summer 1995): 213–30.

26. N. Hudson, "The Violence of Their Lives: The Journal Writing of Two High School Freshmen, *English Journal* 84 (Spring 1995): 65–69.

27. Hooks, *Teaching to Transgress*.

28. Louanne Johnson, *My Posse Don't Do Homework* (New York: St Martin's Press, 1992).

29. Anderson, "Code of the Streets."

30. Hooks, *Teaching to Transgress*; Johnson, "Life after Death."

31. Bomb means potent marijuana.

32. Delpit, *Other People's Children*.

33. The campus now has a part-time counselor who takes up these types of issues with students; during this research, however, her position was not funded and is thus not included.

34. Susan Katz Weinberg, "Where the Streets Cross the Classroom: A Study of Latino Students' Perspectives on Cultural Identity in City Schools and Neighborhood Gangs," paper presented at the annual meeting of the American Educational Research Association, San Francisco, March 1995.

35. Miriam Camitta, "Vernacular Writing: Varieties of Literacy among Philadelphia High School Students," in *Cross-Cultural Approaches to Literacy*, ed. B. Street (pp. 228–46) (Cambridge: Cambridge University Press, 1993), p. 233.

36. A current application of patchwork and mosaic techniques can be seen in hip-hop culture. Radio and dance DJs often "mix" a song with another, or personally add verses or emphases during appropriate "beats" and "breaks." In addition, the art of sampling, or appropriating previously recorded songs, verses, or sounds in order to recreate and record new music, has grown increasingly popular over the last decade. Tricia Rose, *Black Noise: Rap Music and Black Culture in Contemporary America* (Hanover, N.H.: Wesleyan University Press, 1994).

37. Rose, *Black Noise*.

38. While I abhor the term "bitch" as derogatory to women, it remains pervasive in hip-hop culture. I thought it meant a man whose success is due to a female presence, but it refers to someone weak and phony.

39. Dap means respect; duckets, a different spelling of ducats (old European coins), means money.

40. Anderson, "Code of the Streets."

41. An example would be the rap group Public Enemy as the self-proclaimed "Black CNN." In effect, many students get their "information" from sources outside school and it behooves teachers to be aware of what and who their students listen to.

42. Macedo and Freire, *Literacy*.

43. Macedo and Freire, *Literacy*.

44. Thug life can be loosely described, at least since the 1980s, as a lifestyle of hustling, violence, and often illegal activity, underscored by the need to be tough and to be feared. For the purposes of this paper, the pertinence lies in the identification many students feel with popular artists, usually rappers, who personify and promote thug life.

45. The student felt frustrated that the pace could not be quicker, and criticized his peers for not reading more, and faster.

46. Freire, *Pedagogy of the Oppressed*; Shor and Freire, *A Pedagogy of Liberation*.

PART III

In Conclusion: Reflections on the Dilemmas of Urban Education Reform

CHAPTER 10

Gaps, Bridges, and Buffers in the Research, Policy, and Practice of Urban Education: A Dialogue

Theodore R. Mitchell, Carlos Alberto Torres, and Karen A. McClafferty

Hope is the companion of power, and mother of success, for who so hopes strongly has within him the gift of miracles.
　　　　　　　　　　　　　　　　　　　　—Samuel Smiles

CARLOS TORRES (CT). Let me start by asking you, from the perspective of an educational reformer like yourself, what do you think we need to address in dealing with policy and practice in urban education?

TED MITCHELL (TM). I think that we fool ourselves when we think that the problems of urban education can be solved at a structural level or at a policy level. We direct a lot of attention and energy there. But that's really just superstructural, epiphenomena. The real issues and problems in urban education are issues of race and class and power. And those play themselves out by creating a context of hopelessness. First for kids and parents, particularly kids and parents of color, the underclass who feel powerless. Translates into hopelessness. That hopelessness is also a feature of the environment in which many kids find themselves in urban schools. And while many teachers of kids in urban areas are themselves very hopeful of their futures and have gone into the profession precisely to interrupt the destiny of kids who come from environments of powerlessness and hopelessness, after a time it becomes very difficult to keep that hope alive as a professional working in schools. And that hopelessness moves up the system and really begins to infect the structure and the processes of urban schools. So I think that while structure and policy are important, you can't really change the fundamental modes of living and of the development of the psychology of learning, unless you begin to address and have honest conversations about what it means to work in an environment in which most kids don't have hope.

CT. Now, if this nihilism—which is really the counterpart of hopelessness—is so pervasive, I presume it affects not only parents and children in those conditions, but also the teachers that work with them and the overall structure of urban education, including the administrators who face this nihilism everyday. Yet an element of professionalism in teachers and administrators is, sometimes, to address this nihilism and hopelessness by figuring out some technical remedies that could be implemented and hopefully will do some good. In your experience in Los Angeles, have you seen a strategy of purposive, rational, instrumental reason in implementing technical remedies to solve the problems of urban education?

TM. I think that's a very good question. Yes. I think that the issue of technical remedies has a positive and negative side. And the negative side, I think that technical expertise can sometimes mask a variety of different conflicts and contradictions. So some of the technical fixes for schools in Los Angeles and elsewhere have masked fundamentally underlying problems. This very comforting mantra, that is actually a technical mantra, that all children can learn, is on the one hand quite liberating because it says that children from all backgrounds can learn, but if has an underside that is pointed at the children that says that "You can learn," that doesn't take into account the child's context. So a less technocratic mantra might be, "All children can learn and all children come from backgrounds that compromise their ability to learn in a variety of ways." But I would argue that that's true for affluent kids too, but that gets us off track.

I think that there are some very positive elements to some of the technical solutions that have been in place in Los Angeles, and those have two features: I think in an environment of hopelessness, almost any new idea can be the cause for hope. And so there is, in the organizational, sociological perspective, there is sort of a Hawthorne effect at work in almost any technical reform, that it gives people something to pin the remnants of hope to. And this is going to sound nihilistic in a different way, but in some senses, it doesn't matter what the technical fix is. Just so long as there is a flow of potential technical fixes so that teachers and other professionals can hope that by reorienting their practice, they can achieve a result. And they do, for a short period of time. But those technical fixes that don't get at the root issues of race and class and power aren't ever going to change the structure or the process or the experience of education for those kids. Now, I balance the two poles—the positive that I think I've underplayed and the negative that I may have overplayed. I think that there have been some very positive technical fixes in education in Los Angeles having to do with the reengagement of community with schools. And so the decentralization of some elements of school authority from the central district office to the school community engages parents, engages students, engages some small businesses that may literally surround the school. If the project of making the school a better place for kids, for teachers, a more open place for families and communities—that technical fix has had a profound impact because it has reengaged communities with the schools. It has reengaged, in some senses, parents with their children. And that's had a very powerful effect. And I think a positive effect on schooling in Los Angeles.

CT. And this constructive engagement, it refers to a number of options that would be, one of them, charter schools, perhaps there is some discussion of vouchers, there is also discussion of the partition of the district that is too large and unmanageable, limiting those who are accountable in the educational bureaucracy. But I presume there are some discussions on standards for the schools, standards for learning by students, standards for a knowledge floor for the society, standards for teachers, and I presume there must be some connection of this discussion with the role of universities. Could you comment on all of these issues?

TM. I think that you rightly point out the decentralization comes in a variety of flavors. And those are not merely preferences. They're deeply ideologically rooted. And vouchers, as an example, are not about connecting communities with schools or the educational process. Vouchers are about utilizing, submitting education to the logic of the market. Magnet schools are ideologically rooted to the notion that a superordinate goal—focusing on arts, focusing on science—will sweep aside questions of race and class and power, and bring people together on footing of equal interest. And that too is ideologically rooted. Charters are somewhat in between and I think more communitarian in their focus than either of the other two, really coming out of movements, some of them, religious movements in which groups of parents wanted to create schools that matched their own political or social or religious or educational philosophy or ideology. But they are all brought together by the notion that the large urban bureaucracy does not serve the children. And that can be partitioned in any way. The jury on the research is still out on whether these schools are (*a*) effective for the children who attend them and (*b*) whether they are effective in creating environments of increased equity, increased social mobility, increased understanding of difference. The jury, as I say, is out on that.

And so the question about connections to the university is that they could have a profound one at this moment when there are a variety of natural experiments going on in urban education. Natural experiments going on in Los Angeles. What is the educational experience of kids in charter schools as differentiated from kids in the "normal" public school? How do these different variants of decentralization effect issues of equity? And does choice really empower parents? And does competition between these varieties of schooling really raise the level of performance? All of these are fundamental research questions, and I think that it is incumbent on universities, particularly those like us who are deeply embedded in the context of an urban school system, to be doing the research from which we can know as a people about the differential effect of these educational movements. At a different level I think that it's quite critical that we connect with the profession of teaching, the profession of administration in urban schools so that we can be about the project of helping to build hope, helping to maintain hope, to improve the craft and learn from our colleagues in urban schools, so that in turn our training programs can be more effective in providing people the experiences they need to enter into the profession in the challenging environment of urban schools.

KAREN McCLAFFERTY (KM). It really sounds like you were saying that universities should have almost an inquisitive role and a responsive role, and not at all a prescriptive role. Would you agree with that statement?

TM. I think it's a fine balance. I think that over the last fifty years, one of the university's problems has been its prescriptive relationship with public schools. And in particular, its prescriptive relationship with urban schools. For the most part, the environments in which we teach and work aren't the same or even similar to the environments in which most of the teachers in urban schools work. And yet we have been free—too free—to tell teachers in urban schools how to go about doing their business. And so while I think we certainly have things to say *to* teachers in urban schools, and a perspective and a distance that could be valuable to them, I think we have to have a fundamentally inquisitive cast to our relationship with public school teachers, in which we help them interrogate their circumstances and use our distance and perspective to ask questions and then reflect back on research answers in a way that can be useful to them in their craft.

CT. What about standards—the whole discussion about standards?

TM. You're right, and I apologize for missing the whole theme. It was a Freudian slip. One of the things that we do know—and this could probably even tie in—one of the things that we do know from the research that has been done on these decentralized programs as they've occurred around the country is that equity is most seriously at risk when there are not standards that are uniform across the schools for inputs like resources, like teacher quality, like teacher background. And for outcomes—and I know that that's a loaded term—but outcomes in terms of standards to which students should aspire and standards for which schools should prepare students. I'll give you a great example. The University of California has a very prescribed set of admissions requirements—A through F requirements, they're called. They deal with the number of units that students must take in mathematics and social sciences and language to be eligible for admission to the University of California. There are schools in the state of California where it is impossible to move to the university because they don't offer the full range of A through F courses. That's the kind of standard that needs to be maintained throughout the state, throughout the city of Los Angeles, so that students who are engaged in a charter school in one area or a magnet school in the other can still be assured of opportunities afterwards that are even across the board. And so that kind of standard setting is critical to the success of any school system, but particularly to a school system that is more open to variation, more open to decentralization, more open to local control and to family choice.

CT. There is one question that emerges naturally out of the combination of your point that the problems with urban education are based on conflicts around race, class, and power.

KM. And I would add gender which, although it raises a different set of issues, certainly cannot be separated from a discussion of power.

CT. I would agree with Karen's point: Conflicts around class, race, and gender all have differential implications in terms of the relationship between education and power. Yet the alternative is that when we provide standards—argue some scholars and practitioners—we are providing a level playing field in which everybody could measure up to the same situation. But if the inequities are pervasive in terms of race, class, gender and power, are the standards—by definition—going to equalize or make the level playing field even more complicated?

TM. I think that the standards—equal standards with unequal resource allocation condemn the same people who have always been underserved by the educational system, to being underserved in the future. And that's where I think we often in policy terms have the most difficulty with the standards debate. And it's certainly where we have the most difficulty with resource allocations. And I think that we have to, at that point, recall why it is that we have public education in this country. Public education has been miscast in the last several decades as a private good. It's been miscast as an avenue for individual mobility, whereas in fact, historically, it's quite clear that education—public education—in this country is designed for public purposes. And it's designed, as our friend Horace Mann said long ago, to balance the balanced wheel of society. And from that perspective, an unequal investment in those who have been underserved by the educational system is quite consistent with the American view, the historical view of what the public school is and should do. David Labaree's new book—*How to Succeed in School without Really Learning* (1997)—is a great examination of this idea of the increasing privatization of the notion of public schools. And I think that when we look at urban education policy, we get stuck at this very point, of whether the schools exist to serve the public or whether the schools exist to serve the individual and private needs of those students who attend them.

KM. We've tentatively titled this chapter "Gaps, Bridges and Buffers in the Research, Policy and Practice of Urban Education." Do you see those bridges and buffers and gaps as changing?

TM. It's interesting. And I think my comments on the role of the university were my shorthand description of the ideal state. And I think that between where we are and that ideal state, there are many gaps. There are incredible buffers, and there are few bridges. And I think that one of the things we have to be about in schools of education in urban universities is creating bridges. And some of those bridges need to be between practicing professionals in urban schools and the schools of education, where they become our colleagues in this inquisitiveness. And do teacher-driven research that we can help them do because we have the research infrastructure and we can build the sense of colleagueship. At the same time I think it's important for schools of education to build bridges back the other way to the disciplines in the colleges of letters and sciences, where the renewal of those fields—I'm thinking of my own field of history, for example—the renewal of the field of history in the last twenty years has been dramatic, and has been quite powerful, and I would argue potent for the urban schoolteacher. But the buffers are quite high between the historians at a place like UCLA and the history teacher at Jefferson High School in Los Angeles. And so if we can build sort of the two-tiered bridge—one between us and practice and the other between us and discipline fields—I think we'll be able to achieve a much smoother transition of knowledge and of questions. So I think that there's much to be done, there are sociological buffers in terms of the hierarchy of the profession that for too long teachers and professors have been put apart by the perceived hierarchy between what we do in the university and what teachers do, and that creates an enormous boundary between the two practices. Let's be honest. The style of work is very, very different.

CT. We could have started this conversation arguing back and forth on how deep the problems of urban schools are vis-à-vis suburban schools or rural schools. Is there any problem that you find pervasive throughout urban, suburban and rural schools, particularly in the United States?

TM. I would argue that issues of race and class and power and gender permeate all of our social institutions. And schools happen to be particularly poignant places for the expression of those contradictions and those conflicts. So I would say that those run through all of the schools. But, to put a slightly more professional cast to it, I think that teachers in all of those schools suffer from similar isolation from each other, from the ideas of their fields and from the practitioners research—whether it's pedagogic research or discipline field-oriented research. And I think that one of the things that we can do in the university is to break down that sense of isolation. And it's one of the few places where I see an automatic improvement in the quality of life that can be attributed to technology. That the new technologies do provide us with an opportunity to break down distance, to break down the sense of isolation. To create communities, virtual communities around areas of inquiry that can help teachers and help faculty and help students. But I distrust the impetus to create educational software for kids in classrooms. And trust much more the communication potential of the new technology.

KM. I have such concerns about having faith in technology, which seems to be so unevenly distributed—whether it's rural versus urban or lower-income areas versus higher-income areas. It's not something that everyone has access to.

TM. That's where I would draw a quick distinction between the utility of technology for kids and the utility of technology for teachers. And I think your question has in it a very, very correct assessment that if we depend on technology we will essentially again be advantaging those who are advantaged and disadvantaging those who have always been underserved. And so the application of technology in any type of equal sense to that diverse population is going to increase rather than decrease the disparity and outcomes. I think that it's less of a problem for teachers, but I don't want to extrapolate from our sample, but when we sample the student teachers to our program at UCLA, probably only four or five in a given year don't have access to a personal computer of the type that would be required to exchange email with colleagues. And I've long been a proponent of, for UCLA, to require student teachers to have computers. If we require computers, then we're able to include the price of the computer when we compute financial aid packages. In a counterintuitive way, by requiring the computers, we are advantaging those who otherwise wouldn't be able to afford them. But I think that the root issue is we have to worry very much about all attempted technological solutions. And we have to worry about the disparity of access and we have to, at the same time, think about a technological solution, think about a permanent solution to how to erase the lack of access that certain teachers, certain students, certain families have to the technology that's necessary.

CT. That's very interesting. I posed the question on the similarities across the board because one of my perceptions for the need of a sense of renewal is that we lack the notion of a social movement that could propel the schools to fall into line with emerging democratic social utopias, rather than living in this kind of a game of never-ending mirrors, as you were describing in the beginning. And a social utopia that could have been developed in universities as happened in the thirties and forties with reformers of the quality of John Dewey that we all quote so often. What we don't have across the board is this sense of perpetual stimuli because we don't have the social movements. Perhaps we have even seen a decline in social movements.

I just published a book on Paulo Freire, social movements and educational reform in São Paulo entitled *Education and Democracy*. I am impressed with how, using this very simple and straightforward political and pedagogical methodology of having the schools as a unit looking at the community and the needs of the community and building the curriculum around the perceived generative themes of the community, this project of educational reform in itself becomes a social movement. So the interesting thing about the Freire project and São Paulo experience almost seven years ago was that it started with the premise that the new administration would have a strong political view—it was a social democratic administration—that they will take advantage of the social movements to pursue their own policy agenda. They will take advantage of the progressive teaching in the university to link that with the schools, even in the context of a highly bureaucratic municipal system of education. So that was the premise. But the moment that it moved into having the school as the center of attention, that the school would connect with the community to figure out what the needs are, that moment a social movement that was school-based was created.

So you could have a problem in the school like, say, garbage. So garbage was used as the problem in health sciences, very much so, appropriately so. And the students begin to study the implication of garbage dumped in their neighborhoods for their health. But also it was used for writing essays in language courses. It could be used to figure out ways to deal with mathematics in the school. So the teachers got very much caught up with this thing. The administrators in the municipal system liked the model and they were supporting the model. And of course progressive educators in the university jumped in and said, "I was looking for this all my life!" In a way, what was supposed to be, just to how use or take advantage of the social movements—which were quite prevalent at the time in São Paulo—to infuse the school with a new life, the social movement actually took place in the schools. I see neither the social movements propelling the schools into the kind of social reconstructionism approach like in the thirties, nor the social movements beyond the premise of decentralization that could be part of a much greater democratic accord. But I don't see really social movements fighting for issues of equality in the schools or issues of class, race, gender as we were discussing. So, I may be wrong because you are more connected with the current practices in schools than perhaps I am, but what is your sense in terms of social movements impacting school reform?

TM. I think that you're right, that we haven't had a sense of social movement in education since probably the sixties. And we think about the sixties as a period of activism at college campuses and we think that the great book has yet to be written about the social movements of the time. And I think a part of it has to do with this fragmentation and isolation of teachers who don't have those mechanisms to communicate with each other, don't do it well and are under incredible pressure to just sort of do their work. Second is that I think the fact that the decentralization movement has had this cast of being about individual benefit rather than collective benefit has just put the debate about schools into a box that focuses on individual test scores or test scores in schools. Look at the superintendent in Los Angeles who did a very brave thing in identifying the hundred lowest performing schools. But look at the terms in which he expressed the lowest hundred performing schools. They were test scores. And so again the frame of the debate is very instrumental and it's very difficult without significant leadership to generate a social movement that is not just against the specifics, but against the whole frame of an issue. It says, no, no, we're looking at the wrong target. And I think that universities can be faulted for that. That we have not stood up as we should and say the issues aren't simply about student accomplishment or on one or another test score. The issue is about the social purpose of education. And there I think we can lend, not just support for, but leadership to voices in the public schools. Many, many teachers, and obviously many parents want something very different out of the educational experience. The Freirean notion of schools as communities and as a part of communities is, as you say, very generative and very powerful. And there are isolated experiments going on in Los Angeles and elsewhere. One of my favorites was actually in rural Vermont, where the same kind of education took place, as it turns out, around garbage and waste. And if you can measure it, if you can write about it, if you can find out where it came from, and if you can develop ways of thinking about it artistically, you have an entire curriculum.

CT. But of course you cannot have the standards across the board because every curriculum is tailor-made to a particular school.

TM. On the other hand, you can have sophisticated standards at the other end that say, "Do children know how to solve problems? Can they take data and draw inferences from the data and come up with hypotheses?" And if we could develop those kinds of standards about what kids know how to do at the end, then each approach could vary according to the community and appropriate context could be measured at the end to make sure that students have learned about certain things and how to do certain things. But I think, going back to the notion of social movements, I think you've hit exactly on what is lacking in urban education and the kind of approach that would get us to the fundamental issues of race and class and gender and power that we're unable to address as long as we tinker at the policy level without a real core agreement on what schools are for. That's what I see social movements as doing. They're very different from policy talk. Social movements really start with a serious perspective on how things should be and why. And policy talk too easily gets turned by attractive technical solutions.

CT. Precisely. New social movements—like the civil rights movements—they start out of a gesture of moral outrage. And it works because rather than pursuing a particular specific narrow interest, it essentially looks at the role of welfare of a large number of people. I think one of the sadnesses of my experience as a professor in a university of this caliber in the state of California is to understand that the school, the university itself, has become a marionette, has become the subject of a political game. And therefore we have witnessed in the last seven years an assault on affirmative action. We have witnessed a very serious criticism on immigration policies and the life of immigrants. We have witnessed attempts to manipulate very sensitive issues for specific and narrow-minded goals of specific individuals to promote their political careers. So in a way, the most important decisions being made in education in the last seven years were neither connected with learning per se, nor connected with responses to the moral commitments of social movements, but rather the outcome of the specific goals of the specific individuals promoting specific political ideologies of the Right. I will take this as a very sad note.

TM. I would agree with your assessment of the political environment in which universities find themselves. And it's a terrible Hobson's Choice for universities because the ancient agreement that none of us signed on to was that academic freedom was fine as long as academic findings effected the world only in the very long run. And so the more we try to move our work into the world and to have it be a part of the discussions of policy or leadership of social movements, the more we open ourselves up to the curtailment of traditional freedoms by those who say "You're not playing by the rules. Think what you want, but don't act on it." And I think that it's that narrow fine line that universities find themselves on institutionally, and all of us find ourselves on personally. The question—and this may or may not be relevant for the chapter—but the question of whether I should sit for the interview that was in the *LA Times* was something the *Times* and I went back and forth on for two months because of just this word—What can I say, in the opinion section of the *Los Angeles Times*, that will not compromise my colleagues' ability to do their work in an unfettered way in an environment in which institutions are punished for the defensible or indefensible articulations of their members? And I think it puts us all in a very difficult position when we try to act on not only our beliefs but the research that we've done and the actual product of our scholarly activity.

CT. Let me just pose one more question. Coming back to standards, and thinking of the school of education nested in a university of this caliber, and your comments on standards that are applied unfairly to the school of education, the question is what is the role of a school of education in urban environments? The point is that schools of education do a lot of research and teaching similar to what colleges of letters and sciences do. In addition to that, there is a lot of activity, particularly within methods, that is tailor-made to education, to people who teach teachers with a particular learning approach. To people who really go into the communities and try and figure out ways to do educational work and the appropriate pedagogy and so on. In the case of those professors who resemble more what the College of Letters and Sciences do, it is easier to justify their contributions to university scholarship than in the case of those who are in the trenches seeking practical implementation models of teaching, organization, or administration. Then we are faced with a fascinating dilemma. The training of people who are similar to the Letters and Sciences may not be as controversial as training people who will work on the intervention side. Now, if you are an assistant professor, you don't want to be caught in a debate with evaluators who have said that your research is not the quality or the standard, your research has not had the same impact and support. So we have this dilemma that many people feel that when you're an assistant professor you have to conform to the norm mostly to survive and get tenure. When you get tenure, then you get into another process of complex internal co-optation through which all sort of rewards are given, so you proceed to really reproduce yourself again, and this time going for full professor. By the time you are full professor, which probably will be in your mid to late forties, a lot of the energy that you brought as an assistant professor or an associate professor is not wasted or gone, but is not the same energy. Your status in the profession has changed and therefore you don't have to struggle so much to write the right article to be published in peer review. But you have all sorts of limitations and therefore the challenge changes. And eventually for many the connection with the community becomes more and more remote. But of course it's easier for people to evaluate you around the same standards that everybody else evaluates people in universities, when schools of education do quite different work. By the time you are a very prominent member of the profession, you may have all the freedom in the world to do all the sort of things you want connected with the community, connected with the schools, but very rarely do you use it. Because there is a sense of self-fulfilling prophecy: If you get to that point, just keep doing exactly what you were doing before because the academic rewards don't change. As dean of a school of education, as a concerned reformer in urban education, as somebody who started this interview looking at the issue of nihilism, looking at the issue of the loneliness of utopia in the schools, what kind of answer do you have for that scholarly dilemma.

TM. Go into physics. I got more and more depressed as your question went on. Both remembering what it was like to be an assistant professor and thinking how true this dilemma is.

CT. I posed it in a very Weberian fashion, using an ideal type of the professoriate which is a total exaggeration of reality in order to understand reality. I may not totally agree with what I have just said, but I want to elicit your analysis of this issue of differential academic standards and rewards for a professional school like the school of education, which, almost by definition, is closer to answer the needs and demands of concrete communities than perhaps any other unit on campus.

TM. And in the best Weberian sense, it has enough connection to reality to draw from that experience the poignant elements. I think that education isn't just another discipline. It's not like biochemistry which is both the hybrid of and an advance upon two very strong fundamental disciplines—biology and chemistry. Education is that, where one might draw on political science and philosophy as you have done, Carlos. Or history and economics as I have done. And do enough real history and economics to be credible in those fields and to build on them and do something else when thinking about schools of education. But education is also a professional school in most of the places it's practiced. And certainly in the larger settings, education takes place in professional schools, where part of our responsibility as scholars is to figure out how to take our accomplishments in a pure research environment and translate them into practice. And I think we made a mistake in thinking about that, even for assistant professors, as a luxury, as something that one does after one has published the half dozen peer review articles per year. And one of the things that I tried to do as dean is to build that in as a fundamental requirement, to make those translations while the research is being done, rather than thinking of it as an afterthought or part of public service. And, in our own school, discourse is always critical. And a part of our school's promotion process is to divide the writing of one's record into scholarly activity, teaching, and service. And my push for the time I've been here is to include the work that people do as teachers in the scholarly activity portion of the write-up, rather than in the community service part of the write-up. Because to put it in community service puts it in the same category as serving on the buildings and grounds committee. And if it is that, then it will never be an important and core part of what we do.

Now that sounds good. But in reality, the problem with that strategy is that it simply adds to the responsibilities of the junior faculty member. It doesn't substitute. And so the problem that we're having—and I'll be the first to say that we haven't found our way through these things yet—the problem that we're having is that having accomplished the former, adding these contributions to what we expect in scholarly activity, we have not yet figured out how to reduce or even change what we think of as scholarly accomplishment in the area of peer review articles, in the area of grant production, and in the typical measures, the typical standards of scholarly output. And so I think we, at UCLA, and if my conversations with my fellow deans are any indication, we're all in these first-rate schools of education in urban areas, struggling with exactly this same problem of how to define scholarship in a way that doesn't dilute the rigor of the scholarly work that's done but that does allow people to accommodate the professional work and the pure scholarly work, the sort of pure research production work in the same lifetime.

KM. I can tell you from the research that I've been involved with, service is a very vaguely defined concept. Most often, it's perceived as professional service in the form of journal editing or things like that. It's a struggle to define what we mean by teaching, research, and service.

TM. That's really interesting. That's one kind of problem. The other one is that the category isn't research. Again, the discourse is real interesting. There was a reform a number of years ago that has not affected the discourse at all, which was to change the language from *research*, teaching and service, to scholarly activity. And very explicitly, changing that title was the way in which artists were going to be able to talk about exhibits and musicians were going to talk about shows, and people in professional schools were going to be able to talk about their work in developing professionals or working on policy as a part of scholarly activity. But it hasn't penetrated. If left to our own devices, even within the school, we will still do research, teaching, and service.

CT. You are an historian, and you are working extremely hard on reforming urban education. I presume that when you are involved in making decisions you invariably go back to the history of urban education for the right questions and for the historical answers to a given problem. History continues to be with you and informs your judgment and your understanding and perhaps even keeps you alive as an administrator. And I know that you will not disagree with me because in many ways history has done for you what critical philosophy has done for me. But as an historian, what will be the lessons of history in trying to improve the condition of urban education in this country, particularly in Los Angeles?

TM. I think the first is a historiographical conclusion which is that we tend to think at any point in time that the institutions we have are governed by some sort of natural law. And so the first lesson for me of history is that these institutions we call schools were developed at a particular point in time to meet a particular set of needs. And as crazy as they may appear today, they were functional. Or they continue to be functional. And as a historian, talking to policymakers, the important thing for me to convey to them is first the sense of indeterminacy—we can change these things. There is no natural law of schools that says there is a first grade, a second grade, a third grade, a fourth grade, and a fifth grade. Those were constructs to meet a particular set of demands within a particular ideological context at a particular point in time. If we're convinced that the ideological context has changed, that the historical moment has changed, that the needs of society have changed, we can change these institutions. It doesn't make it easy, but it is historically possible, because these were historical and human creations.

The second and contradictory historical thing that I keep thinking about—and I find myself in this situation all the time—is to see how cyclical the issues are. In Los Angeles today we're talking about issues of moving from a more district-oriented board to a board that's elected at large in the community or a board that's appointed by the mayor. At the turn of the century we did the reverse. We moved from a centrally oriented, centrally dominated board to a district-oriented board. And one finds that if you look at the history long enough, you find that in each reform are the seeds of its undoing. Because there is no perfect system. My mentor David Tyack wrote the wonderful book *The One Best System* in which he talked about the progressive era as a time in which people thought they could really get it right and they could develop the one best system that would be the way in which you could do this forever. Well, there is no one best system. But there are persistent issues and they come up, they go away, they come up, they go away. We do things that bring other issues to the fore.

The internal contradictions inherent to many reforms, they take half a century to finally emerge, but when they do, they sort of return us to facing the contradictions themselves. In this case, the question of centralization versus decentralization is the oldest question, it's the question of what kind of expertise is the best kind of expertise to run a school system. Is it the technical expertise that is more easily expressed in central authority or is it a more diffuse expertise that's about the needs of particular communities and the desires of the local population? And if you think it's the local population and community needs, it's the kind of expertise, well, then, you're going to move toward a local board. But those boards tend to be chaotic. They tend to be indecisive. And if what you're after is direction and decisiveness, and so on, again, I would try to move toward centralization. So the circumstances change, and that's the second lesson, that each area of reform has embedded in it contradictions that arise later and then have to be dealt with.

And I think that what that gives me, and I try to convey to other people, is a sense of calm. That we have been here before. That while there is maybe a sense of critical need and emergency to do something, it's not an urgency to create the one best system, but it's a sense of urgency to meet the needs that are facing us today. And then finally to go back to the beginning to where we started. My sense of history does show me over and over again that these fundamental issues of race, of class, of gender and of power remain with us. Much of the cyclical nature of school reform has to do with our need to address, but never to address at a very deep level, the inherent contradictions in capitalist democratic society in which we talk about equality but have social systems that are geared fundamentally around issues of inequality.

KM. An excellent place to end. Thank you, Ted.

CHAPTER 11

Memoirs of Urban Education Policymakers: A Dialogue among Three Former Urban School Superintendents

Harry Handler, Sid Thompson, and Eugene Tucker

with Carlos A. Torres and Karen A. McClafferty

BIOGRAPHIES OF THE PARTICIPANTS

Harry Handler worked for the LA Unified School District for thirty-four years, progressing from substitute teacher to superintendent. He served as superintendent for six years, from 1981 to 1987. He is currently an Adjunct Professor and Special Assistant to the Dean at UCLA in the Graduate School of Education and Information Studies. He has a bachelor's degree from UCLA in mathematics, a master's degree in educational psychology from USC, and a Ph.D. in educational psychology from USC in learning theory, statistics, and measurement.

Sid Thompson has been a senior fellow at UCLA since July of 1997. He had retired as superintendent of the Los Angeles Unified School District, a job he held from 1992 to 1997. He has forty-one years of education experience, all of it K–12. He began in the field as a math teacher, became administrator with the district, and then became superintendent. Mr. Thompson graduated from the U.S. Merchant Marine Academy at

Kings Point where he was a math science major. He came to UCLA for postgraduate work and later received a master's degree from Cal State LA.

Eugene Tucker is a member of the faculty at UCLA, after working twenty-three years as a superintendent of four different school districts in urban, suburban, and rural settings. His most recent assignment—from 1986 to 1992—was as superintendent of the Santa Monica Malibu Unified School District. He describes Santa Monica as "an edge city that has some urban characteristics." For ten years, Dr. Tucker was superintendent of the ABC Unified School District, a suburban school district with some urban characteristics. He was also superintendent of Coachella Valley Unified School District, a rural school district in Riverside County, California. His first superintendency was in a small elementary school district on the outskirts of the city of Los Angeles in the Santa Clarita Valley. Dr. Tucker received three degrees from UCLA: A B.A. in political science, and an M.A. and Ph.D. in education (curriculum studies, administration, and philosophy).

Karen McClafferty earned her Ph.D. from UCLA's Graduate School of Education and Information Studies. Her research focuses on the social role of the educational researcher and the sociopolitical context of the university. She has also done extensive research on urban education and the preparation of teachers for work in multicultural contexts.

Carlos Alberto Torres is a professor of education at UCLA, with a particular emphasis on nonformal education and the political sociology of education. His research interests also encompass the new research in the scholarship of class, race, gender, and the state in a comparative perspective, with a special focus on race relations in the United States and Latin America.

REFLECTIONS ON THE CHALLENGES
OF URBAN EDUCATION

> Experience is never limited, and it is never complete; it is an immense sensibility, a kind of huge spider-web of the finest silken threads suspended in the chamber of consciousness, and catching every air-borne particle in its tissue.
>
> —Henry James

> You can observe a lot by just watching.
>
> —Yogi Berra

KAREN MCCLAFFERTY (KM). We are delighted to have the opportunity to spend some time with you this afternoon and to get a glimpse into your experiences as superintendents in urban school districts. It is a rare opportunity, indeed, to be able to benefit from so many years of experience. Between the three of you, I believe we have close to a hundred years in the schools. Since we felt very strongly about including not only the voice of research but also the very important voice of practice in this book, we could not resist the temptation to include your insights.

CARLOS TORRES (CT). We entitled this chapter of the book, tentatively, "Memoirs from Superintendents in Urban Education." The book, as you have seen in the documentation, deals with the crisis of urban education. We will start with this very, I think, important question. I think it's also a very provocative question. During the time that you were superintendents, given the role and function, you have to handle all sorts of problems. And sometimes you have to be very discreet, extremely diplomatic. You could not always speak up. You were not able to give criticisms that perhaps, now being in academia, you can do. So, given that situation, that the commitments and the situation that you were in as a policymaker, is not any longer present, what were the critical issues that you handled, what were the critical problems that you found? And now you can really speak about it and discuss in detail. We can start from the criticisms and then we can move into the joys more than the sorrows and we can move into the positive achievements that you made or may have found in the last three decades. And of course if you want to do it chronologically, it would be nice. If you can figure out what is going on now compared to the past, it would be very interesting. The question, then, to be brief, is the following: As former superintendents, what kind of criticisms do you have of urban education, in Los Angeles particularly, and in similar areas?

SID THOMPSON (ST). Well, I'll go, I just came out of some of this. The criticisms that I have relate to the process by which board members are elected. The changes in the types of candidates attracted to the board, compared to the way it used to be, are very pronounced. It used to be, when I first started teaching in the system, that the people who were on the board tended to do the job as an avocation. They had jobs all the way from airline pilot to contractor to book reviewer. They did all sorts of things. We've noticed that that's focused and focused to where it is now a much more politicized process. For example, we used to elect our board members at large, and everybody that came into that job represented all students in the system. Hundreds of thousands of students. But they tended to have a global approach to the system. That was changed some years back to representation from subdistricts. And that was a very significant change. It sounds as if it would be more representative, and in a sense it is, but at the same time, it carries with it a lot of, frankly and bluntly, baggage. It carries with it what happens in ward politics. It becomes a matter of "I'm here, and I have a city council person, I have an assembly person, I have a whatever, that are all related to what I represent as a board member." And so that changes the approach.

It is important to note that during that same period of time, we've had a hardening over the years of the approach by the different bargaining units. They realized that the power was with the board members, and they became very active with money and voting support for individual board members. That's had a very critical impact. It's always been there in one form or another, but it's just much more focused. If you look at the LAUSD now, you have not only three teachers on the board, but you have three administrators on the board. And the administrators are in a sense unionized, and so they have their representatives. And I would submit that it takes away from what we had much earlier. The thing that I missed the most in that job was the fact that we seemed to spend an awful lot of time on everything but instruction. We spent time on adult problems. And when I did instruction, I'd almost say "hallelujah, we're talking about youngsters learning." It just didn't happen enough. It didn't focus enough. And I think it's had an effect.

I would also add two things when you talk about urban education. One is, there's a tendency to deal with it as if it's separate and distinct from where the youngsters come from. We know as a nation, we've not addressed issues in their communities as a total problem, we've dealt with it piecemeal. And the problems that are in those communities are reflected in the way kids come to school. And we talk about their reading scores. Some of these youngsters are fortunate that they can just breathe normally, considering what they go through. And we haven't been able to address that. Secondly, we've had an attitude educationally, when we have dealt with instruction, that talks to the problems these urban kids have. They're poor. And there is a lowered expectation. We talk about remediation as if it's stamped on their foreheads. "Remedial." And we have not, to my way of thinking, in any way sufficiently challenged the majority of these youngsters who do have a brain and are coming from all that I referenced as a problem and yet can learn.

GENE TUCKER (GT). Yes, I'd like to pick up where Sid left off. Even though Los Angeles probably represents the extreme of some on these issues, I agree with Sid in terms of the magnitude, the political climate and other issues involved. But we might indicate for example, that we've seen the growing "politicalization" of school boards. An increase in ethnic politics and changes in the nature of people who choose to run or not to run for school boards are some of the areas in which I've seen a very significant change over time. Power politics by the unions definitely have increased significantly, and in my view, not always for the better. A lot of the union issues are adult issues, as Sid indicated, and not focused on what may generally be considered the educational interest of children.

I would also say that there has been a growing tendency over the last several decades of micro-management by boards. In my earlier days as superintendent, boards were more willing to look at broad policy and leave to professional educators the "how to" accomplish goals. This micromanagement has extended beyond boards to legislatures and to governors. Legislative bodies are taking on or politicizing essentially educational issues. For example, taking stances on the politically correct way to teach reading or a politically correct way to teach mathematics. Again, I think we see a shortage of a clear, long-term vision; statements of goals, outcomes, or purposes; and a surfeit of prescription. I've seen this tendency nationally. Power politics accompany the growth of various ethnic groups in communities. Again, many of the political battles are not so much over the very legitimate concern about the needs of all children and the failure of schools to serve adequately children of color, but the sheer pursuit of personal or group power. I don't think there's any question that schools have not served the children of the poor well. Regardless of the ethnicity of the power structure.

HARRY HANDLER (HH). Sid and Gene have done such an outstanding job, I don't have anything left to say.

GT. Since when? (Laughter)

HH. One thought is that the readers may want to go back and read Michael Kirst's research on whether we should have school boards. He has some publications that I think are worth reading. If I may take a slightly different cut at this, it may be helpful. In trying to answer the question that you sent to us, "What are the key problems in urban education in the country?" I wrestled with four words, four concepts. One is the absence of standards. Standards involved for everyone in the enterprise. And I'm not just talking about standards for the program and student performance; standards for the superintendents' behavior, board members' behavior. Responsibilities of parents, legislators, custodians, community leaders, et cetera.

There needs to be a more intensive dialogue on why do the schools exist. What do we expect students to learn? And what are our moral obligations to see that it happens? So standards would be one concept. The other concepts which—and they go together—are *stability* and *consistency*. If one traces what's been happening over the past thirty years, the rules and the slogans are constantly changing without providing the time and the resources to assess the effect. We're a unique quasi-profession—and I can someday elaborate on that if you'd like me to—in that we can always manage to keep our slogans out in front of our performance. Therefore, the people who are supposed to deliver the instructional program aren't certain what's coming next. Why think any of it is important? Eventually it's just going to change the next year. Examples: homogeneous grouping to detracking; from integrated math to traditional math; from whole language to phonics; from decentralization to centralization to charter schools. Consciously or unconsciously as the superintendent, I kept watching this happen and trying to deal with it. We have these four conflicting values: We believe in equality. We believe in efficiency. We believe in liberty. And I added equity, because equity and equality are not the same to me. We try to maximize the effects of all four and it's impossible. If you really want to emphasize equality, you have to give up some efficiency. I can give other examples. So we haven't really found a way to bring about a balance in terms of the four values.

At a more concrete level, my fourth concept is fiscal responsibility. Yes, the schools need more money; yes, teachers should receive higher salaries. No question! But, yes, policymakers and administrators need to show greater fiscal responsibility. That gets back to long- and short-term planning, as mentioned by Gene, along with establishing priorities, and appropriately funding these priorities. As an anecdote, and Sid will recall this, when I became superintendent of the school district, we didn't have a sixth period. I went through the budgets of every manager in the district and concluded that if every manager of a major operation in the school district would reduce his or her expenditures the following year by 10 percent, we could fund the sixth period. That to me ties to what I'm trying to say about priorities and responsibility.

GT. Let me add on one thing. I think Harry mentioned a point that we probably should talk about. He talked about the whole issue of stability and consistency. I think most of us know that without stability in leadership it's difficult to operate even under the best of conditions. In a rapidly changing environment, with changing demands, it becomes even more difficult. The turnover of urban superintendents is amazing. For Sid and Harry to have been in their positions for five and six years respectively, that's amazing, when in many urban areas, the superintendent stays for two or three years at most.

HH. What's the average now, about two?

GT. Maybe two years.

KM. Because the pressure is so overwhelming?

GT. Again, it's because of the changing political winds. Every time a shift of power takes place after a board election, people want a superintendent who might represent a different point of view, philosophy or political position. And then, you also have turnover among board members. You have two things happening—turnover of leadership and a turnover in expectations and demands. As a consequence, teachers and administrators want to wait you out. Why should they change when they don't know what will be expected by the next set of leaders? By the time one superintendent starts to make a change, the next person or group is in power. The change the previous leader wanted is no longer fashionable, no longer considered appropriate. Therefore, there's a lack of consistency. And then you think of the thirteen-year span a child is in an educational system, and the shifts that have taken place within the scope of that child's experience, it is no wonder that significant progress often eludes us.

CT. Now, the shift takes place in the level of the policy. Does it also affect, directly, the school, or does the school have another dynamic?

ST. Don't forget—and Gene hit it right on the head, we all know this as well—we're talking about change at the top. For urban youngsters, the changes at the school level are just as severe. First of all, you have a lot of teachers teaching in there who aren't regularly credentialed. The problems of teaching in an urban setting, the environment and all that, causes turnover, so not only are you turning over at the top, you're turning over at the site. That youngster, and it's a good way to say it, this youngster in twelve to thirteen years of education not only is going through all of those changes at the top but these are policy changes. He also, or she is getting changes at the school level that are probably more upsetting.

HH. Let me provide another example. In 1983, the LA Unified School District opened school with eight hundred classrooms that didn't have teachers.

CT. So what happened?

HH. Substitutes. But that meant that during that year, thousands of youngsters would have a teacher for a week or two and then a different teacher, a week or two, and then a week where there wouldn't be a teacher and they divided up the class.

CT. So the pedagogical bond is never established.

ST. And the teachers were not fully credentialed.

HH. What were the contributing factors? Salaries were very low, and fortunately the State was able to increase salaries. Let me tell you what higher salaries meant. Instead of paying teachers $13,500, we had enough to pay $20,000 a year. Which made it difficult to recruit. But, the point is that there was policy, and you can see how this went from the board to the school. There was a policy that basically said when the teacher told you what part of the city the teacher wanted to work in, then that's where the teacher was assigned. I went to the board and I received support for what became the "Priority Staffing Program" and basically requested a new policy. People are assigned where we need them. And if not, it's okay, get a job in another district. Well, things worked out well. We opened in '84 with only eighty-four classrooms without teachers. So what does that mean? That one shift in policy had an impact on thousands of youngsters. Eighty-four classrooms that didn't have teachers, versus eight hundred classrooms that didn't have teachers. Markedly different.

CT. One of the arguments that has been used particularly by people like Michael Apple and other people looking at changes in the school board is this notion of the stealth campaign in which some factions of the religious right have been using their board appointments to push for very specific agendas. When you are looking at this—the turmoil at the board level and the more belligerent attitude within the school board members, is this situation also happening in the context that you have studied?

GT. I would say that phenomenon is more likely to occur in suburban, as opposed to urban areas. In urban areas you generally have a much larger, more liberal constituency, and you have more people of color who are voting. They are less susceptible to the agenda of the far right. But our colleagues in suburban areas are the ones who describe this phenomenon quite clearly, and it's quite accurate.

ST. That's why a lot of them have been put out.

GT. With the "wrong" belief system on the part of the superintendent, he or she becomes vulnerable.

CT. If you have mustered enough power in a particular district, then you can have almost your own philosophy being played out in that district.

GT. Especially if you can successfully get your supporters to turn out for school elections. School elections in California can either be held with general elections when a larger percentage of people vote, or they can be held in off years. That decision can be made locally. So, if you have an election on odd-numbered years, the off years, then the percentage of people who vote is smaller. The people who vote will tend to be older, without children in school. And, if you have a very well-organized, well-financed special interest group, they can be very successful at winning elections with a relatively small percentage of the electorate. And that's what frequently happens.

KM. Sounds like an enormously frustrating situation. One that must have made it quite difficult to organize the schools in a way that was best for the students. But in those years you must have had some successes—things that you were able to do which you felt simply *worked*.

MICRO-VICTORIES IN URBAN EDUCATION

So when you ask about the victories, I think a lot of them are tiny victories. They're micro-victories. Every once in a while a superintendent will get lucky and have a Board of five to seven people who can work together well.

—Gene Tucker

CT. Yes, let us move into the other side of the coin. You have already mentioned some of your successes. It would be nice always to go back to the real successes, to reminisce. Tell us of something that you have witnessed that worked. Something that works in policy and works in practice. I believe there is a lot of rhetoric going on about whether the schools work or don't work. If you take someone like Gloria Ladson-Billings and her book, *The Dreamkeepers*, about teachers of African American students, a bestseller, sold about 40,000 copies, in which she goes back to the classroom and sees these teachers turning out educated products of people that continue and go on.[1] Or Mike Rose's *Possible Lives*, which is a very exciting way of looking at the schools.[2] So I get a feeling that even in the context of persuasions and the criticisms that you outlined, there are success stories. Could you give us some flavor of that?

ST. The one success that I remember most, that hit me most deeply is not a success yet. But it was a beginning. And it was a matter of saying, when I was the superintendent, how little time was being spent on the curriculum and on the kids. I just found myself going absolutely wild with the fact that my time was effectively co-opted by adult issues. So I went after the instructional program, and I determined whether I could get the teachers to teach the subjects or not, because the numbers of emergency credentialed teachers in the classrooms are just enormous. We had to get the core curriculum to the kids. Some of these schools, 30 percent emergency-credentialed teachers are assigned. How do you have a curriculum with that? But I couldn't change it quickly enough. And if I were to sit there and say I'll be the superintendent for the next fifteen years, I still wouldn't see it. So I just determined, the heck with it, I'll just go for it. I'll take a quantum leap, raise the bar, and see what happens.

And so we got into who was taking algebra, who was taking AP courses, who was taking A through F, and you know who they are. And if you go into the urban schools—the barrios, the ghettos, the combinations of them—you get youngsters who will take those courses and who are academically tough. In spite of whatever they face, they're charging. Those aren't the ones you necessarily have to worry about. You have to nurture, but you don't worry. But it's this huge group of so-called C average, that really aren't. They're better than that, many of them. So one of the things that gave me solace, and I think was good, was to take the old system and say, "Okay, no more. I want to get rid of remedial courses." It sounds dumb. "What do you mean, you're not going remediate anymore?" Remediate, yes. But we don't even want to use the term. Remember what I said about remedial on the forehead. That was just a view of the kids.

KM. Like a stigma.

ST. It's a stigma. You're exactly right. If I can just digress just for a second and tell you that I went to a high school graduation in the valley. Valley High School, mixed. At that school, after the graduation where I spoke— I went out, as I did in all graduations, and talked to the kids. "Okay, what's happening to you, where are you going?" I tell this story wherever I go. I spoke to an African American youngster, a young man, and I said "Son, what are you going to do now?" And he says, "Oh, I don't know." He says, "I just don't know. You know, I've got to figure out—I got through this, and I got my diploma." I said, "Well, did you take algebra?" This kid said to me, "No." I said, "Why, why, why, why didn't you try?" He said, "That's for those people." And he pointed to the white kids. Tragedy.

Well I took him around the side of the building and he and I had what could best be described as a down-home, black-black discussion about this perception of his—we had to communicate. I just couldn't let that youngster go off that way. But it shows you where his thinking was about himself. His self image. That he just didn't have the brain. Anyway, I'm going on and on, but I just want to say this. When I switched and went after the curriculum, when I said we're going to have youngsters going into algebra, we're going to require it, you jump 25,000 kids enrolling over the previous figures in one year, and in that group, 60 percent were Cs, Bs, and As. So they reasonably made it. But what it did for me was once again I was going home and sitting up at night about, "Okay, now we're going to do all of this, and what's going to happen, and what are we going to do about teachers." I was worrying about the delivery of the educational program. So that was a major change for me that's carried a lot of impact.

GT. I don't think that the impression we want to give is that it's all negative. There's a very large number of wonderful teachers and a large number of excellent school administrators, caring people who give and give and give. There are good programs in almost every school—band directors who work sixty hours a week to see that kids get a quality music program, drama teachers, coaches, teachers of every subject and grade level. A majority of our nation's educators really do a tremendous amount for children. But a lot of these achievements are because of the individual and not because of what the system is doing. Maybe the system has let them alone, or, at least, created an environment that has allowed them to do good work.

The structure of schools isolates people. If you isolate a wonderful teacher you are likely to get good outcomes. But an isolated weak or poor teacher is likely throughout his or her career to continue offering instruction at a level that is unsatisfactory. So when you ask about the victories, I think a lot of them are tiny victories. They're micro victories. Every once in a while a superintendent will get lucky and have a board of five to seven people who can work together well. During these times we make tremendous progress. For example, changing the nature of collective bargaining, from a very adversarial model of bargaining to interest-based bargaining, which produced better results for schools and the kids. But with a change in the top leadership (superintendent and board members, union president), as occurred in my experience, conditions can deteriorate very quickly. The board changed, the union leadership changed and the superintendent left. In a few short years, they were back to where they were ten years earlier. People liked what they had, but the nature of the structure allowed it to regress to the earlier unsatisfactory conditions.

I agree with Sid. I think there's some very nice victories such as an increased understanding that more money has to be invested in professional development. I've seen that over the years. I think there is a growing recognition on the part of the total profession, and increasingly among some school board members, that we have to invest more in training the people who work in our system. Our schools can't be better than the quality of the people in our classrooms. So I think that's been a long range victory. I think that there's definitely a growing recognition that we need to do a better job with language minority students. Some progress has been made in this area. The current climate in California, however, is causing us some concern about this issue. We're doing a much better job in meeting the needs of children with disabilities. I think there's no question that statewide we're serving children who were not served well before. I think we're developing a better quality of leaders. Many of our new school principals are better qualified and more instruction-oriented.

RACE AND THE CHALLENGE OF URBAN SCHOOLS

You should be measured by your actions, not your rhetoric.
—Harry Handler

CT. This is really a very useful conversation. Let me pose a question that you have touched upon. There's one area of the conversation to which we're going to move which is one of the concrete interests of Karen about the role of universities in dealing with urban education, but obviously you see a role, since you are here. There are two things I'd like to touch upon before we get into that. One is race relations at the school level. One hypothesis—argued by those such as William J. Wilson—is that the "race problem," put in those terms, the race problem in the U.S. is really a class problem.[3] Not long ago, I think a couple of days ago, I watched a very serious debate at Harvard—Harvard has now recruited perhaps the most outstanding black intellectuals of this country, and all of them were there—and the narrative thread of the seven of them talking at Harvard was what I just stated. The race problem is a class problem.

My question, then, is the following: How would you elaborate on the peculiar "race problem" in Los Angeles, particularly with urban violence associated with that? The second part of the question, which you may want to tackle anyway, is that we have witnessed in the last six years a movement in which the race relations are typically altered because of Proposition 187, Proposition 209, because the affirmative action backlashes and so on.[4] So you were in the trenches, you were really looking at this situation from the inside. What would you say?

HH. You address that in different ways operationally and philosophically. Let me back up a minute so that you understand where I'm coming from. I never saw the superintendency as a person, I saw it as a concept. And I've always felt it a very unfortunate event when people became superintendents and immediately they "owned" the position. Given that philosophic position, perhaps you'll understand where I'm coming from. Number one, you don't deny that there are racial tensions. There are racial tensions. Number two, a number of the efforts to reduce racial tensions have been related to professional development-type activities, focus groups, etc. All of these activities had promise. But they're very limited.

There's no question in my mind that there's such a thing as institutional racism. And institutional racism is not always on the surface. In fact it's the institutional racism which is below the surface that is more dangerous to our society. Did I ever come up with "a solution"? No! Did I have guiding principles that I used in my own personal efforts to try and address some of the issues? Yes. I was the district's principle witness in the desegregation case, and had a number of board members very unhappy with me because I supported integration. But the key point here is, you have to ask yourself, "What do I believe is my role?" You should be measured by your actions, not your rhetoric. You need to accept that whether you like it or not, you are the superintendent. And for the right reasons and the wrong reasons, people take their cues from you.

GT. I would like to comment briefly on racism. It's really interesting, as Sid indicated earlier, you can't separate the child in the school from the child in the community. The community comes into the school, the child brings the community into the school. From my experience, more often than not, students see their schools as safe places. There will likely be some racism in every ethnically diverse group. There will be some territoriality. However, out of a 180–day school year, 178 of those days will be without a major racial incident. My experience has been that when parents hear negative stories, I ask them if they ever visited the campus. They usually have not. Because if they did visit the school, they would see kids pretty much leave school alone. They'll associate with their own friends.

There's not a lot of racial intermixing on most campuses, but neither is there much racial conflict. But when it does happen, it can be very nasty and very difficult. We have to spend a lot of time and energy preparing our administrative and teaching staffs—mostly in high schools and sometimes in middle schools—for potential incidents. Elementary schools are generally free of serious racial incidents.

ST. Yeah, that's what I've found.

KM. So what you're saying—to paraphrase Harry—is that your philosophy or your rhetoric matters little unless the principles are operationalized. And to understand whether or not that's happening, you really need to take a look at what is going on in the schools—the positive and the negative.

HH. I think a key part of that is that you can really see a difference in terms of leadership provided by the principal and the teachers. The bright principal creates activities at the school around common interests. Those common interests—and I'm not just talking about athletics—they bring students together along another dimension. If you're consciously doing that, especially if you're in a high school, it's fantastic the way these young people come together. Now, are you doing something constructive relative to racism? Yes. Are you able to say racism doesn't exist? No. It's there, but now what you're trying to do is every day— that's one of the most frustrating experiences I ever had is when people thought that you could have one period a day for multicultural education and you took care of everything. You create a climate—it's a twenty-four hour a day effort.

GT. Harry is absolutely right. But it's really interesting that most of those opportunities to work with people from mixed groups happen in extracurricular activities. It happens in the athletic program, it happens in the music program, it happens in the drama program. These provide opportunities for youngsters who ordinarily would not interact to work with each other around a common purpose. And today, there's very few administrators who aren't aware of and sensitive to the issue. Where racial interaction is not taking place is in academic classrooms, because of tracking and a whole series of other reasons. Many African American youngsters say "Algebra is not for me" because they don't see many black faces in the algebra classes. And to me that must be one of the next battlegrounds.

ST. I was going to add that as a minority person in the superintendency that one of the great emotional pressures I felt had to do with the African Americans who felt I was "their guy." Now, in the city of Los Angeles as we know, folks live apart. The white population versus the minority population is not a major issue in and of itself except where it's changing in the valley and you have Hispanic movements into many Valley areas. But basically, a more immediate concern right now is the Hispanic/Black. Because there are changes within the neighborhoods where African Americans move out or they see Hispanics moving in and there's a lot of give and take.

And it applies to the superintendency because the pressures I would get were almost daily—"Who are you going to put at that school? I *know* you're going to put an African American, right?" Wrong. Also not just the combination of Hispanic and African American, but you also have the Korean population in Pico Union and west. That's all in that mix. And it's fascinating to see it. Most of the people who live in the greater LA area drive over all that. They're on freeways, never get off. I have one guy who told me, "I didn't realize there was a Koreatown!" I said "Koreatown? That's the largest population of Koreans outside of Seoul!" But the point is that you face on the basis of race, you face not only that from the majority white population—majority U.S. as opposed to our urban schools—but you also face it within ethnic minorities. And so the only way I found I could operate was to work at them and work at them until when they hit me with "You think you ought to make an African American . . . ?" They would apologize, and they would say "Wait a minute, here's what we're saying. We understand that you can't just put blacks in the jobs and all. We know you can't do that. But we want you to at least consider it." Well, okay, that's a start. Because they're coming off of this hard line "you must" to understand the problems. The Hispanics would come to me and they would come in kind of with hat in hand looking at me because they couldn't really fully trust me—they didn't know what I was going to do. After all, he's an African American.

But I made the assignments and I kept that fine balance and I felt, just as Harry had to do and everybody else that's ever thought of this, as you do that, they get to at least understand where you're going to come from. And once they understand that you're not going to play the race role, that you're going to be objective, then they pull back. By the way, Harry, I can't resist. On your institutional racism, it's so true. The African Americans, in that population, you could say the same for the Hispanic populations—going into algebra, when we went into one school we found the vast majority of the African American kids were not taking algebra. When we approached the principal, the principal said, "Well, I know it's tough for the African American kids and the Hispanic kids. They just don't get in there and we haven't enrolled them." But you say, "Let me show you the list. Let me show you these kids who have Bs and As in mathematics prior to the time they could have taken algebra and didn't." And they would immediately say, "Oh, here's John, and here's Mary." If you personalized it, you could just see them with the wheels turning. "Oh my God, I didn't realize it." And then they say to you, "Oh my God, how did that happen? We're not prejudiced!" And I'd say, "No, you're not, but what happens is institutional, with one counselor for six hundred kids, who do they listen to? The middle-class youngster who comes in and says, 'My mom said take algebra, so put me down.' The African American kid, the Hispanic kid? Since they don't raise a ruckus and squeak, they don't get to take it." And the institution tends to accept that.

GT. Maybe this is a segue into another topic. One of the critical issues I see in education is the quality and characteristics of the teaching force. In California our teaching force is a long way from representing the ethnicity of our students. And if you look at who's coming into college now, I don't see in the future teacher pipeline a very diverse population. In urban communities, especially, we're finding an increasingly diverse student population, but still a predominantly white teaching force. And so that suggests to us, that if we think it's important to begin to have a more diverse teaching force, and this speaks to universities, we have to look at how do we do a better job in recruiting and retaining a diverse teaching force. We may need to look at other models for training teachers, ways that are more likely to ensure a more ethnically diverse corps of teachers.

Sid described it beautifully, as did Harry, we have large percentages of unprepared teachers using current training methods—essentially a university model. You get your B.A. degree then you get your teaching credential. The truth of the matter is that people from lower socioeconomic groups cannot defer earning money for that long a period of time. So as a consequence, they're not going into the profession. There's not a lot of evidence to my knowledge indicating that other models cannot also be very effective.

CT. You have any particular hint at what kind of models you are considering?

GT. Yes, I do. I think, for example, we can start looking at what I would call a differentiated staffing model, where people in schools with different levels of training can perform different roles. You might have a fully university-trained person with several years of experience and proven teaching ability who might work with a team that would include people with one or two years of college who would be getting some experience, learning how to perform the teacher's role, working with students or with small groups under the lead teacher's guidance. They would have opportunities to grow and increase their responsibilities over time while they continue their schooling.

If we are thoughtful about it we can create teacher training models that would assure us a more diverse, well-prepared profession. I think that would go a long way to improving our schools and dealing with teacher isolation. Too many unprepared teachers are put in the classrooms. A beginning teacher who comes in unprepared has the same roles and responsibilities as a twenty-year veteran with a proven track record. In an elementary school, they each have thirty children, they each teach for the same length of time each day, they each have the same responsibilities. I like a medical model, for example, which utilizes people in different roles to meet the needs of the patient. I don't know if Harry and Sid agree, but I see this as one of the critical issues in education today. I was reading recently that New York City has 30–40 percent of its teachers who are not fully prepared.

ST. Right, because I think right now, increasingly you hear it takes five years for youngsters to come through here and get a bachelor's degree, then another year, or another whatever, for their teacher certification.

HH. Gene, your program now is a six-year program, isn't it?

GT. They work as full time teachers and are paid during their sixth year while they complete their master's degree.

ST. In my mind, the problem with that system is it takes too long for the person to end up in the classroom to find out if that's what they really want to do. If they don't like kids—and there's nothing wrong with not liking kids, but then they darn sure shouldn't be in front of them. But why should you be waiting that period of time to find out? In other countries—I went to school under the British system when I was little and they used what would be like student teachers much earlier. They still went on to get their degree.

We have teaching assistants in classrooms, but for a different reason. Teaching assistants are in our classrooms because we're providing employment. That really is for the wrong reason. We've been lucky because out of those we've managed to get some darn good teachers. They find out they really like this and they go on and get their degree, and we get them back.

HH. We had a period where we hired a large number of teachers who had emergency credentials. We put together a team of skilled people and had them go in and observe teachers. They didn't know whether the teachers had emergency credentials or not. I wanted to know, "What did you think?" And it was a wash. Which really worried me. Because on the one hand, we say that the non-credentialed teacher isn't prepared. On the other hand, we send experts in to observe, and they can't distinguish. So that says a lot, generates a lot of hypotheses.

The other thing I want to mention is that, as I listen to Gene, and as Gene talked about the medical model, and I understand what Gene's saying and I agree. I know where he's coming from, but it's that kind of problem, when we discuss it, we have to put another hat on. I tried to put the hat on of someone who felt very strongly that the system was unfair, that the system is inequitable. And what I had to wonder about is, will Gene's suggestion lead to white people being in the top positions, such as doctors—and that isn't what you had in mind, but white people being the doctors and the supporting cast being made up of other than white. But what that really says, with a slight modification, you could start after two years of junior college, you could start a career ladder program where people work on their credential, continue to work on their college education, continue to work part time for school districts, and it may take them six or seven years, but then they're fully credentialed teachers.

There's another potential gold mine in the future teacher clubs. There are future teacher clubs in high schools throughout the country, and you can develop curriculum materials in the ninth, tenth, eleventh, twelfth grades. And if you're lucky, you can get out there and get the financial support, you can work with these students to get them financial support while they go to college. If they drop out and aren't in the program, they don't get the financial support. You know you're going to take some losses at the end of the program because some of them aren't going to become teachers. And you can't really say, "I promise you. . . ." But the proportion who do go into teaching is rather rewarding. And it's a small investment. You can really start to prepare people to be teachers and to get them excited about it at an earlier age.

KM. And perhaps in doing that, begin to bring about some changes in the demographic makeup of the teaching force?

GT. Actually, what happens of course in many communities is that the demographic changes are taking place at a faster rate than turnover of teachers. I'll give you some examples. At one time Compton and Inglewood were all white. Within a decade, they became predominantly African American. Within another decade and a half, they became predominantly Hispanic. The power structure remained white for many years after black children were the majority. Now, the power structure is predominantly black, while Hispanics are now the majority. The teaching staff has remained white for a long time, because a teacher's career may span 35–40 years.

So what happens is similar to what occurs at universities. Why are most professors white males? Well, first of all the career of a professor is longer than the career of a teacher. The slow turnover rate provides limited opportunities for women and people of color to enter the professional ranks.

Many people want to see a university staff that reflects the demographic changes. Meanwhile you can't throw out the people who've invested a lifetime making a contribution. Changes will take time. Well, the same is true with the teaching profession. In medicine, for a long time, most doctors were white males. And now, over 50 percent of students in medical school are female. In another decade or two, at least half of the doctors will be female.

Another issue that's important to me in urban education is that given the current structure of schooling, I think that poor, minority children are at a real disadvantage. You think of schooling as primarily being 180 days a year, six hours a day. Children from middle-class families are provided enriched activities in the summertime and supervised activities at the end of the day. Their education continues when school is not in session. Children in urban centers, when not in school, are not likely to be getting rich educational experiences.

ST. TV or the street.

GT. Increasingly, parents are afraid to let their kids play in the street for safety reasons. They keep them at home in front of the television set. So it seems to me that one of the issues we have to think about is the structure of schooling. I think we need to provide rich educational opportunities for more days of the year and more hours per day. Many of these children need more time to accomplish the same high standards that middle-class children in more privileged environments accomplish in less time. So it seems to me that one way of getting at equity is not through equality but by providing more quality learning time and by changing the structure of schooling. Time to learn, that's a critical issue, especially in urban schools.

ST. We're not talking about athletics, per se. But the LA Best program takes an academic approach as recreation—dance, drama—the things they can't do at school normally they do after school. But they also do homework. If the family is disjointed, you might just as well do it where you can do it. And if it's at school, there's nothing wrong with a kindergartner—if I had my magic wand—being two or three more hours in school. What's he going to do? What's she going to do? She's going to be on the street or staring at that tube. Given the option, I'd have them do the after school.

When I was principle at Markham in Watts, right after the riots, they had a federal program, they picked those kids up after school and three bus-loads of them went to Cal State LA. And out at Cal State LA they had drama, they had art, they had subject reinforcement. When they brought them back at seven o'clock in the evening, those kids only had time to get off that bus and go home. They didn't have time to go off romping in the street. Now I'm not saying it has to be like that, but this LA Best, that kind of approach is very beneficial. I told them in Washington, I said if you're talking about the defense budget going down, why don't you take that money and expand the school day. I said that would be a tremendous support to these kids. Not with games. With true academics and the arts and the kinds of things we'd all like to do. It can be done.

BOUNDARIES AND BRIDGES IN URBAN EDUCATION: THE ROLE OF HIGHER EDUCATION

We're going to put ourselves out of business if we don't pull this stuff together and start demonstrating that we really know how to bring about improvement.

—Harry Handler

KM. One of the issues we raise in the introduction to this book is the elimination of boundaries or the bridging of them. Ted Mitchell, for example, in a recent issue of the journal *Daedalus* (1997) describes the changing relationship between the university and its environment—the bridging of what were once very clear distinctions.[5] For me, that ties into the issues of how universities relate to public schools. But it also ties into the issue of community involvement in schools. That's come up in certain points during this discussion, but I'm wondering whether you perceive the opportunity for more community involvement, and how that might happen. I'd also like to know how you perceive the university role in urban school reform.

ST. The community to me, whenever a principal would come in fussing and screaming about "She's a big pain in the neck, she's a big community activist," I couldn't take that. I would say, if they're in there, that's a step we want. So I think for most of us, there are a few crazies out there. That's a given. But most of the people that just drove me crazy were also people who really cared about those kids. They just didn't know what to do about it. And I accepted that challenge in all the different jobs I had. The role for the community is there. The question is whether we have more parent involvement. Not with just bake sales and things, but with curriculum. What it is we expect these kids to learn, and how they can help.

I had a parent—a Hispanic, poor lady, had a number of kids—she said to me, "Mr. Thompson, I don't know the first thing about algebra." And in her way she explained, "I can't even spell it." She said, "So, my kids are taking this stuff. What can I do?" And I think I said, "Let me just be simplistic. When she comes in the door, you shut that tube off and have a particular period of time when she's going to work." And you say "I expect you to work. And I'm going to enforce it." And she says, "But I don't even know how to do it." I said, "You don't have to. When she brings the paper, you don't know what they wrote, but you can tell if they're just messing around! You can see it! So say, 'This is junk, go back and work on it,' you're probably right. Take a chance."

But my point is that there is a real need for that. And we would need another whole hour to talk about community, because I believe in it strongly, and I know these guys do. The other thing I wanted to say about service is that we are so stupid in the way that we deliver services to families, it's incredible. Health, anything, name it. We make them go to what I like to call all those gray buildings. And they can't get there. They're afraid of them, they're afraid to go when they can get there. To me, if you want to impact a parent the most, impact them at the center of what concerns them the most. And that's their kid. If you want to work with a parent who's on aid, and all the rest of it, whatever the aid may be, if you want to really work with that parent, work through the children.

As a high school principal I had a probation officer on campus—huge school, 3,800 kids, 4,000 kids—a probation officer on campus, DPSS working on campus. Why? Because 700 of those kids were on probation. Mostly boys. And when those kids didn't come to school, nobody knew it. A probation officer on campus, when he said, "Charlie, I didn't see you yesterday," that was a lot different to principal Sid, typical "Daddy," saying "You should have been in school." No, no. *He* says, "You be here tomorrow, or you have a problem." I can tell you, it was amazing to me. Attendance just went like this (gestures up) with these kids because nobody's playing with them. One kid with many brothers and sisters, his mother died, DPSS on the job, all those kids taken care of in two hours. I would have spent eight hours trying to find out who to call. So I am a firm believer that we need coordinated approaches to support services. Just absolutely need it. But I want to tell you, there's a huge battle because it's turf. And when I left that school, both workers were taken out. Because "We can't supervise them over there."

GT. I liked what you said—coordinated and school-based. One thing about the university during my few years here is that community-based, school-based work is not deeply valued. There's really a disincentive for the faculty to truly be involved. An assistant professor working for tenure and professional advancement knows there's a hierarchy of values. Research is most valued. At the bottom of that hierarchy is community service.

It seems to me that the university needs to think about or explore ways to reward and encourage faculty to become involved with K–12 schools. I think we have faculty who could make very significant contributions to the work of schools, either at the policy or the operational level. I think a lot of research could be centered around that work. My experience has been that it's problematic for junior faculty to get more involved and many senior faculty don't want to leave their comfort zone.

KM. So, rather than trying to "raise the status" of community service, so to speak, we should focus on a more thorough integration of service and research. It seems like a natural goal for any university with a service mission, but an incredibly challenging one, nonetheless.

HH. I jotted down some notes in anticipation of our conversation and I'll probably address your question in them.

This may sound kind of corny, but we still lack public confidence in public schools. You can't go out and generate a lot of support for these kinds of changes without public support. Then I couple that with lack of understanding of the reason they're called the public schools—and this ties to community. They're called public schools because they belong to the public. That may sound kind of weird, but it's something to keep in mind every day of the week that you work with the public. Those schools belong to the public. So public involvement would seem to me natural. Conflicting needs of the multiplicity of special interest groups has been described. I think more people should read Jonathan Kozol's *Savage Inequalities*.[6] How can we address the question of solutions for the future? I think we have to sustain the national interest in the condition of our schools.

This dialogue and this concern has been going on longer than any of us can remember. Usually it was like a sine curve in calculus, where it's a concern today but tomorrow it isn't. This time it has been very consistent and we better keep it up there. You're in an era now where bottom-up is important. So we balance the two, bottom-up and when there is a need for a decision, someone who has carefully gone through the problem and is willing to take risks associated with decisions, we can't walk away from the community. The research community has provided practitioners with far more knowledge and insight than is being utilized. However, within the research community, there is a lack of consensus regarding what to do. The academics and the practitioners need to reach a consensus regarding "What do we know? What changes should be made?" And working together—practitioner and scholar—how are we going to get it done?

For the past four or five years, I've noticed some progress. If I had a magic wand, I'd say "No more research! We've got to stop right now! We need to regroup and agree on what we think we know, and we've got to go do it." Just, "Time out!" It's not that I don't value the research, and I understand the concept of contributing to knowledge. But we're going to put ourselves out of business if we don't pull this stuff together and start demonstrating that we really know how to bring about improvement.

CT. Strong words. And I appreciate that.

GT. You're going to be out of here. You're not going to be invited back. (Laughter)

THE PASSION OF URBAN EDUCATION

Your reason and passion are the rudder and the sails of your sea-faring soul. If either your sails or your rudder be broken, you can but toss and drift, or else be held at a standstill in mid-seas. For reason, ruling alone, is a force confining; and passion, unattended, is a flame that burns to its own destruction.
—Kahlil Gibran, *The Prophet*

CT. Kahlil Gibran has described reason and passion as the rudder and sails of the soul—one without the other is useless, and the two together are quite powerful. It's very clear to me that there's a fascinating combination here of passion—and I do appreciate passion—and knowledge or reason. And I think when we are talking about this issue, we are not observing dispassionately, like kind of objective scientists, see how the rats are moving, figure out who is losing weight, who is not. And in fact we are part of the rats. When we are observing, we are part of the rats.

But I have one question. You may think that it's a romantic question—I hope you don't think so. But I have been thinking lately about virtues. I think education is always a very noble profession because people are thought of as instilling virtues. The moral commitment, whatever that is. If you were going to list a couple of virtues of a good superintendent, what would they be? In a way, I'm asking you, if you had to get together with a young colleague who is going to be a superintendent, and you want to pass on the baton, then you look at them and say, "Look, there are a couple of things you should know." The question is open.

HH. I just finished with a passionate statement, so . . .

ST. Well, as I think back on the superintendency, there are certain characteristics a person should have. One of them is energy. Because the job is incredibly demanding, and you can't do it on low energy. So you have to be a person who doesn't require nine hours of sleep a night, because you're not going to get it in that job. Although, I know those who do manage to squeak it out. Not here. The other characteristic that I think you must have, especially dealing with board members, is the ability to bring folks together. You have to work for that. Your responsibility is to bring them together. In spite of what I said about what a pain and what they sometimes represent. You have to work with them. So you have to be a communicator. You have to listen and you have to communicate. Now, there are all sorts of things about organization and budget that I won't go into. But the other to me, for a good superintendent, in spite of the fact that we don't necessarily look for this, is an instructional leader. Somebody that is going to lead the district in instruction.

GT. I would add a couple. I certainly would put intellectual honesty at the top of the list. I think that a good superintendent has to know what he or she believes in and have the courage to stand by those beliefs. I think there are times when all of us are pressed against the wall. We have to make those hard decisions which are not popular, but are the right ones for children. A good superintendent has to be really committed to social justice—a person who truly believes that in a democratic society every child deserves access to quality education and who will work to ensure that happens.

I think that a good superintendent has to have qualities that we often attribute to leadership. He or she should have a vision of what could and should be, have the ability to mobilize and engage others in sharing that vision, and empower the people that he or she works with to achieve the outcomes that have been mutually identified.

HH. Virtue. And I only get to pick one. I want to turn it into a game. I only get to pick one. "INTEGRITY."

ST. It sounds like, "Oh, yeah, of course," but no. It is so important.

CT. I think that's an excellent place to stop. It's been a real pleasure. Karen and I would like to thank you profusely.

NOTES

1. Gloria Ladson-Billings, *The Dreamkeepers: Successful Teachers of African American Children* (San Francisco: Jossey-Bass, 1994).

2. Mike Rose, *Possible Lives* (New York: Houghton Mifflin, 1995).

3. See, for example, William J. Wilson, *The Truly Disadvantaged: The Inner City, the Underclass, and Public Policy* (Chicago: The University of Chicago Press, 1987), and William J. Wilson, *The Declining Significance of Race* (Chicago: The University of Chicago Press, 1980).

4. In recent years, California has experienced far-reaching backlash against race-related issues such as immigration and affirmative action. Proposition 187 was a voter initiative aimed at denying social services to undocumented

immigrants in the state. Proposition 209 seeks to end affirmative action in education and hiring. Both were passed by voters.

5. Theodore R. Mitchell, "Border Crossings: Organizational Boundaries and Challenges to the American Professoriate," *Daedalus* 126.4 (1997): 265–92.

6. Jonathan Kozol, *Savage Inequalities: Children in American Schools* (New York: Harper Perennial, 1992).

THE CONTRIBUTORS

Michael W. Apple is John Bascom Professor of Education at the University of Wisconsin, Madison. A former elementary and secondary school teacher and past president of a teachers union, he has worked with educators, unions, dissident groups, and governments throughout the world to democratize educational research, policy, and practice. He has written extensively about the relationship between education and power. Among his most recent books are: *Official Knowledge* (1993), *Education and Power* (1995), *Cultural Politics and Education* (1996), and *Power, Meaning, and Identity* (1999).

Anthony Gary Dworkin is Professor of Sociology at the University of Houston and holds the Ph.D. degree in sociology from Northwestern University. He is past chair of the Department of Sociology at the University of Houston. He is the author of nine books and numerous articles on teacher morale and burnout, student achievement, racial, ethnic, and gender stratification, intergroup relations, and ethnic stereotyping. He is past president of the Southwestern Sociological Association, has served in several elected and appointed positions in the American Sociological Association and other professional associations, and serves on editorial boards and grant review panels in sociology and education. He currently serves as editor of a book series entitled "The New Inequalities," published by the State University of New York Press. Most recently, Dr. Dworkin served on a task force for the Texas Higher Education Coordinating Board, addressing the issues of higher educational access for disadvantaged populations and the maintenance of cultural diversity. He served as principal investigator on the U.S. Department of Education Urban Community Service project described in his chapter.

Pamela Fenning holds a master's and doctorate in School Psychology from the University of Wisconsin, Madison. She has completed a clinical internship at the Devereux Foundation (Pennsylvania), and has worked as a school psychologist with students who evidence significant emotional and behavioral difficulties. Her research and clinical interests involve developing appropriate services for youth who have serious emotional disturbances, evaluating mental health and educational programs within public schools, and implementing discipline policies within school and residential settings.

Harry Handler worked for the Los Angeles Unified School District for thirty-four years, progressing from substitute teacher to superintendent. He served as Superintendent of Schools for six years, from 1981 to 1987. He is currently an Adjunct Professor and Special Assistant to the Dean at UCLA in the Graduate School of Education and Information Studies. He has a bachelor's degree from UCLA in mathematics, a master's degree in educational psychology from University of Southern California (USC), and a Ph.D. in educational psychology from USC, in learning theory, statistics, and measurement.

David Lee Keiser teaches and writes in Berkeley, California. He is currently completing his dissertation at the Graduate School of Education at the University of California at Berkeley while teaching undergraduate courses in multicultural education and poetry. He has published several dialogues about the retraction of affirmative action, in *Social Justice* and *Bad Subjects*, as well as poems in several anthologies. His dissertation, *Stokin' the Fire: Writing Empowerment at an Urban High School*, follows three years of high school teaching, and expands upon the chapter published in this volume.

Karen McClafferty received her M.A. and Ph.D. from the Graduate School of Education and Information Studies at the University of California at Los Angeles. She has worked as a researcher with Children's Television Workshop, developing educational television programming for at-risk youth. Dr. McClafferty is the co-author of several articles on the preparation of teachers for urban schools. Her current research focuses on the sociology of education, with special attention to the social and political context of educational research and the role of higher education in the improvement of urban schools.

Peter McLaren is Professor of Education at the University of California, Los Angeles Graduate School of Education and Information Studies. He has authored, edited, and co-edited over thirty books and monographs on topics that include critical pedagogy, the sociology of education, critical ethnography, critical literacy, and Marxist social theory. His work has been translated in eleven languages. His most recent books include *Schooling as a Ritual Performance* (3rd edition, Rowman and Littlefield, 1999), *Critical Pedagogy and Predatory Culture* (Routledge, 1995), *Critical Multiculturalism* (Westview Press, 1997), and *Che Gue-*

vara and Paulo Freire: An Introduction to the Pedagogy of Liberation (in press, Rowman and Littlefield). Professor McLaren's current interests include globalization, neoliberalism, and Marxist social theory.

Roslyn Arlin Mickelson, a former public high school social studies teacher, is Professor of Sociology and Adjunct Professor of Women's Studies at the University of North Carolina at Charlotte. She received her Ph.D. from the University of California, Los Angeles in 1984. Prior to coming to North Carolina in 1985, she completed a postdoctoral fellowship at the University of Michigan, Ann Arbor's Bush Program in Child Development and Social Policy. Her primary research examines the political economy of schooling and the ways that race, class, and gender shape educational processes and outcomes. Her current research, supported by the National Science Foundation and the Ford Foundation, explores the academic and equity implications of corporate involvement in school reform.

Theodore R. Mitchell is currently serving as Vice President of the J. Paul Getty Trust and Professor of Education at University of California, Los Angeles. He has also served as Vice Chancellor and as Dean of the Graduate School of Education and Information Studies at UCLA. His own research has been in examining educational organizations in an historical perspective. His particular interest is in exploring the ways educational organizations in the United States have resisted or embraced change. He is the author of numerous essays and articles, and is currently completing a book entitled *The Republic for Which It Stands: Liberty, Order, and the Development of Public Schools in America.*

Raymond A. Morrow is Professor of Sociology and Adjunct Professor of Educational Policy Studies at the University of Alberta, Edmonton, where he has taught since 1984. A co-author with Carlos A. Torres of *Social Theory and Education* (SUNY Press, 1995), he has also published extensively in other aspects of social and cultural theory, including a book on *Critical Theory and Methodology* (Sage, 1994) which outlines what is termed an interpretive structuralist research program based in part on the work of Anthony Giddens and Jürgen Habermas.

Marianela I. Parraga, M.Ed., born in Bolivia, is bilingual (Spanish/English) and also has a strong background in French. As a graduate student of Loyola University of Chicago's doctoral program in School Psychology, she has been actively involved as a student representative and as a graduate research assistant. Recently, she was awarded a regional minority scholarship through the Illinois School Psychology Association. Her research interests are in addressing parent-professional communication, developing school discipline policies, and evaluating programs for students in special education. She looks forward to beginning her career in an inner-city school in Chicago.

Margaret K. Purser holds an M.A. degree in sociology from the University of Houston and is president of M. K. Purser Consulting. She is a professional demographer and geographer who built many of the models utilized in the Urban Community Service project described in the chapter and served at one time as a co-principal investigator on the project. School districts, local and regional governments, and businesses rely upon her forecasts for planning and community development.

Ayman Sheikh-Hussin received his Ph.D. degree in economics from the University of Houston and served as the computer specialist on the Urban Community Service project described in the chapter. He is currently in charge of information technology in the Houston office of Communities in Schools, a social service agency working with at-risk youth.

Sid Thompson has been a senior fellow at UCLA since July of 1997. He retired as superintendent of the Los Angeles Unified School District, a job he held from 1992 to 1997. He has forty-one years of education experience, all of it K–12. He began in the field as a math teacher, became administrator with the district, and then became superintendent. Mr. Thompson graduated from the U.S. Merchant Marine Academy at Kings Point, where he was a math science major. He came to UCLA for postgraduate work and later received a master's degree from California State University, Los Angeles.

Laurence A. Toenjes was educated at the University of California at Berkeley (B.A. and M.A., economics) and Southern Illinois University at Carbondale (Ph.D. in economics). Dr. Toenjes has extensive experience in state level education budgeting (Illinois) and school finance analysis (several states, including Texas). During the past three years, while at the University of Houston as a Research Professor in the Department of Sociology, he has participated in projects involving extensive data collection and analysis for many of the school districts in the Houston metropolitan region. He has also worked with numerous state agencies, educational interest groups, task forces, and private groups on education related issues. He served as co-investigator on the Urban Community Service project.

Carlos Alberto Torres is Professor of Education at UCLA's Graduate School of Education and Information Studies and Director of the Latin American Center. He holds a Ph.D. in International Education and Development from Stanford University. He has published numerous books and articles focusing on education in Latin America, with a particular emphasis on nonformal education and the political sociology of education. His research interests also encompass the new research in the scholarship of class, race, gender, and the state in a comparative perspective, with a special focus on race relations in the United States and Latin America.

Eugene Tucker is a member of the faculty at UCLA after working twenty-three years as a superintendent of four different school districts, both urban, suburban, and rural. His most recent assignment—from 1986 to 1992—was as superintendent of the Santa Monica Malibu Unified School District. Dr. Tucker received three degrees from UCLA: A B.A. in political science, and an M.A. and Ph.D. in education (curriculum studies, administration, and philosophy).

Amy Stuart Wells is an Associate Professor of Educational Policy at UCLA's Graduate School of Education & Information Studies. Her research and writing has focused on the role of race in educational policy making and implementation. More specifically, she studies school desegregation; school choice policy, including charter schools; and detracking in racially mixed schools. She received her Ph.D. from Columbia University in Sociology of Education—a joint program between Teachers College and the Graduate School of Arts and Sciences—in 1991. She is author of several journal articles and books, including *Time to Choose: American at the Crossroads of School Choice Policy* (Hill & Wang, 1993); first author with Irene Serna of "The Politics of Culture: Understanding Local Political Resistance in Detracking in Racially Mixed Schools," *Harvard Education Review* (Spring 1996); and first author with Robert L. Crain of *Stepping over the Color Line: African American Students in White Suburban Schools* (Yale University Press, 1997). In 1995, she began a two-year study of charter schools in ten school districts in California funded by the Ford Foundation and the Annie E. Casey Foundation.

Geoff Whitty is the Karl Mannheim Professor of Sociology of Education and Dean of Research at the Institute of Education, University of London. He ran the Urban Education Program at King's College London and was later Dean of Education at Bristol Polytechnic and the Goldsmiths' Professor of Policy and Management in Education at Goldsmiths' College, University of London. He is author of *Sociology and School Knowledge* (Methuen, 1985) and co-author of *The State and Private Education* (Falmer Press, 1989), *Specialisation and Choice in Urban Education* (Routledge, 1993) and *Devolution and Choice in Education* (Open University Press, 1998).

James D. Wilczynski received a M.A. in Clinical Psychology at Xavier University of Ohio. He is currently completing his Ph.D. in School Psychology at Loyola University of Chicago. He previously worked in the Department of Psychiatry at Cook County (Illinois) Department of Corrections. Current areas of interest include working with students with emotional and behavior disorders, developing and evaluating alternatives to suspension programs for regular and special education students, and violence/gang prevention strategies for school settings. He is currently a school psychologist for the Lockport Area Special Education Cooperative in Illinois.

INDEX

New Ethics for the Public's Health

Edited by

DAN E. BEAUCHAMP

Professor Emeritus
Department of Health Policy,
Management, and Behavior
School of Public Health
University at Albany
State University of New York

BONNIE STEINBOCK

Professor
Department of Philosophy
University at Albany
State University of New York

New York   Oxford
OXFORD UNIVERSITY PRESS
1999

Oxford University Press

Oxford   New York
Athens   Auckland   Bangkok   Bogotá   Buenos Aires   Calcutta
Cape Town   Chennai   Dar es Salaam   Delhi   Florence   Hong Kong   Istanbul
Karachi   Kuala Lumpur   Madrid   Melbourne   Mexico City   Mumbai
Nairobi   Paris   São Paulo   Singapore   Taipei   Tokyo   Toronto   Warsaw

and associated companies in
Berlin   Ibadan

Library of Congress Cataloging-in-Publication Data
New ethics for the public's health / edited by Dan E. Beauchamp, Bonnie Steinbock.
p.   cm.   Includes bibliographical references and index.
ISBN 0-19-512438-3—ISBN 0-19-512439-1 (pbk.)
1. Public health—Moral and ethical aspects.   2. Medical policy—Moral and ethical
aspects.   I. Beauchamp, Dan E.   II. Steinbock, Bonnie.
RA652 .N49   1999
174′.2—dc21   99-23617

9 8 7 6 5 4 3 2 1

Printed in the United States of America
on acid-free paper

For

Carole

and

Nick, Sarah, and Sam

New Ethics for
the Public's Health

Preface

New Ethics for the Public's Health is a fresh departure for a textbook on health
policy and ethics. For the first time such a book addresses head-on the public
health issues that are important for the new century. How do we provide access
for all to health care in an era of market forces and managed care? How do we
defend the public's health in the midst of old and newly emergent epidemics
(drug-resistant tuberculosis and Ebola and Hanta viruses)? How do we create a
rational drug policy and health policy, issues that are highly politicized and
increasingly complicated in the context of worldwide immigration and crum-
bling borders? How do we assess the ethics of reproduction in a time of transformation of the family; the meaning of kinship? What are the implications of
the burgeoning of genetic information for the treatment of disease and of privacy, for confidentiality, and for discrimination? What are the rights of undocumented aliens and other strangers to Medicaid and of other public health protections in a time of soaring deficits and shrinking budgets? What are the prospects
for practicing medicine, nursing, social work and public health when "the patient" is not only individuals but, more and more, whole communities?

New Ethics for the Public's Health aims to be very different from typical
medical ethics textbooks. Most texts on medical ethics are edited by philosophers and include articles by philosophers and other health experts who are
philosophically inclined. Their readers include students in courses on medical
ethics. These courses are offered in departments of philosophy or in schools of
medicine and are usually taught by philosophers. Such textbooks have a standard format. After an introductory overview of ethics and philosophy in medicine, the books turn to a long series of topic areas such as the doctor–patient
relationship; the definition of death, abortion, and reproductive technology; the
new biology; emergent ethical issues; and problems in the just allocation of
health care. The focus of the disputes is typically some enduring philosophical
question: When does life begin, or end? What is the meaning of a person? What
are our obligations to future generations? What is the meaning of autonomy in
the doctor–patient relationship? The articles are usually considered to be "classics" or to represent widely admired arguments. The thrust of the text is to
expose the student to contrasting and powerfully argued views on problems
which are deeply disputed or in perpetual conflict and not likely to be resolved

in the near term. Hence the need for (and value in) the philosopher and the instructor to lead the students through the moral thicket and let them choose which arguments they accept, on a reasoned basis.

As we see it, a textbook on ethics and public health needs to be considerably different. In the first place, the ethics of public health concern communities as much as they do individuals. Thus, the focus needs to be on public health's methods and perspective, and a text ought to consider the issues and ethical conflicts that arise from that method or perspective. Philosophers teaching in departments of philosophy may use this text in courses on bioethics or health policy, but it is aimed more directly at public health, social welfare, public policy, and medical schools. Its emphases have been chosen to help students interested in learning about the method and philosophy of public health as viewed from the standpoint of ethics and public health.

This book differs from traditional medical ethics textbooks in another way: It is not based on abstract ethical theory. Unlike modern applied ethics, with roots in utilitarian or contract theory, public health is a pragmatic, somewhat eclectic, approach to real-life problems. Not a philosophy in the same sense as utilitarianism or other ethical theories, public health is more a perspective, one that stresses what practitioners and researchers call the "population" or "community" approach. This approach is built on the communal and contingent bases of knowledge, and on practical and contingent approaches to promoting the common good and social justice. In that it seeks to expand the scope of community health institutions or programs in a liberal democratic society, public health can be viewed as a kind of communitarianism, so long as this is understood as a practical, rather than theoretical, philosophy.

As a perspective, public health is about facing health problems as a group and using organized community approaches to resolve those problems. Its roots lie in the public health campaigns of the 19th and early 20th centuries. Its core method is epidemiology, which is the study of diseases that strike the community or the "people" as a whole. The good it promotes is a common good, one that is aggregate in nature. However, and this is a crucial point for the rest of the text, public health as a method does not *provide first principles*. Public health as a method assumes background principles of community and equality, although these principles are often implicit rather than made explicit in a system of ethics. Its justifications are rooted in legal decisions, in constitutional debates about the state's regulatory powers, and in political debates and controversies on the scope and purpose of democratic government over the individual citizen and the control of markets and the great professions. Protecting the public's health also raises fundamental questions about the duties and obligations owed by citizens to the political community. But the point is that public health must pay careful attention to the larger horizon of community and to the justifications for promoting and protecting the health of the people if it is to prosper and persuade. Empirical methods, even those constructed on a population foundation, are not enough.

The topics in this book differ from other bioethics readers in that they raise fundamental political questions. What is the meaning and scope of community, and the balance between the market and the public realm, in today's modern liberal society, which is so highly individualistic? Does a strong public health policy require a rethinking of the current belief that the market ought to be dominant in most domains to assure an adequate standard of living for all and a high rate of growth? Should safety and the public's health be treated as "market failures," exceptions to the general beneficence of market institutions? Or should the market be captive to the democratic community, subject to oversight by elected and accountable officials? What is the proper balance between the cultural or moral sphere and the public's health given that the former powerfully shapes a community's response to human immunodeficiency virus (HIV), drugs, (including alcohol and tobacco), sex education, and the like? What are the justifications for limiting individual liberty in order to promote the public's health as a common good? And what are the boundaries and limits for free discussion and speech, and for the public's health? Such topics lead the discussion far from the traditional emphases of most applied philosophy and even from its interest in distributive justice. These topics require a consideration of not just what each individual deserves and needs but of what will help whole communities hold together and what will encourage people to consider themselves a community given the powerful forces in health policy (from abortion to national health reform) that tend to pull a community apart.

This book recognizes that not all philosophical issues connected with health are ethical in nature. Social definitions of voluntariness, of risk, and of the causes of public health problems are equally important. Society constantly changes its ways of perceiving public or community problems. Progress is made by changing the perceptions or the "stories" of how drinking and driving, smoking, or HIV and AIDS are caused and prevented. Are our public problems to be conceived of as dominantly individualistic (or market-driven) stories? Are public problems the result of a collapse of morals? Or are these problems rooted in a more complex story about how society is organized and how culture functions? *New Ethics for the Public's Health* seeks to show how the tools of philosophy and analysis are crucial in this process of constructing the new stories of community.

Alcoholism policy provides a good example of this point. For a long time, the prevailing assumption was that excessive drinking is due to the power of alcohol as a societal evil (the Prohibitionist story) or an individual one (whether from a lack of will power, self-deception, or of a "condition" called alcoholism). After Prohibition, alcoholism became defined as a "kind of people" problem, and the locus shifted from the bottle to the person. The simplified version of this story is that alcoholism is located in the person, not the bottle. Today however, most experts acknowledge that both stories—one rooted in moralism and the other in a misguided search for a physiological or psychological explanation for how alcoholism is caused—are seriously defective. A different approach—a public health story—has become more widely accepted despite the fact that it does not seek to answer the question, "What causes alcoholism?" Instead, this new story asks a more practical and answerable question: Can we reduce alcohol problems in society for young people and adults alike through prudent measures such as taxes on alcohol, age limits, and restrictions on advertising?

Of course, new policies that would limit the sale and advertising of alcohol, or tax it more heavily, impose restrictions on the liberty of individuals. Some libertarians will argue that individuals should be free to purchase alcohol at all times, in all places, and at the lowest possible price. For this reason, libertarians are usually at odds with a public health perspective. (This conflict is examined in Chapter 3.) The public health proponent responds that minor infringements on individual liberty that result in significant improvements in aggregate welfare or the common good are justified and are not paternalistic in any objectionable sense.

We attempt to represent differing views and to show how these views clash or agree, but we also attempt to clarify and extend the community perspective on the public's health. Thus, this is a reader with a point of view, yet not one that is devoted exclusively to one view. Our aim is to stimulate students and scholars alike to think about the public's health in a new way, as an issue that requires political and philosophical analysis. We hope that those in epidemiology or health management or medical school working on related issues and facing similar conflicts will find this book both provocative and informative.

Regretfully, for reasons of space, we have eliminated the footnotes to the included articles. Readers who wish to follow up sources should consult the original articles.

We owe thanks to many people. First, we thank our authors and their publishers for graciously allowing us to use their work. We also received generous gifts of time and helpful advice from Lori Andrews (Kent Law School), Mila Aroskar (University of Minnesota), John Arras and Jonathan Moreno (University of Virginia), Ron Bayer (Columbia University), Sissela Bok (Harvard University), Dan W. Brock (Brown University), George Cunningham (California Public Health Department), Signe Dayhoff (Genetic Screening Research Group), Norman Fost (University of Wisconsin), Cynthia Hinton (Emory University), Neil A. Holtzman, Eric Juengst (Case Western Reserve), Erik Parens (The Hastings Center), Karen Rothenberg (Georgetown Law School), and Benjamin Wilfond (National Institutes of Health).

Dan Beauchamp thanks Larry Churchill (University of North Carolina at

Chapel Hill), his colleagues in the New York State Department of Health from 1988 to 1992 during his tenure as a health official, who introduced him to the "real world" of ethical issues in public health, to colleagues in bioethics over the years who have taught him so much, especially Dan Wikler (University of Wisconsin, Madison), Daniel Callahan (The Hastings Center), Ronald Bayer (Columbia University), and to those in the field of alcohol problems and injury, who were instrumental in shaping his ideas about public health, especially James Mosher (the Marin Institute), Larry Wallack (University of California at Berkeley), Robin Room (the Addiction Research Institute, Toronto), Wolfgang Schmidt (formerly of the Addiction Research Institute, Toronto), Alex Wagenaar (University of Minnesota), Steve Teret (Johns Hopkins University), and Milton Terris (*Journal of Public Health Policy*). Finally, a special note of thanks to Bonnie Steinbock for her patience and for making him think harder about the ethics of public health.

Bonnie Steinbock thanks her fellow board members of the now-defunct National Advisory Board of Ethics in Reproduction (NABER); the members of the Hastings Center working groups on maternal–fetal relations, long-term contraceptives, and prenatal testing for disability; and the members of the European Union–sponsored working group on reproductive choice and control of fertility. She has learned much from all of you and had a lot of fun in the process. She also thanks her co-author, Dan Beauchamp, for introducing her to the public health perspective.

Finally, we thank Jeffrey House, our editor at Oxford University Press, who shepherded this book from conception to reality.

Bisbee, AZ   D.E.B.
Albany, NY   B.S.
October 1998

Contents

I

THE SCOPE OF PUBLIC HEALTH
AS ETHICS

INTRODUCTION: ETHICAL THEORY AND PUBLIC HEALTH

THE TURN TO APPLIED ETHICS

About 30 years ago, professional philosophers began to become interested in "applied ethics." This was a major shift in academic philosophy. In the 1920s and 30s, logical positivism taught that ethics could not be done at all, since ethical statements were at best expressions of feeling and at worst arrant nonsense. During the 1950s, the teaching of ethics usually was limited to investigating the meaning of such words as *duty, right,* and *ought.* Discussions of particular ethical problems or policies were considered unphilosophical and best left to theologians and policy makers. A sea change occurred partly as a result of the demand of students in the 1960s for education that was "relevant" and partly as a result of advances in medicine that raised new ethical questions and dilemmas. A number of centers and institutes dedicated to ethics and policy were created where philosophers, often working with individuals in other disciplines, could examine the normative and conceptual issues raised in medicine, law, and other professions.

The result of all this activity has been an extensive literature in bioethics. Bioethicists have written on a wide range of issues including the doctor–patient relationship, confidentiality, informed consent, medical experimentation, the definition of death, euthanasia and physician-assisted suicide, genetic testing and manipulation, abortion, assisted reproduction, and many others. Some of these issues, such as genetic screening and assisted reproduction, can be examined from a public health perspective as well as from the more individualistic perspective typical of biomedical ethics. Some issues, such as alcohol and drug policy or domestic violence, are unlikely to be represented in medical ethics texts. Much of the discussion on these various issues is factual. It focuses on the likely consequences of various policies. Equally important are conceptual tools used to assess both consequences and the means to achieve them. This is where ethical theory has a role to play. There are many different ethical theories. The aim of this Introduction is not to provide a thorough depiction or analysis of all of them. The intention is rather to provide students of public

3

health or public policy who have not had courses in ethical theory with enough background to be able to understand and evaluate the ethical arguments made in this book.

MORALITY, ETHICS, AND MORAL PHILOSOPHY

We start with some terminology. The word *ethics* can be used to refer to the set of rules, principles, values, and ideals of a particular group of people. This is called its descriptive sense. Thus, we might contrast the ethics of the Puritans with the ethics of the Hawaiian Islanders. The word *ethics* can also be used to refer to the systematic study of moral concepts and theories, typically in departments of philosophy. Some philosophers use the term *morality* to refer to ethics in its descriptive sense, that is, concerning the beliefs of particular groups of people about right and wrong, reserving the term *ethics* (or *moral philosophy* or *ethical theory*) for the subject taught in departments of philosophy. However, this usage is not universal, and we use the terms *ethics* and *morality* interchangeably. Students will have to examine the context to determine whether the subject is a group's beliefs about right and wrong or the theoretical study of moral beliefs and concepts.

Theories of morality can be divided roughly into two kinds. *Normative ethics* is primarily concerned with providing a theoretical or foundational basis for how people ought to behave, while *metaethics* is primarily concerned with analyzing the meanings of central ethical terms like *good, right, duty,* and *obligation.* The two are not as rigidly separate as it might at first seem, because normative issues often turn on our interpretation of difficult concepts. For example, an issue in population policy is whether coercive means of reducing population growth are permissible. Clearly, forced abortions and the mandatory contraception of unwilling women are coercive means. But is coercion limited to threats of inflicting harm or can offers and incentives in some contexts also be coercive? For example, it has been charged that laws increasing the welfare payments of women who agree to have Norplant, a long-acting contraceptive, implanted, are a form of coercion. Others reject this label, saying that women who prefer to have more children are not deprived of the payments they would have received. Therefore, they are not harmed or made worse off because of their choice. Nor are they forced to choose the higher welfare payments. The critics of such statutes respond that the "choice" to receive higher payments or have more children is really "no choice," given the poverty in which welfare recipients live. This issue cannot be resolved without a persuasive analysis of the concept of coercion. (Of course, even if incentives are determined not to be coercive, they may be objectionable on a number of other grounds. By the same token, the mere fact that a policy is coercive is not a conclusive reason for regarding it as morally impermissible. Most laws are coercive, but they are not for that reason wrong.)

We see, then, that conceptual analysis is part of ethical and policy analysis. Equally important are normative ethical theories: theories about what makes right actions right (and wrong actions wrong). Such theories are not simply descriptions of what is conventionally considered right or wrong behavior in a particular society or group. Instead, normative ethics attempts to identify and justify basic moral principles and to derive from them guidance for what we ought to do and what kind of people we should strive to become. The basic principles, values, character traits, and so forth can then be applied to specific ethical issues, such as whether there should be mandatory acquired immuno-deficiency syndrome (AIDS) testing in hospitals, when to begin population screening for genetic diseases, and what sort of alcohol and drug policies we should have.

THEORY AND PRACTICE

As we will see, different ethical theories provide different basic principles for deciding what is right or wrong, what should be done or avoided. However, ethical decision making is almost never a matter of automatically applying principles and generating an answer. There are several reasons why this is so. One reason is that the right thing to do often depends on the facts of the case, and these may be difficult to ascertain. For example, at the beginning of the HIV–AIDS epidemic there was much discussion about whether public health officials should close gay bathhouses. Those who argued in favor said that the bathhouses, which were places where men could engage in sex with dozens of partners, were breeding grounds for the spread of disease. Those who opposed said that closing the bathhouses would not change behavior. Men would continue to have multiple partners in more private settings, and the opportunity to educate people about safe sex would be lost. Both sides made a plausible case and it was not obvious which strategy would reduce the spread of AIDS.

Another reason why principles cannot be used to generate solutions in any straightforward way is that they sometimes conflict with one another as well as with other values or goals. For example, an important principle or goal of public health is to reduce the incidence of disease. Genetic diseases can be prevented by screening people to find out who are carriers and then attempting to influence them not to reproduce and thereby pass on genes that cause disease. But it can be argued that any attempt to influence individuals' reproductive decision making violates another important principle, namely, self-determination or autonomy. Which value—the reduction of disease or respect for auton-omy—should take precedence? The answer is not obvious. Thus, even if we could decide which ethical theory is the correct one, the application of that theory to specific practical issues will often be indeterminate or controversial. In any event, there is no consensus about the right ethical theory. This fact is often discouraging to students, who may become cynical about the value of studying moral philosophy. What's the point, if no one can say whether util-itarianism is superior to Kantian ethics, or if both are superseded by contrac-tarianism or virtue ethics or feminist approaches?

We maintain that this disillusionment is unwarranted. The purpose of study-ing moral philosophy is not to discover which ethical theory "has it right"; rather, different ethical theories provide insight into a range of important con-siderations. Utilitarians are right to insist on the relevance of consequences and the importance of securing happiness and well-being, but their critics (noncon-sequentialists) are equally right in insisting that there are other important values, such as justice and self-determination, which cannot be reduced to hap-piness. It seems increasingly likely that no one moral theory is the whole story. Rather, each represents a partial contribution to an extraordinarily complex moral reality.

ETHICS AND RELIGION

For many people, morality is identified with religion. The reasons for this are fairly obvious: All major religions—Judaism, Christianity, Islam, Hinduism, and Buddhism—have ethical teachings associated with them, and the funda-mental ethical tenets of virtually all societies are based on religious teachings. Moreover, many people receive their moral training in religious institutions, such as church, synagogue, or Sunday school. This may lead them to think that ethics *must* be based in religious teaching. However, there is no necessary con-nection between religion and ethics. A person can be ethical and a nonbeliever. A completely secular ethics is perfectly possible, although it undoubtedly will coincide with the teachings of most religions in certain respects.

Moreover, religious tenets themselves can be subjected to moral assessment. For example, the doctrine of purgatory in Christianity was developed in re-sponse to the feeling of many Christians that it was cruel and unfair to commit unbaptized infants to eternal damnation. More recently, some Christian churches have rejected the traditional teachings of Christianity regarding homo-sexuality or the ordination of women, based on moral arguments. Such moral evaluations of religious teachings would be literally impossible if morality were merely a function of religion.

ETHICS AND LAW

Another source of guidance regarding how we should behave is the law. The law may reflect a society's moral consensus on issues such as abortion, surrogate motherhood, or physician-assisted suicide. Interpretation of what the law is often requires normative ethical analysis, as evidenced by legal writings, such as judicial decisions, amicus briefs, and articles by law professors. For example, in the landmark case of *Brown* v. *Board of Education* (347 U.S. 483, 1954), the Supreme Court was faced with the question of whether racially segregated public schools are constitutionally permissible. The Supreme Court decided that segregated schools violate the Constitution, even if the facilities in white and black schools are (as they never were in fact) equal. They are inherently unequal, and so violate the equal protection clause of the Fourteenth Amendment, because the intention and effect of racial segregation is to degrade, stigmatize, and deny equal opportunity to Negro children. The Court's decision was not a narrowly legalistic one, but was based on substantive moral analysis of the concept of equality as it has evolved in the context of American institutions, traditions, and history.

The law may also be viewed as providing limits on what can and cannot be done. For example, federal rules governing medical experiments forbid the use of human subjects without their informed consent or that of a court-appointed surrogate. The rules settle the question of whether an experiment may be done; any study that uses people without their informed consent is impermissible. However, although legal considerations sometimes determine what may or may not be done, and legal considerations are often relevant to moral decisions, the law, no more than religion, does not determine morality. For one thing, just as religious teachings can be criticized on moral grounds, so too can the law. Sometimes this results in changes in the law. For another, it may sometimes be right to violate the law, although determining when this would be justified is obviously a complex ethical issue.

ETHICS AND POLICY

Because of its concern with populations, public health tends to have a macro focus, that is, it tends to be concerned with institutions and policies rather than relations between individuals. To put it another way, public health is a species of public policy. Public policy certainly includes ethical considerations, but it must also consider nonethical factors, such as politics. For example, a single-payer system of health care, such as is found in Canada and Europe, might be the fairest and most efficient system, but it may not be politically feasible in the United States, at least at the present time. Policy makers who ignore political realities do so at their peril. At the same time, existing policies and institutions (like religion and the law) can be criticized on moral grounds. National advisory bodies, such as the President's Commission for the Study of Ethical Problems in Medicine and Biomedical and Behavioral Research or the more recent National Bioethics Advisory Commission, offer recommendations on a range of issues, stressing such moral principles as respect for persons and justice.

As we have seen, ethics is related to, but separate from, religion, law, and policy. Before turning to some of the most influential ethical approaches, we will consider some challenges to ethics.

ETHICAL NIHILISM AND RELATIVISM

A source of cynicism about moral philosophy comes from the conviction—or suspicion—that there is no such thing as *moral reality*. This is known as *ethical nihilism* and it can take several forms. One version of ethical nihilism maintains that morality is simply an illusion, like religion, and something we should get over. This implies that there's nothing really wrong with raping, torturing, and murdering a child. While it is difficult to know how to go about disproving this extreme nihilist claim, it is so far from the experience of virtually everyone that it is even more difficult to take it seriously.

A more plausible version of nihilism claims that morality simply reflects the interests of those in power. This view, originally stated by Thrasymachus in Plato's *Republic*, is also reflected in Marxist theory, as well as in contemporary critical legal theory and postmodernism. It must be admitted that not only the laws and institutions of society, but its moral beliefs, are typically formulated and propagated by people in positions of power. They may impose what promotes their own self-interest on the downtrodden masses while hoodwinking the masses into believing that they are morally required to do what they are told to do. This sort of cynicism about morality seems most plausible in totalitarian regimes. However, even if power is more widely dispersed, as in a democracy, a variation of the criticism can be made. That is, it can be objected that what is claimed to be "objective morality" is nothing but disguised self-interest. Thus, people with well-paying jobs or other sources of income—the *haves*—may view their economic status as something they have worked for, and therefore morally deserve, while the *have-nots* may regard the more fortunate as beneficiaries of an unjust economic system which profits from the existence of an underclass. There is no objectively correct moral answer, according to this version of moral nihilism, but only the self-interest of the respective parties.

We can certainly acknowledge the ability of those in power to control behavior, ideology, and even the interpretation of history. We can also recognize that self-interest may skew people's moral beliefs. It does not follow, however, that morality is *nothing but* the expression of the interests of those in power. An important distinction can be drawn between *conventional morality* or the rules and values currently accepted and promulgated, and *critical* or *ideal* morality, which can be used to assess conventional morality. If morality were just the interests of the powerful, as Marxist theory alleges, it would be literally impossible to condemn on *moral* grounds the behavior and policies of those in power. Yet this is exactly what Marxist and other critics of capitalism attempt to do! The very existence of intelligible social criticism rests on the possibility of a critical or ideal morality which is not identified with the interests of those in power.

A related form of nihilism is *ethical relativism.* Ethical relativism does not say that morality is merely an illusion or something to get over. Nor does it identify morality with the interests of the powerful. Rather, it claims that morality is relative to the mores, values, standards, or rules of a particular culture. What is right for one culture may be wrong for another. Thus, in one culture, premarital sex may be regarded as normal and healthy, while in another it may be regarded as sinful. There is no way to determine which culture is correct about the morality of premarital sex. Indeed, the question does not even make sense because morality is always relative to a particular culture. There is no right and wrong independent of culture.

A major advantage of ethical relativism is its ability to explain the variation in moral beliefs and customs throughout the world. Ethical relativism seems superior to an absolutist conception of morality which maintains that there is one true moral code and that any divergence from that code is immorality. Such a view seems arrogant and presumptuous in the face of the moral diversity of different cultures. Another point in favor of relativism is its recognition that moral beliefs and practices can only be understood within the context of a culture. A practice that at first sight appears irrational or abhorrent may come to make sense when we understand both the material conditions in which it occurs and its symbolic significance. The more we understand a culture, the less likely we are to misinterpret its moral beliefs.

At the same time, ethical relativism has consequences that are difficult to accept. For example, the Nazis thought that Aryans were a superior people and that certain groups—Jews, gypsies, Slavs, etc.—should be deported, enslaved, or exterminated. If ethical relativism is true, then the fact that they believed that it is morally right to exterminate Jews makes it morally right—for them. Ethical relativism rules out the possibility of saying that their behavior was immoral, wicked, and wrong. Is there a way to acknowledge legitimate variations in moral beliefs without proclaiming that whatever people think is right is right—for them?

A first step might be to challenge the seemingly obvious claim that morality differs among cultures. While this may be true in relation to views about (permissible) sex and marriage arrangements, it is less clear that such variation exists as regards basic or fundamental principles of morality, such as the wrongness of lying, stealing, assault, and murder. These acts seem to be universally condemned, undoubtedly because no group can continue to exist where distrust and aggression are the norm. Thus, despite initial appearances, there may be some universal norms due to the very nature of morality as a mechanism enabling people to live together in groups. A second important point is that it does not follow from the mere fact that people in different cultures have different beliefs about morality that their beliefs are correct or justifiable, any more than it follows from the fact that people have different beliefs about the physical world that all their beliefs are equally correct. The mere fact that some people think the world is flat or that disease is caused by devils doesn't make it so (or even "true for them"). It means only that they sincerely (and mistakenly) believe it.

However, ethical relativists may argue that this is precisely the point. While we can offer objective evidence that the world is round, not flat, or that disease is caused by microorganisms, not devils, it is impossible to offer objective evidence about morality. But is this in fact the case? Consider the 19th-century claim that slavery was morally justified. This rested in part on a belief in the intrinsic inferiority of the Africans who were captured and enslaved. It was said that they were incapable of taking care of themselves, incapable of learning, incapable of the emotions their masters felt (such as anguish at the sale of their spouses or children). Not only is this clearly nonsense in hindsight, but it seems that at some level even those who made the claims must have known them to be false. After all, why make teaching a slave to read illegal if slaves are incapable of learning to read?

The point here is that objective, scientific facts play a significant role in moral judgments and constitute a basis for accepting or rejecting moral beliefs. The practice of clitoridectomy or female circumcision provides a good example. This practice, common to certain groups in Africa, is usually performed at puberty, although it may be done on very young children. The girl is held down by older women while her clitoris, or a portion of it, is removed. Anesthesia is not used, and the procedure is done with unsterilized razor blades or knives. In the more radical versions of the procedure, the entire genitalia are removed. The lips of the vulva are sewn up, with only a small hole for urination and menstrual blood. The purpose of clitorectomy is to reduce sexual pleasure and remove the temptation to sexual activity; the vulva is sewn up to ensure that the young woman will remain a virgin until her marriage. In cultures in which the practice is widespread, it may be difficult or impossible for an uncircumcised girl to marry.

Public health professionals and women's health activists around the world have condemned the practice, calling it "female genital mutilation." Not only is it extremely painful when performed, it can have repercussions throughout the woman's life, especially for those subjected to the radical surgery where the entire external genitalia is cut off. Intercourse is more difficult and painful, and childbirth more dangerous. Ironically, those who engage in the practice believe that it is necessary for cleanliness and conducive to fertility. In fact, circumcised women are more susceptible to infection and sexually transmitted diseases and are often rendered infertile. Insofar as the justification for the practice rests on incorrect factual beliefs, it can be rejected without challenging the moral beliefs of those who accept it.

However, the objection to female genital mutilation is not solely based on its adverse health consequences. Feminists also reject the set of beliefs which underlie the practice: that it is wrong for women to experience sexual pleasure, that female virginity must be preserved, that women's bodies are the property of their husbands, that it is permissible to mutilate the bodies of women to keep them meek, submissive, and sexually pure. The contribution of feminism has been to show that such beliefs are endemic to patriarchy and inconsistent with the recognition of women as full human persons entitled to equality and justice.

To summarize, ethical relativism has something to teach us, namely, that human cultures have diverse moral beliefs, many of which are equally valid. Moreover, to understand beliefs that differ from our own, it is necessary to understand them in the context of an entire culture and belief system. But it does not follow that *whatever* people believe is right or immune from moral criticism. Moreover, our own cherished beliefs can also be challenged, something which ethical relativism rules out on principle. In fact, it is only if we *reject* relativism that we can learn from other cultures. For example, we can criticize our own materialistic and wasteful attitudes in contrast with those of most American Indian tribes. Such criticism implies an objective, nonrelativistic standpoint from which we can critically examine our own attitudes and habits as well as those of other cultures.

METHODS FOR RESOLVING OR UNDERSTANDING ETHICAL QUESTIONS

Once we free ourselves from the thrall of ethical relativism, the next question is, How can ethical disagreements be resolved? If ethical progress is possible, how is it possible? On what basis can we arrive at solutions to the problems we face?

An obvious component of understanding and resolving ethical issues in public health is factual information. For example, recombinant DNA technology expands the possibility of screening for genetic disease. A recent issue has been whether there should be mandatory newborn screening for cystic fibrosis (CF).

A host of factual questions arises. For example, what is the accuracy of the proposed test? Will routine or mandatory screening help to identify affected children earlier and improve the treatment of affected newborns? Or will parents become unduly protective of children shown to be affected by pre-symptomatic tests? How much will presymptomatic screening cost and will there be adequate counseling for the parents of affected newborns? Would this be the most effective use of funds to improve the lives of those who have CF?

Sometimes these factual questions are not resolved or even addressed before a policy is put into place. For example, a pilot study of newborn screening for CF was begun in Colorado in 1982, but mandatory screening was legislated even before it was completed! And where a prospective controlled study was done (in Wisconsin), the benefits of routine screening were not demonstrated.[1] This suggests that mass screening programs of newborns and others are some-times driven by political considerations rather than solidly based on scientific evidence. Politicians have an understandable if not always creditable desire to be seen as "doing something," even if that "something" has not been shown to be valuable and could turn out to be harmful. In addition, the role of profit in screening decisions cannot be ignored. As Benjamin Wilfond notes:

> Within weeks of the announcement of the cloning of the cystic fibrosis gene in September 1989, biotechnology companies began marketing the DNA-based test to physicians. Because the initial charge for cystic fibrosis carrier testing was over $200, a mass screening program of pregnant women could have translated into a billion-dollar-a-year industry.[2]

Facts—scientifically based evidence—are crucial to determining good public policy, but facts by themselves cannot indicate which policies should be imple-mented. Facts can influence policy only when the goals to be achieved are delineated. Despite a recognition that goals may differ in different cultures and different communities, there are some goals and principles that have widespread acceptance. These include benefiting individuals (for example, by decreasing disease and improving their health), respect for self-determination, equality, and justice. Of course, the interpretation of these goals and principles is varied, as are beliefs about which policies are most likely to promote them. Moreover, sometimes goals and principles can conflict. When they do, a strategy for prior-itizing them is useful. This is a major reason for the appeal to ethical theory.

ETHICAL THEORIES

Philosophers are often interested in ethical theory as providing a single key to morality. Classical utilitarians regard the maximization of happiness or pleasure as the ultimate goal, and everything else as reducible to happiness. Kantians regard happiness as relatively insignificant morally, and in any event deny that principles like justice or respect for autonomy can be reduced to happiness. Virtue theorists maintain that there has been an overemphasis on right actions and too little attention paid to the kinds of people we should strive to become, while feminists and Marxists claim that power relations are essential to an adequate moral theory. Communitarians deplore the excessively individualistic turn in modern moral philosophy, whether utilitarian or Kantian, and emphasize the importance of shared traditions, values, and goals, as well as the impact of actions and policies on the community considered as a whole rather than as a collection of individuals with separate interests.

Our aim here is not to determine the "correct" moral theory. Indeed, we are dubious that any one moral theory has a monopoly on truth. Probably all of them have something to contribute to the understanding of something as complex and multifaceted as morality. Two of them, utilitarianism and Kantian moral theory, have been dominant in both moral thinking and public policy. At least a rudimentary acquaintance with these theories is essential for understanding the readings in this anthology. However, a third, communitarianism, is particularly appropriate for the aggregate approach to policy exemplified by public health.

UTILITARIANISM

Classical utilitarianism was formulated in the 19th century by Jeremy Bentham and John Stuart Mill, although it built on ideas that go back at least as far as the ancient Greeks. The heart of utilitarianism is "the greatest happiness principle," which holds that actions are right insofar as they tend to promote the greatest happiness of the greatest number, wrong as they tend to promote the reverse.[3]

The first thing to note about the utilitarian tradition is its emphasis on the likely consequences of whatever is under consideration. Actions, policies, motives, and so forth are all judged to be right or wrong, good or bad in terms of their expected consequences. Thus, utilitarianism is a form of consequentialism. Not all consequentialists are utilitarians, but since utilitarianism is the most familiar and influential consequentialist theory, it is the one on which we will focus. Second, the overarching goal to be achieved is pleasure or happiness, where pleasure and happiness are understood, not as transient states of mind or feelings, but rather as total well-being. The theory of value that maintains that pleasure or happiness is the ultimate good is known as *hedonism*. According to hedonism, pleasure is the only thing that is intrinsically good; all other good things—health, knowledge, friendship, love, for example—are desirable because of the happiness they bring. Pain is intrinsically bad, although pain may be good if the experience of pain ultimately brings more pleasure or avoidance of pain. Thus, vaccination is good, even though it hurts, because it avoids the greater harm of serious disease.

Contemporary utilitarians have by and large rejected hedonism, for several reasons. First, happiness is hard to define and even harder to measure. If it is equated to pleasure, considered as episodic sensations, then happiness can be quantified, but it is hard to believe that a life of pleasant sensations is the ultimate good. Happiness is more plausible as the ultimate end if we conceive of it as not limited to pleasant sensations but more globally as the satisfaction of goals contributing to well-being. However, this conception makes quantification and interpersonal comparison, which are essential to utilitarianism, extremely difficult.

Another reason for the rejection of hedonism is that the reduction of all goals and values to happiness, even on the broader interpretation of happiness, is implausible. Knowledge, art, and meaningfulness are all values, and it is far from clear either that these reduce to an aspect of happiness or that these things are valued because they contribute to happiness. They may be valued for themselves, independent of how happy they make people. For these reasons, contemporary utilitarians are more likely to think of the ultimate end not as happiness or pleasure but rather as the satisfaction of individual preferences.

An important question for any moral theory is how it determines which individuals or entities are entitled to moral consideration or moral status. Utilitarians generally consider *sentience,* or the ability to experience pain and pleasure, to be the important feature in deciding who counts or who has moral status. Given a hedonist theory of value, the emphasis on sentience is not surprising. But even preference utilitarians tend to consider sentience an important marker for moral status. This is because nonsentient beings (plants, rocks, buildings) do not have preferences and cannot be happy or unhappy. Thus, sentience is a necessary condition for inclusion in the utilitarian calculus. It is also considered a sufficient condition. That is, if a being suffers, there is no justification for ignoring that suffering, whatever other characteristics it may have or lack. As Bentham said, "The question is not can they reason? Nor can they talk? But can they suffer?"[4] The principle of utility is to be applied not only to all human beings but also, as Mill said, to all sentient creation, as far as is possible.[5] (Some contemporary utilitarians think that it is a good deal more possible than Bentham or Mill were willing to acknowledge. Peter Singer, for example, has argued not merely that animals count, but that they count as much as human beings.[6])

The third point about utilitarianism is that it is a maximizing theory. That is, the right action or policy is the one that achieves the greatest happiness possible. There is only one right action in any situation: the one that maximizes happiness or welfare. Fourth, utilitarianism is an egalitarian theory insofar as it insists that everyone's happiness is to be considered equally.

There are several features that make utilitarianism an attractive theory. One is that it provides a method for deciding which is the right action or policy, namely, the one that produces more good (however this is defined) than other alternatives. Another is that its goals are clearly important ones. What is the point of morality, it may be asked, if not to promote happiness and reduce misery? Surely rules have no intrinsic value unless they achieve good results. Even someone who bases his conception of right and wrong on what God wants must ask *why* God wants us to do certain things and abstain from others. Following the Ten Commandments and the Golden Rule is likely to result in a happier world; this certainly was the way Mill regarded it.[7]

The possibility remains, however, that in certain situations actions which maximize happiness could conflict with other values, such as honesty and fairness. A major objection to utilitarianism is that it could countenance great injustice, such as knowingly condemning an innocent person to prevent mob violence that would result in the deaths of many more innocent persons. Utilitarians respond by saying that this objection fails to consider the total, long-term effects of unjust or dishonest actions. Mill emphasized the destructive effects lying has on trust, saying that these bad effects could rarely, if ever, be outweighed by the good effects to be achieved by deception.[8] Moreover, the temptation to lie is often motivated by self-interest rather than a dispassionate and accurate assessment of the general utility. Recognition of this tendency requires us to adhere in most cases to what Mill called *secondary principles,* such as the rule against lying, as our best bet for achieving the greatest happiness. At the same time, Mill acknowledged that there may be rare instances in which it is justified to break a moral rule—for example, to lie to save a life.

In creating social policy, we often rely on utilitarian reasoning and the notion of the greatest good for the greatest number. For example, a policy requiring that all persons be immunized, with few exceptions, is likely to be most effective in combating communicable diseases. At the same time, it might expose a few, rare, susceptible individuals to vaccine-related damage or even death. Most people would find this acceptable, because the good of universal vaccination outweighs the harm to a few. Nevertheless, the idea that the good of the majority can cancel out the welfare of the few has led to the criticism that utilitarianism devalues individuals and individual rights.

Resistance to utilitarian reasoning can be seen in other examples. Should society compel people to participate in genetic screening or even abortion in order to reduce the number of people born with serious genetic defects? Such a policy would reduce the costs of caring for such individuals and might be rational from a utilitarian standpoint. There is widespread agreement that even if such a policy did promote "the greatest happiness of the greatest number," it would nonetheless be morally unacceptable. As the President's Commission said in *Genetic Screening and Counseling:*

> The chief objection to this argument is that it rests upon a general principle that few, if any, would wish to see consistently implemented—namely, that a person's freedom to make the most intimate choices, and even a person's very existence, depends upon the degree to which social utility is maximized. . . . Rather than finding utilitarianism particularly appropriate in determining social policy on genetics programs, the contrary appears to be the case, in light of the especially strong reasons to preserve individual liberty on matters of medical treatment and reproduction.[9]

It is likely that most utilitarians would opt for a principle of voluntariness with regard to reproductive decisions and try to justify such a principle on utilitarian grounds. Their argument would be that a society in which people's most intimate choices were regulated by state interference would be unlikely to be one that promoted the greatest happiness. Mill himself argued in *On Liberty* that a society that allowed for the greatest amount possible of individual liberty would be the happiest. However, there is no guarantee that this coincidence between the greatest liberty and the greatest happiness will obtain. Policies that are justified on grounds of social utility might conflict with other equally important principles, such as liberty, autonomy, equality, or justice.

KANTIAN ETHICS

Although Immanuel Kant (1724–1804) lived before the classical utilitarians, Kantian ethics is best understood as a critique of the utilitarian approach (which after all was not entirely new with Bentham and Mill).[10] Kant rejected both the theory of value associated with utilitarianism (hedonism) and its consequentialism. In contrast to the utilitarian emphasis on sentience as the basis for moral status, Kant regards the capacity for experiencing pain and pleasure as morally fairly insignificant. Instead, he emphasizes the connection between morality and reason. Reason is what separates man (human beings) from the rest of the animals and what makes us subject to the moral law. Our capacity for rational thought both entitles us to treatment and rights to which animals are not entitled and imposes on us obligations that animals do not have. Animals are not morally required to refrain from murder, theft, and deception. Indeed, these concepts cannot even be applied to animal behavior. Only rational creatures, capable of knowing the difference between right and wrong, can be responsible moral agents.

Of course, the fact that normal adult human beings are capable of rational thought (and thus are moral agents) does not entail that they will always behave morally, that is, in a morally correct fashion. To call people moral agents is not to deny that they may be immoral but rather to say that they are *responsible for* their behavior, that they can be *blamed* for acting wrongly. By contrast, infants, severely retarded individuals, and most animals are not capable of understanding the difference between right and wrong. Whether some primates, such as gorillas and chimpanzees, and perhaps other mammals, such as dolpins, have a moral sense is a debatable point. Nevertheless, even if these animals behave altruistically and reciprocally, it is unlikely that they can be considered moral agents in the way that most humans are. Certainly most animals, like babies and very young children, are not responsible, nor would it be appropriate to blame them for any harm they might cause. Animals can often be trained to act in certain ways by rewards and punishments, but they are not capable of being motivated by moral reasons (such as, "You wouldn't like it if he did that to you").

Kant also objected to consequentialism. It is not the consequences of an act that make it right or wrong. For what happens as the result of what you do is not wholly within your control. It is perfectly possible that doing the right thing will have disastrous consequences and that wrong actions may result in unexpected good results. Basing morality on the consequences makes it altogether too contingent, depriving it of the necessity which Kant regarded as essential to the possibility of morality and a moral law.

Does this mean that Kantian ethics tells us to ignore consequences? If that were the case, we would have to reject Kantian ethics as absurd. In deciding which course of action to take, of course we need to think about the impact on others. Rather, consequences are relevant for Kant only if the proposed action is morally permissible. And the permissibility of an action is not determined by the consequences.

If the permissibility of an action is not determined by its consequences, how is it determined? Or to put the question another way, What makes right actions right and wrong actions wrong? There is widespread agreement that certain actions are wrong, such as lying, stealing, cheating, and harming others. The fundamental question for Kant is *why* these things are wrong. The utilitarian answer is that such actions predictably lead to human misery. Kant considers this answer to be inadequate. He would say that even if no one gets hurt by a wrong action, even if it promotes more happiness than unhappiness, that does not make it right. Lying, stealing, murder are intrinsically wrong; they cannot be made right by their creation of happiness.

Take cheating on examinations, for example. The utilitarian objection is based on the expected bad consequences. Would you want someone who graduated from law school or medical school by cheating to be your lawyer or doctor? Of course not. In addition, cheating quickly becomes insidious and demoralizes those who do not cheat. If "everyone is doing it" and getting away with it, why put the effort into actually learning the material? The negative consequences of cheating are easily demonstrated.

However, these utilitarian objections to cheating could be met in certain circumstances. What if only a few people cheat while most remain honest? It is far from obvious that an isolated instance of cheating will necessarily have more bad effects than good. Nor is it always the case that successful cheating results in an unqualified person posing a risk to others. Imagine, for example, a very good student in a college with an honor code who accidentally comes across the answers to his physical anatomy exam. This gives him the opportunity to "ace" what will certainly be a very difficult exam and improve considerably his chances of getting into a top medical school. Should he use the answers? It seems obvious that this would be wrong but it is not clear that the wrongness stems from the consequences. It cannot be said that cheating in this situation will enable an unqualified student to go on to practice medicine, since we are assuming that the student is qualified. Yet this will not guarantee him a place in medical school, given the competition for admission. Of course, there is the chance that he will be found out, in which case he may be expelled. But what if the chances of anyone finding out that he has seen the answers are extremely low? If no one finds out, then the subsequent demoralization and widespread cheating that are often alleged to be the consequences of particular acts of cheating will not occur. From a consequentialist perspective, the likelihood of the bad effects actually occurring is all-important. Yet most of us do not base the judgment that he should not use the answers on how probable it is that he will be caught, or what the effect on other students will be, or whether he will go on to a brilliant medical career. Instead, if asked *why* it is wrong for him to use the answers even if none of these bad consequences will occur, we are likely simply to say, "It's still cheating." This captures the Kantian idea that the morally relevant consideration is not the consequences of the act but the kind of act it is. An act can have the best consequences—for example, save the most lives, make the greatest number of people happiest—and still be morally wrong.

If consequences do not determine the rightness or wrongness of actions, what then is the mark of right and wrong for Kant? Kant suggests that when we want to know if a proposed action (like cheating on an exam) is morally permissible, the question to ask ourselves is not What are the likely consequences of doing this act? but rather Can I, as a rational agent, consistently will that everyone should act as I am now proposing to act? If we turn this question into an action-guiding principle (what Kant calls a *command* or an *imperative*), we get, "Act only on the maxim of an action that you can consistently will universally." Kant calls this principle the *Categorical Imperative.* What does it mean?

The intuitive idea is that morality requires us not to make exceptions of ourselves. We are not morally permitted to do things that we would regard as wrong if done by others. It does not matter that no one gets hurt as a result. An action is wrong if you cannot consistently will that everyone in this situation act in the way you propose to act.

How is this applied to the example of cheating? A typical misunderstanding is that universalizing the maxim (from "I should cheat" to "Everyone should cheat") would have bad results. If everyone cheated, then exams would be useless, and that would be unfortunate, since exams are a good way to determine who is most qualified. However, this interpretation is not Kantian, but utilitarian, specifically rule-utilitarian, since it is based on the advantage to society of having exams. Kant's point is importantly different. The wrongness of cheating is not based on the social utility of having an examination system. Rather, Kant notes that there is an inherent contradiction in the idea of cheating being adopted as a universal policy. It is this feature that makes it impossible for a rational agent to will such a policy.

What makes cheating as a universal policy self-contradictory? When I consider cheating, I am thinking of acting on something like the following maxim: I should cheat whenever that will enable me to get a better grade. If I apply this universally, it becomes: Everyone should cheat when cheating will enable him or her to get a better grade. In willing this, I am willing two contradictory things:

1. That there be examinations. For if there weren't, I couldn't get a better grade, or indeed any grade at all. Whatever advantage accrues to me from doing well on examinations requires that there be examinations in the first place.

2. That there be no examinations. For if everyone cheated, an examination system could not exist. The very existence of an examination system depends on most people not cheating. If everyone cheated, there would be no point to examinations, and the system would self-destruct.

Someone who refrains from cheating, not out of fear of getting caught, and not even because she thinks that cheating will have bad consequences for everyone, but simply because she recognizes that it is wrong (that is, that it contravenes the Categorical Imperative), acts from the motive of duty. For Kant, only those acts done from the motive of duty have genuine moral worth. Acts done out of sympathy, for example, lack real moral worth, although they are certainly not wrong and indeed should be encouraged.

This is perhaps the hardest aspect of Kantian ethics to understand. Why should not feelings be a source of moral behavior? Why should not an action that derives from sympathy be as morally praiseworthy as one done out of a sense of duty? Kant's answer is that our feelings are not something we can control, and therefore they are not something for which we can be held responsible. Rational agents can be expected to act rightly (that is, consistently with the Categorical Imperative), but not to have certain feelings. Indeed, doing the right thing (sharing one's possessions, helping others) is more praiseworthy if one does it even when one is feeling antisocial and misanthropic.

A central Kantian idea is that persons are ends in themselves, who have values and goals and make choices and decisions. As rational agents, persons have dignity and are entitled to respect. To treat individuals as persons is to respect their values and choices, insofar as these are morally permissible. This means that people must never be treated merely as the means to others' ends. This notion is used to explain the importance of obtaining informed consent from patients and human subjects used in medical and scientific experiments. One of the most blatant examples of the violation of the principle of informed consent occurred in the Tuskegee Syphilis Experiment.

Between 1932 and 1972 the United States Public Health Service (PHS) conducted an investigation into the natural history of untreated syphilis on 399 black men from Macon County, Alabama. The purpose of the experiment was to find out if racial differences affected the course of the disease. The men were led to believe that they were part of a select group receiving special medical care. In fact, they were receiving no care at all for their syphilis.

In 1932, when the study began, there was no effective treatment for syphilis. Victims were usually given arsenic, which had little if any ameliorative, and no curative, effect. It was not until after World War II that penicillin became available as a treatment for syphilis. Therefore, at least at the beginning of the experiment, the men were not deprived of treatment that might have cured them or lessened their symptoms. Indeed, the health of some of the men was undoubtedly improved due to their participation because they got medical care for other conditions that would have gone untreated.

However, the Tuskegee Syphilis Experiment continued until 1972, long after the discovery of penicillin. Men who could have been cured of a devastating disease were allowed to go blind and mad and ultimately die. They were certainly harmed by the withholding of penicillin, and thus the experiment can be condemned on purely utilitarian grounds. It might be countered that, prior to the establishment of Medicaid, the government had no obligation to provide syphilis sufferers with medical treatment, but even if this is true, it certainly had an obligation not to deceive individuals about effective medical treatment in order to get them to participate in the experiment. The Tuskegee Syphilis Experiment is a shameful episode in the history of the Public Health Service, as was acknowledged by President Clinton on May 16, 1997, when he apologized to the few remaining survivors and their relatives.[11] The wrongness was compounded by the harmful effects that occurred when penicillin was available and withheld, but the experiment was wrong from its inception, even before a cure was available. This judgment is best explained in Kantian terms. It is wrong to conduct medical experiments, regardless of their potential social value and independent of the harm that may be inflicted, on persons who have not given their free and informed consent. To use people in this way is to treat them as mere means, rather than ends in themselves.

Public health has a clear utilitarian or consequentialist component. It aims to promote human welfare and reduce human misery, and is solidly based on factual evidence. At the same time, it is limited by Kantian or deontological considerations, such as respect for persons and their rights. The hard questions arise when individual rights clash with the general welfare. Rights-theorists maintain that rights "trump" consideration of the general welfare, but surely this depends on the nature and significance of the right claimed as well as the magnitude of risk to the general population. This issue is particularly important when considering such topics as genetic screening, reproductive decision making, AIDS, and alcohol and drug policy.

COMMUNITARIAN ETHICS

Despite their differences, utilitarianism and Kantian ethics share some presuppositions. Both regard the individual as the focal point of moral concern. Although utilitarianism seeks to promote the greatest happiness of the greatest number, it determines what that is by reference to individual preferences. Kantian ethics also focuses on individuals in its insistence that the rights and dignity of the individual should never be sacrificed for the welfare of the whole. Both ethical approaches also share the idea that since different individuals have different values and different conceptions of the good life, society should remain neutral between these conceptions and not adopt any particular conception to the exclusion of others. The Categorical Imperative, for example, is consistent with many different ways of life. It gives very little positive guidance on how best to live. And while the Principle of Utility instructs us to maximize welfare, it leaves the determination of what constitutes an individual's welfare up to the individual. Mill was particularly insistent that the individual is best positioned to know what is in his or her own interest.

Recently, there has been a reaction to the emphasis on the individual in the dominant ethical theories by a somewhat disparate group of theorists who can be labeled "communitarians." Communitarians reject the notion of timeless, universal ethical truths based on reason. Instead they maintain that our moral thinking has its source in historical traditions of particular communities. Communities are not simply collections of individuals who happen to inhabit the same geographical area. Rather, they are composed of people who share customs, institutions, and values. These provide the starting point from which attempts to solve ethical problems must begin.

Perhaps the most important feature of communitarian ethics for our purposes is its idea of a *common good*. Whereas utilitarianism seeks to promote the welfare of all individuals taken together, communitarianism looks to the *shared* values, ideals, and goals of a community. It asks what kind of community we want to live in and uses this, rather than individual welfare exclusively, as guidance in determining social policy.

A problem for communitarians is that the individuals who make up communities may have very different ideas of what the community should be like. Which vision of "the good life" or "the good society" should prevail? Does not communitarianism, like utilitarianism, threaten a "tyranny of the majority"? In response, communitarians argue that even people with very different values will have shared values. Education is a good example of a shared value. That is, over and above each person's interest in becoming educated, the community as a whole has an interest in seeing that its citizens are educated. This is essential if the society is to be healthy economically, and also for democracy (another shared value of our community) to operate. Undoubtedly, different individuals and groups will have different ideas as to what and how the schools should teach, and these differences will have to be worked out in democratic fashion, which includes private schools, religious schools, and home schooling. Nevertheless, the commitment of the society to educating the young is a shared value.

The health of the public is another shared value. Not only does each individual have an interest in staying healthy, but all of us together share an interest in having a healthy population. Again, we may disagree about the best ways to promote the public's health and over how to weigh individual liberty against the welfare of the whole. Nevertheless, reducing disease, saving lives, and promoting good health are shared values, part of the common good. As public health is fundamentally an effort to promote these shared goals, public health is a species of communitarianism.

Communitarianism challenges the libertarian or market model, which places the highest value on liberty. Liberty here means the absence of restraint, not the liberty to accomplish certain goals, which is often called *positive liberty*. Libertarians see the government as the biggest threat to liberty in the modern state because government controls the means of violence and coercion. They regard the market as the most efficient way to expand liberty for all citizens.

Like libertarians, liberals also place a high value on individual liberty. However, liberty is not the sole value for liberals: Social and economic equality is also a desirable end. Furthermore, liberals do not embrace the market with the same enthusiasm as libertarians. Liberals believe that the government has a significant role to play in regulating the market and offering some form of social safety net which includes health care for the needy, employment and education programs, and pensions to protect the elderly.

Communitarians share with liberals the view that the market needs to be controlled and regulated in order to protect people. But where liberals tend to think solely in terms of harms and benefits to individuals and to insist that individuals determine their own ends and goods, communitarians stress goods that are held or enjoyed in common: clean air and water, the environment, education, and the public's health and safety. These goods cannot be achieved by individual effort alone but must be obtained by collective action and new institutions. Moreover, such collective action and new institutions not only promote the common good but can also strengthen the allegiance of individuals to the community.

Many philosophers have seen the principal issue of public health as that of paternalism, or the intrusion of the state upon individual liberty in order to promote health and safety, such as with requirements that individuals wear seat belts while using automobiles. These kinds of issues were not seen as inherently exciting or as illuminating of the future that was coming for medicine and ethics. Yet the ethical disputes in public health are far more extensive than the debates over paternalism would suggest. What is the nature of the population? Of the community? Does the community share a common good? Who bears the burdens of prevention? Should public health turn away from moralism, the use of the law to promote a specific morality, altogether, even when that morality might reduce the risks of contracting a dread disease? What do all Americans deserve when it comes to health care, and can the market provide affordable health care for all? Should we provide health care for all in a way that recognizes its character as a common good, and in a way that promotes a sense of sharing something in common? What is the ethical relevance of emergent new epidemics and ecological threats, worldwide? These are the issues we turn to in the readings that follow.

NOTES

1. Benjamin S. Wilfond, "Screening Policy for Cystic Fibrosis: The Role of Evidence," Special Supplement, *Hastings Center Report* 25, No. 3 (1995), p. S22.

2. Ibid.

3. John Stuart Mill, Chapter II, "What Utilitarianism Is." *Utilitarianism (1861)*. Edited by George Sher (Indianapolis, IN: Hackett 1979, p. 7).

4. Jeremy Bentham, "An Introduction to the Principles of Morals and Legislation," Chapter XVII, paragraph 4 in Burns and Hart, eds., *The Collected Works of Jeremy Bentham* (London, 1970, p. 283).

5. Mill, *supra* note 3, p. 11.

6. Peter Singer, *Animal Liberation* (New York: Avon Books, 1975).

7. Mill, *supra* note 3, p. 17.

8. Ibid, p. 22.

9. President's Commission for the Study of Ethical Problems in Medicine and Biomedical and Behavioral Research, 1983. Screening and Counseling for Genetic Conditions (Washington, D.C.: Government Printing Office. Chapter 2, pp. 47–48).

10. Kant's best known work on ethics is *Groundwork of the Metaphysic of Morals.*

11. "Clinton Regrets 'Clearly Racist' U.S. Study," *New York Times,* May 17, 1997, A10.

1

POPULATION PERSPECTIVE

Everything in public health ethics begins with the population perspective and with the effort to measure and improve the health status of populations. By "population perspective" we mean the effort to understand the occurrence of disease from a group or community perspective. Whereas in medicine, the patient is an individual person, in public health, the "patient" is the whole community or population. The goal of public health is to reduce disease and early death in populations. Its methodology is epidemiology, a science which uses strategies and methods to determine that which causes the levels, patterns, and etiology of health and disease in communities.

Another facet of the population perspective is that public health measures save *statistical* lives and reduce *rates* of disease within populations. These savings are of real lives and real disease, but the savings cannot be linked to specific persons. No politician can send postcards to particular individuals and claim credit for saving their lives through public health programs they have advocated. What they can and will do is claim credit for improving the health and safety of the whole community, much as they can claim that a new school building or a new bridge benefits the whole community.

The population's health is in this sense a construct of our methods, something built out of the various statistical measures we have developed over time: births, deaths, reports of disease, numbers of people who live in cities, in rural areas, the age distribution of a population, and so forth. When we speak of the health of the population, we are speaking of something real but it is a reality constructed from our methods, abstracted from other elements of our common world.

It is widely appreciated that death and disease are social harms that require governmental action, as with immunization. Less appreciated is the need to understand disease and health risks in different groups in the community: who smokes and who does not, which groups suffer high rates of heart disease and which groups have much lower rates, and why these differences exist. Such information is essential for the prevention of disease.

Still less understood is the way in which health benefits to communities diverge from health benefits to individuals. This central point is made in Geoffrey Rose's classic article, "Sick Individuals and Sick Populations," the first selection in this chapter. As Rose puts it, "A preventive measure which brings much benefit to the population offers little to each participating individual."[1] Rose calls this *the preventive paradox.*[2] It is a paradox because populations are made up of individuals; how, then, can one benefit a population without benefiting the individuals who compose it? Rose is not saying, of course, that populations are made up of anything other than individuals. He *is* saying that improving the health of populations results in disappointingly small improvements to the health of any given individual. For example, the finding that elevated cholesterol levels measured in a population produce elevated rates of coronary artery disease and premature death is a finding about relationships between aggregate or widespread risks and associated rates of disease. Lowering the average level of cholesterol for an entire population would presumably lower the rates of disease and early death and would save thousands of lives. It does not follow, however, that measures to lower the average level of cholesterol would significantly reduce the risk of heart attack for any particular person who is at risk of coronary heart disease. The reason is that there are millions of people who have high levels of cholesterol in their blood. Lowering the average level of cholesterol in the whole population can save thousands of lives while having only disappointingly small reductions of risk for the average individual.

Another example is state and federal seat-belt laws. This legislation clearly saves lives, possibly in the neighborhood of 10,000 lives a year, nationally. This is a lot of lives saved and a significant benefit to the community as a whole. However, this result comes from the wearing of seat belts by well over a hundred million drivers and passengers, each of whom is at a relatively low risk of dying in a highway crash. Wearing a seat belt decreases only marginally any particular person's chance of dying in an automobile accident, which is already low. This does not mean, of course, that there is no reason to wear a seat belt, but rather that the rationale comes from the collective good obtained, the saving of a substantial number of lives, rather than from the benefit to any individual personally.

The social and ecological causes of disease are many and varied, including, for example, nutrition, clean water, the genetic makeup of subgroups, safe housing, access to medical care, and exposure to pathogens. Among other things, epidemiology seeks to explain how the health of populations develops and how disease manifests itself across populations. It asks questions such as, Why has health improved over the past 100 years? Why has tuberculosis reemerged as a serious threat? Why do the Chinese and Japanese have lower rates of heart disease and cirrhosis than, say, Europeans or North Americans?

A fundamental question is how major divisions in the population like race and class shape the health of the total population. Ill health is concentrated among those with low incomes and few social advantages, and these characteristics in turn are concentrated among minority groups like African Americans, Hispanics, and Native Americans. As Vincente Navarro points out in "Race or Class Versus Race and Class," it is hard to distinguish whether the primary factor in producing ill health is race or class; it is likely a combination of both. For example, rates of infant mortality are much higher in the United States than in other industrialized countries, largely due to the existence of a large underclass composed of minorities and poor whites. Understanding institutionalized inequity is part of the effort to understand risks to health and how the public's health can be improved.

Epidemiology is also supposed to develop theories about how the population's health can be explained and improved. In the third selection, Nancy Krieger and Sally Zierler criticize those epidemiologists so focused on the scientific side, on making more accurate and reliable methods for sampling the occurrence of disease and early death, that they neglect the goal of epidemiology—improving the public's health.

Another aspect of causal inference has to do with the way we determine "the cause" of an event. Commonly we ask: Why did this person get sick at this time? Why did this person die of heart disease? But from a population perspective, we have a different purpose. We want to know why this population (or community) has a higher rate of disease than other societies, or why disease rates in a society are on the rise. Which conditions we identify as "the cause" depends in large measure on our purposes.[3] For example, alcoholism has often been viewed as the result of an individual failure to control one's drinking. Those who take a population perspective, however, are more likely to focus on the conditions in society that make excessive drinking likely, from the availability of alcohol to the social practices that encourage heavy or frequent use of alcohol. Similarly, highway crashes have in the past been seen as the result of careless or reckless driving on the part of individuals. After three decades of public health crusades, led by Ralph Nader and others, we now focus more on the safety of automobiles or highways. Individual responsibility is not forgotten, but hazardous driving conditions that affect whole populations are given far more attention than before. The population perspective constructs a new story about how highway injuries occur in society.

NOTES

1. Geoffrey Rose, "Sick Individuals and Sick Populations," *International Journal of Epidemiology* 14 (1985), p. 38.

2. Ibid.

3. For an excellent discussion of the way causes are identified, see H.L.A. Hart and A. M. Honore, *Causation in the Law* (Oxford: Clarendon Press, 1959).

Sick Individuals and Sick Populations

GEOFFREY ROSE

THE DETERMINANTS OF INDIVIDUAL CASES

In teaching epidemiology to medical students, I have often encouraged them to consider a question which I first heard enunciated by Roy Acheson: 'Why did *this* patient get *this* disease at *this* time?'. It is an excellent starting-point, because students and doctors feel a natural concern for the problems of the individual. Indeed, the central ethos of medicine is seen as an acceptance of responsibility for sick individuals.

It is an integral part of good doctoring to ask not only, 'What is the diagnosis, and what is the treatment?' but also, 'Why did this happen, and could it have been prevented?'. Such thinking shapes the approach to nearly all clinical and laboratory research into the causes and mechanisms of illness. Hypertension research, for example, is almost wholly preoccupied with the characteristics which distinguish individuals at the hypertensive and normotensive ends of the blood pressure distribution. Research into diabetes looks for genetic, nutritional and metabolic reasons to explain why some people get diabetes and others do not. The constant aim in such work is to answer Acheson's question, 'Why did *this* patient get this disease at this time?'.

The same concern has continued to shape the thinking of all of us who came to epidemiology from a background in clinical practice. The whole basis of the case-control method is to discover how sick and healthy individuals differ. Equally the basis of many cohort studies is the search for 'risk factors', which identify certain individuals as being more susceptible to disease; and from this we proceed to test whether these risk factors are also causes, capable of explaining why some individuals get sick while others remain healthy, and applicable as a guide to prevention.

To confine attention in this way to within-population comparisons has caused much confusion (particularly in the clinical world) in the definition of nor-

From the *International Journal of Epidemiology,* 14 (1985), 32–38. Reprinted by permission of Oxford University Press.

mality. Laboratory 'ranges of normal' are based on what is common within the local population. Individuals with 'normal blood pressure' are those who do not stand out from their local contemporaries; and so on. What is common is all right, we presume.

Applied to aetiology, the individual-centered approach leads to the use of relative risk as the basic representation of aetiological force: that is, 'the risk in exposed individuals relative to risk in non-exposed individuals'. Indeed, the concept of relative risk has almost excluded any other approach to quantifying causal importance. It may generally be the best measure of aetiological force, but it is no measure at all of aetiological outcome or of public health importance.

Unfortunately this approach to the search for causes, and the measuring of their potency, has to assume a heterogeneity of exposure within the study population. If everyone smoked 20 cigarettes a day, then clinical, case-control and cohort studies alike would lead us to conclude that lung cancer was a genetic disease; and in one sense that would be true, since if everyone is exposed to the necessary agent, then the distribution of cases is wholly determined by individual susceptibility.

Within Scotland and other mountainous parts of Britain there is no discernible relation between local cardiovascular death rates and the softness of the public water supply. The reason is apparent if one extends the enquiry to the whole of the UK. In Scotland, everyone's water is soft; and the possibly adverse effect becomes recognizable only when study is extended to other regions which have a much wider range of exposure. Even more clearly, a case-control study of this question within Scotland would have been futile. Everyone is exposed, and other factors operate to determine the varying risk.

Epidemiology is often defined in terms of study of the determinants of the distribution of the disease; but we should not forget that the more widespread is a particular cause, the less it explains the distribution of cases. The hardest cause to identify is the one that is universally present, for then it has no influence on the distribution of disease.

THE DETERMINANTS OF POPULATION INCIDENCE RATE

I find it increasingly helpful to distinguish two kinds of aetiological question. The first seeks the causes of cases, and the second seeks the causes of incidence. 'Why do some individuals have hypertension?' is a quite different question from 'Why do some populations have much hypertension, whilst in others it is rare?'. The questions require different kinds of study, and they have different answers.

[We can show] the systolic blood pressure distributions of middle-aged men in two populations—Kenyan nomads and London civil servants. The familiar question, 'Why do some individuals have higher blood pressure than others?' could be equally well asked in either of these settings, since in each the individual blood pressures vary (proportionately) to about the same extent; and the answers might well be much the same in each instance (that is, mainly genetic variation, with a lesser component from environmental and behavioural differences). We might achieve a complete understanding of why individuals vary, and yet quite miss the most important public health question, namely, 'Why is hypertension absent in the Kenyans and common in London?'. The answer to that question has to do with the determinants of the population mean; for what distinguishes the two groups is nothing to do with the characteristics of individuals, it is rather a shift of the whole distribution—a mass influence acting on the population as a whole. To find the determinants of prevalence and incidence rates, we need to study characteristics of populations, not characteristics of individuals.

A more extreme example is provided by the population distributions of serum cholesterol levels in East Finland, where coronary heart disease is very common, and Japan, where the incidence rate is low: the two distributions barely overlap. Each country has men with relative hypercholesterolaemia (although their definitions of the range of 'normal' would no doubt disagree), and one could research into the genetic and other causes of these unusual individuals; but if we want to discover why Finland has such a high incidence of coronary heart disease we need to look for those characteristics of the national diet which have so elevated the whole cholesterol distribution. Within populations it has proved almost impossible to demonstrate any relation between an individual's diet and his serum cholesterol level; and the same applies to the relation of individual diet to blood pressure and to overweight. But at the level of populations it is a different story: it has proved easy to show strong associations between population mean values for saturated fat intake *versus* serum cholesterol level and coronary heart disease incidence, sodium intake *versus* blood pressure, or energy intake *versus* overweight. The determinants of incidence are not necessarily the same as the causes of cases.

HOW DO THE CAUSES OF CASES RELATE TO THE CAUSES OF INCIDENCE?

This is largely a matter of whether exposure varies similarly within a population and between populations (or over a period of time within the same population). Softness of water supply may be a determinant of cardiovascular mortality, but it is unlikely to be identifiable as a risk factor for individuals, because exposure tends to be locally uniform. Dietary fat is, I believe, the main determinant of a population's incidence rate for coronary heart disease; but it quite fails to identify high-risk individuals.

In the case of cigarettes and lung cancer it so happened that the study populations contained about equal numbers of smokers and non-smokers, and in such a situation case/control and cohort studies were able to identify what was also the main determinant of population differences and time trends.

There is a broad tendency for genetic factors to dominate individual susceptibility, but to explain rather little of population differences in incidence. Genetic heterogeneity, it seems, is mostly much greater within than between populations. This is the contrary situation to that seen for environmental factors. Thus migrants, whatever the colour of their skin, tend to acquire the disease rates of their country of adoption.

Most non-infectious diseases are still of largely unknown cause. If you take a textbook of medicine and look at the list of contents you will still find, despite all our aetiological research, that most are still of basically unknown aetiology. We know quite a lot about the personal characteristics of individuals who are susceptible to them; but for a remarkably large number of our major non-infectious diseases we still do not know the determinants of the incidence rate.

Over a period of time we find that most diseases are in a state of flux. For example, duodenal ulcer in Britain at the turn of the century was an uncommon condition affecting mainly young women. During the first half of the century the incidence rate rose steadily and it became very common, but now the disease seems to be disappearing; and yet we have no clues to the determinants of these striking changes in incidence rates. One could repeat that story for many conditions.

There is hardly a disease whose incidence rate does not vary widely, either over time or between populations at the same time. This means that these causes of incidence rate, unknown though they are, are not inevitable. It is possible to live without them, and if we knew what they were it might be possible to control them: But to identify the causal agent by the traditional case-control and cohort methods will be unsuccessful if there are not sufficient differences in exposure within the study population at the time of the study. In those circumstances all that these traditional methods do is to find markers of individual susceptibility. The clues must be sought from differences between populations or from changes within populations over time.

PREVENTION

These two approaches to aetiology—the individual and the population-based—have their counterparts in prevention. In the first, preventive strategy seeks to identify high-risk susceptible individuals and to offer them some individual protection. In contrast, the 'population strategy' seeks to control the determinants of incidence in the population as a whole.

The 'High-Risk' Strategy

This is the traditional and natural medical approach to prevention. If a doctor accepts that he is responsible for an individual who is sick today, then it is a short step to accept responsibility also for the individual who may well be sick tomorrow. Thus screening is used to detect certain individuals who hitherto thought they were well but who must now understand that they are in effect patients. This is the process, for example, in the detection and treatment of symptomless hypertension, the transition from healthy subject to patient being ratified by the giving and receiving of tablets. (Anyone who takes medicines is by definition a patient.)

What the 'high-risk' strategy seeks to achieve is something like a truncation of the risk distribution. This general concept applies to all special preventive action in high-risk individuals—in at-risk pregnancies, in small babies, or in any other particularly susceptible group. It is a strategy with some clear and important advantages (Table 1).

Its first advantage is that it leads to intervention which is appropriate to the individual. A smoker who has a cough or who is found to have impaired ventilatory function has a special reason for stopping smoking. The doctor will see it as making sense to advise salt restriction in a hypertensive. In such instances the intervention makes sense because that individual already has a problem which that particular measure may possibly ameliorate. If we consider screening a population to discover those with high serum cholesterol levels and advising them on dietary change, then that intervention is appropriate to those people in particular: they have a diet-related metabolic problem.

The 'high-risk' strategy produces interventions that are appropriate to the particular individuals advised to take them. Consequently it has the advantage of enhanced subject motivation. In our randomized controlled trial of smoking cessation in London civil servants we first screened some 20 000 men and from them selected about 1500 who were smokers with, in addition, markers of specially high risk for cardiorespiratory disease. They were recalled and a random

TABLE 1 Prevention by the 'High-Risk Strategy': Advantages

1. Intervention appropriate to individual
2. Subject motivation
3. Physician motivation
4. Cost-effective use of resources
5. Benefit:risk ratio favourable

half received anti-smoking counselling. The results, in terms of smoking cessation, were excellent because those men knew they had a special reason to stop. They had been picked out from others in their offices because, although everyone knows that smoking is a bad thing, they had a special reason why it was particularly unwise for them.

There is, of course, another and less reputable reason why screening enhances subject motivation, and that is the mystique of a scientific investigation. A ventilatory function test is a powerful enhancer of motivation to stop smoking: an instrument which the subject does not quite understand, that looks rather impressive, has produced evidence that he is a special person with a special problem. The electrocardiogram is an even more powerful motivator, if you are unscrupulous enough to use it in prevention. A man may feel entirely well, but if those little squiggles on the paper tell the doctor that he has got trouble, then he must accept that he has now become a patient. That is a powerful persuader. (I suspect it is also a powerful cause of lying awake in the night and thinking about it.)

For rather similar reasons the 'high-risk' approach also motivates physicians. Doctors, quite rightly, are uncomfortable about intervening in a situation where their help was not asked for. Before imposing advice on somebody who was getting on all right without them, they like to feel that there is a proper and special justification in that particular case.

The 'high-risk' approach offers a more cost-effective use of limited resources. One of the things we have learned in health education at the individual level is that once-only advice is a waste of time. To get results we may need a considerable investment of counselling time and follow-up. It is costly in use of time and effort and resources, and therefore it is more effective to concentrate limited medical services and time where the need—and therefore also the benefit—is likely to be greatest.

A final advantage of the 'high-risk' approach is that it offers a more favourable ratio of benefits to risks. If intervention must carry some adverse effects or costs, and if the risk and cost are much the same for everybody, then the ratio of the costs to the benefits will be more favourable where the benefits are larger.

Unfortunately the 'high-risk' strategy of prevention also has some serious disadvantages and limitations (Table 2).

TABLE 2 Prevention by the 'High-Risk Strategy': Disadvantages

1. Difficulties and costs of screening
2. Palliative and temporary—not radical
3. Limited potential for (a) individual
                         (b) population
4. Behaviourally inappropriate

The first centres around the difficulties and costs of screening. Supposing that we were to embark, as some had advocated, on a policy of screening for high cholesterol levels and giving dietary advice to those individuals at special risk. The disease process we are trying to prevent (atherosclerosis and its complications) begins early in life, so we should have to initiate screening perhaps at the age of ten. However, the abnormality we seek to detect is not a stable lifetime characteristic, so we must advocate repeated screening at suitable intervals.

In all screening one meets problems with uptake, and the tendency for the response to be greater amongst those sections of the population who are often least at risk of the disease. Often there is an even greater problem: screening detects certain individuals who will receive special advice, but at the same time it cannot help also discovering much larger numbers of 'border-liners', that is, people whose results mark them as at increased risk but for whom we do not have an appropriate treatment to reduce their risk.

The second disadvantage of the 'high-risk' strategy is that it is palliative and temporary, not radical. It does not seek to alter the underlying causes of the disease but to identify individuals who are particularly susceptible to those causes. Presumably in every generation there will be such susceptibles; and if prevention and control efforts were confined to these high-risk individuals, then that approach would need to be sustained year after year and generation after generation. It does not deal with the root of the problem, but seeks to protect those who are vulnerable to it; and they will always be around.

The potential for this approach is limited—sometimes more than we could have expected—both for the individual and for the population. There are two reasons for this. The first is that our power to predict future disease is usually very weak. Most individuals with risk factors will remain well, at least for some years; contrariwise, unexpected illness may happen to someone who has just received an 'all clear' report from a screening examination. One of the limitations of the relative risk statistic is that it gives no idea of the absolute level of danger. Thus the Framingham Study has impressed us all with its powerful discrimination between high and low risk groups, but when we see the degree of overlap in serum cholesterol level between future cases and those who remained healthy, it is not surprising that an individual's future is so often misassessed.

Often the best predictor of future major disease is the presence of existing minor disease. A low ventilatory function today is the best predictor of its future rate of decline. A high blood pressure today is the best predictor of its future rate of rise. Early coronary heart disease is better than all the conventional risk factors as a predictor of future fatal disease. However, even if screening includes such tests for early disease, our experience in the Heart Disease Prevention Project (Table 3) still points to a very weak ability to predict the future of any particular individual.

TABLE 3 Five-Year Incidence of Myocardial Infarction in the UK Heart Disease Prevention Project

ENTRY CHARACTERISTIC	% OF MEN	% OF MI CASES	MI INCIDENCE RATE %
Risk factors alone	15	32	7
'Ischaemia'	16	41	11
'Ischaemia' + risk factors	2	12	22
All men	100	100	4

This point came home to me only recently. I have long congratulated myself on my low levels of coronary risk factors, and I joked to my friends that if I were to die suddenly, I should be very surprised. I even speculated on what other disease—perhaps colon cancer—would be the commonest cause of death for a man in the lowest group of cardiovascular risk. The painful truth is that for such an individual in a Western population the commonest cause of death— by far—is coronary heart disease! Everyone, in fact, is a high-risk individual for this uniquely mass disease.

There is another, related reason why the predictive basis of the 'high-risk' strategy of prevention is weak. It is well illustrated by some data from Alberman which relate the occurrence of Down's syndrome births to maternal age (Table 4). Mothers under 30 years are individually at minimal risk; but because they are so numerous, they generate half the cases. High-risk individuals aged 40 and above generate only 13% of the cases.

The lesson from this example is that *a large number of people at a small risk may give rise to more cases of disease than the small number who are at a high risk.* This situation seems to be common, and it limits the utility of the 'high-risk' approach to prevention.

A further disadvantage of the 'high-risk' strategy is that it is behaviourally inappropriate. Eating, smoking, exercise and all our other life-style characteris-

TABLE 4 Incidence of Down's Syndrome According to Material Age

MATERNAL AGE (YEARS)	RISK OF DOWN'S SYNDROME PER 1000 BIRTHS	TOTAL BIRTHS IN AGE GROUP (AS % OF ALL AGES)	% OF TOTAL DOWN'S SYNDROME OCCURRING IN AGE GROUP
< 30	0.7	78	51
30–34	1.3	16	20
35–39	3.7	5	16
40–44	13.1	0.95	11
> 45	34.6	0.05	2
All ages	1.5	100	100

tics are constrained by social norms. If we try to eat differently from our friends it will not only be inconvenient, but we risk being regarded as cranks or hypochondriacs. If a man's work environment encourages heavy drinking, then advice that he is damaging his liver is unlikely to have any effect. No one who has attempted any sort of health education effort in individuals needs to be told that it is difficult for such people to step out of line with their peers. This is what the 'high-risk' preventive strategy requires them to do.

The Population Strategy

This is the attempt to control the determinants of incidence, to lower the mean level of risk factors, to shift the whole distribution of exposure in a favourable direction. In its traditional 'public health' form it has involved mass environmental control methods; in its modern form it is attempting (less successfully) to alter some of society's norms of behaviour.

The advantages are powerful (Table 5). The first is that it is radical. It attempts to remove the underlying causes that make the disease common. It has a large potential—often larger than one would have expected—for the population as a whole. From Framingham data one can compute that a 10 mm Hg lowering of the blood pressure distribution as a whole would correspond to about a 30% reduction in the total attributable mortality.

The approach is behaviourally appropriate. If nonsmoking eventually becomes 'normal', then it will be much less necessary to keep on persuading individuals. Once a social norm of behaviour has become accepted and (as in the case of diet) once the supply industries have adapted themselves to the new pattern, then the maintenance of that situation no longer requires effort from individuals. The health education phase aimed at changing individuals is, we hope, a temporary necessity, pending changes in the norms of what is socially acceptable.

Unfortunately the population strategy of prevention has also some weighty drawbacks (Table 6). It offers only a small benefit to each individual, since most of them were going to be all right anyway, at least for many years. This leads to the *Prevention Paradox:* 'A preventive measure which brings much benefit to the population offers little to each participating individual'. This has been the history of public health—of immunization, the wearing of seat belts

TABLE 5 Prevention by the 'Population Strategy': Advantages

---
1. Radical
2. Large potential for population
3. Behaviourally appropriate

TABLE 6 Prevention by the 'Population Strategy': Disadvantages

1. Small benefit to individual ('Prevention Paradox')
2. Poor motivation of subject
3. Poor motivation of physician
4. Benefit:risk ratio worrison

and now the attempt to change various life-style characteristics. Of enormous potential importance to the population as a whole, these measures offer very little—particularly in the short term—to each individual; and thus there is poor motivation of the subject. We should not be surprised that health education tends to be relatively ineffective for individuals and in the short term. Mostly people act for substantial and immediate rewards, and the medical motivation for health education is inherently weak. Their health next year is not likely to be much better if they accept our advice or if they reject it. Much more powerful as motivators for health education are the social rewards of enhanced self-esteem and social approval.

There is also in the population approach only poor motivation of physicians. Many medical practitioners who embarked with enthusiasm on anti-smoking education have become disheartened because their success rate was no more than 5 or 10%: in clinical practice one's expectation of results is higher. Grateful patients are few in preventive medicine, where success is marked by a non-event. The skills of behavioural advice are different and unfamiliar, and professional esteem is lowered by a lack of skill. Harder to overcome than any of these, however, is the enormous difficulty for medical personnel to see health as a population issue and not merely as a problem for individuals.

In mass prevention each individual has usually only a small expectation of benefit, and this small benefit can easily be outweighed by a small risk. This happened in the World Health Organization clofibrate trial, where a cholesterol-lowering drug seems to have killed more than it saved, even though the fatal complication rate was only about 1/1000/year. Such low-order risks, which can be vitally important to the balance sheet of mass preventive plans, may be hard or impossible to detect. This makes it important to distinguish two approaches. The first is the restoration of biological normality by the removal of an abnormal exposure (eg, stopping smoking, controlling air pollution, moderating some of our recently-acquired dietary deviations); here there can be some presumption of safety. This is not true for the other kind of preventive approach, which leaves intact the underlying causes of incidence and seeks instead to interpose some new, supposedly protective intervention (eg, immunization, drugs, jogging). Here the onus is on the activists to produce adequate evidence of safety.

CONCLUSIONS

Case-centred epidemiology identifies individual susceptibility, but it may fail to identify the underlying causes of incidence. The 'high-risk' strategy of prevention is an interim expedient, needed in order to protect susceptible individuals, but only for so long as the underlying causes of incidence remain unknown or uncontrollable; if causes can be removed, susceptibility ceases to matter.

Realistically, many diseases will long continue to call for both approaches, and fortunately competition between them is usually unnecessary. Nevertheless, the priority of concern should always be the discovery and control of the causes of incidence.

Race or Class Versus Race and Class: Mortality Differentials in the United States

VICENTE NAVARRO

The latest annual report of the US federal government about the health of the US population has created enormous concern about the mortality differentials between whites and blacks. For example, in 1988 life expectancy at birth was 75·5 years for whites but only 69·5 years for blacks. For most causes of death, the death rate in blacks is higher than that in whites, and for many causes of death mortality differentials are increasing rather than decreasing. Alarming reports about these differences have appeared in both the lay press and medical publications. Consequently, it makes sense that the federal government has chosen the reduction of these differentials as one of its top objectives and has called for a "decrease [of the] disparity in life expectancy between white and minority populations to no more than four years."

Although this emphasis on reducing race differentials is undoubtedly very important, another component of the nation's health that is highly relevant to race differentials in mortality has passed unnoticed. The stark fact is that these differentials cannot be explained merely by looking at race. After all, some blacks have better health indicators (including mortality rates) than some whites, and not all whites have similar mortality indicators. Thus we must look at class differentials in mortality in the US, which are also increasing rather than declining. Class is harder to define than race, but the most frequent indicators of social class used for morbidity and mortality statistics in the western industrialised world are occupation, education, and income.

IMPORTANCE OF CLASS DIFFERENTIALS

The US is the only western developed nation whose government does not collect mortality statistics by class. The federal report on health indicators in the

From *The Lancet,* 336 (1990), 1238–1240. Copyright © by The Lancet Ltd. Reprinted by permission of the publisher.

US—*Health, United States, 1989*—tabulates mortality statistics by age, sex, and race but not by class indicators such as income, education, or occupation. With the active encouragement of the European office of the World Health Organisation, most European countries have chosen as the top target in their health policies a reduction, by the year 2000, of the differentials in health status among classes. By contrast, the US is alone among major industrialised nations in not aiming for this goal—in the US, race is used as a *substitute* for class. What the US government seems to ignore is that even if there were no race differentials in mortality, most blacks would still have higher mortality rates than the median or the mean rate in the US population. To understand this point, one has to appreciate that the US has classes as well as races.

How people live, die, and get sick depends not only on their race, gender, and age but also on the class to which they belong. There is empirical information to sustain this position. On one of the few occasions (in 1986) that the US government collected information on mortality rates (for heart and cerebrovascular disease) by class, the results showed that, by whatever indicators of class one might choose (level of education, income, or occupation), mortality rates are related to social class. People with less formal education, with lower income, and belonging to the working class (eg, labourers in the US Census categories of operator and services) are more likely to die of heart disease than are people with more formal education, with higher income, and belonging to the upper classes (eg, managerial and professional).

Mortality Differentials

Figure 1 shows mortality rates for heart disease by occupation. Managerial and professional groups had lower mortality rates for heart disease than did major components of the working class, such as operators and service workers.

Data from the same survey (1986 National Mortality Followback Survey) also show that most of those who died of cerebrovascular disease and all other causes had family incomes of less than $25 000 in 1985 and less than a high school education; the largest proportion of the deceased had worked in technical, sales, and operator occupations—the main occupational groups in the working class. Similar class mortality differentials have been found for breast cancer and for all causes of death.

For both causes of mortality—heart disease and cerebrovascular disease—the class differentials in mortality were larger than the race differentials. The mortality rate for heart disease in blue-collar workers (operators) was 2·3 times higher than the rate in managers and professionals (Figure 1).

Table 23 (age-adjusted death rates for selected causes of death according to sex and race: United States, selected years, 1950–87) of *Health, United States, 1989* shows that for 1986, the heart disease mortality rate for black males was

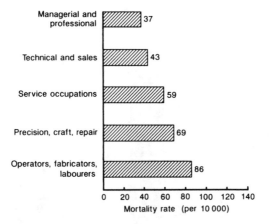

FIGURE 1 Mortality rate for heart disease by occupation, 1986. This figure has been calculated with data from (a) numerator in table 4, ref 7, and (b) denominator in table 627, *Statistical abstract of the United States,* 1988: 376–77 (published by the US Department of Commerce, Bureau of the Census, Washington, DC).

1·2 times higher than for white males, and for black females was 1·5 times higher than for white females.

Morbidity Differentials

Although there are no published data to show mortality rates by class and race, it is likely that the mortality rates for white service workers, for example, are closer to those of black service workers than to those of white professionals. Since there are no data to establish this point, we can look instead at data on morbidity. Morbidity differentials by class are much larger than differentials by race. In 1986, those making $10 000 or less per year reported 4·6 times more morbidity than those making over $35 000, while blacks reported 1·9 times more morbidity than whites. The race differentials were less than half the class differentials. The same report shows that race differentials within each income group are less pronounced than those between income groups. Figure 2 shows the average annual percentage of persons assessing themselves to be in fair or poor health, classified by race and family income. Morbidity rates for blacks making less than $20 000 were much closer to those for whites in the same income group than to those for blacks in income groups greater than $20 000. Similarly, morbidity rates for whites with incomes below $20 000 were closer to those of blacks in the same income group than to those of whites in income groups over $20 000. Whites making under $20 000 had higher morbidity rates than blacks earning over $20 000.

A similar pattern is observed when occupation is used rather than income. Thus blue-collar workers (operators) reported a morbidity rate (9·5%) that was

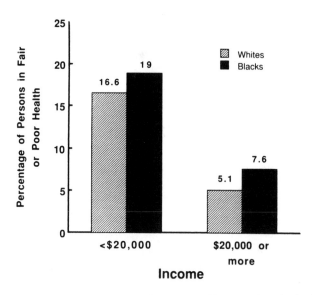

FIGURE 2 Average annual percentage of persons self-assessed to be in fair or poor health, by race and income, 1985–87.

2·9 times higher than that of professionals (3·2%), while blacks reported a morbidity rate 1·9 times higher than that of whites.

Consideration of the annual percentage of persons with limited activity due to chronic conditions rather than self-reported morbidity provides further confirmation. Figure 3 shows, again, that class differentials (measured by income differentials) are larger than race differentials. Moreover, these class differentials have grown larger during the 1980s—even larger than race differentials (figure 4).

DISPARITY OF WEALTH AND INCOME BY CLASS

Within each class (measured by education, income, or occupation), blacks often have worse health indicators than whites. These are the differentials that the US government is targeting for reduction, an important and much-needed task. But the overwhelming majority of blacks (and other minorities) are members of the low-paid, poorly educated working class that have higher morbidity and mortality rates than high-earning, better educated people. The growing mortality differentials between whites and blacks cannot be understood by looking only at race; they are part and parcel of larger mortality differentials—class differentials. In the 1980s, the US witnessed an increased class polarisation of the population, with a reduction of the middle class, a slow growth of the upper and upper-middle classes, and a rapid growth of the low-paid, unskilled working

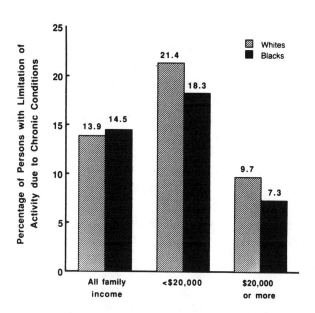

FIGURE 3 Average annual percentage of persons with limitation of activity due to chronic conditions, by race, age, and family income: United States, 1985–87.

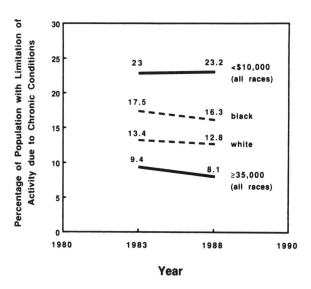

FIGURE 4 Limitation of activity caused by chronic condition, according to income and race, US, 1983 and 1988.

class. Members of the working class are increasingly non-unionised, poorly paid, and part-time, and with a preponderance of minorities and women. The low-earners comprise a heterogeneous group—blacks, Hispanics, whites, men, and women—whose standards of living are rapidly deteriorating because of the growing wealth and income differentials between the upper and lower classes. These social groups belong to the 40% of the population who received only 15·7% of the total income in 1984, the lowest figure since data collection was initiated in 1947. By contrast, the wealthiest 20% received 42·9% of total income, the highest ever. This growing disparity of wealth and income by class mainly, but not exclusively, explains the race differentials in morbidity and mortality.

The growing class differential in mortality rates is not unique to the US. Other countries have noticed that these differentials are not only persistent but growing, and a large national and international debate about the reasons for these class differentials has been initiated. However, in the US there is a deafening silence on this topic. If a prerequisite for finding the right answer is to ask the right question, then it is unlikely that by concentrating solely on race differentials we will ever be able to understand why the health indicators of our minorities are getting worse.

What Explains the Public's Health?—A Call for Epidemiologic Theory

NANCY KRIEGER and SALLY ZIERLER

MR. JORDAN: Is there nothing then but prose, or verse?

PHILOSOPHY-MASTER: No, sir, whatever is not prose, is verse! and whatever is not verse, is prose.

MR. JORDAN: And when one talks, what may that be then?

PHILOSOPHY-MASTER: Prose.

MR. JORDAN: How? When I say, Nicola, bring me my slippers, and give me my night-cap, is that prose?

PHILOSOPHY-MASTER: Yes, sir.

MR. JORDAN: On my conscience, I have spoken prose above these forty years without knowing anything of the matter. . . .

(Jean Baptiste Molière. *Le bourgeois gentilhomme.* 1670)

Epidemiology is a wonderfully ambitious science. It provides a basis for understanding and altering societal patterns of health and disease. These patterns reflect a complex interplay of people's social and biological experience. This interplay integrates the richness and poverty of human life with mechanisms of disease pathogenesis. Understanding this interplay is the fundamental challenge facing epidemiologists. Since our work is to explain what shapes population patterns of disease rather than what makes an individual ill, we have to think consciously about these links. Such thinking we would call the stuff of epidemiologic theory.

Although epidemiologic theory drives much of the work epidemiologists do, we rarely recognize it as such. What we call theory in epidemiology today typically refers to study methodology. Communication of our ideas is explicit about methodologic underpinnings of our study design and analysis. We distinguish multiple ways that error could explain our study results. Assuming that the role of error is not too great, we explain our findings in light of other knowledge about biological, and sometimes social, processes. But where ex-

From *Epidemiology,* 7, January 1996, 107–109. Reprinted by permission of Williams & Wilkins.

plicitly do we name theory to understand the interplay between social and biological processes that shape the public's health?

Our discipline's inattention to epidemiologic theory is relatively new. When epidemiology was first taught in the early 1900s as a self-consciously defined discipline, the first U.S. professor of epidemiology, Wade Hampton Frost, urged development of theories to explain the distribution of disease in populations. Moving away from the more usual focus on natural history of disease in individuals, in 1927 he argued:

> In collecting facts about the distribution of disease, the purpose and view is always to arrive at a better understanding of its nature, sources, means of spread and eventually its control. This implies that the facts must be related to each other in such an orderly way as to establish a theory or philosophy of the disease. . . .

Similar calls for elaborating epidemiologic theory were made in the 1930s in two landmark texts: Major Greenwood's *Epidemics and Crowd Diseases: An Introduction to the Study of Epidemiology,* and Edgar Sydenstricker's *Health and Environment.* These works, synthesizing the epidemiologic knowledge of their times, underscored the importance of social inequalities as determinants of disease in conjunction with biological factors.

In contrast to these researchers, epidemiologists today emphasize creative and effective approaches to modeling causation and explaining effects of error. These approaches have been interpreted as the substance of our field. Notably, as others have observed, we rarely ask: what is the theoretical and ideological basis for conceptualizing and articulating meaningful explanations of the public's health?

EPIDEMIOLOGIC THEORY *vs* THEORIES OF CAUSATION AND OF ERROR

We believe it is useful to distinguish three contexts for theory in our field: (1) epidemiologic theories that frame our etiologic questions, (2) causal theories that form the basis for mathematical models for disease causation, and (3) theories of error that guide our study design, analysis, and interpretation.

What do we mean here by epidemiologic theories *vs* theories of causation and of error? By epidemiologic theories, we refer to interconnected ideas about what explains population health. These theories, by definition, incorporate interdependent social and biological parameters. They organize a complex body of knowledge into coherent interrelations across disease outcomes and make explicit philosophical and ideological assumptions about why, in the words of the noted British epidemiologist Geoffrey Rose, some populations—and not simply some individuals—are sicker than others. Examples of such theories include biomedical, life-style, cultural, behavioral, and social production of disease.

Alternatively, by theories of causation, we refer to interconnected ideas that explain relations among causal effects. These causal relations typically are expressed in the form of schematic or mathematical models that are used in many scientific disciplines. Examples of theoretical constructs relevant to these models include necessary, sufficient, and component causes, and additive and multiplicative effects. And, by theories of error, we refer to interconnected ideas that explain the distribution of error in the design, conduct, and analysis of scientific studies. Operative theoretical concepts include confounding, selection and information bias, misclassification, and random error. The application of these theories of causation and of error to epidemiologic research constitutes the methodologic core of our science.

WHY EPIDEMIOLOGIC THEORY MATTERS

We offer the following example to illustrate the importance of epidemiologic theory. We contrast two distinct theories—life-style and social production of disease—as frameworks for generating hypotheses regarding the single question: what explains the distribution of human immunodeficiency virus (HIV)/AIDS?

A life-style theory explains determinants of population disease occurrence as behavioral clusters or cultural factors that are shared among individuals. This theory has dominated epidemiologic research on HIV, as well as much of the public health agenda for preventing HIV transmission. The first Centers for Disease Control report of unexplained immune suppression that was later named as AIDS proposed a life-style hypothesis: "The fact that these patients were all homosexuals suggests an association between some aspect of a homosexual lifestyle or disease acquired through sexual contact and Pneumocystis pneumonia in this population." Other life-style risk factors named in the epidemiologic literature include "promiscuity", injection drug use, prostitution, or in the case of women not fitting into these categories, "sexual partners of" men who are in defined HIV risk groups. Yet, although the term "life-style" may be used, rarely is the life-style theory named as such. Scholars in other disciplines, however, explicitly identify life-style theory as a major conceptual framework driving epidemiologic knowledge about HIV.

What does it mean to attribute life-style as an explanation for the distribution of HIV within and across populations? Life-style implies that individuals make choices among options, and that these choices are amenable to change given sufficient incentive. Prostitution, for example, is treated as an activity that women choose to engage in, even though the motivation for this choice is rarely ascribed (but is sometimes implied to be a drug habit or desire for "easy money"). Thus, the interconnected explanatory ideas named as life-style theory posit: (1) individuals choose ways of living that have health consequences; (2) what epidemiologists measure on a population level are aggregates of these individual choices, and (3) individualized interventions can alter the distribution of these choices, and ultimately, of disease. These unstated but powerful assumptions are rife within the epidemiologic literature on HIV (and other diseases). Investigators base their study hypotheses, designs, and interpretations on these assumptions. For example, research premised on a life-style framework focuses on inadequate use of condoms (and of sterile needles) as the principal explanation for patterns of HIV incidence within and across different geographic regions.

By contrast, a theory of social production of disease conceptualizes determinants of disease distribution as economic and social relationships forged by a society's political and economic structure. Social groups defined by these relationships are differentially helped or harmed by their position relative to each other. Terms used to convey these relationships include social class, gender and sexism, and race/ethnicity and racism. The imposition of inequalities inherent in these relationships unevenly affects each group's health and well-being.

What would it mean to attribute economic and social relationships as an explanation for the distribution of HIV within and across populations? Surveillance of HIV based on this approach emphasizes the link between increased risk of HIV infection and membership in groups defined by economic deprivation and racial discrimination. Related research explicitly names social policies and political priorities (for example, availability of low-income housing, employment, and affordable education) as critical cofactors in the geographic spread of AIDS in the United States. And, in the case of women and AIDS, theories of social production of disease lead epidemiologists to investigate how gender-based economic inequalities may affect women's ability to determine sexual uses of their bodies. This theory also explains prostitution as an economic survival strategy that has its own political economy. Studies of prostitution and HIV recognize prostitution's complex occupational structure, which includes a range of working conditions affecting risk of exposure to HIV. Reflecting prostitutes' relative material or social deprivation, these conditions include the location of work (on the street, in clubs, brothels, or privately owned homes), characteristics of clients, worker control over agreement to provide services, worker control over what services she or he will provide, and options for protection from physical and sexual violence, as well as from sexually transmitted diseases.

Thus, social production of disease theories provide interconnected explanatory ideas that posit: (1) the relative social and economic positioning of people shapes their exposures, including behaviors; (2) what epidemiologists measure on a population level are attributes of this positioning, and (3) population level interventions shift structural conditions that cause material and social deprivation, and thus alter societal distribution of disease. Hypotheses emerging from this theory propose explanations of HIV transmission in relation to: social class, access to health-related resources, work place conditions, and discrimination based on gender, race/ethnicity, sexual orientation/identity, or other attributes.

EPIDEMIOLOGY AND SOCIETY

As these two contrasting examples suggest, ideas for studies, formation of hypotheses, and emergence of knowledge begin within a theoretical framework. This framework, which we are naming epidemiologic theory, largely determines what we know, what we consider knowable, and what we ignore. We thus argue that epidemiologic theory should be fully acknowledged and debated in our research and training. It is, after all, epidemiologic theory, and not methodology, that distinguishes our discipline from other population-based sciences (for example, demography, quantitative sociology) equally concerned about valid study design, data analysis, and causal inference. Epidemiologic theory also distinguishes our field from other biomedical disciplines because their focus is solely on biological processes (for example, disease pathogenesis), whereas ours is on social and biological pathways that explain the distribution of disease in populations.

And it is the population experience of disease, in actual societies, that is the subject of our investigations. Epidemiologic theory reminds us that our work has a context, and that this context is human society. Ultimately, we are accountable for the knowledge we produce and its effects on the public's welfare.

2

COMMUNITY

The science of public health arose when methods of collecting data and statistical analysis for examining the health of populations were developed. But public health is not simply methods of determining rates of disease in populations. Public health must also be seen as collective action to improve the health of the community. This raises the question: What do we mean by "community"?

Community is one of the most important words in our democratic lexicon, perhaps second only to the idea of the individual. In its most basic meaning, *community* refers to our life together, and the attachments which sustain that life together. A community is not simply a group of people living in close proximity. A community has a life in common which stems from such things as a shared history, language, and values. The term *community* can apply to small groups, such as self-help groups, which share a common goal, or groups formed because of some shared crisis (like AIDS). It can also apply to very large groups, such as a nation which, despite the diversity of its members, has in common political institutions, symbols, and memories.

The term *community* has often been used as part of a critique of the conditions of contemporary life—a critique of industrial capitalism and its world of factories, mines, urban squalor, disease, and social injustice; this sort of generic critique was later broadened in the 20th century to include the scale of mass society and its lack of meaning and shared purpose. For these ills, many blamed the market and the aimlessness of consumer society; others blamed government and its projects, or liberalism and the freedom granted individuals to reject traditional values and go their own way.

Amongst the more egalitarian, *community* became a call to secure a dignified, safe existence for all, including the conditions which make people and communities healthy. Community also serves to unify the political community. The political community is seen as existing to provide security for its members, and security against disease and avoidable death is seen as unifying and making more cohesive the political community. Public health for the past 150 years has constantly altered and expanded its sense of just which health and safety challenges should be viewed as affecting the whole community and deserving of a collective response, including new institutions to guide that response. From the perspective of public health, community involves three closely related ideas:

1. Seeing health risks as common problems that effect the whole community. Seeing health risks as group threats rather than individual ones often results in challenges to the way in which market models of justice view these problems, which range from occupational risks to highway safety to class and race.

2. Using collective measures like regulation, policy, and new institutions to solve those problems. Building new regulation and institutions helps to "institutionalize" health and safety as permanently the responsibility of government at all levels, but especially at the national and state levels.

3. Finding solutions to common problems that strengthen and reaffirm our attachments to the community as a whole and that forge a more cohesive and more meaningful political community.

We have in recent political history in the United States an excellent example of this process of transforming our perception of our public problems and a more meaningful sense of ourselves as a national community. During the 1960s and early 1970s, advocates like Ralph Nader persuaded Congress to pass legislation that made automobiles safer and also made mines and factories safer and water and air cleaner. The success of this legislation caught many by surprise. Politics was supposed to be driven by the actions of organized, powerful interest groups. Advocates speaking on behalf of the whole community were not supposed to represent a real or influential constituency. James Q. Wilson argued that most public policies, before the health and safety legislation of the period, provided benefits to tightly organized and influential groups or powerful, cohesive majorities.[1] The new public health legislation seemed different, however. It conferred benefits on a large, diffuse, and poorly organized group—often the nation as a whole (as with air pollution controls or highway safety). Wilson found this puzzling because, in his words, the public *does not* usually think of itself as a community with common purposes or interests, and because public health legislation usually means painful cost imposed on powerful interests like the automobile industry or the steel industry (air pollution controls in these two examples), it is a wonder that legislation like this ever gets passed at all.

Jack Walker offered a different and more optimistic account of the rise of health and safety legislation. Walker argued that the victory of the public health legislation occurred *because* it expressed a powerful interest of the whole community.[2] Walker argued that such legislation makings cars, highways, mines, and smokestacks safer was attractive to elected officials *precisely because* they affect large numbers of people. Walker believes that the passage of health and safety legislation and the big victory over the automobile industry (the most powerful industry in the United States) constituted the breakthrough that opened the door to public health legislation for the next ten years. While the public that benefits from the policies is large and diffuse, it can be viewed, and can see itself, as possessing shared interests and purposes; in other words, it can see itself as a community that contains all segments of American society, including the most influential and active segments. Today, despite several decades of well-organized opposition to this legislation by business and others, there is little sentiment for making health and safety an entirely local or state issue.

The three selections for this chapter provide different but complementary approaches to the idea of community. In the first selection, Beauchamp argues that the field of public health represents an important if neglected tradition of community: the republican tradition. A republic (like the government of the United States) is a form of democracy that employs representative institutions to achieve common purposes and the common good. The republican tradition in the United States is reflected in our long legal and Constitutional traditions surrounding the development of the regulatory power to promote and protect the public's health. Laws requiring that people wear seat belts, that children be vaccinated before entering school, and that cars have antipollution devices are possible largely because of a republican legacy which permits limits to the rights of property and to individual liberty in order to protect the common good.

In the selection from his book, *Spheres of Justice: A Defense of Pluralism and Equality,* Michael Walzer provides a different but related argument about community. Walzer argues that measures like medical care and public health protections, which promote individual well-being, have another important function, namely, to strengthen individuals' attachment to the community. On this conception of community, a national health plan, for example, not only secures needed medical treatment to individuals but also reaffirms our collective identity as members of a society. In other words, when we face problems as a group and use group methods to solve our problems, we achieve both security for individuals and a stronger sense of community.

In the third selection in the chapter, Jonathan Mann advocates a human rights perspective for public health. A rights perspective is usually seen as individualistic and thus seemingly opposed to a community approach. However, Mann argues in favor of viewing public health as a human rights problem, in part to give it the urgency it deserves. At the same time, taking a public health approach helps to rectify the tendency among medical ethicists to ignore the social foundations of health, including divisions of race and class. While Mann employs a more individualistic discourse than does Walzer or Beauchamp, all three seek to develop health care as a communal responsibility that demands communal action.

NOTES

1. James Q. Wilson, ed., *The Politics of Regulation* (New York: Basic Books, 1980).

2. Jack L. Walker, "Setting the Agenda in the U.S. Senate: A Theory of Problem Selection," *British Journal of Political Science,* 7 (1977), pp. 423–445.

Community: The Neglected Tradition of Public Health

DAN E. BEAUCHAMP

What are the limits of government in protecting the health and safety of the public? As more and more states regulate personal behavior to protect the public health and safety, this question again becomes central. Can there be good reasons for public health paternalism in a democracy? Are health and safety individual interests, or also common and shared ends? . . .

THE MEANING OF THE COMMON GOOD

In one version of democratic theory, the state has no legitimate role in restricting personal conduct that is substantially voluntary and that has little or no direct consequence for anyone other than the individual. This strong antipaternalist position is associated with John Stuart Mill. In his essay, "On Liberty," which has deeply influenced American and British thought for over one hundred years, Mill wrote: "[t]he only purpose for which power can be rightfully exercised over any member of a civilized community, against his will, is to prevent harms to others." The exceptions are children and the incompetent. In this view the common good consists in maximizing the freedom of each individual to pursue his or her own interests, subject to a like freedom for every other individual. In the words of Blackstone, "The public good is in nothing more essentially interested than the protection of every individual's private rights."

In a second version, health and safety remain private interests but some paternalism is accepted, albeit reluctantly. As Joel Feinberg argues, common sense makes us reject a thoroughgoing antipaternalism. Many restrictions on liberty are relatively minor and the savings in life and limb extremely great. Further, often voluntary choices are not completely so; many choices are impaired in some sense. But, as Dennis Thompson contends, even where choices are not

From *The Hastings Center Report,* 15 (1985), 28–36. Copyright © The Hastings Center. Reproduced by permission.

impaired, as in the choice not to wear seatbelts or to take up smoking, paternalism might still be accepted, because the alternative would be a great loss of life and a society in which each citizen was, for many important decisions, left alone with the consequences of his or her choice.

This reluctant acceptance of paternalism leaves many democrats uneasy. Another alternative is to redefine voluntary risks to an individual as risks to others. Indeed, many argue that all such risks have serious consequences for others, and that the state may therefore limit such activities on the basis of the harm principle. Others challenge the category of voluntariness head on, arguing that most such risks, like cigarettes and alcohol use, have powerful social determinants.

The constitutional basis for the protection of the public health and safety has largely been ignored in this debate. This tradition, and particularly the regulatory power (often called the police power), flows from a view of democracy that sees the essential task of government as protecting and promoting *both* private and group interests. Government is supposed to defend both sets of interests through an evolving set of practices and institutions, and it is left to the legislatures to determine which set of interests predominate when conflicts arise.

In the constitutional tradition, the common good refers to the welfare of individuals considered as a group, the public or the people generally, the "body politic" or the "commonwealth" as it was termed in the early days of the American Republic. The public or the people were presumed to have an interest, held in common, in self-protection or preservation from threats of all kinds to their welfare. The commonwealth idea was widely influential among New England states during the first half of the nineteenth century.

The commonwealth doctrine helped shape the regulatory power in Massachusetts and throughout the U.S. The central principles underlying the police or regulatory power were the treatment of health and safety as a shared purpose and need of the community and (aside from basic constitutional rights such as due process) the subordination of the market, property, and individual liberty to protect compelling community interests.

This republican image of democracy was a blending of social contract and republican thought, as well as Judeo-Christian notions of covenant. In the republican vision of society, the individual has a dual status. On the one hand, individuals have private interests and private rights; political association serves to protect these rights. On the other hand, individuals are members of a political community—a body politic.

This common citizenship, despite diversity and divergence of interests, presumes an underlying shared set of loyalties and obligations to support the ends of the political community, among which public health and safety are central. In this scheme, public health and safety are not simply the aggregate of each private individual's interest in health and safety, interests which can be pursued more effectively through collective action. Public health and safety are community or group interests (often referred to as "state interests" in the law), interests that can transcend and take priority over private interests if the legislature so chooses.

The idea of democracy as promoting the common or group interest is captured in Joseph Tussman's classic work on political obligation: "Familiar as it is, there is something fundamentally misleading about the slogan that the aim of government is 'the welfare of the individual' . . . [T]he government's concern for the individual is not to be understood as special concern for *this* or *that* individual but rather as concern for all individuals. Government, that is to say, serves the welfare of the community."

This emphasis on the *public's* health has never meant that the state's power to protect health and safety is unlimited. It has meant that individual liberty and the institutions of the market and private property, operating in the public world, are subject to a developing set of practices designed to defend the common life and the community. Although we call markets "private," all markets operate within the public or common world shared by individual members of the community.

Beyond this public world, which includes the market and collective spheres, there is the private or personal sphere where each individual is devoted to his own. As Hannah Arendt noted, "Throughout his life man moves constantly within what is his *own,* and he also moves in a sphere that is *common* to him and his fellow men. The 'public good,' the concerns of the citizen, is indeed the common good because it is localized in the *world* which we have in common *without* owning it."

It is the private sphere that is problematic for public health. Public health sometimes intrudes into this private sphere in the interest of the health and safety of the community. But, as we shall see in the development of the regulatory or police power, the main thrust has been to focus on the controlling conditions in the public world, particularly by shaping the institutions of the market and private property.

EMERGENCE OF POLICE POWER

In 1850, the Massachusetts Sanitary Commission presented its *Report* to the state legislature. Lemuel Shattuck, a member of the legislature, was the chief author. The guiding definition of public health was set out in the opening pages:

> The condition of perfect *public health* requires such laws and regulations, as will secure to man associated in society, the same sanitary enjoyments that he would have as an isolated individual; and as will protect him from injury from any influ-

ences connected with his locality, his dwelling-house, his occupation, or those of his associates or neighbors, or from any other social causes. It is under the control of public authority, and public administration; and life and health may be saved or lost, and they are actually saved or lost, as this authority is wisely or unwisely exercised.

Shattuck's report clearly accepts the existence of a public realm that is the legitimate object of government intervention to protect the public health, and that requires the alteration of the existing system of property rights and the regulation of the marketplace for its protection.

In Massachusetts, during the same period when the Sanitary Commission's *Report* was issued, a parallel development in legislation and in law sought to alter the system of rights surrounding private property. The goal was to facilitate rapid economic development on the one hand, and at the same time to permit the state to control and monitor that development in order to protect the public's health and safety.

The commonwealth idea was a direct legacy of eighteenth-century American and English radical republican opposition to the Crown, a body of political thought that powerfully shaped the American revolutionary tradition. The primacy of the public or the common good over private interests and the use of the powers of legislation to regulate the economy and protect the health and safety of the community were central to this body of republican thought.

Our root ideas about health and safety policy can be traced to these early state policies. As a leading constitutional scholar, Leonard Levy, has argued: "[T]he police power may be regarded as the legal expression of the Commonwealth idea, for it signifies the supremacy of public over private rights. To call the police power a Massachusetts doctrine would be an exaggeration, though not a great one. [I]t is certainly no coincidence that in Massachusetts, with its Commonwealth tradition, the police power was first defined and carried to great extremes from the standpoint of vested interests."

Apparently, Chief Justice John Marshall was the first to coin the term "police power" in referring to the powers of the states to regulate public health and safety matters in the classic case of *Gibbons v. Ogden* in 1824. Marshall was attempting to clarify the boundary between these powers and the powers of Congress over interstate commerce: "[Police] powers form a portion of that immense mass of legislation which embraces everything within the territory of the state, not surrendered to the general government; all which can advantageously be exercised by the states themselves. Inspection laws, quarantine laws, health laws of every description . . . are component parts of this mass."

The classic definition of the police power was established in *Commonwealth v. Alger* (1851), a decision written by Chief Justice Shaw of the Massachusetts Supreme Court. In this case, Shaw established the basic premises of the police power of the states. His broad definition of this power remains the most influential to this date: "The power we allude to is . . . the police power, the power vested in the legislature by the constitution, to make, ordain and establish all manner of wholesome and reasonable laws, statutes and ordinances, either with penalties or without, not repugnant to the constitution, as they shall judge to be for the good and welfare of the commonwealth, and of the subjects of the same."

In this decision Justice Shaw was ruling on what might seem a minor issue. The case involved a man who owned property on Boston Harbor and who built a wharf that extended beyond a boundary to the public right of way established by the legislature. When the state ordered him to take it down, he went to court, arguing that the legislature had interfered with his property, and that it had not been demonstrated or even argued that his wharf constituted a nuisance or a harm to anyone.

As Levy noted (in referring to another case), great principles are often decided in cases of little factual interest. In the *Alger* decision, Shaw set out the basic premise underlying the police power: "We think it is a settled principle, growing out of the nature of a well ordered civil society, that every holder of property, however absolute and unqualified may be his title, holds it under the implied liability that his use of it may be so regulated, that it shall not be injurious to the equal enjoyment of others having an equal right to the enjoyment of their property in this commonwealth."

To Shaw, the idea of the "common good" implied the health, safety, or welfare of the citizens of Massachusetts. This common interest in health and safety was not adequately protected by common law principles governing the use of property. The common interest in health and safety could only be adequately protected through legislation and regulations affecting the whole people. The common law doctrine regulating the use of property was: *Sic utere tuo ut alienum non laedas* ("Use your own property in such a manner as not to injure that of another").

In *Alger,* Shaw greatly broadened this principle from a case-by-case investigation of whether each citizen had harmed the interest of another, to a broad instrument for the control of property potentially injurious to the interests of the community. As Shaw argued, "Things done may or may not be wrong in themselves, or necessarily injurious and punishable as such at common law, but laws are passed declaring them offenses, and making them punishable, because they tend to injurious consequences."

According to Levy, Shaw "believed that the general welfare required the anticipation and prevention of prospective wrongs from the use of private property." As Ernest Freund argued decades later, the common law of nuisance could deal with evils only after they came into existence: "The police power endeavors to prevent evil by checking the tendency toward it, and it seeks to place a margin of safety between that which is permitted and that which is sure to lead to injury or loss. This can be accomplished . . . by establishing positive standards and limitations which must be observed, although to step beyond them would not necessarily create a nuisance at law."

In perhaps the second most influential police power decision of the nineteenth century, *Munn v. Illinois* (1876), the Supreme Court affirmed these basic principles. The case involved the state of Illinois and its regulation of grain operators' rates in Chicago. Justice Field, arguing for the minority, stated that the market was essentially a private institution: "The business of a warehouseman was, at common law, a private business, and is so in its nature. It has no special privileges connected with it, nor did the law ever extend to it any greater protection than it extended to all other private business."

But Chief Justice Waite, arguing for the majority, disagreed: "Property does become clothed with a public interest when used in a manner to make it of public consequence, and affect the community at large. When, therefore, one devotes his property to a use in which the public has an interest, he, in effect, grants to the public an interest in that use, and must submit to be controlled by the public for the common good, to the extent of the interest he has thus created."

All authorities agree that the police power is very extensive and checked only by express grants of the Constitution to protect basic rights. There is still recurring disagreement on the underlying principle of the regulatory power. Some scholars argue that the basic principle of the regulatory power remains *sic utere*. But other scholars reject this view. For example, Ernest Freund, in one of the most thorough studies of the regulatory power of any period, argues that "[N]o community confines its care of the public welfare to the enforcement of the principles of the common law . . . it exercises its compulsory powers for the prevention . . . of wrong by narrowing common law rights . . . and [through] positive regulations which are not confined to wrongful acts. It is this latter kind of state control which constitutes the essence of the police power."

THE RELEVANCE OF COMMUNITY

This is a crucial issue because on it turns the relevance of the category of the community for the regulatory power. If the regulatory power is simply the enforcement—writ large—of the law that no one should use his or her property in a manner that offends another individual's interests, then the category of community is rendered meaningless. But as W. G. Hastings, another leading scholar of the police power, pointed out, if this power was limited only to prevent harms to others, this doesn't explain why courts uniformly supported the drastic regulation of alcohol by the states. Although judges often pointed to the evil that drinking causes for others than themselves (such as their families or their employers), it was plain to everyone that regulating the "liquor traffic" involved limiting actions that harmed mostly the drinkers themselves. The temperance and prohibition campaigns, first in the 1950s and later at the turn of the century, to control legally and even destroy the alcohol trade provided some of the strongest and clearest rulings of the courts on the police powers.

Perhaps the most significant case testing the constitutionality of state prohibition was *Mugler v. Kansas* (1887). *Mugler* concerned a brewery owner charged with making beer after a state constitutional amendment forbade the manufacture, sale, and use of alcoholic beverages. Plaintiff's counsel argued that the Kansas constitutional amendment was an attempt to regulate purely personal conduct not subject to a compelling state interest. Counsel quoted Mill and the common law principles of *sic utere* as the basic founding principles of the English and American legal tradition. As counsel for the plaintiff argued: "If a state convention or legislature can punish a citizen for manufacturing beer . . . for his own use, then instead of civil liberty, we are living under the most unlimited and brutal despotism known in history. . . . Broad and comprehensive as this [police] power is, it cannot extend to the individual tastes and habits of the citizen, which are confined entirely to himself and have no effect upon others."

The Supreme Court ruled against the plaintiff and held for the state of Kansas. Justice Harlan, writing for the majority, had this to say:

> There is no justification for holding that the State under the guise merely of police regulations, is aiming to deprive the citizen of his constitutional rights: for we cannot shut out of view the fact, within the knowledge of all, that the public health, the public morals, and the public safety, may be endangered by the general use of intoxicating drinks. . . . So far from such a regulation having no relation to the general end sought to be accomplished, the entire scheme of prohibition, as embodied in the [state] constitution and laws of Kansas, might fail, if the right of each citizen to manufacture intoxicating liquors for his own use as a beverage were recognized. . . . Such a right does not inhere in citizenship. Nor can it be said that government interferes with or impairs any one's constitutional rights of liberty or of property. . . . Those rights are best secured in our government, by the observance, upon the part of all, of such regulations as are established by competent authority, to promote the common good.

The Court did not, and could not, pass judgment on the *wisdom* of the state prohibition measures. This judgment, in a republican scheme of government, rests with the legislative body. But the Court did affirm the basic political principles underlying the powers of the states to control and limit the market and private property to protect the health and safety of the citizenry. During the last decades of the nineteenth century, the Supreme Court capitulated to corporate and extreme laissez-faire interests. During this period the Court sought to block the states' power to improve the working conditions for labor, and to facilitate union organization against capital. Even so, the Court continued to uphold striking powers for the states to regulate property when the health and safety of the general citizenry was at stake.

CONTEMPORARY PUBLIC HEALTH PROBLEMS

Several twentieth-century developments have obscured the philosophical roots of the regulatory power, especially as they work to protect the public health. Because the locus of action for protecting the health and safety of the public has swung to the federal government and because the justification for this federal power lies primarily with the commerce clause of the Constitution, the group principle behind public health has tended to be subordinated to the language of individual rights.

The political justification of public health has also tended to be ignored. Most contemporary legal scholars cite the 1905 Supreme Court decision, *Jacobson v. Massachusetts,* as the leading case underlying public health. *Jacobson* dealt with a Cambridge, Massachusetts ordinance requiring compulsory vaccination in a smallpox outbreak. The language of *Jacobson* contains an exemplary and classical defense of the regulatory power, but the facts of the case focus on the control of epidemics, and the overriding necessity for requiring compulsory vaccination to prevent the spread of infection. This has encouraged many scholars to interpret the regulatory power for protecting the public health on the more narrow grounds of preventing injury to others, and to overlook the use of this power to limit liberty in the market or other areas of the public realm, even if such restriction does not protect the interests of other specific individuals.

The two most recent constitutional controversies regarding public health policy and the police power are the fluoridation and the motorcycle helmet controversies. Once again these controversies show the courts willing to accept public health paternalism. However, in the case of the helmet decisions, sometimes the broad principles of the regulatory power have tended to be replaced by spurious legal reasoning.

State supreme courts have unanimously upheld the constitutionality of both measures, and the U.S. Supreme Court has refused to review fluoridation cases, presumably because they pose no threats to constitutional rights. Plaintiffs have argued that fluoridation is an attempt to employ mass medication and constitutes a violation of individual autonomy in an area that is properly private. They have argued that the use of the regulatory power to control private rights was only justified in the past by the threat of contagious diseases. . .

The courts have been less consistent on the question of helmet laws for motorcyclists. Although state supreme courts have unanimously supported the state's power to require helmet usage, the decisions have often introduced as additional justification the danger unhelmeted cyclists pose for others on the road, or the possibility that unprotected cyclists may become wards of the state. . . .

THE LANGUAGE OF PUBLIC HEALTH

What are we to make of this constitutional tradition surrounding the development of the regulatory power for health and safety? What relevance does it have for the policy disputes of today, particularly those concerning the limitation of lifestyle risks?

The constitutional tradition for public health constitutes one of those "second languages" of republicanism that Robert Bellah and his coauthors speak of in their recent book, *Habits of the Heart*. In their book, the first language (or tradition of moral discourse) of American politics is political individualism. But there are "second languages" of community rooted in the republican and biblical tradition that limit and qualify the scope and consequences of political individualism.

Public health as a second language reminds us that we are not only individuals, we are also a community and a body politic, and that we have shared commitments to one another and promises to keep. As the Preamble to the Massachusetts Constitution puts it:

> The end of the institution, maintenance and administration of government is to secure the existence of the body-politic; to protect; and to furnish the individuals who compose it, with the power of enjoying, in safety and tranquility, their natural rights, and the blessings of life. . . . The body-politic is a social compact, by which the whole people covenants with each citizen, and each citizen with the whole people, that all shall be governed by certain laws for the common good.

The danger is that we can come to discuss public health exclusively within the dominant discourse of political individualism, relying either on the harm principle or a narrow paternalism justified on grounds of self-protection alone. By ignoring the communitarian language of public health, we risk shrinking its claims. We also risk undermining the sense in which health and safety are a signal commitment of the common life—a central *practice* by which the body-politic defines itself and affirms its values.

In *Habits of the Heart*, practices are those shared activities that are not purely instrumental and that help shape and affirm the common life. Practices can be religious, aesthetic, or ethical. Public health belongs to the realm of the political and the ethical. Public health belongs to the ethical because it is concerned not only with explaining the occurrence of illness and disease in society, but also with ameliorating them. Beyond instrumental goals, public health is concerned with integrative goals—expressing the commitment of the whole people to face the threat of death and disease in solidarity.

Public health is also a practical science. Spanning the world of science and practical action, it seeks reasonable and practical means of altering property arrangements or limiting liberty to promote the health of the public generally.

These two ideas, the ideas of second languages and of social practices, shed light on why paternalism—at least public health paternalism—plays an affirmative role in the republican tradition. In the constitutional categories for protecting the public health, the regulatory power is to protect not individual citizens, but rather citizens considered as a group, the public health. In this tradition, the public, as well as the community itself, has a reality apart from the citizens who comprise it. Fundamental constituents of the community and the common life are its practices and institutions.

Practices are communal in nature, and concerned with the well-being of the community as a whole and not just the well-being of any particular person. Policy, and here public health paternalism, operates at the level of practices and not at the level of individual behavior. . . .

This suggests that public health paternalism and the language of community on which it is based fit the parent-child analogy very poorly. To Mill, all paternalism was wrong because the individual is best placed to know his own good: "He is the person most interested in his own well-being: the interest which any other person, except in cases of strong personal attachment, can have in it, is trifling. . . . "

But precisely because public health paternalism is aimed at the group and its practices, and not the specific individual, Mill's point is wrong. The good of the particular person is not the aim of health policy in a democracy which defends both the community and the individual. In fact, Mill is wrong twice, because particular individuals are often very poorly placed to judge the effects that market arrangements and practices have on the population as a whole. This is the task for legislatures, for organized groups of citizens, and for other agents of the public, including the citizen as voter.

Mill's dichotomy of either the harm principle or self-protection is too limited; the world of harms is not exhausted by self-imposed and other-imposed injuries. There is a third and very large set of problems that afflicts the community as a whole and that results primarily from inadequate safeguards over the practices of the common life. Economists and others often refer to this class of harms as "summing up problems" or "choice-in-the-small versus choice-in-the-large."

Creating, extending, or strengthening the practices of public health—and the collective goods principle that underlies it—ought to be the primary justification for our health and safety policy. Instead we usually base these regulations on the harm principle. We usually justify regulating the steel or coal industry on the grounds that workers and the general public have the risks of pollution or black lung visited on them, but consumers are not obliged to drink alcohol or smoke cigarettes. While this may be true, in the communitarian language and categories of public health, fixing blame is not the main point. We regulate the steel or coal industry because market competition undervalues collective goods like a clean environment or workers' safety. Using social organization to secure collective goods like public health, not preventing harms to others, is the proper rationale for health and safety regulations imposed on the steel or coal industry, or the alcohol or cigarette industry. . . .

Stengthening the public health includes not only the practical task of improving aggregate welfare, it also involves the task of reacquainting the American public with its republican and communitarian heritage, and encouraging citizens to share in reasonable and practical group schemes to promote a wider welfare, of which their own welfare is only a part. In political individualism, seatbelt legislation or signs on the beach restricting swimming when a lifeguard is not present restrict the individual's liberty for his or her own good. In this circumstance the appropriate slogan is: "The life you save may be your own." But in the second language of public health these restrictions define a common practice which shapes our life together, for the general or the common good. In the language of public health, the motto for such "paternalistic" legislation might be: "The lives we save together might include your own."

Security and Welfare

MICHAEL WALZER

MEMBERSHIP AND NEED

Membership is important because of what the members of a political community owe to one another and to no one else, or to no one else in the same degree. And the first thing they owe is the communal provision of security and welfare. This claim might be reversed: communal provision is important because it teaches us the value of membership. If we did not provide for one another, if we recognized no distinction between members and strangers, we would have no reason to form and maintain political communities. 'How shall men love their country', Rousseau asked, 'if it is nothing more for them than for strangers, and bestows on them only that which it can refuse to none?' Rousseau believed that citizens ought to love their country and therefore that their country ought to give them particular reasons to do so. Membership (like kinship) is a special relation. It's not enough to say, as Edmund Burke did, that 'to make us love our country, our country ought to be lovely.' The crucial thing is that it be lovely for us—though we always hope that it will be lovely for others (we also love its reflected loveliness).

Political community for the sake of provision, provision for the sake of community: the process works both ways, and that is perhaps its crucial feature. Philosophers and political theorists have been too quick to turn it into a simple calculation. Indeed, we are rationalists of everyday life; we come together, we sign the social contract or reiterate the signing of it, in order to provide for our needs. And we value the contract insofar as those needs are met. But one of our needs is community itself: culture, religion, and politics. It is only under the aegis of these three that all the other things we need become *socially recognized needs,* take on historical and determinate form. The social contract is an agreement to reach decisions together about what goods are necessary to our common life, and then to provide those goods for one another. The signers owe

From Chapter 3 (partial) in *Spheres of Justice: A Defense of Pluralism and Equality* by Michael Walzer. Copyright © 1983 by Basic Books, Inc. Reprinted by permission of BasicBooks, a subsidiary of Perseus Books Group, LLC, and also Blackwell Publishers.

one another more than mutual aid, for that they owe or can owe to anyone. They owe mutual provision of all those things for the sake of which they have separated themselves from mankind as a whole and joined forces in a particular community. *Amour social* is one of those things; but though it is a distributed good—often unevenly distributed—it arises only in the course of other distributions (and of the political choices that the other distributions require). Mutual provision breeds mutuality. So the common life is simultaneously the prerequisite of provision and one of its products.

Men and women come together because they literally cannot live apart. But they can live together in many different ways. Their survival and then their well-being require a common effort: against the wrath of the gods, the hostility of other people, the indifference and malevolence of nature (famine, flood, fire, and disease), the brief transit of a human life. Not army camps alone, as David Hume wrote, but temples, storehouses, irrigation works, and burial grounds are the true mothers of cities. As the list suggests, origins are not singular in character. Cities differ from one another, partly because of the natural environments in which they are built and the immediate dangers their builders encounter, partly because of the conceptions of social goods that the builders hold. They recognize but also create one another's needs and so give a particular shape to what I will call the 'sphere of security and welfare'. The sphere itself is as old as the oldest human community. Indeed, one might say that the original community is a sphere of security and welfare, a system of communal provision, distorted, no doubt, by gross inequalities of strength and cunning. But the system has, in any case, no natural form. Different experiences and different conceptions lead to different patterns of provision. Though there are some goods that are needed absolutely, there is no good such that once we see it, we know how it stands *vis-à-vis* all other goods and how much of it we owe to one another. The nature of a need is not self-evident.

Communal provision is both general and particular. It is general whenever public funds are spent so as to benefit all or most of the members without any distribution to individuals. It is particular whenever goods are actually handed over to all or any of the members.* Water, for example, is one of the bare requirements of civil life', and the building of reservoirs is a form of general provision. But the delivery of water to one rather than to another neighbour-

---

*I don't mean to reiterate here the technical distinction that economists make between public and private goods. General provision is always public, at least on the less stringent definitions of that term (which specify only that public goods are those that can't be provided to some and not to other members of the community). So are most forms of particular provision, for even goods delivered to individuals generate non-exclusive benefits for the community as a whole. Scholarships to orphans, for example, are private to the orphans, public to the community of citizens within which the orphans will one day work and vote. But public goods of this latter sort, which depend upon prior distributions to particular persons or groups, have been controversial in many societies; and I have designed my categories so as to enable me to examine them closely.

hood (where, say, the wealthier citizens live) is particular. The securing of the food supply is general; the distribution of food to widows and orphans is particular. Public health is most often general, the care of the sick, most often particular. Sometimes the criteria for general and particular provision will differ radically. The building of temples and the organization of religious services is an example of general provision designed to meet the needs of the community as a whole, but communion with the gods may be allowed only to particularly meritorious members (or it may be sought privately in secret or in noncomformist sects). The system of justice is a general good, meeting common needs; but the actual distribution of rewards and punishments may serve the particular needs of a ruling class, or it may be organized, as we commonly think it should be, to give individuals what they individually deserve. Simone Weil has argued that, with regard to justice, need operates at both the general and the particular levels, since criminals need to be punished. But that is an idiosyncratic use of the word *need*. More likely, the punishment of criminals is something only the rest of us need. But need does operate both generally and particularly for other goods: health care is an obvious example that I will later consider in some detail.

Despite the inherent forcefulness of the word, needs are elusive. People don't just have needs, they have ideas about their needs; they have priorities, they have degrees of need; and these priorities and degrees are related not only to their human nature but also to their history and culture. Since resources are always scarce, hard choices have to be made. I suspect that these can only be political choices. They are subject to a certain philosophical elucidation, but the idea of need and the commitment to communal provision do not by themselves yield any clear determination of priorities or degrees. Clearly we can't meet, and we don't have to meet, every need to the same degree or any need to the ultimate degree. The ancient Athenians, for example, provided public baths and gymnasiums for the citizens but never provided anything remotely resembling unemployment insurance or social security. They made a choice about how to spend public funds, a choice shaped presumably by their understanding of what the common life required. It would be hard to argue that they made a mistake. I suppose there are notions of need that would yield such a conclusion, but these would not be notions acceptable to—they might not even be comprehensible to—the Athenians themselves.

The question of degree suggests even more clearly the importance of political choice and the irrelevance of any merely philosophical stipulation. Needs are not only elusive; they are also expansive. In the phrase of the contemporary philosopher Charles Fried, needs are voracious; they eat up resources. But it would be wrong to suggest that therefore need cannot be a distributive principle. It is, rather, a principle subject to political limitation; and the limits (within limits) can be arbitrary, fixed by some temporary coalition of interests or majority of voters. Consider the case of physical security in a modern American city. We could provide absolute security, eliminate every source of violence except domestic violence, if we put a street light every ten yards and stationed a policeman every thirty yards throughout the city. But that would be very expensive, and so we settle for something less. How much less can only be decided politically.* One can imagine the sorts of things that would figure in the debates. Above all, I think, there would be a certain understanding—more or less widely shared, controversial only at the margins—of what constitutes 'enough' security or of what level of insecurity is simply intolerable. The decision would also be affected by other factors: alternative needs, the state of the economy, the agitation of the policemen's union, and so on. But whatever decision is ultimately reached, for whatever reasons, security is provided because the citizens need it. And because, at some level, they all need it, the criterion of need remains a critical standard (as we shall see) even though it cannot determine priority and degree. . . .

THE EXTENT OF PROVISION

Distributive justice in the sphere of welfare and security has a twofold meaning: it refers, first to the recognition of need and, second, to the recognition of membership. Goods must be provided to needy members because of their neediness, but they must also be provided in such a way as to sustain their membership. It's not the case, however, that members have a claim on any specific set of goods. Welfare rights are fixed only when a community adopts some programme of mutual provision. There are strong arguments to be made that, under given historical conditions, such-and-such a programme should be adopted. But these are not arguments about individual rights; they are arguments about the character of a particular political community. No one's rights were violated because the Athenians did not allocate public funds for the education of children. Perhaps they believed, and perhaps they were right, that the public life of the city was education enough.

The right that members can legitimately claim is of a more general sort. It undoubtedly includes some version of the Hobbesian right to life, some claim on communal resources for bare subsistence. No community can allow its members to starve to death when there is food available to feed them; no government can stand passively by at such a time—not if it claims to be a government of or by or for the community. The indifference of Britain's rulers during the Irish potato famine in the 1840s is a sure sign that Ireland was a colony, a

---

*And should be decided politically: that is what democratic political arrangements are for. Any philosophical effort to stipulate in detail the rights or the entitlements of individuals would radically constrain the scope of democratic decision making. I have argued this point elsewhere.

conquered land, no real part of Great Britain. This is not to justify the indifference—one has obligations to colonies and to conquered peoples—but only to suggest that the Irish would have been better served by a government, virtually any government, of their own. Perhaps Burke came closest to describing the fundamental right that is at stake here when he wrote: 'Government is a contrivance of human wisdom to provide for human wants. Men have a right that these wants should be provided for by this wisdom.' It only has to be said that the wisdom in question is the wisdom not of a ruling class, as Burke seems to have thought, but of the community as a whole. Only its culture, its character, its common understandings can define the 'wants' that are to be provided for. But culture, character, and common understandings are not givens; they don't operate automatically; at any particular moment, the citizens must argue about the extent of mutual provision.

They argue about the meaning of the social contract, the original and reiterated conception of the sphere of security and welfare. This is not a hypothetical or an ideal contract of the sort John Rawls has described. Rational men and women in the original position, deprived of all particular knowledge of their social standing and cultural understanding, would probably opt, as Rawls has argued, for an equal distribution of whatever goods they were told they needed. But this formula doesn't help very much in determining what choices people will make, or what choices they should make, once they know who and where they are. In a world of particular cultures, competing conceptions of the good, scarce resources, elusive and expansive needs, there isn't going to be a single formula, universally applicable. There isn't going to be a single universally approved path that carries us from a notion like, say, 'fair shares' to a comprehensive list of the goods to which that notion applies. Fair shares of what?

Justice, tranquillity, defence, welfare, and liberty: that is the list provided by the United States Constitution. One could construe it as an exhaustive list, but the terms are vague; they provide at best a starting point for public debate. The standard appeal in that debate is to a larger idea: the Burkeian general right, which takes on determinate force only under determinate conditions and requires different sorts of provision in different times and places. The idea is simply that we have come together, shaped a community, in order to cope with difficulties and dangers that we could not cope with alone. And so whenever we find ourselves confronted with difficulties and dangers of that sort, we look for communal assistance. As the balance of individual and collective capacity changes, so the kinds of assistance that are looked for change, too.

The history of public health in the West might usefully be told in these terms. Some minimal provision is very old, as the Greek and Jewish examples suggest; the measures adopted were a function of the community's sense of danger and the extent of its medical knowledge. Over the years, living arrangements on a larger scale bred new dangers, and scientific advance generated a new sense of danger and a new awareness of the possibilities of coping. And then groups of citizens pressed for a wider programme of communal provision, exploiting the new science to reduce the risks of urban life. That, they might rightly say, is what the community is for. A similar argument can be made in the case of social security. The very success of general provision in the field of public health has greatly extended the span of a normal human life and then also the span of years during which men and women are unable to support themselves, during which they are physically but most often not socially, politically, or morally incapacitated. Once again, support for the disabled is one of the oldest and most common forms of particular provision. But now it is required on a much larger scale than ever before. Families are overwhelmed by the costs of old age and look for help to the political community. Exactly what ought to be done will be a matter of dispute. Words like *health, danger, science,* even *old age,* have very different meanings in different cultures; no external specification is possible. But this is not to say that it won't be clear enough to the people involved that something—some particular set of things—ought to be done.

Perhaps these examples are too easy. Disease is a general threat; old age, a general prospect. Not so unemployment and poverty, which probably lie beyond the ken of many well-to-do people. The poor can always be isolated, locked into ghettos, blamed and punished for their own misfortune. At this point, it might be said, provision can no longer be defended by invoking anything like the 'meaning' of the social contract. But let us look more closely at the easy cases; for, in fact, they involve all the difficulties of the difficult ones. Public health and social security invite us to think of the political community, in T. H. Marshall's phrase, as a 'mutual benefit club'. All provision is reciprocal; the members take turns providing and being provided for, much as Aristotle's citizens take turns ruling and being ruled. This is a happy picture, and one that is really understandable in contractualist terms. It is not only the case that rational agents, knowing nothing of their specific situation, would agree to these two forms of provision; the real agents, the ordinary citizens, of every modern democracy have in fact agreed to them. The two are, or so it appears, equally in the interests of hypothetical and of actual people. Coercion is only necessary in practice because some minority of actual people don't understand, or don't consistently understand, their real interests. Only the reckless and the improvident need to be forced to contribute—and it can always be said of them that they joined in the social contract precisely in order to protect themselves against their own recklessness and improvidence. In fact, however, the reasons for coercion go much deeper than this; the political community is something more than a mutual benefit club; and the extent of communal provision in any given case—what it is and what it should be—is determined by conceptions of need that are more problematic than the argument thus far suggests.

Consider again the case of public health. No communal provision is possible here without the constraint of a wide range of activities profitable to individual members of the community but threatening to some larger number. Even something so simple, for example, as the provision of uncontaminated milk to large urban populations requires extensive public control; and control is a political achievement, the result (in the United States) of bitter struggles, over many years, in one city after another. When the farmers or the middlemen of the dairy industry defended free enterprise, they were certainly acting rationally in their own interests. The same thing can be said of other entrepreneurs who defend themselves against the constraints of inspection, regulation, and enforcement. Public activities of these sorts may be of the highest value to the rest of us; they are not of the highest value to all of us. Though I have taken public health as an example of general provision, it is provided only at the expense of some members of the community. Moreover, it benefits most the most vulnerable of the others: thus, the special importance of the building code for those who live in crowded tenements, and of anti-pollution laws for those who live in the immediate vicinity of factory smokestacks or water drains. Social security, too, benefits the most vulnerable members, even if, for reasons I have already suggested, the actual payments are the same for everyone. For the well-to-do can, or many of them think they can, help themselves even in time of trouble and would much prefer not to be forced to help anyone else. The truth is that every serious effort at communal provision (insofar as the income of the community derives from the wealth of its members) is redistributive in character. The benefits it provides are not, strictly speaking, mutual.

Once again, rational agents ignorant of their own social standing would agree to such a redistribution. But they would agree too easily, and their agreement doesn't help us understand what sort of a redistribution is required: How much? For what purposes? In practice, redistribution is a political matter, and the coercion it involves is foreshadowed by the conflicts that rage over its character and extent. Every particular measure is pushed through by some coalition of particular interests. But the ultimate appeal in these conflicts is not to the particular interests, not even to a public interest conceived as their sum, but to collective values, shared understandings of membership, health, food and shelter, work and leisure. The conflicts themselves are often focused, at least overtly, on questions of fact; the understandings are assumed. Thus the entrepreneurs of the dairy industry denied as long as they could the connection between contaminated milk and tuberculosis. But once that connection was established, it was difficult for them to deny that milk should be inspected: *caveat emptor* was not, in such a case, a plausible doctrine. Similarly, in the debates over old-age pensions in Great Britain, politicians mostly agreed on the traditional British value of self-help but disagreed sharply about whether self-help was still possible through the established working-class friendly societies. These were real mutual-benefit clubs organized on a strictly voluntary basis, but they seemed about to be overwhelmed by the growing numbers of the aged. It became increasingly apparent that the members simply did not have the resources to protect themselves and one another from poverty in old age. And few British politicians were prepared to say that they should be left unprotected.

Here, then, is a more precise account of the social contract: it is an agreement to redistribute the resources of the members in accordance with some shared understanding of their needs, subject to ongoing political determination in detail. The contract is a moral bond. It connects the strong and the weak, the lucky and the unlucky, the rich and the poor, creating a union that transcends all differences of interest, drawing its strength from history, culture, religion, language, and so on. Arguments about communal provision are, at the deepest level, interpretations of that union. The closer and more inclusive it is, the wider the recognition of needs, the greater the number of social goods that are drawn into the sphere of security and welfare. I don't doubt that many political communities have redistributed resources on very different principles, not in accordance with the needs of the members generally but in accordance with the power of the wellborn or the wealthy. But that, as Rousseau suggested in his *Discourse on Inequality,* makes a fraud of the social contract. In any community, where resources are taken away from the poor and given to the rich, the rights of the poor are being violated. The wisdom of the community is not engaged in providing for their wants. Political debate about the nature of those wants will have to be repressed, else the fraud will quickly be exposed. When all the members share in the business of interpreting the social contract, the result will be a more or less extensive system of communal provision. If all states are in principle welfare states, democracies are most likely to be welfare states in practice. Even the imitation of democracy breeds welfarism, as in the 'people's democracies', where the state protects the people against every disaster except those that it inflicts on them itself.

So democratic citizens argue among themselves and opt for many different sorts of security and welfare, extending far beyond my 'easy' examples of public health and old-age pensions. The category of socially recognized needs is open-ended. For the people's sense of what they need encompasses not only life itself but also the good life, and the appropriate balance between these two is itself a matter of dispute. The Athenian drama and the Jewish academies were both financed with money that could have been spent on housing, say, or on medicine. But drama and education were taken by Greeks and Jews to be not merely enhancements of the common life but vital aspects of communal welfare. I want to stress again that these are not judgements that can easily be called incorrect.

AN AMERICAN WELFARE STATE

What sort of communal provision is appropriate in a society like our own? It's not my purpose here to anticipate the outcomes of democratic debate or to stipulate in detail the extent or the forms of provision. But it can be argued, I think, that the citizens of a modern industrial democracy owe a great deal to one another, and the argument will provide a useful opportunity to test the critical force of the principles I have defended up until now: that every political community must attend to the needs of its members as they collectively understand those needs; that the goods that are distributed must be distributed in proportion to need; and that the distribution must recognize and uphold the underlying equality of membership. These are very general principles; they are meant to apply to a wide range of communities—to any community, in fact, where the members are each other's equals (before God or the law), or where it can plausibly be said that, however they are treated in fact, they ought to be each other's equals. The principles probably don't apply to a community organized hierarchically, as in traditional India, where the fruits of the harvest are distributed not according to need but according to caste—or rather, as Louis Dumont has written, where 'the needs of each are conceived to be different, depending on [his] caste.' Everyone is guaranteed a share, so Dumont's Indian village is still a welfare state, 'a sort of co-operative where the main aim is to ensure the subsistence of everyone in accordance with his social function', but not a welfare state or a co-operative whose principles we can readily understand. (But Dumont does not tell us how food is supposed to be distributed in time of scarcity. If the subsistence standard is the same for everyone, then we are back in a familiar world.)

Clearly, the three principles apply to the citizens of the United States; and they have considerable force here because of the affluence of the community and the expansive understanding of individual need. On the other hand the United States currently maintains one of the shabbier systems of communal provision in the Western world. This is so for a variety of reasons: the community of citizens is loosely organized; various ethnic and religious groups run welfare programmes of their own; the ideology of self-reliance and entrepreneurial opportunity is widely accepted; and the movements of the left, particularly the labour movement, are relatively weak. Democratic decision-making reflects these realities, and there is nothing in principle wrong with that. Nevertheless, the established pattern of provision doesn't measure up to the internal requirements of the sphere of security and welfare, and the common understandings of the citizens point toward a more elaborate pattern. One might also argue that American citizens should work to build a stronger and more intensely experienced political community. But this argument, though it would have distributive consequences, is not, properly speaking, an argument about distributive justice. The question is, What do the citizens owe one another, given the community they actually inhabit?

Consider the example of criminal justice. The actual distribution of punishments is an issue I will take up in a later chapter. But the autonomy of punishment, the certainty that people are being punished for the right reasons (whatever those are), depends upon the distribution of resources within the legal system. If accused men and women are to receive their rightful share of justice, they must first have a rightful share of legal aid. Hence the institution of the public defender and the assigned counsel: just as the hungry must be fed, so the accused must be defended; and they must be defended in proportion to their needs. But no impartial observer of the American legal system today can doubt that the resources necessary to meet this standard are not generally available. The rich and the poor are treated differently in American courts, though it is the public commitment of the courts to treat them the same. The argument for a more generous provision follows from that commitment. If justice is to be provided at all, it must be provided equally for all accused citizens without regard to their wealth (or their race, religion, political partisanship, and so on). I don't mean to underestimate the practical difficulties here; but this, again, is the inner logic of provision, and it makes for an illuminating example of complex equality. For the inner logic of reward and punishment is different, requiring, as I shall argue later, that distributions be proportional to desert and not to need. Punishment is a negative good that ought to be monopolized by those who have acted badly—and who have been found guilty of acting badly (after a resourceful defence).

Legal aid raises no theoretical problems because the institutional structures for providing it already exist, and what is at stake is only the readiness of the community to live up to the logic of its own institutions. I want to turn now to an area where American institutions are relatively underdeveloped, and where communal commitment is problematic, the subject of continuing political debate: the area of medical care. But here the argument for a more extensive provision must move more slowly. It isn't enough to summon up a 'right to treatment.' I shall have to recount something of the history of medical care as a social good.

THE CASE OF MEDICAL CARE

Until recent times, the practice of medicine was mostly a matter of free enterprise. Doctors made their diagnosis, gave their advice, healed or didn't heal their patients, for a fee. Perhaps the private character of the economic relationship was connected to the intimate character of the professional relationship. More likely, I think, it had to do with the relative marginality of medicine itself. Doctors could, in fact, do very little for their patients; and the common attitude in the face of disease (as in the face of poverty) was a stoical fatalism. Or, popular remedies were developed that were not much less effective, sometimes more effective, than those prescribed by established physicians. Folk medicine sometimes produced a kind of communal provision at the local level, but it was equally likely to generate new practitioners, charging fees in their turn. Faith healing followed a similar pattern.

Leaving these two aside, we can say that the distribution of medical care has historically rested in the hands of the medical profession, a guild of physicians that dates at least from the time of Hippocrates in the fifth century BC. The guild has functioned to exclude unconventional practitioners and to regulate the number of physicians in any given community. A genuinely free market has never been in the interest of its members. But it is in the interest of the members to sell their services to individual patients; and thus, by and large, the well-to-do have been well cared for (in accordance with the current understanding of good care) and the poor hardly cared for at all. In a few urban communities—in the medieval Jewish communities, for example—medical services were more widely available. But they were virtually unknown for most people most of the time. Doctors were the servants of the rich, often attached to noble houses and royal courts. With regard to this practical outcome, however, the profession has always had a collective bad conscience. For the distributive logic of the practice of medicine seems to be this: that care should be proportionate to illness and not to wealth. Hence, there have always been doctors, like those honoured in ancient Greece, who served the poor on the side, as it were, even while they earned their living from paying patients. Most doctors, present in an emergency, still feel bound to help the victim without regard to his material status. It is a matter of professional Good Samaritanism that the call 'Is there a doctor in the house?' should not go unanswered if there is a doctor to answer it. In ordinary times, however, there was little call for medical help, largely because there was little faith in its actual helpfulness. And so the bad conscience of the profession was not echoed by any political demand for the replacement of free enterprise by communal provision.

In Europe during the Middle Ages, the cure of souls was public, the cure of bodies private. Today, in most European countries, the situation is reversed. The reversal is best explained in terms of a major shift in the common understanding of souls and bodies: we have lost confidence in the cure of souls, and we have come increasingly to believe, even to be obsessed with, the cure of bodies. Descartes's famous declaration that the 'preservation of health' was the 'chief of all goods' may be taken to symbolize the shift—or to herald it, for in the history of popular attitudes, Descartes's *Discourse on Method* came very early. Then, as eternity receded in the popular consciousness, longevity moved to the fore. Among medieval Christians, eternity was a socially recognized need; and every effort was made to see that it was widely and equally distributed, that every Christian had an equal chance at salvation and eternal life: hence, a church in every parish, regular services, catechism for the young, compulsory communion, and so on. Among modern citizens, longevity is a socially recognized need; and increasingly every effort is made to see that it is widely and equally distributed, that every citizen has an equal chance at a long and healthy life: hence doctors and hospitals in every district, regular check-ups, health education for the young, compulsory vaccination, and so on.

Parallel to the shift in attitudes, and following naturally from it, was a shift in institutions: from the church to the clinic and the hospital. But the shift has been gradual: a slow development of communal interest in medical care, a slow erosion of interest in religious care. The first major form of medical provision came in the area of prevention, not of treatment, probably because the former involved no interference with the prerogatives of the guild of physicians. But the beginnings of provision in the area of treatment were roughly simultaneous with the great public health campaigns of the late nineteenth century, and the two undoubtedly reflect the same sensitivity to questions of physical survival. The licensing of physicians, the establishment of state medical schools and urban clinics, the filtering of tax money into the great voluntary hospitals: these measures involved, perhaps, only marginal interference with the profession— some of them, in fact, reinforced its guildlike character; but they already represent an important public commitment. Indeed, they represent a commitment that ultimately can be fulfilled only by turning physicians, or some substantial number of them, into public physicians (as a smaller number once turned themselves into court physicians) and by abolishing or constraining the market in medical care. But before I defend that transformation, I want to stress the unavoidability of the commitment from which it follows.

What has happened in the modern world is simply that disease itself, even when it is endemic rather than epidemic, has come to be seen as a plague. And since the plague can be dealt with, it *must* be dealt with. People will not endure what they no longer believe they have to endure. Dealing with tuberculosis, cancer, or heart failure, however, requires a common effort. Medical research is expensive, and the treatment of many particular diseases lies far beyond the resources of ordinary citizens. So the community must step in, and any democratic community will in fact step in, more or less vigorously, more or less effectively, depending on the outcome of particular political battles. Thus, the role of the American Government (or governments, for much of the activity is at the state and local levels): subsidizing research, training doctors, providing hospitals and equipment, regulating voluntary insurance schemes, underwriting the treatment of the very old. All this represents 'the contrivance of human wisdom to provide for human wants.' And all that is required to make it morally necessary is the development of a 'want' so widely and deeply felt that it can plausibly be said that it is the want not of this or that person alone but of the community generally—a 'human want' even though culturally shaped and stressed.*

But once communal provision begins, it is subject to further moral constraints: it must provide what is 'wanted' equally to all the members of the community; and it must do so in ways that respect their membership. Now, even the pattern of medical provision in the United States, though it stops far short of a national health service, is intended to provide minimally decent care to all who need it. Once public funds are committed, public officials can hardly intend anything less. At the same time, however, no political decision has yet been made to challenge directly the system of free enterprise in medical care. And so long as that system exists, wealth will be dominant in (this part of) the sphere of security and welfare; individuals will be cared for in proportion to their ability to pay and not to their need for care. In fact, the situation is more complex than that formula suggests, for communal provision already encroaches upon the free market, and the very sick and the very old sometimes receive exactly the treatment they should receive. But it is clear that poverty remains a significant bar to adequate and consistent treatment. Perhaps the most telling statistic about contemporary American medicine is the correlation of visits to doctors and hospitals with social class rather than with degree or incidence of illness. Middle- and upper-class Americans are considerably more likely to have a private physician and to see him often, and considerably less likely to be seriously ill, than are their poorer fellow citizens. Were medical care a luxury, these discrepancies would not matter much; but as soon as medical care becomes a socially recognized need, and as soon as the community invests in its provision, they matter a great deal. For then deprivation is a double loss—to one's health and to one's social standing. Doctors and hospitals have become such massively important features of contemporary life that to be cut off from the help they provide is not only dangerous but also degrading.

But any fully developed system of medical provision will require the constraint of the guild of physicians. Indeed, this is more generally true: the provision of security and welfare requires the constraint of those men and women who had previously controlled the goods in question and sold them on the market (assuming, what is by no means always true, that the market predates

*Arguing against Bernard Williams's claim that the only proper criterion for the distribution of medical care is medical need, Robert Nozick asks why it doesn't then follow 'that the only proper criterion for the distribution of barbering services is barbering need'? Perhaps it does follow if one attends only to be the 'internal goal' of the activity, conceived in universal terms. But it doesn't follow if one attends to the social meaning of the activity, the place of the good it distributes in the life of a particular group of people. One can conceive of a society in which haircuts took on such central cultural significance that communal provision would be morally required, but it is something more than an interesting fact that no such society has ever existed. I have been helped in thinking about these issues by an article of Thomas Scanlon's; I adopt here his 'conventionalist' alternative.

communal provision). For what we do when we declare this or that good to be a needed good is to block or constrain its free exchange. We also block any other distributive procedure that doesn't attend to need—popular election, meritocratic competition, personal or familiar preference, and so on. But the market is, at least in the United States today, the chief rival of the sphere of security and welfare; and it is most importantly the market that is pre-empted by the welfare state. Needed goods cannot be left to the whim, or distributed in the interest, of some powerful group of owners or practitioners.

Most often, ownership is abolished, and practitioners are effectively conscripted or, at least, 'signed up' in the public service. They serve for the sake of the social need and not, or not simply, for their own sakes: thus, priests for the sake of eternal life, soldiers for the sake of national defence, public [state] school teachers for the sake of their pupils' education. Priests act wrongly if they sell salvation; soldiers, if they set up as mercenaries; teachers, if they cater to the children of the wealthy. Sometimes the conscription is only partial, as when lawyers are required to be officers of the court, serving the cause of justice even while they also serve their clients and themselves. Sometimes the conscription is occasional and temporary, as when lawyers are required to act as 'assigned counsels' for defendants unable to pay. In these cases, a special effort is made to respect the personal character of the lawyer-client relationship. I would look for a similar effort in any fully developed national health service. But I see no reason to respect the doctor's market freedom. Needed goods are not commodities. Or, more precisely, they can be bought and sold only insofar as they are available above and beyond whatever level of provision is fixed by democratic decision making (and only insofar as the buying and selling doesn't distort distributions below that level).

It might be argued, however, that the refusal thus far to finance a national health service constitutes a political decision by the American people about the level of communal care (and about the relative importance of other goods): a minimal standard for everyone—namely, the standard of the urban clinics; and free enterprise beyond that. That would seem to me an inadequate standard, but it would not necessarily be an unjust decision. It is not, however, the decision the American people have made. The common appreciation of the importance of medical care has carried them well beyond that. In fact, federal, state, and local governments now subsidize different levels of care for different classes of citizens. This might be all right, too, if the classification were connected to the purposes of the care—if, for example, soldiers and defence workers were given special treatment in time of war. But the poor, the middle class, and the rich make an indefensible triage. So long as communal funds are spent, as they currently are, to finance research, build hospitals, and pay the fees of doctors in private practice, the services that these expenditures underwrite must be equally available to all citizens.

This, then, is the argument for an expanded American welfare state. It follows from the three principles with which I began, and it suggests that the tendency of those principles is to free security and welfare from the prevailing patterns of dominance. Though a variety of institutional arrangements is possible, the three principles would seem to favour provision in kind; they suggest an important argument against current proposals to distribute money instead of education, legal aid, or medical care. The negative income tax, for example, is a plan to increase the purchasing power of the poor—a modified version of simply equality. This plan would not, however, abolish the dominance of wealth in the sphere of need. Short of a radical equalization, men and women with greater purchasing power could still, and surely would, bid up the price of needed services. So the community would be investing, though now only indirectly, in individual welfare but without fitting provision to the shape of need. Even with equal incomes, health care delivered through the market would not be responsive to need; nor would the market provide adequately for medical research. This is not an argument against the negative income tax, however, for it may be the case that money itself, in a market economy, is one of the things that people need. And then it too, perhaps, should be provided in kind.

I want to stress again that no *a priori* stipulation of what needs ought to be recognized is possible; nor is there any *a priori* way of determining appropriate levels of provision. Our attitudes toward medical care have a history; they have been different; they will be different again. The forms of communal provision have changed in the past and will continue to change. But they don't change automatically as attitudes change. The old order has its clients; there is a lethargy in institutions as in individuals. Moreover, popular attitudes are rarely so clear as they are in the case of medical care. So change is always a matter of political argument, organization, and struggle. All that the philosopher can do is to describe the basic structure of the arguments and the constraints they entail. Hence the three principles, which can be summed up in a revised version of Marx's famous maxim: From each according to his ability (or his resources); to each according to his socially recognized needs. This, I think, is the deepest meaning of the social contract. It only remains to work out the details—but in everyday life, the details are everything.

Medicine and Public Health, Ethics and Human Rights

JONATHAN M. MANN

The relationships among medicine, public health, ethics, and human rights are now evolving rapidly, in response to a series of events, experiences, and struggles. These include the shock of the worldwide epidemic of human immunodeficiency virus and AIDS, continuing work on diverse aspects of women's health, and challenges exemplified by the complex humanitarian emergencies of Somalia, Iraq, Bosnia, Rwanda, and now, Zaire.

From among the many impacts of these experiences, three seem particularly salient. First, human rights thinking and action have become much more closely allied to, and even integrated with, public health work. Second, the long-standing absence of an ethics of public health has been highlighted. Third, the human rights-related roles and responsibilities of physicians and other medical workers are receiving increased attention.

PUBLIC HEALTH AND MEDICINE

To explore the first of these issues—the connections between human rights and public health—it is essential to review several central elements of modern public health.

Medicine and public health are two complementary and interacting approaches for promoting and protecting health—defined by the World Health Organization (WHO) as a state of physical, mental, and social well-being. Yet medicine and public health can, and also must be differentiated, because in several important ways they are not the same. The fundamental difference involves the population emphasis of public health, which contrasts with the essentially individual focus of medical care. Public health identifies and measures threats to the health of populations, develops governmental policies in response

From *The Hastings Center Report*, May–June 1997, 6-13. Copyright © The Hastings Center. Reproduced by permission.

to these concerns, and seeks to assure certain health and related services. In contrast, medical care focuses upon individuals—diagnosis, treatment, relief of suffering, and rehabilitation.

Several specific points follow from this essential difference. For example, different instruments are called for: while public health measures population health status through epidemiological, survey, and other statistically based methods, medicine examines biophysical and psychological status using a combination of techniques, including dialogue, physical examination, and laboratory study of the individual. Public health generally values most highly (or at least is supposed to) primary prevention, that is, preventing the adverse health event in the first place, such as helping to prevent the automobile accident or the lead poisoning from happening at all. In contrast, medicine generally responds to existing health conditions, in the context of either secondary or tertiary prevention. Secondary prevention involves avoiding or delaying the adverse impact of a health condition like hypertension or diabetes. Thus, while the hypertension or insulin deficiency exists, its effects, such as heart disease, kidney failure, or blindness, can be avoided or delayed. So-called tertiary prevention involves those efforts to help sustain maximal functional and psychological capacity despite the presence of both the disease, such as hypertension, and its outcomes, heart disease, stroke, or kidney failure.

Accordingly, the skills and expertise needed in public health include epidemiology, biostatistics, policy analysis, economics, sociology, and other behavioral sciences. In contrast, medical skills and expertise center on the exploration, analysis, and response to the biophysical status of individuals, based principally on an understanding of biology, biochemistry, immunology, pharmacology, pathology, pathophysiology, anatomy, and psychology.

Naturally, the settings in which public health and medicine operate also differ: governmental organizations, large-scale public programs, and various fora associated with developing and implementing public policy are inherently part of public health, while private medical offices, clinics, and medical care facilities of varying complexity and sophistication are the settings in which medical care is generally provided.

Finally, the relationship between the profession and the people with whom it deals differs: in a sense, public health comes to you, while you go to the doctor. And expectations associated with each domain differ: from medicine, individual care and treatment are sought; from public health, protection against broad health threats like epidemic disease, unsafe water, or chemical pollution is expected.

Therefore, public health and medicine are principally distinguished by their focus on collectivities or on individuals, respectively, with a series of subsidiary differences involving methods of work, systems of analysis and measurement, emphasis on primary versus secondary or tertiary prevention, types of expertise and relevant skill, settings in which work is conducted, and client/public relationships and expectations.

Yet obviously, there is substantial overlap. Public health requires a sound biomedical basis, and involves many medical practitioners, whose services are organized in settings such as maternal and child health clinics, or immunization programs. Also, medical practice operates within a context highly influenced and governed by law and public policy. The potentially fluid relationship between public health and medicine is further suggested by recent proposals in this country that certain traditional public health functions be delegated to the private medical sector.

Despite these many differences, people equate medical care with health. Certainly, this basic confusion has informed the recent discussions of health care in the United States; and coverage of health issues in the popular press around the world reflects this perspective, in which access to medical care and the quality of that care are seen as the principal health needs of individuals and populations.

MEDICINE AND HEALTH

Yet the contribution of medicine to health, while undeniably important (and vital in certain situations), is actually quite limited. For example, it is estimated that only about one-sixth of the years of life expectancy gained in this country during this century can be attributed to the beneficial impact of medicine, medical care, and medical research. And it has been estimated that only about 10 percent of preventable premature deaths are associated with a lack of medical care. . . .

The vast majority of research into the health of populations identifies so-called "societal factors" as the major determinants of health status. Most of the work in this area has focused on socioeconomic status as the key variable, for it is clear, throughout history and in all societies, that the rich live generally longer and healthier lives than the poor. Thus, in the United Kingdom in 1911, the age-adjusted standardized mortality rate among members of the lowest social class was 1.6 times higher than for the highest social class. Interestingly, following creation of the National Health Services to ensure full access to medical care, and despite a dramatic change in major causes of death (from mainly infectious to mainly chronic diseases), in 1981 this societal gradient not only persisted, but increased, to a 2.1-fold higher standardized mortality rate among the lowest compared with the highest social class.

A major question arising from the socioeconomic status-health gradient is why there is a gradient. For example, among over 10,000 British civil servants followed for many years, health status and longevity were better for each successive category of civil servants, from lowest to highest. This raises two issues: first, while we believe we can—at least intuitively—explain poor health among the destitute when compared with the rich, associated with a lack of good food, housing, and with poor sanitary conditions, even the lowest class of British civil servants cannot be considered poor. Secondly, why should the civil servants in the next-to-highest group, living in quite comfortable circumstances, experience poorer health than the highest group?

Beyond these unanswered issues, many recent studies have pointed to the limited explanatory power of socioeconomic status, generally measured in terms of current income, years of education, and job classification. Other measures, such as the extent of socioeconomic inequality within a community, the nature, level, and temporal pattern of unemployment, societal connectedness and the extent of involvement in social networks, marital status, early childhood experiences, and exposure to dignity-denying situations have all been suggested as powerful potential components of a "black box" of societal factors whose dominant role in determining levels of preventable disease, disability, and premature death is beyond dispute.

AN ETHICS FOR PUBLIC HEALTH

Public health, although it began as a social movement, has—at least in recent years—responded relatively little to this most profound and vital knowledge about the dominant impact of society on health. To illustrate: we all know that certain behaviors have an enormous impact on health, such as cigarette smoking, excess alcohol intake, dietary choices, or levels of exercise and physical fitness. How these behaviors are conceptualized determines how they will be addressed by public health. The basic question is whether and to what extent these behaviors can be considered, and therefore responded to, as isolated individual choices.

Public health practitioners share a strong belief that important health-related behaviors are substantially influenced by societal factors and context. Yet examining public health programs designed to address the health problems associated with these same behaviors reveals that they generally consist of activities which assume that individuals have essentially complete control over their health-related behaviors. Traditional public health seeks to provide individuals with information and education about risks associated with diet or lack of exercise, along with various clinic-based services such as counseling, or distribution of condoms and other contraceptives. However, while public health may cite, or blame, or otherwise identify the societal-level or contextual issues—which it acknowledges to be of dominant importance, both in influencing individual behavior and for determining health status more broadly—it does not deal directly with these societal factors.

At least three reasons for this paradoxical inaction may be proposed. First, public health has lacked a conceptual framework for identifying and analyzing the essential societal factors that represent the "conditions in which people can be healthy." Second, a related problem: public health lacks a vocabulary with which to speak about and identify commonalities among health problems experienced by very different populations. Third, there is no consensus about the nature or direction of societal change that would be necessary to address the societal conditions involved. Lacking a coherent conceptual framework, a consistent vocabulary, and consensus about societal change, public health assembles and then tries valiantly to assimilate a wide variety of disciplinary perspectives, from economists, political scientists, social and behavioral scientists, health systems analysts, and a range of medical practitioners. Yet, while each of these perspectives provides some useful insight, public health becomes thereby a little bit of everything and thus not enough of anything.

With this background in mind, it would be expected that in the domains of public health and medicine, different, yet complementary languages for describing and incorporating values would be developed. For even when values are shared at a higher level of abstraction, the forms in which they are expressed, the settings in which they are evoked, and their practical application may differ widely.

Not surprisingly, medicine has chosen the language of ethics, as ethics has been developed in a context of individual relationships, and is well adapted to the nature, practice, settings, and expectations of medical care. The language of medical ethics has also been applied when medicine seeks to deal with issues such as the organization of medical care or the allocation of societal resources. However, the contribution of medical ethics to these societal issues has been less powerful when compared, for example, with its engagement in the behavior of individual medical practitioners.

Public health, at least in its contemporary form, is struggling to define and articulate its core values. In this context, the usefulness of the language and structure of ethics as we know it today has been questioned. Given its population focus, and its interest in the underlying conditions upon which health is predicated (and that these major determinants of health status are societal in nature), it seems evident that a framework which expresses fundamental values in societal terms, and a vocabulary of values which links directly with societal structure and function, may be better adapted to the work of public health than a more individually oriented ethical framework.

For this reason, modern human rights, precisely because they were initially developed entirely outside the health domain and seek to articulate the societal preconditions for human well-being, seem a far more useful framework, vocabulary, and form of guidance for public health efforts to analyze and respond directly to the societal determinants of health than any inherited from the past biomedical or public health tradition.

PUBLIC HEALTH AND HUMAN RIGHTS

The linkage between public health and human rights can be explored further by considering three relationships. The first focuses on the potential burden on human rights created by public health policies, programs, and practices. As public health generally involves direct or indirect state action, public health officials represent the state power toward which classical human rights concerns are traditionally addressed. Thus, in the modern world, public health officials have, for the first time, two fundamental responsibilities to the public: to protect and promote public health, and to protect and promote human rights. While public health officials may be unlikely to seek deliberately to violate human rights, there is great unawareness of human rights concepts and norms among public health practitioners. In stark contrast to the large number of bioethics courses available in medical educational settings, a recent survey of all twenty-eight accredited schools of public health in the United States and schools of public health in thirty-four other countries identified only seven formal courses in human rights for the presumed future leaders of public health.

Public health practice is heavily burdened by the problem of inadvertent discrimination. For example, outreach activities may "assume" that all populations are reached equally by a single, dominant-language message on television; or analysis "forgets" to include health problems uniquely relevant to certain groups, like breast cancer or sickle cell disease; or a program "ignores" the actual response capability of different population groups, as when lead poisoning warnings are given without concern for financial ability to ensure lead abatement. Indeed, inadvertent discrimination is so prevalent that all public health policies and programs should be considered discriminatory until proven otherwise, placing the burden on public health to affirm and ensure its respect for human rights.

In addition, in public health circles there is often an unspoken sense that public health and human rights concerns are inherently confrontational. At times, this has been true. In the early years of the HIV epidemic, the knee-jerk response of various public health officials to invoke mandatory testing, quarantine, and isolation did create a major clash with protectors of human rights. Even quite recently, an opinion piece in the *British Medical Journal* purports that excessive respect for human rights crippled public health efforts and is therefore responsible for the intensifying and expanding AIDS epidemic.

However, while modern human rights explicitly acknowledges that public health is a legitimate reason for limiting rights, more recently the underlying complementarity rather than inherent confrontation between public health and human rights has been emphasized. Again in the context of AIDS, public health has learned that discrimination toward HIV-infected people and people with AIDS is counterproductive. Specifically, when people found to be infected were deprived of employment, education, or ability to marry and travel, participation in prevention programs diminished. Thus, recent attention has been directed to a negotiation process for optimizing both the achievement of complementary public health goals and respect for human rights norms.

A second relationship between public health and human rights derives from the observation that human rights violations have health impacts, that is, adverse effects on physical, mental, and social well-being. For some rights, such as the right not to be tortured or imprisoned under inhumane conditions, the health damage seems evident, indeed inherent in the rights violation. However, even for torture, only more recently has the extensive, life-long, family and communitywide, and transgenerational impact of torture been recognized.

For many other rights, such as the right to information, to assembly, or to association, health impacts resulting from violation may not be initially so apparent. The violation of any right has measurable impacts on physical, mental, and social well-being; yet these health effects still remain, in large part, to be discovered and documented. Yet gradually, the connection is being established.

The right to association provides a useful example of this relationship. Public health benefits substantially—even requires—involvement of people in addressing problems that affect them. Because the ability of people concerned about a health problem to get together, talk, and search for effective solutions is so essential to public health, wherever the right to association is restricted, public health suffers. Taking a positive example from the history of HIV/AIDS: needle exchange—the trading-in of needles used for drug injection for clean needles, so as to avoid needle-sharing with consequent risk of HIV transmission—was invented by a union of drug users in Amsterdam. Needle exchange was a classic example of an innovative, local response to a pressing local problem. Needle exchange was not and would have been highly unlikely to have been developed by academics, government officials, or hired consultants! Yet the creative solution of needle exchange and respect for the right of association are closely linked. Thus, in societies in which people generally, or specific population groups, cannot associate around health, or other issues, such as injection drug users in the United States, or sex workers, or gay and lesbian people in many countries, local solutions are less able to emerge or be applied and public health is correspondingly compromised.

A third relationship between health and human rights has already been suggested; namely, that promoting and protecting human rights is inextricably linked with promoting and protecting health. Once again, this is because human rights offers a societal-level framework for identifying and responding to the underlying—societal—determinants of health. It is important to emphasize that human rights are respected not only for their instrumental value in contributing to public health goals, but for themselves, as societal goods of pre-eminent importance.

For example, a cluster of rights, including the rights to health, bodily integrity, privacy, information, education, and equal rights in marriage and divorce, have been called "reproductive rights," insofar as their realization (or violation) is now understood to play a major role in determining reproductive health. From an early focus on demographic targets for population control, to an emphasis on ensuring "informed consent" of women to various contraceptive methods, a new paradigm for population policies *and* reproductive health has recently emerged. Articulated most forcefully at the United Nations Conference on Population and Development in 1994 in Cairo, the focus has shifted to ensuring that women can make and effectuate real and informed choices about reproduction. And in turn, this is widely acknowledged to depend on realization of human rights.

Similarly, in the context of HIV/AIDS, vulnerability to the epidemic has now been associated with the extent of realization of human rights. For as the HIV epidemic matures and evolves within each community and country, it focuses inexorably on those groups who, before HIV/AIDS arrived, were already discriminated against, marginalized, and stigmatized within each society. Thus, in the United States the brunt of the epidemic today is among racial and ethnic minority populations, inner city poor, injection drug users, and, especially women in these communities. In Brazil, an epidemic that started among the jet set of Rio and São Paulo with time has become a major epidemic among the slum-dwellers in the *favelas* of Brazil's cities. The French, with characteristic linguistic precision, identify the major burden of HIV/AIDS to exist among *"les exclus,"* those living at the margins of society. Now that a lack of respect for human rights has been identified as a societal level risk factor for HIV/AIDS vulnerability, HIV prevention efforts—for example, for women—are starting to go beyond traditional educational and service-based efforts to address the rights issues that will be a precondition for greater progress against the epidemic.

Ultimately, ethics and human rights derive from a set of quite similar, if not identical, core values. As with medicine and public health, rather than seeing human rights and ethics as conflicting domains, it seems more appropriate to consider a continuum, in which human rights is a language most useful for guiding societal level analysis and work, while ethics is a language most useful for guiding individual behavior. From this perspective, and precisely because public health must be centrally concerned with the structure and function of society, the language of human rights is extremely useful for expressing, considering, and incorporating values into public health analysis and response.

Thus, public health work requires both ethics applicable to the individual public health practitioner and a human rights framework to guide public health in its societal analysis and response. . . .

At the hypothetical extreme of individual medical care, ethics would be the most useful language. However, to the extent that the individual practitioner is cognizant of the societal forces acting upon the individual patient, societal level considerations may also be articulated in human rights terms. At the other extreme of public health, human rights is the most useful language, speaking as it does directly to the societal level determinants of well-being. Nevertheless, the ethical framework remains critical, for public health is carried out by individuals within specific professional roles and competencies. In practice, of course, positions between the hypothetical extremes of medicine and public health are more common, calling for mixtures of human rights and ethical concepts and language.

PROFESSIONAL ROLES AND RESPONSIBILITIES

The placement of both human rights and ethics and public health and medicine at ends of a continuum suggests also that the interest domains of individuals and organizations can be "mapped" and areas calling for additional attention can be highlighted.

According to this mapping approach, the "French Doctors" movement can be seen as primarily medical, primarily ethics-based, yet with growing involvement in the public health dimensions of health emergencies and in human rights issues raised by these complex humanitarian crises. Similarly, many traditional, medical ethics-based institutes and centers can be placed on this map. At the Harvard School of Public Health, the François-Xavier Bagnoud Center for Health and Human Rights, along with several others, is now focusing on the health-human rights territory. This map also suggests two major gaps in current work: on the ethics of public health, and on the relationships between medicine and human rights.

Where are the ethics of public health? In contrast to the important declarations of medical ethics such as the International Code of Medical Ethics of the World Medical Association and the Nuremberg Principles, the world of public health does not have a reasonably explicit set of ethical guidelines. In part, this deficiency may stem from the broad diversity of professional identities within public health. Yet, curiously, many of the occupational groups central to public health (epidemiologists, policy analysts, social scientists, biostatisticians, nutritionists, health system managers) have not yet developed, or are only now developing, widely accepted ethical guidelines or statements of principle for their work in the public health context. Thus, while a public health physician may draw upon medical ethics for guidance, the ethics of a public health physician have yet to be clearly articulated.

The central problem is one of coherence and identity: public health cannot develop an ethics until it has achieved clarity about its own identity; technical expertise and methodology are not substitutes for conceptual coherence. Or, as one student remarked a few years ago, public health spends too much time on the "p" values of biostatistics and not enough time on values.

To have an ethic, a profession needs clarity about central issues, including its major role and responsibilities. Two steps will be essential for public health to reach toward this analytic and definitional clarity.

First, public health must divest itself of its biomedical conceptual foundation. The language of disease, disability, and death is not the language of well-being; the vocabulary of diseases may detract from analysis and response to underlying societal conditions, of which traditional morbidity and mortality are expressions. It is clear that we do not yet know all about the universe of human suffering. Just as in the microbial world, in which new discoveries have become the norm—Ebola virus, hantavirus, toxic shock syndrome, Legionnaires' disease, AIDS—we are explorers in the larger world of human suffering and well-being. And our current maps of this universe, like world maps from sixteenth century Europe, have some very well-defined, familiar coastlines and territories and also contain large blank spaces, which beckon the explorer.

The language of biomedicine is cumbersome and ultimately perhaps of little usefulness in exploring the impacts of violations of dignity on physical, mental, and social well-being. The definition of dignity itself is complex and thus far elusive and unsatisfying. While the Universal Declaration of Human Rights starts by placing dignity first, "all people are born equal in dignity and rights," we do not yet have a vocabulary, or taxonomy, let alone an epidemiology of dignity violations.

Yet it seems we all know when our dignity is violated or impugned. Perform the following experiment: recall, in detail, an incident from your own life in which your dignity was violated, for whatever reason. If you will immerse yourself in the memory, powerful feelings will likely arise—of anger, shame, powerlessness, despair. When you connect with the power of these feelings, it seems intuitively obvious that such feelings, particularly if evoked repetitively, could have deleterious impacts on health. Yet most of us are relatively privileged, we live in a generally dignity-affirming environment, and suffer only the occasional lapse of indignity. However, many people live constantly in a dignity-impugning environment, in which affirmations of dignity may be the exceptional occurrence. An exploration of the meanings of dignity and the forms of its violation—and the impact on physical, mental, and social well-being—may help uncover a new universe of human suffering, for which the biomedical language may he inapt and even inept. After all, the power of naming, describing, and then measuring is truly enormous—child abuse did not exist in meaningful societal terms until it was named and then measured; nor did domestic violence.

A second precondition for developing an ethics of public health is the adoption and application of a human rights framework for analyzing and responding to the societal determinants of health. The human rights framework can provide the coherence and clarity required for public health to identify and work with conscious attention to its roles and responsibilities. At that point, an ethics of public health, rather than the ethics of individual constituent disciplines within public health, can emerge.

Issues of respect for autonomy, beneficence, nonmaleficence, and justice can then be articulated from within the set of goals and responsibilities called for by seeking to improve public health through the combination of traditional approaches and those that strive concretely to promote realization of human rights. This is not to replace health education, information, and clinical service-based activities of public health with an exclusive focus on human rights and dignity. Both are necessary.

For example, the challenges for public health officials in balancing the goals of promoting and protecting public health and ensuring that human rights and dignity are not violated call urgently for ethical analysis. The official nature of much public health work places public health practitioners in a complex environment, in which work to promote rights inevitably challenges the state system within which the official is employed. Ethical dimensions are highly relevant to collecting, disseminating, and acting on information about the health impacts of the entire range of human rights violations. And as public health seeks to "ensure the conditions in which people can be healthy," and as those conditions are societal, to be engaged in public health necessarily involves a commitment to societal transformation. The difficulties in assessing human rights status and in developing useful and appropriate ways to promote human rights and dignity necessarily engage ethical considerations. For example, beyond accurate diagnosis, beyond efforts to cure, and even beyond the ever-present responsibility for relief of pain, the physician agrees to accompany the patient, to stand by the patient through her suffering, even to the edge of life itself, even when the only thing the physician can offer is the fact of his or her presence. Is this not as relevant to public health? For public health must engage difficult issues even when no cure or effective instruments are yet available, and public health also must accompany, remain with, and not abandon vulnerable populations.

That this work—added to, not substituted for, the current approach of public health—will require major changes in public health reflection, analysis, action, and education, is clear. That it is urgently required, in order to confront the major health challenges of the modern world, is equally clear. . . .

3

PREVENTION AND ITS LIMITS

Public health is known for its stress on preventing disease before it occurs, and doing so through "primary, secondary, and tertiary" prevention.[1] Prevention is the hallmark of public health. Yet the word can quickly become a cliche. We sometimes speak of prevention as if it were a simple and obvious remedy to all social ills, when it is anything but simple or obvious. Readers should be alert to three critical questions in prevention: (1) What is to be prevented? (2) Who is responsible for prevention and who must pay the cost? (3) What level of safety should be the standard for prevention measures?

Preventive measures in public health aim to reduce the exposure of communities to the major hazards of our time. Some of these hazards are diseases: The HIV virus and other viral threats; the recurrence of plague, cholera, and malaria; and gastrointestinal disease caused by deadly parasites and other pathogens are examples. Others are environmental hazards such as air pollution and chemical exposures. Still other hazards have both environmental and behavioral elements, like tobacco and alcohol, and highway crashes. When preventing exposure is not possible, other strategies can be used to protect populations, such as immunization against infectious disease or the use of air bags or seat belts in automobiles.

Reducing exposure to dangers usually necessitates overcoming established conceptions of why epidemics or highway crashes or gunshot injuries occur. These established conceptions focus on the role of particular agents in bringing about the unfortunate result: hence, the term *agent-causality*. In agent-causality the stress is placed upon what the individual did wrong to invite or to accept exposure to dangerous conditions. Someone gets AIDS because he or she had unprotected sex or shared needles. The cause of a workplace accident is the worker's failure to wear safety goggles. The accident was caused by the driver's speeding.

Public health does not deny individual contributions to injury and disease; that would be absurd. However, it is more interested in how hazards might be reduced or mitigated than in blaming individuals. It finds explanations that focus on exposure to risk within populations more helpful than explanations that focus on agent-causality. In exposure (as opposed to agent) causality, the emphasis is less on what individuals do and more on measures to reduce the exposure of whole communities or groups to hazards.

In prevention, the focus is upon the predictable and stable occurrence of disease conditions in society. William Ryan spoke of this perspective a number of years ago: "Adherents of this [public health] approach tended to search for defects in the community and the environment rather than in the individual; to emphasize predictability and usualness rather than random deviance."[2]

Sometimes a measure which seems sensible from an individual standpoint does not reduce risk in the aggregate. One of the more interesting examples comes from the field of injury control. Research indicates that driver education for young people actually results in higher crash rates in this age group.[3] This is surprising because driver education should improve the safety records of young drivers (which is why insurance companies offer a discount on the insurance of teenagers who have taken driver education). However, the incentive for young people to take driver education is the ability to drive at a younger age, say 16 or 17 rather than 18. The mere fact that a greater number of younger, licensed drivers are consequently on the road and exposed to risks, accounts for the increase in the crash rate. The research suggests that states might eliminate the programs in the name of safety.

An emphasis on aggregate harm and exposure to risks suggests an answer to our second question: Who is responsible for taking action to protect the public's health? Responsibility for protecting the public's health is best seen as a collective function, a task of government, because making preventive responsibility an individual matter seldom reduces rates of disease and injury sharply. Cigarette smoking seems the exception, as smoking levels have fallen over the past three decades without massive government regulation. But cigarette advertising was banished from television, there were widely publicized reports from the Office of the U.S. Surgeon General, and the national news media has saturated the public with the dangers of smoking. This, coupled with legal restrictions on smoking in public and increases in tobacco taxes, has sharply cut smoking levels.

The third critical issue in prevention is, How safe should we seek to make the public from the hazards in the workplace, in transportation, or in the environment? This question is difficult, if not impossible, to answer in the abstract, as the answer depends on multiple factors, including the seriousness of the hazard, its prevalence, and the cost of prevention. We cannot give a formula for determining the right level of prevention here but can argue against one way of deciding what risks are acceptable, namely, in terms of individuals' voluntary acceptance of risk. It is sometimes argued that we often voluntarily accept risks that are much more dangerous than other risks that are imposed on us, and from which we, as members of the public, expect government to protect us. For example, we drive automobiles when trains are forced to be much safer. We fly in private planes which are far more dangerous than commercial aircraft. This leads some to suggest that the level of risk individuals are willing to accept in their voluntary choices constitutes a general acceptable level of safety. The implications of such a view are startling. It would mean that airline safety could be allowed to decrease far below the current level, perhaps to the level of automobile traffic. It would allow consumer product safety to decrease in a comparable way, perhaps to the level of risk individuals take when they smoke cigarettes. Because this approach to risk sets the level of safety so low, it is inconsistent with a public health perspective.

The first selection in this chapter, "Public Health as Social Justice," by Dan Beauchamp, was written in the mid-1970s as the Great Society programs were being challenged by a business backlash. The business community resented being forced to carry the burden of making the public safer. Beauchamp analyzes preventive measures such as regulations to control air and water pollution, or to make automobiles and other consumer products safer, in terms of exposure causality and the norms of social justice, showing how this differs markedly from liberal and market models of justice.

This is today an enduring theme in public health—the attempt to persuade democratic bodies to legislate rules for economic production and distribution that are safer. Community public health interests are ranged against powerful, well-organized entities such as corporations and interest groups (like the National Rifle Association). The struggle for the common health and safety is further complicated by the fact that the redistribution of the burdens of health and safety legislation is on behalf of "statistical lives." This resembles a struggle for social justice because the effort is on behalf of the less well-organized and less powerful against the power of the market and its masters.

The second article in this chapter, "Analysis of Cause—Long-cut to Prevention?" by J. H. Renwick, suggests that too much emphasis on the causation of social problems or health problems can be misleading and may distract us from effective measures of prevention. Often we know how to abate (prevent) problems long before we know the causes of problems.

Finally, we turn to the limits to prevention and to the whole idea of community. This is the issue of paternalism. Is it the case that public health, in its zeal to promote the health of the public, goes too far and neglects the rights and interests of the individual?

Paternalism has been a major theme in bioethics. A principal problem facing philosophers who began work in bioethics about three decades ago was the paternalism of American medicine. This gave rise to an entire literature on paternalism in the health field.[4] In the third selection for this chapter, paternalism is defined by Gerald Dworkin as "the interference with a person's liberty of action for reasons referring exclusively to the welfare, good, happiness, needs, interests, or values of the person being coerced." Physicians who seek to promote the individual patient's own good by withholding information (which the physician may think the patient is not qualified to evaluate) or by withholding facts (which the physician may feel might be too painful for the patient), act paternalistically, and indefensibly in the eyes of most bioethicists. The struggle to define a defensible notion of patient autonomy, and to rethink the responsibilities of physicians and other health professionals in honoring that autonomy, has been a major part of the development of biomedical ethics over the past 30 years. This struggle, while not over, has won a respected place for the idea of patient autonomy in American medicine. When philosophers turn to public health and find that its proponents advocate legislation requiring the wearing of motorcycle helmets or seat belts or buying cars with air bags installed, this looks to them like paternalism because the individual's liberty is being restricted to promote his or her own well-being. Influenced by John Stuart Mill's famous essay, "On Liberty,"[5] which is a powerful attack on paternal government, philosophers tend to regard public health as objectionably paternalistic. Indeed, for many in bioethics, public health is synonymous with paternalism.

The term *paternal government* has an interesting history. (The actual term *paternalism* was never used by Mill and seems to be a term of the 20th century.) The idea of paternal government likely first arose in England and dealt with the responsibilities of landed gentry for the welfare of persons who lived on their estates. In this case, the owners and minor nobility were responsible for the well-being and safety of persons who lived on their lands and who were known to them, personally. Thus, paternalism today reminds us of a government which, knowing its citizenry to be unlikely to take care of themselves, passes legislation to require seat belts, to wear motorcycle helmets, and so on. To most people, this idea is anachronistic, condescending, and vaguely insulting because it second-guesses people's own evaluations about what is best for them, treating them like children in need of protection. Most people resent this. They want to be able to make up their own minds and shape their own destiny, even when they make choices that others regard as foolish or unwise.

Mill argued that coercing individuals for their own good was never justified. The sole justification for interfering with a person's liberty was to prevent harm to others. The "harm principle," as it has become known, has been used by some to justify certain public health measures that may seem at first glance paternalistic. On this view, some choices made by individuals impose harms on society even if they do not directly impose harms on specific others. We may call this the *burdens-to-society thesis*. It holds, for example, that individuals who eat fatty foods may think they are harming only themselves, but in truth (or so this argument goes) they are creating future medical bills and higher insurance costs, burdens which all of society has to bear. One article went so far as to argue that the obese impose burdens on society through higher fuel costs, in the form of food and fossil fuels for transportation![6]

A different justification of paternalism focuses on the fact that people sometimes act against their *own* considered judgments about how they ought to act. They overeat when they want to lose weight. They continue to smoke, even though they do not want to get cancer or emphysema. Philosophers call this kind of acting against one's own best judgment "weakness of will." Are coercive measures aimed at getting people to do what they agree they should do, and would do, if only they were not weak-willed, paternalistic? Some argue that they are not, that paternalism inherently involves forcing people to act against their own values, for their own good. Others regard paternalism to counteract weakness of will as a *kind* of paternalism, which may be called "weak" or "soft" paternalism. It seems likely that many public health measures, such as seatbelt legislation, come under the heading of weak paternalism. The legislation forces people to do what they really know they should do but are too lazy or weak-willed to do without the added incentive of a law.

A third approach to the problem of paternalism is to argue that public health measures are not, in fact, paternalistic because the proposed interventions are not aimed at promoting the individual's *own* good. This is the argument suggested by Dan Beauchamp in his article on community and public health in the last chapter. While he termed this form of regulation *public health paternalism,* he means that these limits are not, strictly speaking, classical paternalism. Rather, the legislation in question is aimed at a population and is intended to reduce the rates of premature death and serious injury among that population. Put another way, what is being promoted is the good of the group, not the good of specific individuals.

Because of its emphasis on the good of the group, we can call this the *communitarian perspective.* The communitarian perspective is not vulnerable to the objection that it is condescending or patronizing because the rationale for the coercive measures is *not* that the government knows better than the individual what is in his or her own best interest. It is rather that minor infringements on the liberty of individuals (like buckling up in the car) are justified by the great good that can be accomplished (saving thousands of lives a year). Unlike the burdens-on-society thesis, the communitarian perspective does not blame individuals for imposing costs on society. However, both views justify preventive measures on harm-principle grounds and therefore do not threaten the autonomy of individuals any more than any other harm-preventing measures. The communitarian perspective argues that public health has devised, if not very self-consciously, a theory of individual autonomy that is distinctive and different from the one proposed by Mill in "On Liberty," different from the burdens-on-society thesis, and one that is not a form of soft paternalism, or *paternalism lite*.

NOTES

1. Primary prevention is preventing damaging events from ever occurring. Secondary prevention is reducing the damage or harm from damaging events after they occur (for example, with air bags or seat belts in automobiles). Tertiary prevention is arranging clinical treatment to reduce the level of damage among a population.

2. William Ryan, *Blaming the Victim* (New York: Vintage, 1971 p. 17).

3. Leon S. Robertson, "Crash Involvement of Teenaged Drivers When Driver Education Is Eliminated From High School," *American Journal of Public Health* 70 (1980), pp. 599–603.

4. See Daniel Wikler, "Lifestyles and Public Health," *Encyclopedia of Bioethics, Revised Edition* (New York: Macmillan Library Reference, 1995, v. 3, pp. 1366–69), and Dennis Thompson, *Paternalism in Medicine, Law, and Public Policy*," in Daniel Callahan and Sissela Bok, eds. *Ethics Teaching in Higher Education.* (New York: Plenum, 1980, pp. 245–272). For a defense of paternalism that somewhat resembles the public health position, see Richard Bonnie, "Discouraging Unhealthy Personal Choices: Reflections on New Directions in Substance Abuse Policy," *Journal of Drug Issues* 8 (1978), pp. 199–219. See also Robert M. Veatch, "Voluntary Risks to Health, the Ethical Issues," *Journal of the American Medical Association* 243 (1980), pp. 50–55. See Dan Beauchamp, "Life-Style, Public Health and Paternalism," in S. Doxiadis, ed. *Ethical Dilemmas in Health Promotion.* (London: John Wiley, 1987).

5. J. S. Mill, "On Liberty," in Marshall Cohen, ed. *Philosophy of John Staurt Mill: Ethical, Political, Religious* (New York: Modern Library, 1961, 185–319).

6. B. M. Hannon and T. G. Lohman, "The Energy Cost of Overweight in the United States," *American Journal of Public Health* 68 (1978), 765–767. Others point out that people with poor health habits probably *save* society money in the long run. By dying prematurely, they avoid large medical costs that typically occur at the end of life, as well as Social Security and pension payments. If cost is the issue, perhaps we ought to give smokers a tax break!

Public Health As Social Justice

DAN E. BEAUCHAMP

Anthony Downs has observed that our most intractable public problems have two significant characteristics. First, they occur to a relative minority of our population (even though that minority may number millions of people). Second, they result in significant part from arrangements that are providing substantial benefits or advantages to a majority or to a powerful minority of citizens. Thus solving or minimizing these problems requires painful losses, the restructuring of society and the acceptance of new burdens by the most powerful and the most numerous on behalf of the least powerful or the least numerous. As Downs notes, this bleak reality has resulted in recent years in cycles of public attention to such problems as poverty, racial discrimination, poor housing, un-employment or the abandonment of the aged; however, this attention and inter-est rapidly wane when it becomes clear that solving these problems requires painful costs that the dominant interests in society are unwilling to pay. Our public ethics do not seem to fit our public problems.

It is not sufficiently appreciated that these same bleak realities plague at-tempts to protect the public's health. Automobile-related injury and death; tobacco, alcohol and other drug damage; the perils of the workplace; environ-mental pollution; the inequitable and ineffective distribution of medical care services; the hazards of biomedicine—all of these threats inflict death and dis-ability on a minority of our society at any given time. Further, minimizing or even significantly reducing the death and disability from these perils entails that the majority or powerful minorities accept new burdens or relinquish existing privileges that they presently enjoy. Typically, these new burdens or restrictions involve more stringent controls over these and other hazards of the world.

This somber reality suggests that our fundamental attention in public health policy and prevention should not be directed toward a search for new technol-ogy, but rather toward breaking existing ethical and political barriers to mini-mizing death and disability. This is not to say that technology will never again help avoid painful social and political adjustments. Nonetheless, only the technological Pollyannas will ignore the mounting evidence that the critical barriers to protecting the public against death and disability are not the barriers to technological progress—indeed the evidence is that it is often technology itself that is our own worst enemy. The critical barrier to dramatic reductions in death and disability is a social ethic that unfairly protects the most numerous or the most powerful from the burdens of prevention.

This is the issue of justice. In the broadest sense, justice means that each person in society ought to receive his due and that the burdens and benefits of society should be fairly and equitably distributed. But what criteria should be followed in allocating burdens and benefits: Merit, equality or need? What end or goal in life should receive our highest priority: Life, liberty or the pursuit of happiness? The answer to these questions can be found in our prevailing theories or models of justice. These models of justice, roughly speaking, form the foundation of our politics and public policy in general, and our health policy (including our prevention policy) specifically. Here I am speaking of politics not as partisan politics but rather the more ancient and venerable meaning of the political as the search for the common good and the just society.

These models of justice furnish a symbolic framework or blueprint with which to think about and react to the problems of the public, providing the basic rules to classify and categorize problems of society as to whether they necessitate public and collective protection, or whether individual responsibility should prevail. These models function as a sort of map or guide to the common world of members of society, making visible some conditions in society as public issues and concerns, and hiding, obscuring or concealing other conditions that might otherwise emerge as public issues or problems were a different map or model of justice in hand.

In the case of health, these models of justice form the basis for thinking about and reacting to the problems of disability and premature death in society. Thus, if public health policy requires that the majority or a powerful minority accept their fair share of the burdens of protecting a relative minority threatened with death or disability, we need to ask if our prevailing model of justice contemplates and legitimates such sacrifices.

MARKET-JUSTICE

The dominant model of justice in the American experience has been market-justice. Under the norms of market-justice people are entitled only to those valued ends such as status, income, happiness, etc., that they have acquired by fair rules of entitlement, e.g., by their own individual efforts, actions or abilities. Market-justice emphasizes individual responsibility, minimal collective action and freedom from collective obligations except to respect other persons' fundamental rights.

While we have as a society compromised pure market-justice in many ways to protect the public's health, we are far from recognizing the principle that death and disability are collective problems and that all persons are entitled to health protection. Society does not recognize a general obligation to protect the individual against disease and injury. While society does prohibit individuals from causing direct harm to others, and has in many instances regulated clear public health hazards, the norm of market-justice is still dominant and the primary duty to avert disease and injury still rests with the individual. The individual is ultimately alone in his or her struggle against death.

Barriers to Protection

This individual isolation creates a powerful barrier to the goal of protecting all human life by magnifying the power of death, granting to death an almost supernatural reality. Death has throughout history presented a basic problem to humankind, but even in an advanced society with enormous biomedical technology, the individualism of market-justice tends to retain and exaggerate pessimistic and fatalistic attitudes toward death and injury. This fatalism leads to a sense of powerlessness, to the acceptance of risk as an essential element of life, to resignation in the face of calamity, and to a weakening of collective impulses to confront the problems of premature death and disability.

Perhaps the most direct way in which market-justice undermines our resolve to preserve and protect human life lies in the primary freedom this ethic extends to all individuals and groups to act with minimal obligations to protect the common good. Despite the fact that this rule of self-interest predictably fails to protect adequately the safety of our workplaces, our modes of transportation, the physical environment, the commodities we consume, or the equitable and effective distribution of medical care, these failures have resulted so far in only half-hearted attempts at regulation and control. This response is explained in large part by the powerful sway market-justice holds over our imagination, granting fundamental freedom to all individuals to be left alone—even if the "individuals" in question are giant producer groups with enormous capacities to create great public harm through sheer inadvertence. Efforts for truly effective controls over these perils must constantly struggle against a prevailing ethical paradigm that defines as threats to fundamental freedoms attempts to assure that all groups—even powerful producer groups—accept their fair share of the burdens of prevention.

Market-justice is also the source of another major barrier to public health measures to minimize death and disability—the category of voluntary behavior. Market-justice forces a basic distinction between the harm caused by a factory polluting the atmosphere and the harm caused by the cigarette or alcohol industries, because in the latter case those that are harmed are perceived as engaged in "voluntary" behavior. It is the radical individualism inherent in the market model that encourages attention to the individual's behavior and inattention to the social preconditions of that behavior. In the case of smoking, these preconditions include a powerful cigarette industry and accompanying social and cultural forces encouraging the practice of smoking. These social forces include norms sanctioning smoking as well as all forms of media, advertising, literature, movies, folklore, etc. Since the smoker is free in some ultimate sense to not smoke, the norms of market-justice force the conclusion that the individual voluntarily "chooses" to smoke; and we are prevented from taking strong collective action against the powerful structures encouraging this so-called voluntary behavior.

Yet another way in which the market ethic obstructs the possibilities for minimizing death and disability, and alibis the need for structural change, is through explanations for death and disability that "blame the victim." Victim-blaming misdefines structural and collective problems of the entire society as individual problems, seeing these problems as caused by the behavioral failures or deficiencies of the victims. These behavioral explanations for public problems tend to protect the larger society and powerful interests from the burdens of collective action, and instead encourage attempts to change the "faulty" behavior of victims.

Market-justice is perhaps the major cause for our over-investment and over-confidence in curative medical services. It is not obvious that the rise of medical science and the physician, taken alone, should become fundamental obstacles to collective action to prevent death and injury. But the prejudice found in market-justice against collective action perverts these scientific advances into an unrealistic hope for "technological shortcuts" to painful social change. Moreover, the great emphasis placed on individual achievement in market-justice has further diverted attention and interest away from primary prevention and collective action by dramatizing the role of the solitary physician-scientist, picturing him as our primary weapon and first line of defense against the threat of death and injury. . . .

Public Health Measures

I have saved for last an important class of health policies—public health measures to protect the environment, the workplace, or the commodities we purchase and consume. Are these not signs that the American society is willing to accept collective action in the face of clear public health hazards?

I do not wish to minimize the importance of these advances to protect the public in many domains. But these separate reforms, taken alone, should be cautiously received. This is because each reform effort is perceived as an isolated exception to the norm of market-justice; the norm itself still stands. Consequently, the predictable career of such measures is to see enthusiasm for enforcement peak and wane. These public health measures are clear signs of hope. But as long as these actions are seen as merely minor exceptions to the rule of individual responsibility, the goals of public health will remain beyond our reach. What is required is for the public to see that protecting the public's health takes us beyond the norms of market-justice categorically, and necessitates a completely new health ethic. . . .

SOCIAL JUSTICE

The fundamental critique of market-justice found in the Western liberal tradition is social justice. Under social justice all persons are entitled equally to key ends such as health protection or minimum standards of income. Further, unless collective burdens are accepted, powerful forces of environment, heredity or social structure will preclude a fair distribution of these ends. While many forces influenced the development of public health, the historic dream of public health that preventable death and disability ought to be minimized is a dream of social justice. Yet these egalitarian and social justice implications of the public health vision are either still not widely recognized or are conveniently ignored. . . .

Ideally, then, the public health ethic is not simply an alternative to the market ethic for health—it is a fundamental critique of that ethic as it unjustly protects powerful interests from the burdens of prevention and as that ethic serves to legitimate a mindless and extravagant faith in the efficacy of medical care. In other words, the public health ethic is a *counter-ethic* to market-justice and the ethics of individualism as these are applied to the health problems of the public. . . .

This new ethic has several key implications which are referred to here as "principles": 1) Controlling the hazards of this world, 2) to prevent death and disability, 3) through organized collective action, 4) shared equally by all except where unequal burdens result in increased protection of everyone's health and especially potential victims of death and disability.

These ethical principles are not new to public health. To the contrary, making the ethical foundations of public health visible only serves to highlight the social justice influences at work behind pre-existing principles.

Controlling the Hazards

A key principle of the public health ethic is the focus on the identification and control of the hazards of this world rather than a focus on the behavioral defects of those individuals damaged by these hazards. Against this principle it is often argued that today the causes of death and disability are multiple and frequently behavioral in origin. Further, since it is usually only a minority of the public that fails to protect itself against most known hazards, additional controls over these perilous sources would not seem to be effective or just. We should look instead for the behavioral origins of most public health problems, asking why some people expose themselves to known hazards or perils, or act in an unsafe or careless manner.

Public health should—at least ideally—be suspicious of behavioral paradigms for viewing public health problems since they tend to "blame the victim" and unfairly protect majorities and powerful interests from the burdens of prevention. It is clear that behavioral models of public health problems are rooted in the tradition of market-justice, where the emphasis is upon individual ability and capacity, and individual success and failure.

Public health, ideally, should not be concerned with explaining the successes and failures of differing individuals (dispositional explanations) in controlling the hazards of this world. . . .

Prevention

Like the other principles of public health, prevention is a logical consequence of the ethical goal of minimizing the numbers of persons suffering death and disability. The only known way to minimize these adverse events is to prevent the occurrence of damaging exchanges or exposures in the first place, or to seek to minimize damage when exposures cannot be controlled.

Prevention, then, is that set of priority rules for restructuring existing market rules in order to maximally protect the public. These rules seek to create policies and obligations to replace the norm of market-justice, where the latter permits specific conditions, commodities, services, products, activities or practices to pose a direct threat or hazard to the health and safety of members of the public, or where the market norm fails to allocate effectively and equitably those services (such as medical care) that are necessary to attend to disease at hand.

Thus, the familiar public health options:

1. Creating rules to minimize exposure of the public to hazards (kinetic, chemical, ionizing, biological, etc.) so as to reduce the rates of hazardous exchanges.
2. Creating rules to strengthen the public against damage in the event damaging exchanges occur anyway, where such techniques (fluoridation, seatbelts, immunization) are feasible.

3. Creating rules to organize treatment resources in the community so as to minimize damage that does occur since we can rarely prevent all damage.

Collective Action

Another principle of the public health ethic is that the control of hazards cannot be achieved through voluntary mechanisms but must be undertaken by governmental or non-governmental agencies through planned, organized and collective action that is obligatory or non-voluntary in nature. This is for two reasons.

The first is because market or voluntary action is typically inadequate for providing what are called public goods. Public goods are those public policies (national defense, police and fire protection, or the protection of all persons against preventable death and disability) that are universal in their impacts and effects, affecting everyone equally. These kinds of goods cannot easily be withheld from those individuals in the community who choose not to support these services (this is typically called the "free rider" problem). Also, individual holdouts might plausibly reason that their small contribution might not prevent the public good from being offered.

The second reason why self-regarding individuals might refuse to voluntarily pay the costs of such public goods as public health policies is because these policies frequently require burdens that self-interest or self-protection might see as too stringent. For example, the minimization of rates of alcoholism in a community clearly seems to require norms or controls over the substance of alcohol that limit the use of this substance to levels that are far below what would be safe for individual drinkers.

With these temptations for individual noncompliance, justice demands assurance that all persons share equally the costs of collective action through obligatory and sanctioned social and public policy.

Fair-Sharing of the Burdens

A final principle of the public health ethic is that all persons are equally responsible for sharing the burdens—as well as the benefits—of protection against death and disability, except where unequal burdens result in greater protection for every person and especially potential victims of death and disability. In practice this means that policies to control the hazards of a given substance, service or commodity fall unequally (but still fairly) on those involved in the production, provision or consumption of service, commodity or substance. The clear implication of this principle is that the automotive industry, the tobacco industry, the coal industry and the medical care industry—to mention only a few key groups—have an unequal responsibility to bear the costs of reducing death and disability since their actions have far greater impact than those of individual citizens.

DOING JUSTICE: BUILDING A NEW PUBLIC HEALTH

I have attempted to show the broad implications of a public health commitment to protect and preserve human life, setting out tentatively the logical consequences of that commitment in the form of some general principles. We need, however, to go beyond these broad principles and ask more specifically: What implications does this model have for doing public health and the public health profession?

The central implication of the view set out here is that doing public health should not be narrowly conceived as an instrumental or technical activity. Public health should be a way of doing justice, a way of asserting the value and priority of all human life. The primary aim of all public health activity should be the elaboration and adoption of a new ethical model or paradigm for protecting the public's health. This new ethical paradigm will necessitate a heightened consciousness of the manifold forces threatening human life, and will require thinking about and reacting to the problems of disability and premature death as primarily collective problems of the entire society. . . .

CONCLUSION

The central thesis of this article is that public health is ultimately and essentially an ethical enterprise committed to the notion that all persons are entitled to protection against the hazards of this world and to the minimization of death and disability in society. I have tried to make the implications of this ethical vision manifest, especially as the public health ethic challenges and confronts the norms of market-justice.

I do not see these goals of public health as hopelessly unrealistic nor destructive of fundamental liberties. Public health may be an "alien ethic in a strange land." Yet, if anything, the public health ethic is more faithful to the traditions of Judeo-Christian ethics than is market-justice.

The image of public health that I have drawn here does raise legitimate questions about what it is to be a professional, and legitimate questions about reasonable limits to restrictions on human liberty. These questions must be addressed more thoroughly than I have done here. Nonetheless, we must never pass over the chaos of preventable disease and disability in our society by simply celebrating the benefits of our prosperity and abundance, or our technological advances. What are these benefits worth if they have been purchased at the price of human lives?

Nothing written here should be construed as a per se attack on the market system. I have, rather, surfaced the moral and ethical norms of that system and argued that, whatever other benefits might accrue from those norms, they are woefully inadequate to assure full and equal protection of all human life.

The adoption of a new public health ethic and a new public health policy must and should occur within the context of a democratic polity. I agree with Terris that the central task of the public health movement is to persuade society to accept these measures.

Finally, it is a peculiarity of the word freedom that its meaning has become so distorted and stretched as to lend itself as a defense against nearly every attempt to extend equal health protection to all persons. This is the ultimate irony. The idea of liberty should mean, above all else, the liberation of society from the injustice of preventable disability and early death. Instead, the concept of freedom has become a defense and protection of powerful vested interests, and the central issue is viewed as a choice between freedom on the one hand, and health and safety on the other. I am confident that ultimately the public will come to see that extending life and health to all persons will require some diminution of personal choices, but that such restrictions are not only fair and do not constitute abridgement of fundamental liberties, they are a basic sign and imprint of a just society and a guarantee of that most basic of all freedom— protection against man's most ancient foe.

Analysis of Cause—Long Cut to Prevention?

J. H. RENWICK

Although in biomedical research prevention of a disease is customarily considered complementary to its cause, most of the scientific working hypotheses are framed around testing the supposed cause directly. In some circumstances, however, there are advantages in framing hypotheses around prevention.

I shall consider first the circumstances in which the classical causal hypothesis is more or less adequate. These arise either when a disease situation occurs naturally that superficially resembles a laboratory experiment or when a true experiment is possible in an animal that is acceptable as a valid analogue of man.

The thalidomide incident is an example of the natural or at least unplanned experiment. When thalidomide was taken by pregnant women and a defined range of otherwise rare malformations was observed in many of their offspring but not in the offspring of other women, the hypothesis was proposed that thalidomide was at least a contributory cause of these malformations in humans. Indeed, for any new ailment (disease, malformation or injury), it is simple and effective to state a proposition in the causal mode. As in a classical experiment, a known background situation is modified and an effect produced.

An animal experiment with thalidomide would be an example of the other situation (of adequacy of a causal hypothesis) but only when the test animal is trusted as a valid analogue of man. Rhesus monkeys and certain marmosets are so trusted; the malformations produced in them by this drug are almost identical with those in man. A causal hypothesis even for man, being therefore indirectly testable, can usefully be proposed.

NEED FOR ABATIVE HYPOTHESES

The position is different for ailments to which man has been subject for a long time and for which no convincing animal analogue is available. Unfortunately,

Reprinted by permission from *Nature,* Vol. 246, pp. 114–115. Copyright © 1973 Macmillan Magazines Ltd.

we are in the habit of constructing causal claims about even these ailments although the relevant experiments to test the claims directly would usually be unethical. The causal experiments are therefore impracticable except in imagination. In a 'thought experiment' of this sort, an artificial base-line for the population has to be created. In one example, it could involve the (imaginary) absence of refined sucrose. This basal situation would then be modified (in imagination) by the addition of sucrose and various alimentary disorders would ensue. Such at least is the experiment that seems to be suggested by a causal claim that sucrose is an important factor in the cause of colonic diverticulosis, for example. The hypothesis cannot be tested directly because it is nearly always unethical to increase the risk of ailment in a real experiment.

If we can overcome the habit of allowing cause to dominate our thinking, we have a very simple way of bypassing such a problem. This is to perform a real intervention experiment on a part of the population with its present, known burden of disease. This basal situation is then modified—by some procedure such as reduction of intake of refined sucrose. The degree of abatement of the disease is then the outcome of the experiment. With such an experiment in mind, a preventative hypothesis can be formed that is in principle testable, and there are usually no major ethical objections to an experiment of this sort. Further, the statement can be framed briefly yet accurately in terms of deviation from the present state because the 'present state' is known widely enough for it to require, in many cases, no detailed description. Many intervention experiments of exactly this type are done. The change that I am suggesting is that they should be acknowledged as testing preventative statements and not causal ones.

Preventative statements, when confirmed, will sometimes summon up practical measures to control disease. Any such measure—it may be preventative or therapeutic or both—will be called 'abative' as its purpose is to produce some abatement of the ailment and of its burden to the individual and to society.

NON-RECIPROCAL RELATIONSHIP BETWEEN CAUSE AND ABATIVE

Wherever a necessary-and-sufficient abative measure exists there must, in principle, be a corresponding necessary-and-sufficient cause and *vice versa*. The search for cause or abative then comes to much the same task. But the relationship between cause and abative is not always so exactly reciprocal. For instance, a sufficient abative is one that removes a necessary cause. A somewhat oversimplified example of a 'sufficient abative' would be the banning of rye cultivation to prevent poisoning by the ergot fungus, for which rye is the preferred host. The corresponding causal statement is that rye is the 'necessary cause' of ergot poisoning. As in this example, so in general—an abative measure that

has the property of sufficiency but not of necessity is the counterpart of a cause that is necessary but not sufficient.

The degree of reciprocity is also limited in a more subjective way. Even though abatives, like causes, do interact, the percentage abatement of a disease incidence by a single manipulation is an unambiguous and complete concept. By contrast, the concept of the percentage effect of a single cause is more likely to be misleading unless the interactions with other causes are fully specified. Specifying these interactions by the disclaimer—other things being equal—is rarely adequate.

Few such difficulties apply to statements or hypotheses on abatement. The effects of single causes or abatives are best expressed as percentage change from the initial situation. The effects (causal or abative) may sum to several times the incidence of the disease. This is not awkward if it is abative effects that are being summed since each is operative only potentially and mainly in the future. We are not surprised at the existence of alternative means of prevention nor at the possibility of their interacting, so when the sum exceeds 100% effectiveness, we are not disturbed. But there is a seeming absurdity in the statement, say, that 50% of the present incidence of a disease is caused by each of three factors, x, y, z. For the claim to be explicit, interactions or options must be invoked because, obviously, the realised effect of the three factors combined does not exceed the present overall incidence.

As already noted, intervention studies of abative measure are already an established part of epidemiological practice. For example, there have been non-smoking studies, breathalyser studies, and, on the positive side, fluoridation studies. But the conceptual framework has not been adequately spelled out to my knowledge. In some intervention studies, by a curious inversion, the investigators even imply that causes are being studied rather than abatives. The distinction is worth making as it reflects a difference. Abatement is the aim of medicine; the study of causation of an ailment, say, in experimental animals, is frequently a useful intermediate but may not be an essential one in all cases. Even the very concept of causation can, on occasion, be dispensed with in considering abatement strategies.

REMAINING PROBLEM DISEASES ARE A SELECTED SAMPLE

I suggest that if neither causes nor abatives are yet known—and I shall call such an ailment a problem ailment—causation is probably complex. The more complex the causation, the more likely it is to be currently unknown. In tackling such a problem ailment, then, we would be wise to turn at least some of our attention from causes to abatives. For example, the causal mechanism of carcinoma of the colon is unknown and probably complex. From its geographi-

cal distribution the simple and testable abative measure of a high residue diet has been proposed. From past neglect, simple abatives like this have not always been adequately excluded.

ADVANTAGES OF ABATIVE STATEMENTS

For old-established conditions, three major advantages of abative compared with causal statements have so far been mentioned—direct testability on the human species itself; expressibility in simpler terms; and the opportunity to include a quantitative component that expresses the percentage of prevention anticipated.

This last advantage is well illustrated in the case of road accidents. We should like to make statements such as "20% of accidents in the United Kingdom are caused by alcohol", but such statements are intrinsically misleading because of the interactions: practically no cause operates in isolation. An abative statement that the introduction of the breathalyser laws in the United Kingdom reduced the accident rate by a certain percentage is simpler and open to a smaller range of interpretations.

This example introduces another important advantage of abative propositions. They are directly relevant to the achievement of human goals such as the partial prevention of accidents, and so are directly relevant to decision making in public and private life. The quantitative aspect is the most important in this context, as the predicted advantage has to be balanced against the cost of introducing the abative measure.

It is at least arguable that if the observed association between smoking and lung cancer had led to an abative rather than a causal claim, society's 20 year delay in taking action would have been shorter. The claim would have been directly confirmed by the results now available of non-smoking intervention studies and the question of the identification of the presumed carcinogen(s) could have been deferred. Further, the genetic red herring would have been more clearly recognised for what it is—a matter of intellectual interest but with little practical relevance, in this instance, in decision making.

PERSPECTIVES ON CAUSATION AND ABATEMENT

The properties of abative statements are so attractive that we need to ask why they are rarely made. After all, if prevention of disease is an aim of medicine, why have we departed so completely from the folklore mode of expression exemplified by 'an apple a day keeps the doctor away'? The historian might well find an influence of the philosophy of non-medical science—the domi-

nance of how (does it happen) over how not. Waddington in *The Scientific Attitude* roughly defined science as "the organised attempt of mankind to discover how things work as causal systems". Perhaps the absence of specific mention of abatement in such definitions has been taken to imply that abative statements are less scientific than causal ones, despite the fact that, for both types, the "criterion of truth is experimental" and objective.

Alternatively, did the current emphasis on causation spring from the need of the legal system to apportion blame? Or, equally plausibly, was the need to study epidemics more pressing than the need to study the less dramatic non-epidemic state? The manifest success of laboratory methodology in so many non-human fields undoubtedly played a large part in establishing the habit of thinking in the causal mode. We correctly believe that we have not understood anything at a fundamental level unless we have understood the mechanism of causation. And we often think (incorrectly) that such understanding is a prerequisite of wise action. Kant knew better—that "it is often necessary to make a decision on the basis of knowledge sufficient for action but insufficient to satisfy the intellect".

It is true, even today, that wise action can occasionally be based at least temporarily on empirical knowledge alone and there are many examples of this from the past. From the time of Admiral Wager, scurvy was controlled in the Navy by the provision of citrus fruits before ascorbic acid was known to be a vitamin. Penicillin was used effectively, even before its mode of action was understood; and tobacco avoidance dramatically reduces bronchocarcinoma incidences although we still do not know how.

Decision-making in medicine is more directly concerned with prevention and treatment rather than causation, so we should often express claims in terms of abatement rather than causation as at present. A few scientists disagree. They argue that causation and abatement are simply converse concepts and, at the same time, that one is scientific, the other empirical. Both arguments are rather shallow assessments. Abatement is not always the simple converse of causation. Further, an abative statement can be as scientific and testable experimentally as any other. It may even be just as possible to discover general laws concerning abatement as laws concerning causation.

Abative and causal hypotheses are not mutually exclusive. Indeed, there is a one-to-one relationship between them. The abative statement is usually simpler in practice. This is particularly true for complex problems. And most real-life problems are complex.

Paternalism

GERALD DWORKIN

. . . I take as my starting point the "one very simple principle" proclaimed by Mill in *On Liberty* . . . "That principle is, that the sole end for which mankind are warranted, individually or collectively, in interfering with the liberty of action of any of their number, is self-protection. That the only purpose for which power can be rightfully exercised over any member of a civilized community, against his will, is to prevent harm to others. He cannot rightfully be compelled to do or forbear because it will be better for him to do so, because it will make him happier, because, in the opinion of others, to do so would be wise, or even right."

This principle is neither "one" nor "very simple." It is at least two principles; one asserting that self-protection or the prevention of harm to others is sometimes a sufficient warrant and the other claiming that the individual's own good is *never* a sufficient warrant for the exercise of compulsion either by the society as a whole or by its individual members. I assume that no one with the possible exception of extreme pacifists or anarchists questions the correctness of the first half of the principle. This essay is an examination of the negative claim embodied in Mill's principle—the objection to paternalistic interferences with a man's liberty.

I

By paternalism I shall understand roughly the interference with a person's liberty of action justified by reasons referring exclusively to the welfare, good, happiness, needs, interests or values of the person being coerced. One is always well-advised to illustrate one's definitions by examples but it is not easy to find "pure" examples of paternalistic interferences. For almost any piece of legislation is justified by several different kinds of reasons and even if historically a piece of legislation can be shown to have been introduced for purely paternalistic motives, it may be that advocates of the legislation with an anti-paternalistic outlook can find sufficient reasons justifying the legislation without appealing to the reasons which were originally adduced to support it. Thus, for example, it may be that the original legislation requiring motorcyclists to wear safety helmets was introduced for purely paternalistic reasons. But the Rhode Island Supreme Court recently upheld such legislation on the grounds that it was "not persuaded that the legislature is powerless to prohibit individuals from pursuing a course of conduct which could conceivably result in their becoming public charges," thus clearly introducing reasons of a quite different kind. Now I regard this decision as being based on reasoning of a very dubious nature but it illustrates the kind of problem one has in finding examples. The following is a list of the kinds of interferences I have in mind as being paternalistic.

II

1. Laws requiring motorcyclists to wear safety helmets when operating their machines.
2. Laws forbidding persons from swimming at a public beach when lifeguards are not on duty.
3. Laws making suicide a criminal offense.
4. Laws making it illegal for women and children to work at certain types of jobs.
5. Laws regulating certain kinds of sexual conduct, e.g. homosexuality among consenting adults in private.
6. Laws regulating the use of certain drugs which may have harmful consequences to the user but do not lead to anti-social conduct.
7. Laws requiring a license to engage in certain professions with those not receiving a license subject to fine or jail sentence if they do engage in the practice.
8. Laws compelling people to spend a specified fraction of their income on the purchase of retirement annuities. (Social Security)
9. Laws forbidding various forms of gambling (often justified on the grounds that the poor are more likely to throw away their money on such activities than the rich who can afford to).
10. Laws regulating the maximum rate of interest for loans.
11. Laws against duelling.

In addition to laws which attach criminal or civil penalties to certain kinds of action there are laws, rules, regulations, decrees, which make it either difficult or impossible for people to carry out their plans and which are also justified on paternalistic grounds. Examples of this are:

1. Laws regulating the types of contracts which will be upheld as valid by the courts, e.g. (an example of Mill's to which I shall return) no man may make a valid contract for perpetual involuntary servitude.

2. Not allowing as a defense to a charge of murder or assault the consent of the victim.

3. Requiring members of certain religious sects to have compulsory blood transfusions. This is made possible by not allowing the patient to have recourse to civil suits for assault and battery and by means of injunctions.

4. Civil commitment procedures when these are specifically justified on the basis of preventing the person being committed from harming himself. (The D.C. Hospitalization of the Mentally Ill Act provides for involuntary hospitalization of a person who "is mentally ill, and because of that illness, is likely to injure *himself* or others if allowed to remain at liberty." The term injure in this context applies to unintentional as well as intentional injuries.)

5. Putting fluorides in the community water supply.

All of my examples are of existing restrictions on the liberty of individuals. Obviously one can think of interferences which have not yet been imposed. Thus one might ban the sale of cigarettes, or require that people wear safety-belts in automobiles (as opposed to merely having them installed) enforcing this by not allowing motorists to sue for injuries even when caused by other drivers if the motorist was not wearing a seat-belt at the time of the accident.

I shall not be concerned with activities which though defended on paternalistic grounds are not interferences with the liberty of persons, e.g. the giving of subsidies in kind rather than in cash on the grounds that the recipients would not spend the money on the goods which they really need, or not including a $1000 deductible provision in a basic protection automobile insurance plan on the ground that the people who would elect it could least afford it. Nor shall I be concerned with measures such as "truth-in-advertising" acts and the Pure Food and Drug legislation which are often attacked as paternalistic but which should not be considered so. In these cases all that is provided—it is true by the use of compulsion—is information which it is presumed that rational persons are interested in having in order to make wise decisions. There is no interference with the liberty of the consumer unless one wants to stretch a point beyond good sense and say that his liberty to apply for a loan without knowing the true rate of interest is diminished. It is true that sometimes there is sentiment for going further than providing information, for example when laws against usurious interest are passed preventing those who might wish to contract loans at high rates of interest from doing so, and these measures may correctly be considered paternalistic.

III

Bearing these examples in mind let me return to a characterization of paternalism. I said earlier that I meant by the term, roughly, interference with a person's liberty for his own good. But as some of the examples show, the class of persons whose good is involved is not always identical with the class of persons whose freedom is restricted. Thus in the case of professional licensing it is the practitioner who is directly interfered with and it is the would-be patient whose interests are presumably being served. Not allowing the consent of the victim to be a defense to certain types of crime primarily affects the would-be aggressor but it is the interests of the willing victim that we are trying to protect. Sometimes a person may fall into both classes as would be the case if we banned the manufacture and sale of cigarettes and a given manufacturer happened to be a smoker as well.

Thus we may first divide paternalistic interferences into "pure" and "impure" cases. In "pure" paternalism the class of persons whose freedom is restricted is identical with the class of persons whose benefit is intended to be promoted by such restrictions. Examples: the making of suicide a crime, requiring passengers in automobiles to wear seat-belts, requiring a Christian Scientist to receive a blood transfusion. In the case of "impure" paternalism in trying to protect the welfare of a class of persons we find that the only way to do so will involve restricting the freedom of other persons besides those who are benefitted. Now it might be thought that there are no cases of "impure" paternalism since any such case could always be justified on non-paternalistic grounds, i.e. in terms of preventing harms to others. Thus we might ban cigarette manufacturers from continuing to manufacture their product on the grounds that we are preventing them from causing illness to others in the same way that we prevent other manufacturers from releasing pollutants into the atmosphere, thereby causing danger to the members of the community. The difference is, however, that in the former but not the latter case the harm is of such a nature that it could be avoided by those individuals affected if they so chose. The incurring of the harm requires, so to speak, the active co-operation of the victim. It would be mistaken theoretically and hypocritical in practice to assert that our interference in such cases is just like our interference in standard cases of protecting others from harm. At the very least someone interfered with in this way can reply that no one is complaining about his activities. It may be that impure paternalism requires arguments or reasons of a stronger kind in order to be justified since there are persons who are losing a portion of their liberty and they do not even have the solace of having it be done "in their own interest." Of course in some sense, if paternalistic justifications are ever correct, then we are protecting others, we are preventing some from injuring others, but it is important to see the differences between this and the standard case.

Paternalism then will always involve limitations on the liberty of some individuals in their own interest but it may also extend to interferences with the liberty of parties whose interests are not in question.

IV

Finally, by way of some more preliminary analysis, I want to distinguish paternalistic interferences with liberty from a related type with which it is often confused. Consider, for example, legislation which forbids employees to work more than, say, 40 hours per week. It is sometimes argued that such legislation is paternalistic for if employees desired such a restriction on their hours of work they could agree among themselves to impose it voluntarily. But because they do not the society imposes its own conception of their best interests upon them by the use of coercion. Hence this is paternalism.

Now it may be that some legislation of this nature is, in fact, paternalistically motivated. I am not denying that. All I want to point out is that there is another possible way of justifying such measures which is not paternalistic in nature. It is not paternalistic because as Mill puts it in a similar context such measures are "required not to overrule the judgment of individuals respecting their own interest, but to give effect to that judgment: they being unable to give effect to it except by concert, which concert again cannot be effectual unless it receives validity and sanction from the law."

The line of reasoning here is a familiar one first found in Hobbes and developed with great sophistication by contemporary economists in the last decade or so. There are restrictions which are in the interests of a class of persons taken collectively but are such that the immediate interest of each individual is furthered by his violating the rule when others adhere to it. In such cases the individuals involved may need the use of compulsion to give effect to their collective judgment of their own interest by guaranteeing each individual compliance by the others. In these cases compulsion is not used to achieve some benefit which is not recognized to be a benefit by those concerned, but rather because it is the only feasible means of achieving some benefit which *is* recognized as such by all concerned. This way of viewing matters provides us with another characterization of paternalism in general. Paternalism might be thought of as the use of coercion to achieve a good which is not recognized as such by those persons for whom the good is intended. Again while this formulation captures the heart of the matter—it is surely what Mill is objecting to in *On Liberty*—the matter is not always quite like that. For example, when we force motorcyclists to wear helmets we are trying to promote a good—the protection of the person from injury—which is surely recognized by most of the individuals concerned. It is not that a cyclist doesn't value his bodily integrity; rather, as a supporter of such legislation would put it, he either places, perhaps irrationally, another value or good (freedom from wearing a helmet) above that of physical well-being or, perhaps, while recognizing the danger in the abstract, he either does not fully appreciate it or he underestimates the likelihood of its occurring. But now we are approaching the question of possible justifications of paternalistic measures and the rest of this essay will be devoted to that question.

V

I shall begin for dialectical purposes by discussing Mill's objections to paternalism and then go on to discuss more positive proposals.

An initial feature that strikes one is the absolute nature of Mill's prohibitions against paternalism. It is so unlike the carefully qualified admonitions of Mill and his fellow Utilitarians on other moral issues. He speaks of self-protection as the *sole* end warranting coercion, of the individual's own goals as *never* being a sufficient warrant. Contrast this with his discussion of the prohibition against lying in *Util[itarianism]*.

> Yet that even this rule, sacred as it is, admits of possible exception, is acknowledged by all moralists, the chief of which is where the with-holding of some fact . . . would save an individual . . . from great and unmerited evil.

The same tentativeness is present when he deals with justice.

> It is confessedly unjust to break faith with any one: to violate an engagement, either express or implied, or disappoint expectations raised by our own conduct, at least if we have raised these expectations knowingly and voluntarily. Like all the other obligations of justice already spoken of, this one is not regarded as absolute, but as capable of being overruled by a stronger obligation of justice on the other side.

This anomaly calls for some explanation. The structure of Mill's argument is a follows:

1. Since restraint is an evil, the burden of proof is on those who propose such restraint.
2. Since the conduct which is being considered is purely self-regarding, the normal appeal to the protection of the interests of others is not available.
3. Therefore we have to consider whether reasons involving reference to the individual's own good, happiness, welfare, or interests are sufficient to overcome the burden of justification.

4. We either cannot advance the interests of the individual by compulsion, or the attempt to do so involves evil which outweighs the good done.
5. Hence the promotion of the individual's own interests does not provide a sufficient warrant for the use of compulsion.

Clearly the operative premise here is 4 and it is bolstered by claims about the status of the individual as judge and appraiser of his welfare, interests, needs, etc.

> With respect to his own feelings and circumstances, the most ordinary man or woman has means of knowledge immeasurably surpassing those that can be possessed by any one else. . . .
>
> He is the man most interested in his own well-being: the interest which any other person, except in cases of strong personal attachment, can have in it, is trifling, compared to that which he himself has.

These claims are used to support the following generalizations concerning the utility of compulsion for paternalistic purposes.

> The interferences of society to overrule his judgment and purposes in what only regards himself must be grounded on general presumptions, which may be altogether wrong, and even if right, are as likely as not to be misapplied to individual cases. . . .
>
> But the strongest of all the arguments against the interference of the public with purely personal conduct is that when it does interfere, the odds are that it interferes wrongly and in the wrong place. . . .
>
> All errors which the individual is likely to commit against advice and warning are far outweighed by the evil of allowing others to constrain him to what they deem his good.

Performing the utilitarian calculation by balancing the advantages and disadvantages we find that:

> Mankind are greater gainers by suffering each other to live as seems good to themselves, than by compelling each other to live as seems good to the rest.

From which follows the operative premise 4.

This classical case of a utilitarian argument with all the premises spelled out is not the only line of reasoning present in Mill's discussion. There are asides, and more than asides, which look quite different and I shall deal with them later. But this is clearly the main channel of Mill's thought and it is one which has been subjected to vigorous attack from the moment it appeared—most often by fellow Utilitarians. The link that they have usually seized on is, as Fitzjames Stephen put it, the absence of proof that the "mass of adults are so well acquainted with their own interests and so much disposed to pursue them that no compulsion or restraint put upon them by any others for the purpose of promoting their interest can really promote them." Even so sympathetic a critic as Hart is forced to the conclusion that:

> In Chapter 5 of his essay Mill carried his protests against paternalism to lengths that may now appear to us as fantastic . . . No doubt if we no longer sympathise with this criticism this is due, in part, to a general decline in the belief that individuals know their own interest best.
>
> Mill endows the average individual with "too much of the psychology of a middle-aged man whose desires are relatively fixed, not liable to be artificially stimulated by external influences; who knows what he wants and what gives him satisfaction of happiness; and who pursues these things when he can."

Now it is interesting to note that Mill himself was aware of some of the limitations on the doctrine that the individual is the best judge of his own interests. In his discussion of government intervention in general (even where the intervention does not interfere with liberty but provides alternative institutions to those of the market), after making claims which are parallel to those just discussed, e.g.,

> People understand their own business and their own interests better, and care for them more, than the government does, or can be expected to do,

he goes on to an intelligent discussion of the "very large and conspicuous exceptions" to the maxim that:

> Most persons take a juster and more intelligent view of their own interest, and of the means of promoting it than can either be prescribed to them by a general enactment of the legislature, or pointed out in the particular case by a public functionary.

Thus there are things

> of which the utility does not consist in ministering to inclinations, nor in serving the daily uses of life, and the want of which is least felt where the need is greatest. This is peculiarly true of those things which are chiefly useful as tending to raise the character of human beings. The uncultivated cannot be competent judges of cultivation. Those who most need to be made wiser and better, usually desire it least, and, if they desired it, would be incapable of finding the way to it by their own lights.
>
>   . . . A second exception to the doctrine that individuals are the best judges of their own interest, is when an individual attempts to decide irrevocably now what will be best for his interest at some future and distant time. The presumption in favor of individual judgment is only legitimate, where the judgment is grounded on actual, and especially on present, personal experience; not where it is formed antecedently to experience, and not suffered to be reversed even after experience has condemned it.

The upshot of these exceptions is that Mill does not declare that there should never be government interference with the economy but rather that

> . . . in every instance, the burden of making out a strong case should be thrown not on those who resist but on those who recommend government interference. Letting alone, in short, should be the general practice: every departure from it, unless required by some great good, is a certain evil.

In short, we get a presumption not an absolute prohibition. The question is, why doesn't the argument against paternalism go the same way?

I suggest that the answer lies in seeing that in addition to a purely utilitarian argument Mill uses another as well. As a Utilitarian Mill has to show, in Fitz-james Stephen's words, that:

> Self-protection apart, no good object can be attained by any compulsion which is not in itself a greater evil than the absence of the object which the compulsion obtains.

To show this is impossible; one reason being that it isn't true. Preventing a man from selling himself into slavery (a paternalistic measure which Mill himself accepts as legitimate), or from taking heroin, or from driving a car without wearing seat-belts may constitute a lesser evil than allowing him to do any of these things. A consistent Utilitarian can only argue against paternalism on the grounds that it (as a matter of fact) does not maximize the good. It is always a contingent question that may be refuted by the evidence. But there is also a non-contingent argument which runs through *On Liberty*. When Mill states that "there is a part of the life of every person who has come to years of discretion, within which the individuality of that person ought to reign uncontrolled either by any other person or by the public collectively," he is saying something about what it means to be a person, an autonomous agent. It is because coercing a person for his own good denies this status as an independent entity that Mill objects to it so strongly and in such absolute terms. To be able to choose is a good that is independent of the wisdom of what is chosen. A man's "mode of laying out his existence is the best, not because it is the best in itself, but because it is his own mode."

> It is the privilege and proper condition of a human being, arrived at the maturity of his faculties, to use and interpret experience in his own way.

As further evidence of this line of reasoning in Mill consider the one exception to his prohibition against paternalism.

> In this and most civilised countries, for example, an engagement by which a person should sell himself, or allow himself to be sold, as a slave, would be null and void;

neither enforced by law nor by opinion. The ground for thus limiting his power of voluntarily disposing of his own lot in life, is apparent, and is very clearly seen in this extreme case. The reason for not interfering, unless for the sake of others, with a person's voluntary acts, is consideration for his liberty. His voluntary choice is evidence that what he so chooses is desirable, or at least endurable, to him, and his good is on the whole best provided for by allowing him to take his own means of pursuing it. But by selling himself for a slave, he abdicates his liberty; he foregoes any future use of it beyond that single act.

He therefore defeats, in his own case, the very purpose which is the justification of allowing him to dispose of himself. He is no longer free; but is thenceforth in a position which has no longer the presumption in its favour, that would be afforded by his voluntarily remaining in it. The principle of freedom cannot require that he should be free not to be free. It is not freedom to be allowed to alienate his freedom.

Now leaving aside the fudging on the meaning of freedom in the last line, it is clear that part of this argument is incorrect. While it is true that *future* choices of the slave are not reasons for thinking that what he chooses then is desirable for him, what is at issue is limiting his immediate choice; and since this choice is made freely, the individual may be correct in thinking that his interests are best provided for by entering such a contract. But the main consideration for not allowing such a contract is the need to preserve the liberty of the person to make future choices. This gives us a principle—a very narrow one—by which to justify some paternalistic interferences. Paternalism is justified only to preserve a wider range of freedom for the individual in question. How far this principle could be extended, whether it can justify all the cases in which we are inclined upon reflection to think paternalistic measures justified remains to be discussed. What I have tried to show so far is that there are two strains of argument in Mill—one a straight-forward Utilitarian mode of reasoning and one which relies not on the goods which free choice leads to but on the absolute value of the choice itself. The first cannot establish any absolute prohibition but at most a presumption and indeed a fairly weak one, given some fairly plausible assumptions about human psychology; the second, while a stronger line of argument, seems to me to allow on its own grounds a wider range of paternalism than might be suspected. I turn now to a consideration of these matters.

VI

. . . Let me suggest types of situations in which it seems plausible to suppose that fully rational individuals would agree to having paternalistic restrictions imposed upon them. It is reasonable to suppose that there are "goods" such as health which any person would want to have in order to pursue his own good— no matter how that good is conceived. This is an argument that is used in connection with compulsory education for children but it seems to me that it can be extended to other goods which have this character. Then one could agree that the attainment of such goods should be promoted even when not recognized to be such, at the moment, by the individuals concerned.

An immediate difficulty that arises stems from the fact that men are always faced with competing goods and that there may be reasons why even a value such as health—or indeed life—may be overridden by competing values. Thus the problem with the Christian Scientist and blood transfusions. It may be more important for him to reject "impure substances" than to go on living. The difficult problem that must be faced is whether one can give sense to the notion of a person irrationally attaching weights to competing values.

Consider a person who knows the statistical data on the probability of being injured when not wearing seat-belts in an automobile and knows the types and gravity of the various injuries. He also insists that the inconvenience attached to fastening the belt every time he gets in and out of the car outweighs for him the possible risks to himself. I am inclined in this case to think that such a weighing is irrational. Given his life plans which we are assuming are those of the average person, his interests and commitments already undertaken, I think it is safe to predict that we can find inconsistencies in his calculations at some point. I am assuming that this is not a man who for some conscious or unconscious reasons is trying to injure himself nor is he a man who just likes to "live dangerously." I am assuming that he is like us in all the relevant respects but just puts an enormously high negative value on inconvenience—one which does not seem comprehensible or reasonable.

It is always possible, of course to assimilate this person to creatures like myself. I, also, neglect to fasten my seat-belt and I concede such behavior is not rational but not because I weigh the inconvenience differently from those who fasten the belts. It is just that having made (roughly) the same calculation as everybody else, I ignore it in my actions. [Note: a much better case of weakness of the will than those usually given in ethics texts.] A plausible explanation for this deplorable habit is that although I know in some intellectual sense what the probabilities and risks are, I do not fully appreciate them in an emotionally genuine manner.

We have two distinct types of situation in which a man acts in a non-rational fashion. In one case he attaches incorrect weights to some of his values; in the other he neglects to act in accordance with his actual preferences and desires. Clearly there is a stronger and more persuasive argument for paternalism in the latter situation. Here we are really not—by assumption—imposing a good on another person. But why may we not extend our interference to what we might call evaluative delusions? After all, in the case of cognitive delusions we are prepared, often, to act against the expressed will of the person involved. If a man believes that when he jumps out the window he will float upwards—

Robert Nozick's example—would not we detain him, forcibly if necessary? The reply will be that this man doesn't wish to be injured and if we could convince him that he is mistaken as to the consequences of his action he would not wish to perform the action. But part of what is involved in claiming that a man who doesn't fasten his seat-belts is attaching an irrational weight to the inconvenience of fastening them is that if he were to be involved in an accident and severely injured he would look back and admit that the inconvenience wasn't as bad as all that. So there is a sense in which if I could convince him of the consequences of his action he also would not wish to continue his present course of action. Now the notion of consequences being used here is covering a lot of ground. In one case it's being used to indicate what will or can happen as a result of a course of action and in the other it's making a prediction about the future evaluation of the consequences—in the first sense—of a course of action. And whatever the difference between facts and values—whether it be hard and fast or soft and slow—we are genuinely more reluctant to consent to interferences where evaluative differences are the issue. Let me now consider another factor which comes into play in some of these situations which may make an important difference in our willingness to consent to paternalistic restrictions.

Some of the decisions we make are of such a character that they produce changes which are in one or another way irreversible. Situations are created in which it is difficult or impossible to return to anything like the initial stage at which the decision was made. In particular, some of these changes will make it impossible to continue to make reasoned choices in the future. I am thinking specifically of decisions which involve taking drugs that are physically or psychologically addictive and those which are destructive of one's mental and physical capacities.

I suggest we think of the imposition of paternalistic interferences in situations of this kind as being a kind of insurance policy which we take out against making decisions which are far-reaching, potentially dangerous and irreversible. Each of these factors is important. Clearly there are many decisions we make that are relatively irreversible. In deciding to learn to play chess I could predict in view of my general interest in games that some portion of my free-time was going to be preempted and that it would not be easy to give up the game once I acquired a certain competence. But my whole life-style was not going to be jeopardized in an extreme manner. Further it might be argued that even with addictive drugs such as heroin one's normal life plans would not be seriously interfered with if an inexpensive and adequate supply were readily available. So this type of argument might have a much narrower scope than appears to be the case at first.

A second class of cases concerns decisions which are made under extreme psychological and sociological pressures. I am not thinking here of the making of the decision as being something one is pressured into—e.g., a good reason for making duelling illegal is that unless this is done many people might have to manifest their courage and integrity in ways in which they would rather not do so—but rather of decisions such as that to commit suicide which are usually made at a point where the individual is not thinking clearly and calmly about the nature of his decision. In addition, of course, this comes under the previous heading of all-too-irrevocable decision. Now there are practical steps which a society could take if it wanted to decrease the possibility of suicide—for example not paying social security benefits to the survivors or as religious institutions do, not allowing such persons to be buried with the same status as natural deaths. I think we may count these as interferences with the liberty of persons to attempt suicide and the question is whether they are justifiable.

Using my argument schema the question is whether rational individuals would consent to such limitations. I see no reason for them to consent to an absolute prohibition but I do think it is reasonable for them to agree to some kind of enforced waiting period. Since we are all aware of the possibility of temporary states, such as great fear or depression, that are inimical to the making of well-informed and rational decisions, it would be prudent for all of us if there were some kind of institutional arrangement whereby we were restrained from making a decision which is (all too) irreversible. What this would be like in practice is difficult to envisage and it may be that if no practical arrangements were feasible, then we would have to conclude that there should be no restriction at all on this kind of action. But we might have a "cooling off" period, in much the same way that we now require couples who file for divorce to go through a waiting period. Or, more far-fetched, we might imagine a Suicide Board composed of a psychologist and another member picked by the applicant. The Board would be required to meet and talk with the person proposing to take his life, though its approval would not be required.

A third class of decisions—these classes are not supposed to be disjoint—involves dangers which are either not sufficiently understood or appreciated correctly by the persons involved. Let me illustrate, using the example of cigarette smoking, a number of possible cases.

1. A man may not know the facts—e.g., smoking between 1 and 2 packs a day shortens life expectancy 6.2 years, the costs and pain of the illness caused by smoking, etc.
2. A man may know the facts, wish to stop smoking, but not have the requisite willpower.
3. A man may know the facts but not have them play the correct role in his calculation because, say, he discounts the danger psychologically because it is remote in time and/or inflates the attractiveness of other consequences of his decision which he regards as beneficial.

In case 1 what is called for is education, the posting of warnings, etc. In case 2 there is no theoretical problem. We are not imposing a good on someone who rejects it. We are simply using coercion to enable people to carry out their own goals. (Note: There obviously is a difficulty in that only a subclass of the individuals affected wish to be prevented from doing what they are doing.) In case 3 there is a sense in which we are imposing a good on someone since given his current appraisal of the facts he doesn't wish to be restricted. But in another sense we are not imposing a good since what is being claimed—and what must be shown or at least argued for—is that an accurate accounting on his part would lead him to reject his current course of action. Now we all know that such cases exist, that we are prone to disregard dangers that are only possibilities, that immediate pleasures are often magnified and distorted.

If in addition the dangers are severe and far-reaching, we could agree to allowing the state a certain degree of power to intervene in such situations. The difficulty is in specifying in advance, even vaguely, the class of cases in which intervention will be legitimate. . . .

I have suggested in this essay a number of types of situations in which it seems plausible that rational men would agree to granting the legislative powers of a society the right to impose restrictions on what Mill calls "self-regarding" conduct. However, rational men knowing something about the resources of ignorance, ill-will and stupidity available to the law-makers of a society—a good case in point is the history of drug legislation in the United States—will be concerned to limit such intervention to a minimum. I suggest in closing two principles designed to achieve this end.

In all cases of paternalistic legislation there must be a heavy and clear burden of proof placed on the authorities to demonstrate the exact nature of the harmful effects (or beneficial consequences) to be avoided (or achieved) and the probability of their occurrence. The burden of proof here is twofold—what lawyers distinguish as the burden of going forward and the burden of persuasion. That the authorities have the burden of going forward means that it is up to them to raise the question and bring forward evidence of the evils to be avoided. Unlike the case of new drugs where the manufacturer must produce some evidence that the drug has been tested and found not harmful, no citizen has to show with respect to self-regarding conduct that it is not harmful or promotes his best interests. In addition the nature and cogency of the evidence for the harmfulness of the course of action must be set at a high level. To paraphrase a formulation of the burden of proof for criminal proceedings—better 10 men ruin themselves than one man be unjustly deprived of liberty.

Finally I suggest a principle of the least restrictive alternative. If there is an alternative way of accomplishing the desired end without restricting liberty, then although it may involve great expense, inconvenience, etc., the society must adopt it.

III

MODERN CHALLENGES TO THE PUBLIC'S HEALTH

4

ALCOHOL, TOBACCO, AND OTHER DRUGS

Public health approaches have worked a fundamental change in perspective on the causes and prevention of alcoholism and alcohol abuse. Something similar is taking place with regard to other drugs, including tobacco and the illegal drugs.

There has been a remarkable transformation in this century of our policy toward alcohol, from laissez-faire to national Prohibition to a disease concept of addiction and a more public-health-oriented policy. Today our alcohol policies are an amalgam of these successive eras of prevention; older attitudes persist, unintegrated. A prohibitionist approach is reflected in laws prohibiting the sale of alcohol in some counties, while a more public health approach is seen in imposing state age limits on drinking in order to reduce teenage deaths related to drunk driving. Higher taxes on alcohol to discourage heavy drinking is another example of a public health approach.

Up until the American revolution, there was relatively little interest in officially regulating drinking. The Puritans accepted alcohol, while controlling its use through informal social sanctions, such as those of the local tavernkeepers, the local communities, and the church. Yet the Revolutionary period was a time when drunkenness came to be seen as a rising problem in the towns and cities of the new country. This was intensified by the rise of a new industry: the distilled spirits or whiskey industry among farmers further to the west and inland.

For the next century and a half, Temperance and later Prohibition dominated the American political agenda. The coming of Prohibition in 1917 as a World War I wartime measure, and the institutionalizing of Prohibition with the passage of the Volstead Amendment, are major landmarks in American social and political history. As an experiment in a moralistic approach to alcohol, Prohibition was a serious failure, despite the fact that Prohibition caused drinking to fall precipitously in the United States and to remain low for several decades after repeal. It was a failure because a less restrictive set of measures, like heavy taxation or shorter hours for sale, could have produced the same results in falling drinking levels and declining cirrhosis rates. It was also a failure because its chief aim was less to improve the public's health and instead improve the public morality, to produce the Sober Republic, which would increase well-being in all realms.

Alcoholism, or the concept that heavy drinking is a disease, is one of the legacies of Prohibition. Alcoholism as an idea is based on the "two types of people" theory: There are drinkers who can control their drinking, and alcoholics who can not, and these two groups are fairly fixed in their distribution across the population, with alcoholics constituting a small minority. The idea that drinking behavior is distributed across a population and is constantly changing was not fully appreciated until the late 1960s and early 70s, when researchers began to study the patterning of drinking in the United States.

In the first selection, James Mosher and David Jernigan detail the fundamental shift in thinking about alcohol problems that has occurred in the past three decades, beginning with epidemiological analysis of the relationship between levels of per capita consumption of alcohol and rates of alcohol-related problems like cirrhosis. They describe the growth of a public health perspective inside and outside government circles and how this new conception has changed our stance toward alcohol problems. The public health perspective for alcohol problems is similar to that for other public health problems: The focus is on the distribution of risk and hazard (alcohol) in the whole population and the need for policies that limit and control this hazard. The whole community, including all who drink, bears responsibility for preventing alcohol problems. This new focus shifts attention from drinkers who have a disease and puts far more attention on regulating the sale and price and advertising of alcohol products for the whole community. This new perspective makes limits to consumption of alcohol for everyone a central policy issue. Of course the new perspective is staunchly resisted by the alcohol industry, which prefers to see the problem defined as "treating alcoholism" rather than reducing alcohol consumption (and the profits of the liquor industry) in the whole population.

What about illegal drugs? Is our experience with the prohibition of alcohol such that we should consider legalizing other drugs, like marijuana, heroin, or cocaine? Most public health experts would likely say no, but with considerable hesitance. On one hand, the lesson of the recent decades has been that increasing access to a substance will almost surely increase its consumption. On the other hand, the prohibition of drugs is a very costly and divisive policy in itself. The drug trade takes a terrible social and environmental toll, and the courts and police have been ineffective in combating it, despite the fact that our prisons are filled with people there for drug-related offenses.

Whether we should dismantle part of our national policy against illegal drugs is deeply controversial. Bonnie Steinbock provides a public health perspective on the whole debate over legalizing drugs.[1] As we note in Chapter 6, a public health perspective rejects policies based on moralism. It also demands that any policy be based on empirical evidence. The public health perspective also focuses less on the debate over legalization versus prohibition and more on ways of reducing the harm of using dangerous drugs to individuals and to groups. Steinbock presents a long, sad litany of failures in our current drug policy, including the use of criminal sanctions to discourage even minor drug use and the huge infrastructure we have erected to suppress the trade in drugs. Jails have become overcrowded as long jail sentences have been given for both users and minor drug traffickers. The war on drugs has had a chilling effect on civil liberties, resulting in illicit police searches of vehicles and homes. Based on tips from informants, armed police have burst into apartments in search of drugs, terrifying the inhabitants, who sometimes have nothing to do with drugs. Our drug policy demands cannabis (the active substance in marijuana) not be used to counteract pain and nausea in AIDS and cancer patients. Moreover, we have been ineffective in persuading other nations to reduce the production of drugs, given our inability to curb our domestic consumption.

As Steinbock notes, there are other options to legalization, such as decriminalization or the decision to not arrest and prosecute use of drugs like marijuana, even if laws forbidding their use remain on the books. Several European nations have a more forgiving stance toward those who use drugs; they offer users low-cost drugs or therapy but are strict about the sale or provision of illegal drugs.

The moralistic approach has admittedly had certain benefits. Millions of Americans use little or no alcohol as the result of moral and religious disapproval. Social disapproval is also having an impact on smoking. The decline in smoking in recent decades is not only due to the scare put into the public by a series of Surgeon General reports, but also to the stigmatizing of smokers in our society. Social disapproval is a form of moralism, seeing the smoker as someone who is persisting in a socially condemned practice, a kind of deviancy. While this can go too far, it is nonetheless effective in discouraging people from smoking. The cigarette's long fall from the celluloid lips of Humphrey Bogart and Lauren Bacall to the chilled lips of office workers huddled outside buildings in the winter is a remarkable social transformation ushered in by more than the fear of lung cancer.

In the third selection, Leonard Glantz reviews the debate over regulating advertising for tobacco. This is an important public health issue since tobacco, a legal product, causes far more harm than do illegal drugs. It is important for another reason. The percentage of those smoking tobacco, especially cigarettes, have fallen precipitously since the 1960s, resulting in major declines in heart disease and more recently lung cancer. These declines occurred as a result of aggressive reports by U.S. Surgeons General, as a result of counteradvertising on television and the eventual omission of cigarette advertising on television, and as a result of a constant barrage of public discussion regarding the lethality of smoking.

For these reasons, the battle to control tobacco and smoking has centered on advertising and the media, with some arguing that all advertising for tobacco products should be banned, especially when these advertisements seem targeted at people who are not yet old enough to smoke. (The same issues arise for the promotion of beer by the alcohol industry.) Thus, the question arises: Can the state can legitimately ban advertising for a legal product, one sold in the stream of commerce? Many argue that this would be unconstitutional. As Glantz points out, it may be that the doctrine of "commercial speech," developed by liberal justices on the Supreme Court beginning in the 1970s, may accord advertising, even for dangerous products like alcohol and tobacco, a measure of the protections now granted to ordinary speech in newspapers, television, and elsewhere.

NOTES

1. See also James Mosher and Karen Yanagisako, "Public Health, Not Social Warfare: A Public Health Approach to Illegal Drug Policy," *Journal of Public Health Policy,* 12 (1991), pp. 278–321.

New Directions in Alcohol Policy

JAMES F. MOSHER AND DAVID H. JERNIGAN

INTRODUCTION

An exciting drama is unfolding in the public health field today. As previous reviews have indicated, a new consensus is emerging regarding the prevention of alcohol-related problems, one of our most serious health issues. Built on public health theory and experience, this new alcohol policy movement offers the entire public health field the opportunity to reach new constituencies. In keeping with the nature of the problems it is designed to prevent, the approach cuts across ideological, racial, ethnic, and socioeconomic divisions in our society and provides the means to build a coalition for broad social change in regard to health policy.

As was the case with the antismoking and other public health movements that preceded it, this new alcohol policy movement is opposed by powerful economic and political interests. Classic tactics to divert and blunt health policy reform are now a familiar part of the alcohol field—industry denials of health risks associated with their product; industry-financed research designed to cast doubt on studies documenting adverse consequences of its use; strong-arm lobbying at local, state, and federal levels, including massive contributions to legislators; industry "donations" to a variety of social groups to deter their participation in the reform movement; massive advertising budgets that are used to silence and shape media attention to alcohol problems; and much more. That the tactics have a familiar ring is no coincidence: many alcohol companies are owned by tobacco conglomerates, and draw on that industry's experience in conducting a sophisticated and heavily financed campaign to blunt efforts to prevent tobacco-related disease.

As indicated in previous reviews, implementing the new approaches to alcohol-related problem prevention is not an easy task. The theoretical soundness of the new approaches has been thoroughly documented, and thus this review focuses on both the barriers and promising routes to implementation. Drawing

With permission, from the *Annual Review of Public Health,* Volume 10, © 1989 by Annual Reviews. Also reprinted with the permission of the authors.

on concrete experiences in researching and implementing policy approaches, we argue that the alcohol field is moving into a new implementation stage, requiring new kinds of knowledge and skills. Although much remains to be learned regarding the nature of alcohol problems and the impact of different strategies for their treatment and prevention, and research and programmatic agendas concerning these issues should remain high priorities, it is time for public health advocates to address the challenge of becoming effective in the process of policy change.

Changing policy requires learning to organize new constituencies, becoming effective in the political and economic arena, developing new funding sources, and offsetting the barriers to effective public health reform. It demands as well a coordinated, concerted effort from diverse professionals—researchers and evaluators, program personnel, citizen activists, government administrators, educators, health care providers, health planners, and others. The potential benefits are enormous. Not only do we have a chance to reduce dramatically the tragic toll of alcohol-related problems on society. The approach envisioned here also holds the potential of broadening citizen support and activism on behalf of public health goals and agendas across the board.

The review is divided into four sections: the first section outlines the public health approach to the prevention of alcohol-related problems and documents the consensus that has developed over the last five years regarding this approach. The second section analyzes the barriers to implementation of effective prevention policies. The third section describes current research and activities that address the barriers to change, and the concluding section discusses both lessons learned and future agendas.

THE PUBLIC HEALTH MODEL: ALCOHOL POLICY AND
THE NEW CONSENSUS

The public health field has experienced a revolution in the last 20 years regarding its understanding of alcohol problems. As documented by Room in the 1984 edition of the *Annual Review of Public Health,* this has involved at least three basic conceptual shifts:

1. Change in focus from "alcoholism" to "alcohol-related problems" or "alcohol problems": In the wake of the repeal of Prohibition, researchers and community workers alike increasingly viewed alcohol problems as exclusively due to "alcoholics," whose presumed inherent defect caused their disease. This view divided society into two groups: social drinkers, who suffer no adverse consequences from alcohol consumption; and alcoholics, who had no choice but to abstain to avoid alcohol problems. In this model, prevention activities were limited primarily to early case finding to locate the second group as early as possible. Empirical findings from research studies during the late 1960s and early 1970s undermined these assumptions. Epidemiologic studies found that all parts of the drinking population reported a variety of alcohol problems, and that individuals may drastically change their problematic drinking patterns over time.

2. Renewed emphasis on the diverse health consequences of alcohol use: The focus on the individual alcoholic tended to blind the field to the diverse problems associated with alcohol use—particularly trauma, cirrhosis of the liver, and other long-term health effects such as cancer. Research on alcohol has become increasingly sensitive to alcohol's role as a risk factor in a wide variety of health consequences that include and reach beyond the issue of alcoholism.

3. New attention placed on "alcohol control policy" as an integral prevention strategy: The dominant paradigm that emerged following repeal considered the control of alcohol availability (including the price and physical availability of alcohol, as well as the marketing strategies of the alcohol industry) irrelevant to the incidence and severity of alcohol problems. Alcoholics were assumed to be unaffected by availability, whereas social drinkers, whose consumption might be affected by controls on availability, were assumed to be free of alcohol problems. Indeed, some proponents of this model viewed alcohol controls as potentially counterproductive, stigmatizing alcoholics and creating barriers to the learning of "responsible drinking" norms. As Room has documented, the ferocious and vitriolic condemnation of those propounding even the most mild dissent documents the dominance of this model. Even in the public health field, advocates of control policy faced ostracism and charges that they sought a return to moralistic and prohibitionary alcohol policies.

Again, research findings undercut and eventually discredited this widely held view. As reviewed by Ashley & Rankin, a wide variety of studies have documented the impact of alcohol control variables on health consequences. Contrary to expectations, many control policies affect heavy drinkers more than light and moderate drinkers. The studies do not show uniform results, and differing control strategies have differing impacts. Researchers have found it difficult to measure the impact of relatively modest changes in alcohol availability, and societal and cultural variables must be taken into account. Nevertheless, "taken all together, there is substantial evidence that controls on physical availability can reduce rates of alcohol-related problems, and that the consumption of heavy, as well as moderate drinkers can be reduced".

The Public Health Model

In recent years, alcohol and public health researchers have placed these alcohol control strategies solidly in the public health tradition through the application of the familiar epidemiologic triad of environment-agent-host to alcohol-related problems. In addition to strategies already in place targeting the host—i.e. the individual drinker—with education, deterrence, treatment, and so on, this "public health model" of alcohol-related problems calls attention to the role of environmental factors (the social and physical structures within which alcohol problems occur) and agent factors (the presentation of alcohol, including alcohol packaging, labeling, and price) in the spread of alcohol problems.[1]

The alcohol field has increasingly focused on the interaction of the individual with his or her environment. "Environment" is defined broadly to include not only the physical availability of the agent alcohol, but also the cultural, social, political, and economic arena within which alcohol consumption and alcohol problems take place. According to Wallack,

> In effect, alcohol problems are seen as properties of systems rather than individuals. Individuals are viewed only as they exist in this larger system. Because alcohol problems exist across many different levels of the broader system (i.e. individual, family, peer group, school, community group, societal), prevention efforts must ultimately address all of these levels.

Messages about alcohol consumption abound in every part of the environment. Wallack stresses the importance of making those messages consistent at all levels.

This application of the public health model to alcohol-related problems builds on the research findings discussed above. It recognizes that alcohol problems reach beyond alcoholism. It focuses on populations as well as individuals, and stresses the importance of alcohol availability policies. It also acknowledges the importance of cultural and social norms and their interaction with control policies.

The new approach also creates two important bridges in the field. First, it acknowledges that prevention strategies aimed at individuals are appropriate and needed, provided they take into account and are consistent with strategies for changing problematic environmental factors. Conversely, those working to change environmental factors must be attentive to the impact of and reaction to those changes by individuals. This has helped to defuse some of the unease felt between "control" advocates and health educators. Second, it places treatment/recovery strategies as complementary, rather than opposed, to prevention. Alcoholism recovery, which occurs at the individual level, will be enhanced in a social and physical environment consistent with recovery goals. Concerns re-

---

[1]Alcohol is not always in the agent role in what we term alcohol-related problems. In the case of alcohol-related illnesses, ethanol is the agent, carried by beverage alcohol. In the case of alcohol-related injuries, however, the agent (that which is necessary and sufficient to cause harm to the host) is energy; alcohol is a significant environmental factor increasing the likelihood that an injurious energy exchange will occur.

garding recovery thus must be taken into account as prevention strategies targeting environmental factors are designed. This recognition, which is central to the "social model" recovery movement in California, has helped to overcome the suspicions that historically have separated those involved in recovery and those working for environmental change.

Alcohol Policy and the Public Health Model

Influencing the interaction between the individual and his or her environment involves addressing policy issues—those laws, regulations, formal and informal rules, and understandings that are adopted on a collective basis to guide individual and collective behavior. For the purposes here, the term is not limited to public policy or formal law. Rather it incorporates rules and procedures used by private organizations—commercial and noncommercial—to affect the organizations' members.

Policies at a variety of levels may influence a given situation. For example, a party given at a university dormitory may be subject to state law (no service to underaged persons), university regulation (e.g. a proctor must be present), dormitory regulation (e.g. no guests allowed), and party organizer party planning rules (e.g. no drinking contests). If policies in these overlapping settings are inconsistent, the chances for successful prevention drop significantly. It will be difficult or impossible to establish a moderate drinking norm in a university fraternity that encourages drinking contests and hazing. Such an environment will cause alcohol problems to increase and will undermine the effectiveness of university efforts to educate students about alcohol use.

The public health model, then, involves attention to alcohol policies and their impact on both individuals and their environments. Because the field has historically focused on individual-based strategies, a major contribution of the model is to provide a means for analyzing and addressing environmental factors. Alcohol control policies—the formal laws affecting alcohol availability and price—are an important, but not exclusive, part of this analysis. Numerous new priorities regarding environmental factors have emerged, based primarily on research conducted in the last 20 years:

TAX POLICIES State and federal government policies have resulted in steadily decreasing tax rates. Alcohol prices have fallen 28% relative to inflation since 1967, and the differential pricing between alcohol and other nonalcoholic beverages has practically disappeared. Research relating price and consumption shows this trend to be contrary to public health goals. Other tax policies serve to promote drinking as well, for example, the deduction given to corporations for alcohol purchases, which are assumed to be "ordinary and necessary to the conduct of business".

ADVERTISING AND OTHER PROMOTIONAL PRACTICES OF THE ALCOHOL INDUSTRY The dominant source of information on alcohol in our society comes from the multi-billion dollar promotional efforts of the alcohol industry. Research has shown these messages to be deliberately distorted and deceptive, excluding health information, promoting denial of problems, and targeting groups at high risk for alcohol problems. Huge promotional campaigns overwhelm and contradict the accurate health information available from other sources and inhibit media coverage of alcohol issues. A variety of reforms in advertising practice have been proposed to counteract the impact of the alcohol industry's promotional campaigns. These include bans on alcohol advertisements on radio and television; regulation of advertising content; equal time for health messages on airwaves; and health warning labels on public health containers, on advertisements, and in retail establishments.

Research is equivocal regarding the direct impact of advertising on drinking practices and drinking problems. The industry has used the lack of clear evidence of such an impact as an argument against advertising reforms. The purpose of advertising is to "educate" consumers—affect their beliefs and attitudes—regarding the rewards and benefits of the product. Advertising is not designed to impact consumption directly except on a very long-term basis and in conjunction with other marketing and societal variables. Proving a direct impact is probably impossible given the confounding variables and the long-term strategy involved. From the viewpoint provided by the public health model, however, the degree to which aggressive and deceptive advertising practices cause an inconsistency of messages about alcohol in the environment is a serious problem, which has an adverse impact on other prevention strategies. Proving the direct impact of advertising on drinking practices and problems is thus tangential from the standpoint of a public health model that stresses the need for consistency throughout the environment.

PHYSICAL AVAILABILITY OF ALCOHOL Research has shown a direct link between the physical availability of alcohol and the level of alcohol problems in a society. The regulation of alcohol availability involves a complex set of governmental and private rules and regulations affecting who may serve and sell, where, in what kinds of establishments, in what manner, and at what time. As discussed by Makela et al, the impact of particular reforms is difficult to assess, although research suggests caution in loosening current availability regulations. A recent focus in the field has been to encourage local communities to develop availability regulations that meet the needs and concerns of community members, thus ensuring that regulations have community support. Server intervention, which focuses on the serving practices of both commercial and noncommercial servers, has also been a major focus among alcohol policy advocates (see below for discussion).

SPECIAL PROTECTIONS FOR YOUNG PEOPLE Restricting availability to young people is a major subcategory of control efforts. Research has demonstrated that minimum age drinking laws affect drinking and alcohol-related vehicle crashes among young people. Efforts have been made to regulate industry promotional campaigns on college campuses.

OTHER INSTITUTIONAL TARGETS FOR PREVENTION Social institutions do much to shape the alcohol environment. Beyond the institutions listed above, the agenda for policy change includes the actions of corporations, the military, educational and medical institutions, professional sports, the insurance industry, private foundations, and so on. Corporations have made important strides in developing Employee Assistance Programs to help employees identified as having alcohol problems. Practices in the corporate environment that may foster heavy drinking have come under increasing scrutiny. Alcohol policies on military reservations—notably price promotions—have been targeted. In each institution an agenda for change has been developed, as we have written elsewhere.

These policy agendas, flowing from the public health model, augment and help to shape other activities and priorities found in the alcohol field—adequate recovery services, educational and mass media compaigns, strict drinking-driving laws, and victim assistance programs. Under the model, the comprehensiveness and coordination of the agendas is central. Omitting these environmental influences will severely limit the viability of individual-based strategies. . . .

BARRIERS TO CHANGE: THE CURRENT ALCOHOL ENVIRONMENT

Many agencies and organizations responding to alcohol problems have not adopted the public health model and express fears that the focus on alcohol policy will restigmatize alcoholics and serve as an excuse to abandon treatment priorities. Yet a clear shift in perspective has occurred in this decade, and vocal opposition to this shift has become muted. . . .

The shift in perspective has not, however, been matched by success in achieving alcohol policy reforms. Environmental change requires reform of collective rules and understandings. These rules may be found on an informal or private level or may exist in formal laws and regulations. As discussed below, policy reform has succeeded most often at the local level. Furthermore, these successes tend to be modest and are frequently rolled back by state legislatures overruling local decision-makers. Action at the federal level, except for the legislation encouraging 21-year-old drinking age laws at the state level and the 1988 legislation requiring a health warning on all alcoholic beverage containers, has been notably unsuccessful.

Given a high level of public support and the emergence of a core leadership group, why have efforts to reform alcohol taxes, advertising practices, and availability policies been so unsuccessful? One obvious problem, noted by Room, is that public support is very shallow. The dominant public understanding of alcohol problems remains at the individual level. As Room suggests, a top priority with any alcohol policy reform effort is to focus on public awareness and understanding of the new perspective, which may be more important than whether the reform is actually implemented. Mosher has labeled this public apathy or misunderstanding "societal denial"—a countervailing tendency to deny that alcohol problems are collective problems requiring collective attention and solutions. Rather, the problems are viewed as the "fault" of the individual—as a crime, moral failing, or disease. Thus, although public opinion polls evidence support for alcohol policy reform, that support is easily diverted in the public policy arena.

As Ashley & Rankin point out, the second, more powerful and more profound barrier to implementation involves the alcohol industry and its allies. In part because of the public health field's historical lack of attention to environmental factors, the shape of the alcohol environment since the repeal of Prohibition has largely been determined by the marketing practices of a very powerful and sophisticated industry. As with the tobacco industry, the alcohol industry strongly opposes any attempt to limit marketing practices. Yet these practices are inevitable targets of an environmental approach to prevention. The industry's opposition can be felt not only in the legislatures, but throughout society, fostering continuing societal denial and apathy. Alcohol policy reform, if it is to succeed, must build on a knowledge of the industry, its structure, tactics, strengths, and weaknesses, and how these combine to define and control the current alcohol environment. We now turn to these topics.

Industry Marketing Strategy

The first step in addressing industry tactics is understanding the industry's interest in the alcohol policy debate. Cowan & Mosher have documented the industry's reliance on "total marketing" to maintain and expand its sales and profitability. Total marketing involves first defining the competition. During the last ten years, the industry has defined itself as being part of the "beverage market," competing for "stomach share" with other beverages—soft drinks, tap water, coffee, milk, etc. The beverage industry estimates that Americans drink approximately two quarts of liquid a day, and there is fierce competition among the beverage types (except of course from the "tap water" segment) to maintain and expand market share.

The alcohol industry operates in this "beverage market" by defining the target groups to be reached and developing a marketing plan tailored to each group. The population is broken down by demographic variables: age, sex, race, ethnicity, drinking patterns, etc. Each group so defined receives a distinct marketing effort. The most important group to the industry is the heaviest drinking 10% of the population (a plurality of whom are young men), who consume approximately 57% of all alcohol sold.

The marketing plan for each targeted group has four key components. First, a product is developed suited to the group's tastes, mores, and attitudes. Malt liquor, for example, is a product designed for young black men; fortified wine targets public inebriates; imported scotch is intended to reach upper class men. Wine coolers, one of the newest products on the market, clearly targets young people and women. The industry strongly denies it targets teenagers deliberately; recent polls demonstrate that, whatever the intent, the product has indeed penetrated this market.

The second component involves the promotion of the product that has been developed or identified to its target audience. Sophisticated advertising campaigns are designed to give the product a mythos—a message that ties it to the targeted group's desires, fears, and fantasies. Alcohol promotions are notably lacking in any factual information, particularly regarding potential health consequences. In this context, alcohol advertising is in reality a form of education, one that is dominated by deceptive and irrelevant material. Instead of providing health information, advertising seeks to promote "societal denial," saturating the environment with positive messages. The industry's response in recent years to growing concerns about health and fitness has been to focus promotional campaigns on images of young, physically fit people being active while drinking.

Third, each product in the product line is given a price. The price is set to meet the targeted group's ability and willingness to pay. For upper class and sophisticated drinkers, relatively high prices are expected; for those with limited income or entering the market, such as students, the lowest possible prices are established. Thus, alcohol products have a wide range of prices, but it is of critical importance that the range begin at the lowest price possible. This is particularly important because of the competition with other beverages. A major development in the last 20 years has been the ability of the beer and wine industries to compete in price with soft drinks and other types of nonalcoholic beverages.

Finally, the product needs to be in a place that is easily and widely available to the targeted group. This involves developing new packaging that is suited to the target group and the ability to place the packaging in the appropriate outlets where the group is likely to purchase. Women, for example, do not like to shop in liquor stores, preferring super markets. Thus, for example, in New York the wine industry moved aggressively to change state laws to allow wine coolers, a product targeted to the women's market, to be sold in grocery stores. Again, the competition with other nonalcoholic beverages has led the alcohol industry to become increasingly aggressive in seeking new outlets. From the point of view of the industry, alcohol products need to be as accessible to the target groups as soft drinks if they are to compete effectively.

These four marketing components—product, promotion, price, and place—are carefully coordinated with each other to reach each targeted audience. Thus the marketing plan to reach public inebriates is quite different from the plan for reaching young women. For the former, a very cheap product (fortified wine) is made available primarily in skid row liquor stores. Promotions are done primarily on billboards and in the stores themselves, since the target group is relatively small and does not watch television. Young women, on the other hand, are reached with a sweet, light wine (wine coolers) that avoids an "alcohol" taste, is promoted as a fun, light, healthful beverage, and is sold in grocery and convenience stores.

An understanding of the alcohol industry's marketing strategy helps explain recent trends in alcohol sales. The distilled spirits industry, which has suffered decreased sales over the last ten years, is at a distinct disadvantage. It does not have access to television and radio advertising, and is taxed at a much higher rate than beer and wine, resulting in higher prices relative to the rest of the "beverage market." Both beer and wine producers have suffered stagnated sales in recent years, which the industry attributes to societal concerns for health and fitness and drinking–driving. The industry has avoided an erosion of their markets by developing new "healthful" products—lower calorie beer and wine coolers—that have been very heavily promoted on television and radio and are widely available at low prices.

The ideal social environment from the industry's perspective, then, is one that is saturated with low-cost alcohol and positive alcohol messages, where alcohol is available in a wide and ever expanding array of beverage types, containers, and places of sale. The industry has been remarkably successful in creating this environment since Prohibition. Yet these are precisely the variables that have come under scrutiny in recent years by the public health movement as critical to the prevention of alcohol problems. It is not surprising, then, that reform efforts have met severe resistance from the industry, which feels under siege and views its ability to compete effectively in the beverage market as under attack. . . .

Organizing Local Constituencies

Successful application of environmental approaches to prevention requires the development of organized, educated, and active constituencies at the local level. Public health advocates need to counter industry lobbying with the mobilization of large numbers of people for policy change. Beginning at the local level, this mobilization provides an experiential base for learning about the alcohol environment and about industry tactics. Although many people are concerned over the impact of alcohol on their lives, public consciousness-raising and organizing are usually necessary to channel their interest into action on policy issues. Campaigns at the local level provide a sense of community power and ownership of the alcohol environment. Concerted collective action combats the sense of helplessness that often pervades community discussions of environmental issues. Campaigns build on each other: to a certain degree, whether a particular campaign succeeds matters less than that it sows seeds of awareness and recognition of the utility of community control over the alcohol environment that can be transferred to other policy issues.

Little research as yet documents process or outcomes from community organizing projects. Recent initiatives by major research centers to convene a conference on the implementation of community-based prevention signals a research direction that the field needs to pursue. As mentioned above, most policy successes have been achieved at the local level. Examples from community organizing campaigns already underway indicate the promise this approach holds for policy change. In Mill Valley, California, community organizing efforts recently produced a city ordinance controlling the service of alcohol on city property. At all events serving alcoholic beverages, the ordinance outlaws "no-host" bars; requires nonalcoholic beverage alternatives, low-alcohol beer and wine, and free food be visible and available; and mandates the prominent display of signs about drinking and driving. In Santa Cruz, a decision by law enforcement officials to enforce an ordinance banning drinking on the public beach has contributed to a reduction in police reports and emergency room admissions. San Diego County has instituted a wide variety of environmental policies that are in the process of being evaluated. A comprehensive community organizing project in Castro Valley, California has resulted in a citizen's task force that uses local zoning ordinances to combat proliferation of alcohol outlets. Numerous communities throughout California have successfully organized to mandate point-of-sale warnings about alcohol and birth defects.

Local organizing has intrinsic value in the contributions made toward improvement of the local environment. Local efforts also feed larger organizing agendas. Much about the nature of the alcoholic beverage industry and the policy process can be learned only through the experience of organizing for an apparently simple objective, which then turns out to be connected to a much wider agenda for change. The industry's opposition to birth defect-related warning posters, for example, illustrates a level of callousness to the health impact of alcoholic beverages that often must be witnessed to be believed. Through the experience of confronting the industry on a policy issue, communities can begin to analyze and understand the alcohol environment, and comprehend the contributions of such environmental factors as low excise taxes and widespread availability to alcohol-related problems.

Coalition-Building at the State and Federal Levels

Finally, local organizing provides the basis for the development of much broader coalitions to take on policy issues at the state and federal levels. The warning label issue provides a good example of building on local efforts to mount broad-based statewide and federal campaigns. This issue also exemplifies the potential for health-policy coalition-building that alcohol issues hold. Through the warning label efforts, groups with broad health agendas have become active on alcohol issues, while alcohol-focused organizations have recognized their stake in broader public health issues. Local successes in California have fed into a statewide coalition backing a warning label bill in the state legislature. Led by Consumers Union, the coalition includes entities as diverse as right-to-lifers and Planned Parenthood, as well as the PTA, the California Medical and Nurses Associations, and a host of public and private health and alcohol service delivery organizations.

State and local campaigns both feed into and draw from efforts at the federal level. CSPI and NCA have led the way in organizing two major national coalitions, the National Alcohol Tax Coalition (NATC) and Project SMART. NATC brought the American Association of Retired Persons, the Association of Junior Leagues, the Children's Defense Fund, the National Women's Health Fund, and over 25 other major national organizations together on behalf of excise tax increases. Project SMART, a petition drive that collected over a million signatures in support of equal time for health-oriented counteradvertising on the nation's broadcast media, won the support of the United Methodist Church, Action for Children's Television, Americans for Democratic Action, National PTA, Remove Intoxicated Drivers, and over 20 other national organizations. The recent successful effort to pass warning label legislation at the federal level, again spearheaded by NCA and CSPI, garnered support from over 100 health, consumer action, educational, treatment, and religious organizations. The existence of statewide warning label efforts supported the drive for a federal mandate, while membership in a federal coalition often leads to activism by state-level chapters.

As Room points out, beyond the concrete gains of the coalitions lies the significant contribution that such efforts make to public discourse on alcohol policy. Creating this consciousness-raising about sources and contributors to alcohol-related problems can be as important in the long run as winning a particular alcohol policy reform. This suggests a building block approach, choosing issues on the basis of their ability to raise consciousness and broaden coalitions rather than their ability to ameliorate the problem quickly. Warning labels will have less impact on public education than changes in advertising regulations, but they are politically more accessible and may lay the groundwork for an effective coalition to change advertising practices.

CONCLUSION: LESSONS LEARNED AND FUTURE AGENDAS

The past decade has witnessed a groundswell of support for alcohol policy change. Although major campaigns to raise excise taxes, require health warning labels, and restrict advertising have not yet found success at state or federal levels, much has been learned in the past decade about what a successful movement for alcohol policy change requires. These efforts have done much to raise the consciousness and clarify the goals of the alcohol policy reform movement. The last ten years have produced an efflorescence of research and consensus documents supporting those goals. They are relatively modest and specific. Industry allegations notwithstanding, the movement does not seek the prohibition of alcohol use. As Wallack and others point out, the overall goal is to reduce the risk associated with alcohol use, by altering the environments in which alcohol is available to make abstinence acceptable in all situations, discourage heavy use, and eliminate all use in situations where there is high risk for alcohol-related problems. Because prohibition is not a goal, it is assumed that alcohol-related problems will continue, albeit at significantly lower levels, even if the implementation of this approach to prevention is successful beyond the highest hopes of its proponents. Thus there will continue to be other research activities, lying outside of the realm of primary prevention and adding to our knowledge about treatment and recovery, which will remain important.

In this article we have attempted to outline some of the new knowledge needed to achieve policy reform. A cursory review of the environment permitting harmful actions between host and agent reveals that this environment has been largely determined, not by public health advocates, but by the alcohol industry. Internationally, as in the case of tobacco, the growing concentration of the alcoholic beverage industry and the stagnation of the domestic market are pushing alcohol multinationals to develop markets in the developing countries, exporting their total marketing approach to create the kinds of alcohol environments causing problems in the developed nations. This growing internationalization of alcohol problems only increases the need for effective action on the domestic front.

Familiarity with the industry's definition of the alcohol environment and the tactics used by the industry and its allies to maintain that environment are necessary prerequisites to successful alcohol policy change. The policy agenda articulated in the Alcohol Policy Bill of Rights and elsewhere responds to each of the industry's four P's with prevention strategies designed to create a healthy environment. Successful implementation of that agenda requires a response to the seven areas of industry tactics articulated above that is at least as comprehensive and coordinated as the industry's efforts. Industry attempts to influence legislators must be met by broad-based coalitions dedicated to safeguarding the health of the public. Linkages within the industry and with other industries can be weakened through server intervention, dram shop liability, and research and dissemination on the impact of alcohol problems on industry. The role of industry money in rewarding and punishing allies and opponents, and in improving the industry's image, can be exposed through case studies and through providing organizations and coalitions with experiences and training that demonstrate the function of donations in furthering industry agendas. The tactic of organizing drinkers must be countered by organizing those affected by and concerned about alcohol problems, including recovering people. Finally, sources of funding for research and training on environmental factors must be identified, encouraged, and developed to counter industry-sponsored research.

Prevention research has begun to focus on some of these crucial implementation issues. Research needs to be responsive to and supportive of emerging community agendas for change, and to inform community-based efforts in implementation. Process evaluations and case study analyses of community-based organizing and policy change projects are needed to provide direction to community action. These should be supplemented by outcome studies that document the impact of various policy changes on alcohol-related problems over time. Studies of various institutions and institutional environments, including the alcohol industry but also corporations, professional sports, higher education, the military, and other institutions that may be targets for change or barriers to or promoters of it, are also needed.

Research dissemination needs to take on a new form as well. Most organizations and individuals understand alcohol issues, and are moved to action about them, through a single issue: drinking-driving, alcoholism, injury prevention, domestic violence, etc. The task of implementing the public health approach is to build on these individualized understandings of the problem, shifting people's consciousness of alcohol problems to include an understanding of the importance of environmental forces. Researchers have an important role to play in accomplishing this shift in consciousness by providing a broad range of training and technical assistance activities. These include the development and dissemination of action-oriented informational resources—newsletter articles, action guides, slide and video presentations, information sheets summarizing recent research for the lay public—that introduce environmental issues and provide clear routes for community action. Seminars, conferences, and workshops tailored to the interests of specific groups but introducing broader prevention agendas as well are a high priority. Identification and training of leaders at the local level and the provision of technical expertise to emergent issue-oriented coalitions are also vital roles potentially filled by those with the research expertise to teach others to move with confidence in the face of industry opposition and obfuscation. Finally, researchers need to become active in the funding world, encouraging support of projects that will add to the knowledge base regarding implementation of the new approach.

Several leading alcohol researchers have argued that the current wave of temperance sentiment is merely another in a series of temperance "waves," which inevitably come and go with the tides of history. Although there is undoubtedly some truth to this, the differences between this period in alcohol policy and prevention and previous ones are sufficient to support the argument that we are in a new stage. Never before has the industry been so concentrated in the hands of a few corporations, and so sophisticated in its tactics of opposition to reform. On the public health side, alcohol policy advocates are working from a new understanding of the problem, one that is more comprehensive than earlier formulations, that is based in public health theory and research, and that both seeks more modest goals than past movements and provides the basis for broader coalitions.

What the current wave of temperance sentiment has done is to heighten the immediacy of individual alcohol problems. Alcohol problems grace the covers of major newsweeklies and are profiled in network specials. The challenge to the public health field is to place the problems in a public health perspective, and to organize for permanent policy reform based in that perspective. The breadth of the coalitions that have already been built suggests the potential of a public health approach for reaching new constituencies, raising popular consciousness abut new directions in alcohol policy and new ways to reduce alcohol-related problems, and swelling the ranks of the overall coalition working for a more human health policy in the US.

Drug Prohibition:
A Public-Health Perspective

BONNIE STEINBOCK

THE DRUG PROBLEM

It is estimated that over six million Americans are heavy drug users. Between 1986 and 1988, the number of cocaine addicts in New York City more than tripled, with an estimated total of 600,000 in 1988, most addicted to crack. Although middle-class cocaine use in the United States as a whole is on the decline—it has dropped 22 percent since 1988—Federal officials say that 6.4 million Americans used cocaine last year. In the poorest neighborhoods, cocaine smoking and snorting is on the rise, and a flood of potent heroin is creating new addicts. Drug abuse has caused problems for individuals, families, and society as a whole for years, but the introduction of crack cocaine has made things much worse. Let me mention just a few of the effects attributed to crack in New York City.

- Drug-related crime is far worse than it was twenty years ago. From 1987 to 1988, the number of murders in New York rose 10.4 percent. Police say that drugs, in particular, crack, played a role in at least 38 percent of the 1,867 murders in 1988, compared with a generally constant rate of 20 percent for years.
- Crack contributed to a tripling of cases in which parents under the influence of drugs abused or neglected their children. In 1987, 73 percent of the deaths in abuse and neglect cases resulted from parents abusing drugs, up from 11 percent in 1985.
- Between 1986 and 1988, the number of newborn children in New York City testing positive for drugs—mostly cocaine—almost quadrupled, going from 1,325 to 5,088. Because of crack, in some inner-city hospitals, the number of babies going directly from the hospital into foster homes has

From *Drugs, Morality, and the Law* edited by Steven Luper-Foy and Curtis Brown (Garland Publishing, Inc., 1994). Reprinted by permission.

risen from 2 percent to 15 percent. Urban child-welfare workers estimate that 70 percent of children they see are raised by grandmothers or other relatives after parents abandon them for drugs.

The impact of the crack epidemic on children is perhaps the most heartrending aspect of the drug problem. Other effects of crack, such as the tremendous increase in the prison population—up from 9,815 in New York City in 1985 to over 17,500 in 1989—can be laid to the fact that crack is *illegal*. Legalize addictive drugs, and drug arrests (1.2 million a year in the United States), which are overwhelming the criminal justice system, causing overcrowding in the prisons, and costing billions of dollars, would disappear. Moreover, according to Ira Glasser, Executive Director of the American Civil Liberties Union (ACLU) and a proponent of legalization, three-quarters of "drug-related" homicides are caused by territorial disputes and other incidents relating to the criminal trafficking system. "Only 7.5 percent of the homicides were related to the effects of the drug itself, and two-thirds of those involved alcohol, not crack."

By contrast, the effects of crack on children, both pre- and postnatally, will not be diminished by legalization. Dr. Linda A. Randolph, director of the State Office of Public Health, says that, because of drug abuse, particularly crack, "we are seeing dramatic increases in infant mortality, in congenital syphilis, and in the number of AIDS-infected women who are giving birth." Intensive hospital care for *each* crack baby costs about $90,000. That translates into $2.5 billion annually for the nation.

Crack can have devastating effects on the nervous systems of newborns. T. Berry Brazelton describes the clinical manifestations this way:

> They are either limp and unresponsive or are hyper-sensitive and behave chaotically. They have difficulty receiving and responding to the stimuli of a soothing voice or face. When they are cuddled or rocked, they react with piercing wails and jerky motions. Few people could love these babies. They are likely to suffer later from learning disabilities and to be either hyperactive or emotionally flat. They also tend to be at the mercy of their impulses. The social programs required to educate them will cost billions of dollars.

It should be noted that, although crack is ingested during pregnancy, the harmful effects are imposed on the newborn, the infant, and even the older child. The pregnant crack addict does not risk harm only to herself, but also to the baby she will bear, if she decides not to abort. The term "fetal abuse," often used to describe the use of drugs during pregnancy, is something of a misnomer, since the damage is not confined to the fetus, but is done also to the born child. However one views the fetus, born children have full legal rights, including the right not to be injured prior to live birth. That is why there is no logical contradiction in supporting the right to abortion and maintaining that

women have an obligation not to harm their not-yet-born children through in-
gestion of drugs during pregnancy.

While there is debate among the experts about how bad and long-lasting the
physical damage is to children born to crack users, there is agreement that these
babies are especially susceptible to child abuse. They suffer from neglect because, as one article put it, ". . . people who hardly bother with food for themselves can't be expected to give up precious crack to feed a baby, can they?"
And they are at risk for child abuse because their screaming and nonresponsive-
ness make them unattractive and difficult to care for. As Brazelton asks, "What
would an addicted parent in an addicted environment do to such a baby? The
ingredients for child abuse were all there."

THE LIBERTARIAN APPROACH

Even this brief recounting indicates a major social problem, something with
which society is entitled—even obligated—to concern itself. Yet a libertarian
perspective suggests otherwise. . . .

[L]ibertarian[s] . . . value individual liberty more than any other value. The
libertarian principle can be traced back to John Stuart Mill, who argued in *On
Liberty* that the only purpose for which it was permissible to restrict individual
freedom was to prevent harm to others. A person's own good was never sufficient warrant. Mill's principle has been applied in all sorts of ways: from opposition of seatbelt and helmet laws to opposition to closing gay bathhouses in an
effort to stop the spread of AIDS.

Mill attempted to defend his absolute prohibition against paternalistic intervention on utilitarian grounds, but this has been notoriously unsuccessful. There
is no reason to think that the harm of paternalistic intervention will necessarily
outweigh the benefit to be attained. Philosopher Gerald Dworkin persuasively
argues that it was not utilitarian calculation that led Mill to his absolute rejection of paternalism, but rather a non-contingent, non-utilitarian argument about
what it means to be a person, an autonomous agent. Dworkin says, "It is because coercing a person for his own good denies this status as an independent
entity that Mill objects to it so strongly and in such absolute terms. Dworkin
goes on to argue that some paternalistic intervention can be justified, even on
Millian grounds, namely, restrictions that preserve a wider range of freedom for
the individual in question.

THE PUBLIC-HEALTH APPROACH

Whereas Dworkin can be seen as attempting to justify very limited paternalistic
measures, within a Millian perspective, Dan Beauchamp, a professor of public

health, is a more outright critic of Mill. Beauchamp notes that some restrictions on individual liberty result in considerable social gain. Consider the example of seat belts. Each year roughly forty-five thousand people in the United States are killed in car crashes. Laws requiring the wearing of seat belts or making air bags compulsory would save roughly ten thousand lives a year. That's a lot of lives, a considerable social good. Libertarians object to seat-belt laws as being objectionably paternalistic. Why shouldn't I decide for myself whether to buckle up? Refusing to buckle up doesn't cause "harm to others" and so laws forcing people to use seat belts are not warranted on Millian grounds. But Beauchamp argues that, since the infringement on individual freedom is minuscule, and the social good so great, the intrusion is warranted. He supports "reasonable, minimally intrusive restrictions that yield significant gains in the health and safety of the public."

I think that Beauchamp's public-health approach is far more useful in thinking about the legalization of drugs than the libertarian approach. The libertarian insists that there isn't a drug problem, since trade is a positive sum game, and both parties gain. No one who has any experience with drug abuse and the social upheaval it has caused will agree with that conclusion. Instead of insisting, on ideological grounds, that individuals should have the right to buy whatever they want, regardless of the social costs, we should examine carefully the costs of prohibition and the costs of legalization. This means that the argument about legalization is not primarily a philosophical one. Rather, it is an empirical argument about the likely consequences of different strategies for dealing with the drug problem.

While the public-health approach rejects Mill's absolutist antipaternalism, it entirely agrees with Mill on one thing: the rejection of moralism. Mill argued that legal or social prohibitions on behavior could never be justified simply on the ground that the behavior in question was regarded by the majority as wicked or sinful. He insisted that infringements on individual liberty have to be justified by demonstrating that the conduct in question was likely to cause harm to others.

Of course it is not always easy to settle the question of whether an activity will cause harm to others: the example of violent pornography is a case in point. However, the rejection of moralism at least makes it clear what *kind* of argument is necessary to support coercive intervention. Empirical evidence of injury or the risk of injury is essential. Simply referring to moral principles, no matter how widely accepted, or moral feelings, no matter how strongly held, will not do. Someone who takes a public-health perspective may be willing to consider closing gay bathhouses *if* it is reasonable to think that this will slow the spread of a deadly disease, but will not be willing to infringe on individual liberty because the activities in such places are viewed by many as nasty or evil.

Why does the public-health perspective reject moralism? After all, if it is willing to acknowledge collective or communal values, such as health, why not acknowledge that there can be collective or communal *moral* values? Indeed, aren't free speech, equal opportunity, and the democratic process, which are essential to a democratic republic, *moral* values? Of course. The rejection of moralism does not consist in rejection of or neutrality toward all moral values. Rather, the rejection of moralism consists in opposition to coercion (as opposed to education and persuasion) to eradicate sin and vice or to make individuals morally better.

It might be objected that a public-health approach is based on a false distinction between different kinds of values. On a public-health approach, some government coercion is acceptable for the sake of certain values (for example, those connected to public health) but not others (for example, those related to private sexual behavior). A libertarian might argue that if it is permissible to infringe individual liberty for the sake of social goals, there is no principled reason for insisting that the goals to be achieved must be of a certain kind. If the majority in a society thinks that homosexuality is bad for society, then why shouldn't it pass laws against homosexuality? What justifies coercion for some social goals, but not others? The answer has to do with a certain conception of the common good. The common good should not be understood in terms of whatever the majority values or wants. Such a conception would indeed threaten individual liberty through, in Mill's phrase, "the tyranny of the majority." Rather, I suggest that we think of the common good in terms of what Rawls calls "primary goods": "things which it is supposed a rational man wants whatever else he wants." Health is an example of a primary good. By restricting our conception of the common good to primary goods, we avoid imposing goals and values on individuals that they do not happen to share. However, it may be objected that, even if it is true that everyone has reason to value his or her own health, it does not follow that everyone has reason to value the health of the community. (This was the mistake that Mill is supposed to have made in his proof of the principle of utility.) What if I am not interested in saving ten thousand lives a year? What justifies forcing me to buckle up?

I am not sure that it can be demonstrated that not caring about aggregate welfare or the good of society as a whole is *irrational.* However, the communitarian or republican morality of "We're all in this together" seems to me infinitely preferable to the extreme individualism which is concerned only with individuals' interests and rights. Republican morality balances individual virtues like self-reliance and individual responsibility against community virtues like beneficence, cooperation, and justice. As Dan Beauchamp puts it:

> Beneficence means that we wish the good and welfare of others as well as ourselves, while cooperation and justice mean that we as citizens are disposed to see

that the common welfare is extended to all alike and do not allow our private interests to frustrate achievement of the common good. While the principles of individuality and community can often pull in opposite directions, both principles are needed to assure the fullest development of the individual and his dignity both as an autonomous person and as a member of the political fellowship.

Recognition that there is a common good, as well as the separate welfares of individuals, does not preclude controversy over its nature. Moreover, even when individuals acknowledge a collective good, such as disease prevention, they may differ as to its importance relative to other collective goods. A public-health approach does not demand that we value life and health above all else. It merely supports minimally intrusive restrictions on individual liberty to promote the common good.

A related objection holds that even if it is possible to differentiate among social goods, so that infringement of individual liberty is restricted to primary collective goods, such as health, there is still a danger of imposing majoritarian moral views on individuals, because there is no morally neutral way to characterize even basic goods. All people may want to be healthy, but one's conception of health depends on one's particular moral or religious views. Whether one regards drug use, for example, as "unhealthy" depends on one's views about the body, altered consciousness, pleasure, industriousness, and, in general, the right way to live. It is this inability to characterize, in an objective fashion, basic goods that leads the libertarian to maintain that the assessment about what is worth pursuing should be left to individuals.

I think we can agree that there is an overlap between health and morality without conceding that it is impossible to distinguish the two. Individuals from widely divergent religious and moral backgrounds can agree on whether someone is sick, what disease he or she has, and whether something is a health risk. This suggests that there is a difference between health and morals, which makes it possible, in general, to distinguish arguments and reasons based on health considerations from those based on moral and religious values.

It must be admitted that much of American drug policy has been drenched in moralism. This moralistic attitude is revealed both in regarding addiction as a failure of willpower ("Just say no") and in wildly exaggerated descriptions of the effects of addiction. Here is a description of the effects of heroin from a concurring opinion by Justice Douglas in a 1962 United States Supreme Court decision:

> To be a confirmed drug addict is to be one of the walking dead. . . . The teeth have rotted out; the appetite is lost and the stomach and intestines don't function properly. The gall bladder becomes inflamed; eyes and skin turn a bilious yellow. In some cases membranes of the nose turn a flaming red; the partition separating the nostrils is eaten away—breathing is difficult. Oxygen in the blood decreases; bronchitis and tuberculosis develop. Good traits of character disappear and bad

ones emerge. Sex organs become affected. Veins collapse and livid purplish scars remain. Boils and abscesses plague the skin; gnawing pain racks the body. Nerves snap; vicious twitching develops. Imaginary and fantastic fears blight the mind and sometimes complete insanity results. Often times, too, death comes—much too early in life. . . . Such is the torment of being a drug addict; such is the plague of being one of the walking dead.

Similar lies were propagated about LSD in various newspaper stories, and about marijuana in such films as *Reefer Madness*. The effect, ironically enough, was to persuade a generation that any warnings about drug usage were likely to be completely untrustworthy.

Moralism about drugs is often coupled with hypocrisy about legal drugs. Schoolchildren are taught about the evils of illicit drugs, but the dangers of legal drugs are downplayed or ignored. A recent ad on television depicts a father confronting his child with marijuana found in his room, asking, "Who taught you to do this?" only to be told, "You did, Dad!" The announcer solemnly intones, "Parents who use drugs will have children who use drugs." Yet we don't see ads warning, "Parents who smoke and drink will have children who smoke and drink," despite the fact that far more people die from cigarettes and alcohol than from illegal drugs.

A public-health approach is pragmatic and non-ideological. It rejects moralism, and insists on sound empirical evidence for its claims. It recognizes the values of liberty and privacy, and supports the right of people to make their own choices about how they will live, free from governmental interference. At the same time, it recognizes that private acts can have social consequences. Thus, a public-health approach balances the harm to individuals of coercive laws against the social good to be achieved. It is willing to sacrifice some individual liberty in order to achieve important collective goals, such as the saving of thousands of lives or the eradication of disease.

IMPLICATIONS FOR DRUG POLICY

The Failure of the War on Drugs

There is wide consensus on one thing: the penal approach to the drug problem has been a dismal failure. The United States has poured nearly $70 billion into fighting drugs in the last twenty years, with very little to show for it. The reasons for the failure of the War on Drugs are primarily economic. Illicit drugs are big business. Seventy-nine billion dollars are generated every year by the sale of illicit drugs. Only the Exxon Corporation has higher annual revenues.

In many less-developed countries, drug trafficking, which has provided a new way to earn vast sums of hard currency, is transforming whole economies. In poor Third World countries, coca is one of the few cash crops that grows well, much better than coffee or oranges. In Colombia, Bolivia, and Peru, many farmers have turned from growing food crops to growing marijuana and coca, which make them three or four times as much money a year. In Bolivia, cocaine is estimated to generate as much as ten times the amount of Bolivia's leading official export, tin. Drug traffickers are at least as powerful as the government. They have more money than—and weapons and equipment as least as good as—the armed forces or the police. Moreover, drug traffickers are regarded by much of the populace as benefactors, not criminals. Even with the best will in the world, the government can do little to enforce laws that run counter to the vital economic interests of large numbers of its citizens. And that will is not always present. Mathea Falco, former Assistant Secretary of State for International Narcotics Matters, writes:

> It is very difficult to convince a foreign government to take the serious political and economic risks that are entailed by an all-out campaign against, say, cocaine production when the American public's predilection for cocaine is so well known. And it is virtually impossible to persuade foreign growers of marijuana to stop producing when one American in four has tried the drug—and billions of dollars in profits are being made by marijuana growers in the United States.

Occasionally, the U.S. government has been able to solicit the cooperation of foreign governments to stop production, but often with unexpected results. In 1975, the Mexican government, with American assistance, began a program to eliminate the marijuana crop by spraying it with paraquat. Mexico, then a major supplier to the U.S. market of relatively cheap, low-potency marijuana, effectively destroyed much of the crop. Jamaica and Colombia, previously only minor suppliers of marijuana, quickly stepped up production, producing a plant of much higher potency. In addition, American domestic production of marijuana began to boom. Marijuana is currently the second-largest cash crop in the United States, just after corn and ahead of soybeans.

Throughout the 1980s, the Reagan and Bush administrations acted aggressively in mobilizing the agencies of the federal government in a coordinated attack on the drug supply from abroad and the distribution of drugs within the United States. Total federal spending on the War on Drugs rose from approximately $1 billion to $9 billion during the 1980s. The crackdown yielded record numbers of drug seizures, arrests, and convictions. The Drug Enforcement Administration (DEA), the FBI, and Customs seized nearly half a billion dollars in drug-related assets in 1986. That year, the DEA arrested twice as many drug offenders as in 1982. From the end of 1980 to June 30, 1987, the prison population soared from 329,021 to 570,519. Roughly 40 percent of new prison inmates are incarcerated for drug offenses.

Should we conclude that the War on Drugs was a success? Not at all. None of this activity had any impact on either drug consumption or the drug market.

Domestic marijuana cultivation took off and the black market in cocaine grew to record size. As a result, prices plummeted. Steven Wisotsky, in *Beyond the War on Drugs*: "In 1980–81, a gram of cocaine cost $100 and averaged 12 percent purity at street level. By 1986, the price had fallen to as low as $80 ($50 in Miami), and the purity had risen to more than 50 percent. It rose to 70 percent purity in 1988. Around the nation, crack was marketed in $5 and $10 vials to reach the youth and low-income markets." In hospitals, cocaine-related emergencies rose from 4,277 in 1982 to more than 46,000 in 1988. That trend began to go down in late 1989, but a new Federal report shows a 13 percent increase in hospital emergencies attributed to cocaine in the third quarter of 1991 and a 10 percent increase in emergency room visits from the use of heroin.

This rapid expansion of supply and decline in price occurred despite President Reagan's increasing the federal antidrug enforcement budget from $645 million in fiscal year 1981 to over $4 billion in fiscal year 1987. A third of that budget was specifically devoted to interdiction. Commenting in 1987 specifically upon the interdiction budget, the Office of Technology Assessment concluded:

> Despite a doubling of Federal expenditures on interdiction over the past five years, the quantity of drugs smuggled into the United States is greater than ever. . . . There is no clear correlation between the level of expenditures or effort devoted to interdiction and the long-term availability of illegally imported drugs in the domestic market.

In 1992, the Bush Administration spent nearly $12 billion on drugs, more than double what was spent in Mr. Reagan's last year in office, two-thirds of it going to interdiction. "It reminds me of that cartoon," says Dr. Herbert Kleber, professor of medicine at Columbia University and a former deputy director of the Office of National Drug Control Policy who quit when he couldn't get more money shifted to treatment. "This king is slamming his fist on the table, saying, 'If all my horses and all my men can't put Humpty Dumpty together again, then what I need is more horses and more men.'"

Why has the government continued to pour money and other resources into a failed policy? For the same reason, I suspect, that we stayed in Vietnam. In *The March of Folly*, Barbara Tuchman suggests that "Woodenheadedness . . . plays a remarkably large role in government. It consists in assessing a situation in terms of preconceived fixed notions while ignoring or rejecting any contrary signs. It is acting according to wish while not allowing oneself to be deflected by the facts."

The War on Drugs has not simply failed. It's made things much worse. Steven Wisotsky writes:

It has spun a spider's web of black-market pathologies, including roughly 25 percent of all urban homicides, widespread corruption of police and other public officials, street crime by addicts, and subversive "narco-terrorist" alliances between Latin American guerrillas and drug traffickers. In the streets of the nation's major cities, violent gangs of young drug thugs armed with automatic rifles engage in turf wars. Federal agents estimated in 1988 that more than 10,000 members of "posses" or Jamaican drug gangs were responsible for about 1,000 deaths nationwide. Innocent bystanders and police officers are among their victims.

Another negative effect of the War on Drugs has been a reduction in civil liberties. The Supreme Court has upheld searches without probable cause, warranted searches of automobiles, adopted a "good-faith exception" to the exclusionary rule, and authorized search of "open fields" adjacent to a residence. The power of the police to stop, question, detain, investigate, and search vehicles has expanded significantly. Wisotsky comments, "The net result of the War on Drugs is gradually, but inexorably, to expand enforcement powers at the expense of personal freedom."

The War on Drugs mentality has prevented doctors from making authorized use of many controlled substances having valuable therapeutic applications. In 1984, the House of Representatives killed a bill that would have made injectable heroin available to dying cancer patients suffering severe, intense and intractable pain, when other drugs were ineffective. In California, patients with extremely debilitating cases of rheumatoid arthritis exhibited remarkable pain-free ability when they smoked freebase cocaine. Nevertheless, the government ended the experiment.

Most recently, the fight has centered around the use of marijuana as a medicinal drug. In March 1992, the Drug Enforcement Administration refused to reclassify marijuana as a Schedule II drug so doctors could prescribe it for patients suffering from glaucoma, cancer, muscular sclerosis, and AIDS. A Federal appeals court had ruled the previous April that the government was using illogical criteria in prohibiting the use of marijuana for medical purposes, because the agency had based a conclusion that marijuana had no "currently accepted medical use" on factors like the drug's general availability, its use by a substantial number of doctors, and recognition of its use in medical texts. Since the drug is illegal, the court said, meeting these criteria would be all but impossible.

Robert C. Bonner, chief of the DEA, said that marijuana had not been shown to be as safe and effective as legal alternatives, such as Marinol, a synthetic form of THC, the active ingredient in marijuana. In his response to the appeals court, Bonner said, "Beyond doubt, the claims that marijuana is medicine are false, dangerous and cruel. Sick men, women and children can be fooled by these claims and experiment with the drug. Instead of being helped, they risk serious side effects." Although made in the guise of scientific information, this is pure moralism. As Dr. Lester Grinspoon, an associate professor of psychiatry at Harvard Medical School who is the author of several books on marijuana's medicinal uses, says, "It's absolutely extraordinary that our government is behaving the way it is toward cannibis. They see legalizing it for medical use as a Trojan Horse for recreational use."

There has been a surge in the last year in requests for medical marijuana by AIDS patients, and some advocates argue that this inspired the recent Government actions. "The government is not doing this to protect patients," said Kennington Wall, a spokesman for the Drug Policy Foundation in Washington, which advocates a liberal national drug policy. "They're doing this to protect their political agenda."

Should Drugs Be Legalized?

If the War on Drugs has been a disaster, should drugs be legalized? A simple "yes" or "no" is impossible, partly because different drugs may require different responses, and partly because there are factual issues yet to be resolved. For example, what would be the effect of legalization on access and consumption? Some argue that legalization would have little impact on access, because illegal drugs are already easily available. More than half the high school seniors questioned by University of Michigan researchers in 1991 said that finding cocaine was "fairly easy" or "very easy." Nearly, 40 percent said the same for crack and about a third for heroin.

Others are convinced that, even if illegal drugs are already easy to obtain, legalization would make drugs even more accessible. This would lead to higher addiction rates, and thus worsen the already massive problems faced by the inner city. Many advocates for inner-city communities view illegal drugs as one aspect of the dominant society's oppression of their communities. Legalization "is construed as an expression of disdain for and dismissal of the misery that drugs bring to inner cities," according to Mosher and Yanagisako.

Advocates of legalization think that it will not increase the number of addicts for three reasons. First, although the price of drugs can be expected to go down, this will have little effect on the behavior of addicts who regard drugs as a necessity, not a luxury. Second, there will be little incentive for addicts to try to "hook" others to support their own habits. Third, even if quantity increases, potency will fall. Prohibition leads to stronger and stronger drugs, which are both more concentrated and have higher value. Therefore, even if greater amounts of drugs are consumed under legalization, they are likely to be less harmful to the population.

Advocates of legalization may be right about . . . its . . . effect on consumption and addiction. Still, it should be remembered that *three times* as many Americans abuse alcohol as use illegal drugs. Why? Because alcohol is legal, it

or nonexistent. Sixty-two million Americans have tried marijuana at least
, and roughly 18 million use it regularly. While marijuana is not risk-free
cially for adolescents and pregnant women), there is considerable evidence
it is much less harmful than alcohol. Yet there are approximately one-half
on arrests per year for marijuana, almost all for simple possession or petty
offenses. It is hard to see what social goals require that the criminal justice
m be overburdened in this way.

public-health approach toward drugs would require various measures. First
foremost, it requires continuing education about the benefits and dangers of
legal and illegal drugs. But a public-health approach goes beyond mere
ation. It supports getting tough on the legal drugs by such measures as
ng rid of cigarette vending machines so that cigarettes are not so readily
lable to minors; restricting the hours of sale of liquor; and levying raising
s on these items, commensurate with their social cost—billions of dollars
property damage, disease, and lost productivity. At the same time, the respect
ndividual choice and the rejection of moralism that are part of the public-
th approach require that we remain open to the possibility that some cur-
y illegal but comparatively harmless drugs, such as marijuana, should be
lized. And even if we decide to keep cocaine and heroin illegal, the em-
is should be on treatment. For most of the Reagan years, only about 20
ent of the budget went to treatment and education. This rose to about 30
ent under Bush. Despite Clinton's campaign rhetoric, it is still woefully
equate, according to many experts. Studies indicate that present prevention
treatment efforts reach only 10 percent of alcohol and drug abusers. In
tion, there is also very limited research on which prevention and treatment
rams work. Dr. Herbert D. Kleber, a former deputy director in the Federal
ce of National Drug Control Policy and one of the organizers of the rely created Center on Addiction and Substance Abuse in Manhattan, jokes
t the "four-two-one" syndrome in medical school, meaning that in four
s of medical school, students get two hours of instruction on the nation's
1 health problem, drug abuse. Obviously, this lack of attention must be
essed if we are to combat effectively the drug problem.

NCLUSION

paper does not attempt to answer the complex question of whether drugs
ld be legalized. The answer to that question hinges on various empirical
es, such as whether legalization would increase addiction rates. Instead, my
has been to show that the right approach to the problem of drug addiction
public-health perspective, as opposed to a libertarian approach. . . .
reas the libertarian insists on absolute freedom of choice, regardless of

is easy to buy, it is an accepted part of our culture. If
legal, it seems likely that entrepreneurs would cultivate
package them, and advertise them, just as they do alcohc
to believe that this would result in higher consumption
higher rate of addiction. . . .

Sometimes the argument in favor of legalization is t
what we learned from Prohibition. It is often said th
work": that people went right on drinking in speakeasies
rise of organized crime and led ordinary citizens to lose
fact, by public-health standards, narrowly construed, Prot
Consumption of alcohol fell by more than two-thirds, and
half the level that obtained in 1910. Two years after rep
of alcohol was only one-third of the 1910 level.

Nevertheless, Prohibition was a failure, because it w
restrictive, and repressive. Moreover, it was unnecessary.
". . . most of what we could accomplish in health and sa
could be achieved through more stringent regulation of ₐ
something like ringing a doorbell with a cannon."

It might be argued that it is equally unnecessary to ban
if one is concerned about their impact on the nation's heal
we could legalize or decriminalize the sale of addictive
their availability severely restricted. However, there is an
between alcohol and illicit drugs, and that is simply tha
legal. Millions of Americans have grown up regarding alc
socially acceptable part of life. Having wine in a restauran
dings, and beer at picnics are pleasures of which many An
being deprived. Prohibition of alcohol is politically impos

Because narcotic and opiate drugs have been illegal si
this century, they aren't viewed by most people as some
have a right. *Keeping* drugs illegal would not engender w
resentment, as *making* alcohol illegal would. The questi
makers and ordinary citizens is whether we should opt f
and legalizing addictive drugs. The risks and harms pose
provide a powerful argument against changing the status qu
this reason that Beauchamp supports "a policy that combir
of supply, both here and abroad, with more humane and
ment of users and addicts, even offering some form of mai
native to obtaining drugs in illegal settings."

A pragmatic approach also requires us to distinguish
case for keeping cocaine and heroin illegal is much strong
keeping marijuana illegal. Marijuana is not addictive, that i
cal dependence or withdrawal. Psychological dependence

social costs, the public-health approach balances the values of liberty and autonomy against the values of health and safety. It rejects the uncompromising stances characteristic of both moralism and libertarian ideology. Above all, a public-health approach insists that policies must be based on an honest appraisal of the problem and accurate empirical evidence about what does and does not work to solve it.

Controlling Tobacco Advertising:
The FDA Regulations and the First Amendment

LEONARD H. GLANTZ

INTRODUCTION

On August 28, 1996, the Food and Drug Administration (FDA) published regulations designed to reduce the use of tobacco products (meaning cigarettes and smokeless tobacco) by children. Certain parts of the regulations control the sale of tobacco in that they prohibit sales to individuals under 18 years of age and require sales to be made only in direct face-to-face transactions between the retailer and the consumer, thereby prohibiting sales by vending machines with limited exceptions. Other portions of the rule, in an attempt to limit the attractiveness of tobacco use to young people, regulate the way tobacco products are advertised and promoted. All advertising for these products is limited to the use of the black text on a white background. The only exceptions to this restriction are advertisements appearing in adult magazines or posted in facilities that only adults are permitted to enter. An adult publication is defined as a publication that is read by fewer than 2 million persons younger than 18 and whose readers in this age group constitute 15% or less of the publication's total readership. Furthermore, tobacco product manufacturers are prohibited from manufacturing, licensing, marketing, distributing, or selling any product such as hats or shirts that bears the name, logo, or other indicia of product identification; no tobacco manufacturer or distributor may sponsor sporting, cultural, athletic, musical, or cultural events in which any indicia of its tobacco products are displayed; and no outdoor advertising of tobacco products is permitted within 1000 feet of a playground, elementary, or secondary school. The regulations also require that additional warnings about tobacco's dangers be placed on labels.

These proposed rules raise substantial legal issues. The first is whether the FDA has the jurisdiction to regulate tobacco products at all, a question this

From the *American Journal of Public Health*, 87 (March 1997), 446–451. Reprinted by permission of the American Public Health Association.

paper will not discuss. The second is whether the proposed rules violate the free speech rights of tobacco manufacturers under the First Amendment. This paper will examine the free speech issue in light of recent Supreme Court decisions.

ORIGINS OF THE CONSTITUTIONAL PROTECTION OF COMMERCIAL SPEECH

The specific issue raised by the FDA's regulations is the constitutional protection of commercial speech (speech that proposes a commercial transaction), a murky and evolving area of the law. In 1942 the Supreme Court suggested, without analysis, that commercial speech was not entitled to First Amendment protection. About 3 decades later when the Court next considered this question, it adopted a very different approach. In 1971 (2 years before *Roe v Wade* legalized abortions in all states) a women's health service in New York published an advertisement in a Virginia newspaper stating that abortions were now legal in New York and offering to help women in Virginia obtain abortions. The newspaper publisher was convicted of violating a Virginia law that outlawed the publication of advertisements for abortion services. In *Bigelow v Virginia*, the Court explicitly ruled that commercial speech "enjoys a degree" of constitutional protection. However, it went on to find that the advertisement at issue was not purely commercial; rather, it conveyed information to a diverse audience. For example, the advertisement informed potential law reformers in Virginia that another state had legalized abortion.

The following year the Court dealt squarely with the issue of state regulation of commercial speech. In *Virginia State Board of Pharmacy v Virginia Citizens Consumer Council*, the Court struck down a Virginia statute that outlawed the advertising of prescription drug prices. The issue was "whether speech which does 'no more than propose a commercial transaction' . . . lacks all [constitutional] protection?" The Court answered no, finding that both sellers and buyers have a strong interest in the dissemination of information, and that in a free enterprise economy it is a matter of public interest that commercial decisions be intelligent and well informed. Because commercial speech is constitutionally protected, a state must demonstrate a significant interest to justify abridging the exercise of this right. The state argued that price advertising would reduce the quality of professional pharmacists' services because pharmacists would be forced to reduce their services to meet the prices of discounters. It also argued that price shopping would lead to the loss of the stable pharmacist-customer relationship, making individual attention and monitoring impossible. Finally it argued that advertising would reduce the pharmacist's professional image to that of a mere retailer. In effect, the state argued that drug price advertising was a threat to public health.

The Court was not persuaded by these arguments. It pointed out that professional standards could be better and more directly maintained through direct regulation of pharmacists. The state assumed that low-quality, low-cost pharmacies that advertise would attract unwitting customers. The Court characterized this as a "highly paternalistic approach." Instead, the Court assumed that people would be able to determine where their own best interest lay only if they were well enough informed by opening channels of communication. It pointed out that pharmacists would be allowed to advertise not only the price of drugs but also their superior products and services. The Court concluded, "Virginia is free to require whatever professional standards it wishes of its pharmacists. . . . But it may not do so by keeping the public in ignorance of the entirely lawful terms that competing pharmacists are offering."

The Court also noted that like other speech, commercial speech can be regulated in certain ways. States can regulate the "time, place and manner" of speech in certain circumstances, as well as false or misleading speech.

In subsequent cases, the Court struck down restrictions on lawyer advertising, on the use of "for sale" signs in front of houses, and on contraceptive advertising because these prohibitions infringed on commercial speech. The cases made clear that the Court was giving commercial speech substantial protection while attempting to allow states to regulate it if they could establish a significant enough interest. But the standards to be applied in such a balancing approach were less than clear.

The Court attempted to clarify these standards in *Central Hudson Gas & Electric Corp v Public Service Commission of New York*. In that case, an electric company challenged a New York rule that prohibited electric companies from engaging in any advertising that promoted the use of electricity. The rule's purpose was to further the national policy of conserving energy. The commission also believed that the rule would keep down electric rates because of the way such rates were calculated. The Court applied a four-part test to determine the constitutionality of state restrictions on commercial speech: (1) the speech must concern lawful activity and not be misleading, (2) the asserted governmental interest in restricting the speech must be "substantial," (3) the regulation must "directly advance" the governmental interest, and (4) the regulation must not be more extensive than is necessary to serve the interest.

The Court readily found that selling electricity was a lawful activity and that the proposed advertising was not misleading. It also found that the state's interest in energy conservation and in keeping rates low were substantial, and that there was an immediate connection between advertising and the demand for electricity. Indeed, a monopoly's only reason for advertising would be to increase demand since there are no competitors. However, the Court found that the state's ban on advertising contravened part 4 of the test because it was more extensive than necessary to further the state's energy conservation goals. The electric company argued that the ban prohibited it from advertising products that would lead to more efficient energy use; this included heat pumps, which both sides agreed would greatly improve electric heating. The Court concluded that the state's sweeping ban prevented the company from advertising products that would consume the same amount of energy as alternative sources or actually reduce energy use by diverting demand from less efficient sources.

Several justices who concurred in the outcome questioned the state's authority to ban commercial speech at all. Justices Blackmun and Brennan said, "[We] seriously doubt whether suppression of information concerning the availability and price of a legally offered product is ever a permissible way for the State to 'dampen' demand for or use of the product."

These comments reflect the tension found in these cases. The justices did not disagree that the state has an interest in conserving energy, just as states have an interest in maintaining the quality of pharmacist services. The issue was whether states may further this interest by suppressing speech, which is constitutionally protected, particularly when more direct action can be taken to regulate the activity in ways that would not raise any constitutional problems.

ADVERTISING GAMBLING

The Court gave commercial speech increasing levels of protection, frequently striking down state advertising bans until 1986. That year the case of *Posadas de Puerto Rico v Tourism Company of Puerto Rico* seemed to halt this momentum. Puerto Rico, which permitted casino gambling, prohibited all advertising of the activity that would be accessible to residents of Puerto Rico. Its goal was to reduce residents' demand for casino gambling. In an opinion written by Chief Justice Rehnquist, the Court found that the activity was lawful, the advertising was not misleading, and the state had a substantial interest in reducing the demand for casino gambling by its residents. Further, with regard to part 3 of the *Central Hudson* test, which requires a determination that the advertising ban directly advances the state's interest, the Court found that the legislature's belief that adverising for casino gambling would increase demand was "reasonable" and that such a ban therefore would directly advance the state's interest. The Court also concluded that the ban was no more extensive than necessary to serve the government's interest, and so it also satisfied part 4 of the *Central Hudson* test.

But Justice Rehnquist's majority opinion went further. It argued that the government could ban advertising for any activity that it could prohibit: "It would . . . be a strange constitutional doctrine which would concede to the legislature the authority to totally ban a product or activity, but deny to the legislature the authority to forbid the stimulation of demand for the product or activity through advertising." The Court gave as examples cigarettes, alcoholic beverages, and prostitution. The Court did not seem to require any evidence that the ban on casino advertising would actually have a positive effect. It was willing to defer to the opinion of the legislature without any further evidence, a very low level of review. If this rule were to prevail, governments would have a great deal of latitude to regulate commercial speech because states have wide authority to ban the sale of products and services.

It now appears that the *Posadas* case was an aberration in the Court's commercial speech jurisprudence. After that decision the Court continued to find various bans on commercial speech unconstitutional. In *Rubin v Coors Brewing Company*, the Court struck down a federal law that prohibited beer labels from displaying the alcohol content of the beer. The government contended that such a ban would curb "strength wars" in which brewers would compete for customers on the basis of alcohol content. The Court accepted the government's legitimate interest in trying to prevent excessive consumption of alcohol, but it was not convinced that this approach would directly advance that interest or was no more extensive than necessary. It said that the burden of showing that the regulation furthers the governmental interest in a direct and material way is "not satisfied by mere speculation and conjecture; rather the government body seeking to sustain a restriction on commercial speech must demonstrate that the harms it recites are real and that its restriction will in fact alleviate them to a material degree." The Court rejected the government's concern about strength wars as being based on anecdotal guesses and tidbits. It also rejected the government's argument that the very fact that a brewer brought this type of litigation is proof that advertising increases consumption. The Court said, "Brewers may have many different reasons—only one of which might be a desire to wage a strength war—why they wish to disclose the potency of their beverages." Finally the Court found that there were other, more direct ways to prevent strength wars among brewers, such as the direct regulation of alcohol content in beer, that were "less intrusive" on the manufacturers' First Amendment rights. It is worth noting that in this case the government asked the Court to find that legislatures have broader latitude to regulate speech that promotes "socially harmful activities," and the Court refused to do so.

THE COURT'S 1996 DECISION

The Court's most recent case on commercial speech, *44 Liquormart v Rhode Island*, decided in May 1996, contains a sweeping review of its commercial speech cases and appears to strengthen First Amendment protection for commercial speech. The case concerned the constitutionality of Rhode Island statutes that prohibited publication of the price of any alcoholic beverage in any medium. In previous cases, the Rhode Island Supreme Court upheld the constitutionality of the statute because it served the substantial state interest in "the promotion of temperance." Later, 44 Liquormart, a retail store, placed an advertisement in a newspaper that identified various brands of packaged liquor with the word "WOW" next to pictures of vodka and rum bottles. Concluding that this was a reference to bargain prices, the Rhode Island Liquor Control Administrator assessed a $400 fine.

After paying the fine, the petitioners filed an action in federal district court to have the statutes declared unconstitutional. The judge found that there was a lack of unanimity among researchers regarding the impact of advertising on the consumption of alcoholic beverages. Rhode Island was in the upper 30% of states in the per capita consumption of alcoholic beverages, and alcohol consumption was lower in other states that permitted price advertising. The evidence showed that Rhode Island's ban on liquor price advertising has "no significant impact" on alcohol consumption. Thus, the court ruled that the liquor price ban was unconstitutional because it did not directly advance the state's interest in reducing consumption and was more extensive than necessary.

The case was ultimately appealed to the Supreme Court, which unanimously ruled that the statutes were unconstitutional. While all the justices agreed with the conclusion, not all agreed on the reasons for it. The principal opinion of four justices concluded that the Court developed the commercial speech doctrine to enable states to protect consumers from misleading, deceptive, or aggressive sales practices. In effect, commercial speech is subject to regulation to protect the "fair bargaining process." Thus, it is the state's interest in protecting consumers from "commercial harms" (such as those that would result from false advertising) that justifies regulating commercial speech more than noncommercial speech. But, the opinion said, when the state's purpose for regulating commercial speech has a different goal, the speech involved deserves more First Amendment protection. Restrictions on commercial speech that do not protect consumers from commercial harm often tend to "obscure an 'underlying governmental policy' that could be implemented without regulating speech." The opinion warned, "The First Amendment directs us to be especially skeptical of regulations that seek to keep people in the dark for what the government perceives to be their own good."

The principal opinion found that the Rhode Island price advertising ban "serves an end unrelated to consumer protection." As a result, the ban must be reviewed with "special care." The state must show not only that the ban will advance its interest but that it will do so to a "material degree": that it will "significantly reduce alcohol consumption." The principal opinion then said that the Court can agree with the commonsense notion that lack of advertising would lead to higher prices than would exist if price competition were allowed, and that higher prices might lead to somewhat lower consumption. But in the absence of evidentiary support, the Court cannot find that the advertising ban will "significantly advance" the state's interest in promoting temperance. While the record showed that higher prices might have some effect on the purchasing patterns of temperate drinkers, it did not show that they would "significantly reduce" marketwide consumption or have any effect on abusive drinkers. The liquor stores that brought the suit argued that they would increase their sales by $100 000 per year if they could advertise. The principal opinion interpreted this to mean that the stores would increase their market share by attracting existing alcohol consumers, not by increasing the total number of consumers. The state was not able to identify what price level would lead to a significant reduction in alcohol consumption or how much prices would decline in the absence of a ban. Thus, the Court stated that Rhode Island cannot conclude that advertising leads to increased consumption without engaging in "speculation or conjecture. . . . Such speculation certainly does not suffice when the State takes aim at accurate commercial information for paternalistic ends." Furthermore, the opinion found the restriction on speech to be more extensive than necessary to achieve the state's goal. Accordingly, if the state wished to keep the prices of alcoholic beverages high, it could do so in ways that do not affect speech at all, such as using increased taxation or direct price regulation.

The state, citing *Posadas*, argued that since it could ban the sale of all alcoholic beverages, it could regulate the promotion of the product. The principal opinion conceded that *Posadas* does support the state's argument. However, the opinion found that the *Posadas* case "erroneously performed" the First Amendment analysis and was inconsistent with the rest of the body of law the Court has developed in the commercial speech area. Instead, the opinion said, "in keeping with our prior holdings, we conclude that a state legislature does not have broad discretion to suppress truthful, nonmisleading information for paternalistic purposes that the *Posadas* majority was willing to tolerate." The opinion also explicitly rejected the notion that if a government has the authority to ban an activity it must also have the authority to ban advertising about that activity. The First Amendment forbids government regulation of speech, not conduct. As the opinion put it, "The text of the constitution presumes that attempts to regulate speech are more dangerous than attempts to regulate conduct. . . . As a result the First amendment directs that government may not suppress speech as easily as it may suppress conduct."

The opinion also rejected the state's argument that commercial speech related to "vice" activities should be subject to greater state regulation. Once the state permits products such as alcoholic beverages, lottery tickets, or playing cards to be lawfully purchased, the First Amendment protects speech associated with these items as much as with any other items.

Justice Thomas, who wrote the majority opinion in the 1995 *Coors* case, wrote a concurring opinion even more strongly protecting commercial speech.

He rejected the *Central Hudson* analysis because the principal opinion would seem to uphold the ban on alcohol advertising if it could be proven to be effective. Justice Thomas argued that a state may not further its legitimate interests by "keeping would-be recipients in the dark." He also argued that advertising bans would virtually always fail the fourth prong of the *Central Hudson* test because directly banning, taxing, controlling the price, or otherwise restricting the sale of a product would always be as effective as restricting advertising. This very conservative justice adopted the view of liberal Justice Harry Blackmun in his concurring opinion in *Central Hudson* "that all attempts to dissuade legal choices by citizens by keeping them ignorant are impermissible." Justice Thomas' views on this matter are important because he appears to be the "swing vote" on commercial speech cases.

Four concurring justices took a more limited approach to the issue. They simply noted that the Rhode Island restrictions fail the *Central Hudson* test because the state failed to demonstrate a "reasonable fit" between its ban on alcoholic beverage advertising and its temperance goal. But even these justices said that courts must not accept a state's proffered justification for regulating speech at face value but rather must "examine carefully" or "more searchingly" the state's justification. They made clear that a "closer look" than that taken in *Posadas* is required.

TOBACCO ADVERTISING AND THE FIRST AMENDMENT

The justices' different approaches make it difficult to ascertain definitively the constitutional limits on governmental authority to regulate commercial speech. However, it appears that the commercial speech doctrine is evolving in the direction of affording such speech increased protection. How would the Court view the regulation of tobacco promotion as proposed by the FDA?

The FDA proposal is a combination of bans and restrictions. The distribution of clothing and other paraphernalia with tobacco indicia is entirely banned. Outdoor advertising within 1000 feet of locations frequented by children is banned, but outdoor advertising in other locations is permitted. Advertising in certain publications is limited to black and white text and is therefore regulated but not banned.

In the recent Supreme Court cases, the government has attempted to ban information such as the price of alcoholic beverages or the alcoholic content of the product. These are objective facts that consumers might wish to use in making purchasing choices. Tobacco promotion, however, tends to be more emotive than factual. Joe Camel, people running on the beach, or a hat with the name of a chewing tobacco on it does not provide *information*. Therefore it could be argued that these restrictions do not deprive consumers of information needed to make an informed purchasing choice, a major purpose underlying the protection of commercial speech. The Court, however, has not addressed the relevance of this distinction in the past and has protected advertising that simply lets the consumer know of the existence of a particular product, such as contraceptives.

It is also noteworthy that the Court has been particularly hostile to bans apparently because consumers would not have ready access to the information in question. For example, if alcoholic beverage prices cannot be advertised, the consumer has no easy way to obtain that information. Even with the FDA restrictions, however, tobacco companies will have ample opportunity to make the general public aware of their products.

Further, the FDA's proposal is directed at advertising that might affect children. In all states it is unlawful to sell tobacco products to children, and if it can be shown that the restricted advertising and promotions are directed at children, the restricted speech would be directed at products that are *unlawful* for the target audience to purchase. The First Amendment protects commercial speech only for products that may be lawfully purchased.

There is no doubt that the government can restrict advertisements for tobacco products that are intended for an exclusively child audience. Thus, the government can outlaw such advertisements in the *Weekly Reader*. The issue is whether the proposed regulations are crafted narrowly enough so that the child audience is protected without any undue infringement on the adult audience. Some attempt was made to define the type of publication that the FDA considers to be read by children. However, the agency prohibits the use of other indicia of tobacco products in *all* athletic, artistic, and cultural events, and in many instances this may have virtually no impact on children's use of tobacco. It is unlikely, for example, that substantial numbers of children attend the opera in the evening. Moreover, under these regulations, shirts, hats, and similar promotional items may not be sold or given to adults, not just children. Similarly, the black and white text requirement applies to publications that have adults as the vast majority of readers.

In the past the Court has recognized that states have considerably more authority to protect children than they do adults from what they consider to be offensive material. For example, in *Ginsburg v New York* the Court found that states could adopt different definitions of obscenity for minors and adults. They could also outlaw the sale of material to children under 16 years of age that they could not outlaw for sale to adults without violating the First Amendment. However, the Court did not permit states to outlaw adults' access to such material in order to protect minors. In perhaps a more apt case, the federal government outlawed the mailing of unsolicited advertisements for contraceptives. One argument the government made to support this law was that it would aid parents who desired to keep their children from seeing such mailings. In striking down this statute in *Bolger v Youngs Drug Products Corp*, the Court said,

> This marginal degree of protection is achieved by purging all mailboxes of un-
> solicited material that is entirely suitable for adults. We have previously made clear
> that a restriction of this scope is more extensive than the Constitution permits, for
> the government may not 'reduce the adult population . . . to reading only what is
> fit for children'. . . . The level of discourse reaching a mailbox simply cannot be
> limited to that which would be suitable for a sandbox.

As a result, the government's ability to protect children by regulating advertising that mostly reaches adults is limited.

The prohibition against outdoor advertising as a means of reducing alcohol and tobacco use by children has been litigated. The US Court of Appeals for the Fourth Circuit has upheld the constitutionality of a Baltimore ordinance that bans, with certain limited exceptions, outdoor advertising for alcoholic beverages. The same court also upheld a similar ordinance restricting outdoor tobaco advertising. In upholding these restrictions, the court applied the *Central Hudson* standards. There is no doubt that the state has a substantial interest in reducing the use of alcohol and tobacco by minors. The dispute centered on the means with which to achieve the clearly desirable ends. This court was satisfied that there is a "logical nexus" between the means and the ends chosen by the government to address the problem, and that the proper standard for approval of legislative action is the "reasonableness of the legislature's belief that the means it selected will advance its ends." This, however, is a much lower standard of review than that recently applied by the Supreme Court. Indeed, both of these cases were appealed to the Supreme Court, which vacated and remanded them back to the appeals court for further consideration in light of the *44 Liquormart* case.

On remand, the Fourth Circuit again upheld Baltimore's restrictions on outside advertising for alcoholic beverages. This court, in a two to one decision, upheld the ordinance for three reasons: it was targeted at restricting ads directed at persons under 18 who could not legally buy alcoholic beverages; the state has more power to protect children than adults; and the ordinance was not an outright ban but, in the court's opinion, merely restricted the time, place, and manner of such restrictions. Based on this conclusion, the court also upheld Baltimore's ordinance restricting tobacco advertising. The dissenting judge argued that the *Liquormart* case required a further remand to the trial court for findings of fact to determine if the restrictions on speech would actually further the goal of reducing teenage drinking and whether it would do so to a material degree. It is likely that these cases will return to the Supreme Court.

The standard of review that the principal opinion adopted in *44 Liquormart* presents a serious challenge to the proposed regulations on tobacco advertising and promotion. These regulations are designed to further a governmental policy rather than to protect consumers from commercial harm. This is the regulatory category the principal opinion said should be subject to heightened scrutiny. It is clear from the principal opinion that the Court will no longer assume that there is a connection between advertising and consumption or passively accept the governmental judgment on the matter. In *44 Liquormart*, the Court required evidence that the ban on liquor price advertising would "significantly reduce alcohol consumption," thereby advancing the state's interest to a "material degree." Will the government be able to demonstrate that its proposed regulations will have this sort of impact on underage smoking?

There is considerable evidence that tobacco advertising has an effect on the brand of tobacco that children use. However, the evidence that advertising has a significant impact on smoking initiation is much more equivocal. Even studies that show that there are some effects where tobacco advertising is *totally banned* demonstrate that those effects are relatively small. For the FDA's proposed restrictions to be found constitutional, the FDA will need to demonstrate that restrictions that are not total bans will have a significant effect. For example, it will need to show that restricting billboards within 1000 feet of areas where children congregate but not elsewhere, that prohibiting colorful advertising while permitting black and white advertising, and that prohibiting the indicia of tobacco products on clothing will significantly reduce the use of tobacco by minors. This will be difficult, if not impossible, given the current state of knowledge.

The final hurdle the FDA will need to overcome is to demonstrate that the restriction on speech is no more extensive than necessary to meet its goal. If there are alternative ways to meet the state's goal that would not restrict speech, such restrictions would appear to be more extensive than necessary. The principal opinion in *4 Liquormart* suggested that if the state wished to keep the price of alcoholic beverages high, it should not ban price advertising but rather should increase taxes or directly regulate prices. Tobacco control advocates have already convinced states and the federal government to take action against smoking by minors. Cigarette sales to minors are outlawed, additional taxes have increased prices, educational strategies are used in schools, and anti-tobacco advertising campaigns have been launched. Furthermore, there is some evidence that counteradvertising more effectively reduces rates of smoking than advertising bans. Ironically, the success of such measures is an argument against the need for advertising restrictions as a way of reducing tobacco use by children.

CONCLUSION

The FDA's regulations that affect commercial speech will face a significant constitutional challenge. Whether they will be upheld by the Supreme Court is not clear. The regulations do not totally ban tobacco advertising, which is the type of regulation subject to the Court's strictest scrutiny. It could be argued that they regulate only the "time, place and manner" of tobacco promotion, the type of regulation the Court is more inclined to uphold. On the other hand, the regulations are sweeping, affecting all advertising media, including those that are primarily directed at adults. Furthermore, the effect the regulations will have on children's smoking behavior is far from clear. The trend has been for the Court to be increasingly hostile to governmental restrictions on commercial speech even when the governmental goal is clearly beneficial, such as reducing alcohol consumption.

For those in public health, the protection of commercial speech may be seen as a mixed blessing. The doctrine protects the promotion of alcohol and may well restrict the government's ability to control tobacco advertising. On the other hand, it also protects advertisements for contraceptives, abortion services, and prescription drug prices, all of which were banned by states in the past. The lesson of the constitutional protection of free speech is that one cannot protect speech one approves of and ban speech one dislikes. Those who advocated bans on advertising for contraceptives and abortions felt strongly enough about these issues to convince legislatures and governors to act in their favor. But popular disapproval of speech with a particular content is the reason why there is a First Amendment to protect it. Popular speech needs no protection.

Should the Court strike down the FDA's regulations, there are still many weapons left in the antitobacco arsenal. Certainly the non-speech-related portion of the rule raises no constitutional questions. No constitutional right is invaded by prohibiting vending machine sales, for example. Furthermore, government can act in at least one new way to try to reduce tobacco advertising: it can eliminate tax deductions for the expenses associated with tobacco promotion. It is quite remarkable that the same federal government that is attempting to restrict a particular type of speech indirectly subsidizes that speech by permitting tobacco companies to deduct advertising and promotional expenses from their taxable revenue. There is no doubt that the government could change this rule without raising any substantial constitutional issue. There is no right to a tax deduction. The tobacco industry might argue that such an action would be a deprivation of their rights to equal protection under the law because other industries are permitted to deduct advertising expenses. But such an argument would border on the frivolous. Since there would be no invasion of a fundamental constitutional right, the government would need to demonstrate only that its act was reasonably related to a legitimate goal, a much lower standard than that found in the commercial speech cases. Certainly it would be rational for the government to rescind the indirect subsidization of the promotion of a product that endangers public health as much as cigarettes do. If advertising were made more expensive, there might well be less of it.

If the FDA has jurisdiction over cigarettes, it could also mandate the reduction or elimination of nicotine from this product. This would be a direct means by which it could reduce the negative effects of the drug it wishes to regulate. This move would have a much more direct impact than advertising restrictions, and it also would not raise any constitutional issues.

None of this will come as a surprise to the FDA. The comments accompanying the regulations discuss the First Amendment issue and conclude that the regulations are consistent with the Constitution. The FDA has done a superb job of creating a record to support its position. The Supreme Court will ultimately decide whether that record is good enough to justify the FDA's regulation of commercial speech.

5

INJURY AND VIOLENCE

During the Great Society period, Ralph Nader, William Haddon, Jr., and others argued for transforming injury from a field that viewed injuries as accidents, unpredictable and even inevitable (as "acts of God"), to one that views injuries as exposure-related, predictable, and controllable by communal measures. This transformation focused attention on the field of injury as a communal interest, as one producing savings in lives and prevented injury that benefited the whole community. Again, this shift in focus redefined injury as more than just an individual problem; it was also a community problem. Although specific injuries are a relatively rare occurrence for the individual in a given year (injury is a far more lethal threat when spread over a lifetime), they are common within a community. Most injuries arise from activities that are frequently engaged in by millions of people (like driving an automobile); risks that are, in the short run relatively safe, yet yield overall death and injury tolls that merit public action.

The first selection in this chapter, "Energy Damage and Ten Countermeasure Strategies," is by William Haddon, Jr., a state and federal health official, physician and epidemiologist. (Haddon's term *countermeasure strategy* roughly translates to *preventive strategy*.) Extending the paradigm of communicable disease prevention to chronic disease, Haddon encourages students and practitioners to take a fresh look at just what the range of options might be to prevent a wide range of health problems.

Haddon's typology of injury prevention will strike many as odd. He speaks of humans as *hosts* and hazards as *agents* and of both as they exist in a mediating environment. This shift in orientation is congruent with a shift in contemporary public health and prevention thought, a shift to the notion of *exposure causality*. By stressing the individual as host and by using the idea of *exposure*, which formerly meant infectious expsure to a biological agent, Haddon and others have shifted attention to the field, or environment of risk, that humans together face—risks from exposure to such hazards as the automobile, poorly designed highways, and dangerous work sites containing threats like cotton dust or coal dust. This shift in focus to exposure causality has moved attention away from the exclusive focus on the individual agent and his or her miscalculations or foolishness.

Haddon served as Lyndon Johnson's head of the new National Highway Traffic Safety Administration, one of the first of a whole series of new institutions created during the Great Society to carry public health far beyond the boundaries of the traditional (and conservative) U.S. Public Health Service. Today, injury control is a major component of the field of public health. We have made dramatic progress in cutting the levels of injury, especially on the highways, and even for the category of alcohol-related automobile crashes. For the first time in decades, alcohol-related crashes have fallen below 40% among all crashes, when for decades they remained immovably associated with roughly half of all crashes.

In our second selection, James A. Mercy and his colleagues review the paradigm of injury and suggest extending this model further, to control injuries resulting from violence against persons. Violence is defined as interpersonal violence, "a threatened or actual use of physical force against a person or group that either results or is likely to result in injury or death." They note the high rates of violence committed against young persons. Of primary concern is the high rate of violence associated with homicide in the United States when compared to other nations and the role that firearms play in establishing these rates. Mercy and his colleagues argue that a scientific approach to preventing injuries and death from firearms (as opposed to what he terms the sterile debate over firearm control) will help lower these rates. They suggest that developing "'prosocial' attitudes or beliefs" by the nation's youth will help lower rates of violence in neighborhoods where violence is epidemic, while also seeking to attack the social inequality that may be the fundamental cause of violence. This drive among injury experts is accompanied by a call to lower the role of the criminal sanction as the primary instrument of policy in limiting violence. This focus on controlling violence through controlling the harms associated with handguns and other guns has produced a furious reaction by the National Rifle Association, which is seeking to use its allies in the U.S. Congress to defund that part of the Centers for Disease Control that focuses on handgun violence.

There is little doubt that extending the injury paradigm to interpersonal violence will remain hugely controversial in the years to come, and not the least because it brings public health into collision with perhaps its most potent opponent, the gun lobby.

Regarding limiting the use of the criminal justice system to control violence, Mark Moore in our third selection is skeptical. He welcomes the entry of public health experts into the arena of violence prevention. He notes the usefulness of this new perspective in reshaping our perceptions of how to prevent violence and says that this reshaping is already underway in the notion of "community policing." But he doubts that a public health response can mostly replace the criminal justice sanction. Prevention, he says, is most successful when the causes of a problem are specific and not widespread; however, when they are, this results in an impossibly large landscape on which government must act. The virtue of the criminal justice sanction is that it can be tailored to the actual problem or criminal act of violence itself. Moore's views are especially of interest because, as a national expert on criminal justice, he also chaired a National Academy of Sciences panel in the late 1970s and early 1980s that strongly endorsed implementing a public health perspective for alohol problems and their prevention.

Energy Damage and the Ten Countermeasure Strategies

WILLIAM HADDON, JR.

An important landmark is reached in the evolution of a scientific field when classification of its subject matter is based on the relevant, fundamental processes involved rather than on descriptions of the appearances of the phenomena of interest. In illustration, a fundamental turning point was reached when the debilitation and progressive susceptibility to bruising of shipboard scurvy could for the first time be classified as the process resulting from a deficiency of consumption of something variously present in fruits and vegetables (much later identified as ascorbic acid, vitamin C). In fact, such transition from classifications consisting essentially only of a description of appearances to those based on fundamental processes is basic to scientific progress generally; hence, examples abound from the full gamut of scientific concerns.

Additonal illustrations, among the many, include the classificatory and conceptual transitions that followed recognition:

a. That rocks could be grouped on the basis of the processes involved in their formation—as sedimentary, igneous, metamorphic.
b. That the variations among the Galapagos finches studied by Darwin were the result of differential ecologic processes.
c. That earthquakes were one aspect of tectonic processes.
d. That the epidemic disease of the young which could for decades be described only as 'infantile paralysis' was a rare variant of a commonplace process initiated by infection with one of several similar and previously unknown viruses.
e. That plague was a process in which a specific pathogen, *Pasteurella pestis*, rats, fleas, and people interacted.

From the *Journal of Trauma*, 13 (1973), 321–326. Reprinted by permission of Williams & Wilkins.

EXTRARATIONAL EXPLANATIONS IN THE ABSENCE OF PROCESS KNOWLEDGE

Before such conceptual and hence classification advance, lacking an understanding of process, and therefore of the possibility of human intervention or avoidance, phenomena of concern to people have commonly been attributed to extrarational factors. 'Luck', 'chance', 'accident', 'fate' and similar terms are the hallmarks of such ignorance, and perhaps of a human necessity for explaining it away. The distinction between the way in which people tend to deal with the understood as opposed to the merely known-about is illustrated nicely by the renowned anthropologist Malinowski. He found that Trobriand natives viewed the hazards outside the reef, which they did not understand, in ways more supernatural than they viewed those inside the reef, which they did understand. As he wrote, 'It is most significant that in the lagoon fishing, where man can rely completely upon his knowledge and skill, magic does not exist, while in the open-sea fishing, full of danger and uncertainty, there is extensive magical ritual to secure safety and good results'.

DIVINE PUNISHMENT AS AN EXPLANATION IN THE ABSENCE OF PROCESS UNDERSTANDING

The Book of Job epitomizes another commonplace aspect of human response to undesirable happenings not yet understood—and therefore not yet categorized—in process terms. The events are explained as divine retribution for shortcomings. The suffering of oneself, someone else, or some group occurs because it is divine and well-deserved punishment. Therefore, unless the sin can be expiated by appropriate change in behavior, it may be 'too bad', but there is nothing else to be done to ameliorate the personally or societally undesirable happening unless it is an increase in efforts at human reform.

EXPANDED CLASSIFICATORY SETS AND DIFFERENT SETS

The transition to understanding of underlying, relevant processes commonly results in more than just a relabeling of past groupings. Usually the phenomena previously recognized have been 'the tip of the iceberg', and the recognition of underlying process adds much more. Thus, in the case of what was originally termed 'infantile paralysis', it was found that the infectious process routinely involved hundreds of individuals subclinically for each person ill enough to be diagnosed. Moreover, parallel illustrations are legion, not only from medicine but also widely from other sciences.

For example, understanding the actual nature of earthquakes is to classify them conceptually as one aspect of a far broader range of tectonic processes; and understanding the origins of a butterfly or a clam is to identify it in terms of its life cycle, a process classification. Understanding the process involved in eclipses is to classify them as one aspect of celestial mechanics.

Another frequent result of transition to process-based understanding is regrouping of phenomena not merely in expanded sets, but in new sets that do not bear a one-to-one correlation with the old. As process (or, to use a related [medical] term, etiologic) understanding advanced, the set of phenomena formerly referred to as 'wasting' was in effect, parcelled out to such process-defined sets as tuberculosis, amebiasis, protein deficiency, and a host of others.

More relevant here is to view the process in reverse; that is, from the standpoint of the etiologic or process sets in picking up pieces of many pre-existing descriptive sets.

Thus syphilis, the etiologic set based on the infectious agent, *Treponema pallidum*, picked up parts of previous descriptive sets, such as paresis, gummas, penile lesions, rashes, certain gastric lesions, certain abnormalities of the growing ends of bone, and many others, but not all of those in any one of the earlier descriptive sets. Again, an important point is that there is usually not in such transitions, a one-to-one relationship between the earlier, descriptive ways of looking at the phenomena and those process-based which are substituted for them.

The foregoing is brief background for that which follows, an introduction to the classification of certain widespread, important phenomena defined and grouped in terms of a small number of closely parallel processes. Most of the included phenomena are not yet regarded in process terms by the implicit and explicit classifications still applied to them by most professionals and laymen. Yet there is widespread, implicit, and at least qualitative recognition of the processes themselves, because cultures, past and present, abound in actions directed at changing the outcome of these processes through interventions at specific points in their sequences.

ENERGY DAMAGE PROCESSES

The phenomena of concern are those involved when energy is transferred in such ways and amounts, and at such rates, that inanimate or animate structures are damaged. The harmful interactions with people and property of hurricanes, earthquakes, projectiles, moving vehicles, ionizing radiation, lightening, conflagrations, and the cuts and bruises of daily life illustrate this class.

TEN STRATEGIES FOR REDUCING THESE LOSSES

Several strategies, in one mix or another, are available for reducing the human and economic losses that make this class of phenomena of social concern. In their logical sequence, they are as follows:

The *first* strategy is to prevent the marshalling of the form of energy in the first place; preventing the generation of thermal, kinetic, or electrical energy, or ionizing radiation; the manufacture of gunpowder; the concentration of U-235; the build-up of hurricanes, tornadoes, or tectonic stresses; the accumulation of snow where avalanches are possible; the elevating of skiers; the raising of babies above the floor, as to cribs and chairs from which they may fall; the starting and movement of vehicles; and so on, in the richness and variety of ecologic circumstances.

The *second* strategy is to reduce the amount of energy marshalled: reducing the amounts and concentrations of high school chemistry reagents, the size of bombs or firecrackers, the height of divers above swimming pools, or the speed of vehicles.

The *third* strategy is to prevent the release of the energy: preventing the discharge of nuclear devices, armed crossbows, gunpowder, or electricity; the descent of skiers; the fall of elevators; the jumping of would-be suicides; the undermining of cliffs; or the escape of tigers. An Old Testament writer illustrated this strategy in the context both of the architecture of his area and of the moral imperatives of this entire field: 'When you build a new house, you shall make a parapet for your roof, that you may not bring the guilt of blood upon your house, if any one fall from it'. This biblical position, incidentally, is fundamentally at variance with that of those who, by conditioned reflex, regard harmful interactions between man and his environment as problems requiring reforming imperfect man rather than suitably modifying his environment.

The *fourth* strategy is to modify the rate of spatial distribution of release of the energy from its source: slowing the burning rate of explosives, reducing the slopes of ski trails for beginners, and choosing the re-entry speed and trajectory of space capsules. The third strategy is the limiting case of such release reduction, but is identified separately because in the real world it commonly involves substantially different circumstances and tactics.

The *fifth* strategy is to separate, in space or time, the energy being released from the susceptible structure, whether living or inanimate: the evacuation of the Bikini islanders and test personnel, the use of sidewalks and the phasing of pedestrian and vehicular traffic, the elimination of vehicles and their pathways from community areas commonly used by children and adults, the use of lightning rods, and the placing of electric power lines out of reach. This strategy, in a sense also concerned with rate-of-release modification, has as its hallmark the elimination of intersections of energy and susceptible structure—a common and important approach.

The very important *sixth* strategy uses not separation in time and space but separation by interposition of a material 'barrier': the use of electrical and thermal insulation, shoes, safety glasses, shin guards, helmets, shields, armor plate, torpedo nets, antballistic missiles, lead aprons, buzz-saw guards, and boxing gloves. Note that some 'barriers', such as crash padding and ionizing radiation shields, attenuate or lessen but do not totally block the energy from reaching the structure to be protected. This strategy, although also a variety of rate-of-release modification, is also separately identified because the tactics involved comprise a large, and usually clearly discrete, category.

The *seventh* strategy, into which the sixth blends, is also very important—to modify appropriately the contact surface, subsurface, or basic structure, as in eliminating, rounding, and softening corners, edges, and points with which people can, and therefore sooner or later do, come in contact. This strategy is widely overlooked in architecture, with many minor and serious injuries the result. It is, however, increasingly reflected in automobile design, and in such everyday measures as making lollipop sticks of cardboard and making some toys less harmful for children in impact. Despite the still only spotty application of such principles, the two basic requisites, large radius of curvature and softness, have been known since at least about 400 BC, when the author of the treatise on head injury attributed to Hippocrates wrote: 'Of those who are wounded in the parts about the bone, or in the bone itself, by a fall, he who falls from a very high place upon a very hard and blunt object is in most danger of sustaining a fracture and contusion of the bone, and of having it depressed from its natural position; whereas he that falls upon more level ground, and upon a softer object, is likely to suffer less injury in the bone, or it may not be injured at all . . . '.

The *eighth* strategy in reducing losses in people and property is to strengthen the structure, living or nonliving, that might otherwise be damaged by the entry transfer. Common tactics, often expensively underapplied, include tougher codes for earthquake, fire, and hurricane resistance, and for ship and motor vehicle impact resistance. The training of athletes and soldiers has a similar purpose, among others, as does the treatment of hemophiliacs to reduce the results of subsequent mechanical insults. A successful therapeutic approach to reduce the osteoporosis of many postmenopausal women would also illustrate this strategy, as would a drug to increase resistance to ionizing radiation in civilian or military experience. (Vaccines, such as those for polio, yellow fever, and smallpox, arc analogous strategies in the closely parallel set to reduce losses from infectious agents.)

The *ninth* strategy in loss reduction applies to the damage not prevented by measures under the eight preceding—to move rapidly in detection and evaluation of damage that has occurred or is occurring, and to counter its continuation and extension. The generation of a signal that response is required; the signal's transfer, receipt, and evaluation; the decision and follow-through, are all elements here—whether the issue be an urban fire or wounds on the battlefield or highway. Sprinkler and other suppressor responses, firedoors, MAYDAY and SOS calls, fire alarms, emergency medical care, emergency transport, and related tactics all illustrate this countermeasure strategy. (Such tactics have close parallels in many earlier stages of the sequence discussed here, as, for example, storm and tsunami warnings.)

The *tenth* strategy encompasses all the measures between the emergency period following the damaging energy exchange end the final stabilization of the process after appropriate intermediate and long-term reparative and rehabilitative measures. These may involve return to the pre-event status or stabilization in structurally or functionally altered states.

SEPARATION OF LOSS REDUCTION AND CAUSATION

There are, of course, many real-world variations on the main theme. These include those unique to each particular form of energy and those determined by the geometry and other characteristics of the energy's path and the point or area and characteristics of the structure on which it impinges—whether a BB hits the forehead or the center of the cornea.

One point, however, is of overriding importance: subject to qualifications as noted subsequently, there is no logical reason why the rank order (or priority) of loss-reduction countermeasures generally considered must parallel the sequence, or rank order, of causes contributing to the result of damaged people or property. One can eliminate losses in broken teacups by packaging them properly (the sixth strategy), even though they be placed in motion in the hands of the postal service, vibrated, dropped, piled on, or otherwise abused. Similarly, a vehicle crash, per se, need necessitate no injury, nor a hurricane housing damage.

Failure to understand this point in the context of measures to reduce highway losses underlies the common statement: 'If it's the driver, why talk about the vehicle?' This confuses the rank or sequence of causes, on the one hand, with that of a loss-reduction countermeasure—in this case 'crash packaging'—on the other.

There are, nonetheless, practical limits in physics, biology, and strategy potentials. One final limit is operative at the boundary between the objectives of the eighth and ninth strategies. Once appreciable injury to man or to other living structure occurs, complete elimination of undesirable end results is often impossible, though appreciable reduction is commonly achievable. (This is often also true for inanimate structures, for example, teacups.) When lethal damage has occurred, the subsequent strategies, except as far as the strictly secondary salvage of parts is concerned, have no application.

There is another fundamental constraint. Generally speaking, the larger the amounts of energy involved in relation to the resistance to damage of the structures at risk, the earlier in the countermeasure sequence must a strategy lie. In the ultimate case, that of a potential energy release of proportions that could not be countered to any satisfactory extent by any known means, the prevention of marshalling or of release, or both, becomes the only approach available. Furthermore, in such an ultimate case, if there is a finite probability of release, prevention of marshalling (and dismantling of stockpiles of energy already marshalled) becomes the only, and essential, strategy to assure that the undesirable end result cannot occur.

FOR EACH STRATEGY AN ANALOGOUS OPPOSITE

Although the concern here is the reduction of damage produced by energy transfer, it is noteworthy that to each strategy there is an opposite focused on increasing damage. The latter are most commonly seen in collective and individual violence—as in war, homicide, and arson. Various of them are also seen in manufacturing, mining, machining, hunting, and some medical and other activities in which structural damage, often of a very specific nature, is sought. (A medical illustration would be the destruction of the anterior pituitary with a beam of ionizing radiation as a measure to eliminate pathologic hyperactivity.) For example, a maker of motor vehicles or of aircraft landing-gear struts—a product predictably subject to energy insults—could make his product more delicate, both to increase labor and sales of parts and materials, and to shorten its average useful life by decreasing the age at which commonplace amounts of damage increasingly exceed in cost the depreciating value of the product in use. The manufacturer might also design for difficulty of repair by using complex exterior sheet metal surfaces, making components difficult to get at, and other means. . . .

A SYSTEMIC ANALYSIS OF OPTIONS

It has not generally been customary for individuals and organizations that influence, or are influenced by, damage due to harmful transfers of energy to analyze systematically their options for loss reduction, the mix of strategies and tactics they might employ, and their cost. Yet it is entirely feasible and not especially difficult to do so, although specific supporting data are still often lacking. In fact, unless such systematic analysis is done routinely and well, it is generally impossible to maximize the pay-offs both of loss-reduction planning and of resource allocations.

Such analysis is also needed to consider properly the problems inherent in the use of given strategies in specific situations. Different strategies to accomplish the same end commonly have different requirements; in kinds and numbers of people, in the disciplines involved, in material resources, in capital investments, and in public and professional education, among others. In the case of some damage-reduction problems, particular strategies may require political and legislative action more than others. And, where the potential or actual hazard exists across national boundaries, correspondingly international action is commonly essential.

The types of concepts outlined in this note are basic to dealing with important aspects of the quality of life, and all of the professions concerned with the environment and with the public health need to understand and apply the principles involved—and not in the haphazard, spotty, and poorly conceptualized fashion now virtually universal. It is the purpose of this brief note to introduce the pathway along which this can be achieved.

Public Health Policy for Preventing Violence

JAMES A. MERCY, MARK L. ROSENBERG,
KENNETH E. POWELL, CLAIRE V. BROOME,
AND WILLIAM L. ROPER

A new vision for how Americans can work together to prevent the epidemic of violence now raging in our society has emerged from the public health community. This vision arises from the recognition that, by any measure, violence is a major contributor to premature death, disability, and injury. Fundamental to this vision is a shift in the way our society addresses violence, from a focus limited to reacting to violence to a focus on changing the social, behavioral, and environmental factors that cause violence. From a public health perspective, effective policies for preventing violence must be firmly grounded in science and attentive to unique community perceptions and conditions. Scientific research provides information essential to developing such policies and prevention strategies and methods for testing their effectiveness. Equally critical is the full participation of communities to engender a sense of ownership of this problem and its solutions. Public health seeks to empower people and their communities to see violence not as an inevitable consequence of modern life but as a problem that can be understood and changed. . . .

IMPACT OF INTERPERSONAL VIOLENCE ON THE PUBLIC'S HEALTH

Interpersonal violence can be defined as threatened or actual use of physical force against a person or a group that either results or is likely to result in injury or death. Public health approaches violence as a health issue and consequently uses injuries—both fatal and nonfatal, psychological and physical—to quantify the impact of violence.

On an average day in the United States, sixty-five people die from and more than 6,000 people are physically injured by interpersonal violence. The violent acts appear to be occurring with greater frequency and severity in our society.

From *Health Affairs*, 12 (1993), 7–26. Copyright © 1993 The People-to-People Health Foundation, Inc. All rights reserved. Reprinted by permission.

In fact, the 1980s were arguably the most violent decade of this century, if not in U.S. history. More than 215,000 people died and twenty million more suffered nonfatal physical injuries from violence. Violence also exacts a huge economic toll. The average annual financial costs of medical and mental health treatment, emergency response, productivity losses, and administration of health insurance and disability payments for the victims of assaultive injuries occurring from 1987 to 1990 were estimated at $34 billion, with lost quality of life costing another $145 billion. These grim statistics obscure the disproportionate impact of violence on specific subgroups within our society—most notably, young men, women and children, and the poor.

Youth and Violence

Young people are disproportionately represented among the perpetrators of violence. Arrest rates for homicide, rape, robbery, and aggravated assault in the United States peak among older adolescents and young adults. During the 1980s more than 48,000 people were murdered by youths ages twelve to twenty-four. Interviews with assault victims indicate that offenders in this age range committed almost half of the estimated 6.4 million nonfatal crimes of violence in 1991.

Adolescents and young adults also face an extraordinarily high risk of death and injury from violence. Homicide is the second leading cause of death for Americans ages fifteen to thirty-four and is the leading cause of death for young African Americans. Homicide rates among young American men are vastly higher than in other Western industrialized nations (Exhibit 1). In addition, persons ages twelve to twenty-four face the highest risk of nonfatal assault of any age group in our society. The average age of both violent offenders and victims has been growing younger and younger in recent years.

Violence Against Women and Children

Women are frequent targets of physical and sexual assault by partners and acquaintances. Many of these assaults are fatal. In 1990, 5,328 women died as the result of homicide. Six of every ten of these women were murdered by someone they knew, about half of them by a spouse or an intimate acquaintance. In addition, homicide is the leading cause of death for women in the workplace, accounting for 41 percent of all occupational injury deaths among women during the 1980s. More than 99 percent of assaults on women, however, result not in death but rather in physical injury and severe emotional distress. In 1985 an estimated 1.8 million women were physically assaulted by male partners or cohabitants. In addition, it has been estimated that 1,871 women are forcibly raped each day in the United States. The consequences for women include an

EXHIBIT 1 International Variation In Homicide Rates For Males Ages Fifteen To Twenty-Four, 1988–1991.

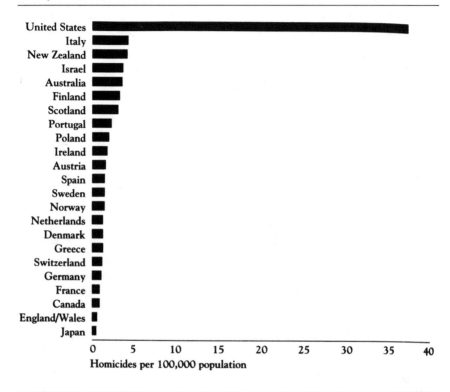

Homicides per 100,000 population

Sources: National Center for Health Statistics, *Vital Statistics,* 1990; and World Health Organization Statistics Annuals, 1990 and 1991.

increased risk of attempted suicide, abusing alcohol and other drugs, depression, and abusing their own children.

Children also are all too frequently the targets of abuse in our society. In 1988 an estimated 1,016 to 2,026 children died from abuse and neglect in the United States. In 1986 a minimum of 1.6 million children experienced some form of nonfatal abuse or neglect. The long-term consequences for abused children include an increased likelihood of depression, poor self-esteem, alcohol and substance abuse, self-destructive behavior, and aggression. These patterns often persist through adolescence and into adulthood. Some, but not all, adults who were abused as children are more likely than other adults to abuse their children and intimate partners and to be arrested for violent crime.

The Impact of Violence on the Poor

The evidence is consistent and compelling that poor people bear a disproportionate share of the public health burden of violence in our society. Homicide victimization rates consistently have been found to be highest in those parts of cities where poverty is most prevalent. In 1991 the risk of becoming a victim of a nonfatal violent assault in the United States was three times greater for persons from families with incomes below $7,500 than for those with family incomes above $50,000.

The Contribution of Firearms

Firearms play a central role in interpersonal violence. In 1990 alone, firearms were used to commit more than 16,000 homicides; an additional 239,400 persons were nonfatally injured duing assaults with firearms. Further, firearms were involved in more than 18,000 suicides, approximately 1,500 unintentional deaths, and an undetermined number of suicide attempts and nonfatal accidents. The lifetime cost of all firearm-related injuries occurring in 1990 was estimated to be $20.4 billion. Firearm-related death rates for women, teenage boys, and young adults are higher now than they ever have been. For young people ages ten to thirty-four, firearms are the second leading cause of death, and one out of five deaths to U.S. teens is due to firearms. In fact, in 1990 more U.S. teenagers died from firearm-related injuries than from all natural diseases combined.

PUBLIC HEALTH CONTRIBUTIONS TO VIOLENCE PREVENTION

Despite the magnitude of this problem, daily reminders in the media, and the imprisonment of an unprecedented proportion of our population, this American tragedy continues largely unabated. We need new solutions. Public health's contributions include placing prevention at the forefront of our efforts, making science integral to identifying and developing effective policies and programs, and integrating the efforts of diverse scientific disciplines, organizations, and communities. Each of these contributions speaks to an existing deficit in our society's response to this problem.

Focus on Prevention

The public health approach brings a strong emphasis and commitment to identifying policies and programs aimed at preventing violent behavior, injuries, and deaths. America's predominant response to violence has been a reactive one—to pour resources into deterring and incapacitating violent offenders by apprehending, arresting, adjudicating, and incarcerating them through the criminal justice system.

This approach, however, has not made an appreciable difference. Although the average prison time served for a violent crime in the United States tripled between 1975 and 1989, there was no concomitant decrease in the level of violent crimes. Removing violent offenders from society by tripling the average sentence for a violent crime, on the other hand, may have prevented 10 to 15 percent of the violent offenses that would have been committed had these prisoners been on the streets. One can only conclude that other forces must be driving the violent crime rate upward. We can either continue to apply increasingly severe penalties and hope to hold our own, or search for additional preventive methods. Even within the criminal justice community there is a movement toward looking for new approaches through community- or problem-oriented policing.

Underlying the public health approach is the strong conviction that violence can be prevented. The wide variation in the homicide rate among developed nations supports this stance. The rate of homicide among males ages fifteen to twenty-four living in developed nations with accurate vital statistics data was more than eight times higher in the United States than in the next-highest country, Italy (37.2 versus 4.3 homicides per 100,000 population in 1988–1991). Even the rate for young white males in the United States—a group more comparable with young Italian males—was more than three times the rate in Italy. The relatively high rates of violence in the United States, therefore, are not an inevitable consequence of economic development. The potential for much lower rates of violence than we are now experiencing also is evident in our own history. Within the United States the homicide rate has varied more than twofold since 1950, ranging from a high of 10.7 per 100,000 in 1980 to a low of 4.5 in 1956.

Perhaps most importantly, although most violence prevention efforts have not been adequately evaluated, at least a few show promise of being successful. Regular visits to the homes of unmarried, poor, teenage mothers by health practitioners have been shown to reduce the incidence of child abuse in a controlled random trial. Providing training in communication, negotiation, and problem solving to middle school youth with behavioral problems has reduced the number of suspensions attributed to violence. The Perry Preschool Project, an educational program directed at the intellectual and social development of preschool children, has been credited with reducing the cost of delinquency and crime, including violence, by approximately $2,400 per child. Laws that prohibit carrying guns in public and that impose a mandatory sentence for crimes perpetrated with a firearm have been found to have small but positive effects on reducing firearm homicides. After passage of the 1977 Washington, D.C., restrictive licensing law that prohibited handgun ownership by everyone but police officers, security guards, and previous gun owners, firearm suicides and homicides declined by 25 percent. Homicide rates remain high and have increased in Washington, D.C., however, indicating that other actions besides restricting handgun ownership are necessary. Thus, despite the fact that we have a great deal more to learn about how to prevent violence, epidemiologic patterns and preliminary evaluation research clearly indicate that it can be prevented.

There exists a broad array of potentially effective intervention strategies through which violence might be prevented. Exhibit 2 presents a listing of examples of these interventions grouped by whether their primary goal is to change knowledge, skills, or attitudes; the social environment; or the physical environment. The efficacy of most of these interventions has not been demonstrated. Nevertheless, they are among the many options to be considered as part of a broad-based, sustained strategy to prevent violence. Among these options, strong emphasis must be placed on addressing the role of social and economic

EXHIBIT 2 Strategies For Preventing Violence And Its Consequences.

STRATEGY TYPE	DESCRIPTION	INTERVENTION EXAMPLES
Change individual knowledge, skills, or attitudes	Deliver information to individuals to Develop prosocial attitudes and beliefs Increase knowledge Impart social, marketable, or professional skills Deter criminal actions	Conflict resolution education Social skills training Job skills training Public information and education campaigns Training of health care professionals in identification and referral of family violence victims Parenting education Mandatory sentences for crimes with guns
Change social environment	Alter the way people interact by improving their social or economic circumstances	Adult mentoring of youth Job creation programs Respite day care Battered women's shelters Economic incentives for family stability Antidiscrimination laws enforced Deconcentrated lower-income housing
Change physical environment	Modify the design, use, or availability of Dangerous commodities Structures or space we move through	Restrictive licensing of handguns Prohibition or control of alcohol sales at events Increased visibility of high-risk areas Disruption of illegal gun markets Metal detectors in schools

deprivation in causing violence. Recent research points to numerous dimensions of poverty that are related to high community rates of violence: high concentrations of poverty, transiency of the population, family disruption, crowded housing, weak local social structure (for example, low organizational participation in comunity life, weak intergenerational ties in families and communities, and low density of friends and acquaintances), and the presence of dangerous commodities or opportunities associated with violence (for example, gun availability and drug distribution networks). If we are to be successful in preventing violence, these fundamental social and economic factors must be addressed.

Public Health Science in Action

Although many scientific disciplines have advanced our understanding of violence, the scientific basis for developing effective prevention policies and programs remains rudimentary. Public health brings something that has been missing from this field: a multidisciplinary scientific approach that is explicitly directed toward identifying effective approaches to prevention.

This approach starts with defining the problem and progresses to identifying associated risk factors and causes, developing and evaluating interventions, and implementing interventions in programs (Exhibit 3). Although the exhibit suggests a linear progression from the first step to the last, in reality many of these steps are likely to occur simultaneously. Information systems used to define the problem also may be useful in evaluating programs. Similarly, information gained in program evaluation and implementation may lead to new and promising interventions.

The first step, defining the problem, includes delineating related mortality and morbidity and goes beyond simply counting cases. This step include obtaining information on the demographic characteristics of the person involved, the temporal and geographic characteristics of the incident, the victim/perpetrator relationship, and the severity and cost of the injury. These additional variables may be important in defining discrete subsets of injuries for which different interventions may be appropriate. For example, prevention of violence between intimate acquaintances is likely to require a different approach than prevention of violence among strangers.

The second step in the public health approach involves identifying risk factors for and causes of injuries. Whereas the first step looks at "who, when, where, what, and how," the second step looks at "why." This step also may be used to define populations at high risk for injury and to suggest specific interventions. Risk factors can be identified by a variety of epidemiologic studies, including rate calculations, cohort studies, and case-control studies.

The next step is to develop interventions based in large part upon information obtained from the previous steps and to test these interventions. Methods for

EXHIBIT 3 Public Health Model Of A Scientific Approach To Prevention.

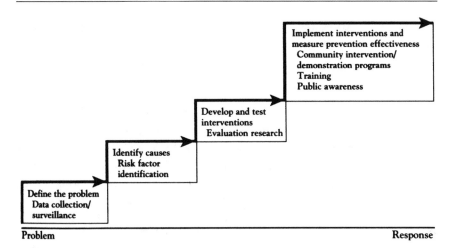

Implement interventions and
measure prevention effectiveness
    Community intervention/
    demonstration programs
    Training
    Public awareness

Develop and test
interventions
    Evaluation research

Identify causes
    Risk factor
    identification

Define the problem
Data collection/
surveillance

Problem   Response

testing include prospective randomized controlled trials, controlled comparisons
of populations for occurrence of health outcomes, time series analyses of trends
in multiple areas, and observational studies such as case-control studies.

The final stage is to implement interventions that have been proved or are
highly likely to be effective. In both instances it is important that data be collected to evaluate the program's effectiveness, particularly since an intervention
that has been found effective in a clinical trial or an academic study may perform differently at the community or state level. Another important component
is determining the cost-effectiveness of such programs. Balancing the costs of a
program against the cases prevented by the intervention can be helpful to policymakers in determining optimal public health practices.

The public health model for a scientific approach to prevention has been
applied to a wide range of noninfectious as well as infectious public health
problems, with a remarkable record of success. Smallpox has been eradicated,
smoking rates have been drastically reduced, and the number of people who die
in car crashes has been reduced by tens of thousands. We believe that this time-
tested, goal-oriented approach will yield similar benefits in the area of violence
prevention. . . .

PRIORITIES FOR PUBLIC HEALTH ANALYSIS AND ACTION

Public health priorities for violence prevention include preventing injuries from
firearms, interrupting the "cycle of violence," developing and evaluating com-

munity approaches to violence prevention, and changing public attitudes and beliefs toward violence. It is believed that attention to these areas offers the greatest chance of saving lives, preventing injuries, and reducing the overall impact of violence on our society.

Preventing Firearm Injuries

Public health has come to see the need for preventing firearm injuries as central to preventing violence, for several reasons. First, firearms are involved in a high proportion of deaths associated with interpersonal violence. In 1990, 65 percent of the more than 24,000 homicides that occurred involved firearms. Further, firearms are involved in approximately 20,000 deaths associated with suicide and unintentional injury each year. Second, studies indicate that firearms have played a key role in the increasing rates of violent death, particularly among youth. For example, recent increases in youth homicide and suicide are almost entirely attributable to increases in homicides and suicides involving firearms. Third, scientific evidence clearly indicates that the presence of a gun in a violent interaction dramatically increases the likelihood that one or more of the participants will be killed; the implication here is that guns are more lethal than other weapons. Fourth, scientific evidence is mounting that access to firearms poses significant risks to owners and their families. For example, in a well-designed study that controlled for other known risk factors, the presence of a gun in a household was found to increase the risk of suicide almost fivefold and the risk of homicide almost threefold. Finally, as previously noted, evaluation research suggests that certain regulatory approaches can prevent deaths involving firearms.

Public health's major contribution in this area has been to advance the scientific understanding of ways in which firearm injuries can be prevented. In fact, public health scientists have been credited with bringing about a "sea-change" in firearm injury research over the past ten years. This scientific approach has spanned the first three stages of the public health model outlined in Exhibit 3. To define the problem, public health scientists have used existing surveillance data to assess the magnitude, characteristics, and impact of the problem on a national, state, and local basis. They are exploring ways to improve the national surveillance of fatal and nonfatal firearm injuries and the monitoring of risky behavior associated with firearm injuries, such as weapon carrying among youth. State and local public health agencies also are developing city and state-wide systems for collecting data on firearm injuries. Public health scientists have helped to identify risk factors by quantifying the risks of gun ownership, looking not only at the risks from guns in the hands of criminals, but also at the risks to gun owners and their families. This research has shown, for example, that for every time a gun kept in the home is used to kill someone in self-defense, it is used forty-three times to kill someone in a criminal homicide, suicide, or unintentional shooting; and if a gun is used in an incident of domestic violence, then the likelihood of one of the two disputants' being murdered is twelve times greater than if another type of weapon were used.

Public health scientists also have been involved in carrying out the third stage of the public health model: testing the effectiveness of interventions. For example, a Detroit ordinance prohibiting the carrying of firearms in public was evaluated and found to have a dampening effect on increases in firearm homicides occurring outside the home. In another example, researchers examining the impact of more restrictive policies toward handgun ownership in Canada found that between 1980 and 1986 the rate of homicide in Seattle, Washington, was 65 percent higher than in Vancouver, British Columbia, and that virtually all of this difference was due to an almost fivefold higher rate of handgun homicide in Seattle. They concluded that a regulatory policy that restricts access to handguns may reduce the rate of homicide in a community.

Although our understanding of the role of firearms in violence has advanced substantially, many questions remain: How frequently are guns used to successfully ward off potentially violent attacks? Do the risks and benefits of firearm possession vary, depending on whether one lives in a rich or poor neighborhood or whether one has children? How do adolescents get guns, and why do they want them? In addition, few interventions to prevent firearm injuries have been evaluated. There is a critical need to assess the value of the numerous intervention strategies that can be, and in some cases are being, adopted. Exhibit 4 lists interventions that focus solely on firearms, grouped by four major prevention strategies.

Addressing firearm-related injuries from a public health perspective helps to reshape the public discussion on firearms in several ways. First, with a firm scientific understanding of the role of firearms in violence, public discussion shifts from a criminal justice debate on "gun control" to a public health discussion of "preventing firearm injuries." The gun-control debate has become so polarized that neither side really seeks to understand the other. As result, there is no middle ground and very little constructive dialogue. By reframing the debate, public health can help to engage many more people in this critically important issue. Second, if scientific information on the health risks of firearms is developed and disseminated, people are empowered to take responsibility and make decisions to reduce the risks for themselves, their families, and their communities.

A third element in reframing the issue of firearm injuries is shifting the focus from an "all-or-none" solution to a broad array of diverse strategies and policies. The remarkable success of public health in preventing motor vehicle injuries exemplifies this approach. Over the past thirty years the United States has invested more than $250 million to discover ways to create safer cars, safer

EXHIBIT 4 Strategies For Preventing Firearm Injuries.

STRATEGY	INTERVENTION
Change how guns are used/stored	Restriction of gun carrying in public
	Mandatory sentences for gun use in crimes
	Owner liability for damage by guns
	Metal detectors in vulnerable places
	Safety education
Affect who has guns	Permissive licensing (for example, all but felons, minors, mentally ill, and so on)
	Waiting periods
	Forbid sales to high-risk purchasers
	Disrupt illegal gun markets
	Combination/electronic locks on guns
Reduce lethality of guns	Protective clothing
	Reduce barrel length/bore size
	Reduce magazine size
	Ban dangerous ammunition
Reduce number of guns	Restrictive licensing (for example, only police, military, guards, and so on)
	Buy back guns
	Increase taxes on guns
	Restrict imports
	Prohibit ownership

Source: Adapted from A.J. Reiss Jr. and J.A. Roth, eds., *Understanding and Preventing Violence* (Washington: National Academy Press, 1993), 272–273.

roadways, and safer drivers. Because of this effort cars now have steering wheels that protect the driver, front ends that crush to absorb impact, safety belts, and air bags; also, many highway systems have eliminated unsafe intersections. All drivers must pass licensing examinations, and we have made great progress in removing drunken drivers from the roads. As a result, the highway driving death rate has decreased markedly, saving more than 243,000 lives. Firearm injuries can be reduced similarly without banning all guns. As with motor vehicle safety, progress can be made by using a variety of approaches that include changes in behavior and environmental modification. . . .

Changing Public Attitudes and Beliefs

Recent experience with public health information and education campaigns for reducing smoking and cardiovascular disease and preventing acquired immunodeficiency syndrome (AIDS) suggests that similar efforts can be important parts of the public health approach to preventing violence. Within the field of injury control, there has been a long-standing debate over the effectiveness of educational efforts to prevent injuries. Early in the history of injury control, many people felt that injuries could be prevented just by telling people to "be careful." Soon, however, critics showed that it was much more effective to change the environment than it was to try to change individual behavior. As a result, many injury-control advocates felt that behavioral change was an ineffective way to prevent injuries. It is clear now, however, that effective injury-control programs—and preventing injuries from violence is no exception—take advantage of both behavioral changes and changes in the environment. For example, to realize the benefits of child safety seats, parents must purchase them and use them correctly.

Public health has now become much more sophisticated in the use of marketing techniques to bring about change. We know that we need to formulate precise objectives, identify target audiences, carefully develop culturally competent messages, and then measure the impact of these marketing efforts on the outcomes of interest. Public health information campaigns for violence prevention must achieve a number of goals. First, they must make people aware of the magnitude and characteristics of the problem of violence today. Second, they must give hope to individuals and communities, informing them that there are things that work and things that people and communities can do to prevent violence. Third, they must mobilize individuals, organizations, and communities to act. Fourth, they must provide information about what works and how to conduct effective prevention programs. And fifth, they must be designed so that we can measure their effectiveness and use that information to constantly improve them.

Most recent attention to violence and the media has been limited to the negative impact of violence in the movies and on television. This has had at least two adverse results. First, opportunities to develop positive uses of the media through social marketing have not been adequately considered. Second, false expectations have been raised about the potential of reducing violence in life by reducing violence in the media.

Popular movies and television contain high levels of violence, and large organizations such as the American Psychological Association and the American Academy of Pediatrics have publicly stated their conviction that violence in the media causes acts of violence in real life. Research has shown that viewing violence on television or in the movies can make children more aggressive and irritable. Researchers have suggested that children today see so much violence on television that they are desensitized to it and may even be encouraged to commit violent acts because of their viewing. There seems little doubt that violence in the media conributes to violence in society. Violence in the media, however, is but one segment, of uncertain size, of the full scope of influences that produce violence in our society. Efforts to reduce media violence should be part of a larger effort to change the many factors contributing to frequent violent behavior in American society. . . .

Violence Prevention: Criminal Justice or Public Health?

MARK H. MOORE

It is difficult to resist being swept up in the enthusiasm for public health approaches to preventing violence. Current levels of violence certainly demand a response. The ones we have made in the past, rooted primarily in the philosophy and practices of criminal justice, seem old, tired and stale—even bankrupt. In contrast, public health approaches seem fresh, optimistic, and full of potential. Most importantly, public health approaches have been extremely successful in engaging new actors—community groups, private enterprise, medical establishments, and social service agencies—in the effort to reduce violence. So, I feel both churlish and counterproductive in raising questions about something that is generally so helpful.

Nonetheless, in the interest of ensuring that society makes the best possible response to violence over the long run, I want to do precisely that: to raise some questions about the public health approach to violence. . . .

PUBLIC HEALTH: SUBSTITUTE FOR OR COMPLEMENT TO CRIMINAL JUSTICE?

Exactly what public health claims in nominating itself to help to solve the nation's violence problem is a little unclear. Sometimes it seems to claim that it represents a comprehensive alternative to criminal justice responses to violence. Thus, James Mercy and colleagues write:

> A new vision for how Americans can work together to prevent the epidemic of violence now raging in our society has emerged from the public health community. . . . Fundamental to this vision is a shift in the way our society addresses violence, from a focus on reacting to violence after it occurs to a focus on changing the social, behavioral, and environmental factors that cause violence.

From *Health Affairs*, 12 (1993), 34–46. Copyright © 1993 The People-to-People Foundation, Inc. All rights reserved. Reprinted by persmission.

This is perhaps the grandest claim and does seem to suggest that the public health approach could replace, or at least subsume, the criminal justice approach to reducing violence. At other times the claims are more modest. They seem to suggest a world in which public health attempts to prevent violence stand alongside criminal justice attempts to respond to the violence that continues despite the best efforts of the public health community to prevent it. . . .

DIFFERENT KINDS OF VIOLENCE

One important limitation of the current public health approach is that it does not focus on all components of the violence problem. For example, Mercy and colleagues begin with a broad definition of "interpersonal violence" and present startling statistics about the total number of people touched by violence each year in the United States. They then move to a more detailed analysis of some particular forms of violence—that involving youth (both as offenders and as victims), and that inflicted on women and children.

The emphasis on these particular kinds of violence is typical of the public health approach. Moreover, it is an important corrective to the traditional focus of the criminal justice system. That system has long neglected the violence occurring in the intimate settings of family and involving either spouses or children. The reasons are that this kind of violence is not always reported to criminal justice agencies and that even if it is reported, the criminal justice response of arrest and prosecution may be neither possible nor desirable to deal with the situation at hand. Thus it has been left to doctors in emergency rooms to reveal the extent of this kind of violence, and to the public health community to develop a wider variety of preventive and crisis responses than are typically imagined by criminal justice agencies. It also has been left to the public health community to increase the priority given to this kind of violence by observing the connection between preventing child abuse and reducing adult criminal violence a generation into the future.

Similarly, although the police certainly will see youth violence, it has been left to the public health community both to establish its importance as the principal threat to the health of young men and to stress preventive rather than control responses. For these reasons, the public health emphasis on these particular forms of violence is helpful.

Yet a person with a criminal justice background cannot help but notice that the focus on youth, women, and children excludes the kind of violence that is in fact most common: the violence that occurs among adult men in robberies, in bars, and in organized criminal enterprises. The simple fact is that the majority of people killed or injured in interpersonal violence in the United States in any given year are adult males—not youth, not women, and not children. These forms of violence attract much of the attention of the criminal justice system; criminal justice responses often seem most appropriate for them.

Thus, in facing the whole problem of violence in society, there is an important complementarity in criminal justice and public health approaches. Each approach sees and emphasizes a somewhat different piece of the violence problem. Either alone would be incomplete.

PREVENTIVE VERSUS REACTIVE APPROACHES

A second claim made by the public health community is that it brings a preventive approach to violence that might replace the reactive approach of the criminal justice system. This is fine rhetoric, useful for mobilizing a crusade. But in important ways it is false.

For one thing, this rhetoric obscures the potential advantages of relying on a reactive rather than a preventive approach. The difficulty with preventive approaches is that precisely because they are preventive, they force one to act on problems and situations that are related only probabilistically to the problem one is really trying to solve. This often means that one has to act in many more places and situations than would be necessary if one were reacting to the essential problem. That poses no difficulty, of course, if the number of places where violence could occur is not all that great, and where the preventive intervention one makes in those places is neither expensive nor intrusive, and is effective in preventing violence in both the short and long runs.

Unfortunately, it is by no means obvious that these conditions always exist. Sometimes the number of people or places where one must intervene to prevent violence increases by several orders of magnitude. Sometimes the need to be in so many places where violence might occur stretches resources so thinly that preventive interventions become too superficial to produce much of a preventive impact at all. . . .

The criminal justice system also has long been interested in intervening early in the lives of those who seem headed for future violence and in doing so through providing assistance and care as well as close control. The juvenile justice system is an old invention of the criminal justice system designed precisely to provide a different, more preventive response to violent acts committed by children and to the conditions in which they live that put them at risk of serious criminal offending in the future. Similarly, for several generations police officers have tried to reduce violence among young males by acting as positive role models, organizing youth athletic leagues, and establishing gang liaison officers.

Somewhat more recently, police departments have adopted some important new tactics designed to prevent crimes through mechanisms other than arrest and prosecution. The idea of "community policing" seeks to use police officers to help communities mobilize their own capacities for self-defense in an attempt to reduce the opportunities and occasions for violence. Similarly, the idea of "problem-solving policing" seeks to identify "hot spots" where violence is particularly likely to occur and to invent responses that make them more peaceable. Typically, the responses do not involve making arrests but instead involve altering the conditions that seem to favor disorder and violence.

Finally, many preventive mechanisms the public health movement imagines relying on to reduce violence may depend on, or be strengthened by, parallel criminal justice efforts. For example, the public health community would like to reduce a particularly important risk factor for violence: children possessing and carrying guns in cities. Achievement of this goal will in all likelihood depend not only on teaching parents to lock up any guns they might have and to keep checking on whether their kids are carrying weapons to school, and not only on regulating licensed gun dealers more closely to ensure that they do not sell guns to children, but also on police efforts to arrest fences who will sell stolen guns to children and gang members whose gun carrying on the streets is forcing other kids to carry guns in self-defense. Similarly, the effort to prevent youthful traffic fatalities associated with drunken driving depended not only on selling the concept of the "designated driver" to youth and on regulating liquor stores more closely, but also on setting up sobriety checkpoints at times and places where drunken driving seemed particularly likely and dangerous. . . . Again, then, the public health approach is seen as an important complement to rather than a substitute for criminal justice approaches to violence. It is not true that one is preventive and the other reactive. They both may be required to produce the desired preventive and control effects.

THE PRACTICAL POTENTIAL OF PUBLIC HEALTH APPROACHES

The ultimate question about the role of public health approaches in dealing with violence is how much of the burden of effective control of violence we can expect them to shoulder. To build confidence in the public health approach, Mercy and colleagues offer several bits of evidence.

First, they point to the fact that the United States has a much higher rate of violence than do other advanced, industrialized nations and that its current level of violence is higher than it has been in the past. These facts are used as "benchmarks" indicating the potential of achieving much lower levels of violence than we now accept. The benchmarks certainly make it plausible that violence can be reduced. But simply observing these facts falls well short of either demonstrating that such levels are now plausible or showing how to produce them. One must make the assumption that the public health approach has the tools to transform the current U.S. culture to that of other countries or to what it once was in this country. That is a fairly large claim.

To make that claim possible, public health advocates produce a second kind of evidence: They point to the success that public health approaches have had in dealing with such problems as smallpox, smoking, and auto accidents. These examples, too, are reassuring and hopeful. But they also fall short of demonstrating that public health methods alone could deal effectively with violence. Indeed, the example of automobile accidents (which is in many ways the closest analogue) might be used to show the potential of public health and criminal justice approaches working together. It may be that the reduction in traffic fatalities owes as much to the criminalization of drunken driving as to safer cars, safer roadways, or increased education about the dangers of drunken driving. . . .

Again, my point is not to deny the essential value of the public health approach. Obviously, there is an enormous difference between programs that reduce violence by saving the lives of both victims and offenders (which the public health approaches tend to do) and programs that reduce violence by saving only the lives of victims (which is how the criminal justice interventions tend to work). My point is simply to tone down the claims of what can be accomplished by public health on its own and to remind people of the continuing need for a criminal justice response. We cannot dismantle the police, prosecutors, and prisons quite yet.

THE INTERNAL COHERENCE OF THE PUBLIC HEALTH APPROACH

What is genuinely exciting about the public health approach (even to a jaded old criminal justice guy like me) is the fact that it does seem to provide a framework for analyzing and acting on the problem that simulates new ideas and, perhaps even more importantly, draws new people into thinking about and acting on the problem of violence. It is significant, I think, that this approach appeals to women and to people of color and gives them a way to participate in the conversation that makes them feel more hopeful, more empowered, and less vulnerable to the suspect machinations of the criminal justice system. It is also wonderful that it attracts people who are trained in the methods of science— who like data, information, and research. And its pragmatic spirit—the resourceful, determined search for anything that will work—is a breath of fresh air into the sterile ideological debates that are strangling the current discussion within criminal justice circles. As a movement, then, the public health initiative is extraordinarily welcome. Still, for all the strengths of the ideas, some important issues will need to be worked out. . . .

THE IDEOLOGICAL BASIS OF BOTH APPROACHES

In the background of the discussion about public health and criminal justice approaches to violence are some important questions about values and ideology that must be acknowledged and discussed openly if practitioners in both fields are to be able to exploit the potential of their diverse approaches. The essential question concerns the role of individual blame and accountability in responding to incidents of "intentional violence."

Obviously, the ideas of individual guilt, blame, and accountability are central to the criminal justice approach to "intentional violence." The moral (as opposed to practical) justification for punishment depends on assuming that individuals are accountable for their own actions and that their degree of culpability depends on whether or not they intended to inflict injury on their fellow citizens. That is generally what is at issue in a criminal trial—not the question of what would be effective in controlling future offending by the particular offender being tried or by the general population. Moreover, that is often an important issue in the mind of the victim of violence and his or her relatives. In short, the criminal justice approach recognizes that society is interested in producing morally appropriate as well as practically effective responses to intentional violence.

In contrast, the public health approaches want to deemphasize and make unnecessary these difficult judgments of moral accountability. They would prefer to get at the problem by attacking the antecedent causes or the risk factors that shape the context of offending rather than the motivations and values of individual offenders. They would prefer to find the causes of violence in society than in the evil intentions of individual offenders. They would prefer to see the problem as one of science and technique rather than of morality and passion. That, at least, is often the way it seems to criminal justice practitioners.

To the extent that these different moral intuitions exist, or seem to exist, they tend to widen the differences between the two communities. Criminal justice practitioners see the public health community as apologists for misbehavior. Public health practitioners see the criminal justice practitioners as wrathful avengers, more interested in venting their emotions than in achieving practical effects.

To get over this hurdle, it is important for each side to acknowledge the truth of what the other side has to say. It is true that intentionally injuring a fellow citizen is morally offensive and should be responded to with moral indignation as well as with a practical plan for reducing violence in the future. It also is true that some offenders are bad and dangerous. And although society or cruel fate may have played an important role in making them that way, there is precious little that can be done about it now. This much must be granted to criminal justice practitioners by public health practitioners.

On the other hand, it also is true that many instances of violence that turn up in the criminal justice system, including some of the most serious, are produced by relatively ordinary citizens who find themselves in extremely provocative circumstance, not by dangerous, determined offenders. This in no way excuses the conduct. But it does temper society's just response. It also is true that there may be some important ways that society could work on the conditions that give rise to violence and, through that work, save both the offender and the victim. To the extent that such interventions are possible, they should be pursued enthusiastically, for they are always to be preferred to the sad business of prosecuting offenders after the fact. That much must be granted to public health practitioners by criminal justice practitioners.

Indeed, this latter point is particularly urgent, for it is the public health approach that now needs encouragement. And it is the public health approach that constitutes the new and promising frontier. For all my quibbles, I am delighted that it has arrived when it has. We need it desperately.

6

AIDS AND OTHER NEWLY
EMERGENT DISEASES

With the appearance of the HIV and AIDS epidemic, many were caught by surprise. The age of epidemics was thought to be ending. Smallpox had been eradicated throughout the world. Tuberculosis was on the decline in many places. Polio had been defeated in the industrial societies. While tuberculosis, plague, polio and other threats like malaria and cholera still raged throughout the world, many experts expected that these scourges would be eliminated or sharply reduced in the near future. AIDS should have served as a warning against this optimism, but for most experts, it did not. This was because AIDS in the West and especially in the United States was an epidemic first among the gay and intravenous drug-taking communities. Because HIV infection and AIDS were seen as a disease transmitted through the sexual practices of gay men, or by injecting drugs with contaminated needles, the fight against it was seen as being as much a battle against discrimination and moralism as a battle against a frightening new epidemic.

The use of the law to proscribe behavior on moral grounds, even if the behavior does not harm individuals, is known as *legal moralism.* Legal moralism has cultural and religious origins but its deepest roots are in purity rituals: avoidance rituals designed to make the environment and the community safe from the threat of uncleanness and contamination. Modern public health, which uses laws and regulations to save lives and prevent disease, has long been entangled with legal moralism, which uses the same measures to protect society against behavior that is viewed in some quarters as "offensive, degrading, vicious, sinful, corrupt, or otherwise immoral."[1] These morals offenses "included mainly sex offenses, such as adultery, fornication, sodomy, incest and prostitution, but also a miscellany of nonsexual offenses,"[2] such as the desecration of a corpse. From the first the debate over AIDS and HIV policy has been entangled with the controvesies surrounding the belief that society is entitled to proscribe behavior regarded as sinful or wicked.

Moralism is opposed to a public health perspective because it believes epidemics to be the result of moral dissolution. It makes the victims of epidemics, rather than the disease itself, the threat to society. Camus said it well, in the words of Dr. Rieux in *The Plague*: "All I maintain is that on this earth there are pestilences and there are victims, and it is up to us as much as possible, not to join forces with the pestilences."[3]

In the campaign to forge a coherent, nonmoralistic policy against the AIDS epidemic in the United States, a number of states—New York, New Jersey, and Massachusetts among them—constructed elaborate protections for people with HIV and AIDS which prevented traditional public health notification procedures and partner notification from coming into play. In general, AIDS was treated as an "exception" to the regime normally used by state and local public health agencies to monitor the outbreak and spread of communicable diseases such as tuberculosis or other sexually transmitted diseases. These laws were passed over the objections of many medical groups and other segments of the public who pointed out that such policies left many spouses and others unprotected.

In the first selection for this chapter, Chandler Burr notes the contradictions inherent in AIDS exceptionalism. For example, it has been argued that partner notification would be ineffective, in the case of HIV and AIDS, because those who were infected had so many partners. Yet partner notification has been used for many other sexually transmitted diseases where the infected individuals had hundreds of sexual contacts. Another reason for treating HIV as an exception to the communicable disease regime was the absence of effective treatment. With the arrival of new drug treatment therapies that seem to slow the progression of the disease, this rationale no longer holds. For these and other reasons, Burr urges an end to AIDS exceptionalism, a suggestion which appears to be taking hold. For example, in New York, mandatory reporting legislation has recently been passed.

In the second selection, Bayer and Dupuis review traditional public health policies such as testing, case reporting, and partner notification in the context of the resurgence of tuberculosis. Unless TB patients faithfully take their medications, even after they are no longer symptomatic, it will be impossible to suppress the disease, prevent its spread, and prevent the appearance of drug-resistant strains of tuberculosis. Treating those with active tuberculosis is especially difficult because many are without symptoms. Further, because they are so often poor, homeless, or addicted to intravenous drugs, it is difficult to maintain contact with them and assure that they are following their treatment regime. This has led some to advocate the use of coercive measures, including confinement, as necessary to combat this new public health menace. As new drugs and treatment regimens are developed, the same arguments may be used with regard to people with HIV and AIDS. However, given the many infected people who desperately want treatment but are unable to pay for it or to get into clinical trials, it seems unlikely that coercive measures are the solution to the AIDS epidemic.

We may come to a different conclusion about the dangers of coercion with the emergence of a whole new cast of epidemic diseases. We have noted the optimism of the 1960s and 1970s about the prospect of eliminating epidemics altogether, at least in the coming decades. AIDS was the great exception. But then, suddenly, new diseases (or at least diseases little known in the West) came tumbling out of the back closets of the world: the Hanta virus, Lassa fever, the Ebola virus, mad cow disease, a new variant of bubonic plague in India, the return of cholera to South America, and the reemergence of dengue fever, malaria, and yellow fever. Of course, many of these diseases had remained major killers in the world outside of the western developed one, but they hadn't received much attention in the western news media. When virologists began to speak of newly emergent viruses, "new" often meant something old that turns up in a new place.

Joshua Lederberg, in the third selection for this chapter, offers a powerful if short analysis of the precarious position humans occupy within the ecosystem. He says that "[W]e have too many illusions that we can, by writ, govern the remaining vital kingdoms, the microbes, that remain our competitors of last resort for dominion of the planet." He argues that "The opening of wild lands to human occupation also has exposed people to unaccustomed animal viruses, to zooneses," and that we should not let our preoccupation with the AIDS epidemic "obscure the multiplicity of infectious disease that threaten our future." He goes on to say that "we share a common vulnerability to these scourges. No matter how selfish our motives, we can no longer be indifferent to the suffering of others."

In our fourth selection, Paul R. Epstein provides a more detailed discussion of the environmental stresses and instability that are likely underlying the appearance of new diseases or old diseases in new places, and of our common vulnerability to new threats. Cholera likely arrived in the Americas because of discharges of bilge water from southeast Asian freighters. Once here, cholera found great algal blooms ready to amplify and broadcast the threat, along with ships that moved goods to the U.S. gulf coast. Some experts warn that the appearance of vast algal blooms throughout the world signal a fundamental ecological threat for the spread of disease and ecosystem instability. Weather shifts such as El Niño events likely have led to periods of intense rains in desert regions and consequent upsurges in vectors (deer mice) for Hanta virus and plague, and the subsequent infection and deaths from these diseases among U.S. residents. Epstein argues for increased monitoring of precarious environmental regions and close cooperation among climatological, wildlife, and public health experts, groups that seldom have coordinated in the past.

It remains to be seen how these new diseases and epidemics will alter the balance of power in the struggle to protect the community and to preserve the rights of individuals. Many will argue that these new threats will never be conquered unless and until the basic human rights of decent housing, clean water, the ability to limit family size, and basic medical care are secured for all humans everywhere, and until growth and the despoiling of the ecology is checked. Others will argue that, in addition to these basic protections, communities will of necessity have to protect themselves against infected individuals and groups through the classic public health methods of reporting of cases, notification, and the provision of treatment where available.

NOTES

1. Edwin M. Schur and Hugo Bedau, *Victimless Crimes* (Englewood Cliffs, NJ: Prentice-Hall, 1974, p. 90).
2. Joel Feinberg, *Social Philosophy* (Englewood Cliffs, NJ: Prentice-Hall, 1973).
3. *The Plague*, trans. Stuart Gilbert (New York: Modern Library, 1948, p. 229).

The AIDS Exception: Privacy vs. Public Health

CHANDLER BURR

Epidemiology, which encompasses both the systematic study of infectious disease and the implementation of the means to contain it, is something of a medical oddity. As dependent on statisticians and politicians as it is on medical-care providers, and often used at times of desperation, by practitioners who have been accorded police and in certain cases military powers, epidemiology has sometimes had to strike a balance between the harshness that may be required to control infectious diseases and the civil liberties of people whose rights may be subject to abridgement.

Since the turn of the century, with the introduction in this country of bacteriological testing and the establishment of boards of health, standard public-health measures have been deployed against infectious diseases. These measures, leaving aside the extreme step of holding people in quarantine, have typically included at least some of the following: *routine testing* for infection, often undertaken without explicit patient consent; *reporting* to local health authorities of the names of those who test positive for infection; *contact tracing*, or the identification of any people who may have been exposed to infection; and *notification* of these possibly infected people that they may have been exposed. Some combination of these four practices has been commonly applied against outbreaks of infectious diseases, including typhoid, diphtheria, and tuberculosis, and against upsurges in sexually transmitted diseases. It would be surprising if, out of all the viruses and bacteria that can do us significant harm, one was exempted from the scope of these measures. It would be even more surprising if the one chosen pathogen was responsible for an epidemic that today constitutes the leading cause of death among all Americans aged twenty-five to forty-four.

This very thing has, of course, happened, largely in order to accommodate civil-rights concerns. The practie of traditional public health has been to a great degree suspended for acquired immune deficiency syndrome and for human immunodeficiency virus, the virus that causes it. Although various

From *The Atlantic Monthly,* June (1997), 57–67. Reprinted by permission of the author.

traditional public-health steps are being taken against AIDS and HIV, in differing combinations from state to state, the result is a chaotic patchwork—one that is inadequate, a growing number of critics say, to the task of containing and eradicating AIDS.

"We have convinced ourselves," Ralph Frerichs, a prominent epidemiologist at the University of California at Los Angeles, wrote in a recent issue of the journal *Epidemiology*, "that the fight for survival can be waged in a way that is socially acceptable but not always biologically credible." Many public-health officials, he contended, "have remained steadfast in their commitment to programs and approaches that have hidden the identity of HIV carriers but have failed to halt viral transmission"—a commitment that is in the end bound to prove self-defeating, "making winners of the virus but losers of people."

THE PRICE OF COOPERATION

What is known in the field of public health as AIDS exceptionalism has been maintained in legally and programmatically direct ways and also in complex and subtle ways. Its origins are not difficult to ascertain.

When AIDS first surfaced, in the early 1980s, it was indisputably a disease of urban male homosexuals (and, to a far lesser extent, of intravenous-drug users). Public-health authorities, faced with a fatal, communicable disease whose method of transmission they did not understand, desperately needed the cooperation of the infected—as they would in any epidemic. In the case of AIDS, however, the infected eventually became disinclined to cooperate. "In the first months and years of the epidemic," the journalist Elinor Burkett, the author of *The Gravest Show on Earth* (1995), recalled not long ago, "people with AIDS died in the hallways of hospitals, where nurses wouldn't touch them. They were kicked out of their apartments. Insurance companies canceled their policies. Their bosses fired them. They had no idea how to get Social Security disability payments or Medicaid."

The discovery of HIV, and the development of a test that could detect it, brought matters to a head. In the aftermath of anti-gay persecution and even violence, the price exacted by a terrified gay community for cooperation in even a rudimentary public-health effort was ironclad anonymity. In 1985, shortly before the federal government was to announce the licensing of the first test for detecting HIV, the National Gay Task Force and the gay civil-rights group Lambda Legal Defense and Education Fund filed a petition in federal court to delay this action, pending a legal guarantee that the test would not lead to widespread screening aimed at gay men. They then put pressure on the Food and Drug Administration, which along with the federal Centers for Disease Control (now the Centers for Disease Control and Prevention, and henceforward referred to as the CDC) had been made aware of eager queries from school districts hoping to use the HIV test to identify and fire gay teachers. The FDA quickly acceded to the demand that the HIV test be used not to screen and identify *people* for HIV infection in systematic campaigns but only to screen the blood in blood banks.

Out of the threat that the HIV test posed to privacy grew a rigid resistance to almost all HIV testing without consent—and a public-health approach to combating AIDS characterized by considerable delicacy. The FDA's agreement to restrict how the HIV test could be used resolved, temporarily, a political problem. Left unanswered, as Randy Shilts, in his book *And the Band Played On* (1987), observed, was "the broader public health question of how you can control a disease if you decline to find out who is infected." Shilts went on, "In this poisoned atmosphere, the nuances of long-term consequences for control of the infection fell low on the list of gay concerns."

The result, ultimately, was the effective suspension of traditional public-health procedures for AIDS, which is to say, there would be no routine testing for HIV; the reporting of the names of the HIV-infected would be required only in some places, and would miss the epidemic's hotspots; and contact tracing and notification would as a result be greatly handicapped, and in many places pursued in desultory fashion if at all, often in the face of opposition. All efforts were to be voluntary—dependent on educational outreach and persuasion rather than on systematic procedures. "U.S. officials had no alternative but to negotiate the course of AIDS policy with representatives of a well-organized gay community and their allies in the medical and political establishments." Ronald Bayer, a professor at the Columbia University School of Public Health, wrote in a critical retrospective some years ago, "In this process, many of the traditional practices of public health that might have been brought to bear were dismissed as inappropriate."

A number of opportunities present themselves for the routine testing of people for various diseases by public institutions, routine testing being defined as testing that can be performed without a person's explicit consent. Pregnant mothers are routinely tested for tuberculosis, hepatitis B, and syphilis; testing for chlamydia and group-B streptococcus is also common under certain circumstances. Newborn babies are routinely tested, without the mothers' permission, for phenylketonuria and hypothyroidism. Patients admitted to hospitals may undergo a variety of blood tests, depending on their symptoms, the tests being performed as a matter of course, without necessarily informing the patient or asking explicit permission. Although a patient can at any time refuse to undergo a routine test, he or she does not have to be specially notified that the test is being done or given a specific opportunity to refuse.

HIV testing, in contrast, is almost always voluntary—which means it is done either at an anonymous-testing site or with a person's explicit permission (and which usually means also that the person being tested must sign a release). At the federal level HIV testing is required only of immigrants entering the country, foreign-service and military personnel, and federal-prison inmates. At the state level routine testing is prohibited everywhere except under narrowly defined circumstances. Marcia Angell, the executive editor of *The New England Journal of Medicine*, and a proponent of routine testing in some form, says, "Having to ask specifically has a huge effect, and it is a clear difference between AIDS and many other diseases."

Making even certain subpopulations the target of routine testing would turn up large numbers of infected people who currently escape detection. In a 1992 *New England Journal of Medicine* article Robert Janssen and his colleagues at the Division of HIV/AIDS at the National Center for Infectious Diseases recommended voluntary targeted testing for HIV in certain hospitals, a policy well short of routine testing and yet one that has been implemented virtually nowhere. They wrote,

> We estimate that about 225,000 HIV-positive persons were hospitalized in 1990, of whom only one third were admitted for symptomatic HIV infection or AIDS. Routine, voluntary HIV testing of patients 15 to 54 years old in hospitals with 1 or more patients with newly diagnosed AIDS per 1,000 discharges per year could potentially have identified as many as 110,000 patients with HIV infection that was previously unrecognized.

Testing that is merely voluntary may also miss populations that disproportionately need to be reached. The people least likely to have the virus are the most likely to say yes to a test, and the people most likely to have it are the most likely to say no. In one study infection rates were 5.3 times as high among people who refused HIV testing as among people who consented to it.

One might ask, How could a study give the infection rate of those who refused the HIV test? The answer demonstrates the methods that researchers—in this case, at the New Mexico Health and Environment Department—must employ in order to obtain data without violating personal rights as protected by law. Voluntary, anonymous HIV tests were offered over a three-month period to all patients visiting a sexually-transmitted-disease clinic. Eighty-two percent of the patients consented to being tested for HIV. To determine the rate of HIV infection among those who did not consent to testing, researchers located serum that had been taken from these patients for syphilis testing, removed all identifying information, and then tested the serum for HIV.

Exceptionalists argue that routine testing will "drive AIDS underground"—make people avoid the health-care system altogether. There is no empirical proof that this will or won't occur to a greater extent than it already does, under a voluntary regime. Ultimately one must ask whether people who would go underground because of perceived self-interest should dictate policy—and also whether such people would cooperate in disease-prevention efforts under any circumstances.

Why does testing matter? The most basic epidemiology holds that early knowledge of where a virus is moving—into which populations—is essential to slowing its spread. Even if a disease cannot be cured, knowing who the infected people are may help prevent the transmission of the disease to other people. Geneviève Clavreul, a California-based consultant to the International Cancer and AIDS Research Foundation, says that because of testing and reporting restrictions the California Department of Public Health is in essence "flying blind" in its epidemiological tracking. By law or regulation, cases of certain sexually transmitted diseases and of many other infectious diseases must be reported to state departments of health, and the names of the infected are in most cases provided and are always held in confidence. HIV is the exception. Although the disease called AIDS must be reported by name in all fifty states, infection with HIV, the virus that causes AIDS, need not be; only twenty-six states mandate the (confidential) reporting by name of positive test results for HIV, and these states tend to be ones with modest caseloads. Twelve states— including California and New York, by far the two worst-afflicted states—have no broad reporting requirements for HIV.

Requiring the reporting of AIDS but not HIV seems equivalent to requiring, say, that full-blown cases of hepatitis B be reported but not any newly detected infections with the hepatitis virus. Actually, it is worse. The incubation period for hepatitis B is usually two or three months, whereas the period between infection with HIV and a diagnosis of AIDS is often longer than ten years. This means that during all this time HIV-positive people can be both infectious and outside the public-health system. The disease is further privatized by the HIV home-testing kits now on the market, which to yet one more degree put testing and reporting into the hands of individuals.

As noted, state public-health practices mandate that certain sexually transmitted diseases be reported; in part to avoid reporting HIV some states have decided not to classify HIV as a sexually transmitted disease—even though the primary mode of HIV infection is, of course, sexual. As of 1995 only twelve states had classified AIDS and HIV infection as sexually transmitted diseases. Only sixteen states had even classified them as communicable diseases. Treating AIDS and HIV infection as exceptions, twenty-three states, including New York and California, had classified them as a separate category of disease. A report prepared for the CDC by Georgetown University and Johns Hopkins University's Program on Law and Public Health observes of this situation: "Disease-specific legislation may thwart public health goals by generating separate policies, programs, and procedures for diseases that may share common behavioral risk factors and require a unified approach for treatment and prevention."

Beyond issues of testing and reporting lies the issue of partner notification. "Partner notification" is the term used by the CDC to describe a spectrum of outreach efforts. One such effort is contact tracing, also called "provider referral," in which doctors or public-health officials locate partners of infected people (if the infected people are willing or able to provide names) and notify them of possible infection; the name of the known infected person is always kept confidential. At a further remove on the spectrum is "patient referral," in which infected people locate and notify partners on their own. Only thirty-three states have laws that explicitly allow doctors or public-health officials to notify the sex or needle-sharing partners of those with AIDS or infected with HIV. Only four states (Arkansas, North Carolina, South Carolina, and Oregon) have statues requiring notification.

All states technically have something that they can point to as a "partner-notification program," having such a program being a prerequisite for obtaining certain federal funds. But the effectiveness of partner-notification programs varies widely, for reasons relating as much to how the programs are implemented as to what specific steps they call for: the real difference is between states, such as Colorado and North Carolina, that actively strive to find and notify partners primarily through provider referral, and states, such as New York and California, that tend to rely on patient referral, deferring the responsibility of notification of the infected.

As one would expect, there seems to be a marked contrast between the effectiveness of well-established partner-notification programs in which provider-referral services are made available, and that of programs in which infected people themselves do the notifying if they are so inclined. One study found that active partner-notification programs offering provider-referral services get 30 to 90 percent (depending on the city or state) of people who have tested positive to cooperate in contacting those they may have infected. Ninety percent or more of those contacted agree to be tested. However, programs in which notification is left up to the infected achieve a cooperation rate of less than 10 percent. It should be noted also that by virtue of the fact that trained public-health personnel in most instances make the notifications in provider-referral cases, testing information and counseling are made readily available to possibly infected contacts. Programs that notify primarily through provider referral find a larger proportion of other infected people, and find them earlier. The sooner a person knows of his or her infection and begins treatment, and the higher that person's T-cell count when treatment begins, the better the prognosis. In a recent study conducted at a Los Angeles AIDS clinic the average T-cell count in HIV-positive women who entered the clinic through active provider-referral partner notification was found to be 411; the average for all other women entering the clinic was 157. ("T-cell count" refers to the number of T-helper cells, a kind of white-blood cell that is essential to the proper functioning of the cellular immune system; HIV attacks and kills these cells. The T-cell count is closer to 1,000 in a healthy person, though the healthy range is subject to considerable variability. A T-cell count under 200 is one of the criteria for a diagnosis of AIDS.)

Does an absence of routine testing, reporting, and notification mean that a lot of undiscovered AIDS and HIV cases are festering in the larger society? Yes. According to the CDC, the number of Americans infected with HIV is as high as 900,000; of these, the CDC estimates, perhaps half are unaware of their infection. At least a quarter of all people in whom AIDS was diagnosed from 1990 to 1995 in Los Angeles County first became aware of their infection when they came to hospitals or clinics with advanced symptoms, having never previously been tested for HIV. In all likelihood such people had been HIV-positive for years. Most cancer, diabetes, or high-blood-pressure patients have been tested for these medical problems, know their status, and have begun treatment well before admission to a hospital with advanced symptoms. The situation with AIDS means, as one Los Angeles AIDS clinic director observed during a recent interview, that "something is really wrong." Because the lifetime cost of treating HIV is so high (estimated in 1993 to be $119,000 per patient), the CDC has concluded that AIDS and HIV notification programs pay for themselves if only one in eighty notifications prevents a new HIV infection by indicating to the notified person that a change in behavior is warranted.

AIDS has been so thoroughly exempted from traditional public-health approaches that civil libertarians have defeated in court attempts by health authorities to notify the spouses of people who have died of AIDS that their husbands or wives were HIV-infected. During the first years of the disease, legislation urged by civil libertarians prohibited physicians and public-health officials from notifying even the spouses of living people who had tested positive for HIV, some of whom continued to have unprotected sex with their partners. In some states laws have been enacted making partner notification by a physician at best discretionary under tightly defined circumstances.

National legislation on spousal notification, passed last year, mandates that states make a "good-faith effort" to notify at-risk spouses. However, in effect the law applies only to states that already require the names of infected people to be reported. And in any event, the matter of partner notification when the partners are (or were) married addresses, of course, only a small part of the AIDS problem.

WRONGHEADED RATIONALES

How has AIDS exceptionalism been justified? In the mid-1980s four arguments were regularly heard for exempting AIDS from standard public-health practices. 1) There had never before been a disease that seemed to constitute a de facto marker for homosexuality, with all the social stigma that this label carries. 2) The confidentiality of testing would inevitably be violated, precisely because AIDS is more stigmatized than any other disease. 3) Given the large number of sex partners of many of those who have become HIV-infected, contact tracing would be ineffectual. 4) Because there is no cure for AIDS, and no treatment to render the infected uninfectious, it was pointless to report HIV infection as is done for other infections.

However legitimate the civil-liberties issues it sought to address may have been more than a decade ago, the exceptionalist orthodoxy is now fundamentally wrongheaded as a matter of good public health and medicine.

The argument that AIDS is a unique marker for homosexuality is incorrect, and always was so. Rectal gonorrhea in men has been almost exclusively a disease of the gay population, and is a more reliable marker for homosexuality, if anyone were looking for such a marker, than AIDS ever was. And yet cases of rectal gonorrhea have appeared for decades, by name and date, in confidential case reports sent to state public-health departments.

The argument that confidentiality will inevitably be violated has met a serious counter-argument in the form of reality: the experience of Minnesota and Colorado, which have since 1985 mandated the confidential reporting by name of both HIV and AIDS cases. As of the end of last year, for example, Colorado health authorities had received the names of 5,723 people with AIDS and of 5,137 additional people infected with HIV. There have been no breaches of confidentiality. As noted, twenty-six states now require confidential reporting of all HIV cases by name. A single intentional breach of confidentiality in the CDC's AIDS surveillance system is known to have occurred (in Florida).

As for discrimination, the federal Americans with Disabilities Act (ADA), passed in 1990, a decade after the beginning of the AIDS epidemic, prohibits discrimination based on HIV status. In addition, the federal Vocational Rehabilitation Act of 1973, state discrimination laws, and state constitutions have all been interpreted by courts as protecting people from exactly the sort of discrimination that AIDS exceptionalists claim is inevitable. And courts have in most cases ruled that being infected with HIV constitutes a disability according to the legal definition of the term, even when the infected person is asymptomatic. "We've done more or less everything that can be done on the legislative front to protect people from discrimination on the basis of HIV status," says Chai Feldblum, an associate professor at Georgetown University Law School and one of the principal architects of the ADA. "The laws are there."

The argument that contact tracing will prove to be ineffectual because many of those infected with HIV have had a large number of sex partners ignores the fact that many of those infected with syphilis and gonorrhea, other diseases for which gay men are at increased risk, have also had a large number of sex partners, and yet contact tracing has been standard procedure for these diseases for decades.

The argument that name reporting is pointless because there is no treatment has always been open to question on a number of grounds. Yes, the statement may have a certain logic from the perspective of a given infected individual concerned only about his or her fate. But if infected people can be identified, education and counseling may at the very least prompt changes in their behavior which will diminish the risk that they go on to infect others: contact tracing, in turn, extends the possibility of risk-diminishing behavioral change even more widely. Knowing who is infected is essential in helping to prevent new infections, even if the infected person himself cannot be helped.

In any event, evidence shows that new medical treatments are making HIV less infectious than ever. The latest treatments are astonishingly promising for at least some of the infected population.

Some 15 to 30 percent of HIV-infected pregnant women pass the virus on to their infants. Early treatment with zidovudine, or AZT, for the woman during pregnancy and for the infant after birth, can cut the proportion to eight percent. A new class of drugs called protease inhibitors is likely to cut the rate even further, if the drugs are used early. The key word is "early"—which means testing pregnant mothers, not just newborn babies. The American Medical Association now recommends that HIV testing be made mandatory for pregnant women. Gay and AIDS activists have denounced this recommendation.

Protease inhibitors, which in some cases have reduced the level of HIV in the bloodstreams of the infected to undetectable levels, have revolutionized care for many patients. "I think we already have the capability to make HIV infection a chronic, manageable disease like diabetes in patients who can afford the therapy and who can take it with one-hundred-percent compliance," says Joel Gallant, the director of the Moore HIV Clinic at the Johns Hopkins University School of Medicine. Protease inhibitors have provoked debate as to their long-term effectiveness, their ability to withstand viral resistance, and their price (the protease inhibitor Invirase costs approximately $7,000 for a year's supply), and also, as Gallant has noted, because of the fastidiousness required for effective administration. But the fact remains that the exceptionalist argument that no treatment is possible is losing whatever force it had.

The benefits of knowing who is infected are still more compelling today than they were in 1992, when the CDC AIDS laboratory chief Donald Francis, writing in the *Journal of the American Medical Association* in favor of more aggressive testing and the channeling of the infected into prevention and counseling programs, brought up "the ability to deliver important new products produced by scientific research." He wrote,

> Should the day come when a vaccine or therapeutic drug becomes available, a
> system for immediate delivery to those in greatest need would be required. There is
> no system by which to do that now. But if all infected persons were being followed

up in an early intervention program, delivery would be straightforward. In my opinion, early intervention should be given the highest national priority.

The fact that AIDS is not easily transmissible (it is a hundred times less infectious than hepatitis B, and incomparably less contagious than an airborne disease like tuberculosis) provides further impetus to discover who is and is not HIV-infected. The knowledge that a given person is infected, if it means that the person takes any preventive measures at all, is much more valuable in the case of AIDS than it is for other diseases.

REMEDY-RESISTANT POLITICS?

Despite such developments, attempts to alter the public-health approach to AIDS, though on occasion successful, have met with fierce opposition. A case in point occurred in the spring of 1995, when Gary Ackerman, a liberal Democratic congressman from New York, introduced a bill with 220 co-sponsors to "unblind" a national infant-testing program for HIV run by the CDC as a way of monitoring HIV-infection rates in women. Since 1988 the CDC had been "blind-testing" infants for HIV in forty-five states—using blood samples, collected at birth, from which all identifying tags had been removed. Testing for HIV in this way meant that the CDC knew how many infants carried their mother's HIV antibodies but not who they or their infected mothers were. Mothers, therefore, were being sent home without being informed that they and in some cases their children were infected with a fatal virus. The CDC had no choice in the matter, being legally prevented from testing without informed consent. Under the Ackerman bill mechanisms were to be instituted so that if an infant tested positive, those doing the testing would have a way of knowing who that infant was, and its mother could be informed.

The response to this proposed legislation was immediate. Virtually every gay and AIDS group, including Gay Men's Health Crisis, the AIDS Action Council, and the National Association of People With AIDS, along with the ACLU and prominent public-health experts at leading universities, opposed the bill, largely on the grounds that unblinding the tests would do nothing to help prevent HIV transmission from mothers to their infants and would violate the privacy inherent in such an anonymous surveillance study, potentially scaring pregnant women away from seeking proper prenatal care. The intensity of feeling with which such measures have been opposed should not be underestimated. Ackerman's bill was modeled on a bill introduced in the New York State Assembly by the Democratic legislator Nettie Mayersohn to unblind the anonymous infant-testing program in New York. Mayersohn, a pro-choice, feminist old-line liberal who in 1989 had been named Legislator of the Year by the New York State chapter of the National Organization for Women, was labeled a "fascist" by individuals associated with the AIDS lobby. (Last June, three years after Mayersohn introduced her original legislation, the New York legislature passed a bill allowing the state to institute mandatory HIV testing of newborns and to notify parents of the test results. Newborn testing began last February.)

In the matter of the Ackerman legislation, the head of the CDC informed Ackerman that if the bill were not withdrawn, the CDC would suspend the infant-testing program altogether. Ackerman gave no credence to this threat by a public-health agency, because the infant-testing program was demonstrably useful in tracking the prevalence and trajectory of heterosexual AIDS. But the CDC program was indeed suspended. Public-health authorities thus lost even this imperfect means of monitoring one aspect of the epidemic.

In response to the CDC's suspension of testing, Ackerman joined forces with Tom Coburn, a Republican congressman and a Christian conservative from Oklahoma, to draft new legislation that has become known as the "Baby AIDS Compromise." The legislation was enacted last May as part of a larger bill, the Ryan White CARE Reauthorization Act. The compromise requires state health-care workers to offer counseling and voluntary HIV testing to pregnant women who have not previously been tested for HIV. States that by March of 2000 do not meet certain goals with respect to the voluntary HIV testing of pregnant women or to HIV incidence among newborns will have to implement a manda-tory infant-testing program or lose some federal AIDS funding.

The ultimate question for AIDS exceptionalism is this: Do the disease-con-tainment and disease-prevention measures of traditional public health—the measures from whose full force AIDS has been significantly shielded—work? The answer given to this question by AIDS exceptionalists as well as tradi-tionalists seems to be yes. Joel Gallant, for example, opposes routine involun-tary testing for HIV and aggressive partner notification, but not on medical grounds; rather, he fears the potential for employment and insurance discrimi-nation, domestic abuse, and breaches of confidentiality. He maintains that he would otherwise favor traditional public-health procedures for the fight against AIDS, particularly routine testing.

Lee Reichman, the executive director of the National Tuberculosis Center and a physician on the staff of the New Jersey Medical School who cares for AIDS patients, cautions that given the course that the evolution and politics of the disease have taken, traditional public-health measures by themselves may no longer be feasible, in part because of the possibility that they will drive the infected underground. As noted, this is an exceptionalist article of faith. But Reichman goes on: "Traditional public health is absolutely effective at control-ling infectious disease. It should have been applied to AIDS from the start, and it wasn't. Long before there was AIDS, there were other sexually transmitted diseases, and you had partner notification and testing and reporting. This was routine public health at its finest, and this is the way STDs were controlled."

In the months ahead a national debate may well be joined over rescinding the exceptional public-health status of AIDS, owing in part to a bill introduced by Tom Coburn, the Oklahoma congressman. Coburn's bill, the HIV Prevention Act of 1997, would establish confidential HIV reporting nationwide. It would require states to inform anyone who has been exposed to HIV. It would require that all people accused of sexual offenses be tested for HIV. And it would allow health-care providers to test a patient for HIV before performing a risky invasive medical procedure. The Coburn bill contains a number of other provisions and also two nonbinding "sense of the Congress" resolutions, one urging states to criminalize the intentional transmission of HIV, the other affirming the principle that strict confidentiality must be observed in carrying out the bill's provisions. (A companion bill has been introduced in the Senate.) "The fact is that epidemiology works," Coburn says, "and public-health policies work to control disease, and they work by identifying vectors of infectious disease, and you notify people at risk. If you don't do that, you can't control the disease. And that's what we've not done with HIV."

The AIDS Action Council—a group "dedicated solely to shaping fair and effective AIDS policy," in the words of its literature—has denounced the Coburn bill as "an attempt to federalize policies that do nothing but stigmatize and punish people living with HIV/AIDS." The act, in the view of the council, "replaces education and personal responsibility with 'Big Brother' intrusion and control." In previous statements the council has characterized measures like the ones now proposed as "failed policies that do nothing to prevent any more Americans from becoming infected with HIV."

It is hard to see how traditionalist policies can be said to have "failed" with AIDS, since they have not been systematically tried. Be that as it may, some skepticism toward legislation like Coburn's is warranted. Conservatives representing themselves as public-health advocates are certainly vulnerable to a charge of hypocrisy. Coburn's bill does not address one of the exceptionalists' central criticisms: that although traditional procedures will identify more infected people, conservatives are not prepared to offer any plan for helping those infected people (many of whom have no health insurance and little education, and many of whom are homeless) after they have been identified. The Coburn bill offers no new funds for the state public-health departments that would be obliged to carry out its testing and reporting provisions. A traditionalist approach to AIDS will cost money, and those who advocate such an approach should be making the case that more money is needed.

Exceptionalists also point out, correctly and bitterly, that the hatred directed against homosexuals, and the discrimination they experience at the hands of anti-gay conservatives, among others, are responsible in the first place for the very exceptionalist policies that conservatives like Coburn now so strongly oppose. Coburn's own outlook gives one pause. It was Coburn who elicited condemnation and ridicule when he criticized the airing on network television last winter of *Schindler's List,* complaining about the depiction of violence and frontal nudity.

As noted, epidemiology has sometimes had to weigh the issue of civil rights against the issue of effective disease control. The time has come to consider anew how these factors should tip the scales. We do not, of course, have an absolute guarantee that traditional epidemiology applied to AIDS and HIV would markedly bolster the success of public-health, efforts. But such a guarantee is hardly required. Marcia Angell, of *The New England Journal of Medicine,* observes, "Nobody can document or prove that traditional methods of control would work better at containing AIDS, because nobody has done what would be necessary to get such proof—studying two populations, one in which traditional methods are applied and one in which they aren't. The reason no one has done this is that it is impossible. It is impossible because it's unethical and logically unworkable. So, as in many things in life, the default position is common sense. And I have no doubt, given the track record of these methods in controlling other diseases that if, for example, we screened all expectant mothers, we could prevent AIDS in many cases. And if we traced partners, we would prevent AIDS in many cases. And if we routinely tested in hospitals, we would prevent AIDS in many cases."

Ralph Frerichs, of UCLA, framed the matter like this in the course of an interview: "Historically, public health has always transcended the legal system, much like the military. When you have an outside threat, you can suspend the normal rules of society. Traditionally, we epidemiologists have been granted full responsibility, but society has eroded that and we now talk about respecting the rights of human individuals who have disease-causing viruses, bacteria, and so on, which makes it increasingly difficult to stop the spread of these diseases. This is society's choice. But this is de facto granting rights to the viruses and to the bacteria. And when epidemics are presented this way, as a matter of rights, the public has a harder time distinguishing the infection from the infected. The virus is our enemy, not the person with the virus, but at the same time that person harbors the virus, and we need to take a series of steps to prevent that virus from moving to another person.

"In AIDS, as in all epidemics, there is a tradeoff between emphasizing detection of the virus and the civil-rights violations that detection engenders. Given that we have not pushed for aggressive testing, reporting, and partner notification, it appears that our society is willing to accept a higher amount of HIV infection to avoid interfering with the rights of HIV-infected people."

Earlier this year the Centers for Disease Control and Prevention reported that largely because of gains in life expectancy among the infected, annual deaths from AIDS had registered a significant decline for the first time since the onset of the epidemic. That they have done so is hardly grounds for complacency. It is evidence, however, that medical interventions make a palpable difference—and is all the more reason to start subjecting AIDS, from a public-health perspective, to more systematic procedures.

In the end AIDS would be unlikely to prove resistant to good basic public-health policies. It may survive if it can circumvent good sense.

Tuberculosis, Public Health, and Civil Liberties

RONALD BAYER AND LAURENCE DUPUIS

INTRODUCTION

Tuberculosis, a scourge referred to in the seventeenth century as the "captain of all these men of death," has returned to plague contemporary America, just when medical and public health measures seemed poised to consign the disease to the pages of history. In 1989, the Center for Disease Control's Advisory Council for the Elimination of Tuberculosis established a goal of eliminating tuberculosis in the United States by 2010. But as early as 1985, the long trend of declining tuberculosis cases had already reversed itself, and by 1992, there were 52,000 more cases than would have been expected had the downward trend continued.

The dramatic return of this disease poses serious questions about the failures of public health policy during the 1970s and 1980s. The new epidemic has also forced a reappraisal of the legal and ethical implications of disease-control measures that might be marshaled to combat the spread of contagious disease. This selection first briefly reviews the medical and epidemiological background of the current tuberculosis epidemic and the influence of AIDS on traditional approaches to disease control. The remainder . . . focuses on the specific ethical and legal questions surrounding tuberculosis control, with a particular emphasis on the civil-liberties implications of four approaches to disease control: the provision of supportive services to encourage patients to complete therapy; the use of directly observed therapy to monitor adherence to therapy; the involuntary detention of noncompliant patients; and the forced administration of tuberculosis medications.

THE RETURN OF TUBERCULOSIS

Tuberculosis is a communicable disease caused by *Mycobacterium tuberculosis,* an organism that is most commonly transmitted by inhaling airborne droplets expelled by the cough of a person with infectious tuberculosis. In most cases, people infected with *M. tuberculosis* do not develop clinical disease, but remain noninfectious, asymptomatic carriers. Among infected persons with noncompromised immune systems, there is an estimated 5–10% *lifetime* risk of developing clinical disease. People with both *M. tuberculosis* and HIV infection, by contrast, have a 5–10% *annual* risk of developing clinical disease. Clinical disease most commonly affects the lungs, but may affect other sites as well. Treatment of active disease ordinarily involves taking several drugs, at least two to three times per week, for a period of 6–9 months. Such treatment is generally highly effective, and results in long-term cure in about 95% of cases. Treatment of HIV-infected tuberculosis patients, however, is complicated by the unusually rapid progression from initial infection to active disease, which results in a high incidence of treatment failure and mortality.

Tuberculosis was among the leading causes of death in western society throughout the nineteenth century and remains one of the most common infectious diseases worldwide. Approximately one third of the global population carries *M. tuberculosis*, 8 million new cases are reported annually, and each year nearly 3 million die from the disease. In the United States, however, the prevalence of the disease declined steadily, beginning in the early part of the century and continuing until the mid-1980s. The historical decline in TB morbidity and mortality has been attributed to a number of factors. Prior to the introduction of antibiotic therapy in 1946, the decline in tuberculosis probably was the result of improvements in nutrition and housing that accompanied rising wages and improved living standards in the first half of the century, as well as specific public health interventions—such as education, isolation, and quarantine—that contained the spread of the disease. From 1953, the year after the introduction of the antituberculosis drug, isoniazid, through 1984, the number of tuberculosis cases reported decreased from 84,304 to 22,255, an average decline of 5% per year.

Despite the overall decline in tuberculosis in the United States, the disease continued to be a significant problem among people of color and in low-income communities. For example, in 1984, when the tuberculosis case rate had dropped to 9.4 new cases per 100,000 population in the United States, the case rate in central Harlem—a predominantly African-American community with high rates of poverty—was 90.7 per 100,000.

Beginning in 1985, the downward trend in reported cases of tuberculosis in the United States was reversed. From 1985 through 1991, the number of reported TB cases increased 18%. The HIV epidemic is certainly a major factor in the resurgence of tuberculosis. In New York City, nearly 50% of tuberculosis patients in 1988–89 were also infected with HIV; this suggests that many reported cases are the result of reactivation of latent infection in immune-suppressed individuals. While reactivation of latent disease has contributed to the increase in reported tuberculosis cases, recent studies indicate that more than one third of active cases in New York City and San Francisco are the result of recent transmission. Dramatic cutbacks in public funding and in facilities for TB control and treatment, as well as increasing poverty, homelessness, over-crowded housing and drug abuse have all played critical roles in the emerging epidemic.

The resurgence of tuberculosis is primarily afflicting those disadvantaged communities where the disease had persisted despite the overall national de-cline. From 1985 through 1990, the number of tuberculosis cases increased dramatically among Hispanics, African-Americans, and Asian/Pacific Islanders, while reported cases among non-Hispanic whites continued to decline. By 1990, the TB case rate in central Harlem approached 200 per 100,000, approx-imately 4 times the New York City rate and 20 times the national rate. These are also the communities, that have borne much of the weight of the continuing HIV/AIDS epidemic.

Exacerbating the ominous increase in tuberculosis is the emergence and pro-liferation of strains of the disease that resist one or more of the medications typically used to treat TB patients. In a national survey of culture-positive TB cases reported in the first quarter of 1991, investigators found that 9.5% of cases were resistant to rifampin and/or isoniazid, two of the safest and most effective first-line antituberculosis drugs, and that 3.5% of cases were resistant to both drugs. A study in New York City found that 19% of culture-positive cases during April 1991 were resistant to both rifampin and isoniazid. Multi-drug-resistant tuberculosis (MDR-TB) is considerably more difficult and expen-sive to treat than nonresistant disease, and is associated with much greater mor-tality, particularly among patients infected with HIV. In a report on 171 carefully treated and monitored non-HIV patients with multidrug-resistant dis-ease, only 56% of the patients had successful drug-therapy outcomes (negative sputum cultures without relapse) and 37% died, about half from tuberculosis. In investigations of nine outbreaks of multidrug-resistant tuberculosis in hospitals and prisons, the CDC found mortality rates ranging from 72% to 89%. Between 20% and 80% of the cases in those outbreaks were HIV infected.

The rise of multidrug-resistant tuberculosis is ultimately attributable to in-adequate drug therapy, which results either from inappropriate treatment by the physician or poor adherence to recommended therapy by the patient. Al-though the current system for tracking rates of treatment completion is inade-quate, available data indicate that in some of the cities hardest hit by drug-resistant strains of tuberculosis, completion rates have been dismally low. For example, in New York City between 1986 and 1990, only 53.6% of patients completed six continuous months of therapy, whereas San Francisco, Dallas, and El Paso all had completion rates above 90% during the same period. At one location in New York, 89% of tuberculosis patients were lost to follow-up before they had completed therapy. Although drug-resistant strains initially develop as a result of inadequate therapy, it must be underscored that such strains can be transmitted directly to previously healthy individuals. One study in New York concluded that most patients with drug-resistant tuberculosis did not acquire drug-resistant disease through inadequate treatment of a susceptible strain, but were initially infected with a drug-resistant strain transmitted to them by another person.

DISEASE CONTROL AFTER AIDS

Responses to the resurgence of tuberculosis must be understood in the context of the AIDS epidemic, which has shaped popular as well as professional conceptions of the appropriate public health approaches to epidemic disease.

As the public policy responses to AIDS took shape in the United States and in other democratic nations, a consensus emerged against using coercive state interventions long associated with the practice of public health. Rather, a voluntaristic strategy took hold that focused on eliciting the cooperation of those at risk for HIV infection. Mass education, voluntary testing and counseling, the protection of the rights of privacy of those with HIV, and the prohibition against unwarranted acts of discrimination were essential elements of this approach. The roots of this strategy, broadly endorsed by public health officials at the federal, state, and local levels, were many. HIV transmission typically takes place in intimate or secretive settings between consenting adults during sexual intercourse or drug use, not through casual contact. Public health and clinical medicine have no magic bullet to cure the disease; only voluntary personal risk-reduction behavior is effective in preventing further transmission. AIDS primarily affects marginalized populations—gay and bisexual men, intravenous drug users, social and ethnic minorities—with a long history of suspicion about the intentions and practices of government. The shaping of AIDS policy was singularly affected by the capacity of one of these groups—urban, middle-class gay men—to articulate their concerns about the dangers of using the AIDS epidemic as a pretext for undermining their hard-won, but still fragile, rights of privacy and liberty.

But tuberculosis is not AIDS. It is an airborne disease that can be transmitted to contacts who may be largely unaware that they are being placed at risk, or who may be unable to take precautions to protect themselves. Unlike AIDS, tuberculosis is generally curable. Even drug-resistant tuberculosis may be treated effectively, particularly in cases where the disease is susceptible to at least one of the first-line medications. The availability of effective therapy makes it possible to interrupt the spread of infection to the general population through medical intervention with the individual patient. Finally, while legislation and practice surrounding AIDS reflected the transformation that had occurred in American constitutional law over the previous three decades, which had expanded the rights of the individual to challenge the exercise of state authority, TB surveillance and control were still governed "by antiquated laws that predate modern concepts of constitutional law and the need for a flexible range of public health powers."

It is an unfortunate irony that AIDS and tuberculosis—the former a new threat that has evoked a radical rethinking of public health practices stressing principles of voluntarism, the latter an ancient threat, the control of which epitomized the coercive tradition in public health—have been superimposed upon each other for epidemiological and biological reasons. The resurgence of tuberculosis in the midst of the AIDS epidemic challenges us to revisit the legal and ethical principles that guide public health practices and to navigate a course between a return to broad and relatively unfettered coercive state action and a reliance on solely voluntary measures that may not prove sufficient to protect vulnerable communities.

THE ETHICAL AND LEGAL FOUNDATIONS OF TUBERCULOSIS CONTROL

The threat of tuberculosis to the public health provides the ethical and legal basis for government intervention in decision-making regarding an individual's health care. In contemporary ethical theory, and in biomedical ethics, strong emphasis is placed on the rights of the individual and on principles of autonomy and self-determination. But as central as those values are, the legitimacy of limiting them has long been recognized. Although conflict does exist about the nature and justification of those limits, there is no controversy in liberal democratic cultures over the principle that when the exercise of one person's freedom may result in harm to another, the state may intervene. Known as the "harm principle," this universally recognized limitation on autonomy was given its most potent expression by the nineteenth-century philosopher John Stuart Mill:

> [T]he only purpose for which power can be rightfully exercised over any member of a civilized community, against his will, is to prevent harm to others. His own good, either physical or moral, is not a sufficient warrant.

This principle clearly provides an ethical foundation for establishing public health programs designed to require those with communicable diseases to behave in ways that are likely to reduce the risk of transmission. It is sufficiently robust to justify requiring those with infectious tuberculosis to avoid public places where exposure to others would occur, and to authorize state action to enforce such requirements.

The public health authority to limit individual freedom when disease threatens has long been recognized in constitutional jurisprudence. Nearly ninety years ago, in *Jacobson v. Massachusetts,* a case that centered on the question of compulsory vaccination, the Supreme Court held that the U.S. Constitution permitted states to enact "such reasonable regulations . . . as will protect the public health and the public safety" as long as such efforts did not "contravene the Constitution of the United States, nor infringe any right granted or secured by that instrument." *Jacobson* also reiterated the rule that courts should give deference to a state's exercise of the police powers designed to protect the public health. Such measures could be invalidated only if they had "no real or substantial relation" to their ostensible goals. This extraordinary deference to government action prevailed throughout much of the 20th century, persisting as late as the 1960s. The past three decades of constitutional development, however, particularly in the area of involuntary confinement of psychiatric patients, have seen increased scrutiny of the exercise of the police powers, raising questions about the constitutionality of statutes relating to communicable disease and tuberculosis control, many of which were enacted before the profound shift in the balance between individual liberties and state authority.

Although the law gave considerable latitude to public health officials, virtually all TB control measures were focused on the necessity of identifying, treating, and limiting the activity of those whose tuberculosis was infectious. In 1992, the Centers for Disease Control undertook a broad review of state laws governing tuberculosis control, and found that 43 states provided for the quarantine of TB patients within their own homes, 35 specifying that the quarantine should last until the person was no longer infectious. Forty-two states permitted the commitment of TB patients to treatment facilities, 24 permitting such confinement until the individual no longer posed a health threat to others.

The resurgence of tuberculosis and the emergence of drug-resistant strains among inadequately treated patients have compelled public health officials to recognize the necessity of efforts to assure that patients with tuberculosis be treated beyond the period of infectiousness until they are cured. In 1992, a panel meeting under the auspices of the United Hospital Fund of New York made the attainment of "treatment until cure" the centerpiece of its recommendations. The Advisory Council for the Elimination of Tuberculosis underscored the necessity of treatment until cure in its 1993 report on the status of TB control laws throughout the United States.

The ethical, legal, and constitutional principles that justify public health efforts to control tuberculosis seem broad enough to justify efforts to assure that all patients with tuberculosis are treated until cured. Legal commentators have endorsed the goal of treatment until cure, as have advocates acting on behalf of individuals with HIV infection and AIDS. There has been sharp controversy, however, over the nature of the public health interventions that might be employed to achieve the goal of treatment completion, and the extent to which the legal and ethical principles that guide medical and public health practice should constrain the exercise of those interventions.

ETHICAL AND LEGAL ISSUES IN ENHANCING
PATIENT ADHERENCE TO TREATMENT

Although there may be exceptions, patients diagnosed with acute infectious tuberculosis tend to be compliant with treatment because of the desire to be rid of the unpleasant symptoms of the disease—weakness, fever, cough, and night-sweats. Much more complex is the attainment of compliance during the post-acute phase of tuberculosis, when symptoms no longer motivate the patient to take his or her medication. Poor patient compliance with treatment is not unique to tuberculosis, although failure to complete therapy for many other diseases does not have the same dire individual and public health consequences.

Any effective approach to improving adherence to therapy must be sensitive to the obstacles to treatment that face the economically disadvantaged and socially marginalized people among whom tuberculosis is most common. The prevalence of homelessness, drug abuse, alcoholism, and psychiatric comorbidity are factors that must be considered in shaping policies to enhance treatment completion. Brudney, who has been particularly concerned with tuberculosis among the homeless, has written:

> Homelessness, by definition, means lack of permanent shelter. Whether a person lives on the streets, wanders from one SRO to another, or moves in and out of a congregate facility, medical care is rarely his or her first priority. The daily search for food and shelter belie the possibility of an organized schedule, appointment keeping or routine medical ingestion as is necessary with TB treatment. Alcoholism, drug dependence and psychiatric disturbances affect anywhere from 50 to 90 percent of the homeless, and the notion that persons so affected can remember and comply with clinic appointments and medication regimens is laughable.

In ethics there is a dictum that states "ought implies can." A person cannot be held morally accountable for failing to adhere to ethical or legal standards if he or she cannot do so, or if he or she faces insuperable obstacles to adherence. This ethical principle compels us to recognize that the elimination of impediments that impinge on the capacity of an individual to cooperate in his or her own care for tuberculosis is essential. This is especially so given the prospect of the imposition of compulsory measures and the potential loss of liberty for those who are not compliant. What are the practical implications of "ought implies can"?

The goal of treatment completion and the ethical norms that should shape the measures used to attain that goal require that homeless individuals not be discharged from hospitals to the streets or to chaotic and often dangerous mass shelters after treatment for their acute infectious tuberculosis. They cannot reasonably be expected to comply with their care unless they are provided with a secure residence and, in many instances, with other social supports. That is also true of prisoners with tuberculosis whose sentences come to an end before their treatment has been completed. Individuals with drug or alcohol addiction must be provided with referrals and access to treatment programs. So too must individuals with psychiatric illnesses that could impair their capacity to comply with long-term, often complex, treatment regimens. Unfortunately, hospital discharge plans rarely, if ever, assure access to such supportive services that facilitate treatment. The provision of such services will be costly, but will ultimately be less costly than the consequences of treatment failure—the spread of tuberculosis and the potential development of drug-resistance. Furthermore, effective outpatient services are less costly than the confinement of patients in secure facilities.

The ethical requirement that the government provide supportive services to enhance the prospect of compliance may find legal expression in the constitutional principle that requires the state to use the least restrictive means possible to achieve its goals when individual liberties are at stake. More than three decades ago the U.S. Supreme Court held in *Shelton v. Tucker:*

> Even though the governmental purpose be legitimate and substantial, that purpose cannot be pursued by means that broadly stifle fundamental personal liberties when the end can be more narrowly achieved. The breadth of legislative abridgment must be viewed in the light of less drastic means for achieving the same basic purpose.

In *Lessard v. Schmidt,* a Federal District Court decision handed down in 1972, the implications of this standard were further defined. The state "must bear the burden of proving (1) what alternatives are available; (2) what alternatives were investigated; and (3) why the investigated alternatives were not deemed suitable."

Public health authorities now generally recognize that it is preferable, from both an ethical and a practical perspective, to make affirmative efforts to encourage voluntary compliance with health precautions before resorting to coercive action. In the context of tuberculosis, federal, state, and local health authorities acknowledge the importance of providing social supports and other "enablers"—such as car fare, meals, and even small cash payments—for undergoing care. However, it remains unclear whether what is accepted in principle will be put into practice by health officials. Also unclear is whether a court would *legally* require the state to expend public resources to enhance the prospect of compliance with TB therapy before taking more coercive action.

For some advocates for patients with tuberculosis, the case for requiring the provision of services before depriving a patient of liberty is clear. The New York City Tuberculosis Working Group, for example, has argued:

> In deciding whether the prescription against forced detention had been overcome by clear and convincing evidence, the court would consider any evidence of mitigating circumstances including failures by the City to provide services or benefits to which the patient was entitled. . . . It is unethical, illegal, and bad public policy to detain "non-compliant" person's before making concerted efforts to address the numerous systematic deficiencies that make adherence to treatment virtually impossible for many New Yorkers.

From the perspective of the Working Group, the government that fails to provide adequate social supports for the most vulnerable loses the legal as well as the moral authority to threaten with a deprivation of liberty those whose behavior poses a health risk.

However, poor public policy—even unethical public policy—is not necessarily unconstitutional. A court would have to consider whether a failure on the part of the government to provide a particular service—for example, a stable apartment, as opposed to a bed in a dangerous shelter—renders an effort to impose restrictions on individual liberty constitutionally suspect. At a time when government resources are limited, a court would also have to consider whether the claims of those with tuberculosis, who are threatened with a deprivation of liberty, are always to be given precedence over those who are equally needy but who do not have tuberculosis. Must the state always give priority to those with tuberculosis who find themselves on long waiting lists for drug treatment? Or for minimally decent living conditions? Must they be given priority over those who may have waited for extended periods and who may be quite desperate, perhaps even more desperate? The legal question posed here is whether the doctrine of the least restrictive alternative, which initially served as a negative limit on government action (i.e. the state cannot hospitalize if outpatient care would have been as effective), can also be interpreted to impose positive obligations on government, such as an obligation to provide social supports that may facilitate compliance? . . .

DIRECTLY OBSERVED THERAPY

Among the strategies designed to enhance patient compliance is directly observed therapy (DOT), a practice that involves having the patient take his or her medications in the presence of a health care provider or other responsible third party. First proposed for individuals with poor records of treatment adherence and for those whose demographic or psychological profile suggested a high risk of treatment failure, directly observed therapy has emerged as a standard of care. Recently, the Centers for Disease Control and Prevention, a number of prominent physicians, and others have recommended that all tuberculosis patients be placed on a regime of directly observed therapy, at least in localities where rates of completion fall below an acceptable level. Indeed, the Advisory Council for the Elimination of Tuberculosis calls for DOT in areas where treatment completion falls below 90%.

The primary rationale for the administration of medications under direct supervision is the recognition that nonadherence is common among patients who must take medication over an extended time period. In the case of tuberculosis, such noncompliance has the grave consequence of leading to drug resistance and reactivation of clinical disease. The CDC recommends that DOT "be considered for all patients because of the difficulty in predicting which patients will adhere to a prescribed treatment regimen." In addition, the recommendation for universal, rather than selective, DOT is motivated by a desire to avoid discrimination based on race, social class, and other factors that providers may perceive to have an effect on compliance.

The practice of directly observed therapy has been efficacious from a public health perspective. It has contributed to increasing rates of treatment completion. In addition, a recent study in Texas found substantial declines in the rates of drug resistance and relapse after the institution of a county-wide program of universal directly observed therapy. The rate of primary drug resistance (i.e. the patient contracted a drug-resistant strain from another person) decreased from 13.0 percent to 6.7 percent, while the rate of acquired resistance (i.e. a patient's initially drug-sensitive strain became resistant, probably due to a treatment failure) declined from 14.0% to 2.1 %. The relapse rate declined from 20.9% to 5.5%.

From an ethical, legal, and constitutional perspective, the important question is not who should be *offered* the support of DOT, but rather, when may DOT be *imposed* by the state.

Faced with the dramatic rise of multidrug-resistant tuberculosis and data that suggested very high rates of treatment failure, Iseman, Cohn & Sbarbaro put forth a public health argument for universal directly observed therapy.

> We believe it is time for entirely intermittent directly observed treatment programs to be used for all patients. Some will argue that it will be impossible to treat every patient with directly observed therapy and that many people with tuberculosis do comply with treatment and would be offended by having to submit to direct observation while they swallow-medications. Unfortunately, the literature is replete with studies demonstrating . . . that professionals are not able to distinguish the compliant from the noncompliant in advance.

Given the price of failure, in morbidity, mortality, and the cost of treating resistant strains of TB, they conclude, "we cannot afford not to try it." The case for universal directly observed therapy, at least at the outset of treatment, has also been made by the United Hospital Fund Working Group on Tuberculosis and HIV. It too was concerned by the failure of other approaches to achieve high rates of treatment completion and by the inability of professionals to predict treatment adherence. Though fully aware of the burdens that DOT would entail for some individuals, the working group concluded that, on ethical and legal grounds, universal DOT was desirable:

> The fact that all start their post-hospitalization treatment under a common program of supervision should help to reduce the stigma of treatment and create an effective public health plan for the control of TB. Such an approach will also limit the extent to which initial treatment decisions violate the principle of justice which seeks to preclude acts of invidious discrimination.

The call for universal directly observed therapy has provoked sharp opposition. First, it has been argued that such an effort would entail an enormous waste of scarce resources. Funds that could best be used to provide services to those most in need would be diverted to the supervision of those who would be compliant on their own. But most critically, universal directly observed therapy has been challenged as an unethical intrusion upon autonomy, as "gratuitously annoying"; as a violation of the constitutional requirement that the least restrictive alternative be used; and as contrary to the requirements of the Americans With Disabilities Act that decisions involving restrictions on those with disabilities be based on an individualized assessment. The Policy Director for the Gay Men's Health Crisis, D. Hansel, has written:

> I cannot see how mandatory directly observed therapy can be reconciled with the principle of the least restrictive alternative in the exercise of governmental power, since it would require the imposition of a coercive treatment regime in a class of people without any showing that they, as individuals will fail voluntarily to follow a course of medical treatment. Nor does it comport with basic Constitutional due process principles, which require an individualized determination before state sanctions are imposed.

Legal commentators too have generally rejected mandatory, DOT as overly broad and thus violative of constitutional principles. However, this opposition to *universal* DOT should not be construed as a rejection of *mandatory* DOT in all cases. Even advocates for patients' civil liberties accept mandatory, court-ordered DOT in cases of clear noncompliance, especially when the alternative appears to be involuntary confinement.

In its 1993 revision of the New York City Health Code, the City's Board of Health rejected universal mandatory DOT and instead authorized the Commissioner of Health to impose DOT on patients who were noncompliant with treatment during the noninfectious stage of their illness.

DETENTION OF NON-COMPLIANT PATIENTS

As noted earlier . . . ethical, legal, and constitutional principles have long recognized the authority of the state to confine individuals with infectious tuberculosis when they pose a threat to the health of others. This power to deprive an individual of his or her liberty in the name of public health has vested public health officials with an authority that, from the perspective of the individual, may be indistinguishable from that wielded by the criminal justice system. Yet until relatively recently, the protections accorded to defendants in criminal prosecutions have not been extended to those viewed as a threat to the public health. As late as 1966, a California appellate court upheld the confinement of a TB patient pursuant to a law that provided virtually no procedural protections for the patient. In its ruling, the court, quoting an earlier case, stated:

> Health regulations enacted by the state under its police power and providing even drastic measures for the elimination of disease . . . in a general way are not affected by constitutional provisions, either of the state or national government.

This broad deference to the legislature and to the exercise of public health powers would come to look archaic just a few years later, as the jurisprudence of confinement underwent a radical revision in the wake of a series of far-reaching constitutional challenges to the power of the state to confine patients with psychiatric disorders to mental hospitals. By 1979, Chief Justice Burger would state in *Addington v. Texas:*

> This Court has repeatedly recognized that civil commitment for any purpose constitutes a significant deprivation of liberty that requires due process protection. Moreover, it is indisputable that involuntary commitment to a mental hospital . . . can engender adverse social consequences to the individual. Whether we label this phenomena "stigma" or choose to call it something else is less important than that we recognize that it can occur and that it can have a very significant impact on the individual.

It was on the basis of such developments in mental health law, rather than as a result of challenges to the actions of public health officials in responding to tuberculosis cases, that it became possible to assert successfully that TB patients be accorded the procedural protections guaranteed by the Constitution. In 1980, in the only reported appellate court decision to date upholding the procedural rights of a tuberculosis patient, the Supreme Court of Appeals in West Virginia articulated a standard that expressly followed the developments in mental health law. The state's Tuberculosis Control Act was ruled unconstitutional because it did not guarantee the right to counsel, did not provide for the right to cross examine, confront and present witnesses, and failed to hold the state to the stringent "clear and convincing" standard of proof required by *Addington.*

Although the West Virginia decision is not controlling in other states, the social transformation in the legal and political context within which issues of confinement were considered in the 1970s and 1980s did shape policy and practice in the United States. . . .

This expansion on the conceptions of who posed a threat to the public health, driven by concerns about MDR-TB, represented a move of great significance. No longer did the person to be confined have to represent an immediate threat of transmission. Rather it was the *prospect* of reactivation and the *prospect* of the development of drug-resistance that provided the grounds for state intervention. Here the concept of "threat" was informed by the population-based concerns of public health. It was concern about the collective consequence of permitting many individuals to conduct themselves in a way that posed some threat that motivated the extension of public health powers to reach noninfectious TB patients. But this was a calculus far different from one that would center on the potential risk posed by a given individual. Nevertheless, legal commentators have, by and large, agreed that "confinement until cure would probably be found constitutional for noninfectious patients who did not adhere to treatment."

A striking reflection of the expansion of the concept of what constitutes a public health threat was the adoption in 1993 of treatment until cure regulations by the New York City Board of Health. Under the newly enacted Section 11.47 of the City's Health Code, the Commissioner may confine an individual for whom there is a "substantial likelihood, based on such person's past and present behavior, that he or she cannot be relied upon" to complete treatment. Under the amended code, a court review must be accorded to a confined patient within five business days, and even if the individual does not request release, the Department of Health must seek judicial review within the first 60 days of detention, and subsequently at 90-day intervals. Upon requesting release, the confined individual is entitled to a lawyer, and, if too poor to afford counsel, must be provided with one at public expense. . . .

FORCED MEDICATION

Remarkably, the very New York Health Code that extended the scope of the Commissioner's authority to isolate noncompliant patients despite their noninfectious status states that the regulations are "not to be construed to permit or require the forcible administration of any medication without a prior court order." In part, this restraint is simply a reflection of prevailing constitutional doctrines that recognize the rights of psychiatric patients, even criminally or civilly committed patients, to refuse treatment. It also reflects the importance of general principles of autonomy and informed consent. At the heart of judicial rulings that have established the right to refuse medication is the assumption that individuals may retain the right to some self-determination even when confined because they pose a risk to themselves or others. In *Rivers v. Katz,* the

New York Court of Appeals held that a civilly committed patient can be compelled to accept medication only after a judicial determination that the individual lacked the capacity to make a reasoned decision about the particular treatment. The determination of capacity was to be made at a hearing at which the patient was afforded representation by a lawyer.

What holds for a patient whose mental capacities are impaired is certainly true for those who are confined for tuberculosis, where no assumption about such impairment can be made. A decisionally capable patient may choose to forgo treatment even at the risk of death. That is the bedrock of the principle of informed consent. But such a patient does not have the right to endanger others. That is the bedrock of the statutory authority to confine noncompliant TB patients. It is, of course, possible that in a given case the refusal to accept medication may reflect psychiatric impairment. Under such circumstances, and after appropriate judicial review, compulsory treatment of the psychiatric disorder might be undertaken to enhance the prospect that the patient would be able to make an informed judgment about whether to cooperate in the treatment of his or her tuberculosis. But the ultimate paradox may remain: The state may confine a noncompliant individual because of the failure to undergo treatment, but may not impose treatment on the confined patient. This paradox underscores the fundamental limits of state power in a liberal society: The government may act to protect the public, but not to protect the competent individual from, his own willful, perhaps foolish, choices.

CONCLUSION

From both an ethical and legal perspective, the state has an obligation to assure that the population is protected against the ravages of infectious disease. That responsibility in the context of tuberculosis is best exercised by the development of programs and strategies designed to facilitate the identification and treatment of those with disease. In large measure, the central public health goals can be achieved by encouraging the cooperation of patients with tuberculosis. The expanded provision of directly observed therapy, indeed the establishment of directly observed therapy as a standard of care, may also be crucial. There will, however, be occasions when recourse to coercion will be necessary to protect the public health. Such occasions come at a price both because of the public costs of confinement and the individual's loss of liberty. But acknowledging that it may be necessary to rely on coercion should not be confused with making compulsion the centerpiece of a tuberculosis program. For pragmatic and principled reasons, coercion must be viewed as a last resort.

Much has been learned since the resurgence of tuberculosis took a place on the national agenda in the early 1990s. It has become clear that the rise in the number of cases, and, more centrally, the increase in the number of multidrug-resistant cases stemmed, at least in part, from the erosion of the public health infrastructure and the intensification of poverty and overcrowding in urban areas. With public alarm providing the motivation, governmental expenditures on TB control rose sharply. Those funds made possible a rapid expansion of local health department initiatives, including the broadening of voluntary directly observed therapy. In New York City, for example, the number of TB patients receiving directly observed treatment increased from fewer than 100 in 1991 to more than 1200 in 1993. The fruits of those efforts may be reflected in 1993 statistics, which for the first time in eight years on a national level and the first time in 14 years in New York City indicate that new cases of tuberculosis declined. It is too soon to know whether these numbers represent a trend or a statistical adjustment. But what is certain is that if stabilizing or declining tuberculosis cases provoke another cycle of budgetary retrenchment, the foundations for yet another upsurge in cases will have been laid. This time history will repeat itself not as tragedy but as farce.

Medical Science, Infectious Disease, and the Unity of Humankind

JOSHUA LEDERBERG

The ravaging epidemic of acquired immunodeficiency syndrome has shocked the world. It is still not comprehended widely that it is a natural, almost predictable, phenomenon. We will face similar catastrophes again, and will be ever more confounded in dealing with them, if we do not come to grips with the realities of the place of our species in nature. A large measure of humanistic progress is dedicated to the subordination of human nature to our ideals of individual perfectability and autonomy. Human intelligence, culture, and technology have left all other plant and animal species out of the competition. We also may legislate human behavior. But we have too many illusions that we can, by writ, govern the remaining vital kingdoms, the microbes, that remain our competitors of last resort for dominion of the planet. The bacteria and viruses know nothing of national sovereignties. In that natural evolutionary competition, there is no guarantee that we will find ourselves the survivor.

Some of the great successes of medical science, including the "miracle drugs," the antibiotics of the 1940s, have inculcated premature complacency on the part of the broader culture. Most people today are grossly overoptimistic with respect to the means we have available to forfend global epidemics comparable with the Black Death of the 14th century (or on a lesser scale the influenza of 1918), which took a toll of millions of lives.

Visualize human life on this planet as mirrored in the microcosm of a culture of bacteria; a laboratory test tube can hold ten billion cells, twice the human population of the globe. More than 70 years ago, Frederick William Twort and Felix d'Herelle discovered that bacteria have their own virus parasites, the bacteriophages. It is not unusual to observe a thriving bacterial population of a billion cells undergo a dramatic wipeout, a massive lysis, a sudden clearing of the broth following a spontaneous mutation that extends the host range of a single virus particle. A hundred billion virus particles will succeed the bacteria;

From the *Journal of the American Medical Association,* 260 (August 5, 1988), 684–685. Reprinted by permission of the American Medical Association.

but their own fate now is problematic, as they will have exhausted their prey (within that test tube). Perhaps there are a few bacterial survivors: mutant bacteria that now resist the mutant virus. If so, these can repopulate the test tube until perhaps a second round, a mutant-mutant virus, appears.

Such processes are not unique to the test tube. The time scale, the numerical odds, will be different. The fundamental biologic principles are the same.

Humans are more dispersed over the planetary surface than are the "bugs" in a glass tube; there are more diverse sanctuaries, and we have somewhat fewer opportunities to infect one another. The culture medium in the test tube is more hospitable to virus transmission than is the space between people (with the exceptions of sexual contact and transfusion). The ozone shield still lets through enough solar ultraviolet light to hinder aerosol transmission, and most viruses are fairly vulnerable to desiccation in dry air. The unbroken skin is an excellent barrier to infection; the mucous membranes of the respiratory tract are much less so. Our immune defenses are a wonderfully intricate legacy of our own evolutionary history. This enables machinery for producing an indefinite panoply of antibodies, some one of which is (we may hope) a specific match to the antigenic challenge of a particular invading parasite. In the normal, immune-competent individual, each incipient infection is a mortal race between the penetration and proliferation of the virus within the body and the evolution and expansion of antibodies that may be specific for that infection. Previous vaccination or infection with a related virus will facilitate an early immune response. This in turn provides selective pressure on the virus populations, encouraging the emergence of antigenic variants. We see this most dramatically in the influenza pandemics, and every few years we need to disseminate fresh vaccines to cope with the current generation of the flu virus.

Many defense mechanisms, inherent in our evolved biologic capabilities, thus mitigate the pandemic viral threat. Mitigation also is built into the evolution of the virus; it is a Pyrrhic victory for a virus to eradicate its host! This may have happened historically, but then both the vanquished host and the victorious parasite will have disappeared. Even the death of the single infected individual is relatively disadvantageous, in the long run, to the virus compared with a sustained infection that leaves a carrier free to spread the virus to as many contacts as possible. From the perspective of the virus, the ideal would be a nearly symptomless infection in which the host is oblivious of providing shelter and nourishment for the indefinite propagation of the virus' genes. Our own genome carries hundreds or thousands of such stowaways. The boundary between them and the "normal genome" is quite blurred. Not much more than 1% of our DNA can be assigned specific physiological functions; most of it is assumed to be a "fossil" legacy of our prior evolutionary history, DNA that is today parasitic on the cell. Further, we know that many viruses can acquire genetic information from their hosts, which from time to time they may transfer to new ones. Hence, intrinsic to our own ancestry and nature are not only Adam and Eve, but any number of invisible germs that have crept into our chromosomes. Some confer incidental and mutual benefit. Others of these symbiotic viruses or "plasmids" have reemerged as oncogenes, with the potential to mutate to a state that we recognize as the dysregulated cell growth of a cancer. This is a form of Darwinian evolution that momentarily enhances the fitness of a cell clone at the expense of the entire organism. Still other segments of "nonfunctional" DNA are available as reserves of genetic potential for further evolution, in a sense more constructive for the individual and the species.

At evolutionary equilibrium we would continue to share the planet with our internal and external parasites, paying some tribute, perhaps sometimes deriving from them some protection against more violent aggression. The terms of that equilibrium are unwelcome: present knowledge does not offer much hope that we can eradicate the competition. Meanwhile, our parasites and ourselves must share in the dues, payable in a currency of discomfort and precariousness of life. No theory lets us calculate the details; we can hardly be sure that such an equilibrium for earth even includes the human species even as we contrive to eliminate some of the others. Our propensity for technological sophistication harnessed to intraspecies competition adds a further dimension of hazard.

In fact, innumerable perturbations remind us that complex systems often fluctuate far from equilibrium—each individual death of an infected person is a counterexample. Our defense mechanisms do not always work. Viruses are not always as benign as they would be if each particle had the intelligence and altruism to serve the long-term advantage of the group.

Fears of new epidemics as virulent as those of the past have been modified by the expectation that modern hygiene and medicine would contain any such outbreaks. There is, of course, much merit in those expectations. Influenza in 1918 was undoubtedly complicated by bacterial infection that now can be treated with antibiotics; vaccines, if we can mobilize them in time, can help prevent the global spread of a new flu. However, the impact of technology is not all on the human side of the struggle. Monoculture of plants and animals has made them more exposed to devastation. The increasing density of human habitations as well as inventions such as the subway and the jet airplane that mix populations all add to the risks of spread of infection. Paradoxically, improvements in sanitation and vaccination sometimes make us the more vulnerable because they leave the larger human herd more innocent of microbial experience.

The opening of wild lands to human occupation also has exposed people to unaccustomed animal viruses, to zoonoses. Yellow fever has sustained reservoirs in jungle primates, and the same source is the probable origin of the human immunodeficiency virus in Africa. It is mystifying that yellow fever has not become endemic in India, where competent mosquitoes and susceptible people abound. We will almost certainly be having like experiences from the "opening" of the Amazon basin.

Our preoccupation with acquired immunodeficiency syndrome should not obscure the multiplicity of infectious diseases that threaten our future. It is none too soon to start a systematic watch for new viruses before they become so irrevocably lodged. The fundamental bases of virus research can hardly be given too much encouragement. Recombinant DNA, still a scare word in some quarters, is our most potent means of analyzing viruses and developing vaccines. Such research should be done on a broad international scale to both share the progress made in advanced countries and amplify the opportunities for field work at the earliest appearance of outbreaks in the most afflicted areas.

The basic principles of vaccination were established long ago, but practical means of production of vaccines for viral afflictions like polio had to await the cell and tissue culture advances of the 1950s. The most celebrated example, smallpox, also has the oldest historical roots. That success has encouraged other proposals for the eradication of other infectious agents. Rarely do we have the understanding of its natural history needed to calibrate the feasibility of the goal. This will strain our basic knowledge of the genetics and evolution of the etiologic agents.

For example, our stratagems on malaria, gonococcus, and human immunodeficiency virus are all confounded by the poorly understood capacity of the viruses to undergo further antigenic evolution. We know a bit more about influenza, but not enough to give us more than a few weeks or months of lead time merely to respond to its perennial variations.

As one species, we share a common vulnerability to these scourges. No matter how selfish our motives, we can no longer be indifferent to the suffering of others. The microbe that felled one child in a distant continent yesterday can reach yours today and seed a global pandemic tomorrow. "Never send to know for whom the bell tolls; it tolls for thee."

Emerging Diseases and Ecosystem Instability: New Threats to Public Health

PAUL R. EPSTEIN

INTRODUCTION

The 1980s marked the return of infectious diseases to front stage. Of course, infectious diseases never disappeared outside the West. Today, many direct contagions, such as tuberculosis, multidrug resistant tuberculosis, pertussis, and diphtheria, and those involving vectors and animal reservoirs such as yellow fever, malaria, and dengue, are undergoing redistribution. Indeed, the present period of unprecedented ecological change and the growing economic and social crises that are driving vast movements of hosts are together contributing to the resurgence of old pests and the appearance of new ones. Important components in this rapid evolution are the vulnerabilities of ecosystems and instabilities in climate.

The Centers for Disease Control and Prevention (CDC) has launched a program to monitor and mitigate emerging diseases by focusing on the evolution of new pathogens and the reemergence or redistribution of old ones. The range of issues involved were recently reviewed and were the subject of an interdisciplinary workshop in Woods Hole, Mass, sponsored by Harvard School of Public Health New Disease Group in November 1993.

Two new diseases of 1993—a virulent viral strain appearing in the United States and a novel cholera variant bursting upon the scene in Asia—are cause for alarm and demand pause for reflection. But once the precise agents have been identified, a deeper comprehension of the web of environmental, social, and host factors from which they have emerged, and of the breakdowns in "natural" controls on species abundance that they represent, can reveal a great deal about the "health"—the stability, resilience, diversity, and vigor—of Earth's life-support systems.

From the *American Journal of Public Health,* 85 (1995), 168–170. Reprinted by permission of the American Public Health Association.

THE HANTAVIRUS

In the southwestern United States, hantavirus infection has been confirmed in 94 persons in 20 states with 48% mortality (Dr J. Woodall, New York State Department of Health, personal communication, October 10, 1994). In Louisiana, a variant close to but distinct from the "four-corners" strain killed a bridge worker; a "cousin" hantavirus was found in a Floridian (who survived) and remains present in local cotton rats (*Sigmodon hispidus*); another variant was found in Indiana; and in February 1994, a 22-year-old student in Rhode Island died of possibly another variant.

The sudden appearance of an unexpected and lethal clinical presentation (hantavirus pulmonary syndrome), caused by viruses that have perhaps long existed at low levels in rodent populations and were previously associated with distinctly different clinical entities, raises important questions. Was the related virus that was identified in 1983 by serology and polymerase chain reaction in similar mouse populations in the Southwest as virulent then for humans as it is today, or is the current high mortality indicative of a new strain? Are the extreme virulence and new cell tropism (pulmonary versus renal and hemopoietic) also signs of a novel variant? Or has an extant viral agent been amplified through changes in rodent ecology, and have conditions helped select and disseminate a highly virulent variant?

An Evolving Agent?

In the past, hantaviruses have been associated with hemorrhagic fever with renal syndrome and perhaps with chronic nephropathy. Four distinct hantaviruses of the family *Bunyaviridae*—Hantaan, Puumala, Seoul, and Prospect Hill—have been identified, and several others have been described in Southeast Asia and in Europe. In the 1950s, Hantaan virus caused Korean hemorrhagic fever with renal syndrome in thousands of United States and United Nations troops, although the etiology remained obscure until 1976. Puumala virus, carried in the European bank vole (*Clethrionomys glareolus*), produces a milder neuropathia epidemica in Scandinavia and the Balkans, as does Seoul virus in Asia. During the 1980s, hantaviruses were isolated from domestic rats in Texas; from deer mice (*Peromyscus maniculatus*) and humans in California, Colorado, and New Mexico; and from a meadow vole captured on Prospect Hill, Md. To date, this last has been unassociated with human disease. The current variant was named Muerto Canyon virus after the locale of recognition, which prompted some Native Americans to contest the name; it has been since designated "Sin Nombre."

Hantaviruses, apparently asymptomatic in rodents and transmitted in their saliva and excreta, may be associated with hypertension and chronic renal disease in the United States. However, the 1993 appearance was the first outbreak of acute illness associated with the hantavirus in the United States, and its flulike presentation, followed swiftly by acute respiratory distress syndrome, is unique. In the four-corners area, *P. maniculatus,* which is widespread in North America, appears to be the primary reservoir host (as it is for Lyme disease [*Borrelia burgdorferi*]), while another close relative may harbor the Louisiana strain. The CDC has issued guidelines for minimizing indoor and outdoor exposure to all rodents.

Reports of new *Hantavirus* isolates from new areas of Europe suggest that other hantaviruses are present in other geographically isolated rodent populations (Dr S. S. Morse, Rockefeller University, personal communication, March 1994). The identification of Puumala virus (normally found in voles) in the house mouse (*Mus musculus*) in Yugoslavia suggests that interspecies transfer of hantaviruses can occur under suitable conditions. Because emerging infections often arise in areas undergoing ecological or demographic change, the former Yugoslavia, beset by war and economic breakdown, is a critical region and deserves close monitoring.

A Changing Environment

A likely scenario in the southwestern United States is that heavy rains following 6 years of drought caused pine nuts and grasshoppers to flourish, thereby nourishing deer mice. Then, driven from underground burrows by flooding, a swollen population of natural hosts (a 10-fold increase from May 1992 to May 1993) enhanced the chance for the virus to thrive and be passed on. Thus, whatever the hantavirus' route of entry into the human population, alterations in nutrient supplies and in the ratio of prey with *Peromyscus* predators (owls, snakes, coyotes, and cats) created selection pressures for the emergence or amplification of an apparently new variant of *Hantavirus.*

A Navajo chief reflected, "We suffer for we have not taken better care of the earth" and "our people have lost harmony with nature." The landscape and diversity of animals in the region, where rainwater channeled from rocky outcrops once irrigated the fields, have declined from overgrazing and deforestation. But large climatological swings and a year of great storms (witness the blizzards and the floods of 1993 and 1994) may reflect even greater instability in Earth's natural systems.

Weather patterns and jet streams across North and South America, western Europe, Asia, and Africa are strongly influenced by the Pacific Ocean warming center. El Niño events, which begin at Christmastime, determine patterns for a year and have, until recently, occurred about twice a decade. Warmer seas evaporate quickly, yielding greater precipitation over some areas and drought in others. The strength of the 1992/93 El Niño was unexpected, and the endurance of $+2$ to 3°C anomalies in ocean temperatures into summer was unprecedented. Because the persistence of negative South Pacific sea-level pressures that drive El Niño now spans over 4 years (an occurrence without analogue in the historical record), and warming is predicted to continue at least through the 1994/95 winter, weather patterns have become particularly erratic and volatile (i.e., unstable).

Leading climatologists have projected more frequent El Niño events, with greater variation in storm frequency, onset, intensity, and duration, accompanying a continued increase in greenhouse gases. The ocean is a "global thermostat," explains Rachel Carson in *The Sea Around Us,* and the warming atmosphere transfers heat to the oceans for worldwide distribution. It is the global "conveyor belt" of warm Gulf Streams moving north, and of deep, cold southward currents, that may have stalled (or reversed directions) to produce the rapid climate swings of the past, as disclosed in Greenland ice-core records.

Monitoring El Niños, temperature, wind, and precipitation patterns, and biodiversity has enormous implications for surveillance of disease vectors and reservoirs; indeed, the widespread resurgence of infections may have profound implications for future fossil fuel and forestry policies.

A NOVEL VARIANT OF CHOLERA

In India and Bangladesh, a new variant of cholera erupted in January 1993. By mid-April, the novel form of *Vibrio cholerae*—armed with cholera enterotoxin plus a colonizing gene and bearing a previously undetected antigen (O139)— had invaded Calcutta (15 000 cases, 230 dead) and saturated Dhaka (600 cases per day at peak). The novel strain, dubbed "O139 Bengal," which is considered more hardy than biotype El Tor in terms of its environmental adaptation (Dr R. B. Sack, Johns Hopkins University School of Hygiene and Public Health, personal communication, April 1994), is spreading in Thailand and Pakistan and is present in 10 Southeast Asian nations (R. Cash, MD, Harvard School of Public Health, personal communication, May 1994). Its epidemiological spectrum, infecting adults and children, indicates the absence of cross-immunity between it and El Tor, the agent of the ongoing seventh pandemic that left Asia in 1961. One case has been imported into the United States, but the "anastomoses" between water supplies and sanitation requisite for endemicity are largely absent, save for the Mexico-US border region.

The Algal Reservoir

Aquatic plants, seaweeds, and freefloating phyto- and zooplankton can harbor vibrios in viable but nonculturable, sporelike forms, as demonstrated by fluorescent antibody and polymerase chain reaction techniques. (Note that O139 Bengal has not been tested in this regard, but there is no reason to suspect that its affinity for algae and weeds is different from that of other O1 and non-O1 vibrios.) The growth of marine and freshwater photosynthesizers is prompted by nitrogen-rich wastewater, fertilizers, acid rain, and runoff soil (eutrophication). Wetlands and mangroves ("nature's kidneys") filter out nitrates and phosphates. While inputs are increasing, the filtration systems are being lost to development and aquaculture, diking and drilling. Concurrently, fish stocks (predators of plankton) are in decline in 14 of the world's 17 major fishing grounds. In addition, climate-related warmer sea surface temperatures also increase algae growth by (1) augmenting photosynthesis and algal metabolism, (2) increasing nutrient-rich coastal upwelling, and (3) shifting the community of organisms toward more toxic species ("red tides," fish and shellfish poisoning), which are in turn less palatable to grazers. Indeed, planktonologists postulate a "global epidemic" of coastal algal blooms that may well represent one of the first biological signals of global change (Dr T. J. Smayda, University of Rhode Island School of Oceanography, personal communication, June 1994).

Other Vibrios

El Tor *V. cholerae* may have arrived in the Americas in the ballast and bilgewater of ships coming from Asia, there finding abundant algal blooms for amplification; from there it hitchhiked in Latin American ship hulls to the US Gulf Coast. And in the Gulf, another vibrio (*Vibrio vulnificus*), found in oysters, has caused deaths in Florida residents with preexisting liver disease.

Sanitation and water supplies—environmental conditions inside national boundaries—have been the primary focus of public health interventions (and are certainly not meant to be minimized by this analysis). However, it may be that widespread changes in coastal ecology are generating "hot systems" in which mutations (random, perhaps adaptive—bacteriophage, ultraviolet-B light, or chemically initiated) are being selected and amplified under new environmental pressures and then transferred to human populations through the food chain (fish and shellfish). In addition to O139 Bengal, more antibiotic-resistant forms of *V. cholerae* O1, biotype El Tor, have emerged; and in Peru a chlorine-defiant "rugose" variant has surfaced (perhaps related to intermittent disinfection), adding a new mixture of cholera organisms to penetrate poor populations that have little access to potable water.

As threats to marine resources, food safety, and sustainable yields result in direct costs to fishing communities, marine biologists are becoming increasingly concerned for the overall health of marine ecosystems. The new variant of *V. cholerae* intrudes upon planned trials of an oral recombinant vaccine, and although it took the seventh pandemic 30 years to become global, we may expect a more rapid dissemination of O139 Bengal, the agent of an eighth world pandemic. An early warning system—monitoring algal blooms (guided by remote sensing), fish, and shellfish samples for vibrios—is feasible.

CONCLUSIONS

The links between the environment and health may be direct (from toxins to heat waves or cold spells) or indirect (involving intermediate species as vectors and/or reservoirs). At the 1993 Wood Hole conference, participants from the CDC and the World Health Organization, and from universities and institutes in the United States and abroad, concluded that a major impediment to disease monitoring and detection was the fragmentation of epidemiology and scientific disciplines. In response, a new framework is emerging, one that incorporate meteorological mean values (i.e., the climate regime) and anomalies, ecosystem-based findings, molecular epidemiological techniques, *and* surveillance of indicator species (e.g., rodents, insects, and algae) and health outcomes. Integrating surveillance of biological indicators that carry disease—that is, of rapid responders that are therefore sensitive indicators of perturbed environments—is key. It was fortuitous that an ecological station in Sevilleta, NM, was monitoring deer mice, and our knowledge of the marine food web comes from microbiologists, oceanographers, and ichthyologists—groups that do not readily coordinate their findings and data. Geographic information and mapping systems offer a new methodology to integrate systems by overlaying and fusing data sets.

Focusing on critical regions where life-support systems such as water and soil fertility are fragile can also improve monitoring. Land-use changes (deforestation for farming) leading to shifts in rodent species, combined with an influx of nonimmune workers, are apparently related to five emerging arenaviruses in Latin America (Lassa in several nations, Junin in Argentina, Machupo in Bolivia, Guaranito in Venezuela, and Sabiá in Brazil), all of which are associated with hemorrhagic fevers and high case fatality. Many new and resurgent diseases reflect bioclimatic conditions permissive for parasite and pest persistence, and the emergence of hantavirus in a US terrestrial setting, as well as the evolution and spread of cholera in the marine environment, provide illuminating case studies for future health monitoring and environmental management.

Finally, while social, political, and economic factors are not the immediate focus of this paper, they are clearly integral to the condition and management of the environment, for therein lie the driving forces of global change (the cumulative effects of local inputs and transformations) and the inequitable distribution of exposures, vulnerabilities, and access to treatment. Just as the 19th-century confluence of urban epidemics (tuberculosis, cholera, and smallpox) gave rise to modern epidemiology and sanitary reform, so too must the emergence and resurgence of infectious diseases today stimulate interdisciplinary, comparative, and collaborative epidemiology, as well as a renewed focus on primary prevention—that is, on the forms of development and the fossil fuel–based economies that drive global change.

The health professions and teaching institutions must reach across scientific disciplines to study the implications of accelerated environmental change. As interpreters to the public of the impacts of global change, the medical and public health professions can assume an influential role in policies that address our common safety. Finally, risk assessment of anthropogenic activities—from chemical contaminants to development practices—must include indirect ecological effects, to best ensure that the untoward impacts of our interventions do not overwhelm the direct effects intended.

7

JUSTICE AND HEALTH CARE

Justice in the allocation of health care is a topic that could easily demand a book of readings on its own. What should be done about the 40 million uninsured in the United States? Should "high-tech" and expensive medical measures be used to extend the life of the very elderly? Should they be used to save very premature infants with dubious prognoses? What would be a fair allocation of organs for donation? Should people whose habits (heavy smoking or drinking) contributed to their need for organ donation be considered on a par with those with healthier lifestyles? How can we control health care spending, and whose responsibility is it to pay for health care? Individuals? Employers? The government? We cannot cover all these important issues in this chapter. What we can do is touch on a few critical issues concerning the future direction of health care in the United States and the prospects for universal access.

It must be acknowledged up front that some people, especially libertarians, do not agree that justice requires that all citizens receive health care. While this is certainly a possible philosophical position, which we discuss below, it is clearly a minority view. For most people, the fact that 40 million Americans lack health insurance contradicts the ideal of "liberty and justice for all." At the same time, the United States has just tried unsuccessfully, yet again, to pass a national health plan. We need to understand the causes for this failure.

On the political front, the American public seems receptive to a scheme for providing universal coverage. The experience with the Clinton plan and the furious storm of opposition it generated from the insurance industry and the Republican Party reveals that the public can be frightened off, at least temporarily. This should not surprise us. The public in democracies is usually reserved in its judgment when vast new schemes for social improvement are offered. The Canadians, for example, passed their national health plan in two stages, between the late 1950s and the late 1960s, and the national electorate was split almost evenly over the issue of a private plan versus a government scheme. The government scheme won in Parliament, and subsequently public support for the Canadian system grew rapidly.[1] Today, despite the difficulties

Canada has undergone—the threat of a secession by Quebec and a very deep recession in this decade, forcing cutbacks in medical spending—support for Medicare (the name of their national plan) remains quite high.

On the question of what went wrong in the United States, almost no expert believes that public opposition was the fundamental barrier to passage of the Clinton plan.[2] Most believe that the opposition of organized interests, primarily small business and the insurance industry (which feared that it might be eliminated by the new plan), helped glue together opposition from Republicans and conservative Democrats.

The Clinton plan accelerated the shift in the United States toward a more competitive health care system and toward managed care, a shift that is in keeping with the promarket balance of political forces that prevail in Washington, D.C. Managed care does this by managing the amount and quality of care received by patients via entry-level doctors and health maintenance organizations (HMOs). Managed care seeks to save money by keeping patients out of hospitals when they don't need it and by putting them in cheaper but equally effective therapies. As an idea it has been around since before World War II. It first got its big push to national attention when President Nixon introduced legislation in the early 1970s to help HMOs spread and to head off a push toward universal health care. And later the idea was altered to include the idea that HMOs would control costs by competing with other HMOs, each offering the same level of comprehensive benefits (with the poor supported by the government).

In the first selection, Amy Gutmann examines the ethical foundations for health care access for all. She considers (and rejects) the libertarian thesis that health care is a preference like any other good and that markets allocate preferences adequately enough. In this view, it is no more the business of government to provide people with health care than it is the business of government to provide people with houses and automobiles. Instead people should be free to spend their income as they choose, whether on health insurance or consumer goods. A market approach to health care is best. As Gutmann points out, some libertarians would support providing more income to the poor to assure more equity in market transactions. But libertarians reject the wholesale application of one system for all as inefficient, as a violation of people's basic right to dispose of their income as they see fit, and as deeply paternalistic. In addition, Richard Epstein, a leading libertarian, argues that universal access is inefficient and wasteful.[3] Viewing health care as a right is not only prohibitively expensive, it rewards the sick and self-indulgent while punishing the healthy and the active. The libertarian view is in the minority in the United States and it is almost nonexistent as a view in other western democracies. In Canada, Germany, France, England, and the Scandinavian countries, health care, like education, is regarded as a public good and is publicly provided for all, although the terms of this public arrangement vary considerably. Moreover, the cost of health care overall is far lower than in the United States. We might add that this approach promotes "hanging together" by the electorate in defense of the common system. Thus a national health plan tends to promote social cohesion around the matter of security against illness and the lack of medical care. Most in these other countries recognize that assuring health care for all is expensive, but they also are well aware that the cost of health care in their countries (Canada, England, France, Germany) is far lower overall than it is in the United States, and public support for continuing these policies remains very high. One of the most important features of the drive to pass a national health insurance plan, and (earlier) to pass Medicare and (even earlier) Social Security, was to strengthen the national community at the expense of the regional and racial fault lines that hobbled the United States in its search for a wider equality.[4]

The Gutmann piece was written long before the failure of the Clinton plan but it still remains a classic argument for a national or universal health care system. A principal feature of her argument is that a one-class health care system, one for the rich, the middle classes and poor alike, promotes a health care system that caters to the needs of the better off as well as the poor, and this will strengthen the overall system level of benefits. Gutmann for practical political reasons acknowledges that a one-class system could not go so far as to forbid the rich from purchasing more health care outside the system, spending out-of-pocket.

Larry Churchill, in our second selection, paints a future in which the market dominates our common life for medicine, and it should raise many questions about the direction of present policies. Churchill suggests that a market-driven system not only undermines principles of justice and the ideal of equality in health care; it also endangers the welfare of patients and weakens trust in physicians. When physicians work for health plans which are not accountable to the electorate, conflicts of interest are inevitable, especially in for-profit plans.

In the third selection, Bradford Gray analyzes the future of trust in physicians in a new era of medical care. A critical question for the future of medicine is whether it will remain a profession in charge of its own destiny. Will physicians who work for HMOs be allowed to set policy for patients in a way consistent with the values of medicine as a profession? Gray argues that trust was already declining for physicians in the traditional fee-for-service settings. Managed care can and should be made to increase the trust patients have for physicians, through codes of ethics, forms of ownership (nonprofit versus profit), and so forth. Gray suggests that it is likely that some form of corporate medicine will be the future of the United States, and the challenge is to marry that future with a medicine that serves the society as well as the corporation. Some will doubt that this can be done.

New threats to the public's health, such as those we discussed in the last chapter, may put a national health plan back on the political agenda. In the last selection for this chapter Phyllis Freeman and Anthony Robbins take up this issue. Freeman and

Robbins argue that public health policy must be a central part of any national health care reform. State departments of health will need to work far more closely with private physicians in forging an effective prevention policy. This cooperation is especially needed if we are to identify new and emergent threats to health, from new hazards in the workplace to new threats from communicable diseases. Epidemic diseases and a whole new host of threats from viral and bacterial pathogens worldwide provide unparalleled opportunities for the spread of infection. These dangers may force us to reconsider a national health plan for reasons of self-protection than out of a concern for justice for all.

NOTES

1. For discussion of this shift in popular opinion in Canada, see Dan Beauchamp, *Health Care Reform and the Battle for the Body Politic* (Philadelphia, PA: Temple University Press, 1996, pp. 43–44).

2. See Haynes Johnson and David S. Broder, *The System: The American Way of Politics at the Breaking Point* (Boston: Little Brown, 1996). Johnson and Broder focus on the difficulties of mobilizing majority support in a badly fragmented political system at the top, plus organized opposition from small business and the insurance industry. See Jacob S. Hacker, *The Road to Nowhere* (Princeton, NJ: Princeton University Press, 1997); Theda Skocpol, *Boomerang: Clinton's Health Security Effort and the Turn Against Government in U.S. Politics* (New York: W.W. Norton, 1996); and Dan Beauchamp, *Health Care Reform and the Battle for the Body Politic. supra.* note 1.

3. Richard Epstein, *Mortal Peril: Our Inalienable Right to Health Care?* (Reading, MA: Addison-Wesley, 1997).

4. Samuel H. Beer, "In Search of a New Public Philosophy," in Anthony King, ed. *The New American Political System.* (Washington, DC: American Enterprise Institute for Public Policy Research, 1978, pp. 5–44).

For and Against Equal Access to Health Care

AMY GUTMANN

There is a fairly widespread consensus among empirical analysts that access to health care in this country has become more equal in the last quarter century. Agreement tends to end here; debate follows as to whether this trend will or should persist. But before debating these questions, we ought to have a clear idea of what equal access to health care means. Since equality of access to health care cannot be defined in a morally neutral way, we must choose a definition that is morally loaded with a set of values. The definition offered here is by no means the only possible one. It has, however, the advantage not only of clarity but also of having embedded within it strong and commonly accepted liberal egalitarian values. The debate is better focused upon arguments for and against a strong *principle* of equal access than disputes over definitions, which tend to hide fundamental value disagreements instead of making them explicit.

An equal access principle, clearly stated and understood, can serve at best as an ideal toward which a society committed to equality of opportunity and equal respect for persons can strive. It does not provide a blueprint for social change, but only a moral standard by which to judge marginal changes in our present institutions of health care.

My purpose here is not only to evaluate the strongest criticisms that are addressed to the principle, ranging from libertarian arguments for more market freedom to arguments supporting a more egalitarian principle of health care. I also propose to examine the sorts of theoretical and practical problems that arise when one tries to defend an egalitarian principle directed at a particular set of institutions within an otherwise inegalitarian society. Since it is extremely unlikely that such a society will be transformed all at once into an egalitarian one, there ought to be room within political and philosophical argument for reasoned consideration and advocacy of "partial" distributive justice, i.e., of principles that are directed only to a particular set of social institutions and

From the *Milbank Memorial Quarterly, Health and Society,* 59 (1981), 542–560. Reprinted by permission of Blackwell Publishers.

whose implementation is not likely to create complete justice even within those institutions.

THE PRINCIPLE DEFINED

A principle of equal access to health care demands that every person who shares the same type and degree of health need must be given an equally effective chance of receiving appropriate treatment of equal quality so long as that treatment is available to anyone. Stated in this way, the equal access principle does not establish whether a society must provide any particular medical treatment or health care benefit to its needy members. I shall suggest later that the level and type of provision can vary within certain reasonable boundaries according to the priorities determined by legitimate democratic procedures. The principle requires that if anyone within a society has an opportunity to receive a service or good that satisfies a health need, then everyone who shares the same type and degree of health need must be given an equally effective chance of receiving that service or good.

Since this is a principle of equal *access,* it does not guarantee equal *results,* although it probably would move our society in that direction. Discriminations in health care are permitted if they are based upon type or degree of health need, willingness of informed adults to be treated, and choices of lifestyle among the population. The equal access principle constrains the distribution of opportunities to receive health care to an egalitarian standard, but it does not determine the total level of health care available or the effects of that care (provided the care is of equal quality) upon the health of the population. Of course, even if equality in health care were defined according to an "equal health" principle, one would still have to admit that a just health care system could not come close to producing an equally healthy population, given the unequal distribution of illness among people and our present medical knowledge.

PRACTICAL IMPLICATIONS

Since the equal access principle requires equality of effective opportunity to receive care, not merely equality of formal legal access, it does not permit discriminations based upon those characteristics of people that we can reasonably assume they did not freely choose. Such characteristics include sex, race, genetic endowment, wealth, and often, place of residence. Even in an ideal society, equally needy persons will not use the same amount or quality of health care. Their preferences and their knowledge will differ as will the skills of the providers who treat them.

A One-Class System

The most striking result of applying the equal access principle in the United States would be the creation of a one-class system of health care. Services and goods that meet health care needs would be equally available to everyone who was equally needy. As a disincentive to overuse, only small fees for service could be charged for health care, provided that charges did not prove a barrier to entry to the poorest people who were needy. A one-class system need not, of course, be a uniform system. Diversity among medical and health care services would be permissible, indeed even desirable, so long as the diversity did not create differential access along nonconsensual lines such as wealth, race, sex, or geographical location.

Equal access also places limits upon the market freedoms of some individuals, especially, but not exclusively, the richest members of society. The principle does not permit the purchase of health care to which other similarly needy people do not have effective access. The extent to which freedom of the rich must be restricted will depend upon the level of public provision for health care and the degree of income inequality. As the level of health care guaranteed to the poor decreases and the degree of income inequality increases, the equal access standard demands greater restrictions upon the market freedom of the rich. Where income and wealth are very unevenly distributed, and where the level of publicly guaranteed access is very low, the rich can use the market to buy access to health care goods unavailable to the poor, thereby undermining the effective equality of opportunity required by an equal access principle.

The restriction upon market freedoms to purchase health care under these circumstances creates a certain discomforting irony: the equal access principle permits (or is at least agnostic with respect to) the free market satisfaction of preferences for nonessential consumer goods. Thus, the rigorous implementation of equal access to health care would prevent rich people from spending their extra income for preferred medical services, if those services were not equally accessible to the poor. It would not prevent their using those same resources to purchase satisfactions in other areas—a Porsche or any other luxurious consumer good. In discussing additional problems created by an attempt to implement a principle of equal access to health care in an otherwise inegalitarian society, I return later to consider whether advocates of equal access can avoid this irony.

Hard Cases

As with all principles, hard cases exist for the equal access principle. Without dwelling upon these cases, it is worth considering how the principle might deal with two hard but fairly common cases: therapeutic experimentation in medicine, and alternative treatments of different quality.

Each year in the United States, many potentially successful therapies are tested. Since their value has not been proved, there may be good reason to limit their use to an appropriate sample of sick experimental subjects. The equal access principle would insist that experimenters choose these subjects at random from a population of relevantly sick consenting adults. A randomized clinical trial could be advertised by public notice, and individuals who are interested might be registered and enrolled on a lottery basis. The only requirement for enrollment would be the health conditions and personal characteristics necessary for proper scientific testing.

How does one apply the principle of equal access when alternative treatments are each functionally adequate but aesthetically or socially quite disparate? Take the hypothetical case of a societal commitment to adequate dentition among adults. Replacement of carious or mobile teeth with dentures may preserve dental function at relatively minor cost. On the other hand, full mouth reconstruction, involving periodontal and endodontal treatment and capping of affected teeth, may be only marginally more effective but substantially more satisfying. The added costs for the preferred treatment are not inconsiderable. The principle would seem to demand that at equal states of dental need there be equal access to the preferred treatment. It is unclear, however, whether the satisfaction of subjective desire is equivalent to fulfillment of objective need.

In cases of alternative treatments, proponents of equal access could turn to another argument for providing access to the same treatments for all. A society that publicly provides the minimal acceptable treatment freely to all, and also permits a private market in more expensive treatments, may result in a two-class system of care. The best providers will service the richest clientele, at the risk of inadequate treatment for the poorest. Approval of a private market in alternative treatments would rest upon the empirical hypothesis that, if the publicly funded level of adequate treatment were high enough, few people would choose to short-circuit the public (i.e., equal access) sector; the small additional free market sector would not threaten to lower the quality of services universally available.

Most cases, like the one of dentistry, are difficult to decide merely on principle. Proponents of equal access must take into account the consequences of alternative policies. But empirical knowledge alone will not decide these issues, and arguments for or against a particular policy can be entertained in a more systematic way once one exposes the values that underlie support for an equal access principle. One can then judge to what extent alternative policies satisfy these values.

SUPPORTING VALUES

Advocates of equal access to health care must demonstrate why health care is different from other consumer goods, unless they are willing to support the more radical principle of equal distribution of all goods. Norman Daniels provides one foundation for distinguishing between health care and other goods. He establishes a category of health care needs whose satisfaction provides an important condition for future opportunity. Like police protection and education, some kinds of health care goods are necessary for pursuing most other goods in life. Any theory of justice committed to equalizing opportunity ought to treat health care as a good deserving of special distributive treatment. Equal access to health care provides a necessary, although certainly not a sufficient, condition for equal opportunity in general.

A precept of egalitarian justice that physical pains of a sufficient degree be treated similarly, regardless of who experiences them, establishes another reason for singling out certain kinds of health care as special goods. Some health conditions cause great pain but are not linked to a serious curtailment of opportunity. The two values are, however, mutually compatible.

A theory of justice that gives priority to the value of equal respect among people might also be used to support a principle of equal access to health care. John Rawls, for example, argues that without self-respect "nothing may seem worth doing, or if some things have value for us, we lack the will to strive for them. . . . Therefore the parties in the original position would wish to avoid at almost any cost the social conditions that undermine self-respect."

Conditions of Self-Respect

It is not easy to determine what social conditions support or undermine self-respect. One might plausibly assume that equalizing opportunity and treating similar pains similarly would be the most essential supports for equal respect within a health care system. And so, in most cases, the value of equal respect provides additional support for equal access to the same health care goods that are warranted by the values of equal opportunity and relief from pain. But at least some kinds of health care treatment not essential to equalizing opportunity or bringing equal relief from pain may be necessary to equalize respect within a society. It is conceivable that much longer waiting time, in physicians' offices or for admission to hospitals, may not affect the long-term health prospects of the poor or of blacks. But such discriminations in waiting times for an essential good probably do adversely affect the self-respect of those who systematically stand at the end of the queue.

Some of the conditions necessary for equal respect are socially relative; we must arrive at a standard of equal respect appropriate to our particular society. Universal suffrage has long been a condition for equal respect; the case for it is independent of the anticipated results of equalizing political power by granting every person one vote. More recently, equal access to health care has similarly become a condition for equal respect in our society. Most of us do not base our self-respect on the way we are treated on airplanes, even though the flight attendants regularly give preferential treatment to those traveling first class. This contrast with suffrage and health care treatment (and education and police protection) no doubt is related to the fact that these goods are much more essential to our security and opportunities in life than is airplane travel. But it is still worth considering that unequal treatment in health care, as in education, may be understood as a sign of unequal respect even where there are no discernible adverse effects on the health or education of those receiving less favored treatment. Even where a dual health care system will not produce inferior medical results for the less privileged, the value of equal respect militates against the perpetuation of such a system in our society.

CHALLENGES

Equality of opportunity, equal efforts to relieve pain, and equal respect are the three central values providing the foundation of support for a principle of equal access to health care. Any theory of justice that gives primacy to these values (as do many liberal and egalitarian theories) will lend prima facie support to a health care system structured along equal access lines.

We are now in a position to consider alternative values and empirical claims that would lead someone to challenge, or reject, a principle of equal access to health care. These challenges also enable us to elaborate further the moral and political implications of the principle.

Proponents of the Market

The most radical and vocal opposition comes from those who support a pure free market principle in health care. A foundation of support for the free market principle is the idea that the relative importance of satisfying different human desires is a purely subjective manner: we can distinguish between one person's desire for good medical care and another person's desire for a good Beaujolais only by the price they are willing to pay for each. If no goods are special because there is no way of ranking desires except by individual processes of choice, then what better way than the unconstrained market to allow us to decide among the smorgasbord of goods society has to offer?

Health care goods and services are likely to be more equally allocated through the market if income and wealth are more equally distributed. Several defenders of the market as a means of allocating goods and services also support a moderate degree of income redistribution on grounds of its diminishing marginal utility, or because they believe that every person has a right to "basic minimum." Neither rationale for redistribution takes us very far toward a principle of equal access to health care. If one retains the basic assumption that human preferences are totally subjective, then the market remains the best way to order human priorities. Only the market appropriately decentralizes decision-making and eliminates all nonconsensual exchanges of goods and services.

Although a minimum income floor under all individuals increases *access* to most goods and services, even at a higher level than that supported by Friedman and others, a guaranteed income will be inadequate to sustain the costs of a catastrophic illness. An exceptionally high guaranteed minimum might result in almost universal insurance coverage at a fairly high level. Supporters of free market allocation do not, however, press for a very high minimum for at least two reasons. They fear its effects on incentives, and they cannot justify a high guaranteed income without admitting that there are many expensive goods that are essential to all persons, and are not just mere consumer preferences.

The first reason for opposing an exceptionally high minimum is probably a good one. A principle approaching equality of income and wealth is likely to have serious disincentive effects on productive work and investment. There are also better reasons for treating health care as a special good, a good that society has an obligation to provide equally to all its members, than there are for equally distributing most consumer goods.

A significant step beyond the pure free market principle is a position that preserves the role of the market in allocating different "packages" of health care according to consumer preferences, but concedes a role for government in supplying every adult with a "voucher" of a certain monetary value redeemable exclusively for health care goods and services. Proponents of health vouchers must assume that there is something special about health care to justify government in taxing its citizens to provide universally for these goods, and not all others. But if health care is a more important good, because it preserves life and expands opportunity, then what is the rationale for effectively limiting the demand a sick but poor person can make upon the health care system? Why should access to health care be dependent upon income or wealth at all?

Opponents of equal access generally imply that more than minimal access will unjustly curtail the freedom of citizens as taxpayers, as consumers, and as providers of health care. Let us consider separately the arguments with regard to the many citizens who are taxpayers and consumers, and the few citizens who are providers of health care.

The Charge of Paternalism

Charles Fried has argued that equal access to health care is a particularly intrusive form of paternalism toward citizens. He claims further that "apart form a rather general commitment to equality and, indeed, to state control of the allocation and distribution of resources, to insist on the right to health care, where that right means a right to equal access, is an anomaly. For as long as our society considers that inequalities of wealth and income are morally acceptable, . . . it is anomalous to carve out a sector like health care and say that *there* equality must reign."

Would an equal access system necessarily be intrusive or paternalistic in its operation? A national health care system simply cannot be said to take away the income entitlement of citizens, since citizens are not entitled to their gross incomes. We can determine our income entitlements only after we deduct from our gross income the amount we owe the state to support the rights of others. To the extent that the rationale of an equal access principle is redistributive, those individuals who otherwise could not afford certain health care services will experience an expansion of their freedom (if we assume an adequate level of social provision). Of course, part of the justification of a national health care system is that it would also guarantee health care coverage to people who could afford adequate health care but who would not be prudent enough to save or to invest in insurance. Even if we accept the common definition of paternalistic actions as those that restrict an individual's liberty so as to further his or her interest, we still have to assess the assertion that this (partial) rationale for an equal access system entails a restriction of individual liberty. Unlike a law banning the sale of cigarettes or forcing people to wear seat belts, the institution of a national health care system forces no one to use it. If a majority of citizens decide that they want to be taxed in order to ensure health care for themselves, the resulting legislation could not be considered paternalistic: "Legislation requiring contributions to some cooperative scheme (such as medical care) . . . is not necessarily paternalistic, so long as its purpose is to give effect to the desires of a democratic majority, rather than simply to coerce a minority who do not want the benefits of the legislation." It is significant in this regard that for the past twenty years the Michigan survey of registered voters has found a consistent and solid majority supporting government measures designed to ensure universal access to medical care.

The charge of paternalism levied against an equal access system is therefore dubious because it is extremely difficult, if not impossible, to isolate the self-protectionist rationale from the redistributive and the democratic rationales. Those who object to a national health care system on the grounds that it is coercing some people for their own good forget that such a system still could be justified as a means to avoid the threat to a one-class system that exempting the rich would create. To condemn such a system as paternalistic would commit us to criticizing all legislation in which a democratic majority decides to protect itself against the wishes of a minority when exemption from the resulting policy would undermine it. Other critics wrongly assume that people have an entitlement to the case equivalent of the medical care to which society grants them a right. People do not have such an entitlement because taxpayers have a right to demand that their tax dollars are spent to satisfy health needs, not to buy luxuries. Indeed, our duty to pay taxes is dependent upon the fact that certain needs of other people must be given priority over our own desires for more commodious living.

Other Restrictions

Nonetheless, two restrictions upon consumer freedom are entailed in an equal access system. One is the restriction imposed by the taxation necessary to provide all citizens, but especially the poorest, with access to health care goods. This restriction does not raise unique or particularly troublesome moral problems so long as one believes that the freedom to retain one's gross income is not an absolute right and that the resulting redistribution of income to the health care sector increases the life chances and thereby the effective freedom of many citizens.

But there is a second restriction of consumer market freedom sanctioned by the equal access principle: the limitation upon freedom to buy health care goods above the level publicly provided. Aside from reasserting the primary values of equality, there is at least one plausible argument for such a restriction. Without restricting the free market in extra health care goods, a society risks having its best medical practitioners drained into the private market sector, thereby decreasing the quality of medical care received by the majority of citizens confined to the publicly funded sector. The lower the level of public provision of health care and the less elastic the supply of physicians, the more problematic (from the perspective of the values underlying equal access) will be an additional market sector in health care.

Without an additional market sector, would the freedom of physicians and other providers to practice wherever and for whomever they choose be unduly restricted? The extent of such restrictions will also vary with the level of public provision and with the diversity of the health care system. Public funds already are crucial to providing many physicians with basic income (through Medicare and Medicaid fees), research opportunities through the National Institutes of Health (NIH), and . . . with hospitals and other institutions in which to practice (through the provisions of the Hill-Burton act). In place of the time and resources now directed to privately purchased add-ons, an equal access system would redirect providers toward meeting previously unserved needs. These types of redirections of supply and redistributions of demand are commonly accepted in other professions that are oriented toward satisfying an important public interest. The legal and teaching professions are analogous in this regard. The equal access principle, strictly interpreted, however, adds another restriction, a limitation upon private practice that supplies health care goods not equally accessible to the entire population of relevantly needy persons. This restriction upon the freedom of providers does not have an analogue in the present practice of law or of education, although the arguments for equal access to the goods of these professions might be similar. And so, one's assessment of the strength of the case for such a restriction is likely to have implications beyond the health care system.

It is hard to see why one ought to prevent people, rich or poor, from spending money upon health care goods while permitting them to spend money on consumer goods that are clearly not essential, and perhaps even detrimental to health. One reason might be the possible systemic effect, mentioned above, that such additional expenditures would deprive the less advantaged of the best physicians. The freedom of providers as well as consumers would have to be restricted in order to curtail this effect. But beyond this empirically contingent argument for restricting any market in health care goods that are not equally accessible to all, the strict limitations upon market freedom in "extra" health care goods are hard to accept if one believes that medical services are at least as worthy items of expense as other consumer goods. One could argue that physicians ought to be free to meet the demand for additional medical goods, especially when that demand is a substitute for demand for less important goods.

This criticism illuminates a more general problem of attempting to equalize access to any good in an otherwise inegalitarian society. The more unequal the distribution of income and wealth within our society, the more likely that the freedom of consumers and providers to buy and sell health care outside the publicly funded sector will result in inequalities that cannot properly be regarded merely as the product of differences in consumer preferences. Therefore, in an inegalitarian society, we must live with a moral tension between granting providers the freedom to leave the publicly funded sector and achieving more equality in the satisfaction of health care needs.

A principle of equal access to health care applied within an otherwise egalitarian society might give little or no reason to restrict the freedom of providers or consumers. One argument often voiced against a publicly funded system that permits a marginal free-market sector is that the government is a less efficient provider of goods than are private parties. But the equal access principle does not require that the government directly provide medical services through, for example, a national health service. Government need only be a regulator of the use and distribution of essential health-care goods and services. This is a role that most people concede to government for many other purposes deemed essential to the welfare of all individuals.

Government regulation may, of course, be more expensive and hence less efficient than government provision of health care services of similar extent and quality. The tradeoff here would be between the additional market choice facilitated by government regulation of private providers and the decreased public cost of government provision. Despite utilitarian claims to the contrary, no simple moral calculus exists that would enable an impartial spectator to determine where the balance of advantage lies. Philosophers ought to cede to a fairly constituted democratic majority the right to decide this issue. What constitutes a fair process of democratic decision-making is an important question of procedural justice that lies beyond the scope of this paper.

Liability for Voluntary Risks?

Another important criticism of the equal access principle cuts across advocacy of the free market and government regulation of health care. Supporters of both views might consistently ask whether it is fair to provide the same level of access for all people, including those who voluntarily adopt bad health habits, and who quite knowingly and willingly take greater-than-average risks with their lives and health. Even if it might be unjust not to provide health care for those people once the need arises, why would it not be fair to force those who choose to drink, smoke, rock climb, and skydive also to bear a greater burden of their ensuing medical costs than that borne by people who deliberately avoid these risky pursuits? An equal access principle seems to neglect the distinction between voluntary and nonvoluntary health risks in its eagerness to ensure that all people have an equal opportunity to receive appropriate health care.

Gerald Dworkin extensively and convincingly argues that it would not be unfair to force individuals to be financially liable for voluntarily undertaken health risks, but only under certain conditional assumptions. These include our ability 1) to determine the relative causal role of voluntary versus nonvoluntary factors in the genesis of illness; 2) to differentiate between purely voluntary behavior and what is nonvoluntary or compulsive; and 3) to distinguish between genetic and nongenetic predispositions to illness. For example, to satisfy the first condition one would have to determine the relative causal role of smoking and environmental pollution in the genesis of lung cancer; to fulfill the second, one must know when smoking (or drinking or obesity) is voluntary and when it is compulsive behavior; and to satisfy the third condition, one must distinguish among those who smoke and get cancer, and those who smoke and do not. In addition, so long as there are no good institutional mechanisms for monitoring certain risky activities or for differentiating between moderate and immoderate users of unhealthy substances, qualifying the equal access principle to take account of voluntary health risks is likely to create more unfairness rather than less. Finally, given great inequalities in income distribution, the poor will be less able to bear the consequences of their risky behavior than will the rich, creating a situation of unfairness at least as serious as the unfairness of equally distributing the burdens of health care costs between those who voluntarily impose risks upon themselves and those who do not. With respect to the health hazards of overeating and obesity, for example, the rich have recourse to expensive programs of weight control unavailable to the poor. Since we have such scanty knowledge of situations when sickness can be attributable to voluntary health risks, criticisms of the equal access principle from this perspective have more weight in principle than they do in practice.

Equal Access to All Health Goods

All criticisms considered so far are directed at the equal access principle from a perspective suggesting that government involvement and public funding of health care would be too great and the role of the market too small in an equal access system. Now let us consider a powerful criticism of the principle for including too little, rather than too much, in the public sector. The criticism can be posed in the form of a challenge: if one crucial reason for supporting a principle of equal access is that health goods are much more essential than many other goods because they provide a basis for equalizing opportunity and relieving substantial pain, then why not require a government to provide equal access to *all* those health goods that would move a society further in the direction of equalizing opportunity and relieving pain for the physically and mentally ill? Without pretending that our society could ever arrive at a condition of absolute equality of health (or therefore strict equality of opportunity), proponents of this principle could still argue that we should move as far as possible in that direction.

In a society in which no tradeoffs had to be made between health care and other goods, equal access to *all* health goods might be the most acceptable principle of equity in health care. Of course, we do not live in such a society. Given the advanced state of our medical and health care technology, and the prevalence of chronic degenerative diseases and mental disorders in our population, a requirement that society provide access to every known health care good would place an enormous drain upon social resources.

Costliness per se is not the main issue. The problem with the principle of equal access to all health goods is that it demands an absolute tradeoff between satisfaction of health care needs and other needs and desires. The simplest argument against this principle is that other needs, such as education, police protection, and legal aid, will be sacrificed to health care, if the principle is enforced. But this argument is too simple. A proponent of equal access to all health goods could consistently establish some priority principle among these goods, all of which satisfy needs derived in large part from a principle of equal opportunity. The weightier counterargument is that, above some less-than-maximum level in the provision of opportunity goods, it seems reasonable for people to value what, for want of a better term, one might call "quality of life" goods: cultural, recreational, noninstrumental educational goods, and even consumer amenities. A society that maximized the satisfaction of needs before it even began to provide access to "quality of life" goods would be a dismal society indeed. Most people do not want to devote their entire lives to being maximally secure and healthy. Why, then, should a society devote all of its resources to satisfying human *needs?*

Democracy and Equal Access

We need to find some principle or procedure by which to draw a line at an appropriate level of access to health care short of what is socially and techno-logically possible, but greater than what an unconstrained market would afford to most people, particularly to the least advantaged. I suspect that no philosoph-ical argument can provide us with a cogent principle by which we can draw a line within the enormous group of goods that can improve health or extend the life prospects of individuals.

This problem of determining a proper level of guaranteed social satisfaction of need is not unique to health care. Something similar can be said about police protection or education in our society. Philosophers can provide reasons why police protection and education are rightly considered basic collective needs and why they should be given priority over individual consumer preferences. But no plausible philosophical principle can tell us what level of police protec-tion or how much education a society ought to provide on an egalitarian basis.

The principle of equal access to health care establishes a criterion of distribu-tion for whatever level of health care a society provides for any of is members. And further philosophical argument might establish some criteria by which to judge when the publicly funded level of health care was so low as to be unfair to the least advantaged, or so high as to create undue restrictions upon the ability of most people to live interesting and fulfilling lives. The remaining question of establishing a precise level of priorities among health care and other goods (at the "margin") is appropriately left to democratic decision-making. The advantage of the democratic process in determining the precise level of health care provision is that citizens have an equal and collective voice in deter-mining a decision that, according to the equal access principle, ought to be mutually binding. Citizens not only reap the benefits; they also share the bur-dens of the decision to expand or limit access to health care.

There is yet another advantage to this procedural method of establishing a fair level of health care provision. If the democratic decision will be binding upon all citizens, as the equal access principle assumes it must be, then one might expect the most advantaged citizens to exercise more political pressure to increase access to health care and hence increase the opportunity of the least advantaged above the level that they could afford in a free market system, or in a system where the rich were not included within the publicly funded health care sector. One finds some evidence to support this hypothesis in comparing the relative immunity from budget cutbacks of the program under universal entitlement of Medicare compared with the income-related Medicaid program. Of course, if costliness to the taxpayer is one's only concern, this added political pressure for health care expenditures is a liability rather than a strength of a one-class system. But from the perspective of equal access, the cost of a two-class system, one privately and one publicly funded, is an inequitable distribution of quantity and quality of care according to wealth, not need. The added nonproductive costs required merely to keep the two classes apart are seldom taken into account. And from the perspective of those supporters of an equal access principle who also want to increase the total level of health care provision, the two-class system threatens to work in the opposite direction, siphoning off the pressure of citizens who have a disproportionate share of political influence. A democratic decision, the results of which are constrained by the principle of equal access, will give a relatively accurate reading of what most people believe to be an adequate level of health care protection. The major disadvantage of the equal access constraint is that the decision of the majority or its representatives binds everyone, even those people who want more than the socially mandated level of health care.

Given the great economic inequalities of our society, it is politically impossible for advocates of equal access to fulfill their task. No democratic legislator could possibly succeed in winning support for a proposal that restricted market freedom as extensively as a strict interpretation of the equal access principle requires. And it probably would be a mistake to insist upon strict philosophical standards: one thereby risks throwing the possibility of greater access to health care for the poor out with the insistence upon curtailing access for the rich.

CONCLUSION

I began by arguing that a principle of equal access to health care was at best an ideal toward which our society might strive. I shall end by qualifying that statement. A sufficiently high level of public provision of health care for all citizens and a sufficiently elastic supply of health care would significantly reduce the threat to universal provision of quality health care of a private market in extra health care goods, just as a very high level of police protection and education reduces the inequalities of opportunity resulting from purchase of private bodyguards or of private school education by the rich.

In the best of all imaginable worlds of egalitarian justice, the equal access principle would be sufficiently supported by other egalitarian social and economic institutions that a market in health care would complement rather than undercut the goals of equal respect and opportunity. But philosophers ought to resist basing their political recommendations solely upon a model of the best of all imaginable worlds.

Market Meditopia: A Glimpse at American Health Care in 2005

LARRY R. CHURCHILL

> *Images of the future are usually only caricatures of the present.*
> *Perhaps this picture of the future of medical care will also prove*
> *to be a caricature. Whether it does depends on choices that Amer-*
> *icans have still to make.*
>
> —Paul Starr
> *The Social Transformation*
> *of American Medicine*

Market forces, unleashed to work their magic after the demise of federal health reform in 1994, continue to dominate the organization and financing of health care. While the number of managed care organizations proliferated in the late 1990s, the smaller and less well-funded companies found it difficult to compete. Many smaller insurance companies sold their health care holdings and returned to their traditional life, fire, and auto insurance products. Shortly after the turn of the century, a handful of very large health care corporations remained and had captured most of the market. These organizations provided comprehensive and integrated health services products, from birthing centers to hospice care.

The key to the success of these corporate winners, in addition to their size, was their skill in risk selection, that is, their ability to avoid persons with complicated and expensive illnesses. Since 30 percent of the population uses more than 90 percent of all health services in any given year, the successful health care corporations succeeded by being sure they had as few of that heavy-utilizing 30 percent as possible.

Early in the twenty-first century, testing for genetic markers for some of the most devastating and costly diseases became sufficiently reliable to be widely used, although effective therapies for most of these diseases were not yet available. Even though the information from genetic tests remains officially confidential, insurers often found a means of access to some of this information, and this enhanced the already quite sophisticated methods by which actuaries predicted which groups would be "undesirable" from a cost perspective. Since genetic markers for diseases are used to exclude persons or treatments under "preexisting condition" clauses, those excluded in this new way became known

From *The Hastings Center Report,* 27 (January, February 1997), 5–6. Copyright ©The Hastings Center. Reproduced by permission of The Hastings Center and the author.

as GEPPEs (genetically predisposed persons). GEPPEs are currently lobbying for recognition and a redress of their grievances under the Americans with Disabilities Act.

The rate of increase in the number of uninsured—roughly one million per year—has continued unabated since 1995, mainly because of small employers dropping health insurance coverage for their employees. Also, in 1998 Medicaid funding for the uninsured was sharply curtailed as the administration and standard-setting for the program was given over entirely to the states. While some states, such as New York and California, continued their programs using roughly the old federal model for benefits, other states, such as Texas and Florida, altered the priorities of their programs dramatically, moving the funding away from poor women and children and placing it in long-term nursing and custodial support for the elderly. An additional ten million persons lost their insurance coverage for health care between 1998 and 2003 because of these Medicaid changes.

The cumulative result was sixty million uninsured persons in the United States, roughly 24 percent of the population, in 2004.

While there have been sporadic movements toward major reform of the health care system, the lobbying power of corporate health care organizations in Washington has never been stronger. Reform movements, led largely by poor and lower middle-class citizens, with disproportionate representation of minorities and females, have had little effect. Corporations have sought to quell the occasional expressions of bad conscience over the exclusion of poor citizens through periodic gestures of medical philanthropy, sometimes on a grand scale. For example, as a grass roots movement for health reform seemed to be gaining steam in 2003, the number of "free" heart transplants for indigent patients rose dramatically, peaking during the fourth quarter. These "Christmas heart" recipients were prominently displayed as "poster patients" in several health care organizations' advertising campaigns about community service in December 2003. Still, most political observers attributed the loss of momentum for reform to the absence of an effective lobbying effort in Washington.

The most recent serious effort at reform occurred in conjunction with the 2004 presidential and congressional elections. At that time, the impetus for reform was fueled in part by the findings of a study done by the Institute of Medicine, and in part by a series in the *New York Times*. The Institute of Medicine study indicated that the health status of Americans had fallen further behind Europeans and Canadians in rates of cancer, coronary artery disease, stroke, infant mortality, and several other measures. Although the reform movement didn't come close to succeeding, it scared the health care establishment enough to lobby Congress for new ways of reporting health statistics. Under the new system, the health indicators of the uninsured are deleted before any official international comparisons are made. This practice of segmenting health statistics was widely hailed as fairer, since it compares insured citizens of one country with insured citizens of another, without the confounding effects of including the medically indigent.

The *New York Times* series appeared in September 2004 and dramatized the plight of Herbert and Jane Spencer. Herbert, 55 and a computer analyst, was made redundant in the "right-sizing and consolidation" of the small firm for which he worked when it was purchased in December 2003. While he did receive some severance benefits, they did not include health insurance. The new year proved to be a disastrous one for the Spencers. Jane was diagnosed with breast cancer in January, requiring a series of surgical and radiation treatments. Herbert had increasing problems with depression, largely due to his wife's illness and his own inability to find employment. Then in May, as Jane was on the rebound from her treatments, she was injured in an automobile accident and spent two weeks in the hospital and several months in rehabilitation. Most of the *Times* series focused on Herbert's frustrating efforts in dealing with the bills for his wife's care, in the midst of being shunted from one health care provider to another in search of effective and affordable psychiatric help for himself. His frustration was underscored by a suicide attempt in late July. By August the Spencers' savings had been exhausted, and they sold their house to pay medical bills.

The *Times* series won a Pulitzer Prize and was later published as a paperback. It also brought the Spencers to the attention of community agencies, and some of the Spencers' problems were dealt with, at least temporarily. Yet the story of the Spencers—the story of impoverishment through medical bills—occupied the national consciousness for only a few weeks. By October the polls indicated that the Spencers had been all but forgotten and political candidates, sensing that this issue had run its course, shifted their campaign speeches away from health care reform issues.

Over the last ten years the consumer rights movement in health care has increased its momentum, largely because of the fears of patients that managed care would mean less quality for them and higher profits for business. Advocacy groups for particular patients, such as Alzheimer patients, AIDS patients, and cystic fibrosis patients, have been particularly vocal and effective in protecting the interests of their constituents. The overall impact of this intensified consumer rights advocacy on the uninsured, however, has been minimal at best. While consumer advocacy groups have been effective for their respective groups, they have not been interested in making common cause with the medically indigent more generally.

While a background concern about the high number of uninsured has persisted, one of the chief dampening factors for political action to correct this problem has been a widely held and deeply seated belief that those without health services are probably less deserving. Personal responsibility for health behaviors has been a constant theme of health educators, professionals, and public figures for several decades. While smoking, beef-eating, and excess alcohol consumption are tolerated among the insured, these practices are frequently cited as a reason for not including the uninsured in a program of care. One watershed event in this lack of sympathy was a speech by the Surgeon General at the turn of the millennium. Her speech linking "moral character" and "health behaviors" was intended to promote good health practices. The result, however, was to correlate personal responsibility and health status so closely that the (uninsured) sick are often seen as reaping the just deserts of their "profligate living."

Health care corporations have made several proposals to provide health services to the uninsured, seeing this large group as another source of business. However, since the uninsured typically are chronically ill, unemployed, or work for modest wages, few of them have sufficient funds to buy into the existing systems of care. Federal and state governments have to date been unwilling or unable to subsidize this care. The continuing high cost of the Medicare program—in spite of reforms to Medicare in 1997, 1999, and 2003—is usually cited as the chief reason for the federal government to stay out of the health care business. Any proposal to raise taxes to benefit the uninsured is considered a political death wish.

The impact of corporate capitalism on health care costs over the past decade has been mixed. Aggressively managed care, under corporate leadership, showed substantial cost reductions during the late 1990s. Careful selection of risks, along with increased co-payments and deductibles, helped to hold down the costs for buyers of services and provided handsome profits for corporations selling health care products. These cost reductions, however, turned out to be short-lived. Skills for rational technological assessment turned out to be less than those for risk selection. As new medical technologies came on line the popular demand for them grew, and the costs of health care began to rise again at a pace that equated cost escalations of the 1970s and 1980s. While the uninsured are using fewer health services than ever before, the services they do use are still provided in the most expensive venues, emergency rooms and intensive care units. For the fiscal year ending October 2005, costs are running at one and one-half times the general inflation rate and consume 21 percent of the gross domestic product.

The phrase "market meditopia" first appeared in an editorial in *The Economist* in the spring of 2005 and has gained wide currency as a shorthand description of the peculiar American proclivity for seeking utopian levels of health through unregulated marketing of medical services. While *The Economist* editorial used this phrase as an ironic indictment of U.S. health policy, American politicians have picked up the phrase as if it were a distinctive American virtue, or a sign of American genius in health policy. Governors in some southern states have begun to campaign for reelection on a platform to extend the reach of market forces even further by eliminating Medicaid completely. As one governor put it, "We have a duty to end the vicious cycle of medical dependence that has enslaved our fellow citizens and sapped their energy for individual health care responsibility." Last week the AMA endorsed market meditopia as essential to protect "the best health care system in the world."

Trust and Trustworthy Care in the Managed Care Era

BRADFORD H. GRAY

Sick people, the physician Eric Cassell observed, are "people who are forced to trust." Trust on the part of patients has long been viewed as fundamental to therapeutic relationships. Patients' willingness to accept medical advice and services has rested on trust in physicians' technical competence and adherence to a fiduciary ethic that held that the physician's responsibility was to put the patient's interests above self-interest. Ethical codes have long encouraged physicians to be trustworthy by discouraging exploitation of patients' vulnerability. Such ethical ideals have been enforced mainly through professional socialization and self-regulation, which are rooted in societal faith in the fiduciary ethic.

The development of third-party payment in fee-for-service medical care also involved trust—between payers and physicians. Payers were not present when services were rendered, and physicians' assessments of patients' needs triggered the flow of dollars from third-party payers to all types of providers. Payers had little choice but to trust those assessments until ways to monitor and assess the appropriateness of services emerged.

Managed care shifts much control over the flow of dollars and patients from physicians to large organizations that have strong economic goals and the power to influence patient care in pursuit of those goals. This combination of purpose and power is a major source of doubts about the trustworthiness of these organizations, particularly because they reduce the power of health professionals who profess adherence to the fiduciary ethic. Thus, even though managed care can reduce the amount of unnecessary and inappropriate care, critics can point to a variety of ways in which managed care might undermine trust, and trustworthiness, in medical care.

Is a decline in trustworthiness an inevitable aspect of managed care, or might new modes of trustworthiness supplant more traditional forms? In this paper I argue that trust in the fiduciary ethic was declining even before the rise of managed care, that patients' need for trustworthy care is undiminished, and that managed care can operate in ways that merit patients' trust. This trustworthiness may, paradoxically, have its basis in accountability structures that emphasize monitoring and auditing rather than trust in physician autonomy. An important question is whether, and under what circumstances, managed care might make care more trustworthy, not less. To answer that question, I evaluate four alternatives for enhancing the trustworthiness of managed care.

THE EROSION OF TRUST IN FEE-FOR-SERVICE CARE

Critics of managed care often evoke an idealized image of the past, but there is a long history of skepticism about the trustworthiness of doctors, especially under fee-for-service medicine. Early in this century George Bernard Shaw railed against surgeons: "[T]he more appalling the mutilation, the more the mutilator is paid." Voices also have been raised within the profession for more than a century about the pernicious effects of economic conflicts of interest on medicine's performance and public image.

For both patients and payers, trust in the competence and fiduciary ethic of physicians and health care institutions has been strained in recent decades by exploding health care costs, accompanied by much publicity about malpractice crises, fraud and abuse, inexplicable variations in patterns of care and high levels of inappropriate services, and an efflorescence of medical commercialism and conspicuous conflicts of interest. Payers and the attentive public came to understand that services received by patients can be a function of much more than their objective medical needs and that the choice of a physician or hospital can affect care and its outcomes. Professional self-regulatory mechanisms have been widely criticized for ineffectiveness regarding such matters.

Ironically, the fiduciary ethic, as sometimes interpreted by doctors, contributed to payers' desire for alternatives to trust, as when physicians viewed their obligations to patients as including the manipulation of third-party payers' rules to obtain payment for ineligible services. At one time this meant hospitalizing some patients unnecessarily so that services would be covered by their hospital insurance. More recently it has meant "gaming" utilization review systems and payment rules to obtain payment for services deemed by payers to be unnecessary, inappropriate, cosmetic, or experimental. In such ways the fiduciary ethic, thought essential to trust in the doctor/patient relationship, became a source of distrust in the doctor/payer relationship.

Efforts to find alternatives to dependence on trust have developed in recent decades. Patients now routinely seek second opinions, obtain services from "alternative" practitioners, and consume journalistic lists of "the best" physicians and hospitals. More fundamental changes have occurred among purchasers of care, with the embrace of managed care. Cost control is key to the economic success of managed care organizations. Available tools include gatekeepers, practice guidelines and utilization review, and payment methods that discourage the provision of additional services. Health maintenance organizations (HMOs) and preferred provider organizations (PPOs) also can use data on the performance of physicians and other providers to form and manage their networks.

CONTINUING NEED TO PROTECT PATIENTS' INTERESTS

Managed care is a response of purchasers to problems in the doctor/patient/payer nexus. Managed care does not, however, eliminate patients' vulnerability or their need for trustworthy care. An industry of outcomes research, practice guidelines, and utilization review has developed to address the competency aspect of trustworthiness, but the fiduciary aspect has received much less organized attention.

It is apparent, however, that high ethical standards are essential to protecting patients' interests, even in (or perhaps especially in) the era of managed care. For example, the successful operation of utilization management programs relies heavily on physicians' willingness to speak for the patient's interests when threatened by an unsound review decision. A need also exists for adherence to patients' interests within HMOs that use any of the available cost management tools. For example, if physicians were simply to follow their incentives as gatekeepers in individual practice associations (IPAs), major problems would ensue for patients. An orientation toward serving patients' interests among the medical policymakers within managed care organizations also may help to assure that organizations' practice guidelines, medical standards, and review procedures appropriately emphasize patients' needs.

The growth of managed care has itself added sources of doubt regarding the physician's fiduciary ethic as a guardian of the patient's best interests. Managed care has reduced physicians' autonomy in ways that have been widely decried in the profession. Critics charge that the fiduciary ethic is undermined by some managed care methods. They point to conflicts of interest introduced by some compensation arrangements, situations that divide physicians' loyalties, intrusions of external parties into the doctor/patient relationship, and implementation of rules that limit the alternatives that doctors can offer patients.

Physicians' power also has been reduced by their growing dependence on relationships with HMOs and PPOs for a flow of patients, whereas they once depended primarily on satisfactory relationships with existing patients or colleagues. This client or colleague dependency, as Eliot Freidson termed it, may not always have influenced physicians in ways that served patients' best interests, but organization dependency has introduced a powerful new influence into medical care: pressure for physicians to practice in ways that satisfy organizations and their economic interests.

In light of patients' vulnerability, more attention is warranted to the fit between managed care and the fiduciary aspect of medical professionalism. How might continued viability of the fiduciary ethic be assured when the health care system is becoming increasingly price-competitive and dominated by large organizations that have strong economic interests? Sole reliance on the ethical standards of individual physicians seems insufficient, not only because of the loss of confidence in the strength and consistency of such standards within the profession but also because of disparities in power between individual physicians and managed care organizations.

POTENTIAL SOURCES OF TRUST IN MANAGED CARE

Among the ways that the fiduciary ethic might be encouraged in managed care are (1) developing effective ethical standards in the managed care industry, (2) populating the field with mission-oriented nonprofit organizations, (3) increasing physician control within managed care organizations, and (4) using market-oriented solutions involving monitoring, measuring, and public disclosure of the performance of managed care plans.

Ethical Standards

Codes of ethics and statements of ethical ideals are commonplace among professional associations in health care. Their manifest purpose is to provide ethical guidance to members of the profession, although it is uncertain how much and how uniformly behavior is affected. A second purpose is to assure outsiders (potential patients, purchasers, and regulators) that the profession stands for high ethical principles.

The American Medical Association (AMA) has had a code of ethics for 150 years, and its Council on Ethical and Judicial Affairs regularly publishes opinions on ethical issues. Its guidelines on conflicts of interest reflect the fiduciary ethic, holding that "under no circumstances may physicians place their own financial interests above the welfare of their patients" and that "the primary objective of the medical profession is to render service to humanity."

Such an ethical orientation, which is characteristic of professional associations, has not been adopted by organizational providers of health care or their trade associations. Perhaps the closest version is in the American Hospital Association's (AHA's) Patient's Bill of Rights, which dates from the early 1970s. The "rights" imply that hospitals are responsible for treating patients and their privacy respectfully, providing information about treatment, and allowing patients to refuse recommended treatment. The closest the Bill of Rights comes to the fiduciary ethic is in its carefully qualified right to expect a hospital, "within its capacity and policies," to make a "reasonable response" to a patient's request for "appropriate and medically indicated care and services."

Within the managed care industry, statements about ethical responsibilities of providers have been slow to develop and are framed in terms of patients' rights rather than caregivers' obligations. Economic conflicts of interest are not addressed or even acknowledged. Moreover, the language frequently has a contractual flavor and is stated in reciprocal terms, with patients' responsibilities enumerated along with their rights. Of course, since plans are subject to state insurance regulation or federal regulation under the Employee Retirement Income Security Act (ERISA) (or both), their obligations to enrollees are indeed contractual: An open-ended obligation such as the fiduciary ethic is alien to the legalistic relationship between insurers and the insured, in which specificity, precedent, and equity are key considerations.

Changes are occurring regarding managed care organizations' acknowledgment of ethical issues. As recently as late 1994 I was told by the Group Health Association of America (GHAA), the American Managed Care and Review Association (AMCRA), and the American Association of Preferred Provider Organizations (AAPPO) that they had no standards of ethics for member organizations. I received similar responses from such leading nonprofit managed care organizations as Kaiser Permanente, Harvard Community Health Plan, and The HMO Group. Perhaps the youth, rapid evolution, fragmentation, or competitiveness of the managed care industry explains this inattention to ethical ideals. Or perhaps industry leaders and the large purchasers with whom they deal are skeptical about voluntary ethical standards. Or perhaps the industry's priorities have been elsewhere, such as in the development of data systems and other management tools that might protect the interests of patients more effectively than would ethical standards alone.

LATEST DEVELOPMENTS Demand is growing for ethical standards in managed care, with developments on several fronts. In early 1995 the National Health Council (NHC), an association of disease-oriented organizations, not managed care organizations, adopted a set of principles for managed care that were stated in terms of patients' rights and responsibilities. Notably, the number of requests for the document was much greater than anticipated by the NHC, which had to go back to press after 10,000 copies were distributed.

The "Accreditation Standards for Managed Care" that were implemented in 1995 by the National Committee for Quality Assurance (NCQA) cover some pertinent topics, including patients' rights and grievance procedures. To meet accreditation requirements, health plans must adopt their own statement of members' rights and responsibilities that cover matters specified by the NCQA, including access to information, grievance procedures, confidentiality, and so forth. The language is contractual in nature (for example, specifying matters about which enrollees are entitled to information) and contains none of the "best interest of the patient" language that characterizes the fiduciary ethic. . . .

In sum, ethical standards are not well established in the managed care industry and devote little or no attention to the problems addressed by the fiduciary ethic, particularly the conflict-of-interest problem and its resolution in favor of the patient. Moreover, both the limited credibility of associational philosophies and industry accreditation standards as predictors of behavior and the contractual "rights and responsibilities" formulations of the standards that exist suggest that ethical codes within the managed care industry are not a replacement for a fiduciary ethic implemented by physicians with patient care responsibility. Nor are they so intended. Even so, the increasing organizational attention in the managed care field to the problems for which medicine's fiduciary ethic has been a response is a development worth following. . . .

Role of Nonprofits

If medical practice has become organization-dependent, might the ownership form of the organization on which physicians are dependent make a difference? Compatibility between the medical profession and nonprofit health care organizations has been noted in the past by a number of observers. Some have seen it negatively, such as the economists in the 1970s who attributed the predominance of nonprofit hospitals in this country to the power of physicians and the ease with which they could manipulate a nonprofit institution to serve their ends, which were assumed to be economic. However, the link can be viewed more favorably because of an affinity of purposes and moderation of the inevitable tensions between professional prerogatives and organizational requirements. This may seem naïve to persons who are familiar with the conflicts that often typify relationships between medical staffs and hospital administrations. But, at least in ideals, nonprofit health care institutions, like members of the medical profession, are expected to be animated by values other than profit or self-interest.

The nonprofit organizational form and the medical profession's normative emphasis on ethical behavior may serve similar purposes: to facilitate trust and discourage exploitation of vulnerable patients. I have already discussed this with regard to the medical profession, but some parallels with the nonprofit form are worth noting.

Seeking to explain why organizations in certain fields tend to be nonprofit, the legal scholar Henry Hansmann has suggested that the nonprofit organization helps to solve problems of distrust that arise in fields in which purchasers lack the information needed to monitor or evaluate the services provided by sellers. Such

purchasers may prefer to deal with nonprofit organizations since they are prohibited from distributing profits and, therefore, have less incentive to exploit their
informational advantages vis-à-vis purchasers. Nonprofits thus may play a trust-
enhancing role in economic relationships in which informational asymmetries are
present. Interestingly, Hansmann questioned the need for the nonprofit form in
health care because the interests of vulnerable patients are protected by physicians
who adhere to the fiduciary ethic. The possibility that health care organizations
could undermine the physician's fiduciary ethic was not considered.

AFFINITY WITH PROFESSIONAL IDEALS The claim of an affinity between medical
professionalism and the nonprofit form has plausibility but requires qualification. First, the empirical side of the claim is not well documented. Research a
decade ago found some indications that for-profit hospitals were actually more
responsive to physicians than were nonprofits, as measured by physicians' presence on boards and their reports of administrative responsiveness. However,
this was in the era before diagnosis-related groups (DRGs), when the incentives
of profit-oriented hospitals and physicians who believed that "more is better"
were aligned.

Other research provides some support for the hypothesized compatibility between the nonprofit form and professional ideals. For-profit hospitals have been
more likely than nonprofit hospitals to pressure physicians to act in ways that
served the hospital's economic interests—in this case, not to admit Medicaid
patients. The incentive systems used by for-profit HMOs have greater influence
on physicians than do the incentives of nonprofit HMOs, although the reasons
are not wholly clear. There also is some evidence that for-profit HMOs tend
to spend less of the premium dollar on medical care than do nonprofits. The
values implied by this would presumably be consistent with the values of those
who provide patient care. For-profit health plans have headed the list of plans
with high levels of complaints and disenrollments among Medicare enrollees,
whereas the lowest levels on both measures have been in nonprofits.

This evidence is hardly dispositive of the question of whether there is an
affinity between medical professionalism and the nonprofit form, and much
more research is needed on ownership forms and physicians' roles in managed
care.

SHRINKING SHARE OF HMO MARKET The second problematic aspect of the suggestion that the nonprofit form in managed care might be more trustworthy in a
fiduciary sense is that as managed care enrollment has grown over the past fifteen
years, the largely nonprofit field has been transformed: More than two-thirds of
plans are now for-profit, and a majority of enrollees are in for-profit plans. About a
third of nonprofit HMOs converted to for-profit status over the past fifteen years.

(Notably, the current surge of interest in managed care reform is commonly framed in terms of concern about HMOs' profit-oriented behavior.)

Despite their shrinking share of the HMO market, nonprofits provide valuable leadership activities and lessons in organizational performance. For example, of twenty-one HMOs designated as "exceptional quality" by GTE in its *Health Care Consumer Guide* for employees, twenty were nonprofits, as were sixteen of the twenty-one HMOs listed on *U.S. News and World Report's* "Honor Roll" of HMOs with high standards for preventive care. The continued viability of the nonprofit form in managed care merits public policy concern.

POLICY POSSIBILITIES The prevalence of different forms of ownership in managed care has been largely due to governmental policies in the past. Government—as purchaser, regulator, and funder—could do much to encourage the continued availability of nonprofit alternatives in the field. For example, Medicaid managed care has stimulated many nonprofit health centers and hospitals that traditionally have served the poor to move into the world of capitated medical care; they may need both technical assistance and capital if they are to survive. On the regulatory front, flexibility is needed in rules about tax exemptions, speed is needed in response to exemption requests, and greater skepticism might be warranted in response to requests for nonprofit conversions to for-profit status. (On the other hand, it is important that tax exemptions have a meaningful basis, which suggests greater attention to issues of governance and community benefit in managed care.) Finally, insofar as access to capital is driving decisions of existing nonprofits to convert or causing new HMOs to be formed as for-profits rather than nonprofits, government could act to enhance nonprofit plans' access to capital.

Physician Influence Within Managed Care

The oft-stated concern that managed care replaces a fiduciary ethic with an incompatible business ethic implies that managed care might be more trustworthy if the influence of physicians within managed care organizations were enhanced. Physician influence can include complete or shared ownership of a firm, complete or shared ownership of a physician group that contracts with managed care organizations, or a strong voice within managed care organizations.

Intuitions differ regarding whether physician control may enhance managed care organizations' commitment to the fiduciary ethic, and evidence is now sparse. There is some evidence that physicians' influence within managed care organizations may increase, not decrease, the organization's willingness to exert pressure on individual physicians. Thus, my research with Mark Schlesinger and Krista Perreira found that utilization review organizations with high levels of physician control were particularly willing to interfere with practicing physicians' autonomy. This could be compatible with the fiduciary ethic if it enhances appropriateness and quality of services. We also found that review organizations in which physicians had comparatively great influence were more likely to act in an agency capacity toward patients, as indicated by their organization's willingness to intervene (with the patient, hospital, or state authorities) in instances in which problematic care came to light.

Another interesting clue comes from James Robinson and Lawrence Casalino's study of six large medical groups in California that were paid by capitation. These physician-controlled groups had 40 percent lower hospital utilization rates than those in commercial HMOs in California and about half of the national HMO rates for both Medicare and commercial plans. Clearly, simplistic assumptions that physician control of managed care will translate into more extensive services are not correct. How the low rates of hospital use comport with the fiduciary ethic is not clear.

The hypothesis that the fiduciary ethic of the medical profession can be transmitted to managed care organizations via physician control of such organizations is intriguing. It suggests a means for sensitively separating the beneficial and dubious aspects of practitioner autonomy from each other, discouraging nonrational or economically motivated practices while providing the flexibility needed to respond to patients' individual needs. The question is, Does it work that way?

Role of Purchasers and Market Forces

Large purchasers have become very interested in measuring the performance of health plans. Private purchasers took the lead, but interest is growing among governmental purchasers. Important developments include the creation and adoption within the managed care industry not only of accreditation standards and mechanisms but also of standards regarding data that plans should collect and report about services to enrollees. The Health Plan Employer Data and Information Set (HEDIS) is rapidly gaining acceptance as a standardized means for collecting and reporting data on health plan performance.

Increasingly, employers are seeking performance information from HMOs, collecting plan-specific satisfaction data from enrollees, and making this information available to employees. In some instances, the information is published, as with the 1994 and 1995 data on federal employees' satisfaction with more than 200 HMOs in the Federal Employees Health Benefits Program (FEHBP). In other instances, the information is made available to beneficiaries for their use in choosing a health plan. For example, the information given to Xerox employees about the plans from which they may choose includes coverage and costs, whether the plan is accredited by the NCQA, the percentage of primary care physicians who are board-certified, the average waiting time for urgent and emergency care, member satisfaction and the percentage of enrollees who would recommend the plan to family and friends, immunization rates for two-year-olds, the percentage of adults ages forty to sixty-four who have had a cholesterol test in the past five years, the percentage of women ages fifty-two to sixty-four who have had a mammogram in the past two years, the percentage of women ages twenty-one to sixty-four who have had a Pap test in the past three years, and hospital admission rates for asthma patients ages two to nineteen.

Much better monitoring of physician and hospital performance exists in many managed care organizations than ever existed in the traditional fee-for-service system. Anecdotes suggest that when employees are given such information about alternative plans, they tend to move toward efficient, high-quality plans and that HMOs strive to improve performance. . . .

CONCLUSION

Managed care has become a lightning rod for ethical concern. Yet managed care also offers solutions of a sort to ethical problems that existed in the world of unmanaged fee-for-service medicine. Some aspects of managed care—strongly profit oriented plans and powerful physician incentives—seem to exacerbate concerns about ethics and trustworthiness. Greater ethical sensitivity in the managed care industry, preservation or enhancement of a nonprofit sector within the industry, appropriate involvement of physicians, and improvement of monitoring and reporting on the performance of managed care plans might mitigate such concerns.

A system based on trust in the competence and fiduciary ethic of individual physicians is being replaced by a system based on alternatives to trust. Hopes about trustworthiness of physicians' patient care decisions are increasingly being supplemented by evidence. An ideal system would reward physicians who provide excellent care and have high ethical standards. This may be a direction in which managed care is moving, although it is difficult to tell. For the foreseeable future, the new methods of accountability should be viewed as supplements, not alternatives, to trustworthy physicians who adhere to the fiduciary ethic.

The ethical obligations of physicians are more clearly defined than are the obligations of institutions. Building a strong, patient-centered ethic in organizations is one of the great challenges facing managed care. Perhaps the most appropriate starting point is to build institutional settings that allow the fiduciary ethic of health professionals to exist and flourish.

National Health Care Reform Minus Public Health: A Formula for Failure

PHYLLIS FREEMAN AND ANTHONY ROBBINS

INTRODUCTION

Because renewed energy for health care reform springs from perceptions of risk that center more on economic than on physical vulnerabilities, so too do the remedies. Detailed attention from dozens of consultants to cost containment and to financing universal access to medical services has obscured what should be a decisive distinction between proposals. Do they attend to improving health and reducing disease or only to paying for diagnosis and treatment for those already ill?

Proposals now under serious consideration by the Congress would guarantee Americans payment for doctor visits and hospital services. A great start! But none promises to integrate the medical care system with the public health structure and assure participation of medical care providers in those functions necessary to detect and respond early to health threats. If we accept the pervasive perception that universal access to medical services will address all important health needs, we will miss a magnificent chance to prevent disease—and to hold off unnecessary medical care expenditures. Moreover, if we do not get this right now, the door of political opportunity may not open for a second chance for many years.

Impending health care reform could take advantage of the extensive medical services system, at little additional cost, to accomplish many previously unattainable health goals for the nation, but nothing about the planning process or debate so far makes that outcome seem likely. Repeated references during the debate on health care reform to "access to prevention services" belie a failure to understand the difference between insuring personal health services and assuring public health gains. The distinction is a strategic one. Public health is grounded in the Constitutional authority to protect the health and safety of the entire population. In contrast, medical care is oriented to the needs of the indi-

From the *Journal of Public Health Policy,* 15 (1994), 261–282. Reprinted by permission of the publisher.

vidual. Medical services can be preventive, curative or palliative. Good medical care can have a favorable effect on public health even if the services were not offered as features of a population-based strategy. But our nation will never achieve optimal health from our enormous investments in the medical care system without explicitly integrating public health guidance and accountability into the reform of medical care management and finance. Medical care is an element of public health, but the sheer enormity of the medical care system means that it is seen as being separate.

Attention to public health authority has waned. Few professionals remaining in the states or in the Public Health Service can imagine how to marry the tremendous momentum for reform of the medical care industry to a public health strategy designed to achieve gains in public health. Yet each state needs to make use of the expanding federal role in health care reform and of the state's Constitutional police powers to regulate aspects of medical practice that would achieve health benefits for all. The federal health care reform law should make it possible.

Public health reaches far beyond the current popular notion of prevention, which focuses on individual lifestyle rather than on social, economic, and environmental hazards that few individuals can avoid without strong protective legislation and enforcement by the state. Chemical hazards in workplaces, polluted air and water in residential communities, contaminated food in supermarkets and restaurants, and spread of infectious diseases by people, animals and food all pose health risks that can be reduced more efficiently by public health interventions than by medical care. Even when costly medical services can diminish or cure the harm to individuals caused by environmental exposures, other deadly threats remain for which medical care is impotent regardless of how much the individual or society would be willing to spend. . . .

UNIVERSAL SICKNESS INSURANCE POSING AS COMPREHENSIVE HEALTH CARE REFORM

Why has the debate about health care reform neglected public health? Health insurance is a necessity for every American. It buys medical services and avoids personal financial disaster. The ultimate purpose of health care reform as currently debated in the United States is to pay for insurance against the costs of illness. This narrow focus on sickness insurance misses opportunities to improve health, yet it is perfectly tuned to the concerns of the public. . . .

Those who foot the bill for medical care—government, non-government insurers, employers, and citizens—are all engaged in efforts to reduce their financial responsibility and to shift the burden to others. Government tinkers with eligibility rules and benefit limitations for Medicaid to limit spending growth.

Under these pressures Oregon initiated rationing for Medicaid patients, limiting recipients to those medical services the state deemed most cost-effective. No similar limits have been placed on insurance plans for the more affluent. Insurance companies raise premiums, screen out applicants and limit coverage. This reduces workers' ability to change jobs when a "preexisting condition" may be grounds for exclusion from the new employer's group plan—if there is one. Employers in the squeeze are likely to increase each employee's contribution or to cut health benefits from the package. According to a 1991 *New York Times* poll, one-third of those with family incomes below $15,000, and more than one-half of those with incomes above $30,000, had been subjected to this practice within the previous year. . . .

No proposal before the Congress approaches reform from a public health perspective. Yet, if we fail to build into the reformed structure of medical services a way to guarantee those measures that can improve health and dampen the need for medical services, it will be a formula for failure. The costs of unnecessary disease will burden the medical care system, and the health of our people will improve far more slowly.

BEYOND INSURANCE: INCORPORATING BETTER HEALTH INTO REFORM

To achieve the full health potential of the one trillion dollars already spent in the health care sector we need to recognize additional ways to improve health, protect life and make effective use of our medical care resources.

The reformers started down one promising path when they anticipated incorporating in the benefit package a class of personal health services known to have positive impact on the health status of the population. Within this class there are two distinct categories: 1) medical services which are protective for the community as well as for the individual, such as immunizations or treatment for tuberculosis, and 2) those which tend to improve health when provided systematically to all at risk. Screening and treatment for high blood pressure or cancer of the cervix are examples. Reformers talk about reaching optimal coverage for these services through quality control mechanisms, such as "report cards." Today our coverage for pap smears and high blood pressure detection is rarely complete, even in managed care settings. Under health care reform, if the quality control approach works, we are likely to see improved preventive services. But will we see successful control of tuberculosis, toxic exposures, and other public health threats?

In 1983, the Centers for Disease Control was planning a campaign to eliminate tuberculosis. Effective antibiotics were available to render each TB patient noninfectious. All that was needed was a systematic way to screen, treat and monitor several thousand people. Yet without organized and accountable medical services, state tuberculosis programs in health departments had no way to insist that providers of personal health services help. Ten years later the situation is far more grave. Resistant TB organisms are increasingly common, rendering antibiotics ineffective, and the national objective has slipped from elimination to control. If medical practitioners had been engaged in the tuberculosis elimination plan that was proposed in 1983, today our nation might not be searching for over a half billion dollars of new money to control the spreading epidemic of multidrug-resistant tuberculosis which so threatens health care workers and others.

In such programs success in public health terms depends on how public health makes use of the medical care system. Public health authorities should be able to deputize health plans and practitioners, engaging them in managing treatment to protect individuals and the community. Success in the face of challenges to health like tuberculosis remains unlikely under reform. Medical care lacks a tradition of reaching out to patients in need of care who may not seek it. Thus we remain unlikely to provide these people with the therapy to treat themselves and protect the community around them. Society as a whole will suffer little if physicians wait for patients to seek medical care for most problems, but we all pay for missed public health opportunities. Later in this paper we use immunization to illustrate how doctors can become more effective protagonists of public health in a reformed scheme.

Fundamental public health information systems and intervention strategies—the health care analogs of smoke alarms and fire fighting—should be integrated into the health reform bundle. Epidemiology, research and public health information systems are not personal health services. They do not slip easily into an existing niche in medical insurance schemes—the benefit package. But public health systems should be so embedded in reform that they cannot be uncoupled from medical care now or in the future. If cohesion is not assured at the start we will consume our limited resources caring for the equivalent of increasing numbers of smoke and burn victims as preventable problems spread—unnecessarily.

The medical care system can do more than respond with targeted treatment. Medical practitioners can and should strengthen public health capacity by detecting in individuals medical problems which might have been preventable if discovered earlier, and reporting such occurrences to the authorities responsible for controlling further exposures. For example, when a physician discovers that a patient with a neuropathy is suffering from solvent poisoning from his job in a plastics plant, it should be standard practice to report the event and the danger to public health authorities who may be able to protect fellow workers. Similarly for lead poisoning, rat bites, and exposures to environmental toxins, the medical practitioner must be linked to public health authorities who can intervene at the source as well as directing populations to early treatment.

Reporting of disease is critical for public health, yet there is no reliable system in place to ensure that doctors will report suspicious cases or that public health authorities will investigate them in the field and in the laboratory and act to prevent additional illnesses. Everywhere diseases are under-reported because physicians do not see themselves as part of a public health system to prevent disease, except for the patients in their own practice. Too often physicians do not make the effort to comply with state reporting requirements because in caring for sick patients they may not see the cumulative consequences of failure to report—or the benefits of public health interventions.

Practitioners can respond to public health information as well as provide it. For example, research may reveal that certain chemicals and physical agents cause cancer, but only many years after initial exposure. For individuals exposed to carcinogens, screening and monitoring may save their lives. Bladder cancer caused by azo dye exposures in the textile industry, as an example, can often be cured if detected early. None of the health care reform proposals as yet incorporates a systematic way to identify, contact and offer early treatment to all those at risk. No plan yet contemplates making health plans a clinical arm of the public health departments. At best, plans will be graded for their success in providing preventive services, such as pap smears, to everyone in the plan for whom the test is appropriate.

Optimal public health gains will be more difficult to achieve if populations remain outside the reformed medical care system, that is, if they are not enrolled. From the public health point of view, a policy decision to leave some individuals outside the health care system does not remove their contribution to health or disease in the United States. Yet Congress is already debating just how *universal* health care reform should be, further evidence of inattention to medical care's role in public health. If the Congress chooses to limit insurance for health services to some categories of residents, its members should recognize that there is no economic or health justification for withholding payment and limiting access to those measures which protect the community from the spread of preventable problems.

The precise list of the services for delivery to populations at risk and to populations posing risks to others can be argued about and revised over time as health conditions change and knowledge grows. Similarly, the specific data needed from providers to bolster epidemiological information systems and research will evolve. But all these activities which unify public health and medical practice into an effective and efficient health care system cannot be grafted onto reform after organizational, management and financing mechanisms have been legislated. Instead, the overall design needs to contemplate how to use enrollment, management and finance components as incentives, checks and balances to improve performance and health. . . .

PUBLIC HEALTH AUTHORITY—A NEGLECTED
FOUNDATION FOR REFORM

The need to protect the health of the public will not disappear with health care reform. Public health authority will still exist in the states, even if this topic is neglected in federal health care reform legislation. To protect the public, states should be able to harness the medical care system's highly trained workforce, capable laboratories, linked records system, and billions of contacts with the population.

Authority to regulate human behavior to avoid harm and to enhance health, called the "police power," is contained in Article X of the United States Constitution. The framers included this power among those "not delegated to the United States by the Constitution, nor prohibited by it to the States," thus among those "reserved to the States respectively, or to the people."

States began establishing authority in boards of health more than a century ago, and expanded their activities through state and local health departments. Quarantine of people capable of spreading communicable diseases, searches of housing, restaurants and factories for health hazards, seizures of dangerously mislabeled goods, injunctions to refrain from or engage in certain acts, and licensure of practitioners and of facilities to enforce minimum standards of practice have all been sanctioned by courts as legitimate efforts to protect the public's health.

A measure of federal health regulation began early under the "commerce clause" of the Constitution. Federal interventions in health have expanded in this century. Food and drug laws, and worker, environmental and consumer protections have invoked federal preemption of state authority. Many federal health programs offer grants and financial incentives to the states. The dominant force is financial assistance under the Social Security and Public Health Service Acts to encourage states to expand services for special populations such as children, the poor, the elderly, and migrant workers. . . .

No one asserts that states can protect the public's health without assistance. The tools for improving public health, such as surveillance and information systems, research and development for new diagnostic tests, vaccines and therapies depend on national investment and coordination. Health care reform must assure continued support for the National Institutes of Health, the Centers for Disease Control, the Food and Drug Administration, and programs at the Department of Labor and Environmental Protection Agency created to protect the public health. Yet no health care reform proposal explicitly takes advantage of state public health authority and the federal institutions that support it. Where private medical service providers deliver the bulk of services, public health officials should remember that the states have the Constitutional authority to define the public health and to regulate providers to protect the public health. Where the incentives in the medical care system prove insufficient to protect the public health, states can and should insist on effective and efficient use of resources.

The federal government has resources essential to helping states meet the public health and medical needs of their residents. Federal programs in the Public Health Service should retain and expand their roles in setting health goals for the nation. Federal health care reform legislation should allocate a proportion of medical care funds to states for core public health functions and use the federal guidelines to assure compatible data collection, epidemiological research and reporting systems—and sufficient scope of effort and competence to provide the basis for holding medical practices accountable to public health goals.

Reform legislation should reaffirm the states' Constitutional power to protect the public health, giving them the needed financial and managerial leverage to use the restructured health care system, including its private sector participants, to reach public health objectives. States should translate national health targets into local ones and assist medical practices to improve and contribute to state-wide and national gains. Beyond management systems and rewards, the states will need to use their public health authority to regulate medical practice. When attempting to alter physician behavior, it is "especially important that physicians perceive the proposed changes as beneficial to patients (or at least not harmful)." Thus it will be particularly important for public health regulation to be developed and evaluated in conjunction with the medical care system, rather than imposed from the outside.

States' primary contribution under reform will be public health leadership, technical assistance to medical providers, core public health regulatory systems, and management techniques to squeeze the most health from each medical dollar. Many health departments are unprepared in one of two ways. Some have little experience with regulating medical services, and concentrate regulatory efforts on health hazards in the community. The very idea that such a health department could provide wise guidance and exercise an important measure of control over medical resources may seem incredible. Other departments are principally providers of medical services for the poor and neglect broad-based, strategic public health interventions. These departments seem poorly equipped to exercise regulatory control for the benefit of the whole population. But as poorly equipped as the states may be, they remain the only entities with broad public health authority. National reform architects have neglected to reinforce these powers or to propose any statutory substitute at the federal level.

IMMUNIZATION

To illustrate the risks we face if we bungle health care reform and to suggest the shape of a solution, immunization serves as a useful example. This is a challenge President Clinton is already confronting. The basic public health authority of states can be used to make medical services achieve public health objectives. Failures and subsequent success in the United Kingdom suggest that it will be possible, even before National Health Care Reform is enacted, to know whether the Clinton administration and Congress have recognized the public health element.

Immunization fits perfectly into a reformed medical care system. It is a personal health service, like diagnosis or treatment, but is best understood as a public health strategy to reduce the burden of treatment costs and of disease for society as a whole. If, as our nation designs health care reform, we fail to require that public health interventions like immunization reduce the burden of disease, we will pay for avoidable doctor and hospital visits and escalate the tension around rationing of medical care for the ill.

A fundamental difference separates public health programs prescribed for populations from decisions of individuals to seek treatment. Immunization, for example, generates greatest savings only when it is applied so completely that disease outbreaks are averted altogether. Short of "herd immunity" (a high level of immunity in the population that reduces disease transmission), the unprotected—unvaccinated individuals and those in whom vaccine failed to stimulate immunity—remain vulnerable.

Historical lessons about immunization, starting with Edward Jenner, the inventor of the vaccine against smallpox, should guide reform. Jenner realized that simply administering vaccine to patients seeking medical care would not fulfill his dream of global eradication. Although Jenner understood them intuitively in 1796, two lessons need to be relearned: First, only systematic immunization of entire populations protects society from epidemics. Second, however central the role played by medical practitioners in administering vaccines, an explicit, population-based strategy must exist to assure participation by physicians and immunization of *everyone* who may be at risk. No society has achieved the public health benefit of vaccines simply by waiting for individuals to seek immunization, even where "access" and payment were guaranteed.

In 1979 the U.S. Public Health Service set national goals, asking each state to increase immunization rates for children from 60 to at least 90 percent. A crucial element of the strategy was federal pressure on states to enact and enforce laws requiring full immunization before a child can enter school. The striking operational success of this first systematic program, measured by the number of children fully immunized at school entry, masked a design failure revealed in the 1980s. The initial strategy focused on school age children whose immunization status could be checked on their first day in school. There was no comparable "check point" or enforcement plan for younger children who were not entering school.

About half of preschool children, especially those aged 0–2, remained incompletely immunized. A measles epidemic in 1989–91 brought the error of omission to the front pages of American newspapers. The U.S. Public Health Service acknowledged that a two-year epidemic had resulted in more than 55,000 reported cases of measles, more than 130 measles-related deaths, and 11,000 hospitalizations. President Clinton estimated the hospital costs alone at $20 million for an epidemic that $1 million worth of public health could have prevented. If past experience holds, for every measles death there will be three additional children with permanent brain damage who will continue to add costs to the medical care system throughout their lives. The epidemic was diagnosed as due to failure to immunize preschool children on time.

For immunization monitored at school entry, public health agencies could rely on practitioners and clinics to immunize children identified to need vaccine. Without a tracking and notification system to alert health authorities and families for each immunization visit, there was no population-based accountability for infants and toddlers, as at school entry. In the 1980s diminished federal public health funding, increasing vaccine prices, and increasing demand on public clinics compounded the problem. Even families who sought immunizations for their preschoolers could not always find them.

A reformed medical care system could cure these flaws and assure timely immunization of preschoolers (and adults, too), but only if practitioners are held accountable to a national public health strategy. Everyone must be guaranteed payment for services and a regular place to seek them. Moreover every person should be enrolled in a medical plan or practice which can be held responsible for the results—full and timely immunization of all enrollees. The difference between guaranteed "access" to medical care for those who seek it, and accountability of medical practices to public health authorities to render services that may never be sought by the consumer, is decisive. Bearing the distinction in mind, immunization is not the only public health service which can make use of a reformed medical care system.

When delivery of vaccines is fully integrated into a universal medical care program, public health support will be required as much as ever. We must assure that cases of vaccine-preventable disease are reported to public health authorities so that vaccine failures can be detected and flaws in the delivery system investigated and remedied. Disease surveillance based on competent laboratories will be needed to detect emerging and re-emerging infections. Our capacity to vaccinate with safe and effective vaccines will also depend on government research and development, and regulation. As a public health tool and because they have usually provided less return on investment than pharmaceuticals, vaccines are unlikely to attract sufficient investment without government assistance.

It is not clear that health care reformers understand the difference between clinical and public health laboratories, and no reform proposal acknowledges the difference or incorporates the public health function in its scheme. Public health laboratories perform tests to determine threats to the population even if there will be no diagnostic or therapeutic benefit to the individual from whom a sample is drawn. For example, we now have an effective vaccine for H flu type B, a disease which causes meningitis, predominantly in young children. When the vaccine was introduced in the state of Massachusetts it reduced the incidence of the disease by 70% in the first year. Similar results have occurred wherever the vaccine has been delivered universally.

There is no vaccine for other types of H flu, or for the nontypeable strains which also may cause invasive disease. With increased use of the H flu type B vaccine the relative importance of the other types and nontypeable strains is increasing as public health officials attempt to distinguish disease caused by strains against which there is no vaccine from failures of the vaccine to protect vaccinated children against type B. Similarly it is laboratory testing which allows public health officials to identify outbreaks which can be quelled by immunizing children who may have missed one or all doses of the type B vaccine.

Because there may be no clinical benefit to the individual patient to determine the particular strain, many clinical laboratories do not perform the tests. In the absence of a funded public health laboratory or of public funds to pay a clinical lab for this function, the lab may bill the patient or the patient's insurer, either of whom may refuse to pay the claim because the typing test does not enhance treatment. With increasing emphasis on cost containment, clinical labs are likely to avoid such testing. But most medical care reformers have not appreciated the distinction nor have they made provision to assure that technically competent laboratories handle public health testing—and guarantee remuneration. Public health officials also worry that cost containment-conscious physicians concerned only with their individual patients may not think to order these sorts of tests or to provide samples to their colleagues in public health laboratories. Many states are doing less of this sort of testing as appropriations shrink—or are less equipped to produce reliable results as the technology available in public facilities lags behind the clinical labs.

UNITED KINGDOM EXPERIENCE

Should one doubt that attention to public health strategies is needed when planning health care reform, consider the history of immunization in Britain. Failure of public health authorities to intervene in the National Health Service and of medical practitioners to practice public health subjected Britons to forty years of unnecessary exposure to vaccine-preventable disease.

The British adopted their version of national health care reform in 1947 by establishing the National Health Service. Its designers made the erroneous assumption that universal access to and payment for medical services would suffice. It took forty-four years before they understood the flaw in their original blueprint and were able to correct it. We need not replicate that misjudgment.

Since 1947 basic medical services in England have been provided by general practitioners, salaried by the National Health Service. Since the start every child was on the list of a general practitoner paid and equipped to provide recommended immunizations. The vaccines were available free to doctor and patient which eased the process. Even so, in the 1960s children unimmunized against pertussis fueled the spread of frightening epidemic disease. Whooping cough outbreaks were evident in hospital admission rates. How was this happening with universal, fully paid access to medical services?

The answer was almost too simple: medical practitioners left to their own devices were not very good at public health. Even where they administered vaccines to children whose families sought them at appropriate intervals, physicians did not seek out all those on their lists who came in late or not at all. Doctors saw only the individual child, rarely encountering the broader consequences of missed immunizations. In the absence of data showing that practitioners were giving preventive services principally to patients who sought them, never reaching many who remained at risk, epidemic pertussis erupted before health authorities knew national rates of immunization were too low to maintain herd immunity. Even assigning every child to a doctor had not guaranteed high levels of immunization coverage.

Belatedly the national public health agency (Department of Health) asserted leadership and enlisted the medical care system (National Health Service) in a joint effort to avert further epidemics. In April 1990 the Department set targets and reviews for all levels of operation of the NHS. This time they assured good results.

By 1991 immunization coverage in England rose from a national average of approximately 70 percent to an unprecedented high of 90 percent for children in every age group. . . .

Because success was so impressive, new target levels have been set to raise coverage levels to 95 percent of all children. British public health authorities have made doctors a contributing part of the national immunization effort, and today no one suggests that a separate public health program is required to achieve universal childhood immunization as public health guidance and support has purposefully been integrated into daily medical practice.

Childhood immunization is a powerful example, but other public health objectives can be realized as well—if we articulate the strategy and assign to the medical services delivery system those tasks its medical practitioners can perform most effectively and efficiently. Together, the federal government and the states should build a system in which:

- medical services providers detect, obtain necessary laboratory confirmation, and report cases of disease in a prescribed manner, helping public health inspectors and investigators find and control sources of exposure in the community;
- medical services providers respond promptly with early diagnostic testing and treatment when individuals at high risk (or their characteristics) are identified by public health workers in the community;
- medical services providers reach every member of the population who can benefit individually or when "treatments" are needed to protect others;
- medical services providers know if their interventions are succeeding and if new or different health problems threaten our people.

CONCLUSION

An expanded prescription would require the reformed medical care system to perform certain functions systematically that in the past have been optional for medical practitioners or left to health departments by default. The challenge to reformers is to rebuild the core public health capacity of the states to create a competent national system, and to assure that the medical services that we will pay for under health care reform perform certain functions critical to the health of the public. How can we know that the federal reformers are incorporating every intervention that can improve health and hold off unnecessary expenditures? Do they have a thorough analysis of how medical services will contribute to public health? And if so, does their analysis indicate which of these services require assistance and guidance from public health departments? Have they made sure in each instance to *secure* resources for the public health component as well as for medical services?

   This advice is not new, but it is timely. Seventy-five years ago, a warning about inattention to public health agencies was issued to the Medical and Chirugical Faculty of Maryland. It must be heeded today as we reform medical care:

> With the appropriations for health insurance running into millions of dollars annually it goes without saying that legislative bodies will not materially increase the appropriations for their health departments. Owing to this fact, there is a decided probability of sickness insurance acts endangering the very existence of State health departments by absorbing all of the funds available for health work. Our statesmen and lawmakers must, therefore, be careful that proper and ample provisions are made for health machinery in any sickness insurance act.

IV

NEW TECHNOLOGY AND THE PUBLIC'S HEALTH

8

REPRODUCTIVE ISSUES

The right of individuals to decide whether and when and how often to have children has been held to be a basic human right. Procreative liberty[1] can be defended on several grounds. Classic liberals stress the right of individuals to make intimate and private decisions, especially those that reflect religious or spiritual values, without government intervention.[2] In the United States, the Supreme Court has held that a fundamental constitutional right of privacy[3] protects the right of individuals to use birth control and to terminate pregnancies prior to viability.[4] Feminists stress the essential connection between the ability of women to control their fertility and equality.[5] Public health professionals consider access to contraceptives and family planning to be an intrinsic part of women's health care, because of the health risks associated with too many pregnancies and births. Unintended and unwanted pregnancies also result in children who may not be properly cared for. All of these factors contribute to a general recognition of the right of individuals to avoid reproduction, including a right to have access to contraception and abortion. Indeed, many in public health view the legalization of abortion as the greatest advance since penicillin.[6] At the same time, the topic of abortion remains controversial and divisive. Precisely for that reason, it is represented in virtually every textbook on medical ethics, in numerous applied ethics collections, and in several collections devoted solely to abortion.[7] Rather than cover this well-trod ground, we have decided to focus, not on the right to avoid procreation, but rather the right *to have children.* This is the flip side of procreative liberty—the affirmative right to have offspring, and therefore not to be subjected to forced contraception, sterilization, or abortion. Although this too is generally regarded as also part of the right of privacy, nevertheless, from time to time, proposals are made to limit the reproductive freedom of various groups. For example, bills have been introduced to encourage (some would say "force") women on welfare to use Norplant, a long-acting contraceptive. At least one judge made the use of Norplant a condition of probation for a woman who pled guilty to child abuse. Another judge sentenced a couple convicted of sexually molesting the woman's son to ten years in prison, but offered them probation if the woman (not the man!) would consent to a tubal ligation.[8]

All of these proposals have been roundly criticized, on a variety of grounds, not least of which is that they infringe individuals' rights to reproduce. Undoubtedly, such proposals sometimes have punitive and moralistic motives (see Chapter 4), but they also reflect a plausible view that individuals ought, if possible, to refrain from reproducing if they are unable or unwilling adequately to care for children, or if conditions are such that the children would be likely to have lives of extreme suffering or deprivation.[9] The right to procreate is not an absolute right and needs to be balanced in light of both parental and social responsibility. At the same time, proposals to restrict the right to reproduce need to be evaluated in light of the history of forcible sterilization of the "feeble-minded." This sordid chapter in U.S. history is chillingly recounted in the first selection by Philip Reilly. As Reilly points out, some of those who were sterilized were actually not mentally retarded. Many were poor or members of minority groups, or institutionalized for other reasons. Moreover, sterilization programs were often instituted not to protect children from abusive or incompetent parents but out of the belief that some individuals or "races" are inferior and ought not to reproduce. The legacy of eugenics has implications not only for reproduction but also for genetics (covered in Chapter 9).

Over the last few decades, reproductive medicine has made huge strides. Assisted reproductive technologies (ART), from the relatively "low tech" (fertility drugs) to the more "high tech" (*in vitro* fertilization or IVF), enable some infertile individuals to have children they could not have had in the past. New techniques and improvements of existing techniques are being made all the time. At the same time, ART is very expensive, imposes physical and emotional burdens, and has a relatively low success rate, all of which make it unlikely to help more than a small proportion of infertile individuals. Using "the lens of public health," Elizabeth Heitman suggests that a better approach to the problem of infertility includes increased and expanded research on infertility, public education about the effect of sexually transmitted diseases (STDs) on fertility, and increased access to preventive measures against and treatment of STDs.

Some people have wondered why we should be concerned with infertility in a world that is already overpopulated. There is general agreement among experts that overpopulation is a problem, but there is a split in the population field between two different approaches. On one side are those who see overpopulation as the primary problem, because it is thought inevitably to lead to poverty, famine, disease, environmental catastrophe, and social unrest, especially in developing countries. Those who take this approach, which is sometimes labeled "zero population growth," are often willing to impose coercive measures, if necessary, to prevent these disasters.

On the other side are those who advocate a human development approach to population in which reproductive health, improving the status of women, and protecting individual rights are central objectives. This approach holds that allowing individuals to make their own procreative choices and empowering them to carry out these choices is the way to solve the problem of overpopulation. Human development advocates maintain that improving the quality of life of people in poorer countries will lead to population stabilization, as it has in richer countries. Moreover, they point out that coercive policies to limit population often turn out to be ineffective and even counterproductive. Finally, human development advocates do not regard overpopulation as the main problem. They maintain that most resource depletion and environmental damage stems less from population increases in poorer nations than from overconsumption in richer ones. Reducing population by itself will not address these harms.

Further complicating the area of population studies is the complexity of the question of ideal population size, an issue brought out in the selection by Joel E. Cohen. According to Cohen, the question, "How many people can the earth support?" is not a question like, "How old are you?" That is, it does not have a definitive correct answer. How many people at what standard of living? For how long? With what safety net in case of natural disasters? Only after we understand the multitude of issues behind the "deceptively simple" question, "How many people can the earth support?" can we begin to ask which approach to population policy, the "zero population growth" or the human development approach, is most likely to be effective. Readers of this book will also want to ask which approach best reflects a public health perspective.

NOTES

1. "Procreative liberty" is the term John Robertson uses in his book, *Children of Choice: Freedom and the New Reproductive Technologies* (Princeton University Press, 1994), to describe the right to have, or not have, offspring.

2. For a powerful statement of the liberal position, see Ronald Dworkin, *Life's Dominion* (New York: Alfred A. Knopf, 1993).

3. The expression "fundamental constitutional right" is no longer commonly used. Instead, the justices refer to "protected liberty interests." See, for example, *Griswold v. Connecticut*, 381 U.S. 479 (1965); *Roe v. Wade*, 410 U.S. 1134 (1973).

4. See, for example, Susan Sherwin, *No Longer Patient: Feminist Ethics and Health Care* (Philadelphia, PA: Temple University Press, 1992, pp. 99–116); and Rosalind Pollack Petchesky, *Abortion and Woman's Choice: The State, Sexuality, and Reproductive Freedom* (Boston, MA: Northeastern University Press, 1985).

5. Not all public health officials regard abortion as a public health triumph. For some, those who consider abortion to be the killing of innocent children, the legalization of abortion is undoubtedly regarded as a public health catastrophe. Former Surgeon General C. Everett Koop is a notable example. How one regards abortion, then, is not simply a matter of taking a public health perspective but also depends largely on one's views about the moral status of the fetus.

6. See, for example, John D. Arras and Bonnie Steinbock, eds., *Ethical Issues in Modern Medicine,* 5th ed. (Mountain View, California: Mayfield, 1998), and Susan Dwyer and Joel Feinberg, *The Problem of Abortion,* 3rd ed. (Wadsworth, 1997).

7. All of these cases are discussed in my article, "The Concept of Coercion and Long-Term Contraceptives," in Ellen H. Moskowitz and Bruce Jennings, eds. *Coerced Contraception? Moral and Policy Challenges of Long-Acting Birth Control* (Washington, D.C.: Georgetown University Press, 1996, pp. 53–78).

8. For a defense of this view, see, for example, John D. Arras, "AIDS and Reproductive Decisions: Having Children in Fear and Trembling," *Milbank Quarterly* 68, no. 3 (1990), pp. 353–382, and Bonnie Steinbock and Ron McClamrock, "When Is Birth Unfair to the Child?," *Hastings Center Report* 24, No. 6 (1994), pp. 15–21.

9. See Sissela Bok, "Population and Ethics: Expanding the Moral Space," in Gita Sen, Adrienne Germain and Lincoln Chen, eds. *Population Policies Reconsidered* (Cambridge, MA: Harvard University Press, 1994, pp. 15–26).

The Resurgence of Eugenics

Philip R. Reilly

As we have seen, in the first two decades of this century a remarkable number of sterilization laws were enacted, and about thirty-two hundred institutionalized persons were subjected to eugenic sterilization. The bulk of this activity took place from 1909 to 1913, and legislative voting records suggest that the laws had wide support. However, eugenic sterilization programs were actually implemented only in those states in which key persons, such as superintendents of state hospitals, were supportive. Except in California and several Midwestern states, relatively few residents of institutions were sterilized. During World War I, many of the laws were struck down by the courts, and for a time (1918–22), no new sterilization statutes were enacted.

Despite the demise of most of the laws, the number of institutionalized persons who were sterilized each year in the United States continued to rise. This was largely due to the California program. From January 1, 1918, until December 31, 1920, there were 1,150 sterilizations performed upon persons in six California state hospitals for the insane, roughly one for every six persons admitted. About three hundred retarded persons were also sterilized at the Sonoma State Home, an institution with a capacity of twenty-two hundred residents. During those three years, approximately 80 percent of all eugenic sterilizations carried out in the United States were performed in seven institutions in one state.

Despite the quiescence of sterilization programs virtually everywhere except California, the sterilization movement soon made a remarkable comeback. A small number of eugenicists capitalized effectively on the national concern over the dramatic postwar influx of immigrants from Southern and Eastern Europe and growing uneasiness about the northern migration of American blacks. The resurgence of sterilization programs was closely tied to the popular demand to limit immigration. The eugenicists' argument that hordes of immigrants would weaken the American gene pool provided part of the intellectual rationale for

From Chapter 6 in *The Surgical Solution: A History of Involuntary Sterilization in the United States* by Philip Reilly (The Johns Hopkins University Press, 1991). Reprinted by permission of the publisher and the author.

the restrictive Immigration Act of 1924. It is no accident that a second wave of state sterilization laws, targeted at a different threat to the "race," were enacted at the same time.

The issues discussed at the Second International Congress of Eugenics, which met at the American Museum of Natural History in New York City in September 1921, reflect this dual concern. Authorities in genetics, medicine, and eugenics presented 108 papers. Fifty-three reported on laboratory genetics or pedigree studies that documented the inheritance of human traits; 55 addressed the biological and social consequences of marriages between persons of different ethnic backgrounds. As the papers, including those such as "Some Notes on the Negro Problem," "The Problem of Negro-White Intermixture," and "Inter-marriage with the Slave Race" suggest, there was special concern about miscegenation. Nor was that concern limited to eugenic circles. During the first quarter of this century, many states enacted laws that were intended to tighten already existing limits on interracial marriage.

The roots of antimiscegenation law are deeply set in the soil of American history. As early as 1630, only a few years after Negroes were brought to Virginia, the governor's council declared that Hugh Davis, a white man, was to be whipped publicly for "abusing himself to the dishonor of God and shame of Christians by defiling his body in lying with a Negro." In 1662, the state's general antifornication statute was amended to include heavier penalties if the guilty parties had also violated racial boundaries. In tracing Virginia legislative history (which is typical of the South), one finds an unswerving preoccupation with preserving those boundaries. A law enacted in 1787 declared that "every person who shall have one-fourth part or more of Negro blood shall be deemed a mulatto." There the color line held until 1910 when the state legislature, responding to increasing intermarriage between whites and blacks, declared that any person whose ancestry was one-sixteenth Negro was of that race. Many Americans feared that dilution of the ancestral stock by mulattoes and blacks threatened the nation's future. According to one authority, between 1890 and 1910 the "colored" population increased by 81 percent, while the Negro population increased by only 22.7 percent.

In Virginia the legislature responded by passing legislation titled "An Act to Preserve Racial Integrity." The key feature of this law, the most powerful legal obstacle to interracial marriage erected since the Civil War, was to define a "white" person as one "who has no trace whatsoever of any blood other than Caucasian." Officials charged with issuing marriage licenses were ordered not to do so until they had "reasonable assurance that the statements as to color of both man and woman are correct." Existing interracial marriages were declared void regardless of the state in which they had been licensed, and interracial cohabitation was declared a crime. There was one exception to the anti-miscegenation policy. The "Pocahontas exception," written in deference to the large number of persons who claimed to be descendants of Pocahontas and John Rolfe, permitted a white to marry "a person with one-sixteenth or less of the blood of an American Indian." At least two other states, Georgia and Alabama, followed Virginia's lead and defined as white only those persons whose genealogy was untainted. . . .

Although many ardent proponents of eugenic sterilization believed that it would reduce the prevalence of crime, most early twentieth-century American criminologists flatly rejected this neo-Lombrosian thesis. For example, in his book, *Criminology* (1918), Maurice Parmelee asserted that Lombroso was "rather ignorant of the modern science of biology, and especially of the theory of heredity." Parmelee argued that what Lombroso had called "atavistic" traits were in reality examples of arrested development caused by an inhospitable environment. He admitted that hereditary factors sometimes figured in criminal conduct, but overall, he saw little value in sterilization as a means of reducing crime.

Six years later, when Edwin Sutherland, a criminologist working at the University of Illinois, published his textbook, the vestiges of Lombrosian thought were sparse indeed. Sutherland wrote that "criminality as such cannot be inherited. If any trait is inherited which predisposes to crime, we do not know what it is. Even in the case of the feeble-minded and insane, it is not clear that their abnormalities are inherited, in the strict sense of the word, in a very large proportion of cases and, in addition, it is not clear that people with such difficulties are more prone to commit crimes than other people." Sutherland concluded that there was "no evidence that criminality would be reduced appreciably" by sterilization laws.

Some contemporary journalists, however, advanced a more titillating view. For example, during 1924 and 1925 French Strother, editor of *World's Work,* a popular tabloid, wrote five articles on the biological basis of crime. These pieces illustrate how eugenics was portrayed for the lay reader. One article, "The Cause of Crime: Defective Brain," was a profile of Harry Olson's work as chief justice of the Chicago Municipal Court. Strother quoted Olson as asserting that "practically all criminals are mentally abnormal." In 1914, convinced that it was time to use scientific methods in the service of crime prevention, Olson had founded the Psychopathic Laboratory. He instructed its director, Dr. William Hickson, a psychometrician, to develop "tests of character" to identify criminals. A decade later Strother reported that Hickson had discovered that dementia praecox (schizophrenia) was the cause of nearly all crimes, a finding that he promised would revolutionize criminology. Hickson's conclusions supplied Judge Olson, a staunch eugenicist, with exactly the mechanistic view of aberrant behavior that he sought. On returning from a tour of European psychology laboratories, Hickson reported to Olson that he had learned a new method of screening for criminal tendencies. He was convinced that nine out of ten criminals were mentally abnormal, and that he could identify more precisely the specific types of defects that led to crime. He suggested to reporters that the Chicago Police should round up the city's one hundred toughest characters and that those found by Psychopathic Laboratory tests to be abnormal should be committed *before* they harmed society.

Another of Strother's articles, "The Cure for Crime," was a strident argument to "stop the breeding of mental defectives" as quickly as possible. A third, which purported to be a primer on heredity, illustrated Mendelian inheritance by discussing the gene for Jewish facial appearance. Analyzing "all possible Jewish-Gentile crosses," Strother advised his readers that "all children of a Jew and a Gentile will look like Gentiles, that if a pure Gentile marries a half-Jew, all the children will look like Gentiles, and that if a half-Jew marries a half-Jew, one child of every four will look like a Jew and the other three will look like Gentiles." Unfortunately, more people probably read Strother's article in one week than read genetics textbooks in an entire year.

The tireless efforts of a few prominent eugenicists like Judge Olson, who oversaw the work of thirty-six other judges, helped to keep prosterilization arguments viable during the years just after defeats in the courts. Olson flatly condemned the view in academic criminology circles that there was no persuasive evidence for the heritability of criminal tendencies. In his 1925 presidential address to the Eugenic Research Association, he asserted: "Crime prevention, finally, is seen to be the weeding out of defective stocks, and it is the first step in the eugenics program."

EUGENICS SOCIETIES

As Americans grew more discontented with the huge influx of immigrants in the postwar years, many people became interested in the problem of racial vigor. In dozens of towns across America, small groups of citizens organized to ponder this and other eugenic questions. Two of these organizations, the American Eugenics Society and the Human Betterment Foundation, attained some prominence. Although it is difficult to assess their impact on sterilization policy, there is no doubt that they published pamphlets, provided speakers, and worked assiduously to keep eugenics proposals, especially sterilization, alive as newsworthy topics.

Although the American Eugenics Society was not incorporated until 1926, it was started shortly after the Second International Congress of Eugenics met in New York City in September 1921. If the First International Eugenics Congress, which had convened in London in 1912, reflected the eugenic thinking in Great Britain, the New York City meeting showed that a group of committed eugenicists had emerged in the United States. Dr. Henry Fairfield Osborn, president of the American Museum of Natural History, was chosen by his American colleagues as president of the Second International Congress, Madison Grant was elected treasurer, and the tireless Laughlin worked as chairman of the Exhibits Committee. After the congress closed, several prominent Americans, wanting to do more than maintain a committee affiliated with the London-based International Commission on Eugenics, formed the Eugenics Society of the United States of America.

By March 1923 this New York-based group, which changed its name to the American Eugenics Society (AES) in 1924, was sufficiently cohesive to be lobbying in Albany against legislation that it felt would have dysgenic effects. With strong support from the New York Charities Aid Association (an organization abhorred by hard-core eugenicists), two New York legislators had introduced a bill providing special educational assistance for "retarded" children (defined as those who were learning at a level that was three or more years below that expected for their age). The Austin-Cole Bill proposed providing state funds to stimulate the schools to hire more teachers to work in special education. A memorandum prepared by Laughlin for the AES about this bill described the proposed program as unequivocally "anti-eugenic," siphoning tax dollars that would be better spent on the gifted. He suggested lobbying to amend the law so that the retarded children could be sterilized. "Otherwise," he feared, "the education of the defective will bolster him or her up to the reproductive period and will make it more possible for him or her to become a parent than would be possible if he or she were less well trained." Despite the efforts of the AES, the bill became law.

In the mid-twenties Irving Fisher, a professor of public policy at Yale, was the driving force behind the AES, which then maintained its headquarters in New Haven. Fisher enlisted a zealous but unsophisticated eugenicist named Leon Whitney to be the society's secretary. Whitney, a wealthy farmer and an avid dog breeder, had undergone an almost mystical conversion to eugenics, giving up his comfortable country life to plunge into a new career. In 1928 he published *The Basis of Breeding* (dedicated to Laughlin), a volume intended to educate laypersons about genetics. One key eugenics activity that Whitney extolled in his book was to sponsor "fitter family" contests. These contests frequently took place at fairs in the Midwest: judges reviewed human pedigrees to determine the most eugenically positive families, just as the best cattle, chickens, and pigs competed for blue ribbons. He also helped the AES to construct a "Eugenics Catechism," a pamphlet of questions and answers about eugenics, and to launch the publication of a periodical called *Eugenics.* . . .

Gosney first learned of the eugenics movement from a newspaper article that announced the opening of the Eugenics Record Office in Cold Spring Harbor in 1910. He wrote to Charles Davenport to learn more, and his interest soon became advocacy. By 1920, Gosney had become convinced that the crucial undertaking in eugenics would be to educate young people about the importance of mate selection. But despite his offers of financial support, he was unable to persuade any university to sponsor his unique educational plan. Thwarted in his first effort, Gosney turned his attention to the study of negative eugenics. He decided to analyze the history of sterilization in California. In 1926 Gosney organized a council of advisers, including Dr. J. H. McBride, a member of the state Commission on Immigration and Housing, and Paul Popenoe, a sociologist who edited the *Journal of Heredity,* to begin a detailed examination of how sterilization of thousands of California's defectives had affected the state. During this period his interest became a conviction, and in 1929 he created the Human Betterment Foundation (HBF), a nonprofit corporation intended to foster eugenics.

From the inception of the California sterilization study Gosney turned to Laughlin for advice. Laughlin provided him with copies of the forms that he used to record and store eugenic data at the ERO and urged him to visit the state hospitals, advice probably given because Laughlin knew the frightening impact that large numbers of poorly housed feeble-minded persons could have on an inexperienced person. A few weeks later Gosney wrote Laughlin that McBride and Popenoe were visiting institutions around the state and that he was gathering the support of physicians and government officials for undertaking a much larger study of sterilization. In reply, Laughlin sent the names and addresses of fifty-two persons whom he knew had been released from California hospitals after being sterilized so that Gosney could conduct a follow-up investigation on the long-term effects of vasectomy.

In March of 1926 Gosney and Laughlin formally agreed to collaborate. From Gosney's perspective, at least, there was ample reason to do so: "It appears to me that there will be great value in having two independent and parallel studies of this topic. The whole project of sterilization is continually under attack, and is certain to be attacked still more vehemently if we proceed with an educational campaign on its behalf. To meet these attacks, we will need all the ammunition available, and it seems unquestionable that a single investigation would be less effective than a double investigation."

By May 1927 Gosney had assembled an impressive list of consultants to the sterilization study. They included David Starr Jordan, chancellor of Stanford University, Lewis Terman, the nation's most prominent psychometrician, and S. J. Holmes, the Berkeley geneticist. Over the next few months the HBF consultants approved eighteen reports on the medical, psychological, economic, and legal dimensions of California's long-running (1909–27) sterilization program. Collectively these reports, all of which were published during the next three years, constituted the first comprehensive "proof" that sterilization was cost-effective and posed no significant medical harm to the institutionalized persons at whom it was aimed. Popenoe, who wrote many of the papers, reassured readers that the data revealed no evidence of discrimination because of race or ethnicity, and that two-thirds of those paroled after sterilization did "reasonably well" outside of the institutions. By 1928 his work was sufficiently well regarded that he was invited to address the annual meeting of the American Bar Association on the topic of sterilization and criminality. *Sterilization for Human Betterment,* published by Gosney and Popenoe in 1929, was the first comprehensive discussion of sterilization aimed at the lay reader. They argued that under a scientifically applied sterilization program, "the number of mentally defective persons in the community could be reduced by perhaps as much as half in three or four generations."

In 1930 the HBF began to conduct an annual survey of state sterilization programs. Like Dr. Sharp before World War I and Harry Laughlin in the 1920s, during the 1930s Edward Gosney and Paul Popenoe were the chief propagandists for and scorekeepers of eugenic sterilization in America. For example, in 1935 the HBF mailed over forty thousand pamphlets containing their sterilization survey results to professors at 436 colleges in every state and several foreign countries. During 1935, Gosney even convinced Harry Chandler, publisher of the *Los Angeles Times,* to run a column, "Social Eugenics," in the paper's Sunday magazine.

By the late 1920s Gosney's name had begun to appear on the letterheads of the various eastern eugenics groups. In 1932 he was invited to speak at the Third International Congress on Eugenics in New York City. He must have regarded this as a signal honor, for despite his age and poor health, he took the long train ride across America. His speech at this last great gathering of eugenicists rejected the belief that segregation or involuntary contraception could effectively limit reproduction by defectives. He was convinced that any technique other than sterilization would result in the births of many more defective persons. The HBF was quite active until Gosney's death in 1942, when it too ceased to exist. . . .

One of the most colorful and zealous (if ineffective) eugenicists of the 1930s was a Kansas City businessman named J. H. Pile. In 1938, extremely concerned by the sharply declining birth rate that the Depression fostered, Pile set up the Eugenic Babies Foundation. It was intended to increase reproduction by women "above the average in intellect" and to deny parenthood to "chronic paupers, confirmed criminals, feeble-minded and insane persons." Pile, who hoped for an endowment of one hundred million dollars, launched a campaign to enlist the United States Chamber of Commerce and the various eugenics societies in his cause. He frequently wrote to the AES. However, Huntington and Osborn eschewed involvement with radical groups, and they decided to "steer clear of Mr. Pile." Pile's utopian fantasy should not, however, be dismissed too quickly, While his proposals were ridiculed in the United States, German officials were initiating *Lebensborn,* a program that involved kidnapping eugenically desirable children from Poland and elsewhere, and setting up special homes where the sturdiest German girls were urged to become pregnant by select German soldiers and bear their "superior" babies.

In 1939 the AES was courted by another would-be eugenic philanthropist. After his graduation from Princeton at the turn of the century, James G. Eddy made a fortune in the lumber industry. He later founded the Institute for Forest Genetics, which contributed substantially to that field and earned the support of the Carnegie Institute. In 1938 Eddy approached Laughlin, offering to support a human heredity clinic that would alert couples to the risk of bearing defective babies. Laughlin carried the plan to the directors of the Carnegie Institute (a mistake, since he was in disfavor), who rejected it as being too removed from basic research. Eddy then asked if the AES would consider operating such a clinic for which he would provide one-half the first year's budget. Although Osborn admired Eddy, he and Huntington agreed that a "marriage reference bureau" was too limited an operation for the AES. Just a few years later the Dight Institute at the University of Minnesota started a similar clinic that was perhaps the nation's first genetic counseling center.

Although the 1930s saw a general shift of emphasis toward programs that enhanced principles of positive eugenics, some groups continued to push for sterilization. The mandate of the Sterilization League of New Jersey . . . which began in Princeton in 1934, was to put "a check on the reproduction of defectives." The president was T. L. Zimmerman, a former judge of the juvenile and Domestic Relations Court in Bergen County. For nearly a decade the league lobbied arduously but unsuccessfully for a sterilization law. Despite repeated legislative defeats at home, the league was a tireless propagandist for eugenic sterilization.

THE SECOND WAVE OF STERILIZATION LAWS

After a peak in 1913, when five new states adopted sterilization laws, legislative activity slowed significantly. From 1918 until the end of 1922, only Washington was added to the ranks, while seven other state laws were invalidated. But in 1923 there was a resurgence of legislative activity, and eugenic sterilization laws were enacted in Oregon, Montana, Delaware, and Michigan. Virginia adopted a sterilization law the following year, and in 1925 the legislative floodgates opened. Nine state legislatures passed bills, and seven were enacted (two were vetoed). Of these Idaho, Utah, Minnesota, and Maine enacted their first eugenic sterilization laws. At the end of 1925, enabling legislation to support sterilization programs was law in seventeen states.

Advocates had learned from the mistakes made in earlier legislative efforts. For example, after carefully analyzing the constitutional infirmities of the early laws, Laughlin drafted a model eugenic sterilization bill that purported to safeguard the procedural rights of the persons to whom it might be applied, and that satisfied the Equal Protection Clause. The bill required the state eugenicist to conduct surveys to identify persons who were "potential parents of socially inadequate offspring." Such surveys would canvass the entire population, not merely the residents of state institutions, without regard to "personality, sex, age, marital condition, race or possessions." If the state eugenicist determined that an individual was a potential parent of socially inadequate offspring and a candidate for involuntary sterilization, the statute required a hearing, followed automatically by a jury trial and the right of appeal. Although no state enacted the precise text of Laughlin's bill (a draft of which was approved by the American Bar Association Committee on Sterilization), many of its features were incorporated into new bills. The phrase "potential parent of socially inadequate offspring" was widely copied.

What was the attitude of state officials in regard to implementing these new statutes? An unpublished manuscript, entitled "Sterilization of the Unfit Degenerates," which contains the results of a survey of state officials conducted in 1925 by the Rhode Island State Library, sheds some light on this question. For example, the Connecticut state librarian responded that he found no evidence of eugenic sterilizations performed in that state's institutions during the prior ten years.

The executive director of the Delaware Board of Charities, J. Hall Anderson, reported that without benefit of legislation (but with the consent of the families), he had authorized the sterilization of four patients. Anderson strongly advocated a broad sterilization law to cover "cases outside of Institutions," but noted that "in the present state of political opinion it would probably be impossible to get the Legislature to sanction such a drastic measure." This comment was made just when many legislatures were passing compulsory sterilization laws, suggesting that public opinion drew the line firmly at the institution's portals.

Officials in Kansas, a state that adopted a very aggressive sterilization policy in the mid-1920s, worried that the public might be offended by overzealous application of the law. Charles S. Huffman, a member of the Board of Educational, Charitable and Correctional Institutions, noted that "the larger number of protests come from those of the Catholic faith who claim it is against their religious teachings to interfere with nature." Catholic opposition to sterilization became quite active during the mid-1930s. Nevertheless, Kansas was one of the first states whose officials explicitly adopted a policy of sterilizing "most all feeble-minded, institutionalized women patients of the childbearing age."

Just as they had in the past, opponents of involuntary sterilization laws launched a constitutional attack on the flurry of new laws. The battle was joined in two states, Michigan and Virginia. The Michigan law, which contemplated sterilizing "idiots, imbeciles, and the feeble-minded, but not the insane," was not limited to institutionalized persons. Shortly after an order by the Wayne County Probate Court that one Willie Smith should be sterilized by "vasectomy or X-ray," his guardian *ad litem* challenged the law. On June 18, 1925, the Supreme Court of Michigan ruled that the statute was "justified by the findings of Biological Science," and was "a proper and reasonable exercise of the police power of the state." The high court also held that a section of the law that exempted from sterilization wealthy feeble-minded persons who could pay for the care of their children was a violation of the Equal Protection Clause. Nevertheless, the Michigan decision, the first by a state supreme court to uphold a eugenic sterilization law, was a major victory for the pro-sterilization forces.

The constitutional challenge to the Virginia law, which was ultimately decided by the Supreme Court of the United States, had the largest impact on eugenic sterilization programs. Early in 1924 the Virginia legislature, noting that "heredity plays an important part in the transmission of insanity, idiocy, imbecility, epilepsy and crime," overwhelmingly passed an involuntary sterilization bill (the Senate voted 30–0; the House, 75–2). The law, which gave the superintendents of five state institutions the power to petition a special board for permission to sterilize those inmates whom they believed it would benefit, was signed by the governor on March 20, 1924.

On January 23, 1924, an eighteen-year-old woman named Carrie E. Buck, the illegitimate daughter of an allegedly feeble-minded woman named Addie Emmet, who had been adopted by a Charlottesville family at the age of four, was committed to the State Colony for Epileptics and Feeble-Minded. Always a problem child, Carrie, who was said to have a mental age of nine and an I.Q. of about 50, had recently given birth to an illegitimate child who was also allegedly feeble-minded. Fearing that Carrie would bear more children in the State Colony, Dr. A. S. Priddy, the superintendent, petitioned for sterilization. Realizing that the law would eventually be challenged, state officials were eager to make this the test case. In searching for an expert witness, they asked the advice of Judge Olson, who recommended Harry Laughlin. Although he never saw the patient, on the basis of his review of her records Laughlin concluded that Carrie was part of the "shiftless, ignorant and worthless class of anti-social whites of the South." He noted that her sexual immorality was "a typical picture of the low-grade moron," and that the possibility of her feeble-mindedness being due to nonhereditary causes was "exceptionally remote."

On September 10, 1924, the board approved the sterilization of Carrie Buck. A young attorney named R. G. Shelton was appointed as her guardian, and he immediately appealed to the Circuit Court of Amherst County, Virginia. The case was argued on November 18, 1924, and Laughlin's deposition was submitted into evidence. On April 13, 1925, Judge Bennet Gordon upheld the constitutionality of the law and ordered that Carrie be sterilized within ninety days.

The record that the proponents of the law compiled was impressive. Besides the testimony of Laughlin, they secured the support of Dr. J. S. DeJarnett, superintendent of the largest state institution in Indiana, and Dr. Arthur Estabrook, a colleague of Laughlin's at Cold Spring Harbor who specialized in pedigree analysis and who had worked as a eugenics adviser to the state of Indiana. Shelton secured *no* experts to testify on Carrie Buck's behalf. In upholding the decision of the local court, the Virginia Supreme Court of Appeals rejected Carrie's argument that the law violated the Equal Protection Clause of the Constitution. Judge Jesse P. West ruled that the statute constituted a reasonable kind of class legislation that was intended to *benefit* the persons who would be sterilized. The decision was affirmed without dissent.

On February 6, 1926, Carrie Buck appealed to the United States Supreme Court. Although the highest court had refused to hear arguments on the validity of sterilization laws in the past, this time it permitted the appeal, and the case was argued in the autumn. In his brief, Shelton presciently warned that if the law was upheld, "A reign of doctors will be inaugurated and in the name of science new classes will be added, even races may be brought within the scope of such a regulation and the worst forms of tyranny practiced." This is, of course, a capsule summary of Nazi eugenics.

On May 2, 1927, by vote of 8 to 1, the Supreme Court upheld the Virginia involuntary sterilization law. Justice Oliver Wendell Holmes, eighty-six years old at the time, wrote the brief majority opinion. In now famous words, Holmes asserted: "It is better for all the world, if instead of waiting to execute degenerate offspring for crime, or to let them starve for their imbecility, society can prevent those who are manifestly unfit from continuing their kind. The principle that sustains compulsory vaccination is broad enough to cover cutting the Fallopian tubes."

Dismissing the objection that the Virginia statute violated the Equal Protection Clause by treating institutionalized persons differently from those not in institutions as "the last resort of constitutional arguments," Holmes, whose published letters strongly suggest that he was a eugenicist, opened the doors to eugenic sterilization in the United States. Justice Butler, the only dissenter, did not file an opinion. Although the resurgence of sterilization laws had been under way for four years when *Buck v. Bell* was decided, the Supreme Court ruling greatly boosted the pace at which sterilization programs were enacted and implemented. During the next few years the number of states with sterilization laws jumped from seventeen to thirty, and the number of sterilizations performed on institutionalized persons rose substantially. The subsequent fifteen years (1927–42) were a triumphant period for those who embraced hereditarian hopes for social progress.

Infertility As a Public Health Problem: Why Assisted Reproductive Technologies Are Not the Answer

ELIZABETH HEITMAN

Since the late 1970s, remarkable technological developments in the medical treatment of infertility have received tremendous public attention. Almost simultaneously, both the lay and medical press have announced that impaired fertility is a significant health problem in the United States, what some have called an "epidemic of infertility." The lay press commonly cite the alarming statistic that one out of every twelve couples, and as high as one in six in some age groups, is unable to have children. But while the new sub-specialty of reproductive medicine has grown into a multibillion dollar enterprise, the public health dimensions of infertility have received relatively little attention.

In this time of increased interest in preventive and primary care medicine and efforts to develop community priorities for health services, public health perspectives warrant particular consideration. Regrettably, public health's traditional research and strategic agendas in the area of reproduction have left significant gaps in our understanding of the causes, prevention, and treatment of infertility and its implications for health planning, education, and policy. Moreover, public health policies and rhetoric on family planning ironically may appear to support the widespread use of the very sort of high-tech interventions that public health advocates typically consider too costly and ineffective for widespread use.

This article examines the phenomenon of infertility and efforts to address it through the lens of public health. Specifically, it considers how various imprecise and incomplete conceptual definitions skew the epidemiological data on infertility in ways that exaggerate the proportion of infertile couples whom assisted reproductive technologies might help. The article then explores what is known about infertility among segments of the population that have been

From the *Stanford Law & Policy Review,* 6 (1995), 89–102. Copyright © 1995 by the board of Trustees of the Leland Stanford Junior University. Reprinted by permission.

largely overlooked, and why assisted reproductive technologies are not an effective means of addressing their conditions. Finally, this article suggests how new public health policies and community-oriented measures can complement or replace the current emphasis on expensive, high-tech interventions for the treatment of infertility.

THE SCOPE OF PUBLIC HEALTH

Organized community efforts to prevent disease, promote physical and mental health, and address threats to the well-being of communities distinguish public health from clinical medicine. Public health practitioners often express their ethical goals as the protection of the common good and the reduction of health-related inequalities across populations. Public health policies have often concentrated specifically on the poor and others with limited access to medical services. Yet while public health efforts are ultimately intended to benefit individuals, their emphasis on community welfare presupposes that community interests may override individuals' personal interests. This precept can create ethical tension between practitioners and policymakers in public health, who focus on the community as a whole, and those in clinical medicine, who focus on the identified patient.

Perhaps the best known activities of public health are the monitoring of the population's health status and the collection of health statistics. The epidemiological, statistical, and environmental functions of both governmental and nongovernmental public health organizations play a crucial role in health-related research, health planning, and the control of disease at every level of society. Equally important to public health, however, are the less prominent dimensions of health education and community mobilization, the development and evaluation of health policy, and the assessment of health services. A comprehensive approach to infertility must involve each of these disciplines.

EPIDEMIOLOGY AND INFERTILITY

The field of epidemiology measures the distribution, dynamics, and determinants of health and disease in and across populations. These data often provide the basis for disease control, health planning, and health policy formation. Other than studies on environmental and disease-based threats to fertility, public health researchers in reproductive health have typically studied patterns of community fertility, examining population-based birthrates and their determinants rather than the distribution, dynamics, or determinants of the ability to conceive or carry a pregnancy to term. Prior to the development of medical technologies for assisted reproduction, there was virtually no public health literature on infertility.

Definitions, Presuppositions, and Conceptual Issues

Although extensive statistics on worldwide fertility exist, little comprehensive epidemiological data is available on the actual prevalence or causes of infertility. One major reason for this paucity of information on infertility is that, until recently, it has simply not been considered a public health problem. Since the turn of the century, and particularly since the availability of contraceptives, epidemiological efforts and public health concern about reproduction have focused on fertility as a *threat* to the health of women, their children, and society. This response has been particularly directed toward nonwhite and poor women, and women in developing nations. Epidemiologists, health educators, and policymakers have understood the control of fertility to mean its restriction, not its enhancement. Today, the field of public health is dominated by concern for the improvement of women's personal standard of living, and that of their communities, through the stabilization or limitation of reproduction.

Other conceptual considerations also affect the data on infertility in ways that are important for health planning and policy. Differences in the essential terminology used across the literature pose one obstacle to integrating the work of clinical reproductive health specialists and epidemiologists. Classically, the word *fertility* connotes *actual childbearing,* whereas *fecundity* refers to *reproductive ability.* However, *infertility* means *diminished capacity for conception* whereas *infecundity* means the *total inability to reproduce.* Nonetheless, the terms fertility and fecundity are often used as equivalents, and fecundity/infecundity are almost never used in the lay or clinical literature. The phrases *diminished* or *impaired* fecundity and fertility add to the definitional confusion.

In most clinical publications, *infertility* typically refers to a couple's inability to conceive after one or more years of unprotected intercourse, and assumes that neither partner is surgically sterile. This latter distinction may complicate the comparison of clinical reports with broader statistical data, which may include surgical sterilization as one type of infertility. *Primary infertility* refers to the inability to conceive a first child; *secondary infertility* refers to the inability to conceive additional children after one or more live births. Despite these distinctions, the legal, ethical, and sociological literature on infertility has associated almost all forms of involuntary childlessness, including a woman's inability to carry a conceptus to live birth, with infertility. Moreover, despite a growing literature on male infecundity, most of the focus remains on the experiences and treatment of women's infertility. Lay perspectives on the issue may further cloud the terminology; in some cultural contexts, the idea of infertility may also include a woman's failure to bear sons.

An epidemiological issue that is vital to health planning and policy is the appropriate definition of normal, healthy, or appropriate fertility. In 1975, a World Health Organization (WHO) report on the epidemiology of infertility suggested that worldwide a five percent rate of infertility might be a human norm. A clear and consistent definition of fertility is necessary as the baseline for classifying and addressing unhealthy fertility. To date, none exists that can be used in policy to address *both* subfertility and superfertility for *both* populations and individuals.

Part of the problem is the complex biology of fertility. But any definition of healthy or appropriate fertility will also be charged with moral and political implications. Definitions of healthy fertility affect the options of the "unhealthy," and are problematic whether they relate to superfertility or infertility. Many proponents of population control claim that couples and individuals have a right "to decide freely and responsibly on the number and spacing of their children," and have a right of access to family planning information and services to ensure that freedom. This contention suggests that the choice to procreate is the fundamental ethical issue underlying worldwide efforts to control fertility.

However, the rhetoric of reproductive choice and access to medical services seldom includes claims for a right to reproduce, except in terms of freedom from governmental intervention. Although U.S. federal policies require that public facilities providing family planning services also offer basic medical services to assist conception, the treatment of infertility is only rarely mentioned under the umbrella of family planning services. There are also few public infertility clinics in the United States.

For most researchers and policymakers in the field of population control, definitions of "appropriate" fertility are based on the replacement birthrate (2.1 children per woman), population-based average used in national reproductive policy and health education campaigns. As the birthrates in most democratic, industrialized nations have fallen below the replacement rate, this figure has also been linked with such other public health and human rights goals as education and political freedom. However, where specific numerical targets have been applied to individuals, as in the People's Republic of China, public health and human rights advocates have sharply criticized the accompanying governmental interference in personal choice.

Although the concept of replacement has been used to justify a couple's religious or patriotic duty to procreate, it has not been used in policy to support an infertile couple's right to have children. Moreover, the standards of both reproductive choice and replacement affect policy options regarding society's duties to individuals whose fertility has been impaired by the "natural lottery" of disease and disability. In a clinical context, any diagnosis of infertility implies a disease state that, for medical reasons, should be treated. However, even among clinicians there is no consensus on what treatment is adequate or who should pay for such treatment.

In the spring of 1994, the issue of access to infertility treatment at public expense gained considerable attention in New York and Massachusetts when reviews of state-funded health programs revealed that indigent women and men had received drug treatment, surgery, and artificial insemination for infertility under Medicaid. In Massachusetts, the policy debate focused on efforts to reform the welfare program. The dispute was short lived; taxpayer opinion was overwhelmingly against funding. State administrators soon prohibited Medicaid from underwriting such treatment. The public objected most strongly to coverage for the treatment of secondary infertility: 63% of the 260 women receiving fertility drugs in the preceding year already had 1 or more children, and 2 had 8 children each. Critics of the program insisted that the desire to have children was not a medical problem, and that treating infertility at state expense worked against society's interest in preventing the birth of children who would be dependent on public assistance.

In contrast, New York's ongoing debate has focused on the "scandal" of providing specialized treatments when essential primary care services are not available. This broader policy issue of prioritizing medical treatments covered by the state has troubled both public officials and private policy analysts concerned with the just allocation of resources. Recent efforts at health care reform have not adequately addressed the availability of infertility services, perhaps due to the intense debate over access to government-funded abortion. Again, without a clear definition of healthy fertility, neither the scope and meaning of impaired fertility as a public health problem nor the appropriate governmental response can be addressed conclusively.

Defining the "reproductive years," particularly for women, poses another definitional challenge to epidemiology. Definitions of women's reproductive capacity have traditionally been relevant only during the period between menarche (the onset of menses) and menopause, roughly ages fifteen to forty-four. Although a man's reproductive capacity extends throughout his adult life, a man's fertility is effectively limited by his partner's menopause. This distinction has blurred and become politically volatile as in vitro fertilization (IVF) with donor oocytes (female egg) eliminates menopause as the upper age boundary for women's fertility, and the falling age of puberty extends the lower boundary. France has already outlawed the use of IVF with oocyte donation to redress the effects of menopause. French legislators claimed that the natural course of a woman's reproductive life should not be artificially extended. Women's rights advocates and infertility researchers have argued, however, that women should have the option to bear children for as long as they wish, both because of today's longer life expectancy and more active old age, and as a matter of gender equity.

A final consideration involves defining the population for purposes of conducting reproductive health studies. This is perhaps the most serious challenge for public health research on infertility. A number of public health investigators have observed that the recent epidemiological interest in infertility has been due less to a concern about the condition as a public health problem than to the marked increase in infertility consultations that began in 1972. In the United States and elsewhere in the industrialized world, the causes of infertility have been measured primarily by clinicians and epidemiologists affiliated with infertility clinics. As a result, the research population has consisted almost exclusively of those people already seeking medical diagnosis and treatment for childlessness, and the needs and interests of these individuals have shaped the collection of demographic data on infertility.

Reliance on projections from patient data is partly due to methodological constraints, as infertility is a medical diagnosis that can be established only after a thorough medical evaluation. However, this data cannot reflect the more general concerns of community-based perspectives on reproductive health or disease prevention and control. Because most couples seeking high-tech treatment for infertility have been affluent whites, published studies typically do not reflect the traditional public health concern for under-served and at-risk populations. Experts have questioned the validity of inferring population-based infertility rates from the experiences of a narrow spectrum of clinic patients. Nonetheless, little has been done to elaborate the differences between the experiences and needs of this group and those of the public at large. Such clarification is essential to making future epidemiological research on infertility widely applicable.

The Population-Based Data

In 1976, the Center for Health Statistics conducted the National Survey of Family Growth (NSFG), the first direct, population-based study of infertility carried out in the United States. The study was repeated in 1982 and 1988. The 1982 NSFG surveyed 7,969 women between the ages of 15 and 44 regarding their reproductive history. This study has been the cornerstone of the U.S. literature on the epidemiology of infertility. Its results form the primary basis of the 1988 report on infertility by the Congressional Office of Technology Assessment (OTA), probably the most widely cited publication in the field. Advance data from the 1988 NSFG have been available since late 1990, but the survey's results are not yet reported in full.

Using personal interviews, the 1982 NSFG examined the fecundity, use of contraception, dates and outcomes of any pregnancies, marriages, use of family planning and infertility services, and demographics of a national sample of women between fifteen and forty-four years old. From this survey, researchers estimated that nationally approximately 4.5 million, or 8.4% of the 53.6 million married women of childbearing age had an impaired ability to have children. Approximately half of these women, 1.9 million, had no children; 2.6 million had 1 or more previous births. When these figures included those surgically sterilized, infecund couples constituted 13.9% of the study's population.

The 1988 interviews with 8,450 women echo the 1982 figures. In 1988, the NSFG projected that 4.9 million women, 15 to 44 years of age, or 8.4% of the 57.9 million married women of childbearing age nationwide, had impaired fecundity. Of this total, 2.2 million were classified as having primary infertility and 2.7 million as having secondary infertility. While a specific figure excluding surgically sterilized couples is not yet available, commentaries accompanying the data suggest that the 1982 rate of 13 to 14% remains applicable because there was no significant change in the rates of impaired fecundity in any category.

Claims about an epidemic of infertility first arose from the 1982 NSFG's finding that rates of primary infertility had doubled since the National Fertility Study in 1965. In reality, the overall infertility rate for couples had remained relatively constant, growing only 0.6% from 13.3% in 1966 to 13.9% in 1982. However, rates for women in some age groups had increased. In particular, the percentage of infertile women between ages 35 to 39 rose from 18.4% to 24.6%, and the rate among women ages 20 to 24 more than doubled, from 3.6% in 1965 to 10.6% in 1982. Epidemiologists have pointed out repeatedly that the rise in the number of childless women over age thirty-five is not surprising in light of the large increase in the population of women over age thirty-five during the period, coupled with the "baby boom" generation's postponement of childbearing. However, the enormous publicity surrounding the treatment of infertility among women over thirty-five and the ethical and legal controversy over IVF and commercial surrogacy created the popular perception that infertility had increased dramatically across the board.

Despite the assurances of epidemiologists that "there is no epidemic" of infertility, NSFG data suggest several areas in which public health problems do exist. First, there are significant disparities in the rates of infertility among women of different demographic backgrounds. Second, the reasons for the prevalence of impaired fecundity among young women is unclear, and what is known is not fully explained by changes in the size of the cohort. And third, the apparent stability of rates of impaired fecundity generally, despite the greater availability and use of a variety of treatments for infertility, calls into question both the effectiveness of these technologies and their role in infertility policy.

ETHNIC AND SOCIOECONOMIC DIFFERENCES IN INFERTILITY The 1982 NSFG, providing the most recent data organized by race and socioeconomic group, reported the prevalence of infertility among black couples (excluding the surgically sterile) across women's age groups to be roughly twenty-one percent. This figure is 1.5 times greater than the rate of 13% reported among white couples. The most recent data available also suggest that women with less than a high school education (a standard measure of lower socioeconomic status) are more likely to be part of an infertile couple than are their more educated counterparts.

The causes of the higher rate of infertility among blacks are not known. A number of researchers have suggested that there may be an important correlation with black women's higher reported incidence of pelvic inflammatory disease (PID), a leading cause of infertility worldwide. The 1982 NSFG found that black women were about twice as likely to have been treated for PID as were white women, and that both whites and blacks were more likely to have been treated than Hispanic women. Although the percentage of women treated for PID did not vary statistically with income, women with only high school educations were more likely than college-educated women to have been treated. These data may also seriously underestimate the effects of PID on the fertility of black women, because a considerable proportion of women with PID do not seek treatment.

The documented prevalence of infertility among black couples suggests that black women should constitute a considerable proportion of those seeking infertility services. However, the opposite is true: infertile nonwhite women appear to seek reproductive services much less often than their white counterparts. Only thirty percent of both black and Hispanic women reporting impaired fecundity in the 1988 NSFG, as compared with forty-seven percent of white women, had sought some form of infertility service, including simple medical advice on becoming pregnant.

The high percentage of infertility among black women that is attributed to PID also suggests that these women might be candidates for surgery to repair blocked fallopian tubes or for IVF. Nonetheless, only 12.8% of black women in the NSFG had sought specialized infertility services (including ovulatory drugs, artificial insemination, surgery or other intervention for blocked fallopian tubes, or IVF), compared with 17% of Hispanics and 27.2% of whites. Socioeconomic status also plays a role, as only 8% of poor women (0 to 149% of poverty level) had sought specialized fertility services, compared with 32% of affluent women (400 + % of poverty level).

Insurance coverage, not discussed in the NSFG, impacts heavily on access to specialized reproductive services. Many people with excellent health insurance may discover that their policies exclude treatment for infertility beyond a diagnostic work-up or perhaps surgical intervention to repair damaged organs. While at least eight states now require insurance companies to cover or offer coverage for IVF as part of any policy that includes pregnancy-related services, many basic health insurance policies do not always cover pregnancy. Doctors who know of a couple's financial constraints and limited insurance coverage may not refer them to fertility clinics. Moreover, both private clinics and state-funded medical school clinics typically have eligibility criteria for prospective IVF couples that include such socioeconomic factors as a "stable" marriage, sufficient education to comply with treatment regimens, and the financial resources to provide "adequately" for a child. Each of these factors may weigh against the poor, as well as against nonwhite couples whom clinic personnel may assume to be more financially at risk.

Even if treatment for infertility were readily accessible to poor and nonwhite couples, their use of such services might still depend on the extent to which they perceive infertility to be a medical problem. The belief that pregnancy is not a medical condition is considered a significant barrier to the use of prenatal services by poor, black, and Hispanic women. These women receive significantly less prenatal care compared to middle-class whites. Even less is known about the psychosocial experiences of infertile nonwhite and poor women than is known about their rates of impaired fertility. Discovering couples' motives for seeking infertility services has dominated the question of how demographic variables affect perceptions of infertility and responses to it.

Many middle-class white women experience infertility as a frustrating foreclosure of choice. They seek to regain personal control over their lives and bodies through medical intervention. By contrast, many poor and nonwhite women who have endured other hardships and who consequently may not focus on issues of personal control, may experience infertility more in terms of general adversity. If infertility is one in a series of negative, seemingly irreversible events in a woman's life, she may be more likely to attribute it to fate or God's will than seek to address it through science. Women with such beliefs are less likely to seek medical treatment irrespective of their rates of infertility.

IMPAIRED FERTILITY AMONG YOUNG ADULTS AND TEENAGERS The prevalence of infertility among young women is not as well documented as that of women over age twenty-five. Nonetheless, the available data suggest that impaired fecundity among women ages fifteen to twenty-four is a considerable problem. The 1982 NSFG reported that between 1965 and 1982 the rate of infertility (excluding surgical sterilization) among married women ages 15 to 19 rose from 0.06% to 2.1%, and from 3.6% to 10.6% for women ages twenty to twenty-four. Unfortunately, the NSFG's focus on married women and changes in the age categories make population wide inferences difficult.

The most recent NSFG found that the rate of impaired fecundity among married women ages 15 to 24 dropped from 8.8% in 1982 to 7.6% in 1988. However, because the 1988 NSFG does not use the same age-groups as the 1982 report, it is difficult to interpret the prevalence of infertility among women twenty to twenty-four, whose infertility rates had increased so dramatically in the previous cycle. Moreover, by focusing exclusively on married women, the

NSFG does not address the fecundity of the large numbers of unmarried, sexually active women in this age-group. Particularly among young black women, a greater proportion of whom experience motherhood without marriage, impaired fertility may be a real concern.

Much of the increase in infertility among young women has been attributed to an increased incidence of chlamydia and gonorrhea, sexually transmitted diseases (STDs) which can lead to PID and occlusion of the fallopian tubes. The rates of sexually transmitted diseases have increased across all age and demographic groups. This increase appears to be especially significant for black adolescents and young adults. These groups typically have limited access to the medical care that can prevent the serious health consequences of STDs. Rising infertility rates among young black women appear to be one of the most serious effects of PID resulting from untreated STDs.

THE EFFECTIVENESS AND COSTS OF REPRODUCTIVE TECHNOLOGIES The lack of change in the prevalence of infecundity and infertility reported in the United States over the past two decades raises a serious challenge to the role of clinical infertility treatment in reproductive health policy. Most specialized infertility treatments (ovulation-inducing drugs, artificial insemination, tubal surgery, and IVF) attempt to redress childlessness rather than to cure biological infertility per se. If, as the data suggest, assisted reproductive technologies have had little effect on rates of infertility or on the differentials among subgroups, it is difficult to justify their apparent primacy among interventions against infertility. It is even harder to rationalize any future widespread application at public expense.

The effectiveness of reproductive technologies depends on whether their effects are measured in terms of live births or improved natural procreative capacity. Couples who successfully conceive and deliver a child using assisted reproductive techniques may still be considered infertile for epidemiological purposes if they remain unable to procreate without medical assistance. If the policy question is how best to resolve childlessness among the infertile rather than how best to address its biological causes, the answers may differ greatly.

As is typical of most high-tech medical interventions in the United States, the major infertility treatments were not well evaluated before they were adopted into widespread practice. In the past few years, however, clinical studies and technology assessments have suggested that even measured in terms of individual births following infertility treatment, the demonstrated effectiveness of specialized techniques has not been high. For example, using the delivery of a live infant as the measure of successful treatment, researchers report that the most effective use of IVF (to treat tubal blockage) has a marginal success rate of only 10 to 15 live births per 100 women over as many as 6 cycles. The reported effectiveness of IVF for the treatment of low sperm count, endometriosis, and advanced maternal age has varied across clinical studies. While some clinics claim success rates of fifteen to twenty percent, the comprehensive analysis performed by the Canadian Royal Commission on New Reproductive Technologies concluded that there is no clear indication of IVF's effectiveness for these conditions.

Beyond the issue of effectiveness, the costs and potential unwanted side effects of assisted reproductive technologies raise further questions about their widespread application and their potential coverage by public health policies. Three recent evaluations of the direct charges and indirect economic consequences of infertility treatment concluded that the costs of induced ovulation, tubal surgery, and IVF are too great to ignore in the formation of public policy.

Although the charge for a single treatment cycle may be as low as a few hundred dollars for fertility drugs and several thousand dollars for IVF, the cumulative cost for a successful delivery after such interventions is dramatically higher. In 1991, the average hospital delivery charge for mother and infant in one Boston teaching hospital was slightly under $10,000. Although total hospital charges do not reflect total costs, this figure is profoundly less than the costs of a live birth after tubal surgery, projected at $85,000. Similarly, the costs of a live delivery range from $50,000 to $72,727 when IVF is used for tubal occlusion and from $160,000 to $800,000 when IVF is used to overcome the combination of male-factor infertility and advanced maternal age. The average range for IVF generally is $66,667 to $114,286. Moreover, the eighty-five to ninety percent of couples who do not achieve pregnancy or live birth despite multiple interventions may incur the bulk of these costs as they undergo treatment.

One element often overlooked in the greater cost of delivery associated with assisted reproductive technologies is the cost of multiple-gestation pregnancies, which may be ten to thirty times more likely with the use of ovulation-inducing drugs and the implantation of more than one embryo. The growing use of infertility treatments nationwide has been associated with a marked rise in the number of multiple-gestation pregnancies and an attendant incidence of related complications and costs for mothers and babies. Counting only the hospital charges for delivery and subsequent care of mother and infant, studies have estimated the cost per baby of twins at $18,974 and of triplets at $36,588.

Assisted reproductive technologies also carry significant non-economic costs. The social costs of higher morbidity and mortality among infants from multiple-gestation pregnancies are occasionally compounded by the tragic need for "selective reduction," the abortion of one or more fetuses when multiple gestation itself threatens the lives of the woman and/or all of her would-be progeny. Moreover, there is growing evidence that ovulation-inducing drugs may be linked to an increased risk of ovarian cancer, especially for those women who ultimately never conceive.

Even when the physical costs are few, the psychological consequences of infertility treatment may be quite burdensome. Many commentators have observed that the use of reproductive technologies often involves a tragic medicalization of women's (and men's) experiences of procreation, and creates false hopes for biological parenthood. Particularly for those couples who never conceive, the resulting anxiety, confusion, and shame of failure can be devastating.

Infertile couples reportedly willing to try and to pay "almost anything" to create their own baby are not unlike many chronically ill Americans searching for a cure. Their choice to pursue high-cost and marginally effective treatment at their own expense is an essential freedom afforded by the private health care system in the United States. However, the public health policy goal of reducing health-related inequalities across the population does not require that society underwrite the universal pursuit of low-probability outcomes.

While standards of appropriate intervention and coverage have been more difficult to establish in the United States than in countries with nationalized health care, reform of the United States' system will depend on the establishment of such standards and the demonstrated effectiveness of specific interventions. The challenge for policymakers is to evaluate the benefits of biological parenthood, to weigh the costs and effectiveness of intervention against those benefits, and to assess the results with respect to essential health services. It was in this context that the Clinton administration excluded IVF from its standard health insurance package and the Canadian province of Ontario restricted IVF coverage to use for bilateral tubal blockage.

In the absence of widespread insurance or governmental coverage of specialized reproductive services, those couples who cannot afford to pay for treatment may never gain access to the technologies. Governmental decisions that simply limit the availability of these technologies would perpetuate not only the current inequity in access to specialized procedures but also the narrow clinical view of infertility as a disease that demands a high-tech cure. It is essential that comprehensive health policy on infertility also incorporate a preventive element. By promoting research and education on the *causes* of infertility, and providing programs to modify or prevent behaviors that increase infertility-causing disease, the need for infertility treatment could be reduced and the medical services provided more effectively.

RECOMMENDATIONS FOR POLICY AND RESEARCH

Increased and expanded research on infertility is essential if this complex problem is to be resolved. The lack of comprehensive epidemiological data on the prevalence and causes of infertility compromises both the value of what is known and the manner in which that knowledge is used to form policy. In 1988, the OTA suggested that the federal government improve the collection of data on infertility by expanding the NSFG's sample and the frequency of follow-up surveys. Populationwide statistics on infertility are still badly needed to form public policy, because the absence of data limits the political voice of groups whose problems affect all of society. Future demographic studies must be crafted carefully because their design can influence not only the interpretation of issues, but also the identification of key players and the definition of their roles and needs for many years.

The usefulness of future research will also depend on the standardization of definitions and methods in the epidemiology of infertility. For example, the definition of groups included in an expanded study of infertility must consider both the statistical and political meaning of "significant population." To maximize the applicability of data to both medical and public health intervention, classification should consider:

- strictly biological/genetic factors that appear to be important for fertility and its impairment;
- socio-cultural beliefs and practices, such as late marriage or the acceptance of adolescent parenthood, that may have important biological consequences for fertility; and
- socio-cultural beliefs and practices that affect the perception of infertility and the use of medical services.

Each of these factors must also be examined with regard to their relationship to race, ethnicity, and socioeconomic status.

Importantly, additional epidemiological research is also needed to study the relationship between the spread of sexually transmitted diseases and the incidence of infertility. One of the OTA's first recommendations on addressing infertility was that Congress establish a national data collection system to study chlamydia and PID. To date, no such database exists, and we may in fact have a less clear picture of the prevalence and consequences of STDs than we had before the OTA report. Because infertility caused by PID appears to disproportionately affect poor and nonwhite women, and because such infertility may be perceived as the result of sexual behavior that some would consider immoral, this research has not had the moral appeal of providing treatment for the "innocent" and "responsible" women whose infertility stems from other causes. Yet without such data it is difficult to separate the preventable from the unpreventable causes of infertility.

Together with increased and re-focused research into the epidemiology of infertility, changes in policy are also essential. As discussed earlier, the prevention of infertility has received very little attention in either practice or in policy. The general emphasis on treatment over prevention is a noted consequence of Americans' desire for a technological "quick fix" to problems. This search for immediate solutions is coupled with an unwillingness to invest in less tangible, future effects of prevention where only statistical persons are at risk. This emphasis is illustrated by the reality that less than one percent of the nation's aggregate health expenditures are spent on preventive public health activities, despite their typically greater effectiveness and lower cost. Where treatment is difficult, expensive, or largely ineffective, however, the importance of prevention grows. Infertility is a classic example demonstrating why the need for prevention is central to comprehensive health policy.

In 1993 the Canadian Royal Commission on New Reproductive Technologies confronted these issues and recommended the establishment of a centralized, integrated, national preventive strategy to address infertility. While the differences in the U.S. health care system make centralized oversight unlikely, an integrated strategy on prevention is still necessary. Efforts to prevent infertility should take place at four levels:

- education
- access to preventive health services
- access to treatment for STDs
- ongoing evaluation and research of the successful approaches to reduce the risk and incidence of infertility.

Education

Although public education about sexually related matters continues to be a politically volatile topic, the OTA's primary recommendation for Congressional involvement in the prevention of infertility was to increase the public's understanding of PID and the STDs that cause it. Community clinic-based educational campaigns on sexual and reproductive health may be particularly valuable among populations where childbearing is central to a woman's identity. However, such programs should also actively target men as potential carriers of infertility-causing STDs. In addition to their current emphasis on the prevention of HIV and unwanted pregnancy using barrier contraceptives, these educational programs should stress that barrier methods have the additional advantage of protecting future fertility. This approach is consistent with campaigns that present birth control as a means of increasing a woman's reproductive choices, as barrier contraceptives protect the choice to bear children in the future.

Across the country, the principal site for public health education is the school. Health education classes typically include material on sexuality, reproduction, and sexually transmitted diseases, including HIV. Although the timing of school-based sex education varies tremendously among communities, experts advocate educational programs beginning in elementary school as part of a comprehensive strategy to reduce the incidence of teen pregnancy, STDs, and HIV. This approach may help to reduce infertility among young women, as the increased rate of sexual activity among preteens suggests that education in middle school may occur too late to prevent some PID-related infections.

However, in spite of the intellectual appeal of educational efforts, there is controversy over the effectiveness of sex education in the schools because there has been no demonstrated decrease in teen pregnancy or STDs in communities with even the most comprehensive programs. At the same time programs that teach only abstinence do not seem to have any significant effect either. Experience with integrated community approaches to sex education suggests that multilateral efforts may be more successful. Providing a combination of factual knowledge about sexual issues, help in developing interpersonal and decision-making skills, and social support for responsible behavior has been shown to reduce the incidence of teen parenthood. Especially in communities where adolescent parenthood is accepted, such educational programs may make a convincing case for both abstinence and "safe sex" by stressing that unprotected intercourse *threatens* one's future ability to have children. Such a unified approach may be the key to an effective educational strategy targeting preventable infertility.

Increased Access to Preventive Health Services

Beyond education, increased access to preventive measures against PID-induced infertility, particularly the greater availability of barrier contraceptives, is an essential aspect of a comprehensive public health campaign. For adult patients of public family planning clinics, the emphasis on birth control and assumptions about women's willingness or ability to use more active forms of contraception have led to an increased use of Norplant (time released contraceptive placed in the arm for up to five years) and Depo-Provera (hormone shot contraceptive lasting three months) over both the Pill and diaphragms. But with any of these types of contraception, women must be encouraged to also use a barrier method to protect against both conception and STDs. The "female condom," intended to give women the power to protect themselves against both pregnancy and STDs, has met with little acceptance. The use of traditional condoms with other forms of contraception may be abandoned unless women have equally easy access to both. Similarly, STD clinics, which treat primarily male patients, should provide condoms cheaply or free of charge as part of their treatment. In doing so, clinics should also emphasize the protection of fertility to add weight to current warnings about HIV and the personal benefits of using condoms.

Efforts to distribute condoms in public schools have prompted heated criticism from religious authorities and conservative political activists who claim that the easy availability of contraceptives is a tacit approval of adolescent sexual activity. Nonetheless, educational programs that teach adolescents the social and developmental skills necessary to postpone sexual activity, and programs to protect young people from STDs and their consequences, must acknowledge the early age at which many adolescents already engage in sexual intercourse. The practice of making condoms available would recognize and confront this reality.

Access to Treatment for STDs

Access to diagnosis and treatment of infertility-causing STDs is both essential to any personal health care package and integral to any meaningful public health system. Attention to the diagnosis and effective treatment of STDs can significantly reduce the incidence of infertility from PID and the potential demand for reproductive services. Typically, treatment consists of low-tech antibiotics which are simple and inexpensive to administer. Contact tracing of persons infected with chlamydia and gonorrhea, a traditional dimension of public health efforts to track and control the spread of STDs, may also play an important role in advancing this treatment strategy.

Ongoing Evaluation and Research

Measuring the effects of prevention and identifying the relevant variables is a complex process that may make the success of preventive health campaigns difficult to ascertain in the short term. Population-based research on the prevention of infertility will require policymakers' patience to view successes in the long-term. A long-range outlook is necessary if the educational and treatment programs under study are to remain in place until their goals, methods, and outcomes can be evaluated.

Whether focused on school-based, clinic-based, or community-based education, health educators need to determine which strategies work for specific populations and why. In particular, more research is needed into the often-acknowledged gap between awareness of health risks and associated behavior. Studies examining the effectiveness of condom distribution among various populations from various sites are needed to establish which variables affect the actual use of condoms once they have been made available. Research into the prevention of HIV also affords an important opportunity to evaluate measures to control the STDs that affect fertility. Finally, evaluation of treatment programs for STDs must explore whether emphasis on the treatment of men, whose symptoms appear earlier and more markedly, can improve the prevention of infertility among women. Such an integrated research agenda can enhance policy for the treatment of infertility in several ways by indicating the areas in which preventive strategies do not work and thus where medical efforts to understand the causes of infertility must be redoubled. This knowledge can then illuminate those situations in which prevention is indeed the key to eliminating infertility.

How Many People Can the Earth Support?

JOEL E. COHEN

On April 25, 1679, in Delft, Holland, the inventor of the microscope, Antoni van Leeuwenhoek, wrote down what may be the first estimate of the maximum number of people the earth can support. If all the habitable land in the world had the same population density as Holland (at that time about 120 people for every square kilometer), he calculated, the earth could support at most 13.4 billion people—far fewer than the number of spermatozoans his lenses had revealed in the milt of a cod.

In subsequent centuries, van Leeuwenhoek's estimate has been followed by dozens of similar calculations. Around 1695 a Londoner named Gregory King estimated that the earth's "Land If fully Peopled would sustain" at most 12.5 billion people. In 1765 a German regimental pastor, Johann Peter Süssmilch, compared his own figure (13.9 billion) with the estimates of van Leeuwenhoek, the French military engineer Sébastien Le Prestre de Vauban (5.5 billion) and the English writer and cartographer Thomas Templeman (11.5 billion).

In recent decades estimates of maximum population have appeared thicker and faster than ever before. Under the rubric of "carrying capacity" they crop up routinely in environmental debates, in United Nations reports and in papers by scholars or academic politicians trained in ecology, economics, sociology, geography, soil science or agronomy, among other disciplines. Demographers, however, have been strangely silent. Of the more than 200 symposiums held at the 1992 and 1993 annual meetings of the Population Association of America, not one session dealt with estimating or defining human carrying capacity for any region of the earth. Instead, professional demographers tend to focus on the composition and growth of populations, restricting their predictions to the near term—generally a few decades into the future—and framing them in conditional terms: *If* rates of birth, death and migration (by age, sex, location, marital status and so on) are such-and-such, *then* population size and distribution will be so-and-so.

From *The Sciences,* November/December 1993, pp. 18–23. Based on the book, *How Many People Can the Earth Support?* by Joel E. Cohen. Copyright © 1995 by Joel E. Cohen. Reprinted by permission of the author and the publisher, W. W. Norton and Company.

Such conditional predictions, or forecasts, can be powerful tools. Projections by the U.N. show dramatically that *if* human populations continued to grow at 1990 rates in each major region of the world, *then* the population would increase more than 130-fold in 160 years, from about 5.3 billion in 1990 to about 694 billion in 2150. Those figures are extremely sensitive to the future level of average fertility. If, hypothetically, from 1990 onward the average couple gradually approached a level of fertility just one-tenth of a child more than required to replace themselves, world population would grow from 5.3 billion in 1990 to 12.5 billion in 2050 and 20.8 billion in 2150. In contrast, if (again hypothetically) starting in 1990 and ever after couples bore exactly the number of children needed to replace themselves, world population would grow from 5.3 billion in 1990 to 7.7 billion in 2050 and would level off at around 8.4 billion by 2150.

The clear message is that people cannot forever continue to have, on average, more children than are required to replace themselves. That is not an ideological slogan; it is a hard fact. Conventional agriculture cannot grow enough food for 694 billion people; not enough water falls from the skies. The finiteness of the earth guarantees that ceilings on human numbers do exist.

Where are those ceilings? Some people believe that any limit to human numbers is so remote that its existence is irrelevant to present concerns. Others declare that the human population has already exceeded what the earth can support in the long run (how long is usually left unspecified). Still others concede that short-term limits may exist, but they argue that technologies, institutions and values will adapt in unpredictable ways to push ceilings progressively higher so that they recede forever. The differences of opinion are buttressed by vast disparities in calculation. In the past century, experts of various stripes have made estimates of human carrying capacity ranging from less than a billion to more than 1,000 billion. Who, if anybody, is right?

For several years I have been trying to understand the question, "How many people can the earth support?" and the answers to it. In the process I came to question the question. "How many people can the earth support?" is not a question in the same sense as "How old are you?"; it cannot be answered by a number or even by a range of numbers. The earth's capacity to support people is determined partly by processes that the social and natural sciences have yet to understand, partly by choices that we and our descendants have yet to make.

In most of its scientific senses, *carrying capacity* refers to a population of wild animals within a particular ecosystem. One widely used ecology textbook defines it as follows: "Number of individuals in a population that the resources of a habitat can support; the asymptote, or plateau, of the logistic and other sigmoid equations for population growth." Even within ecology, the concept of carrying capacity has important limitations. It applies best under stable conditions and over relatively short spans of time. In the real world, climates and habitats fluctuate and change; animals adapt to their conditions and eventually evolve into new species. With each change, the carrying capacity changes, too.

When applied to human beings, the concept becomes vastly more volatile. I have collected twenty-six definitions of human carrying capacity, all published since 1975. Most of them agree on a few basic points—for instance, that the concept refers to the number of people who can be supported for some period (usually not stated) in some mode of life considered plausible or desirable. Most of the definitions recognize that ecological concepts of carrying capacity must be extended to allow for the role of technology. Most also agree that culturally and individually variable standards of living, including standards of environmental quality, set limits on population size well before the physical requirements for sheer subsistence start to become an issue.

In other respects, however, the definitions vary widely or even contradict one another. How long must a population be sustainable? Does it make sense to speak of local or regional carrying capacity—or do trade and the need for inputs from outside any specified region imply that only a global scale will do? More fundamental, how constraining are constraints? Some definitions deny the existence of any finite carrying capacity altogether, holding that human ingenuity will win out over any natural barriers; others acknowledge that the limits are real but recognize that human choices, now and in the future, will largely decide where those limits fall.

In my opinion, that last point—the interplay of natural constraints and human choices—is the key to making sense of human carrying capacity. The deceptively simple question "How many people can the earth support?" hides a host of thorny issues.

HOW MANY PEOPLE AT WHAT AVERAGE LEVEL OF MATERIAL WELL-BEING?

The human carrying capacity of the earth will obviously depend on the typical material level at which people choose to live. Material well-being includes food (people choose variety and palatability, beyond the constraints imposed by physiological requirements); fiber (people choose cotton, wool or synthetic fibers for clothing, wood pulp or rag for paper); water (tap water or Perrier or the nearest river or mud hole for drinking, washing, cooking and watering your lawn, if you have one); housing (Auschwitz barracks, two men to a plank, or Thomas Jefferson's Monticello); manufactured goods; waste removal (for human, agricultural and industrial wastes); natural-hazard protection (against floods, storms, volcanoes and earthquakes); health (prevention, cure and care); and the entire range of amenities such as education, travel, social groups, solitude, the arts, religion and communion with nature. Not all of those features are captured well by standard economic measures.

HOW MANY PEOPLE WITH WHAT DISTRIBUTION OF MATERIAL WELL-BEING?

An ecologist, an economist and a statistician went bow hunting in the woods and spied a deer. The ecologist shot first, and his arrow landed five meters to the left of the deer. The economist shot next, and her arrow landed five meters to the right of the deer. The statistician looked at both arrows, looked at the deer, and jumped up and down shouting: "We got it! We got it!"

Estimates of human carrying capacity rarely take into account the scatter or distribution of material well-being throughout a population. Yet paying attention to average well-being while ignoring the distribution of well-being is like using an average arrow to kill a deer. People who live in extreme poverty may not know or care that the global average is satisfactory, and the press of present needs may keep them from taking a long-term view. For example, thanks to genetic engineering, any country with a few Ph.D.s in molecular plant biology and a modestly equipped laboratory can insert the genes to create stronger, more disease-resistant, higher-yielding plants. If every region has the scientific and technical resources to improve its own crop plants, the earth can support more people than it can if some regions are too poor to help themselves.

HOW MANY PEOPLE WITH WHAT TECHNOLOGY?

The complexities of technological choices often disappear in heated exchanges between environmental pessimists and technological optimists:

Ecologist: When a natural resource is being consumed faster than it is being replenished or recycled, an asset is being depleted, to the potential harm of future generations.

Technologist: If new knowledge and technology can produce an equivalent or superior alternative, then future generations may turn out to be better off.

Taxpayer: Which natural resources can be replaced by technology yet to be invented, and which cannot? Will there be enough time to develop new technology and put it to work on the required scale? Could we avoid future problems, pain and suffering by making other choices now about technology or ways of living? *[No answer from ecologist or technologist.]*

The key to the argument is time. As Richard E. Benedick, an officer of the U.S. Department of State who has also served with the World Wildlife Fund, worried:

While it is true that technology has generally been able to come up with solutions to human dilemmas, there is no guarantee that ingenuity will always rise to the task. Policymakers must contend with a nagging thought: what if it does not, or what if it is too late?

HOW MANY PEOPLE WITH WHAT DOMESTIC AND INTERNATIONAL POLITICAL INSTITUTIONS?

Political organization and effectiveness affect human carrying capacity. For example, the United Nations Development Program estimated that developing countries could mobilize for development as much as $50 billion a year (an amount comparable to all official development assistance) if they reduced military expenditures, privatized public enterprises, eliminated corruption, made development priorities economically more rational and improved national governance. Conversely, population size, distribution and composition affect political organization and effectiveness.

How will political institutions and civic participation evolve with increasing numbers of people? As numbers increase, what will happen to people's ability to participate effectively in the political system?

What standards of personal liberty will people choose?

How will people bring about political change within existing nations? By elections and referendums, or by revolution, insurrection and civil war? How will people choose to settle differences between nations, for instance, over disputed borders, shared water resources or common fisheries? War consumes human and physical resources. Negotiation consumes patience and often requires compromise. The two options impose different constraints on human carrying capacity.

HOW MANY PEOPLE WITH WHAT DOMESTIC AND INTERNATIONAL ECONOMIC ARRANGEMENTS?

What levels of physical and human capital are assumed? Tractors, lathes, computers, better health and better education all make workers in rich countries far more productive than those in poor countries. Wealthier workers make more wealth and can support more people.

What regional and international trade in finished goods and mobility in productive assets are permitted or encouraged? How will work be organized? The invention of the factory organized production to minimize idleness in the use of labor, tools and machines. What new ways of organizing work should be assumed to estimate the future human carrying capacity?

HOW MANY PEOPLE WITH WHAT DOMESTIC AND INTERNATIONAL DEMOGRAPHIC ARRANGEMENTS?

Almost every aspect of demography (birth, death age structure, migration, marriage, and family structure) is subject to human choices that will influence the earth's human carrying capacity.

A stationary global population will have to choose between a long average length of life and a high birthrate. It must also choose between a single average birthrate for all regions, on the one hand, and a demographic specialization of labor on the other (in which some areas have fertility above their replacement level, whereas other areas have fertility below their replacement level).

Patterns of marriage and household formation will also influence human carrying capacity. For example, the public resources that have to be devoted to the care of the young and the aged depend on the roles played by families. In China national law requires families to care for and support their elderly members; in the United States each elderly person and the state are largely responsible for supporting that elderly person.

HOW MANY PEOPLE IN WHAT PHYSICAL, CHEMICAL AND BIOLOGICAL ENVIRONMENTS?

What physical, chemical and biological environments will people choose for themselves and for their children? Much of the heat in the public argument over current environmental problems arises because the consequences of present and projected choices and changes are uncertain. Will global warming cause great problems, or would a global limitation on fossil-fuel consumption cause greater problems? Will toxic or nuclear wastes or ordinary sewage sludge dumped into the deep ocean come back to haunt future generations when deep currents well up in biologically productive offshore zones, or would the long-term effects of disposing of those wastes on land be worse? The choice of particular alternatives could materially affect human carrying capacity.

HOW MANY PEOPLE WITH WHAT VARIABILITY OR STABILITY?

How many people the earth can support depends on how steadily you want the earth to support that population. If you are willing to let the human population rise and fall, depending on annual crops, decadal weather patterns and long-term shifts in climate, the average population with ups and downs would include the peaks of population size, whereas the guaranteed level would have to be adjusted to the level of the lowest valley. Similar reasoning applies to variability or stability in the level of well-being; the quality of the physical, chemical and biological environments; and many other dimensions of choice.

HOW MANY PEOPLE WITH WHAT RISK OR ROBUSTNESS?

How many people the earth can support depends on how controllable you want the well-being of the population to be. One possible strategy would be to maximize numbers at some given level of well-being, ignoring the risk of natural or human disaster. Another would be to accept a smaller population size in return for increased control over random events. For example, if you settle in a previously uninhabited hazardous zone (such as the flood plain of the Mississippi River or the hurricane-prone coast of the southeastern U.S.), you demand a higher carrying capacity of the hazardous zone, but you must accept a higher risk of catastrophe. When farmers do not give fields a fallow period, they extract a higher carrying capacity along with a higher risk that the soil will lose its fertility (as agronomists at the International Rice Research Institute in the Philippines discovered to their surprise).

HOW MANY PEOPLE FOR HOW LONG?

Human carrying capacity depends strongly on the time horizon people choose for planning. The population that the earth can support at a given level of well-being for twenty years may differ substantially from the population that can be supported for 100 or 1,000 years.

The time horizon is crucial in energy analysis. How fast oil stocks are being consumed matters little if one cares only about the next five years. In the long term, technology can change the definition of resources, converting what was useless rock to a valuable resource; hence no one can say whether industrial society is sustainable for 500 years.

Some definitions of human carrying capacity refer to the size of a population that can be supported indefinitely. Such definitions are operationally meaningless. There is no way of knowing what human population size can be supported indefinitely (other than zero population, since the sun is expected to burn out in a few billion years, and the human species almost certainly will be extinct long before then). The concept of indefinite sustainability is a phantasm, a diversion from the difficult problems of today and the coming century.

HOW MANY PEOPLE WITH WHAT FASHIONS, TASTES AND VALUES?

How many people the earth can support depends on what people want from life. Many choices that appear to be economic depend heavily on individual and cultural values. Should industrial societies use the available supplies of fossil fuels in households for heating and for personal transportation, or outside of households to produce other goods and services? Do people prefer a high average wage and low employment or a low average wage and high employment (if they must choose)?

Should industrial economics seek now to develop renewable energy sources, or should they keep burning fossil fuels and leave the transition to future generations? Should women work outside their homes? Should economic analyses continue to discount future income and costs, or should they strive to even the balance between the people now living and their unborn descendants?

I am frequently asked whether organized religion, particularly Roman Catholicism, is a serious obstacle to the decline of fertility. Certainly in some countries, church policies have hindered couples' access to contraception and have posed obstacles to family planning programs. In practice, however, factors other than religion seem to be decisive in setting average levels of fertility for Roman Catholics. In 1992 two Catholic countries, Spain and Italy, were tied for the second- and third-lowest fertility rates in the world. In largely Catholic Latin America, fertility has been falling rapidly, with modern contraceptive methods playing a major role. In most of the U.S. the fertility of Catholics has gradually converged with that of Protestants, and polls show that nearly four-fifths of Catholics think that couples should make up their own minds about family planning and abortion.

Even within the church hierarchy, Catholicism shelters a diversity of views. On June 15, 1994, the Italian bishops' conference issued a report stating that falling mortality and improved medical care "have made it unthinkable to sustain indefinitely a birthrate that notably exceeds the level of two children per couple." Moreover, by promoting literacy for adults, education for children and the survival of infants in developing countries, the church has helped bring about some of the social preconditions for fertility decline.

On the whole the evidence seems to me to support the view of the ecologist William W. Murdoch of the University of California, Santa Barbara: "Religious beliefs have only small, although sometimes significant, effects on family size. Even these effects tend to disappear with rising levels of well-being and education."

In short, the question "How many people can the earth support?" has no single numerical answer, now or ever. Human choices about the earth's human carrying capacity are constrained by facts of nature and may have unpredictable consequences. As a result, estimates of human carrying capacity cannot aspire to be more than conditional and probable: if future choices are thus-and-so, then the human carrying capacity is likely to be so-and-so. They cannot predict the constraints or possibilities that lie in the future; their true worth may lie in their role as a goad to conscience and a guide to action in the here and now.

The following beautiful quotation from *Principles of Political Economy,* by the English philosopher John Stuart Mill, sketches the kind of shift in values such action might entail. When it was written, in 1848, the world's population was less than one-fifth its present size.

> There is room in the world, no doubt, and even in old countries, for a great increase of population, supposing the arts of life to go on improving, and capital to increase. But even if innocuous, I confess I see very little reason for desiring it. The density of population necessary to enable mankind to obtain, in the greatest degree, all the advantages both of cooperation and of social intercourse, has, in all the most populous countries, been obtained. A population may be too crowded, though all be amply supplied with food and raiment. It is not good for man to be kept perforce at all times in the presence of his species. A world from which solitude is extirpated, is a very poor ideal. . . . Nor is there much satisfaction in contemplating the world with nothing left to the spontaneous activity of nature; with every rood of land brought into cultivation, which is capable of growing food for human beings; every flowery waste or natural pasture ploughed up, all quadrupeds or birds which are not domesticated for man's use exterminated as his rivals for food, every hedgerow or superfluous tree rooted out, and scarcely a place left where a wild shrub or flower could grow without being eradicated as a weed in the name of improved agriculture. If the earth must lose that great portion of its pleasantness which it owes to things that the unlimited increase of wealth and population would extirpate from it, for the mere purpose of enabling it to support a larger but not a better or a happier population, I sincerely hope, for the sake of posterity, that they will content to be stationary, long before necessity compels them to it.
> It is scarcely necessary to remark that a stationary condition of capital and population implies no stationary state of human improvement. There would be as much scope as ever for all kinds of mental culture, and moral and social progress; as much room for improving the Art of Living, and much more likelihood of its being improved, when minds ceased to be engrossed by the art of getting on. Even the industrial arts might be as earnestly and as successfully cultivated, with this sole difference, that instead of serving no purpose but the increase of wealth, industrial improvements would produce their legitimate effect, that of abridging labour. . . . Only when, in addition to just institutions, the increase of mankind shall be under the deliberate guidance of judicious foresight, can the conquests made from the powers of nature by the intellect and energy of scientific discoverers, become the common property of the species, and the means of improving it and elevating the universal lot.

9

GENETIC SCREENING, TESTING, AND THERAPY

Perhaps no other field in health care has advanced as rapidly in the last few years as genetics. Rapid breakthroughs in genetic research, a $3 billion federal Human Genome Project that will map and sequence the genetic makeup of humans, and advances in molecular biology are all contributing to this genetic revolution. According to one commentator, "Conservative estimates are that some 50,000 gene markers will be developed as a result of molecular biology and translated into easy-to-employ biochemical assays, genetic tests, new drugs, and genetic therapies."[1]

Genetic screening can be done to identify those who have, or are likely to develop, a disease, although they are as yet asymptomatic, or it can be done to identify carriers, that is, those who will not develop the disease but who could pass it to offspring. Screening can be done on an entire population, or it can be targeted to some subset, such as an ethnic group at high risk for a particular disease. The most pervasive form of screening currently practiced is neonatal screening, for example, for phenylketonuria (PKU), a metabolic disorder which causes severe mental retardation if not treated with a special, and extremely restrictive, diet. Prenatal screening can identify fetuses with hereditary conditions, which may lead to treatment after or even before birth. Most commonly, however, the detection of genetic disease in fetuses results in abortion.

The genetic defects which cause many single-gene disorders, such as Huntington disease (HD) and cystic fibrosis (CF), have already been discovered, and screening tests have been developed. However, diseases caused by the malfunction of a single gene are relatively rare. The most prevalent diseases—and thus the ones most important from a public health perspective—result from a complex interaction of genetic and environmental factors. Screening for multifactorial diseases, such as breast and ovarian cancer, prostate cancer, coronary artery disease, diabetes, hypertension, Alzheimer's disease, and some forms of mental illness, may be on the horizon.

Genetic testing can contribute to the prevention or reduction of disease. For example, genetic testing of presymptomatic individuals enables them to benefit from early intervention (if it is available). Prenatal genetic testing can help at-risk couples avoid the birth of a seriously ill baby. However, genetic testing could also result in stigmatization and discrimination. For example, information about a person's genetic predisposition to disease might be used by insurance companies to deny coverage or increase premiums. A number of states have passed laws that prohibit insurance companies from doing this.[2]

Another problem with genetic testing is that there are literally thousands of inherited conditions: how should society, insurers, the medical profession, and drug companies decide which tests should be developed and offered? As more and more markers for genetic diseases are discovered, there is increased pressure for genetic testing, due in part to the emergence of a biotechnology industry with a financial interest in testing. Unless it is done appropriately, genetic screening may not yield useful information or improve the public's health. Elias and Annas comment:

> The optimal genetic screening program would only be initiated after adequate public education, with community support and involvement in the program; those screened would be informed of the purpose of the screening and give consent; confidentiality would be maintained; results would be conveyed through nondirective counseling; screening tests would be inexpensive, simple, and accurate; there would be sufficient qualified personnel and laboratory facilities for required follow-up; and the program would provide means of self-assessment.[3]

A good example of a successful population screening program is screening in the Jewish community for Tay-Sachs disease (TSD). The devastating nature of the disease, combined with the lack of a therapy or cure, made it a good candidate for prenatal and carrier screening. Since testing for Tay-Sachs began in the 1970s, there has been a greater than 90% reduction in the incidence of the disease in the Jewish population in the United States and Canada.

However, screening for genetic disease has not always been beneficial, and sometimes has caused great harm. The story of sickle cell disease is a case in point. Law professor Patricia King writes:

> Sickle cell screening programs were often mandated by state legislatures, in contrast to voluntary screening programs for Tay-Sachs disease, which primarily affects Jews. Only after the passage of the National Sickle Cell Anemia Control Act in 1972, which required that federal funds be used in voluntary programs, was the movement toward mandatory laws halted. These programs developed in an ad hoc fashion with disastrous consequences for the African-American community. Inadequate provisions for confidentiality led to stigmatization and discrimination in employment and insurance. As a result of inadequate education and counseling, the difference between sickle cell trait and sickle cell disease was poorly understood by those affected and the general community.[4]

Other problems in mass screening stem from the reliability of the test and the dual problems of false negatives and false positives. Consider newborn screening for PKU, mandated by most states. As Norman Fost points out in the first selection in this chapter, the Guthrie test identified some children with a variation of abnormal phenylalanine metabolism as having PKU when they were not in fact at risk for retardation. Moreover, since the severely restrictive PKU diet itself can cause brain damage, the mass screening program caused some children who would have been of normal intelligence to become retarded.

Abby Lippman discusses another problem raised by prenatal genetic testing, namely, that it "prevents" genetic disease by eliminating fetuses who have certain genetic traits. "Prenatal diagnosis," she writes, "presupposes that certain fetal conditions are intrinsically not bearable." While this is undoubtedly true of the severest diseases, like Tay-Sachs, it is not the case for some of the most common conditions for which prenatal diagnosis is performed, such as Down syndrome, spina bifida, or cystic fibrosis. Individuals living with these conditions may object to prenatal testing because they think it suggests that they should never have come into existence, that their lives are not worth living. Many in the disability community argue that resources would be better spent on making society more accommodating of those with disabilities rather than on screening programs aimed at preventing the births of people likely to be disabled.

Some feminists also object to prenatal testing because they do not believe that it has improved the lot of women or enhanced their choices. Instead, the routinization of prenatal testing makes the "decision" to be tested, and to abort if the fetus is affected, a foregone conclusion. As Lippman notes, "Society does not truly accept children with disabilities or provide assistance for their nurturance. Thus, a woman may see no realistic alternative to diagnosing and aborting a fetus likely to be affected." Lippman does not totally reject prenatal testing, but she does advocate a closer look at the assumptions that motivate it.

Another aspect of the "dark side of genetic screening" is the potential it has to be used not only to prevent serious disease, but to select against relatively minor medical conditions, such as near-sightedness or hay fever. Will there be pressure on prospective parents to have a "perfect baby"? Genetic screening might also be used to prevent the births of people with nonmedical conditions, such as homosexual orientation, which some scientists think has a significant genetic component. Should such tests be developed and made available to people who want them? Some argue that this would be an inappropriate use of technology, one that would contribute to prejudice and discrimination against homosexuals.[5] A related fear is that prenatal testing and genetic engineering might be used, not for the prevention of disease, but for enhancement: to create children who are stronger, smarter, taller, or better looking. Many consider this to be a "new eugenics" and almost as scary as the old eugenics.

The last selection, by LeRoy Walters and Julie Gage Palmer, comes from their book, *The Ethics of Human Gene Therapy*. (Readers interested in understanding the science of genetic disease and how gene therapy works are advised to consult this excellent book.) Gene therapy attempts to treat diseases that result from errors in the structure or function of genes by adding new genes to cells or by substituting new genes for original malfunctioning genes. Sickle cell anemia, cystic fibrosis, rheumatoid arthritis, familial hypercholesterolemia, coronary artery disease, various cancers, and AIDS are among the diseases that might someday be successfully treated with gene therapy. Gene therapy in humans has so far been limited to somatic cell gene therapy. Because somatic cell gene therapy affects only nonreproductive cells, none of the genetic changes produced by somatic cell gene therapy will be passed on to the patient's children. At present, somatic cell gene therapy is still in the experimental stage. While the prospects hold great promise, it remains true that "no approach has definitely improved the health of a single one of the more than 2,000 patients who have enrolled in gene therapy trials worldwide."[6] Nevertheless, somatic cell gene therapy is accepted in principle as no more problematic than any other experimental therapy.

Germ-line gene therapy involves a therapeutic genetic alteration in germ-line or reproductive cells, and is usually done on zygotes or preimplantation embryos. It has several advantages over somatic cell gene therapy. First, in the treatment of genetic diseases, such as CF, which affect many different organs, somatic cell therapy might require several different procedures to accomplish delivery to the various cell types involved. By contrast, germ-line gene therapy would allow the addition of a properly functioning gene to all of the affected cell types in one fell swoop.[7] Second, because germ-line gene therapy would be performed at the earliest stages in human development, it could prevent damage that might occur during fetal development. Third, because germ-line gene therapy alters reproductive cells, any changes would be transmitted to the patient's offspring, if any. Thus, germ-line therapy offers the attractive possibility of reducing the incidence of certain inherited diseases, such as CF, in the human gene pool.

At the same time, the ability to introduce permanent changes into the genome is regarded by many people as making germ-line gene interventions ethically unacceptable. In addition to fear of unalterable mistakes being introduced into the gene pool, critics are concerned about the potential for abuse of the technology to enhance healthy individuals. Such concern, in part, informed a bioethics convention produced by the Council of Europe in 1997 that gathered signatures from twenty-two European states. This convention says that genetic manipulation may be undertaken for purposes of prevention, diagnosis or therapy—but only if it does not aim to introduce a permanent modification in the genome.[8]

Walters and Palmer consider the arguments for and against germ-line gene therapy and conclude that voluntary programs are ethically acceptable in principle. They note that in order to accomplish the permanent elimination of genes that cause disease, germ-line gene therapy would have to be given not only to individuals who suffer from the disease but to healthy carriers of defective genes as well. In their book, Walters and Palmer concede that screening and treating healthy carriers would be an "ambitious public-health program" but maintain that it is "not an entirely unrealistic prospect," noting that programs of a similar scale have been carried out to counteract infectious disease such as tuberculosis and small pox.[9] We leave it to the reader to decide whether germ-line gene therapy ought to be permanently and universally banned, or welcomed as the next contribution to public health.

NOTES

1. Philip J. Boyle, "Shaping Priorities in Genetic Medicine," Special Supplement, *Hastings Center Report* 25, no. 3 (1995), p. S2.

2. Robert Pear, "States Pass Laws to Regulate Uses of Genetic Testing," *New York Times,* October 18, 1997, A1.

3. Sherman Elias and George J. Annas, *Reproductive Genetics and the Law* (Chicago: Yearbook Medical, 1987, p. 54).

4. Patricia A. King, "The Past as Prologue: Race, Class, and Gene Discrimination," in George J. Annas and Sherman Elias, eds. *Gene Mapping: Using Law and Ethics as Guides* (New York: Oxford University Press, 1992, p. 99).

5. Udo Schuklenk, Edward Stein, Jacinta Kerin, and William Byne, "The Ethics of Genetic Research on Sexual Orientation," *Hastings Center Report* 27, no. 4 (1997), pp. 6–13.

6. Theodore Friedmann, "Overcoming the Obstacles to Gene Therapy," *Scientific American* (1997), p. 96.

7. LeRoy Walters and Julie Gage Palmer, *The Ethics of Human Gene Therapy* (New York: Oxford University Press, 1997, p. 62).

8. Meredith Wadman, "European States Outlaw Permanent Changes," *Nature* (1998), *http://www.nature.com/Nature2.*

9. Walters and Palmer, *supra* note 7, p. 63.

Ethical Implications of Screening Asymptomatic Individuals

NORMAN FOST

There is nothing new about screening asymptomatic individuals. It has become more common as health supervision and prevention have become a larger part of medical practice. Individual patients are routinely screened for hypertension, diabetes, and urinary tract infection. Mass screening of school children for intelligence, visual problems, and scoliosis are familiar activities.

Nor is genetic screening new. Mass screening of newborns for phenylketonuria (PKU) began decades ago, and has long been supplemented by tests for other genetic disorders such as maple syrup urine disease, and more recently, hemoglobinopathies. Adults have long been screened for sickle cell disease or trait.

What is new is the rapid growth of laboratory tests for genetic disorders. Molecular biology and the Human Genome Project are increasing the ability to identify genetic disorders and predisposition to disease at a dizzying pace, and each disorder and test has its own unique complexities. The discovery of the gene for cystic fibrosis was a remarkable achievement but not surprising. What was surprising was the discovery that there was not one mutation but hundreds, raising a variety of unanticipated scientific questions and complicating familiar ethical and legal questions about population screening.

Much has been made of the distinction between *screening* and *testing*. The former, as defined by Holtzman in this volume, generally refers to a program aimed at a defined population, often under public auspices. The latter generally refers to a procedure performed on an individual in a doctor-patient relationship. I do not find this distinction a particularly useful one in considering the ethical issues. All screening programs involve performing a test on individuals. If the program is voluntary, then at least minimal standards for consent are implied and the issues overlap substantially with what is called testing. Conversely, some forms of testing are so widespread as to constitute a standard of

From *FASEB Journal*, 6 (1992), 2813–2817. Reprinted by permission of the publisher and the author.

practice and have become de facto screening programs. The central question is what ethical principles and policies should guide proposals to perform a test on an asymptomatic individual or population of individuals.

The principles that should guide genetic screening have been identified with broad consensus for nearly 20 years. Studies and reports from the National Academy of Sciences Institute of Medicine, the President's Commission for the Study of Ethical Problems in Medicine and Biomedical and Behavioral Research, and the Hastings Center are remarkably homogeneous in their conclusions and recommendations. More recently, considerations of presymptomatic screening programs for specific disorders, such as cystic fibrosis and HIV infection, have rediscovered the same principles. The participants in these committees and reports typically include scientists, clinicans, lawyers and ethicists, advocates, and skeptics. Two factors are constant: agreement on the principles that should guide screening and the recurrent appearance of screening programs that ignore these principles.

A BRIEF HISTORY OF GENETIC SCREENING: TWO CASE STUDIES

Mass population screening for genetic disorders in asymptomatic individuals has been conducted for four purposes: presymptomatic detection of disorders for which effective *treatment* is thought to be available; *reproductive counseling,* particularly when effective treatment is not available; *research,* including studies of prevalence or natural history, or to recruit individuals into experimental treatment studies; and *inclusion or exclusion,* particularly for decisions regarding insurance employment. Two case studies will be reviewed to illustrate the ethical problems that arise.

Screening for Treatment: Phenylketonuria

The basic biochemistry of this rare inborn error of metabolism has been understood for more than 60 years. By 1960 it was clear that early detection and institution of a diet restricted in phenylalanine could ameliorate and possibly prevent the severe brain damage that developed in nearly all affected children. The development of the Guthrie test made it possible to screen all newborns cheaply and efficiently, and the development of an inexpensive and palatable milk created the opportunity to make PKU a model for preventing mental retardation. Aided by the leadership of a president passionately concerned about retardation—John F. Kennedy—state statutes were passed mandating newborn screening and referral to treatment centers.

In its early days, there was imperfect knowledge about the many variations of abnormal phenylalanine metabolism and about use of the diet. As a result, some children with variants of hyperphenylalaninemia who were not at risk for retardation were started on the diet. Because severe restriction of this essential amino acid could cause brain damage as surely as could excess, some children were made retarded by the program, and a smaller number died from complications of severe malnutrition. Despite a plea from the American Academy of Pediatrics Committee on Nutrition that mandatory screening be stopped, the program continued and expanded.

Later advances in the understanding of phenylalanine metabolism clarified the indications for treatment and its appropriate limits, but another complication appeared. The survival of women with PKU to reproductive age created a cohort of potential mothers at risk for causing even more extensive damage to potentially normal infants. High serum phenylalanine is one of the most potent teratogens known, causing retardation or structural malformations in 90% of exposed fetuses. As most affected fetuses would not be at risk for PKU, and because one affected mother could give birth to many damaged children, the net potential effect of the newborn screening and treatment program could be an increase in severely damaged children. Such damage can theoretically be prevented if mothers at risk maintained normal serum phenylalanine throughout pregnancy, but such a diet is onerous and must be initiated soon after conception.

In summary, several lessons were learned from the PKU program that should be expected in any screening program whose primary purpose is presymptomatic treatment.

1. *Genetic disorders, like all diseases, are heterogeneous.* There is probably no single-gene disorder, in the sense that phenotype will be determined by a single gene. This is certainly the case when the screening test is a gene product, rather than the gene itself, as such products may be controlled by a number of genes. The disease may be caused by many mutations, as in cystic fibrosis, with widely varying clinical manifestations. Even when there is a single mutation, as in sickle cell disease, the clinical course may be variable, affected by other genes and environmental factors, so that not all individuals will have a similar need for treatment and may not respond similarly to treatment. Treatment that may be lifesaving for some individuals may be unnecessary for others, so that risk/benefit considerations will vary among individuals.

2. *Screening/treatment programs are experiments until benefits and risks have been defined in well-designed studies.* There is broad acceptance for the principle that experimental drugs should be subjected to more rigorous oversight than standard treatment, as risk/benefit ratios are unknown and more likely to be adverse. Moreover, patients cannot meaningfully consent to interventions if there is inadequate information on their benefits and risks. Although drugs, and more recently, devices, have been highly regulated for these reasons, new surgical procedures, laboratory tests, and their attendant treatments have generally not been subjected to high standards of review.

3. *Political factors and zeal can obscure critical thinking.* The rush to institute mass PKU screening was the product of a "PKU lobby," consisting of well-meaning and passionate advocates for the retarded, including families with personal experience with PKU, as well as scientists and the President of the United States. The normal scientific caution that accompanies new tests and treatments was brushed aside, and critics were either dismissed as obstacles in the campaign or their skepticism was suppressed.

4. *Mandatory programs are hard to stop.* The impulse to mandate screening for PKU was understandable given the rarity of the condition. The normal diffusion of scientific information to the general practitioner is slow, and advances regarding a disease that affects 1 in 10,000 infants is not likely to attract immediate attention. But the extraordinary step of mandating treatment should create a special standard for proving its safety and efficacy. As news of the complications and complexities began to trickle in over a decade or more, there was little enthusiasm to return to the legislatures to admit error or to ask that the program be reconsidered. Even when the safety and effectiveness of the PKU had been established, compliance did not necessarily correlate with the presence of mandatory screening: some states with voluntary screening have higher rates of compliance than those that mandate screening.

Screening for Reproductive Counseling: Sickle Cell Disease

Although the molecular basis of this autosomal recessive disorder has been understood longer than any other, effective treatment has remained elusive. Inexpensive and accurate tests for heterozygotes have long been available, and widespread screening was stimulated by the availability of federal funds in the 1970s. Couples found to be carriers had several options: *1)* Abstain from having children; *2)* adoption; *3)* artificial insemination (or later, egg donation) from a donor known not to be a carrier; *4)* illegitimacy, i.e., natural insemination by a donor other than the woman's primary partner; *5)* informed "gambling," i.e., choosing to have natural children as an informed choice; or *6)* prenatal diagnosis and selective abortion.

Most of these alternatives were either unavailable or unappealing to many couples who were screened and found to be at risk, but because the tests were inexpensive and had very low error rates, widespread screening was thought to offer potential benefits to some clients with little or no risk. As with PKU screening, the risks began to become apparent after widespread screening, not as part of prospective studies. They can be classified in two categories: confusion and stigmatization.

CONFUSION Confusion by the clients themselves was common, typically involving a failure to understand the difference between sickle trait (the carrier state) and sickle cell disease (the homozygous condition) or a failure to understand basic elements of probability and reproductive risks. The confusion between trait and disease was aggravated by the reality that sickle trait is associated with morbidity and even mortality under some conditions. Misunderstanding of probability is a more widespread problem, and is related to the general lack of public education on the subject. This confusion was not due to negligent or apathetic counseling. Experienced and dedicated counselors were surprised and frustrated at their inability to educate effectively.

Confusion could also occur in the minds of others. Many states required sickle screening as a condition of entry into elementary school. This served no apparent public health purpose nor did it offer any clear benefit to prospective students, because the vast majority with sickle cell disease would already have been diagnosed by that age, and those with sickle trait had little to gain from genetic counseling while in elementary school. The muddled motives of these programs can be appreciated from a Massachusetts statute that authorized "tests on every child susceptible to the disease known as sickle cell trait . . ." or a District of Columbia law that required sickle screening as a condition of school entry "to prevent and control the spread of communicable diseases." The Dupont Company was discovered to be discriminating on the basis of sickle trait because of an unproven belief that such persons were at higher risk for workplace-related disability. Life insurance companies denied coverage to applicants with sickle trait, without evidence of shortened life expectancy compared with other applicants matched for race and socioeconomic status.

STIGMATIZATION Stigmatization refers to an undesirable social consequence of being labeled. Like confusion, this can occur within the mind of the person screened or by others.

Self-stigmatization refers to adverse consequences of being labeled despite accurate understanding of the information. Although everyone carries lethal recessive genes, ignorance may be bliss and the actual knowledge of it can be distressing and lead to behavioral consequences. The normal inhibitions in sexual relations may be aggravated by the awareness that one is carrying a lethal gene.

Stigmatization by others includes discrimination by employers and insurers. The Air Force Academy excluded African-Americans with sickle trait because of concerns over service-connected disability. This policy was not entirely without reason, as persons with sickle trait are at risk for life-threatening sickling at high altitudes, due to low oxygen tensions, although many thought the actual risk for Air Force recruits had been exaggerated. Couples at risk for producing offspring with sickle cell disease do put health insurers at risk for higher costs. A small self-insured employer may be seriously burdened by one such family. Discrimination on the basis of risk has been central to commercial insurance. Most health insurance is purchased by groups, so that individuals are protected from discrimination on the basis of genetic risk. Companies have not found it economically prudent to screen applicants for individual policies, but results from screening tests obtained for other purposes may not be concealed and increasing awareness of such data has led to discrimination.

In addition to insurance and employment problems, screening led to unexpected discovery of illegitimacy. Counselors were often unprepared for this potential calamity, and women were generally unaware that testing could result in such disclosures. Meaningful efforts to obtain informed consent were uncommon.

The net result of federal funding for mass sickle screening, along with mandatory state screening laws, led to a backlash. Because the gene is concentrated in African-Americans in the U.S., screening programs were racially targeted. As persons being screened came to realize that the benefits were unattractive or unavailable, screening was perceived as having more risks than benefits for many individuals. Prenatal diagnosis was not generally available when screening programs were initiated and at their peak. The racial orientation of the programs, along with concerns about the risk/benefit ratio, led to suspicions of genocide.

The problems with sickle screening were not prominent in a national Tay-Sachs program targeted at Jewish couples. This program featured extensive education before screening was offered and rigorous standards for consent and post-test counseling. Follow-up studies showed high levels of satisfaction, with little stigmatization. Some of these differences can be attributed to the higher educational level of the target population; the absence of any medical significance to the carrier status, reducing the risks for confusion; and the availability of prenatal diagnosis. Thalassemia programs in Sardinia and the Greek Cypriot community in Great Britain also had wider acceptance.

In summary, there were several lessons from the sickle experience that should be anticipated in any widespread screening program whose primary purpose is reproductive counseling.

1. As with treatment programs, *screening programs for reproductive counseling are experiments with unknown benefits and risks.* Well-designed pilot studies are needed to demonstrate that pre-test information can be effectively communicated; that laboratory and counseling errors can be minimized; and that post-test counseling is available.

2. *Informed consent* should be a central feature of such programs. Whether any benefits exist for a given client and whether the possible benefits are worth the risks are value judgments that can be made only by the prospective client. Disclosure should include, when appropriate, the possibility of loss of insurance and employment as well the risk of uncovering illegitimacy.

3. *Screening programs may be driven by political considerations.* A major factor in the federal funding of sickle screening was a political promise by President Nixon in anticipation of political support from African-American leaders. Sickle screening did not emerge from the communities most affected nor from advocacy by leaders in medicine. The availability of money attracted physicians and community leaders. As with PKU screening, enthusiasm exceeded considerations of science or public health. In a study in Greece, widespread sickle screening and counseling had no apparent effect on the birth incidence of infants with sickle cell disease.

4. *Justifications for mandatory screening should be scrutinized.* As with PKU screening, screening was mandated prior to demonstrations of need or benefit. These programs eventually were either repealed or unenforced. In addition to the mandatory programs for entry into school, there were premature proposals to screen newborns without careful consideration of risks and benefits. Many years later, well-designed prospective studies demonstrated the effectiveness of early treatment in preventing serious infection in infants with sickle cell disease, although many of these programs have not adequately addressed the problems associated with identifying infants with sickle trait or other unusual hemoglobinopathies.

WHAT IS SPECIAL ABOUT GENETIC SCREENING?

Presymptomatic screening is central to contemporary medical practice, including the routine annual history and physical examination, urinalysis, and multiphasic laboratory screening. The ethical problems identified in the PKU and sickle stories are not unique to genetic screening. All presymptomatic screening presents the possibility for benefits and risks, generally unknown until they have been studied, and is of uncertain value outside a patient's choice based on his or her unique values. It is primarily the tremendous power of recombinant DNA technology that expands the potential of screening. The difference from the past is quantitative, but on such a scale as to raise the possibility of a major change in traditional premises and practices.

Some experts predict that the Human Genome Project will not simply identify the sequence of the human genome but make available to each individual a record of his/her particular genome, including all mutations with accompanying descriptions of the benefits and risks of testing for the associated disorders. The availability of such information would seem incompatible with traditional notions of informed consent. It is almost beyond comprehension that a typical American consumer, with an 8th-grade reading level, could evaluate such an encyclopedia of information and make an informed choice about whether to undergo prenatal diagnosis and selective abortion, or face an even more complex array of choices regarding gene therapy.

These problems are further complicated by the enormous opportunities for profit in genetic technology. The discovery of the gene for cystic fibrosis created an immediate potential market of at least $1 billion. The opportunity for profit has always coexisted in medicine, but the close involvement of practitioners with commercial genetic laboratories is radically different from the health care system of 20 years ago. The rapid growth of complex profitable technology is occurring in a climate of relatively little regulation, so that concerns about quality control are magnified.

Finally, the new technology creates special problems in a country whose citizens are dependent on their employers for health insurance. Such employers are understandably concerned and motivated to reduce the costs of producing goods and services; employees at high risk for expensive illness themselves or their offspring can threaten the economic survival of a business. The ability to screen prospective employees for such risks will certainly be used if it can be shown to be cost effective. Federal law restricts employers from discriminating on the basis of handicap, but it is unclear whether or how much this will limit the ability of employers to use genetic testing to deny employment.

The discovery of the gene for cystic fibrosis is again illustrative. This remarkable breakthrough created immediate hope for prevention or treatment of the most common serious genetic disease in North America. At the very least, it seemed evident to some that pregnant women should be offered the opportunity to be tested, even though the initial mutation discovered accounted for only 70% of abnormal chromosomes. The American Society of Human Genetics and a National Institutes of Health (NIH) workshop recommended that widespread testing not be initiated before pilot studies had demonstrated the safety and efficacy of a screening program. The challenge of effective counseling was complicated by the discovery of more than 150 mutations, collectively accounting for only 85% of affected individuals; by the high costs of a nationwide screening program; and by uncertainty of the public health benefit of such expenditures. At least three federal agencies—the Institute of Medicine, the Office of Technology Assessment, and the Ethical, Legal, and Social Issues Program of the National Center for Human Genome Research—are sponsoring major studies of the policy implications, but screening appears to be expanding despite the absence of studies as to its effectiveness, toxicity, costs, or benefits. Pilot studies funded by NIH had just begun in late 1991.

The controversy surrounding heterozygote screening for cystic fibrosis has been accompanied by disagreement about the justifications for presymptomatic screening of newborns. Colorado began such a program in an uncontrolled fashion years before a prospective controlled study was begun in Wisconsin, and contrary to recommendations of the Cystic Fibrosis Foundation. The Wisconsin study has yet to show any benefits 6 years after the first cohort began receiving presymptomatic treatment.

CONCLUSIONS

The principles that should guide genetic screening—whether for presymptomatic treatment, reproductive counseling, or research—have been well delineated without substantial disagreement for almost 20 years.

1. Screening programs should be thought of as experiments, with unknown benefits and risks, until well-designed pilot studies with clearly stated goals have demonstrated efficacy, safety, and costs.

2. Individuals should have the right to decide for themselves whether or not to be tested. This requires the informed consent of the patient or his or her representative.

3. Mass screening programs are often driven by political considerations or a desire for profit. Policy should include review by those without vested interests, including representatives from the communities most affected.

4. Mandatory programs are extremely difficult to modify, especially vulnerable to political motives, and not necessarily the most effective way to bring clearly beneficial services to the appropriate individuals.

5. Programs of demonstrated efficacy constitute expenditures of limited health care resources, which must be weighed against other potential uses of such funds.

Prenatal Genetic Testing and Screening: Constructing Needs and Reinforcing Inequities*

ABBY LIPPMAN

PRENATAL DIAGNOSIS: A TECHNICAL AND A SOCIAL CONSTRUCTION

Of all applied genetic activities, prenatal diagnosis is probably most familiar to the general population and is also the most used. Prenatal diagnosis refers to all the technologies currently in use or under development to determine the physi(ologi)cal condition of a fetus before birth. Until recently, prenatal diagnosis usually meant amniocentesis, a second trimester procedure routinely available for women over a certain age (usually thirty-five years in North America) for Down syndrome detection. Amniocentesis is also used in selected circumstances where the identification of specific fetal genetic disorders is possible. Now, in addition to amniocentesis, there are chorionic villus sampling (CVS) tests that screen maternal blood samples to detect a fetus with a neural tube defect or Down's syndrome, and ultrasound screening. Despite professional guidelines to the contrary, ultrasound screening is performed routinely in North America on almost every pregnant woman appearing for prenatal care early enough in pregnancy. And although ultrasound is not usually labeled as "prenatal diagnosis," it not only belongs under this rubric but was, I suggest, the first form of prenatal diagnosis for which informed consent is not obtained.

Expansion of prenatal diagnosis techniques, ever widening lists of identifiable conditions and susceptibilities, changes in the timing of testing and the

---

*Prenatal diagnosis, the focus of much of this paper, is troublesome for all women, users and critics alike. In no way do I intend my remarks about it to reflect on women who have considered or undergone testing; criticism of the technologies is not to be read as criticisms of them. Women considering childbearing today face agonizing issues I was fortunate enough not to have to confront, and I can only admire their resilience and strength.

From the *American Journal of Law & Medicine,* XVII (1991), Parts III (19–36) and V (44–49). Reprinted with permission of the American Society of Law, Medicine & Ethics and Boston University School of Law and the author.

populations in which testing is occurring, and expanding professional definitions of what should be diagnosed *in utero,* attest to this technology's role in the process of geneticization. But these operational characteristics alone circumscribe only some aspects of prenatal diagnosis. Prenatal diagnosis as a social activity is becoming an element in our culture and this aspect, which has had minimal attention, will be examined in depth.

Prenatal Diagnosis and the Discourse of Reassurance

Contemporary stories about prenatal diagnosis contain several themes, but these generally reflect either of two somewhat different models. In the "public health" model, prenatal diagnosis is presented as a way to reduce the frequency of selected birth defects. In the other, which I will call the "reproductive autonomy" model, prenatal diagnosis is presented as a means of giving women information to expand their reproductive choices. Unfortunately, neither model fully captures the essence of prenatal diagnosis. In addition, neither acknowledges the internal tension, revealed in the coexistence of quite contradictory constructions of testing that may be equally valid: 1) as an assembly line approach to the products of conception, separating out those products we wish to develop from those we wish to discontinue; 2) as a way to give women control over their pregnancies, respecting (increasing) their autonomy to choose the kinds of children they will bear; or 3) as a means of reassuring women that enhances their experience of pregnancy.

The dominant theme throughout the biomedical literature, as well as some feminist commentary, emphasizes the last two of these constructions. A major variation on this theme suggests, further, that through the use of prenatal diagnosis women can avoid the family distress and suffering associated with the unpredicted birth of babies with genetic disorders or congenital malformations, thus preventing disability while enhancing the experience of pregnancy. Not unlike the approach used to justify caesarean sections, prenatal diagnosis is constructed as a way of avoiding "disaster."

The language of control, choice and reassurance certainly makes prenatal diagnosis appear attractive. But while this discourse may be successful as a marketing strategy, it relates a limited and highly selected story about prenatal diagnosis. Notwithstanding that even the most critical would probably agree prenatal diagnosis *can be* selectively reassuring (for the vast majority of women who will learn that the fetus does not have Down syndrome or some other serious diagnosable disorder), this story alone is too simplistic. It does not take account of why reassurance is sought, how risk groups are generated and how eligibility for obtaining this kind of reassurance is determined. Whatever else, prenatal diagnosis *is* a means of separating fetuses we wish to develop from those we wish to discontinue. Prenatal diagnosis does approach children as consumer objects subject to quality control.

This is implicit in the general assumption that induced abortion will follow the diagnosis of fetal abnormality. This assumption is reinforced by the rapid acceptance of chorionic villus sampling (CVS), which allows prenatal diagnosis to be carried out earlier and earlier in pregnancy when termination of a fetus found to be "affected" is taken for granted as less problematic. The generally unquestioned assumption that pre-implantation diagnosis is better than prenatal diagnosis also undermines a monotonic reassurance rhetoric. With pre-implantation (embryo) diagnosis, the selection objective is clear: only those embryos thought to be "normal" will be transferred and allowed to continue to develop. Thus, embryo destruction is equated with induced abortion. In perhaps the most blatant example, Brambati and colleagues have proposed the combined use of *in vitro* fertilization, gamete intrafallopian transfer, chorionic villus sampling and fetal reduction to "avoid pregnancy termination among high risk couples" [sic], and have stated that the "fetus was reduced" when describing a situation in which this scenario actually occurred.

Thus, while no single storyline is inherently true or false, the reassurance discourse appears to mask essential features of genetic testing and screening that are troubling. Reassurance—for pregnant women or for geneticists—notwithstanding, the story is more complex. Prenatal diagnosis necessarily involves systematic and systemic selection of fetuses, most frequently on genetic grounds. Though the word "eugenics" is scrupulously avoided in most biomedical reports about prenatal diagnosis, except when it is strongly disclaimed as a motive for intervention, this is disingenuous. Prenatal diagnosis presupposes that certain fetal conditions are intrinsically not bearable. Increasing diagnostic capability means that such conditions, as well as a host of variations that can be detected *in utero,* are proliferating, necessarily broadening the range of what is not "bearable" and restricting concepts of what is "normal." It is, perhaps, not unreasonable to ask if the "imperfect" will become anything we can diagnose.

While the notion of reassurance has been successfully employed to justify prenatal testing and screening as responses to the problems of childhood disability, we need to question both the sufficiency and the necessity of its linkage to prenatal diagnosis. At best, reassurance is an acquired, not an inherent, characteristic of prenatal diagnosis. Even if testing provides "reassurance," it is of a particular and limited kind. For example, although the fetus can be shown not to have Down syndrome, most disabilities only manifest themselves after birth. Further, it is not the (only) way to achieve a global objective of "reassuring" pregnant women. Indeed, it may even be counterproductive. This becomes clear if one reconstructs the notion of reassurance. Assuming it is an acceptable objective of prenatal care, are there ways to reassure pregnant women desiring "healthy" children that do not lead to genetic testing and control?

Data from the United States Women, Infants and Children program leave little doubt that "low technology" approaches providing essential nutritional, social and other supportive services to pregnant women will reduce the low birth weight and prematurity responsible for most infant mortality and morbidity today. Providing an adequate diet to the unacceptably large number of pregnant women living below the poverty line would clearly "reassure" them that their babies were developing as well as the babies of wealthier women. Similarly, allocation of funds for home visitors, respite care and domestic alterations would "reassure" women that the resources required to help them manage their special needs were readily available without financial cost, should their child be born with a health problem. It would also be "reassuring" to know that effective medication and simplified treatment regimes were available or being developed for prevalent disorders. Reassurances such as these may be all that many pregnant women want. Not only would these alternative approaches provide "reassurance" with respect to (and *for*) fetal disability, they would diminish a woman's feeling of personal responsibility for a child's health, rather than "exacerbate" it as does prenatal diagnosis.

Genes may contribute to the distribution of low birth weight and prematurity in North America, and likely some investigators will seek their location and the order of their DNA base sequences on the human gene map. The social and economic inequalities among women with which they are associated, however, are already well "mapped"; the "location" of women who are at increased risk is well known; the "sequences" of events leading to excessively and unnecessarily high rates of these problems have been well described. From this perspective, *gene* mapping and sequencing may be irrelevant as a source of reassurance in view of the most pressing needs of pregnant women. Even if genes were shown to be related to these problems, it must be remembered that the individuals to whom reassurance will be provided, as well as the concerns chosen for alleviation, rest on social, political and economic decisions by those in power. Such choices require continued analysis and challenge.

Constructing the "Need" for Prenatal Diagnosis

While reassurance has been constructed to justify health professionals' offers of prenatal diagnosis, genetic testing and screening have also been presented in the same biomedical literature as responses to the "needs" of pregnant women. They are seen as something they "choose." What does it mean, however, to "need" prenatal diagnosis, to "choose" to be tested? Once again, a closer look at what appear to be obvious terms may illuminate some otherwise hidden aspects of geneticization and the prenatal diagnosis stories told in its voice.

We must first identify the concept of need as itself a problem and acknowledge that needs do not have intrinsic reality. Rather, needs are socially constructed and culture bound, grounded in current history, dependent on context and, therefore, not universal.

With respect to prenatal diagnosis, "need" seems to have been conceptualized predominantly in terms of changes in capabilities for fetal diagnoses: women only come to "need" prenatal diagnosis after the test for some disorder has been developed. Moreover, the disorders to be sought are chosen exclusively by geneticists. In addition, posing a "need" for testing to reduce the probability a woman will give birth to a child with some detectable characteristic rests on assumptions about the value of information, about which characteristics are or are not of value and about which risks should or should not be taken. These assumptions reflect almost exclusively a white, middle-class perspective.

This conceptualization of need is propelled by several features of contemporary childbearing. First, given North American culture, where major responsibility for family health care in general, for the fetus she carries and for the child she births, is still allocated to a woman, it is generally assumed that she must do all that is recommended or available to foster her child's health. At its extreme, this represents the pregnant woman as obligated to produce a healthy child. Prenatal diagnosis, as it is usually presented, falls into this category of behaviors recommended to pregnant women who would exercise their responsibilities as caregivers. Consequently, to the extent that she is expected generally to do everything possible for the fetus/child, a woman may come to "need" prenatal diagnosis, and take testing for granted. Moreover, since an expert usually offers testing, and careseekers are habituated to follow through with tests ordered by physicians, it is hardly surprising that they will perceive a need to be tested. With prenatal diagnosis presented as a "way to avoid birth defects," to refuse testing, or perceive no need for it, becomes more difficult than to proceed with it. This technology perversely creates a burden of not doing enough, a burden incurred when the technology is *not* used.

A second feature, related to the first, is that women generally, and pregnant women specifically, are bombarded with behavioral directives that are at least as likely to foster a sense of incompetence as to nourish a feeling of control. It is therefore not surprising that a search for proof of competence is translated into a "need" for testing; external verification takes precedence over the pregnant woman's sense of herself. Evidence that the fetus is developing as expected may provide some women with a sense that all is under control (although this suggestion has not been studied empirically to the best of my understanding). Personal experience is set aside in favor of external and measured evidence. Moreover, given that a pregnant woman is more and more frequently reduced to a "uterine environment," and looked upon as herself presenting dangers to the fetus (especially if she eats improperly, smokes, drinks alcoholic beverages, takes medications, etc.), being tested becomes an early warning system to identify whether this "environment" is adequate. Women who share these suspicions and doubt that they can have a healthy baby without professional aid are likely to subject themselves to tests that are offered.

Third, prenatal diagnosis will necessarily be perceived as a "need" in a context, such as ours, that automatically labels pregnant women thirty-five years and over a "high risk" group. Although this risk labeling is, itself, socially rather than biologically determined, women informed that they are "at-risk" may find it hard to refuse prenatal diagnosis or other measures that are advertised to be risk-reducing. Once again, however, this "need" does not exist apart from the current context that created it by categorizing homogeneously those thirty-five and older who are pregnant as "at-risk." Mere identification of one's self as a member of a "high risk" group may influence the interpretation of an absolute risk figure and the acceptance of a test. In this light, the additional screening and testing possibilities generated by genome projects are likely to expand greatly the ranks of those deemed "needy." As the number of factors or people labeled as risks or at-risk increases, so, too, will offers of intervention.

Fourth, as prenatal diagnosis becomes more and more routine for women thirty-five years and older in North America, the risks it seems to avoid (the birth of a child with Down syndrome) appear to be more ominous, although the frequency of Down syndrome has not changed. This, too, may have a framing effect, generating a "need" for prenatal testing among women in this age group. Interestingly, however, this perception may inadvertently influence both the implementation and efficiency of proposed screening programs designed to supplement risk estimates based on maternal age with information from maternal blood samples. Having been socialized during the past fifteen to twenty years to view age thirty-five and over as the entry card to prenatal diagnosis, and convinced that once past this birthday they are "at risk," how will women beyond this age respond when blood test results remove them statistically from those in "need" of prenatal diagnosis? Will there be lingering doubts, and their sequelae, or will it be as easy to remove a risk label as it has been to affix one? What about the younger women who will have become prematurely aged (that is, eligible "by age" for prenatal diagnosis though not yet thirty-five)? As the title of a recent book phrases it, are pregnancy screening and fetal diagnosis *Calming or Harming?* We neither have the data necessary to answer this question, nor do we give priority to studies that would be informative. Instead, we proceed as if calming were a foregone conclusion. Programmatic changes such as these, no less than those subsequent to developments in genomics, underline how risk groups and needs are generated and constructed.

Fifth, on the collective level, prenatal diagnosis is generally presented as a response to the public health "need" to reduce unacceptably high levels of perinatal mortality and morbidity associated with perceived increases in "genetic" disorders. This reduction is of a special kind, in that prenatal diagnosis does not *prevent* the disease, as is usually claimed. Yet, even this "need," ostensibly based on "hard" data demonstrating the size of these problems, is constructed. For example, geneticists say "their" kinds of diseases are increasing as the prevalence of infectious diseases decreases, making genetic intervention seem appropriate. But others construe the same data as evidence of an increase in the "new morbidity" of pediatrics (developmental delays, learning difficulties, chronic disease, emotional and behavioral problems, etc.), the problems of concern in *their* specialty. Clearly, what one counts, emphasizes and treats as "evidence," depends on what one seeks as well as on the background beliefs generating the search. The numbers are then tallied, justifying a "need" to do something.

Moreover, unacceptably high rates of morbidity generate all sorts of "needs." Reducing these solely to biomedical problems hides the range of potential responses that might be considered.

Viewing needs and demands as cultural creations within a social context leads to doubts that assumptions of "free choice" with respect to the actual use of prenatal diagnosis are appropriate. It also clarifies why it is not fruitful to think that there may be a conflict between women who want prenatal diagnosis and critics who do not want them to have it. Not only does this polarization misinterpret the critics' position, it fails to recognize, for example, that prenatal diagnosis cannot really be a choice when other alternatives are not available, or that accepting testing as "needed" may be a way for a woman to justify going through what is a problematic experience for her. Society does not truly accept children with disabilities or provide assistance for their nurturance. Thus, a woman may see no realistic alternative to diagnosing and aborting a fetus likely to be affected.

Parallel to the creation of a woman's "need" for prenatal diagnosis is the development of health professionals' "need" for technological solutions to problems of malformation. Thus, geneticists increasingly choose to use and develop prenatal diagnosis to deal with problems of malformation excluding, if not precluding, consideration of other approaches. They "need" to employ these technologies, and in doing so they establish professional norms about how much is needed. Individual decisions about when a woman needs testing accumulate, and rapidly establish new standards for the profession. The routine use of ultrasound to monitor all pregnancies is probably the most obvious example. Regardless of the driving forces for dependency on this technology, the result is the construction of a particular "need": the basic "need" to know the gestational age of the fetus; the additional "need" to demonstrate that the pregnancy is progressing "normally." And the "needs" grow.

"Needs" for prenatal diagnosis are being created simultaneously with refinements and extensions of testing techniques themselves. In popular discourse— and with geneticists generally silent witnesses—genetic variations are being increasingly defined not just as problems, but, I suggest, as problems for which there is, or will be, a medical/technical solution. With but slight slippage these "problems" come to be seen as *requiring* a medical solution. This again hides the extent to which even "genetic" disease is a social/psychological experience as much as it is a biomedical one. This process is likely to accelerate as gene mapping enlarges the numbers of individuals declared eligible for genetic testing and screening. Given the extent of human variation, the possibilities for constructing "needs" are enormous.

Prenatal Diagnosis and the Social Control of Abortion and Pregnancy

The third element in the prenatal discourse that I will consider here stems from the often told story that testing is an option that increases women's reproductive choices and control. This claim has had much attention in the literature and I will examine it only with respect to how some features of prenatal diagnosis do increase control, but allocate it to someone other than a pregnant woman herself. This is most apparent in the context of abortion.

Without doubt, prenatal diagnosis has (re)defined the grounds for abortion—who is justified in having a pregnancy terminated and why—and is a clear expression of the social control inherent in this most powerful example of geneticization. Geneticists and their obstetrician colleagues are deciding which fetuses are healthy, what healthy means and who should be born, thus gaining power over decisions to continue or terminate pregnancies that pregnant women themselves may not always be permitted to make.

To the extent that specialists' knowledge determines who uses prenatal diagnosis and for what reasons, geneticists determine conditions that will be marginalized, objects of treatment or grounds for abortion. Prenatal diagnosis is thus revealed as a biopolitical as well as a biomedical activity. For example, an abortion may only be "legal" in some countries if the fetus has some recognized disorder, and the justifying disorder only becomes "recognizable" because geneticists first decide to screen for it. Fuhrmann suggests that in Europe, in fact, geneticists significantly influenced legislators establishing limits within which abortion would be at all permissible, by arguing that access to abortion be maintained through a gestational age that reflected when results from amniocentesis might be available. One wonders where limits might have been placed had first trimester chorionic villus sampling been available *before* amniocentesis? Would they have been more restrictive?

Other potential participants in what should be an intensely personal matter for "control" include insurance companies and governments. If either funds genetic screening programs or covers the cost of treatment for conditions diagnosable *in utero,* they may claim a say in determining which tests are carried out, and what action the results entail. Recently circulated reports about a health maintenance organization planning to withdraw medical coverage for a woman who could have avoided the birth of a child with cystic fibrosis if she had "chosen" to abort the pregnancy after the prenatal diagnosis was made, gives substance to concerns about changes in the locus of control. While this kind of abuse of power grabs headlines—and gets discounted as something regulations can prevent—there are more subtle forms of control that achieve the same ends and actually result from seemingly benevolent regulations and public policies. For example, newborn screening for Phenylketonuria (PKU) is carried out in the United States with universal approval. However, in only four states are health insurers required to cover the cost of the special foods children with PKU need. What choices/control does a woman have in this context? What are her options if prenatal diagnosis for PKU is offered? It would not be unreasonable to believe that a pregnant woman who learns that the fetus has the genes for PKU and does not see this as a reason for abortion may feel compelled to terminate her pregnancy because she could not herself finance the special diet her child would require after birth. Such pressures (explicit and implicit) exerted on a woman to abort a pregnancy following the prenatal diagnosis of some problem that makes her unable to keep a pregnancy she wants reveals another way in which social control over abortion may be genetically based.

Policy decisions establish control, too, in the guise of guidelines for seemingly straightforward features of prenatal screening and testing programs. For example, it has been shown that parents' decisions about pregnancy termination for the same chromosome abnormality are influenced by whether or not fetal anomalies are visualized on ultrasound. Even *who* does the counseling associated with prenatal diagnosis can influence what a woman does after learning of a fetal chromosome abnormality; rates of induced abortion are higher when obstetricians relate the results of testing than when geneticists do. Similarly, the interval between prenatal diagnosis counseling and testing is of consequence. This is demonstrated clearly in the reported association between the rates of amniocentesis utilization and the interval between counseling and testing: the shorter the interval, the greater the use. Pressure from state policies establishing when (as well as how) genetic counseling will be provided to screening program participants may be covert, but this does not prevent it from being controlling. In sum, prenatal testing and screening may provide control. But for whom? To what ends? For whose benefit? . . .

CONCLUSION

There are an unlimited number of ways to tell stories about health and disease, and an extensive vocabulary exists for telling them. Yet today, an increasing number of these stories are being told in the same way and with the same language: genetics, genes and genetic technologies. These genetic presentations of health, disease and ways to deal with them are grounded in the political and social context of the storytellers. My concern has been to decipher some of the stories about prenatal genetic screening and testing, and to reveal alternative constructions and interpretations to those already written.

Prenatal testing and screening, as has been repeated throughout this text, are most often presented as ways to decrease disease, to spare families the pain of having a disabled child and to enhance women's choice. The best-selling stories about them speak of reassurance, choice and control. As has also been suggested, this discourse presents a child born with some disorder requiring medical or surgical care as (exhibiting) a "failure." This failed pregnancy theme is reinforced in counseling provided to these families when counselors emphasize how most fetuses with an abnormality abort spontaneously during pregnancy, are "naturally selected," as it were, and how prenatal testing is merely an improvement on nature.

Just as there are several ways to construe reassurance, choice and control, the birth of a child with a structural malformation or other problem, "genetic" or otherwise, can be presented in other than biomedical terms. Is the story claiming that the pregnancy has malfunctioned (by not spontaneously aborting), resulting in a baby with a malformation, any "truer" than the story suggesting that *society* has malfunctioned because it cannot accommodate the disabled in its midst? Social conditions are as enabling or disabling as biological conditions. Why are biological variations that create differences between individuals seen as preventable or avoidable while social conditions that create similar distinctions are likely to be perceived as intractable givens?

While "many people don't believe society has an obligation to adjust to the disabled individual," there is nothing inherent in malformation that makes this so. Consequently, arguing that social changes are "needed" to enable those with malformations to have rich lives is not an inherently less appropriate approach. Actually, it may be more appropriate, since malformation, a biomedical phenomenon, requires a social translation to become a "problem." Expanding prenatal diagnostic services may circumvent but will not solve the "problem" of birth defects; they focus on disability, not on society's discriminatory practices. They can, at best, make only a limited contribution to help women have offspring free of disabilities, despite recent articles proposing prenatal diagnosis and abortion as ways to "improve" infant mortality and morbidity statistics. Thus, as sociopolitical decisions about the place of genetic testing and screening in the health care system are made, it will be important to consider how problems are named and constructed so that we don't mistakenly assume the story told in the loudest voice is the only one—or that the "best seller" is best.

Unarguably, illness and disability *are* "hard" (difficult) issues, and no one wants to add to the unnecessary suffering of any individual. But being "hard" neither makes illness or disability totally negative experiences, nor does it mean they must all be eliminated or otherwise managed exclusively within the medical system. Women's desire for children without disability warrants complete public and private support. The question is how to provide this support in a way that does no harm.

To date, support has been constructed to comprise genetic screening and testing. This construction is, in many ways, a result of the current system of health-care delivery in North America and the economic pressures on it. At a time when cost-containment is a dominant theme and a primary goal of policy makers, identifying those with, or susceptible to, some condition and preventing the occurrence of the anticipated condition seem to "make sense." It coincides, too, with the risk-benefit approach currently applied to most social and environmental problems. It corresponds with middle-class attitudes toward planning, consumers' rights and quality. But while this approach seems to "make sense," it does not suffice as a justification for the use of these technologies. Though it is more than twenty years since the first fetal diagnosis of Down syndrome by amniocentesis, we do not yet know the full impact of prenatal testing and screening on women's total health, power and social standing.

When amniocentesis was introduced, abortion subsequent to a diagnosis of fetal abnormality was presented as a temporary necessity until treatment for the detected condition could be devised. Advocates assumed that this would soon be forthcoming. With time, however, the gap between characterization and treatment of disease has widened. New information from efforts at gene mapping will certainly increase the ability to detect, diagnose and screen, but not to treat. A human gene map will identify variations in DNA patterns. Genes that "cause" specific disease, as well as those associated with increased susceptibility to specific disorders, will be found. Simultaneously, prenatal screening and testing are evolving in a context where a "genetic approach" to public health is gaining great favor. All the variations that will be mapped can become targets of prenatal testing. Which targets will be selected in the quest for improved public health? And who will determine that they have been reached? Given the extraordinary degree of genetic variability within groups of people, what does "genetic health" actually mean—and does it matter?

For society, genetic approaches to health problems are fundamentally expensive, individualized and private. Giving them priority diminishes incentives to challenge the existing system that creates illness no less than do genes. With prenatal screening and testing in particular, the genetic approach seems to provide a "quick fix" to what is posed as a biological problem, directing attention away from society's construction of a biological reality *as* a problem and leaving the "conditions that create social disadvantage or handicap . . . largely unchallenged."

Justice in the domain of health care has several definitions, but only one is generally employed in contemporary choice-and-control stories of genetic screening and testing. In these stories, justice is defined by the extent to which testing and screening programs are available and accessible to all women. Distributive justice is the goal: fair treatment requires access for all.

This definition seems insufficient. Access involves more than availability, even broadly defined. Not all individuals can respond similarly even to universally "available" services and, even if they can, unfairness and injustice may continue. Thus, perhaps we need to introduce other concepts of justice when thinking about prenatal testing and how these programs contribute to, or diminish, fairness in health and health care for women (and others). Do they ensure good for the greatest number (social justice) given all the causes of perinatal morbidity and mortality? Do they recognize and seek to correct past discrimination (corrective justice) given current and historically-based inequities in health? Will they level the playing field for women, for the poor?

One approach to justice is not necessarily better than another. In fact, depending on the circumstances, each one might be seen as "better." We need to keep these multiple routes to fairness in mind as we determine those to whom we wish to be fair and that for which fairness will be sought. For instance, human relationality may be as worthy of guarantees and respect as human autonomy; "individual good" is not always synonymous with "common good," though social responsibility need not become paternalism. There are choices to be made and the choices will reflect our values and ideology. How we choose our culture (by the routes we take) is no less problematic than how we choose our children, and consequences from both will be among our legacies.

Addressing these choices will itself be "hard," and will require we recognize and grapple with disjunction between goals and needs—perhaps even "rights" —on the social and on the individual levels. What seems to be appropriate or best for the individual may not be so for the collectives to which we all belong. We need urgently to address these contradictions now, using our energies to situate, understand and maybe even in some way resolve them, rather than keep them at the periphery of our vision. We must confront the possible need to choose between what is unfortunate and what is unfair in the distribution and reduction of risks to health and well-being. We must also acknowledge how our compassion for an individual's situation may harm women's health in general if addressing private needs dislocates provisions required for the public or solidifies existing inequities in women's position. This disjunction is not unique to genetic screening and testing, but is certainly echoed with force in this area.

This disjunction will make dialogue about the place of prenatal diagnosis in women's health care especially difficult (and, on occasion, tense). However, this only underscores the need to avoid premature closure of discussion and to avoid reducing it to sterile debates between "pros" and "cons." The issue is *not* between experts promoting technology and Luddites trying to retard science. It is not between women who "want" prenatal diagnosis and women who don't want "them" to have it. It is not a dispute between advocates of prenatal diagnosis who are seen as defending women's already fragile rights to abortion and critics who are said to be fueling "right to life" supporters seeking to impose limits on women (and their choices). All of these themes are being played out, but to focus on them is to create false polarities and to trivialize the possible advantages and disadvantages of these technologies when trying to deal with women's health concerns. Moreover, it incorrectly decontextualizes these technologies, severing their essential relatedness to time and place and isolating them from the broader health and social policy agenda of which they are a part.

Consequently, it is imperative that we continue to listen to the stories being told about prenatal testing and screening with a critical ear, situate them in time and place, question their assumptions, demystify their language and metaphors and determine whether, and to what extent, they can empower women. These technologies warrant social analysis. Not to examine repeatedly the tales and their tellers will be to abdicate responsibility to the generations that present and future genetic screening and testing programs will, or will not, allow to be born. A perspective that makes us responsible for the future effects of our current activities, the well-intentioned and the unintended, may stimulate the imaginative re-vision required so that we consider not just "where in the world" we are going with the new genetics, but where we want to go and whether we in fact want genetics to lead us there.

Germ-Line Gene Therapy

LEROY WALTERS AND JULIE GAGE PALMER

ETHICAL ISSUES

An Earlier Stage of the Discussion: *Muller versus Lederberg*

The ethical debate over intentionally introducing genetic changes into the human germ line through advanced biomedical techniques goes back at least to the 1920s and 1930s and the writings of classical geneticists J.B.S. Haldane and H. J. Muller. The discussion was renewed in the late 1950s and early 1960s, with two of the chief protagonists being H. J. Muller and molecular biologist Joshua Lederberg. Muller advocated the improvement of the gene pool through voluntary programs of assisted reproduction—specifically artificial insemination using semen from donors who had what Muller viewed as the best combination of physical, intellectual, and moral qualities. (Egg donation was not a technical possibility in the 1960s, as it is today. Given his general advocacy of women's rights, Muller would surely have approved the equal participation of women in this voluntary program for improving the human gene pool.) At a symposium held in London in November 1962, Joshua Lederberg criticized Muller's proposal for its lack of precision and for the very slow progress that Muller's plan for guided evolution would deliver. In Lederberg's words,

> The recent achievements of molecular biology strengthen our eugenic means to achieve [human survival]. But do they necessarily support proposals to transfer animal husbandry to man? My own first conclusion is that the technology of human genetics is pitifully clumsy, even by the standards of practical agriculture. Surely within a few generations we can expect to learn tricks of immeasurable advantage. Why bother now with somatic selection, so slow in its impact? Investing a fraction of the effort, we should soon learn how to manipulate chromosome ploidy [number of sets of chromosomes], homozygosis [the union of gametes that are identical for one or more pairs of genes], gametic selection, full diagnosis of heterozygotes, to accomplish in one or two generations of eugenic practice what would now take ten or one hundred.

From Chapter 3 in *The Ethics of Human Gene Therapy* by LeRoy Walters and Julie Gage Palmer (Oxford University Press, 1997). Reprinted by permission of the publisher.

Even 30+ years after Lederberg's statement there are many "tricks" that molecular biologists have not yet learned about genes, chromosomes, and cells. The chief trick that remains elusive is guiding new genes to precise locations where they can replace malfunctioning genes. Also, in the 1990s we are less likely to *begin* our discussions of germ-line genetic intervention by thinking of global effects on human evolution. We are much more likely to begin by considering specific diseases and decisions that are likely to be faced by couples who are deciding whether or not to have children. The thinking of those couples will be focused, first and foremost, on the welfare of their children and perhaps on the welfare of their children's children as well.

A Preliminary Question: Should This Issue Be Discussed at All?

In September of 1992 a distinguished physician–scientist, Dr. James V. Neel, appeared before the NIH RAC [National Institutes of Health Recombinant DNA Advisory Committee] to discuss spontaneous and induced germ-line mutation. Dr. Neel argued that it would be premature for the RAC to discuss the scientific and ethical questions surrounding germ-line gene therapy. His precise message, as summarized in a 1993 editorial, was the following:

> The Committee's desire to prepare itself for future developments would under most circumstances be laudable, but for a Committee with this visibility and prestige to begin to consider the subject of germ-line therapy in an organized fashion at this time would send the wrong vibes to the scientific, ethical, and political communities. Such an action might appear to imply the belief that the Committee would be seriously considering this prospect within the terms of office of present Committee members. Given the tremendous issues at stake, and even with the utmost attempt on my part to anticipate the amazing speed of advances in the field of molecular genetics, I could not imagine serious organized discussions of this subject by such a group within the next 20 or 30 years. (Individuals will, of course, express their views as they please.)

Dr. Neel carefully avoids urging individuals, like the present authors, to refrain from discussing the topic of germ-line gene therapy. On the other hand, he clearly thinks that it would be a mistake for public advisory committees like the RAC to engage in anticipatory discussions of this subject. We respectfully disagree. In our view, the years from 1983 through 1988, during which the RAC looked ahead to the first hypothetical somatic-cell gene-therapy proposals, were very profitably devoted to anticipating what the new technology might mean and to developing "points to consider," or very general guidelines, for somatic cell therapy proposals. In a similar way, given the research advances outlined in the earlier part of this chapter, we think that both individuals and public advisory committees would be wise to begin the discussion of this important topic sooner rather than later. If proposals for human application of germ-line gene therapy are delayed because of technical obstacles, or if research moves in unanticipated directions that must then later be taken into account, the risks of premature discussion are low. On the other hand, if a technical breakthrough occurs that makes germ-line gene therapy feasible, the anticipatory discussion of the topic may turn out to have been essential for the calm formulation of rational oversight policies. . . .

Major Ethical Arguments in Favor of Germ-Line Gene Therapy

In this and the following section we will analyze the major ethical arguments for and against germ-line gene therapy. For this analysis we will make the optimistic assumption that germ-line intervention methods will gradually be refined until they reach the point where gene replacement or gene repair is technically feasible and able to be accomplished in more than 95% of attempted gene transfer procedures. Thus, the following analysis presents the arguments for and against germ-line intervention under the most favorable conditions for such intervention.

A first argument in favor of germ-line intervention is that it may be the only way to prevent damage to particular biological individuals when that damage is caused by certain kinds of genetic defects. . . . [O]nly genetic modifications introduced into preimplantation embryos are likely to be early enough to affect all of the important cell types (as in retinoblastoma), or to reach a large enough fraction of brain cells, or to be in time to prevent irreversible damage to the developing embryo. In these circumstances the primary intent of gene therapy would, or at least could, be to provide gene therapy for the early embryo. A side effect of the intervention would be that all of the embryonic cells, including reproductive cells that would later develop, would be genetically modified.

A second moral argument for germ-line genetic intervention might be advanced by parents. It is that they wish to spare their children and grandchildren from either (1) having to undergo somatic cell gene therapy if they are born affected with a genetic defect or (2) having to face difficult decisions regarding possibly transmitting a disease-related gene to their own children and grandchildren. In our first scenario, admittedly a rare case, two homozygous parents who have a genetic disease know in advance that all of their offspring are likely to be affected with the same genetic disease. In the second scenario, there is a certain probability that the parents' offspring will be affected or carriers. An assumption lying behind this second argument is that parents should enjoy a realm of moral and legal protection when they are making good-faith decisions about the health of their children. Only if their decisions are clearly adverse to the health interests of the children should moral criticism or legal intervention be considered.

A third moral argument for germ-line intervention is more likely to be made by health professionals, public-health officials, and legislators casting a wary eye toward the expenditures for health care. This argument is that, from a social and economic point of view, germ-line intervention is more efficient than repeating somatic cell gene therapy generation after generation. From a medical and public health point of view, germ-line intervention fits better with the increasingly preferred model of disease prevention and health promotion. In the very long run, germ-line intervention, if applied to both affected individuals and asymptomatic carriers of serious genetic defects, could have a beneficial effect on the human gene pool and the frequency of genetic disease.

A fourth argument refers to the roles of researchers and health professionals. As a general rule, researchers deserve to have the freedom to explore new modes of treating and/or preventing human disease. To be sure, moral rules set limits on how this research is conducted. For example, animals involved in the preclinical stages of the research should be treated humanely. In addition, the human subjects involved in the clinical trials should be treated with respect. When and if germ-line gene therapy is some day validated as a safe and effective intervention, health care providers should be free to, and may have a moral obligation to, offer it to their patients as a possible treatment. This freedom is based on the professional's general obligation to seek out and offer the best possible therapeutic alternatives to patients and society's recognition of a sphere in which health professionals are at liberty to exercise their best judgment on behalf of their patients.

A fifth and final argument in favor of germ-line gene therapy is that this kind of intervention best accords with the health professions' healing role and with the concern to protect rather than penalize individuals who have disabilities. This argument is not simply a plea for protecting all embryos and fetuses from the time of fertilization forward. Both authors of this book think that abortion is morally justifiable in certain circumstances. However, prenatal diagnosis followed by selective abortion and preimplantation diagnosis followed by selective discard seem to us to be uncomfortable and probably discriminatory halfway technologies that should eventually be replaced by effective modes of treatment. The options of selective abortion and selective discard essentially say to prospective parents, "There is nothing effective that the health care system has to offer. You may want to give up on this fetus or embryo and try again." To people with disabilities that are diagnosable at the prenatal or preimplantation stages of development the message of selective abortion and selective discard may seem more threatening. That message may be read as, "If we health professionals and prospective parents had known you were coming, we would have terminated your development and attempted to find or create a nondisabled replacement."

This argument is not intended to limit the legal access of couples to selective abortion in the case of serious health problems for the fetus. We support such access. Rather, it is an argument about what the long-term goal of medicine and society should be. In our view, that long-term goal should be to prevent disability and disease wherever possible. Where prevention is not possible, the second-best alternative is a cure or other definitive remedy. In cases where neither prevention nor cure is possible, our goal should be to help people cope with disability and disease while simultaneously seeking to find a cure.

Major Arguments Against Germ-Line Gene Therapy

First, if the technique has unanticipated negative effects, those effects will be visited not only on the recipient of the intervention himself or herself but also on all of the descendants of that recipient. This argument seems to assume that a mistake, once made, could not be corrected, or at least that the mistake might not become apparent until the recipient became the biological parent of at least one child. For that first child, at least, the negative effects could be serious, as well as uncorrectable.

Second, some critics of germ-line genetic intervention argue that this technique will never be necessary because of available alternative strategies for preventing the transmission of diagnosable genetic diseases. Specifically, critics of germ-line gene therapy have sometimes suggested that preimplantation diagnosis and the selective discard of affected embryos might be a reasonable alternative to the high-technology, potentially risky attempt to repair genetic defects in early human embryos. Even without in vitro fertilization and preimplantation diagnosis, the option of prenatal diagnosis and selective abortion is available for many disorders. According to this view, these two types of selection, before embryos or fetuses have reached the stage of viability, are effective means for achieving the same goal.

The third argument is closely related to the second: this technique will always be an expensive option that cannot be made available to most couples, certainly not by any publicly funded health care system. Therefore, like in vitro fertilization for couples attempting to overcome the problem of infertility, germ-line gene therapy will be available only to wealthy people who can afford to pay its considerable expense on their own.

The fourth argument builds on the preceding two: precisely because germ-line intervention will be of such limited utility in preventing disease, there will be strong pressures to use this technique for genetic enhancement at the embryonic stage, when it could reasonably be expected to make a difference in the future life prospects of the embryo. Again in this case, only the affluent would be able to afford the intervention. However, if enhancement interventions were safe and efficacious, the long-term effect of such germ-line intervention would probably be to exacerbate existing differences between the most-well-off and the least-well-off segments of society.

Fifth, even though germ-line genetic intervention aims in the long run to treat rather than to abort or discard, the issue of appropriate respect for preimplantation embryos and implanted fetuses will nonetheless arise in several ways. After thoroughgoing studies of germ-line intervention have been conducted in nonhuman embryos, there will undoubtedly be a stage at which parallel studies in human embryos will be proposed. The question of human embryo research was recently studied by a committee appointed by the director of the National Institutes of Health. Although the committee specifically avoided commenting on germ-line intervention, its recommendation that certain kinds of human embryo research should be continued and that such research should be funded by NIH provoked considerable controversy. Critics of the committee's position would presumably also oppose the embryo research that would be proposed to prepare the way for germ-line gene therapy in humans. Their principal argument would be that the destruction or other harming of preimplantation embryos in research is incompatible with the kind of respect that should be shown to human embryos.

Even after the research phase of germ-line genetic intervention is concluded, difficult questions about the treatment of embryos will remain. For example, preimplantation diagnosis may continue to involve the removal of one or two totipotential cells from a four- to eight-cell embryo. While the moral status of totipotential human embryonic cells has received scant attention in bioethical debates, there is, at least a plausible argument that a totipotential cell, once separated from the remainder of a preimplantation embryo, is virtually equivalent to a zygote; that is, under favorable conditions it could develop into an embryo, a fetus, a newborn, and an adult. This objection to the destruction of totipotential embryonic cells will only be overcome if a noninvasive genetic diagnostic test for early embryos (like an x-ray or a CT scan) can be developed. Further, even if a noninvasive diagnostic test is available, as we have noted above, a postintervention diagnostic test will probably be undertaken with each embryo to verify that the intervention has been successful. Health professionals and prospective parents will probably be at least open to the possibility of selective discard or selective abortion if something has gone radically wrong in the intervention procedure. Thus, germ-line genetic intervention may remain foreclosed as a moral option to those who are conscientiously opposed to any action that would directly terminate the life of a preimplantation embryo or a fetus.

The sixth argument points to potential perils of concentrating great power in the hands of human beings. According to this view, the technique of germ-line intervention would give human beings, or a small group of human beings, too much control over the future evolution of the human race. This argument does not necessarily attribute malevolent intentions to those who have the training that would allow them to employ the technique. It implies that there are built-in limits that humans ought not to exceed, perhaps for theological or metaphysical reasons, and at least hints that corruptibility is an ever-present possibility for the very powerful.

The seventh argument explicitly raises the issue of malevolent use. If one extrapolates from Nazi racial hygiene programs, this argument asserts, it is likely the germ-line intervention will be used by unscrupulous dictators to produce a class of superior human beings. The same techniques could be also used in precisely the opposite way, to produce human-like creatures who would willingly perform the least-attractive and the most-dangerous work for a society. According to this view, Aldous Huxley's *Brave New World* should be updated, for modern molecular biology provides tyrants with tools for modifying human beings that Huxley could not have imagined in 1932.

The eighth and final argument against germ-line genetic intervention is raised chiefly by several European authors who place this argument in the context of human rights. According to these commentators, human beings have a moral right to receive from their parents a genetic patrimony that has not been subjected to artificial tampering. Although the term "tampering" is not usually defined, it seems to mean any intentional effort to introduce genetic changes into the germ line, even if the goal is to reduce the likelihood that a genetic disease will be passed on to the children and grandchildren of a particular couple. The asserted right to be protected against such tampering may be a slightly different formulation of the sixth argument noted above—namely, that there are built-in limits, embedded in the nature of things, beyond which not even the most benevolent human beings should attempt to go.

A Brief Evaluation of the Arguments

In our view, the effort to cure and prevent serious disease and premature death is one of the noblest of all human undertakings. For this reason the first pro argument—that germ-line intervention may be the only way to treat or prevent certain diseases—seems to us to be of overriding importance. We also find the third pro argument to be quite strong, that a germ-line correction, if demonstrated to be safe and effective, would be more efficient than repeated applications of somatic cell gene therapy. In addition, the final pro argument about the overall mission of the health professions and about society's approach to disabilities seems to us to provide a convincing justification for the germ-line approach, when gene replacement is available.

Our replies to the objections raised by critics of germ-line intervention are as follows:

1. *Irreversible mistakes.* While we acknowledge that mistakes may be made in germ-line gene therapy, we think that the same sophisticated techniques that were employed to introduce the new genes will be able to be used to remove those genes or to compensate for their presence in some other way. Further, in any sphere of innovative therapy, a first step into human beings must be taken at some point.

2. *Alternative strategies.* Some couples, perhaps even most couples, will choose the alternative strategies of selective abortion or selective discard. In our view, a strategy of attempting to prevent or treat potential disease or disability in the particular biological individual accords more closely with the mission of the health sciences and shows greater respect for children and adults who are afflicted with disease or disability.

3. *High cost, limited availability.* It is too early to know what the relative cost of germ-line intervention will be when the technique is fully developed. In addition, the financial costs and other personal and social harms of preventable diseases will need to be compared with the financial costs of germ-line gene therapy. It is at least possible that this new technology could become widely diffused and available to many members of society.

4. *Use for enhancement.* Prudent social policy should be able to set limits on the use of germ-line genetic intervention. Further, some enhancements of human capabilities may be morally justifiable, especially when those enhancements are health related. We acknowledge that the distribution of genetic enhancement is an important question for policy makers. . . .

5. *Human embryos.* In our view, research with early human embryos that is directed toward the development of germ-line gene therapy is morally justifiable in principle. Further, we acknowledge the potential of a totipotential cell but think that the value of a genetic diagnosis outweighs the value of such a cell. We also accept that, if a serious error is made in germ-line gene therapy, terminating the life of the resulting embryo or fetus may be morally justifiable. In short, there is a presumption in favor of fostering the continued development of human embryos and fetuses, but that presumption can in our view be overridden by other considerations like serious harm to the developing individual or others and the needs of preclinical research.

6. *Concentration of power.* We acknowledge that those who are able to use germ-line intervention will have unprecedented ability to introduce precise changes into the germ lines of particular individuals and families. However, in our view, it is better for human beings to possess this ability and to use it for constructive purposes like preventing disease in families than not to possess the ability. The central ethical question is public accountability by the scientists, health providers, and companies that will be involved with germ-line intervention. Such accountability presupposes transparency about the use of the technology and ongoing monitoring process aimed at preventing its misuse.

7. *Misuse by dictators.* This objection focuses too much attention on technology and too little on politics. There is no doubt that bona fide tyrants have existed in the 20th century and that they have made use of all manner of technologies—whether the low-tech methods of surgical sterilization or the annihilation of concentration camp inmates with poison gas or high-tech weapons like nuclear warheads and long-range missiles—to terrify and to dominate. However, the best approach to preventing the misuse of genetic technologies may not be to discourage the development of the technologies but rather to preserve and encourage democratic institutions that can serve as an antidote to tyranny. A second possible reply to the tyrannical misuse objection is that germ-line intervention requires a long lead time, in order to allow the offspring produced to grow to adulthood. Tyrants are often impatient people and are likely to prefer the more instantaneous methods of propaganda, intimidation, and annihilation of enemies to the relatively slow pace of germ-line modification.

8. *Human rights and tampering.* It is a daunting task to imagine what the unborn and as-yet-unconceived generations of people coming after us will want. Even more difficult is the effort to ascribe rights to human beings. Insofar as we can anticipate the needs and wants of future generations, we think that any reasonable future person would prefer health to serious disease and would therefore welcome a germ-line intervention in his or her family line that effectively prevented cystic fibrosis from being transmitted to him or her. In our view, such a person would not regard this intervention as tampering and would regard as odd the claim that his or her genetic patrimony has been artificially tampered with. Cystic fibrosis was not a part of his or her family's heritage that the future person was eager to receive or to claim.

Would Germ-Line Gene Therapy Be, or Lead to, a Eugenics Program?

We can perhaps best approach this question by imagining a future world in which the global elimination of a genetic disease by means of germ-line gene therapy is technically feasible.

> The year is 2055, and a definitive genetic cure for the mutations that cause cystic fibrosis (CF) has recently been discovered, tested, and perfected. This target-specific mode of gene therapy takes a properly functioning gene to the site of the mutation, splices out and destroys the malfunctioning gene, and replaces it with the properly functioning gene. The new technique can be applied equally well to somatic and germ-line (sperm or egg) cells.
>
> The World Health Organization (WHO) has recently announced a global program to eradicate all CF mutations from the human gene pool. The program is modeled on the earlier campaign to eliminate smallpox. All at-risk persons will be required to undergo testing and, if found to be affected or heterozygous, to accept genetic treatment of both their somatic and reproductive cells. WHO estimates that

the global campaign will succeed within 35 years, at the most, and that the effort, when completed, will save $40 billion annually (in 2050 dollars) in the world health budget.

This hypothetical situation is extrapolated from past and present programs aimed at controlling serious infectious diseases. These programs include the worldwide campaign that eliminated smallpox, as well as state-based programs of mandatory immunization against such diseases as measles and polio.

A first issue raised by this hypothetical is whether it is reasonable to draw an analogy between infectious disease and genetic disease. Proponents of the analogy point to the transmissibility of disease in both cases and argue that the mere direction or mode of transmission—horizontal or vertical—is less important than the spread of disease. Opponents of the analogy point out that, while some infectious diseases are transmitted by intimate behavior, all genetic disease transmission occurs in the context of reproduction, one of the most intensely personal and private spheres of human life.

Second, we are not told in the hypothetical whether a voluntary program of genetic screening and gene therapy for CF has been tried and has failed. If it has not been tried, the burden of proof for the proponent of a mandatory program is heavier. Yet there may be plausible arguments, based on cost or the number of decades required to reach the goal in a voluntary program, for the moral preferability of the mandatory approach in this case and all relevantly similar cases. If a voluntary program has been tried and has failed because of public inertia or unreasonable resistance, a mandatory program might seem to be morally justifiable in this case, even to a civil libertarian, as a reasonable means to a highly desirable end.

Here we as coauthors see no alternative to drawing a sharp, clear moral and public-policy line. In our view, state intervention in reproductive decisions by individuals and couples is virtually always wrong and virtually always counterproductive as a public policy. We would apply this strong preference for voluntary public-health programs to several current technologies, for example, maternal serum alpha-fetoprotein screening to detect neural tube disorders, prenatal testing of HIV-infected pregnant women and postnatal testing of their infants, and newborn screening for genetic disease. In the same way we would apply this preference to the future hypothetical possibility of germ-line genetic intervention. Thus, we would support the *offering* of diagnostic testing and germ-line gene therapy to all adults. In our view, the vast majority of individuals and couples would eagerly participate in such a program, just as the vast majority of parents consent to newborn testing in states where free choice in this matter is respected. However, we regard state intervention to compel people to accept germ-line genetic intervention in their reproduction as a violation of a basic human right.

Would a voluntary germ-line program that aimed to reduce the incidence of one or more genetic diseases in human populations be a eugenics program? Much depends on whether the term *eugenics* is employed as a morally neutral, descriptive term or as a term that already includes in its very meaning a negative moral judgment, like the words "murder" and "rape." The coercive and discriminatory eugenics programs adopted in the United States and Nazi Germany in the first half of the 20th century are rightly condemned as immoral. The question remains, however, whether there is a place for the notion of a morally justifiable eugenics program—one that is strictly voluntary and firmly based on reliable genetic technologies. In our view, the word "eugenics" has been so tainted by the discriminatory, coercive practices of multiple nations in this century that it cannot be rehabilitated. Thus, we would want to use a different and probably more cumbersome formulation to describe such a program, for example, "a voluntary program to reduce the incidence of genetic disease through germ-line genetic intervention."

Finally, we note that the kind of public-health program outlined in this scenario would only be feasible if safe, reliable methods for effecting precise genetic changes in human sperm (or sperm-producing) cells and human egg cells within the bodies of adults are developed. Any technique that depends on in vitro fertilization and in vitro gene repair will be much too expensive to be used on a population-wide basis.

The Continuing Relevance of the "Points to Consider" and General Ethical Principles

The preceding chapter on somatic cell gene therapy discussed seven questions that are currently asked by the NIH RAC as it reviews somatic cell proposals. These questions are contained in a guidance document called the "Points to Consider." The questions can be summarized as follows:

1. What is the disease to be treated?
2. What alternative treatments are available?
3. What is the potential harm of the intervention?
4. What is the potential benefit of the intervention?
5. How will the selection of patients be conducted in a way that is fair to all candidates?
6. How will the voluntary and informed consent of patients (or their parents or guardians) be solicited?
7. How will the privacy and confidentiality of patients be preserved?

In our view, these questions will be relevant to germ-line gene therapy proposals, but their emphasis will shift in important ways. In answering question 2, future researchers may need to discuss not only alternative *treatments* but also alternative strategies to prevent the transmission of genetic disorders to future generations. The options of preimplantation diagnosis and selective discard and of prenatal diagnosis and selective abortion will surely be discussed in this context. Questions 3 and 4 will also be pertinent but with an important shift in emphasis. If germ-line gene therapy is performed on early human embryos, the principal risks will be to the embryo and the embryo's potential descendants, not to the genetic parents of the embryo. Even if the parents have their sperm and egg cells treated in vivo by means of gene therapy, it is more likely that something will go wrong in the offspring than in the parents themselves. Similarly, the benefits of germ-line intervention will accrue primarily to, the genetically repaired embryo and the embryo's future children rather than to the parents. Thus, the focus of the benefit–harm calculus will be expanded to include multiple future generations within a particular family, and both parents and researchers will know that their decisions will have long-term genetic effects.

The third and fourth questions will be broadened in another respect, as well. Some critics of germ-line genetic intervention have raised ethical objections to *ever* employing this technique on grounds of the serious social harm that might ensue. While the same critics have also been concerned about somatic cell gene therapy, their principal focus has been germ-line approaches. Thus, researchers proposing to undertake germ-line gene therapy, or at least the review bodies evaluating such proposals, will need to take into account a much broader range of nonmedical consequences. . . .

The Authors' Conclusion

Ultimately, the moral case for or against germ-line gene therapy must be established by good reasons. In our evaluation of the pro and con arguments and in our discussion of eugenics, we have attempted to indicate why we find voluntary programs of germ-line genetic intervention to be ethically acceptable in principle. We think that this strategy should be employed only when gene replacement or gene repair is a validated technique. In addition, we are hopeful that techniques will be developed for repairing sperm and egg cells in the bodies of prospective parents before fertilization occurs. Finally, we find both the goal of preventing disease in a particular individual and the goal of preventing the transmission of genetic disease to the individual's descendants to be worthy rationales for this intervention.

Index

AIDS. *See also* Epidemics, newly emergent; Tuberculosis
and civil liberties, 88–91, 211–224, 228
as disease of homosexual males and drug-injecting addicts, 212–213
as exception to communicable disease control, 208, 211–224, 217–218
and gene therapy, 342
opposition of gay community to routine testing for, 213–215, 220–222
partner notification and, 211, 216–217
rationale for exempting testing, reporting, and notification, 217–220
testing for and reporting, 5, 211–217
and tuberculosis, 228–229
Alcohol policy. *See also* Drugs (Ilegal); Tobacco policy
and alcohol industry, 142–145
and disease concept of alcoholism, 132, 136–137
Prohibition, 131–132
public health perspective on, 132–149
state prohibitions laws, 62–64
Annas, George, 340
Assisted reproductive technologies. *See also* Infertility
effectiveness and cost of, 323–325
and multiple gestation, 324
Report of Canadian Royal Commission on, 327
risks of, 324–325

Bentham, Jeremy, 13–14. *See also* Ethical theories
Buck, Carrie (*Buck* v. *Bell*), 312–313. *See also* Eugenics

Community. *See also* Provision, communal
and the common good, 21–22, 57–59
and the common life, 68–69
as critique of modern life, 53
definitions of, 53–54, 68
as living together to secure safety and welfare, 68–72
and membership, 68–71
and needs, 68–71
and police (regulatory) power, 59–64
and provision, 68–82
and redistribution, 73–75, 105–109
and social justice, 105–109

Drugs (illegal)
consequences of legalizing or decriminalizing illegal drugs, 160–163
failure of penal approach ("War on Drugs"), 156–160
and libertarian perspective on legalization, 152
public health perspective toward, 152–156
as public problem, 132–133, 150–163

Elias, Sherman, 340
Epidemics, newly emergent. *See also* AIDS
cholera, new variants of, 247–248
and ecosystem instability, 240–250
factors in new epidemics, 240–243
globalization of epidemics, 240–250
hantavirus, 245–247
Equal access to health care principle. *See also* Justice
arguments against equal access, 260–263
defining, 256–257